Guide to Manuscript Revision

ab	....	Spell out abbreviation (M 7b)
adv	....	Use abverb form (U 2c)
agr	....	Make verb agree with subject (or pronoun with antecedent) (U 3a, U 3b)
ap	....	Use apostrophe (M 2b)
cap	....	Capitalize (M 2a)
coh	....	Strengthen coherence (C 1d)
coll	....	Use less colloquial word (U 2a)
CS	....	Revise comma splice (M 4a)
d	....	Improve diction (W 4)
dev	....	Develop your point (C 1b)
div	....	Revise word division (M 7a)
DM	....	Revise dangling modifier (U 3c)
frag	....	Revise sentence fragment (M 3b)
FP	....	Revise faulty parallelism (U 4c)
gr	....	Revise grammatical form or construction (U 1)
awk	....	Rewrite awkward sentence (U 4a)
lc	....	Use lower case (M 2a)
MM	....	Shift misplaced modifier (U 3c)
P	....	Improve punctuation (M 3-6)
#	....	New paragraph (C 1b)
no #	....	Take out paragraph break (C 1b)
ref	....	Improve pronoun reference (U 3b)
rep	....	Avoid repetition (U 4a)
shift	....	Avoid shift in perspective (U 4b)
sl	....	Use less slangy word (U 2a)
sp	....	Revise misspelled word (M 1)
st	....	Improve sentence structure (U 4)
t	....	Change tense of verb (U 1a)
trans	....	Provide better transition (C 2c)
W	....	Reduce wordiness (U 4a)

American English Today

Hans P. Guth   *General Editor and Senior Author*

Edgar H. Schuster   *Contributing Author, 7-9*

Contributing Authors, 7 and 8
Muriel Blatt, Los Angeles Harbor College
Stella Johnston, Baltimore County Public Schools

Consultants
Nettye Goddard, San Jose Unified School District
William Slothower, San Jose State College

Graphic Advisor
Herbert Zettl, San Francisco State College

American English Today

The Growth of English

12

WEBSTER DIVISION/McGRAW-HILL BOOK COMPANY
St. Louis   New York   San Francisco   Dallas   Atlanta

Editorial Contributions and Development:	**Brian K. McLaughlin**
	Evalyn Kinkead
Editing and Styling:	Richard Lynch
	Genny Boehmer
Design:	Virginia Copeland
	Nancy Steinmeyer
Production:	Bert Henke

5 6 7 8 9 10   KPKP   79 78 77 76 75 74 73 72

PREFACE

About the Series

American English Today, Grades 7-12, offers materials for meaningful work in English at every level of junior and senior high school. Each volume offers work in the following areas:

(1) WORDS. The basic asset of a good speaker and writer is his love of language. The first chapter in each volume builds the student's *interest in words;* it helps him develop the habit of watching them in action. The student systematically develops his control over the vocabulary of English as he studies the relations between words and things, words and ideas, and words and other words.

(2) GRAMMAR. In each book, one chapter is devoted to the English sentence. Carefully planned work in modern grammar extends the student's understanding and control of the structural resources of English sentences. These chapters help to develop the student's sentence sense. They provide him with *cumulative sentence-building practice,* bringing together the most relevant contributions from different schools of linguistic scholarship.

(3) USAGE. At a time when this area of English instruction is often slighted, the series offers *a positive modern approach to usage.* One basic obligation of English teachers is to make sure that non-standard English will not hold their students back. A second basic obligation is to help their students move confidently from the informal standard English of casual conversation to the more formal standard English appropriate to serious writing and speaking. Experienced teachers know that an error-centered approach, relying on highly technical grammatical analysis, cannot help most students reach these goals. In this series, usage is taught positively, in a carefully planned program that emphasizes essentials and builds skill and confidence through extensive oral and written practice.

(4) COMPOSITION. The backbone of the series is its *strong sequential composition program.* In each volume, a program of writing units involves the student in worthwhile assignments, guides him through the process of writing, and leads to the sense of achievement that becomes an incentive to more challenging work. Short examples of good professional and student writing and longer *prose models*

demonstrate what good writing is and how it can be produced. Instead of perpetuating an artificial division between "expository" and "creative" writing, the series stresses the creative and imaginative elements in expository prose.

(5) MECHANICS. Instruction in spelling, punctuation, and manuscript form provides *clear guidelines to the conventions of written English.* The mechanics chapter in each volume, rather than listing miscellaneous do's and don'ts, helps the student to understand the role of these conventions in context. The standards set in these chapters reflect the best modern practice.

(6) SPEECH. An important part of using English well is being able to hold one's own in the give and take of discussion, being able to speak effectively to a group. Throughout the series, *systematic instruction in oral English* develops the student's articulateness, his power to organize, his sense of purpose.

(7) RESOURCES. The final chapter in Volumes 10-12 offers instruction in the use of the dictionary and the library, letter writing, application for admission to college.

Readers of the series will note the following special features:
—*The materials promote learning that combines purposeful direction by teacher and textbook with active participation by the student in the process of discovery.* Text and exercises throughout involve the student in testing, applying, and elaborating the concepts presented. Inductive "Further Study" sections at the end of each chapter call for independent exploration by the student.
—*Though each chapter focuses on one major area of English, these areas are not taught in isolation.* Sample sentences and exercise materials in the language chapters are often drawn from *literature.* Special emphasis throughout the series is on areas like sentence building or the rhetoric of the sentence, which build a bridge between the teaching of language and writing. Exercise materials often use content from *related areas* of English and are often structured to illustrate and reinforce principles of composition.
—*The series reflects in its design a unified and balanced definition of English as a subject.* Regardless of changing fashions and specialized interests, teachers of English share certain basic responsibilities and commitments. In the wake of the movements and controversies that have swept over the teaching of English in recent decades, a broad new *consensus* is emerging. To help give shape and expression to that consensus has been the authors' ambition and inspiration.

About This Book

Volume 12, *The Growth of English,* offers materials in language and composition for students whose previous training has prepared them for more mature and challenging work. Rather than being a mere review or "sourcebook," this book provides the framework for a true capstone course.

Special features of the book are as follows:

—Throughout, the book offers a *coherent overview* of materials in language and composition that in earlier years are covered in more partial and exploratory fashion. The volume provides a complete stock-taking of the concepts and skills that together determine the student's understanding and mastery of English.

—The book provides the student with the fuller understanding of language that comes from a knowledge of its *history* and its role in our culture. The student sees American English in perspective by studying it against the background of its past and in relation to British and World English.

—The book helps the student develop the sense of *style* that makes communication effective. Throughout, it provides him with models and practice that strengthen his control of apt, accurate, forceful words; of a mature sentence style; and of the full range of formal and informal English.

—The work in language throughout the book is closely integrated with the student's study of *literature.* He constantly sees language at work in excerpts from the best writers. In studying the history of the language, he works with Shakespeare's English and other literary sources. An important part of his composition work is devoted to writing about literature.

—The work in composition stresses the relationship between writing and the student's own *experience and thought.* It explores the kind of thinking that gives structure and meaning to experience. More extended prose models enable the student to see how a writer thinks through his subject in a structured piece of writing.

A NOTE ON TERMINOLOGY: The authors have made a special effort to ensure that terms drawn from linguistics and rhetoric will prove intelligible to the student—and that they will *remain* meaningful as he moves from one book to another, and from one level of schooling to the next. Wherever possible, the authors have chosen terms *close to common usage* and widely used in authoritative textbooks in school and college. The authors have not made use of systems of diagraming that vary drastically from one school of thought to another and from one book to the next. The terminology in the chapters on grammar and composition is in close harmony with that used in the most widely adopted modern textbooks for courses in college English.

TABLE OF CONTENTS

CHAPTER 4   **COMPOSITION**   **271**

PROSE MODELS

A WORD ABOUT LANGUAGE

Language is man's greatest invention and most precious possession. Without it, trade, government, family life, friendship, religion, and the arts would be either impossible or radically different. How we use language, and how well, has much to do with what kind of people we are. Much of what we call education in one way or another helps us extend our understanding and mastery of language.

As you extend your own understanding and mastery of language, you should remember these basic principles:

(1) *Language has a history.* Language is the way it is for the same reason a mountain or a giant redwood is the way it is: the forces working on it from time immemorial have so shaped it over the centuries. Some of the most *recent* history of our language we can still trace: We can tell when our ancestors first became acquainted with a paved "street," taking from the Romans both the thing, and its name. We can show that our word *silly* a thousand years ago meant "blessed." But much else in our language — the words, and how they are put together in sentences — has roots going back into distant prehistory:

Language, man's greatest intellectual accomplishment, is immeasurably ancient. We may be fairly sure that man was already making use of the complicated and highly systematized set of vocal sounds which go to make up language when the woolly-haired rhinoceros and the mammoth roamed the earth. Archaeologists have shown that man was using tools in those far-off prehistoric days, a fact which presupposes his ability to hand down knowledge of their construction and use to his descendants.

—Thomas Pyles, *The Origins and Development of the English Language*

(2) *Language is a highly structured system.* Our own language we learn the natural and easy way — by constant exposure to it as children. But when we learn a *second* language in school, we are impressed by how much there is to it. Just as the study of anatomy and biochemistry impresses us with the marvelous complexity of the human organism, so the study of language impresses us with the complexity of the speech patterns constructed by the human brain. As in the human organism, the parts of a sentence are not a mere jumble. They mesh in intricate ways. Linguists studying the languages of so-called primitive peoples have found their ways of talking fully as rich and complicated as ours:

Out of a relatively small group of sounds — fewer than a hundred — that any normal person can learn to produce can be made hundreds of thousands of words, which in turn can be combined according to the rules of grammar into a virtually endless number of different sentences. All languages have this complex, many-layered structure. That is what makes them adequate to the needs of their users. Contrary to some popular impressions, the word and sentence structure of the language of the most primitive peoples is highly complex. Anyone who undertakes to study an American Indian language, with its long, intricately complicated word structure and its delicate nuances of grammar, many of them very different from those we are used to in English, discovers immediately how preposterous is the widespread notion that the first Americans communicated largely by grunts, by sign-language, and by smoke signals.   —W. Nelson Francis, *The English Language*

(3) *People judge one another on the basis of language.* One of the most noticeable things about a person is the way he talks. If he talks the way *we* do, he is one of us; if he talks differently, we

may be amused, or suspicious. We may consider his way of talking ignorant, or ill-bred. Modern students of language have tried hard to counteract such judgments. Just as a redhead may be no more emotional than other people, so the person who says "he don't" and "you was" may be no less intelligent than the one who speaks *standard* English. Much nonstandard English was at one time part of the language of the best writers, and can be found in Chaucer's poems and Shakespeare's plays. Schools teach standard English for two major reasons:

— Before radio and television helped to level speech differences, *regional dialects* could drift apart until they became a real barrier to communication. A speaker or writer who wants to be heard outside his family and neighborhood must be able to use the kind of language that is *current everywhere*.

— In the United States, as in most European countries, the standard language has become the badge of the educated person and a symbol of *social and economic status*. It is essential for success in school and office:

> Even though there is nothing inherently "wrong" or "bad" about using a nonstandard dialect, there are times when it can harm the person who uses it. . . . Undemocratic and unfair as it may seem, the fact is that standard English is "front door" English. And American schools are committed to the task of making it possible for every citizen to enter by the front door if he wishes to do so.
> —Virginia F. Allen, "Teaching Standard English as a Second Dialect"

(4) *Most of our thinking is done in and through language.* Vague notions take definite shape as we try to formulate them in exact words. Key terms help us pin down important distinctions — between "direct" and "representative" democracy, or between "freedom" and "license." To think an argument through, and to check it step by step, we like to have it in front of us, written down. Language assists and guides us in our thinking, but it may also *mis*guide us. It tends to move in well-worn ruts, and may keep us from trying *new* ideas, from striking out in new directions. Old slogans, old formulas may survive even though they no longer fit new situations. Then, as one writer has said, "the words stay put while the world spins away beneath." Part of our task in using

language is to keep it alive and flexible, so that it can do justice to the world around us, and to our own authentic experience.

(5) *Writing developed late in the history of language.* Writing developed late in man's history as an attempt to preserve the records, laws, myths, and heroic legends that in illiterate societies had passed from mouth to mouth, from the father to the son:

> However man started to talk, he did so a breathtakingly long time ago, and it was not until much later that he devised a system of making marks in or on wood, stone, and the like to represent what he said when he talked. Compared with language, writing is a newfangled invention, although certainly none the less brilliant for being so. . . . The earliest writings (in Sumerian) go back only about five thousand years, but man had been talking . . . for hundreds of thousands of years.
> —Thomas Pyles, *The Origins and Development of the English Language*

Writing has its own history, and its own traditions. Written language is not a mere partial record of speech, like a tape recording. Some things, like the tone of voice, the knowing wink, the reassuring smile, are filtered out as speech is written down. But other things are *added*. Writing gives us a chance to develop a *considered* opinion, to construct an argument that will *hang together*. It enables us to reach a large audience, and to make what we say last. By and large, writing is more serious, more public, and more permanent.

CONTENTS

CHAPTER ONE

Words:
OUR CHANGING LANGUAGE

The history of words is part of the history of man.

Man learned early in his history that word power is as important as muscle power. Leaders of half-trained and poorly equipped armies, but with a gift for inspiring words, have triumphed over formidable enemies. Some books—the New Testament, Karl Marx's *Das Kapital*—have recharted the future of humanity. In the less solemn framework of our own lives, we witness the power of words every day. We do not really need a magic word to open doors for us—just the right word at the right time.

What discourages us when we try to develop our power over words is that there are so many of them—literally hundreds of thousands of words. We hardly seem to make a dent when we study them in miscellaneous word lists of ten or twenty. One way to give meaning and direction to the study of words is to look at them from a *historical perspective*. When paying attention to the history behind the words we study, we profit in several important ways:

(1) Word history helps us *organize* our study of words. Knowledge of the history of English will enable us to see the relations between *scribe, script, describe, prescribe, scrivener, description,* and a host of other words that are rooted in a common past.

(2) Word history helps explain the bewildering *richness and variety* of our word resources. It helps explain how we came to acquire not only a set of related words like *people, populace,* and *population* (all derived from the same Latin root), but also the many *different* words that we use when

— we call the lore of a people its *folk*lore;
— we call different members of a people *country*men or compatriots;
— we say that the members of a people have a common *nationality;*
— we say that their descendants share the same *ethnic* background.

(3) Word history helps explain the *overtones* and associations of words. It helps us recognize the distinctive flavor of

— *learned words,* that came to us through books: *hypothesis, axiomatic, compendium;*
— *literary words,* that live on in the language of poets: *damsel, chevalier, prowess;*
— *fashionable words,* that are dear to newscasters and journalists: *defense posture, rolling readjustment, escalation.*

W 1 *The History of English*

Our language is the result of centuries of change.

Language does not stand still. The farther we go back in our reading, the more we become aware of the distance English has traveled since it was first spoken in the British Isles. When we go back a hundred years, what we read begins to seem old-fashioned:

> He *bethought* himself of his native valley, and resolved to go back *thither.* . . . People were the more ready to believe that this must *needs* be the fact. . . . The effect was no less high and beautiful when his human *brethren* were the subject of his verse. (Hawthorne)

When we go back five or six hundred years, what we read becomes hard to follow:

For sely is that deth, soth for to seyne,
That, ofte ycleped, cometh and endeth peyne.

For happy is that death, to say it plain,
That, often called for, comes and ends our pain.

(Chaucer)

When we go back a thousand years, what we read seems like a different language:

Hafa nū ond geheald hūsa sēlest,
gemyne mǣrpo, mǣgen-ellen cyð,
waca wið wrāþum!

Have now and hold of houses the best,
Bear glory in mind, sing the courage of heroes,
Beware of the foe!　　　　　*(Beowulf)*

As we study the history of our language, we encounter several different kinds of change:

(1) Over the centuries, every language shows *slow, gradual changes* in pronunciation, in the meaning of words, and in grammatical rules. Shakespeare apparently pronounced *reason* like *raisin*, and *grease* like *grace*. He rhymed *good* and *food, mood* and *blood*. Chaucer pronounced *see* somewhat like our modern *say*, and *mine* like our modern *mean*. Over the centuries, the English vowels have shifted from one pronunciation to the other, most of them several times. Similar gradual shifts have taken place in the meaning and forms of words. Chaucer's *sely* is the same word as modern *silly*, but in his time it meant "blessed." *Cometh* and *endeth* have changed their *-th* ending to *-s*. Some changes affect only a single word, but many, like the loss of the final *-th*, affect whole categories — thousands of words.

(2) Over the centuries, separated areas develop *different dialects* of the same language. Changes in pronunciation or in grammar may not spread evenly throughout the territory where a language is spoken. In England, as in France and Germany, the traveler may hear a slightly different kind of language as he goes from one village to the next. In some parts of Virginia and Canada, *house* still has a *u*-sound as in *you*, rather than the standard sound, as in *now*. When dialects go their separate ways over many centuries, they become

different languages. At one time, Dutch and English were dialects no farther apart than Boston English and New Orleans English are today.

(3) As people migrate to new territories, or develop new ways of life, their language changes to *adjust to what is strange and new*. English settlers in Australia needed words for the kangaroo, the wombat, and the boomerang. In the nineteenth century, the railroads brought into being a whole new vocabulary, from *locomotive* and *sleeper* to *switchman* and *caboose*.

(4) A language may be completely submerged or radically altered by *armed conquest*. After the Romans conquered France and Spain, only the Basques, inhabitants of isolated mountain country, preserved their native speech. The other conquered peoples gradually learned to speak varieties of Latin that over the centuries developed into modern French and Spanish. England was conquered by the French-speaking Normans in 1066. Eventually, English again became the language of government and literature, but in the process it absorbed many thousands of French words.

(5) Close *cultural contacts* make words travel from one language to another. Modern French has taken over many English words along with things imported from Britain and the United States: *le parking, le dancing, le football, le jazz, le snack*. English has imported much of the language of French cooking: *entrée, soufflé, sauté, hors d'oeuvres, dessert*.

W 1a The Major Stages

Scholars have traced the growth of our language from its Indo-European origins through Old English and Middle English to modern times.

When we check the history of a word in a dictionary, we frequently encounter the following abbreviations: *IE* for Indo-European, *Skt* for Sanskrit, *OE* for Old English, *ME* for Middle English, *L* for Latin, *F* for French. To understand the significance of these labels, we must know something about the four major stages in the history of our language:

INDO-EUROPEAN

A SIMPLIFIED FAMILY TREE

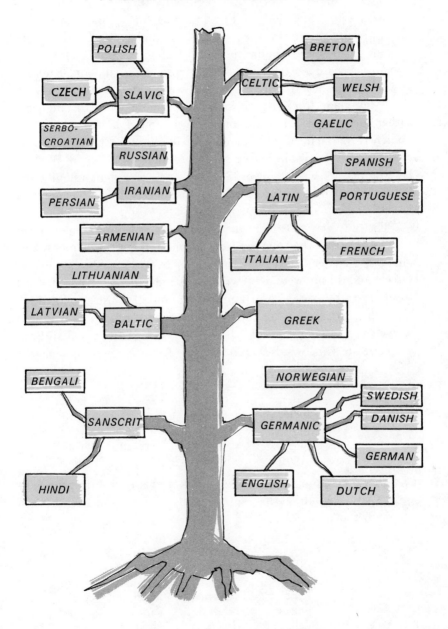

(1) *English, like most European languages, derives from the common Indo-European stock.* Language scholars in the eighteenth and nineteenth centuries proved a striking thesis about the origin of most of the languages of Europe: The farther back these languages were traced in their earliest written records, the more obvious their basic similarities in vocabulary and grammatical structure became. Early forms of English, German, and Russian, as well as classical Latin and Greek, were found to be parts of a single **language family,** derived from a common parent language. Other members of the same family were found in Asia. The best known is **Sanskrit,** an old language of literature and religious worship. It plays in India a role similar to that of Latin in Western civilization. Its written records, going back over a thousand years before the birth of Christ, show it to have been strikingly similar in its early stages to its European cousins.

The only way to explain the close kinship of all these languages is to assume that they derived from a common **Indo-European** language spoken (but never written down) two thousand years before Greek and Latin were first written. Some languages *not* derived from Indo-European are Hungarian and Finnish (related to Turkish); the Hebrew of the Old Testament (related to Arabic); as well as the languages of Africa, the Pacific, and the Far East.

Here are some words shared by many Indo-European languages:

SANSKRIT	GREEK	LATIN	GERMAN	ENGLISH
pitār-	patēr	pater	Vater	father
mātr	mētēr	mater	Mutter	mother
bhratār-	phratēr	frater	Bruder	brother
srd	kardia	cord-	Herz	heart
yuga	zygon	jugum	Joch	yoke

The basic number words in many of the Indo-European languages are **cognate** forms — "born together" — going back to a common root:

SANSKRIT	GREEK	LATIN	GERMAN	ENGLISH
dvau	dyo	duo	zwei	two
trayas	treis	tres	drei	three
sapta	hepta	septem	sieben	seven
nava	ennea	novem	neun	nine
dasa	deka	decem	zehn	ten

Our word *serpent* is related to the Sanskrit word *sarpati,* "he creeps"; our *mad* (for "insane") to Sanskrit *methati,* "he hurts." Our word *pentagon,* from the Greek word for "five," is related to Sanskrit *pantcha,* "five," and the Persian *pentcha,* "hand." The modern Indian word *maharaja,* descended from Sanskrit, is related to the Latin words for "great king" — *magnus rex.*

To judge from words found in all or most Indo-European languages, the people who spoke the common parent language
— lived in an area where birch, beech, oak, and willow grew; where wolf, bear, beaver, eagle, and owl were found (perhaps an area along the Baltic coast of Germany and Poland);
— had dogs; raised pigs, cattle, and goats; raised grain crops;
— lived before the discovery of iron but after the invention of the wheel (perhaps about three thousand years before the birth of Christ).

As these people spread over a larger area, different groups developed their own dialects, which later became separate languages. As the result of migration and conquest, these languages spread through an area from Ireland to India, from Iceland to Italy and Greece. Major subdivisions of the original Indo-European language include

CELTIC — in Julius Caesar's time the language of England and France;

GERMANIC—splitting up later into English, Dutch, German, Danish, Swedish, and Norwegian;

LATIN — splitting up into Italian, French, Spanish, and Portuguese;

GREEK — the language of the *Iliad* and *Odyssey,* parent of modern Greek;

SLAVIC — splitting up into Czech, Polish, Russian, and Serbo-Croatian (the language of modern Yugoslavia);

PERSIAN — the language of modern Iran;

SANSKRIT — parent of modern Hindi and Bengali.

(2) *Old English was brought to Celtic England by Germanic invaders.* The Old English period stretches roughly from A.D. 450 to 1100. Toward the end of the fifth century A.D., Germanic tribes from the Continent invaded Britain. Over a period of two hundred years, they gradually subjugated and settled most of the country.

The fate of the native Celts and their language was similar to the fate, centuries later, of the North American Indians and their now almost extinct languages. Where not killed or enslaved, the Celts were pushed back into the western and northern parts of the British Isles. There, varieties of the Celtic language survived until modern times:

— **Welsh** is spoken (and heard in church, or on radio and television) by half a million people in Wales. We are reminded of Welsh when we see in print Welsh names like *Llanystumdwy* or *Llewellyn* (*Lloyd* is a more familiar Welsh name).

— **Gaelic** is still known in the Scottish highlands. English has taken over such Gaelic words as *ingle* ("flame," "fireplace") and *cairn* ("memorial pile of stones").

— In modern Ireland, an attempt was made to revive *Erse* as a national language to symbolize the country's hard-won independence from England.

Much ancient Celtic lore survives in the romances about King Arthur and the Knights of the Round Table — whose historical counterparts were Celtic Britons fighting the Germanic invaders. Except for a few words like *crag* and *hog*, the language of the Celts is represented in Modern English mostly in the names of towns and rivers and lakes: *London, York, Dover, Thames, Avon, Loch Lomond*.

The Germanic tribes conquering the Celts came across the North Sea from Denmark and West Germany. They were
— the **Angles,** after whom England and English were named;
— the **Saxons,** whose name survives in the names of several English counties: *Essex, Sussex, Wessex* (for East, South, and West Saxony);
— the **Jutes,** who settled in the southeastern tip of England, in Kent.
These tribes spoke **Old English,** existing in several dialects that were close cousins of Dutch and the Low German dialects of northern Germany. Even today, many English and German words are very similar:

ENGLISH:	hand	finger	water	house	bring	drink
GERMAN:	Hand	Finger	Wasser	Haus	bringen	trinken

Old English first appeared in writing after the arrival of Christian missionaries from Rome in 597. We find it in translations from the Bible, religious tracts, early histories, and records of Germanic poetry, such as the epic *Beowulf* — all written down by Christian clerics. Here is a sample from an early Old English manuscript (modern *th* has been substituted for the corresponding Old English letters) :

Thā Apollonius thaet gehierde, he tham gehiersumode and
(When Apollonius that heard, he them obeyed and

eode forth mid tham menn, oth thaet he becom to thaes cyninges
went forth with the men, till that he came to the king's

healle. Tha eode se mann in beforan to tham cyninge and cwaeth,
hall. There went the man in before to the king and quoth,

"Se forlidena monn is cumen, the thu aefter sendest, ac he
"The shipwrecked man has come that you after sent, but he

ne maeg for scame in gan buton scrude."
not will for shame in go without clothes.")

Notice that most of the words in this passage survive in slightly changed form in Modern English. Even strange looking words turn out to be familiar: *scrude,* the word for "clothes," is our modern word *shroud. Buton,* the word for "without," is our modern *but.*

Much of the basic vocabulary of English to this day is of Old English, Germanic stock. In the eighth century, a second wave of Germanic invaders began to raid the coast of England: the Vikings or "Norsemen" from Denmark and Norway. After much fighting, they settled in the northeastern part of England and gradually blended with the Anglo-Saxon population. Many words from their Scandinavian dialects, called **Norse** in most dictionaries, reinforced the common Germanic stock of English. Here are some words brought to England by the Norsemen:

broth, cast, cut, die, egg, fellow, give, hit, leg, sister, skill, skin, skirt, sky, take, wing

(3) *In Middle English, we find the Germanic base of English overlaid by thousands of French words as the result of the Norman Conquest.* The Normans were descendants of Viking raiders who

had settled in northern France and had acquired a northern French dialect. William, Duke of Normandy, in 1066 at the Battle of Hastings, made good a far-fetched claim to the English throne. He soon conquered all of England and stamped out all opposition. Norman noblemen took over the land; Norman clergymen took over the highest posts in the church. The language of the king's court, of government, law, and literature, for several centuries was French.

Meanwhile, English was still spoken by the common people. In their dealings with their French-speaking betters, they gradually learned thousands of French words. These became a permanent part of the language, with the process of gradual absorption and assimilation of French words continuing all through the **Middle English** period, roughly from A.D. 1100 to 1500. At first, the words taken over were related to the aristocratic way of life and the political role of the new overlords:

court, castle, baron, noble, countess, servant, messenger, feast, minstrel, juggler, tower, privilege, prison, peace, standard, treason, treasure, war

But gradually English took over thousands of words for all aspects of life. Many of these simply *replaced* older English words:

uncle, envy, prince, witness, crime, army, mercy, disease, poor, reward, praise, pray, receive

Other French words provided *doubles* for English words that survived:

ENGLISH:	might	wish	hearty	bough	help	begin
FRENCH:	power	desire	cordial	branch	aid	commence

Still other French words joined their English doubles, but with some *difference in meaning*. *Ox, pig, calf,* and *sheep* (English) became (French) *beef, pork, veal,* and *mutton* as they turned into meat on the table. Can you see the differences in meaning and use in the following pairs?

ENGLISH:	stool	board	doom	seethe	house
FRENCH:	chair	table	judgment	boil	mansion

English pushed out French as the language of politics and literature in the fourteenth century. Chaucer wrote his *Canterbury*

Tales in English, and they were read and understood by nobleman and citizen alike. The Norman aristocrats had become Englishmen, but at the same time much of the English vocabulary had become French. In the process, the language had moved much closer to Modern English. Here is a city ordinance in Middle English, with spelling and punctuation slightly modernized. Words taken over into English from French have been italicized — notice *how many* of these there are. Can you, with the help of your classmates, make out what the city fathers are concerned about?

> The *Mair* and Aldermen *chargen,* on the kynges behalf and this *Cite,* that no *manere persone,* of what *astate, degre,* or *condicion* that euree he be, *duryng* this holy tyme of Christemes, be so *hardy* in eny wyse to walk by nyght in eny *manere* mommyng, pleyes, *enterludes,* or eny other *disgisynges,* with eny *feynyd* berdis, *peyntid visers, disfourmyd* or *colourid visages* in eny wyse, up *peyne* of *enprisonement* of her bodyes, and makyng *fyne* aftir the *discrecion* of the *Mair* and Aldermen (A.D. 1418)

(4) *Early Modern English shows the results of the many centuries when Latin was the language of church, education, and science.* Early Modern English survives in the King James Version of the Bible and in the plays of Shakespeare and his contemporaries. One notable feature is its rich fund of learned and technical words borrowed from Latin, and to a lesser extent from Greek. Latin had been the language of the medieval (Roman Catholic) church. The authorized Roman Catholic version of the Bible, the Vulgate, was (and still is) in Latin. Schools and universities taught Latin so that students could study philosophy, literature, and medicine. Most books printed in Europe before 1500 were in Latin. In the sixteenth and seventeenth centuries, Greek was widely studied as the language of Homer, Aristotle, and Plato; Latin was studied as the language of Vergil, Ovid, and Cicero. Early modern science used Latin as an international language.

Here are typical Latin words that came into the language before and during Shakespeare's time:

agile, allusion, considerable, conspiracy, contempt, custody, exist, genius, gesture, index, infinite, innate, meditate, nervous, picture, polite, rational

Like the earlier borrowings from French, such Latin words contributed tremendously to our fund of **synonyms** — words with the same or very similar meaning:

ENGLISH	LATIN
dear	expensive
childhood	infancy
madman	lunatic
skill	dexterity
trip	excursion
feeling	emotion
fear	terror

Together with earlier arrivals from French, we often get *sets of three* with similar or identical meaning:

ENGLISH	FRENCH	LATIN
ask	question	interrogate
fire	flame	conflagration
rise	mount	ascend
wrath	rage	fury
make bigger	enlarge	magnify
understanding	reason	intelligence
meek	humble	abject

Often the French and Latin doubles in such sets go back to the same common root. Typically, the French word has *developed* from Latin the way the word *sure* developed from an earlier Latin word represented by our English *secure:*

ENGLISH	FRENCH	LATIN
breakable	frail	fragile
kingly	royal	regal
sunder	sever	separate

Here is a sampling of Early Modern English — lines from the Psalms in the Authorized King James Version. Words taken into English directly from Latin have been italicized:

> Judge me, O Lord, according to my righteousness, and according to mine *integrity* that is in me. . . . The Lord hath heard my *supplication;* the Lord will receive my prayer. . . . For they have consulted together with one *consent:* they are *confederate* against thee. (1611)

EXERCISE 1 Check a dictionary or encyclopedia to identify the following *Indo-European languages:* Provençal, Yiddish, Hittite, Urdu, Bulgarian, Gothic, Romany, Creole, Roumanian, Plattdeutsch. (Your teacher may ask you to identify each of these in a sentence or two, or to prepare a more detailed report on *one* of them.)

EXERCISE 2 Does your dictionary point out the close kinship between words from the *same Indo-European root?* What can you find out about the connection among the words in each of the following groups? (Use a collegiate dictionary if one is available.)

1. hound, canine, cynicism
2. hearty, cordial, cardiac
3. hundred, centenary, hecatomb
4. four, quadrangle, tetralogy
5. father, patrician, patriot
6. bearing, transfer, metaphor
7. foot, pedestrian, tripod
8. wheel, cultivate, cycle
9. tooth, dentist, orthodontics
10. five, quintuplets, pentagon

EXERCISE 3 [Optional] In each of the following pairs, a word going back to Old English is paired with a word *from the same root* and borrowed from Latin. Notice that in each pair of words the initial sounds (which at one time must have been the same) are now different. In each case, the first sound of the *English* word shows a sound shift that helped set English apart from its more distant Indo-European cousins. Sum up which sounds changed, and to what. After each sound change that you identify, give the examples from the list below.

	ENGLISH	LATIN		ENGLISH	LATIN
1.	father	paternal	13.	break	fraction
2.	foot	pedicure	14.	brother	fraternal
3.	three	tripod	15.	guest	host
4.	tooth	dental	16.	heart	cordial
5.	flat	place	17.	garden	horticulture
6.	two	dualism	18.	thin	tenuous
7.	fee	pecuniary	19.	horn	cornucopia
8.	toe	digit	20.	corn	grain
9.	timber	domestic	21.	ten	December
10.	thirst	torrid	22.	bite	fission
11.	thumb	tumor	23.	clay	glue
12.	fleece	plume	24.	hound	canine

EXERCISE 4 [Optional] For several of the following, can you find the *German* word derived from the same root? In each pair, the first sound of the German word shows a sound shift that helped set German apart from English. Four initial sounds are illustrated here: *d, t, p, th.* For how many of these can you find out what change took place as German drifted apart from English? (Have someone who knows German *pronounce* the words for you.)

do, tongue, day, plow, thick, dance, tooth, plum, pluck, thin

EXERCISE 5 What is the meaning and history of the following *Celtic* words?

bard, druid, eisteddfod, Gawain, shamrock, banshee, colleen, pibroch, Guinevere, Bryn Mawr

EXERCISE 6 English absorbed from *Norse* many words, from common Germanic stock, that serve as doubles to words that were already part of Old English. In each of the following pairs, which is the original Old English word (mark it *OE*); which is from Norse (mark it *N*)? What difference, if any, is there in use or meaning?

1. no/nay
2. whole/hale
3. shatter/scatter
4. ditch/dike
5. shirt/skirt
6. shot/scot
7. shriek/screech
8. edge/egg (on)

EXERCISE 7 In each of the following pairs, the second is a double that came into English from *French*. What difference, if any, is there in meaning or use?

1. ask/demand
2. stench/odor
3. luck/fortune
4. deep/profound
5. work/labor
6. forehead/front
7. shun/avoid
8. feed/nourish
9. game/venison
10. hide/conceal

EXERCISE 8 In each of the following sets of three, the first word is from *Old English*, the second from *French*, and the third from *Latin*. What are the differences in meaning or in use? Does your dictionary show that the French and Latin word go back to the same root? (Select *five* of these sets.)

1. deem/judge/adjudicate
2. folk/people/population
3. follow/pursue/prosecute
4. hallowed/sacred/consecrated
5. evil/malign/malignant
6. evildoer/malfeasance/malefactor
7. want/poverty/pauperism
8. leaf/foil/folio
9. reckon/count/compute
10. draw out/portray/protract

EXERCISE 9 Many words derived from Old English have almost exact *synonyms* derived from Latin. Examples are *mankind/humanity, manly/virile, onlooker/spectator.* Find ten such pairs.

EXERCISE 10 The words in the following pairs ultimately go back to the same *Latin root.* Point out *differences* in meaning that set the words in each pair apart.

1. population/populace
2. delight/delectation
3. male/masculine
4. appease/pacify
5. penance/penitence
6. obedience/obeisance
7. loyal/legal
8. fancy/fantasy
9. master/magistrate
10. nourish/nurture

EXERCISE 11 The following is the beginning of the Book of Psalms in the *Early Modern English* of the King James Version. Check the origin of the italicized words. How many go back to Old English? How many came into English from French? How many came into English directly from Latin? (Use a collegiate dictionary if you can.)

Blessed is the *man* that *walketh* not in the *counsel* of the *ungodly,* nor *standeth* in the *way* of *sinners,* nor *sitteth* in the *seat* of the *scornful.*

2 But his *delight* is in the *law* of the *Lord;* and in his *law* doth he *meditate day* and *night.*

3 And he shall be like a *tree planted* by the *rivers* of *water,* that *bringeth* forth his *fruit* in his *season;* his *leaf* also shall not *wither;* and whatsoever he doeth shall *prosper.*

4 The ungodly are not so: but are like the *chaff* which the *wind driveth* away.

5 Therefore the *ungodly* shall not stand in the *judgment,* nor *sinners* in the *congregation* of the *righteous.*

6 For the *Lord knoweth* the *way* of the *righteous:* but the *way* of the *ungodly* shall *perish.*

Language changes to meet new needs and fit new situations.

Language is not a closed system, finished once and for all. New things and new institutions bring with them new words. When Germanic tribes first encountered Roman civilization, their language took over from the Romans ways of talking about streets and cities and armies. When Christian missionaries came into England, they brought with them a new vocabulary of belief and ritual. When Americans developed their own independent institutions, they created a whole new language of politics.

When we look back over such changes, we realize how much our language is a *living record* of our history. At the same time, we realize how much the meaning of a word is intertwined with the historical circumstances that gave rise to it. The following information about the word *slave* and its synonyms shows how closely meaning may be tied up with the traditions or institutions to which a word originally referred:

> **slave** (slāv) *n.* **1.** One whose person is held as property; a person in slavery; a bondsman; serf. . . . [<F *esclave* < Med. L *slavus*, orig., Slav; because many Slavs were conquered and enslaved] — **Syn.** (noun) 1. *Slave, bondman, serf, thrall, vassal,* and *peon* denote a person under subjection to another, or under his domination. A *slave* is wholly the property of another; in ancient warfare, captives often became the *slaves* of their conquerors. A *bondman* is bound by a contract to render service to another, but enjoys a degree of liberty denied the *slave*. A *serf* is bound to live and work on a landed estate; he may come under a new master when the estate is sold or inherited. *Thralls* and *vassals* were different types of *bondmen* in the feudal system. *Thralls* were bound to personal service in a household. A *vassal* might be the master of his own business; he owed his lord service in warfare in return for the lord's protection within his domain. *Peon* is usually associated with Spanish-American countries, and refers to a person so ridden by debt or poverty that he is a virtual *serf*. With the passage of slavery in most countries, these words are rarely used in their literal senses, except in historical writing, but they are widely used in extended sense to denote one who is under the dominating influence of another.

—Standard College Dictionary

Here are some elements in our vocabulary that mirror important influences in the history of our culture:

— *the language of worship*

When the Anglo-Saxons converted to Roman Christianity (A.D. 600-1000), they took over much of its Latin and Greek vocabulary of doctrine, ritual, and administration:

altar, angel, apostle, candle, chalice, church, creed, deacon, disciple, epistle, martyr, mass, nun, pope, priest, psalm, shrine

— the language of government

During the thirteenth and fourteenth centuries, when a French-speaking Norman nobility dominated government, law, and administration, English absorbed from French many terms like the following:

alliance, authority, duke, government, homage, majesty, parliament, realm, revenue, sovereign, statute, treason, treaty

— the language of learning

Our language of science and scholarship is heavily indebted to the sixteenth-century revival of ancient Greek literature and learning, part of the general "Renaissance" of the cultures of classical antiquity. Here are some originally Greek terms familiar to the student of literature:

apostrophe, drama, emphasis, epilogue, episode, hypothesis, paragraph, paraphrase

— the language of colonization

During the fifteenth and sixteenth centuries, Spain and Portugal pioneered in the discovery and conquest of new overseas territories. Here are terms for features and products of the New World, with some words that had come into Spanish or Portuguese from American Indian sources:

alligator, cannibal, canoe, chocolate, cocoa, hammock, hurricane, maize, potato, tobacco, tomato

— the language of navigation

During the seventeenth century, Holland was a great maritime power, rivaling England. The Dutch being close neighbors, many Dutch terms were taken over into English:

aloof, boom, bowsprit, buoy, cruiser, dock, freight, keel, lighter, pump, skipper

— the language of trade

In the seventeenth century, Italy led in the development of modern banking and commerce. Terms like the following go back to Italian:

capital, commercial, discount, dividend, insurance, investment

— *the language of the American way*

For over a century, our language has coined a succession of **Americanisms** to describe new features of our changing way of life. Here are some examples:

basketball, brownstone, coed, gangster, mortician, motel, nickelodeon, pin-up, prefab, Rotarian, rustler, sundae, technicolor

EXERCISE 12 After the number of each of the following words, write the name of the *language from which it came into English*. Be prepared to explain in class what you could find about the original meaning of the word, or about the historical circumstances or cultural contacts that brought it into our language. (Use a collegiate dictionary if one is available.)

1.	alphabet	*6.*	caravan	*11.*	etiquette	*16.*	pundit
2.	bamboo	*7.*	clan	*12.*	fetish	*17.*	ski
3.	banana	*8.*	coffee	*13.*	matinee	*18.*	sloop
4.	buccaneer	*9.*	coolie	*14.*	patio	*19.*	soviet
5.	budget	*10.*	czar	*15.*	poltergeist	*20.*	trek

EXERCISE 13 What can you find out about the original or literal meaning of the following *biblical* terms? From what language is each derived? (Your teacher may ask you to write a sentence or two about *five* of these words.)

amen, cherub, evangel, exodus, genesis, hallelujah, hosanna, Lucifer, shibboleth, sabbath

EXERCISE 14 What is the original meaning of the following terms from *Greek and Roman history and literature?* How does the origin of the word help explain its current meaning? (Your teacher may ask you to write a sentence or two about *five* of these words.)

barbarian, candidate, forum, laconic, mentor, ostracize, panic, patrician, plebeian, spartan

EXERCISE 15 French was the language of the *age of chivalry,* of knighthood and romance. Select *ten* of the following words. After the number of each word, write a word or phrase explaining its meaning. How many of the words have you encountered in your reading of literature inspired by the French romances of the Middle Ages?

1.	barbican	*6.*	fief	*11.*	minstrel	*16.*	prowess
2.	chevalier	*7.*	goblet	*12.*	pinnacle	*17.*	puissance
3.	dalliance	*8.*	joust	*13.*	plume	*18.*	stratagem
4.	damsel	*9.*	lute	*14.*	paramour	*19.*	travail
5.	fealty	*10.*	mastiff	*15.*	palfrey	*20.*	turret

EXERCISE 16 How well do you know the *language of music?* From what language is each of the following words derived, and what does it mean? (Your teacher may ask you to write a sentence or two about *five* of these words.)

cantata, contralto, crescendo, ensemble, falsetto, libretto, lieder, maestro, primadonna, repertoire

EXERCISE 17 What is the history of the following terms from the language of *English and American politics?* (Your teacher may ask you to write a sentence or two about *five* of these words.)

Tory, Whig, abolitionist, emancipation, carpetbagger, filibuster, gerrymander, suffragette, caucus, vigilante

EXERCISE 18 [Optional] Have you ever investigated the origin of familiar *first names?* Can you find a dictionary that gives the source and original meaning of the following? (Select *ten.* Your teacher may ask you to write a sentence or two about each.)

Catherine, Cecily, Charles, Donna, Edgar, Edith, Elizabeth, Fred, Gregory, Harold, Jack, John, Joseph, Judith, Margery, Matthew, Michael, Natalie, Theresa, Walter, William

W 1c Semantic Change

Over the centuries, words change their meanings.

Words do not stand still. They shift in meaning, lose some of their old uses, and find unexpected new applications. *Wit* once meant intelligence in general; today it often means a gift for clever, amusing talk. *Hound* once stood for any kind of dog but came to stand for a special kind of hunting dog later. A good dictionary gives us a feeling for the original or core meaning of a word, and for some of the ways it has changed or branched out. The following entry gives us a feeling for how the meaning of *nice* shifted gradually from "ignorant" and "foolish" through "finicky" to "pleasing" and "respectable":

> **nice** \'nĭs\ *adj* |ME, foolish, wanton, fr. OF, fr. L *nescias* ignorant, fr. *nescire* not to know, fr. *ne-* not + *scire* to know| **1**: showing fastidious or finicky tastes : REFINED **2**: marked by or demanding delicate discrimination or treatment *nice* distinction **3 a**: PLEASING, AGREEABLE <*nice* time> <*nice* person> **b**: well-executed <*nice* shot> **4a**: socially acceptable : WELL-BRED <offensive to *nice* people> **b**: VIRTUOUS, RESPECTABLE <*nice* girl>

—Webster's New Students Dictionary

Studying such entries, we find mirrored several major kinds of changes:

(1) *Old words adapt to new experience.* As our way of life changes, we often stretch the meaning of an old word to fit the new facts:

shoot originally "hurl" or "throw" (related to *scoot*); came to mean "fire a gun" after firearms replaced spears and other "thrown" weapons

broadcast originally "scatter seed with a wide circular motion," the way a farmer used to at sowing time, walking down the field; came to mean "transmit (and thus disseminate widely) by radio"

(2) *Words shift gradually by small logical steps, often reaching a point far removed from their original meaning.* Here is a rough outline tracing the gradual shifts in the history of some familiar words:

meal time > time for eating > food

pretty tricky > clever > comely > beautiful

curious careful > inquisitive > strange

weird fateful > supernatural > odd

plausible worthy of applause > persuasive > deceptive

(3) *Almost all of our more common words have branched out from a common core to develop multiple meanings and applications.* For the verb *run*, a widely used high school dictionary distinguishes fifty-five meanings, not counting its use in combinations like *run across* or *run short*. Can you see how the following words branched out into various related meanings?

shop	1. workshop 2. store 3. factory
hand	1. part of body 2. handwriting 3. applause 4. cards dealt a player 5. laborer
magazine	1. storehouse 2. storehouse for powder or ammunition 3. periodical
fraternity	1. brotherhood by blood 2. brotherly feeling for mankind 3. closely knit social organization
short	1. short circuit 2. short film

(4) *As words change, some of their older meanings go out of use.* If we still occasionally encounter these meanings, we call them **archaic.** If they have gone out of use altogether, we call them **obsolete.** Shakespeare uses the word *fond* in its archaic sense of "foolish." The reader of earlier English and American literature must be alert to words with meanings no longer in common use. Here are some examples from Crevecoeur's *Letters from an American Farmer,* first published in 1782:

> We are all animated with the spirit of an *industry* which is unfettered and unrestrained . . . (diligent work)
> A pleasing uniformity of decent *competence* appears throughout our habitations . . . (enough to live on)
> There he sees . . . a farmer who does not *riot* on the labor of others . . . (live luxuriously)
> I know it is fashionable to *reflect on* them, but I respect them . . . (blame)

Change in meaning, technically known as **semantic** change, often moves in predictable directions. A word extends its range to related areas, with occasional jumps made plausible by an analogy between the old and the new thing the word covers. Here are some of the less common directions that semantic change may take:

— SPECIALIZATION

A word may *narrow* its range. *Ill,* originally "bad" or "evil" in a more general sense, has come to mean primarily "sick." The broader meaning survives in *ill-bred* and *ill-advised.* Lady Macbeth says that her husband is "not without ambition but without the *illness*" that should attend it — without the *evil,* or readiness for evil, that is needed to make ambition successful. Here are some examples of such narrowing:

wife	originally "woman" (married or unmarried), as still in *midwife, fishwife;* now narrowed to "married woman"
captain	originally the same word as *chieftain:* generally a "leader"; then narrowed to the commander of a ship or a company
starve	originally "die"; then narrowed to "die of hunger"
meat	originally "food"; narrowed to food from the meat of animals

—— PEJORATION

Words that originally stand for something good or indifferent may gradually shift to express disapproval. *Accident* originally meant any accidental or chance happening. It has come to stand for unfortunate accidents, mishaps, mischances. Change in the opposite direction would be "melioration": *Knight* originally meant "youth" but was upgraded to mean "feudal nobleman." Here are some examples of pejoration:

gossip	godparent > idle, malicious talker
knave	boy > rascal
silly	happy > blessed > simple-minded > foolish
lewd	layman > ignorant > licentious
varlet	young vassal > young servant > worthless fellow

—— TRANSFER

A name may be transferred from one thing to another by often roundabout processes of association. Here is how one proper name came to stand for something else:

> *Stogy,* for instance, calls to mind the Conestoga wagon and the part it played in the amazing westward push early in the nineteenth century. . . . *Conestoga* was the name of an Iroquoian tribe, now long extinct; the tribal designation was applied to a valley in Lancaster County, Pennsylvania, where the large covered wagon which was the principal means of westward transportation before the introduction of railroads seems to have originated. The early Conestoga wagoners rolled long cigars for smoking on their trips, and such a cigar was called a *conestogy* (which is merely the earlier pronunciation of *Conestoga,* like *Iowy* for Iowa); this was subsequently clipped to *stogy.*
>
> —Thomas Pyles, *Words and Ways of American English*

EXERCISE 19 Check your dictionary for the *original meaning* of the following words. Answer each question in a word or phrase.

1. What was originally stored in a *barn?*
2. What was the original occupation of a *hussy?*
3. Does a *husband* have to be a married man?
4. What was the original occupation of a *lady?*
5. What were the original duties of a *marshal?*
6. What was the most basic privilege of a *lord?*
7. Why would it originally have been hard to "pocket" a *fee?*
8. What did the *gentle* in "gentleman" originally stand for?
9. What kind of stories did a *jester* originally tell?
10. What animal is alluded to in the word *chivalry?*

EXERCISE 20 Answer the questions about each of the following words in a sentence or less. (Or your teacher may assign different parts of this exercise to different members of the class.)

1. What is the buried *original meaning* of each: *Halloween, handicap, disaster, dandelion, inveigle?*
2. What are three major *different current meanings* for each of the following nouns: *foot, crown, pipe, train, paper?*
3. How does the history of each of the following illustrate *pejoration: ban, casualty, censure, idiot, predicament?*
4. How does each of the following illustrate *transfer* from a proper name to a more general meaning: *atlas, cereal, dunce, marathon, vandalism?*

EXERCISE 21 Each of the words italicized in the following passages illustrates a *meaning no longer in common use.* Write down the word and after it the meaning that fits the context. (Number the words from 1 through 20.)

1. Bless you, fair *dame!* I am not to you known,
   Though in your state of honor I am *perfect.*
   I *doubt,* some danger does approach you nearly:
   If you will take a *homely* man's advice,
   Be not found here; *hence,* with your little ones.
   (Macbeth, Act IV, Sc. 2)

2.   Say from *whence*
   You owe this strange *intelligence?* or why
   Upon this *blasted* heath you stop our way
   With such prophetic greeting?
   (Macbeth, Act I, Sc. 3)

3.   Let the gods so *speed* me as I love
        The name of honor more than I fear death.
                                (*Julius Caesar,* Act I, Sc. 2)

4.   I am as constant as the Northern Star
        Of whose true-fixed and resting quality
        There is no *fellow* in the firmament.
                                (*Julius Caesar,* Act III, Sc. 1)

5.   Were I so minded
        I here could pluck his highness' frown upon you
        And *justify* you traitors.
                                (*Tempest,* Act V, Sc. 1)

6.   But let it pass, and think it is of *kind*
        That often change doth please a woman's mind.
                                (Sir Thomas Wyatt)

7.   If I forget thee, O Jerusalem, let my right hand
        forget her *cunning.*   (Psalms)

8.   All who know that shire are very well acquainted
        with the *parts* and merits of Sir Roger. He is a gentle-
        man that is very *singular* in his behavior. . . .
        He has all his life dressed very well, and remembers
        habits as others do men.   (Sir Richard Steele)

9.   Let us raise a *standard* to which the wise and honest
        can *repair.*   (George Washington)

10.   When I first *cheapened* my lodgings, the landlady
        told me that she hoped I was not an author.
                                (Samuel Johnson)

11.   The voice I hear this passing night was heard
        In ancient days by emperor and *clown.*
                                (John Keats)

12.   Oh London tunes are new tunes, and London books
        are wise,
        And London plays are *rare* plays, and fine to country
        eyes.   (John Masefield)

EXERCISE 22   [Optional]   What can you find out about the connection in *origin and meaning* among the members of each of the
following groups?

1. ward, warden, guardian   *6.* bank, bench

2. money, mint   *7.* cattle, chattel, capital

3. blame, blaspheme   *8.* final, fine, finance

4. Jupiter, jovial   *9.* cadet, cad, caddie

5. ballad, ballet, ballroom   *10.* canine, canary

W 2 *Word Resources*

As the result of its varied history, English offers us a rich choice of vocabulary resources.

Everyone has at some time felt at a loss for words. Instead of saying clearly and forcefully what is on his mind, he has felt in-articulate, tongue-tied. Whatever the reason for such lack of fluency, it is not likely to be a deficiency in our language. The language at our disposal is the very opposite of poverty-stricken. As the result of constant enrichment over the centuries, it offers us a wealth of resources that we can hardly ever fully exploit. Typically, we have not just *one* word but a *cluster* of words for each meaning and shade of meaning. We don't simply have to "read" a message, we can "decipher" it, "pore over" it, in order to "make it out." When we travel, the result may be a "trip," a "journey," a "voyage," an "excursion," a "jaunt," a "tour"; or even, if we are very lucky, an "expedition," a "cruise," or a "safari." A "word hoard" like the famous *Roget's Thesaurus* lists after key ideas dozens and sometimes hundreds of closely related words:

food	*nourishment, nutriment, sustenance, nurture, provender, provisions, ration, diet, comestibles, victuals, edibles, viands*
repetition	*iteration, reiteration, duplication, recurrence, tautology, redundancy, echo, encore, refrain, recapitulation, reverberation*
freedom	*liberty, independence, autonomy, emancipation, franchise, immunity, exemption, elbowroom, laissez faire*

How can you make this wealth of resources serve your own purposes as a speaker and writer? Obviously, there is no magic formula for acquiring a mastery of words. The most basic require-ment is *constant exposure*. No one ever became a great musician by occasionally pecking out a tune on the piano. The promising future musician *lives with* music and all it stands for, getting it into his bones. Similarly, the promising speaker and writer *lives with* words. He reads and listens — not just when an "assignment" makes him, but whenever he can. He practices — talking to himself, writing imaginary letters to editors, doing imitations of great orators (and of his teachers).

Develop an interest in words as words. Language does not serve people well who remember it only when they need it. The great masters of our language learned as young people to marvel at the sounds and shapes of words, to collect them the way we collect stamps or coins. A true craftsman uses tools that are useful but at the same time in their own way beautiful. A first-rate speaker and writer knows how to make language serve his purpose. At the same time, he shares the poet's delight in its power to capture the color, the warmth, and the zest of life.

W 2a Accurate Words

**Make full use of the common stock of words,
using words with just the right shade of meaning.**

Learning to use fully the resources of our language is not really a matter of learning "big words." First in importance is learning to use fully and accurately our common stock — words that are part of the common language shared by laymen and scholars alike. To develop your knack for finding the right word, you will first of all have to start watching *language at work* in everyday life. Make the following pieces of advice part of your word-watcher's guide:

(1) *Look for specific words.* Learn to call birds and trees by their right names. Pay attention to what a mechanic or carpenter calls the tools of his trade. General words are convenient because they cover much ground: "Birds fly." But specific words carry more information; they give identity to things and set one apart from the other. We come closer to the *real* bird when we do not simply call it a bird but a robin, a hummingbird, a sparrow, a buzzard, a bluejay, a quail.

GENERAL: *tool*
SPECIFIC: drill, wrench, gauge, chisel, plane, lever, wedge

GENERAL: *fish*
SPECIFIC: trout, salmon, cod, haddock, shad

A writer with a command of specific words *takes in more* than one always content with a handy general label. To George Orwell, for instance, in *1984*, a pen is not just a pen; there are important *distinctions* to be made:

GENERAL: He took a pen and started to write.
SPECIFIC: Winston fitted a nib into the penholder and sucked it to get the grease off. The pen was an archaic instrument, seldom used even for signatures, and he had procured one, furtively and with some difficulty, simply because of a feeling that the beautiful creamy paper deserved to be written on with a real nib instead of being scratched with an ink pencil.

(2) *Look for words that make expression concrete.* Some words appeal strongly to our senses. They conjure up shapes and colors. They make us hear sounds or feel textures. Such words with a strong **sensory** dimension help us re-create the actual feel of concrete experience. A colorless word like *drink* provides basic information. But a concrete word like *guzzle, sip,* or *slurp* makes us see (and hear!) the person taking a drink.

COLORLESS: *eat*
CONCRETE: swallow, nibble, gobble, bolt, munch, gnaw, devour

COLORLESS: *shout*
CONCRETE: bellow, bawl, halloo, whoop, scream, screech, shriek, bark, growl, yawp

In the following passage, can you point out the words that make the reader see the actual movements, and hear the cries, of the birds in flight?

He watched their flight; bird after bird: a dark flash, a swerve, a flash again, a dart aside, a curve, a flutter of wings. He tried to count them before all their darting quivering bodies passed: six, ten, eleven: and wondered were they odd or even in number. Twelve, thirteen: for two came wheeling down from the upper sky. They were flying high and low but ever round and round in straight and curving lines and ever flying from left to right, circling about a temple of air.

He listened to the cries: like the squeak of mice behind the wainscot: a shrill twofold note. But the notes were long and shrill and whirring, unlike the cry of vermin, falling a third or a fourth and trilled as the flying beaks clove the air.

—James Joyce, *A Portrait of the Artist as a Young Man*

(3) *Choose the synonym with the right shade of meaning.* No two words are simply interchangeable. **Synonyms** are words that mean almost the same — but not quite. *Discard* and *spurn* are synonyms of *reject.* But we discard things rather casually; we reject something more deliberately, and we spurn something with indignation. A good dictionary points up such differences, often in "synonymies" following the regular dictionary entry:

> **Syn.** *v.* **1. Roam, rove, ramble** mean to wander. **Roam** means to go about here and there as one pleases over a wide area, with no special plan or aim: *The photographer roamed about the world.* **Rove** usually adds the suggestion of a definite purpose, though not of a settled destination: *Submarines roved the ocean.* **Ramble** particularly suggests straying from a regular path or plan and wandering about aimlessly for one's own pleasure: *We rambled through the shopping district.*

—*Thorndike-Barnhart High School Dictionary*

> **syn** LONG, YEARN, HANKER, PINE, HUNGER, THIRST mean to have a strong desire for something. LONG implies a wishing with one's whole heart and often a striving to attain; YEARN suggests an eager, restless, or painful longing; HANKER suggests the uneasy promptings of unsatisfied appetite or desire; PINE implies a languishing or a fruitless longing for what is impossible; HUNGER and THIRST imply an insistent or impatient craving or a compelling need

—*Webster's Seventh New Collegiate Dictionary*

(4) *Develop an ear for the right idiom.* An **idiom** is a characteristic way of saying things; typically its meaning is more than the sum of its parts. We have to know the customary use of the whole phrase to recognize the difference between "doing good" and "doing well." By merely looking up *keep* and *hold* in a dictionary, a foreigner could not guess that we idiomatically say "keep in mind" rather than "hold in mind." Unidiomatic English provides us with information that we can decipher, but it moves in such wooden fashion that listening or reading becomes a strain.

Command of idiom not merely helps us convey the right meaning, but helps us convey it naturally, deftly, with ease. Some dictionaries provide an exceptionally full account of the idioms in which a word is used:

by a head, 1. in *horse racing*, etc., by the length of the animal's head; hence, 2. by a very small margin.

by (or down by) the head, in *nautical usage,* with the bow deeper in the water than the stern.

come to a head, 1. to be about to suppurate, as a boil. 2. to culminate.

give one his head, to let one do as he likes.

go to one's head, 1. to confuse, excite, or intoxicate one. 2. to make one vain or overconfident.

hang (or hide) one's head, to lower one's head or conceal one's face in or as in shame.

head and shoulders above, definitely superior to.

head off, to get ahead of and cause to stop or turn away; intercept.

head over heels, 1. tumbling heels over head, as in a somersault. 2. deeply; completely. 3. hurriedly; impetuously; recklessly.

heads up! [Colloq.], look out! be careful!

keep one's head, to keep one's poise, self-control, etc.; not become excited or flustered.

keep one's head above water, 1. to remain afloat; not sink. 2. to keep oneself alive, out of debt, etc.

lay heads together, to consult or scheme together.

lose one's head, to lose one's poise, self-control, etc.; become excited or flustered.

make head, to make headway; go forward; advance.

make head or tail of, to understand: usually in the negative.

on (or upon) one's head, as one's burden, responsibility, or misfortune.

one's head off, a great deal: preceded by a verb, as, he talked *his head off*.

out of (or off) one's head, [Colloq.], 1. crazy. 2. delirious; raving.

over one's head, 1. *a)* too difficult for one to understand. *b)* so that one cannot understand. 2. in spite of one's prior claim. 3. without consulting one; to a higher authority.

put heads together, to consult or scheme together.

take it into one's head, to conceive the notion, plan, or intention.

turn one's head, 1. to make one dizzy. 2. to make one vain or overconfident.

—Webster's New World Dictionary

The first-rate speaker or writer may seem to have a natural gift for hitting the apt word, the happy phrase. But in fact he is likely to have developed his natural talent by much patient effort. He is likely to *try out* different words. He is likely to tinker with a key sentence, going back to it again and again until he hits upon the words that fit just right.

EXERCISE 23 One reason we can learn about language from the poet is that he uses *more* of it than we ordinarily do. In the following poem from Walt Whitman's *Song of Myself*, point out words that point more *specifically* to objects and places than vaguely generalized description could. Point out all words that are exceptionally *concrete* — words exceptionally successful in making us see, hear, and feel what the poet is trying to describe.

Stretch'd and still lies the midnight,
Two great hulls motionless on the breast of the darkness,
Our vessel riddled and slowly sinking, preparations to pass to
the one we have conquer'd,
The captain on the quarter-deck coldly giving his orders
through a countenance white as a sheet,
Near by the corpse of the child that serv'd in the cabin,
The dead face of an old salt with long white hair and care-
fully curl'd whiskers,
The flames spite of all that can be done flickering aloft and
below,
The husky voices of the two or three officers yet fit for duty,
Formless stacks of bodies and bodies by themselves, dabs of
flesh upon the masts and spars,
Cut of cordage, dangle of rigging, slight shock of the soothe
of waves,
Black and impassive guns, litter of powder-parcels, strong
scent,
A few large stars overhead, silent and mournful shining,
Delicate sniffs of sea-breeze, smells of sedgy grass and fields
by the shore, death-messages given in charges to survivors,
The hiss of the surgeon's knife, the gnawing teeth of his saw,
Wheeze, cluck, swash of falling blood, short wild scream, and
long, dull, tapering groan.
These so, these irretrievable.

EXERCISE 24 Select three of the following words. For each, write down *five* synonyms that are at the same time more specific and more concrete. For instance, for *speak* substitute verbs that point to a certain kind of speaking and at the same time make us hear the sound of it, or make us visualize the speaker.

1. speak   *2.* sing   *3.* run   *4.* noise   *5.* thin

EXERCISE 25 How good are you at recognizing the *shades of meaning* that distinguish one synonym from another? For *five* of the following groups, explain in a sentence or two what sets the words apart from one another.

1. snatch — grab — seize	*6.* pronounce — enunciate — recite
2. utter — broach — air	*7.* primitive — barbaric — crude
3. instruct — educate — train	*8.* serious — earnest — solemn
4. quick — prompt — agile	*9.* calm — serene — placid
5. squirm — fidget — writhe	*10.* tremble — sway — totter

EXERCISE 26 Select (A) or (B). Write a roughly synonymous word or phrase for the part italicized in each of the listed *idiomatic expressions:*

(A)

1. *as good as* new
2. a *good* thrashing
3. *make good* a promise
4. a coupon *good for* two dollars
5. it was all *to the good*
6. it's a *good* ten miles
7. complaining *does no good*
8. the warranty *is good for* ten years
9. the machine *is good for* another ten years
10. *good* intentions

(B)

11. a *run-of-the-mill* performance
12. we *had the run of* the ship
13. let me *run down* the facts
14. different from *the common run*
15. *run* a risk
16. there was *a run on* the bank
17. we *ran out of* gas
18. he let the illness *run its course*
19. give someone *a run for his money*
20. let's *run for it*

EXERCISE 27 For each of the following, write down three *familiar idioms* using the word.

1. heart 2. mind 3. hand 4. finger 5. track

W 2b The Broader Range

Broaden your knowledge of the vocabulary of serious discussion, always seeing new words in context and in connection with words related in history or in meaning.

To talk about art or science or political theory, we need words for distinctions, concepts, institutions. Reading a serious magazine article requires a more complex vocabulary than ordering a hamburger. Much of our formal education in effect equips us with the vocabulary of serious discussion and adult literature. A truly educated person does not use big words to give himself airs. He does not try to impress by always substituting *augment* for *grow, impediment* for *obstacle,* and *disparate* for *unlike.* Instead, he develops his grasp of the kind of language he needs to deal with statements like the following:

(Biography) The company commander was a very strict and peppery *martinet. Reserved, punctilious, impeccable,* and *severe,* he was held in the greatest awe.

(History) At the time the Constitution was being framed, Europe had rulers that can be called *benevolent despots.* Yet the founders of this nation preferred freedom to *paternalism.*

(Social Science) "Social Engineering" is a *mechanistic* concept. It deals with individuals not as *unique* beings of *diverse* gifts and *infinite* worth, but as structural units to be built into a planned society.

(Art) Nothing is as *tyrannical* as a reigning style. It is a *juggernaut* destroying everything in its path. It brushes aside former styles which were equally *imperative.*

When we check the sources of the words that thus go beyond everyday talk, we find that the great majority of them came into English from the traditional languages of education and scholarship: *Latin and Greek.* Many came to us from Latin through French, and others from the many other languages with which English has had cultural contacts. But most by far go back to Latin and Greek. To extend your command of such words, develop the following habits:

(1) *Do not study unfamiliar words in isolation but relate them to the context that helps give them meaning.* Our minds are illsuited to the retention of bit-facts, of unrelated items. Fix your attention not on the word alone, but on how it is used. Often the statement of which the word is a part furnishes important clues to its meaning. Robert Frost says, "My object in living is to unite / My *avocation* and my vocation." We gather from the context — from what surrounds the word — that *avocation* stands for

something that is not *automatically* part of one's profession or trade but is more likely *opposed* to it. *Avocation* very likely means something like "hobby" or "interest."

Here are some familiar kinds of *context clues:*

— *definition* or paraphrase that translates the word, sometimes following the word at some distance in the same sentence or paragraph:

> The influence of technology on our ways of thinking is ever more apparent to the *anthropologist* — the student of man.

— one or more *synonyms* appearing in extended discussion of the same idea:

> The fanatic commits himself wholeheartedly to an idea, *dogmatically* rejecting all questions that might lead him to change his mind. (attitude that suits a fanatic)

— one or more *examples* that point to the general idea they illustrate:

> Humanity has found it hard to escape a familiar *predicament* — too much brawn with too little brain. (something undesirable)

— details that furnish the *elements* for a definition:

> Man is a *paradox* — half dust, half spirit. (something mixed of contradictory elements)

— contrasting elements that point to their *opposite:*

> Today, even brutal dictatorships render lip service to *humanitarian* principles. (the opposite of brutal)

(2) *Try to relate unfamiliar words to familiar Latin or Greek roots. Innate* means "inborn"; the same root is used in *prenatal* ("before birth") and *native* ("someone who was born here"). Such cross-references serve us as a peg to hang a new word on; they serve us as a crutch in getting from the familiar to the new. Do not expect such associations to work as a magic key. Often the same root appears in a different *form* and is not easily recognized. Would you have recognized the idea of "being born again" in *renascent?* Often a literal translation of a Latin root does not give us the exact *meaning. Legible* does not quite mean "readable"; *eloquent*

does not quite mean "outspoken"; *manufactured* no longer means "handmade."

Here is a review of some of the more helpful Latin and Greek roots. How does knowing the root help you understand and remember the words given as examples?

LATIN

ann-, enn-	year	annual, centennial, perennial
aqu-	water	aquarium, aquatic, aqueduct
audi-	hear	audition, auditorium, inaudible
capit-	head	capital, decapitate, per capita
carn-	flesh	carnal, incarnation, carnivorous
cred-	believe	credible, credulous, credo
culp-	guilt	culpable, culprit, exculpate
curr-	run	current, concurrent, precursor
doc-	teach	doctor, docile, doctrine
duc-	lead	duct, conducive, induction
equ-	alike	equal, equitable, iniquity
fac-	make	facile, manufacture, factitious
flor-	flower	florist, flora, florid
fus-	pour	profuse, diffuse, effusive
gress-	march	progress, aggressive, retrogression
jur-	swear	juror, perjure, conjure
laps-	fall	relapse, collapse, elapse
loqu-	talk	eloquent, colloquial, colloquium
magn-	large	magnitude, magnify, magnificent
man-	hand	manual, manuscript, manicure
meter-	measure	barometer, chronometer, thermometer
min-	small	minimum, diminutive, diminish
noc-	harm	noxious, innocuous, innocent
pos-	put	compose, depose, impose
port-	carry	portage, deport, transport
prehend-	grasp	apprehend, prehensile, comprehend
rupt-	break	rupture, disrupt, interrupt
sanct-	holy	sanctuary, sanctify, sanctity
sci-	know	science, prescient, omniscience
scrib-	write	scribe, inscribe, proscribe
sec-, sequ-	follow	sequel, consequence, persecute
temp-	time	temporary, temporal, contemporary
ten-	hold	tenant, tenet, tenure
tract-	draw	extract, protracted, distract
urb-	city	urban, urbane, interurban
verb-	word	verbal, verbatim, verbiage
vit-	life	vitality, revitalize, vitamin

anthrop-	*man*	anthropology, philanthropy, misanthrope
bibli-	*book*	bibliography, bibliophile, bible
bio-	*life*	biology, biographer, antibiotic
chron-	*time*	anachronistic, synchronized, chronological
cosm-	*universe*	cosmos, cosmic, cosmopolitan
geo-	*earth*	geography, geology, geocentric
graph-	*write*	stenographer, orthography, graph
hydr-	*water*	dehydrate, hydraulic, hydroelectric
morph-	*form*	amorphous, metamorphosis, morphology
path-	*feel*	sympathy, empathy, antipathy
phil-	*friend*	philanthropy, anglophile, philosophy
phob-	*enemy*	phobia, xenophobia, anglophobe
phon-	*sound*	symphony, euphony, phonology
psych-	*mind*	psychology, psychotic, psychiatry
pyr-	*fire*	pyre, pyromaniac, pyrotechnics
sphere-	*ball*	spherical, hemisphere, atmosphere
therm-	*heat*	thermometer, thermostat, thermal

(3) *Pay attention to how familiar Latin and Greek prefixes (and suffixes) change the meaning of different roots.* It is true that a prefix like *per-* expressed a number of different relationships, not always easily recognized in the modern English word. But word study does become easier and more profitable when we habitually associate groups of words like the following:

> precursor (forerunner), predict (foretell), premonition (foreboding), resist (withstand), restrain (withhold), retreat (withdraw)

Knowing that *inter* often means "between" does provide a bridge among the words in the following group:

> interrupt, interpose, interact, interstice, interval

Here is a review of some of the more helpful Latin and Greek prefixes:

LATIN

ab-	*away*	absent, abduct, abstemious
ante-	*before*	antedate, antebellum, anterior
circum-	*around*	circumvent, circumnavigate, circumspect
co-, con-	*together*	concord, conspire, convene
contra-	*against*	contradict, contravene, contraband
de-	*down*	depose, deject, detract

dis-	apart	dissent, disperse, dismember
ex-	out of	extract, exhume, expunge
inter-	between	intercede, intervention, interval
post-	after	posterity, postscript, postmortem
pre-	before	precede, preamble, prelude
pro-	forward	progress, projection, provident
re-	back	reject, recede, regenerate
sub-	under	submerge, subjugate, subterranean
trans-	beyond	transcend, transfuse, transitory

GREEK

a-	without	ahistorical, amorphous, anonymous
anti-	against	antipathy, antidote, antithesis
auto-	self	automatic, autograph, autonomy
eu-	beautiful	euphony, eulogy, euphemism
hemi-	half	hemisphere, hemistich
hetero-	different	heterogeneous, heterodox, heterosexual
hyper-	excessive	hypercritical, hypersensitive, hyperbole
mon-	one	monarch, monogamy, monotone
ortho-	right	orthodox, orthography, orthodontics
pan-	all	panorama, panchromatic, pantheism
poly-	many	polygon, polygamy, polytheism
syn-, sym-	together	synchronize, synthesis, symposium

A few Latin *suffixes* have meanings that often help us master new words:

-cide	killer	parricide, fratricide, suicide
-esce	grow, become	coalesce, convalesce, putrescent
-fy	make	magnify, glorify, vilify

EXERCISE 28 How extensive is your command of the vocabulary of serious discussion and literature? Use the following exercise as a *diagnostic test*. The italicized words, derived from Latin or Greek, are from a short story by Mary McCarthy. After the number of each word, put the letter for the choice *closest to it in meaning*.

1. *anomalous*   a. unnamed   b. irregular   c. new
2. *interlocutor*   a. talks to one   b. investigator   c. interrupter
3. *impeccable*   a. faultless   b. speechless   c. breathless
4. *cynosure*   a. censure   b. fault   c. eye-catcher
5. *surreptitious* a. secret   b. sensitive   c. repeated
6. *cathartic*   a. heating   b. cooling   c. purging
7. *vibrant*   a. diminishing   b. vigorous   c. growing
8. *perfunctory*   a. unheard of   b. thorough   c. routine

9.	*alienated*	a. accustomed	b. estranged	c. disbanded
10.	*discretion*	a. wise choice	b. bad luck	c. intuition
11.	*compulsive*	a. repellent	b. cautious	c. obsessed
12.	*solicitude*	a. solitude	b. stubbornness	c. care
13.	*preordained*	a. chaotic	b. predestined	c. doomed
14.	*ostensible*	a. ugly	b. alleged	c. imaginary
15.	*protagonist*	a. champion	b. wanderer	c. adviser
16.	*inopportune*	a. illegal	b. unopposed	c. ill-timed
17.	*supererogatory*	a. superfluous	b. excellent	c. horrible
18.	*overt*	a. in the open	b. in the dark	c. by mistake
19.	*intrinsic*	a. absolute	b. inherent	c. dependent
20.	*conjugal*	a. daring	b. militant	c. marital

EXERCISE 29 The following words, all derived from *Latin,* are from the opening chapters of John Knowles' novel *A Separate Peace.* Select *ten.* After the number of each word, write a word or phrase that has roughly the same meaning.

1. sedate
2. perpendicular
3. tacit
4. nondescript
5. capacious
6. crucial
7. contentious
8. salient
9. detectable
10. irate
11. apprehension
12. prodigious
13. regimen
14. invincible
15. inane
16. inured
17. insidious
18. latent
19. inebriating
20. exuberant

EXERCISE 30 The following words, all derived from *Greek,* are from William Faulkner's short novel *The Bear.* After the number of each word, write a word or phrase that has roughly the same meaning.

1. anachronism
2. epitome
3. apotheosis
4. myriad
5. anonymity
6. mentor
7. stethoscope
8. archaic
9. hemisphere
10. lethargic

EXERCISE 31 After the number of each sentence, put the letter for the choice closest in meaning to the italicized word. Be prepared to explain in class how the *context of the word* helps you to understand and remember its meaning.

1. In the era of the hydrogen bomb, power politics are as *obsolete* as oxcarts on Broadway.
   a. dangerous   b. outdated   c. familiar
2. The countless patriotic speeches of World War I made many people suspicious of *grandiloquent* words.
   a. bombastic   b. new   c. indecisive
3. The Russian diplomats were jovial at the banquet but very *truculent* at the conference table.
   a. friendly   b. talkative   c. stubborn
4. The founder of the firm had been motivated not by just ordinary greed but by a monumental *rapacity*.
   a. kindness   b. pride   c. extreme greed
5. The dictator's former friends had turned into his most *implacable* enemies, rejecting all thought of compromise.
   a. unforgiving   b. unexpected   c. blameworthy
6. Frequent bombings had *obliterated* all traces of human habitation.
   a. erased   b. changed   c. accentuated
7. The men listened to the speech with a *rapt* expression, fully absorbed in the glorious vision of a better tomorrow.
   a. bored   b. doubtful   c. entranced
8. The suspect was beginning to show the effects of lack of sleep and *incessant* questioning.
   a. unceasing   b. occasional   c. infrequent
9. The pilot gingerly guided the boat through the *treacherous* waters.
   a. dangerous   b. quiet   c. deep
10. Scientific research proves previous findings false as often as it *corroborates* them and proves them true.
    a. contradicts   b. bears out   c. records

EXERCISE 32   After the number of each phrase, put the letter of the meaning that matches most closely the italicized word. Be prepared to explain in class how *context* helps guide your choice.

1. was treated with insult and *contumely*
2. ready to stop any *incipient* rebellion
3. reluctant to help his *impecunious* relatives
4. confronted with *incontrovertible* facts
5. represented a pleasure-loving, *decadent* aristocracy
6. went on to a *corollary* of his conclusion
7. pleaded for more *rapport* between employer and employee

8. smiled at my *ingenuous* remarks
9. already stiff requirements becoming more *stringent*
10. much of his music was merely *derivative*

a. just beginning
b. not original
c. deteriorating
d. contempt
e. naive

f. further implication
g. harmony
h. demanding
i. poor
j. not to be refuted

EXERCISE 33 After the number of each word, write down the meaning of the *Latin root* contained in it. Be prepared to show how it helps explain the meaning or use of the word.

1. recluse
2. pugnacious
3. onerous
4. reclaim
5. gregarious

6. pacify
7. puerile
8. succumb
9. ubiquitous
10. infallible

EXERCISE 34 After the number of each group of words, write down the meaning of the *Latin root* that they share. Be prepared to show how it helps explain the meaning or use of the words in the group.

1. conspicuous, perspicuous, introspection
2. excrescence, crescendo, crescent
3. insane, sanitation, unsanitary
4. animate, unanimous, pusillanimous
5. interlude, prelude, elude
6. verdict, contradict, predict
7. fugitive, centrifugal, refuge
8. uniform, unison, unify
9. prescribe, proscribe, conscription
10. elaborate, laborious, laboratory

EXERCISE 35 How good are you at telling apart words from Latin and Greek that are *closely related in meaning?* Choose *ten* of the following groups. In a sentence or two, explain the differences in meaning that set the words in each group apart. Be prepared to point out the role of Latin and Greek roots and prefixes that you recognize.

1. colossal — gigantic — immense
2. benign — benevolent — beneficent
3. hostile — antagonistic — recalcitrant
4. cryptic — secretive — enigmatic
5. contract — covenant — pact
6. revolution — insurrection — mutiny
7. terse — taciturn — succinct
8. fatuous — verbose — unctuous
9. fastidious — judicious — meticulous
10. ludicrous — incongruous — absurd
11. pretend — dissemble — simulate
12. regret — remorse — contrition
13. hesitate — vacillate — procrastinate
14. accompany — escort — conduct
15. relent — surrender — succumb
16. postpone — defer — suspend
17. expostulate — rebuke — repudiate
18. dismay — repugnance — revulsion
19. practical — feasible — expedient
20. reiterate — recapitulate — paraphrase

EXERCISE 36 Of the *Latin and Greek roots* listed in this section, select the five that you have most frequently found useful in your own reading and writing. For each, list three more words beyond those given as examples in this book.

EXERCISE 37 [Optional] How well can you distinguish words close enough in appearance to become *pairs and snares?* In a sentence each, indicate the difference in meaning for *five* of the following pairs.

1. fortuitous — fortunate
2. luxurious — luxuriant
3. deprecate — depreciate
4. definite — definitive
5. illustrated — illustrious
6. discrimination — recrimination
7. congenital — congenial
8. familiar — familial
9. personal — personable
10. poignant — pungent

Learn how to master and use the technical terms of a profession or field of knowledge.

Few people can work or study profitably without the ability to handle exact technical terms. A mechanic who wants to order parts must know their exact technical names. A dermatologist cannot simply say, "There is something wrong with your skin"; he must have a large and exact vocabulary for different skin conditions. A student who wants to study the history of architecture in medieval Europe must learn the names of many structural and ornamental parts of many different kinds of buildings.

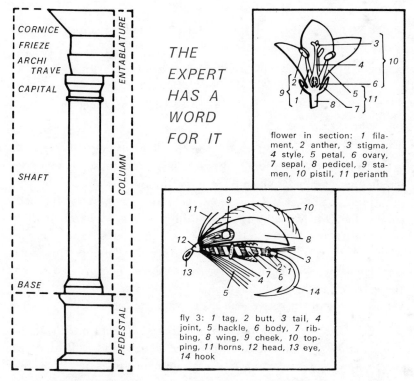

THE
EXPERT
HAS A
WORD
FOR IT

flower in section: *1* filament, *2* anther, *3* stigma, *4* style, *5* petal, *6* ovary, *7* sepal, *8* pedicel, *9* stamen, *10* pistil, *11* perianth

fly 3: *1* tag, *2* butt, *3* tail, *4* joint, *5* hackle, *6* body, *7* ribbing, *8* wing, *9* cheek, *10* topping, *11* horns, *12* head, *13* eye, *14* hook

Notice how the technical terms used in the following dictionary entry enable us to talk exactly about how a fluorescent lamp operates and is put together:

fluorescent lamp *n* : a tubular electric lamp having a coating of fluorescent material on its inner surface and containing mercury vapor whose bombardment by electrons from the cathode provides ultraviolet light which causes the material to emit visible light

fluorescent lamp: *1* anode, *2* stem press, *3* base pins, *4* exhaust tubes, *5* cathode

—*Webster's Seventh New Collegiate Dictionary*

Whenever you deal with a technical or scholarly field, you can save yourself much wasted effort by taking note of important terms and getting their exact bearings. Here are typical technical terms that you might encounter in different fields of study:

BIOLOGY: chrysalis, chromosome, microorganism, pistile, ectoplasm, thorax

MECHANICS: flywheel, inertia, fulcrum, ratchet, caliper, filament, gyroscope, crankshaft, sprocket

ARCHITECTURE: transept, cloister, portico, nave, apse, colonnade, pediment, flying buttress

To make technical terms serve you well, remember the following *cautions:*

(1) *Never use a technical term merely to impress or to parade your learning.* A mechanic uses *carburetor* because "gadget for vaporizing gasoline and mixing it with air" is too much of a mouthful. A physician uses anatomical terms for parts of the body so that he can attend to the medical problem at hand, without being distracted by the taboos that cluster around more familiar words. A botanist uses Latin terms to identify plants because their popular names often vary. In each case the person who invests the extra effort in mastering the technical terms gets something *in return* — a gain in convenience, or exactness, or efficiency.

(2) *Make your technical terms manageable and intelligible for a lay audience.* Try not to spring several new and difficult terms on them in the same sentence. Weave into your texts the definitions, explanations, and reminders that help make new terms meaningful and familiar. Can you see how in the following passage an eminent scientist *helps* the lay reader with key technical terms?

Here in the Paleocene occurred the first great radiation of the placental mammals, and among them were the earliest *primates* — the zoological order to which man himself belongs. Today, with a few unimportant exceptions, the primates are all *arboreal* in habit except man. For this reason we have tended to visualize all of our remote relatives as tree dwellers. Recent discoveries, however, have begun to alter this one-sided picture. Before the rise of the true *rodents,* the highly successful order to which present-day prairie dogs and chipmunks belong, the environment which they occupy had remained peculiarly open to exploitation. Into this zone crowded a varied assemblage of our early relatives.

—Loren Eiseley, *The Immense Journey*

EXERCISE 38 Select *ten* of the following technical terms. What *fields* do they represent? What does each term mean? Which of these would you expect a high school graduate to know?

ecology, millennium, Deuteronomy, counterpoint, fleur-de-lis, brochure, joist, analgesic, habitat, syllogism, promontory, quadruped, assizes, requiem, solstice, chiaroscuro, colophon, cornice, animism, protoplasm

EXERCISE 39 Examine the use of technical terms in the following passages adapted from magazine articles intended for the *educated general reader*. Explain all italicized words.

1. A great deal of contemporary art is incomprehensible. The personal interpretation of nature is being replaced by a private set of *ideographs,* a kind of *calligraphy,* to which the ordinary man has no key.

2. The Taj Mahal is a *mausoleum* in India erected by Shah Jehan to the memory of his favorite queen. It is *octagonal* in form; the gilt crescent at the *apex* of its dome is two hundred and seventy feet from the ground level. This mausoleum is *inlaid* with jasper, cornelian, turquoise, agate, onyx, amethysts, and sapphires. The *sarcophagus* of the sultana is in a vault directly under the center of the building. There is no part of the exterior, except the dome, that is not covered with *arabesques* and inscriptions in black marble on the polished white of the surface.

3. At the beginning, statements by the Communist students in the discussions were *polemical,* and their vocabulary was studded with phrases about imperialists and Western aggressions. They had been taught a *dialectical* mode of argument in which there were two sides, one of which was always wrong. But the defense

and *exegesis* of a "Western" point of view was difficult, since there was no clear definition of what the West included. The *simplistic* notion of a virtuous, noncolonial East and a malignant, imperialist West disintegrated under discussion.

EXERCISE 40 Technical terminology need not be dry and pedantic. The *shoptalk* of many a specialized trade is rich and colorful. Study the following sample of papermaking lingo. Where do the technical terms seem to come from? (If you can, set up a few major categories.) What makes some of these terms expressive or colorful?

Wood chips and cooking liquors are fed into the pulp mill digesters. Contents of the digester are steamed to temperature and then held there for a period during which the wood chips are converted to pulp. When the proper degree of cooking has been achieved, the blow valve is opened and the digester contents are forced out under pressure; this is known as "blowing the cook." The pulp is forced into blow pits or cyclones, and the noncombustible gases are allowed to escape — sometimes through a vomit stack.

Slush pulp needs further treatment before it can be used in papermaking; it is usually put through a knotter, over a screen and through a centricleaner to remove shives and dirt, and then is thickened on a decker. . . . Usually, several kinds of pulp are blended and this stock then passes through one or more of a series of beaters and/or refiners; one widely used refiner is called a jordan. The final mixture of materials from which paper is to be made is called the furnish.

The first part of the paper machine is the head box, a feed trough for pulp, extending across the whole machine. At the bottom of the head box is the holey roll, which keeps the furnish agitated. The slice, a narrow opening in the head box, distributes a thin stream of pulp across the Fourdrinier wire, which is the heart of papermaking; it is a continuous open mesh wire screen traveling over a long series of rolls. Pulp first strikes the wire at the breast roll; it is next carried over a series of table rolls for drainage and then over flat boxes or suction boxes, to the vacuum couch (pronounced kootch) roll, which further removes excess water.

After the couch, the wet, newly formed web of paper is transferred to the pick-up felt, which may carry it through one or more press-sections for further water removal. Then it enters the dry end of the machine, where the paper web, about 30 percent dry, weaves over a long series of drums or cans, internally heated, and finally to the calendar stack, which is a series of pressure rolls.

Testers at the dry end measure physical properties to see if the paper meets specifications. They tonk the roll with a stick to see if it is sound, and if not, slab off or cull the defective part and throw it down the broke hole.

When slab stock is made, the paper is trimmed with a guillotine, fanned for the quick count and inspected. Then, if the sheet is free of slime spots and the paper is not wormy, crushed, cockled or chain-wrinkled, it is ready for sale.

REVIEW EXERCISE   Study the italicized words in the following selection. Use your dictionary where necessary. Which of the words are *unfamiliar* to you? Find the meaning that fits the context. Which are familiar words *used in unfamiliar ways?* Make a special list of these. Which are *technical terms* of special interest to the student of language?

Pidgin is an old and *legitimate* language. Although today it is ignored, *derided,* and marked for *extinction,* still it quietly continues to gather *converts* throughout a good part of the world. Most people would be surprised to learn that Pidgin is not just a *quaint relic* of the past, or the *comic-relief* dialogue in *Terry and the Pirates,* but a language both *viable* and valuable.

To be sure, Pidgin's limited vocabulary can *engender* some *laughable* quotations, such as the oft-reprinted description of a piano by a New Guinea native: "Him fella big box, you fight him, he cry." Or the *classic* announcement by a Chinese servant that his master's prize sow had given birth to a *litter:* "Him cow pig have kittens."

But Pidgin's seemingly *imprecise* vocabulary can be almost poetic at times. There could hardly be, in any language, a friendlier definition of a friend than the Australian *aborigine's* "him brother belong me." Or consider his description of the sun: "lamp belong Jesus." Pidgin can be *forthright,* too. An *Aussie* policeman is "gubmint catchum-fella." Whiskers are "grass belong face."

The earliest recorded form of Pidgin was the *polyglot jargon* with which the *Crusaders* made themselves understood on their eleventh-century *expeditions* to the Holy Land. But the Pidgin that survives today was born on the China coast three hundred years ago. The crewmen of the merchant *vessels* and trading posts were *disinclined* to bother learning Chinese, and the Chinese saw little sense in the *involved* grammatical *locutions* of the traders' languages. They compromised by *adopting* the Westerners' words and *adapting* them to Chinese *syntax.* The resultant *goulash* became known to both parties as "business" language, or, because the closest a Chinese could come to pronouncing business was "bishin" or "bijin" — *eventually* Pidgin.

The Pidgin of the coast trade gradually became an *amalgam* of English and Portuguese words (these two nationalities being the earliest traders), of Chinese words, and a sprinkling from other languages — all of them *subtly transmuted* by the *vagaries* of pronunciation. Thus we have the word "cumshaw" — *ubiquitous* in the Orient — meaning *gratuity* or bribe or rake-off. The expression was originally "come ashore money" — a sailor's tip to the *launch* boatman. "Savvy," meaning to *comprehend*, is a *corruption* of the Portuguese *sabe*.

—from Gary Jennings, "Pidgin: No Laughing Matter"

W 3   *Meaning*

Language does not merely convey information; it carries emotion, imagination, and thought.

One basic function of language is to carry information. It is like a map that points not only to objects and people but also to events in progress, important background facts, and coming attractions. When we study the meaning of a word, we call the part that *points to something* the **denotation** of the word. Denotation is the most businesslike, the most useful, kind of meaning. When we assemble a model engine, we want the instructions to point clearly to parts that are actually there. Technical reports and how-to-do-it instructions are typically written in informative, *denotative* language.

But information is not all there is to language. When we study meaning, we find *how much else there is to language* besides straightforward information. **Semantics** is the branch of language study that explores the *different dimensions* of meaning. Here are some of the added dimensions of meaning that the semanticist must keep in mind:

(1) *Words often reflect personal preference.* Language is often less like an impersonal map than like a guide with strong personal feelings. It is as if a map kept saying "Chinese restaurant here (I

like it!)" and "Dutch family living there (never did like that kind of people)." When a man calls a house a "shack," we learn something about *how he feels* about the house. The personal attitudes suggested by a word make up its **connotation**. Most people naturally use strongly *connotative* language when talking about politics, taxes, or juvenile delinquents.

(2) *Words often have a strong imaginative element.* The word *helicopter* points directly to the thing; *whirlybird* points to the thing but at the same time makes us see it as a huge bird with whirling wings. The first word is literal; the second **figurative**. To the literal-minded person, figurative language always seems to be taking a *detour*. But when it gets to its destination, it usually does so in a more striking, a more telling way than literal language can. The most memorable writers are those who like William Blake naturally use a figurative style, always exploiting striking comparisons and analogies:

> Prudence is a rich, ugly old maid courted by Incapacity.
> The tigers of wrath are wiser than the horses of instruction.

(3) *Words often reflect the way we sort out and interpret experience.* The word *mammal* is not the name of any real animal we can point to. It stands for a *logical category* that zoologists have made up. If we compare experience to a large, well-stocked museum, only part of our language points to the actual exhibits. Much of our language provides the rooms and shelves and pigeonholes that we need to keep the exhibits in an intelligible order. The farther away this sorting process takes us from first-hand experience, the more **abstract** our words become. *Justice* is a large abstraction, providing us with a shelf on which we find many familiar and some unexpected exhibits. Of such abstractions we soon learn to ask: What range of phenomena is this term supposed to cover? How useful is this classification?

W 3a Connotative Words

Use words in full awareness of their overtones and connotations.

Language conveys feelings as well as information. *Robert* and *Bobby* refer to the same person, but they express a different *atti-*

tude; they imply a different *relationship.* Some words are affectionate; some are contemptuous. We call what the word stands for its denotation; we call the attitude it implies its **connotation.** The most important distinction is between attitudes of approval and disapproval, between favorable and unfavorable connotations.

A good dictionary shows that language *judges as well as reports. Project,* as a synonym of *plan,* tends to imply approval or admiration. Other synonyms, like *scheme,* tend to imply disapproval or opposition:

> **SYN.—plan** refers to any detailed method, formulated beforehand, for doing or making something (vacation *plans*); **design** stresses the final outcome of a plan and implies the use of skill or craft, sometimes in an unfavorable sense, in executing or arranging this (it was his *design* to separate us); **project** implies the use of enterprise or imagination in formulating an ambitious or extensive plan (they've begun work on the housing *project*); **scheme,** a less definite term than the preceding, often connotes either an impractical, visionary plan or an underhand intrigue (a *scheme* to embezzle the funds).

> *—Webster's New World Dictionary*

Of a whole battery of synonyms, few may turn out to be neutral:

FAVORABLE:	chuckle, smile, guffaw
UNFAVORABLE:	snicker, cackle, smirk
FAVORABLE:	lad, youngster, youth
UNFAVORABLE:	brat, juvenile, punk
FAVORABLE:	firm, resolute, resolved, determined
UNFAVORABLE:	stubborn, dogmatic, obstinate, doctrinaire

An effective speaker or writer is sensitive to connotations the way a first-rate cook is sensitive to differences in flavor, or the way a painter is sensitive to shades and hues. He is aware not only of the judgments that words imply, but also of the whole *range of associations* that determine our reactions:

> We take Cunning for a sinister or crooked wisdom. And certainly there is a great difference between a cunning man and a wise man, not only in point of honesty, but in point of ability. (Sir Francis Bacon)

> *Reputation, prestige,* and *esteem* seem hardly fitting as synonyms of *honor,* despite what the dictionary says, for they don't seem to carry the gilt edge that brightens the word "Honor." (Student paper)

When you are saying that someone is a "civil" man you are not merely saying that he is polite. You are saying that this polite and thoughtful man, aware of his own rights and dignity, and the rights and dignity of others, is a good citizen. Civility means good citizenship, for *civic, civil,* and *civilization* come from the same Latin root. Our ancestors, therefore, meant that decent manners are a requirement of decent citizenship, and so one of the cornerstones of civilization.

In studying the connotations of words, remember the following points:

(1) *Different meanings of the same word may carry different connotations.* The word *discriminate* is an unfavorable term when a social scientist applies it to biased, unfair behavior. It is a favorable term when it is used by an art critic to mean "be discerning, make fine distinctions." The favorable meaning is used in expressions like "I wish he would be more *discriminating* in his choice of ties."

(2) *The same word may have different connotations in different contexts.* The word *wise* is favorable in "wise man" but unfavorable in the slang term "wise guy." We have different attitudes toward the smartness in "smart move" and "smart aleck." Notice that the word *style* suggests admiration in some contexts but not in others:

NEUTRAL: American cars are known for their frequently changing *styles.*

FAVORABLE: This car really has *style.*

(3) *The connotations of a word may differ for different audiences.* To the ordinary city-dweller, *primitive* implies a deplorable lack of modern conveniences and refinements. But to many lovers of modern art (and to many nature lovers), *primitive* implies something powerful, genuine, or unspoiled

(4) *Often, the connotations of a word have changed during its history.* We now apply *artificial* mainly to things we reject, but it once meant "done with great art or skill." A *natural* once was someone raw and unpolished, an idiot. Here are some words to watch for in reading the literature of earlier periods:

sanctimonious	Today, the word points the finger at insincere or overdone, unctuous piety. But Prospero in Shakespeare's *Tempest* solemnly speaks of the "sanctimonious ceremonies" or *holy* rites of marriage for his daughter.
suburb	Today, suburban living is associated with affluence and leisure. But in Shakespeare's time, the suburbs were often the most *disreputable* parts of town:

Dwell I but in the *suburbs*
Of your good pleasure? If it be no more,
Portia is Brutus' harlot, not his wife.

(*Julius Caesar*, Act II, Sc. 1)

fellow	*Fellow* was often used to imply a *low,* common person:

Worth makes the man, and want of it the *fellow*.

(Alexander Pope)

Your use of connotative words tests your command of language in two important ways:

— How good is your *ear* for language? If you have a good ear for words, you will avoid sentences like the following, where the connotations of important words clash with the intended meaning:

In the past, I always *looked forward* to my English classes with regret.
He has *subjected* us to many profitable hours of lecture and discussion.

— How sensitive are you to the reactions of your *audience?* A word with offensive connotations, thoughtlessly used, can undo the good done by an eloquent speech. Contemptuous terms for nationalities or races will alienate not only the groups involved but also outsiders of good will. Do you remember incidents where you have seen this happen?

The feelings stirred up by words can range from mild amusement to black destructive anger. Awareness of the connotations of words gives us a proper respect for the power of words for good, and for evil.

EXERCISE 41 In each of the following pairs, one word clearly implies an unfavorable judgment. After the number of each pair, put the letter for the more *negative* term. Be prepared to discuss the full implications of both terms in class.

1. (a) colorful   (b) gaudy
2. (a) impetuous   (b) rash
3. (a) gloat   (b) rejoice
4. (a) worship   (b) idolatry
5. (a) appeasing   (b) conciliatory
6. (a) blustering   (b) assertive
7. (a) obedient   (b) obsequious
8. (a) do-gooder   (b) humanitarian
9. (a) attentive   (b) officious
10. (a) ogle   (b) stare

EXERCISE 42   In each of the following pairs, which is the *stronger* word? After the number of the pair, put the letter for the stronger or more emphatic term. Be prepared to explain what the stronger word adds to the meaning it shares with the weaker one. (Your classmates may disagree with you on the connotations of some of these terms.)

1. (a) suffering   (b) agony
2. (a) threat   (b) menace
3. (a) triumph   (b) victory
4. (a) savage   (b) wild
5. (a) old   (b) ancient
6. (a) gigantic   (b) big
7. (a) terror   (b) fear
8. (a) dried out   (b) parched
9. (a) fertile   (b) prolific
10. (a) warped   (b) twisted

EXERCISE 43   How do the synonyms in each of the following groups *differ in connotation?* Be prepared to discuss fully the reactions people might typically have to the different words in each group. (Your teacher may ask you to select *three* of these groups and write a paragraph about each.)

1. intelligent — clever — shrewd — sly
2. vagrant — drifter — wanderer — bum
3. secret — furtive — discreet — underhanded
4. coddle — spoil — pamper — humor

5. gossip — chatterbox — tattletale — blabbermouth
6. eccentric — character — oddball — crank
7. forthright — blunt — brazen — bluff
8. filch — steal — pilfer — loot
9. gang — peer group — clique — club
10. fashion — fad — vogue — craze

EXERCISE 44 [Optional] Explore as fully as you can the differences in connotation between the members of each pair:

human—humane; female—feminine; male—masculine; mother—matron; womanly—womanish; manly—mannish; childish—childlike; catty—kittenish; rural—rustic; ancient—antique

EXERCISE 45 Study the following poem by John Masefield. For which of the italicized words or phrases in the poem can you find a possible synonym with a *different* connotation? How, in the poem as a whole, does the poet make *familiar* connotations serve his purpose? Where does he go *counter* to established connotations?

A Consecration

Not of the princes and *prelates* with *periwigged* charioteers
Riding triumphantly *laureled* to *lap* the *fat of the years,* —
Rather the scorned — the rejected — the men hemmed in with the
     spears;

The men of the *tattered* battalion which fights till it dies,
Dazed with the dust of the battle, the *din* and the cries,
The men with the broken heads and the blood running into their eyes.

Not the *be-medaled* Commander, beloved of the throne,
Riding *cock-horse* to parade when the *bugles* are blown,
But the *lads* who carried the koppie and cannot be known.

Not the ruler for me, but the ranker, the *tramp* of the road,
The *slave* with the sack on his shoulders pricked on with the goad,
The man with too weighty a *burden,* too weary a load.

The sailor, the stoker of steamers, the man with the clout,
The chantyman bent at the halliards putting a tune to the shout,
The drowsy man at the wheel and the tired look-out.

Others may sing of the wine and the wealth and the *mirth,*
The *portly* presence of *potentates* goodly in girth; —
Mine be the dirt and the *dross,* the dust and *scum of the earth!*

Theirs be the music, the colour, the glory, the gold;
Mine be a handful of ashes, a mouthful of mould.
Of the *maimed,* of the halt and the blind in the rain and the cold —
Of these shall my songs be fashioned, my tales be told.

—John Masefield, *Poems*

W 3b Figurative Words

Exploit the resources and avoid the pitfalls of figurative language.

Figurative language conveys meaning *by comparison.* When we run out of words for different shapes, we say what a shape is *similar to:* "pear-shaped," "oval" (egg-shaped). When we say that a speaker "echoes" Thomas Jefferson, we use the *analogy* between words coming back to us from a mountain and words coming back from someone who has read them in a book. Literally, we uproot trees; figuratively, we uproot people, or traditions.

Far from being the special property of poets, figurative words are a basic feature of all language. Everyday language is shot through with *familiar figurative expressions* for ideas like the following:

to get by, survive	keep one's head above water; keep the wolf from the door; ride out the storm; save one's skin; pull through; fall on one's feet; roll with the punches; squeeze by
to be successful	find a place in the sun; have arrived; be in; strike it rich; have got it made

Much of our more formal vocabulary preserves *buried figurative expressions* that no longer bring to mind the original comparison:

accumulate	"put in a heap"
arrive	"come to shore"
assuage	"to make sweeter"
bias	"a sloping surface, inclined to one side"
egregious	"standing out from the herd"
recalcitrant	"one who kicks"

Occasionally, we read a passage that graphically reminds us of the original figurative meaning of a familiar expression:

Having reached the camp, about ten o'clock, we kindled our fire and went to bed. . . . We had first rolled up a large log some eighteen inches through and ten feet long, for a *backlog,* to last all night, and then piled on the trees to the height of three or four feet, no matter how green or damp.

(Thoreau)

The following *kinds of figurative language* each extend the reach of language in a somewhat different way:

SIMILE — a short comparison that *explicitly* compares one thing to another. It often uses words like *like, as if,* or *as though:*

The evening air was pale and chilly and after every charge and thud of the footballers the greasy leather orb flew *like a heavy bird* through the grey light.   (James Joyce)

METAPHOR — a compressed comparison actually *substituting* one thing for another. It lets the reader or listener make the necessary translation from the figurative to the literal:

In the changing *skies* of our republic some *stars* will set, while other *lights* seen to be *planets* will glow more brightly as the heavens become bare around them. (literally not about *stars* but about political *leaders*)

ALLUSION — a compressed reference to something in *history, legend, or mythology.* It asks the listener or reader to work out for himself the implied parallel:

met his Waterloo   (after a promising career was finally decisively defeated, like Napoleon at the battle of Waterloo in 1815)

won a Pyrrhic victory   (gained victory at an excessive cost leading to later defeat, like the Greek king Pyrrhus in fighting the Romans in the third century B.C.)

SYMBOL — something specific that acquires a more *general significance,* standing as one representative example for many similar cases:

Expect poison from the standing water.   (William Blake)

Figurative words add tremendously to the *power of language,* since they speak not just to our intellect but to the whole of our personality:

(1) Figurative language *extends our command over shades of meaning,* allowing us to say much with few words. Notice the *implications* carried by some of the figurative synonyms of the literal term *center:*

core (we get to it by clearing away less important matter)
hub (everything revolves around it)
heart (tremendously powerful and precious, the center of life)

(2) Figurative language *speaks directly to our senses.* It gives life and body to ideas, making us visualize what normally we only think. The following passage gives us a more immediate picture of the stock market before the great crash than any literal description could:

> The market was *like a wild river* that year, *breaking through all the dams* of prudence and common sense.
>
> (John P. Marquand)

(3) Figurative language directly *speaks to our feelings;* it makes us share in attitudes and emotions. How would you describe the feelings communicated by the following passage?

> Keep me as the *apple of the eye,* hide me under the *shadow of thy wings,* from the wicked that oppress me.
>
> (Psalms)

(4) Figurative language *serves as an aid to thought.* An illuminating analogy often makes us realize things we had previously ignored. When someone speaks of "the *ocean* of air," we are made to see how air surrounds us everywhere, that without it we are like fish out of water.

To make figurative language serve you well, remember the following *cautions:*

— For figurative language to be effective, the implied *analogy must fit:*

APT: Beneath the thick crust of our actions, the heart of the child remains unchanged. (A crust may indeed build up gradually without destroying what is underneath.)

INEPT: Education provides the foundation upon which an individual is to be built. (Education *develops* an individual who already exists, who is not really built *after* education provides a foundation.)

— Several *analogies should reinforce each other,* whereas in a **mixed metaphor** they tend to cancel each other out:

CONSISTENT: Legends are the slowly perfected fruit from a shoot of imagination grafted onto a tree of fact. (The tree, the shoot, and the fruit are all part of the same **sustained metaphor.**)

MIXED: He decided not to fall for the bait of easy money the way his father had. (Fish do not *fall* for bait but *rise* to it.)

— *Fresh analogies command attention,* whereas **clichés** have lost their original humorous or dramatic quality as the result of too frequent repetition:

FRESH: A platitude is a jellyfish withering on the shore of the sea of thought. (Ambrose Bierce)

All poetry is dipped in the dyes of the heart. (Edith Sitwell)

TRITE: He came from the *wrong side of the tracks.*
We looked at it with a *jaundiced eye.*
I intend to make it *crystal clear.*
He rode into office on the President's *coattails.*
Everyone left in a *mad rush.*

EXERCISE 46 In one sentence each, explain the *origin* of *five* of the following figurative expressions:

dark horse, a jerkwater town, jackpot, an unfrocked priest, give short shrift, hamstring someone, a sounding board, in the doldrums, get the hang of it, hue and cry

EXERCISE 47 Modern American English uses many *sports metaphors* from football or baseball: *fumble the ball, be off base, strike out.* Which older or less familiar sports and games are represented by the following figurative expressions? What is their meaning?

allure, there's the rub, checkmate, crestfallen, retrieve, worry, foible, haggard, gambit, pawn

EXERCISE 48 What are the *symbolic associations* of common colors? Collect as many common expressions using major colors as you can, for instance *white lie, white elephant, blue mood, greenhorn, see red.* Interpret and present your findings. (Your teacher will tell you whether to present your material in a short paper or as an oral report.)

EXERCISE 49 In one sentence each, explain *five* of the following *allusions:*

tantalize, Trojan horse, tilting at windmills, Achilles' heel, Cassandra-like warnings, send to Coventry, Spartan simplicity, Procrustean methods, play Cupid, sell down the river

EXERCISE 50 Investigate the metaphorical uses made in *everday language* of one major area of experience. For instance, investigate expressions making metaphorical use of animals (to strain at a *gnat*), or of sailing (walk the plank), or of parts of the body (be all *ear*). Present your findings in a short paper or as an oral report.

EXERCISE 51 Evaluate the use of figurative language in the following passages. After the number of each passage, put the appropriate abbreviations: *E* for effective; *M* for mixed metaphor; *T* for too trite. Be prepared to defend your choices in class.

1. Poems are peculiar plants, and nobody knows much about what makes them germinate.
2. The man I love will have to realize that life is more than peaches and cream.
3. The medical field has climbed from the very bottom to make it what it is today.
4. There must come a time, in every generation, when those who are older secretly get off the train of progress, willing to walk back to where they came from, if they can find the way.

    (Eric Sevareid)
5. A theme topic that might die on its feet in the wrong circumstances may catch fire when assigned at the right time.
6. Some students are content with a college that offers an assembly-line education, with the student at the end stamped "B.A., certified fit for corporate consumption."
7. Any student who wants to succeed will have to burn the midnight oil.
8. Teachers who rely on classic comics to acquaint students with great writers are using a sugar-coated crutch.
9. The function of witty women has always been to prick the balloon of masculine self-inflation.
10. He plunged into the course with vigor and interest as the portal to a life's career.

EXERCISE 52 Rewrite each sentence, using figurative language. Express the same idea more *concretely,* more *forcefully,* or more *dra-*

matically. Make sure the rewritten sentence makes the reader visualize a real day, a real rain, a real person. To make your examples convincing, try not to *strain* for effect — avoid "putting it on too thick."

EXAMPLES: The sailboat moved very slowly.
The sailboat was fanned along by the faintest of breezes.
A heavy rain began to fall.
The rain came down like a solid sheet of water.

1. It was very hot.
2. He worked hard washing dishes in a restaurant.
3. It was an exceptionally dark night.
4. A strong wind made the treetops move back and forth.
5. The old man ran down the street as fast as he could.
6. The train went noisily through the tunnel.
7. I spent hours studying for the exam.
8. The newcomer acted stand-offish.
9. There was snow everywhere.
10. By and large, Americans enjoy freedom of speech.

EXERCISE 53 [Optional] Discuss as fully as you can the use of figurative language in the following passages. How apt, how consistent, how fresh are the figurative expressions used? How fully can you trace their implications, and their probable effect on the reader?

1. Only once do I remember my father having breathed a word of complaint about his fortunes to me, and that for a passing moment. Only once did he lift his visor in my sight.
(Sir Winston Churchill)

2. Words may be likened to checks drawn on a bank, worth nothing as paper, but valuable insofar as they represent cash in the bank. Words are "cashed" when we are directed to the things and events they stand for. (Lionel Ruby)

3. If General Grant was not the great man so many thought, he was a native growth from American soil, endowed like his age with a dogged will and a plodding energy, and he gave his country what he had. Though the branches of the tree were ungainly and offered too hospitable shelter to unseemly birds of the night, the gnarly trunk was sound at the heart. (Vernon Louis Parrington)

4. The language of the street is always strong. What can describe the folly and emptiness of scolding like the word *jawing*? . . . And I confess to some pleasure from the stinging

rhetoric of a rattling oath in the mouths of truckmen and teamsters. How laconic and brisk it is by the side of a page of the *North American Review*. Cut these words and they would bleed; they are vascular and alive; they walk and run.

(Emerson)

W 3c   Abstract Words

Learn to give body to abstract terms, and to limit their scope.

Language helps us find our way in our environment. **Specific** words do so by giving us the name and address of actual things and events: "the second large elm as you come down Vine Street from the corner of Market"; "the big shark Jim caught off the coast of California in September." **Abstract** words help us sort out the innumerable specific things we observe into logical categories. The more comprehensive the category, the more abstract the word. The most specific words are proper names, which actually identify a single individual. The most abstract words are words like *time* and *life,* which cover a tremendous amount of ground.

Here are some related words, going from the specific toward the more and more abstract:

Rover — terrier — dog — mammal — vertebrate — animal — life
Jim — neighbor — Southerner — American — man — primate

Our use of abstractions shows how skillful we are in sorting out the things in the world around us. When they are unskillfully used, abstract words are a poor guide. Language is like a well-stocked library displaying on innumerable shelves the treasures of experience. Abstract words serve us as a cataloguing and numbering system that works well only part of the time. Here are some familiar *shortcomings of abstract language:*

— Abstract terms often *overlap.* There is often no clear demarcation between adjoining shelves. Scientists take pains to *limit* their classifications. A whale for instance is an aquatic animal propelling itself by a caudal fin. But whale is excluded from the scientific definition of *fish,* since it breathes and reproduces like a mammal. In ordinary language, the demarcations are often less exact. Is "wit" more or less the same as "sense of humor"? Or is it true, as one writer said, that "wit is a lean creature with sharp inquiring nose, whereas humor has a kindly eye and comfortable girth"?

— Abstract terms *differ in meaning from user to user.* What the word *moral* means depends on the ethical standards of the person who uses it. To the military man, killing the enemy is a moral duty. To the pacifist, it is a moral duty *not* to kill. To one person, it may seem "fair" that students doing poorly should get *additional* help. To another person, "fair treatment" means that everyone should have an exactly *equal* amount of assistance.

— Abstract terms sometimes *stand for nothing* clearly discernible in the world of experience. They direct us to an empty shelf. For a long time, the word *instinct* was used as a catchall term to describe what guided migratory birds, or what guided the bat in flight between wires strung in a darkened room. In the case of the bat, the real guidance system turned out to be a kind of "sonar" similar to radar. The bat uses sound waves bouncing back from obstacles in its path to guide it in its flight.

To keep abstract language from becoming arbitrary or misleading, we have to *anchor it firmly to firsthand experience.* Abstract words are powerful devices for organizing reality, but they do poorly on their own. An undeveloped abstraction is like a head without a body, like a general staff without troops.

Try the following to give visible body and shape to ideas — in other words, to *make the abstract concrete:*

(1) Make it a habit to follow up a general statement with a *specific example:*

ABSTRACT: Gang members find it hard to accept the traditional *recreation* offered by community agencies.

SPECIFIC: They find it more exciting to roam the streets than to *play Ping-Pong* at a Youth Center.

(2) Provide the *detailed elaboration* that shows what an idea means in practice:

ABSTRACT: Without his creative intelligence, man would still be at his most *primitive* level of development.

DETAILED: He would be no more than a species of primate *living on seeds, fruit, roots, and uncooked flesh, and wandering naked through the woods and over the plains like a chimpanzee.*

(3) Use a striking *figurative analogy* to make an abstract idea graphic and immediately clear:

ABSTRACT: His writing deliberately avoids the obvious and makes a cult of *subtlety.*

FIGURATIVE: He is too ready to throw aside in contempt the valuable haystack *in a fine search for a paltry needle.*

(4) Use a *relevant quotation* to show what an idea has meant in the life of an actual person:

ABSTRACT: Typically, even a great artist's motives are partly *disinterested* and partly *commercial.*

AUTHENTIC: As Mahalia Jackson once said, "I've been singing now for almost forty years, and most of the time I've been *singing for my supper* as well as *for the Lord.*"

(See also the section on "Definition" in Chapter Four, "Composition.")

EXERCISE 54 How competently is the italicized abstract word handled in each of the following passages? Have the pitfalls of abstract language been avoided? What has been done to anchor the term to firsthand experience?

1. Consumer research has revealed the *complexity* of the buyer's motives rather than conscious hypocrisy. People say that they want sensible cars "just for transportation," but they buy glamorous cars that make them feel adventurous.

2. Nature administers impartial *justice.* The strong and determined triumph; the incompetent are weeded out.

3. To do something really well, a person must be guided at least in part by *disinterested* motives. Hemingway once said: "There are bullfighters who do it just for the money — they are worthless. The only one who matters is the bullfighter who feels it, so that if he did it for nothing, he would do it as well."

4. Nineteenth-century America believed in *individualism.* If everyone would get on with his particular job, the hidden hand would take care of the universal harmony.

5. The appointment of women to cabinet positions is long overdue. This way the government will profit from women's *intuition.*

6. The ethical requirements of great religious movements are often too rigid for the ordinary person. *Abstinence* is a good thing when practiced in moderation.

7. *Individualism* was the belief that everyone should paddle his own canoe, especially on the high seas.

8. *Loyalty* means an unconditional commitment. People temperamentally inclined to question and to criticize cannot be really loyal.

9. Mr. Fitzhugh is an *authority* on Greece, having given a slide lecture on his recent trip there to several local clubs.

10. Television *glorifies* the glamorous bully. It makes mama-loving Robin Hoods out of such murderous devils as Jesse and Frank James, and obnoxious gunmen of usually decent officers.

EXERCISE 55 Use each of the following abstract terms *in a sentence* in which you anchor it to concrete experience. Employ different possible means of giving body and shape to an abstract idea: *public spirit, integrity, creativity, dedication, loyalty.*

EXERCISE 56 Select three short passages in which a *speaker or writer* seems exceptionally successful in giving concrete meaning to a familiar abstract idea. Be prepared to present and discuss these passages in class.

W 4 Effective Diction

An effective user of the language knows how to be brief, blunt, and direct.

The effective speaker or writer enjoys the changing spectacle of language, but he also knows how to *put language to work.* He knows how to choose the words that will do the job. Rather than using words to impress, he uses them to make a point. Rather than become entangled in words, he uses them to convey forcefully his intended meaning.

Use the following advice as a guide to effective **diction,** that is, effective word choice:

(1) *Use words economically.* One accurate word is better than two woolly ones. Much wordiness is the result of **padding,** of words used without conviction in hopes of filling an empty space:

Verbs greatly contribute to the meaning of the English language.

The automobile is here to stay.

Unnecessary duplication of words is **redundancy:** "Forward progress" is redundant, because it is not possible to make *backward* progress. "Basic essentials" is redundant, because what is basic is *always* essential. Can you see what makes for wordiness in the following?

REDUNDANT: All of a sudden it happened overnight.

REDUNDANT: The average voter is usually not interested in economics.

REDUNDANT: Physical education develops one's physical body control and coordination.

(2) *Use words no bigger than your subject.* The use of big words for trivial things is **jargon.** Jargon results when someone tries to impress us by always using the longer, the more technical, the more scholarly word. Use technical words where they are necessary, but fight the temptation to use a fancy word when a plain one will do:

FANCY	PLAIN	FANCY	PLAIN
conceptualize	think	methodology	method
anomalous	strange	hypothesize	guess
implement	put in effect	effectuate	bring about
escalate	step up	ambivalent	contradictory
dichotomy	split	epiphany	revelation

Practice trimming pretentious statements down to size by translating them into plain English:

JARGON: Debating *polarizes* a class into *dichotomized* groups for the exploration of *discussable* issues.

PLAIN ENGLISH: Debating splits a class into opposing groups for discussion.

JARGON: It is *imperative* that nursing *personnel* be offered improved *monetary incentives.*

PLAIN ENGLISH: We should give nurses more money.

(3) *When necessary, be blunt and direct.* It is true that sometimes we have to gloss things over in order to be tactful. We have to evade a direct question in order to be kind. There is something

brutal and final about the word *crippled;* there is something encouraging, as well as an implied promise to be of assistance, in the word *handicapped.* But we merely trick ourselves and others if we always use beautiful words for ugly things. Pretty words for not so pretty things are **euphemisms.**

Do you recognize some of the following euphemisms?

EUPHEMISM	BLUNT
low-income group	poor
senior citizens	the aged
long illness	cancer
problem child	troublemaker
be ill	vomit
financial trouble	bankruptcy
mortuary	funeral home

When language becomes too elaborate, too fancy, too roundabout, it becomes a barrier between you and your audience. Learn to ask yourself periodically: What exactly am I trying to say?

EXERCISE 57 What exactly is each of the following sentences trying to say? Rewrite each sentence in *plain English.* Be prepared to explain what made the sentence wordy, pretentious, or roundabout.

1. The amount of exercise engaged in by an individual is determined by the cultural group with which he is associated.
2. John is inclined to take the property of others without permission and tends to stretch the truth.
3. Modern mountain climbers plan walks that are not commensurate with their stamina.
4. Bad behavior pertaining to hospitality was shown against Odysseus.
5. During my childhood years, I was not physically well coordinated.
6. A youth may feel severity of depression at being scorned because his tie is not of the latest fashion.
7. After a smoke, I usually berate myself for having so indulged.
8. The purpose of taking the life of a criminal is aimed at deterring others from the commission of the crime.
9. My projected employment as a gardener did not materialize, as we could not agree on a suitable remuneration.
10. Children in compacted urban areas are in dire need of improved educational opportunities.

EXERCISE 58 There are various ways in which language can come between the writer and his audience. In each of the following passages, what *distracts* the reader from the subject at hand? Be prepared to discuss each passage in detail.

1. The last chapter of the book is an illogical finale to a story whose whole modus operandi was tragedy. The hero's outcome could not possibly reach so blissful a conclusion. He was a member of the quintuplet whose fate could end in nothing less than despair.

2. From angels through witches, women have been at home in the air for millenniums! And now, for milady's eyes only, X Airlines offers Plane & Fancy — 62 pages of timely travel information for women on the go, written by women in the know! Here you'll find travel bits and tidbits ranging from dreams to schemes, tots to tipping, weights to wardrobes — plus pertinent pointers on planning, packing, proposals, pets, and pallet pampering.

3. I finally left my boon companions to return to my humble abode, for I had to rise bright and early the next A.M. to return to the pursuit of filthy lucre, earning the coin of the realm necessary to the obtaining of life's necessities.

EXERCISE 59 [Optional] In a dictionary of usage, find an article dealing with a major obstacle to effective diction. Consult H. W. Fowler, *Modern English Usage,* or one of its recent adaptations; Evans and Evans, *A Dictionary of Contemporary American Usage;* Strunk and White, *The Elements of Style;* or a similar authoritative guide to effective style. Choose a problem of diction for which you can find examples in current American English. Prepare a report in which you discuss the problem you have chosen, adding examples from your own current listening and reading. (Your teacher will tell you whether to present your findings in a short paper or as an oral report.)

FURTHER STUDY: English Literature

The reading of imaginative literature truly tests our knowledge of our mother tongue. The poetry of Shakespeare and Milton takes us back to early forms of Modern English, impressing on us the shifts in vocabulary and meaning that have occurred over the centuries. The novels of Charles Dickens and Thomas Hardy take us into an everyday world remote in time and space, with its own vocabulary of politics and business, its own shoptalk and small talk. But above all, the great poet, novelist, or playwright is a *master* of language. He exploits its full range. He mobilizes its potential for nuance, for allusion, for metaphorical implication.

The following assignments will lead you to explore the range of words, and of word uses, that awaits the American reader of English literature.

Assignment 1 How far can you go back in the history of our language and still read and understand what you find? The following passage is from the *fifteenth century* — part of Sir Thomas Malory's retelling of the stories of King Arthur and the Knights of the Round Table. What difficulties does its vocabulary offer to the modern reader? Pay special attention to the italicized words: Some are French words that had recently come into English at this stage of the language. Some are English words that have since dropped out of use. (Note that modern *i* is here often spelled *y;* modern *o* is sometimes spelled *oo.*)

> And never was there seen a more *doolfuller bataylle in* no crysten londe. For there was but russhyng and rydyng, fewnyng and strykyng, and many a grymme worde was there spoken eyder to other, and many a dedely stroke. But ever kyng Arthur rode thorughoute the bataylle of syr Mordred many tymes and dyd ful nobly as a *noble* kyng shold, and at al tymes he faynted never; and syr Mordred that day put hym in *devoyr* and in grete *perylle.* And thus they faughte alle the longe day and never *stynted* tyl the noble knyghtes were layed to the colde erthe; and ever they faught stylle tyl it was nere nyghte, and by that tyme was there an hondred thousand layed deed upon the *down.* Thenne was Arthur *wode wrothe* oute of *mesure,* whan he sawe his peple so slayn from hym. Thenne the kyng loked a-boute hym, and thenne was he *ware* of al hys *hoost* and of al his good knyghtes were lefte no moo *on lyve* but two knyghtes; that one was syr Lucan de Butlere, and his broder, syr Bedwere. And they were *ful sore* wounded. "Jhesu mercy," sayd the kyng, "where are al my noble knyghtes *becomen?* Alas, that ever I shold see thys dolefull day, for now," sayd Arthur, "I am come to myn ende."   —Sir Thomas Malory

Assignment 2 Much nineteenth-century English poetry and fiction takes us to a *rural setting* not yet changed by mechanization. The farmer still plows and sows and harvests according to a centuries-old rhythm. In the following passages, explain all terms that have become strange for the modern city dweller.

LANGUAGE HAS A HISTORY

LATIN
The Arch of Titus in the Roman Forum (Alinari)

SANSCRIT
Babylonian Cylinder proclaiming
the rebuilding of the temple of
the sun god
(Metropolitan Museum of Art)

EGYPTIAN
Egyptian hieroglyphics
(WHO photo by Paul Almasy)

GREEK
A funeral stone in the National
Museum, Athens (Alinari)

1. Who hath not seen thee oft amid thy store?
     Sometimes whoever seeks abroad may find
   Thee sitting careless on a granary floor,
     Thy hair soft-lifted by the winnowing wind;
   Or on a half-reaped furrow sound asleep,
     Drowsed with the fume of poppies, while thy hook
       Spares the next swath and all its twinéd flowers:
   And sometime like a gleaner thou dost keep
     Steady thy laden head across a brook;
     Or by a cider-press, with patient look,
       Thou watchest the last oozings, hours by hours.

                              —John Keats, "To Autumn"

2. The agricultural and pastoral character of the people
   upon whom the town depended for its existence was shown by
   the class of objects displayed in the shop windows. Scythes,
   reap-hooks, sheep-shears, bill-hooks, spades, mattocks, and
   hoes at the ironmonger's; beehives, butter-firkins, churns,
   milking stools and pails, hay-rakes, field-flagons, and seed-lips
   at the cooper's; cart-ropes and plough-harness at the saddler's;
   carts, wheel-barrows, and mill-gear at the wheelwright's and
   machinist's; horse-embrocations at the chemist's; at the glov-
   er's and leather-cutter's, hedging-gloves, thatcher's knee-caps,
   ploughman's leggings, villager's pattens and clogs.

                    —Thomas Hardy, *The Mayor of Casterbridge*

Assignment 3 The following passages are examples of literary
English through the centuries. Examine the italicized words and other
words that might cause difficulty for the modern reader. Pay special
attention to *familiar words used in unfamiliar ways.*

1. When the right virtuous Edward Wotton and I were at
   the Emperor's Court together, we *gave* ourselves *to* learn
   horsemanship of John Pietro Pugliano, one that with great
   commendation had the place of an *esquire* in his stable. And
   he, according to the fertileness of the Italian *wit,* did not only
   afford us the demonstration of his practice, but sought to en-
   rich our minds with the contemplations *therein* which he
   thought most precious. But with none I remember mine ears
   were at any time more *loaden,* than when (either angered
   with slow payment, or moved with our learner-like *admiration*) he exercised his speech in the praise of his *faculty.*
   He said, soldiers were the noblest *estate* of mankind, and
   horsemen the noblest of soldiers. He said they were the
   masters of war and ornaments of peace; speedy goers and

strong *abiders;* triumphers both in camps and courts. *Nay,*
to so unbelieved a point he proceeded, as that no earthly
thing bred such *wonder* to a prince as to be a good horseman.
                    —Sir Philip Sidney, *An Apology for Poetry* (1595)

2. And be not jealous on me, *gentle* Brutus:
Were I a common *laughter,* or did use
To *stale* with ordinary oaths my love
To every new *protester,* if you know
That I do fawn on men and hug them hard,
And after *scandal* them; or if you know
That I *profess* myself in banqueting
To all the *rout,* then *hold* me dangerous.
                    —Shakespeare, *Julius Caesar,* Act I, Sc. 2 (1599)

3.   Having pursued the history of a pun, from its original to
its downfall, I shall here define it to be a *conceit* arising
from the use of two words that *agree* in the sound, but differ
in the sense. The only way therefore to try a piece of *wit,* is
to translate it into a different language: If it bears the test
you may *pronounce* it true, but if it vanishes in the experiment you may conclude it to have been a pun. In short, one
may say of a pun as the *countryman* described his nightingale,
that it is *vox & praeterea nihil,* a sound, and nothing but a
sound.   —Joseph Addison, *The Spectator* (1711)

4. It is in truth *iniquity* on high
    To cheat our sentenced souls of *aught* they *crave,*
And *mar* the *merriment* as you and I
    Fare on our long *fool's-errand* to the grave.

Iniquity it is; but pass the can.
    My *lad,* no pair of kings our mothers bore;
Our only *portion* is the *estate* of man:
    We want the moon, but we shall get no more.

If here today the cloud of thunder *lours,*
    Tomorrow it will *hie* on far *behests;*
The flesh will grieve on other bones than ours
    Soon, and the soul will mourn in other breasts.
                    —A. E. Housman, "The Chestnut Casts His Flambeaux"

Assignment 4 Literature makes us take a new look at familiar
things and ideas. It helps us break through the crust built up by
habit. In each of the following passages, the italicized term is a
familiar word used with unfamiliar associations or implications. How

successfully does the author *go counter to the established connotations* of the term? Explain in detail how each passage departs from familiar ways of using the key term and other related words.

Your teacher may ask you to select a short passage from your current reading that similarly modifies familiar connotations. Prepare to present it to the class for discussion and comparison.

1. Extreme busyness, whether at school or college, kirk or market, is a symptom of deficient vitality; and a faculty for *idleness* implies a catholic appetite and a strong sense of personal identity. There is a sort of dead-alive, hackneyed people about, who are scarcely conscious of living except in the exercise of some conventional occupation. Bring these fellows into the country or set them aboard ship, and you will see how they pine for their desk or their study. They have no curiosity; they cannot give themselves over to random provocations; they do not take pleasure in the exercise of their faculties for its own sake; and unless Necessity lays about them with a stick, they will even stand still. It is no good speaking to such folk: they cannot be idle, their nature is not generous enough: and they pass those hours in a sort of coma, which are not dedicated to furious moiling in the gold-mill.

—R. L. Stevenson, "An Apology for Idlers"

2. When shall the saner softer polities
Whereof we dream, have sway in each proud land
And *patriotism,* grown Godlike, scorn to stand
Bondslave to realms, but circle earth and seas?

—Thomas Hardy, "Departure"

3. You tell me, doubt is Devil-born.

I know not. One indeed I knew
    In many a subtle question versed,
    Who touched a jarring lyre at first,
But ever strove to make it true;

Perplexed in faith, but pure in deeds,
    At last he beat his music out.
    There lives more *faith* in honest doubt,
Believe me, than in half the creeds.

He fought his doubts and gathered strength,
    He would not make his judgment blind,
    He faced the specters of the mind
And laid them; thus he came at length

To find a stronger faith his own,
    And Power was with him in the night,
    Which makes the darkness and the light,
And dwells not in the light alone.

—Alfred, Lord Tennyson, "In Memoriam"

Assignment 5   Some writers use very *bold figurative language,* calling our attention to analogies or parallels we would not usually notice. Other writers use more conventional or predictable figures of speech. Discuss the figurative language in each of the following literary passages. Is it familiar or unexpected? Is it plausible or far-fetched? How do different kinds of figurative language affect the reader?

1. This rudeness is a sauce to his good wit,
   Which gives men stomach to digest his words
   With better appetite.   (Shakespeare)

2. O who shall, from this dungeon, raise
   A soul enslaved so many ways?
   With bolts of bones, that fettered stands
   In feet; and manacled in hands.
   Here blinded with an eye; and there
   Deaf with the drumming of an ear.
   A soul hung up, as 'twere, in chains
   Of nerves, and arteries, and veins.
   Tortured, besides each other part,
   In a vain head, and double heart.

   (Andrew Marvell)

3. 'Tis education forms the common mind;
   Just as the twig is bent the tree's inclined.

   (Alexander Pope)

4. At last, when she judged it to be the right moment, Mrs. Mooney intervened. She dealt with moral problems as a cleaver deals with meat.   (James Joyce)

5. The reef enclosed more than one side of the island, lying perhaps a mile out and parallel to what they now thought of as their beach. The coral was scribbled in the sea as though a giant had bent down to reproduce the shape of the island in a flowing, chalk line but tired before he had finished.

   (William Golding)

CONTENTS

CHAPTER TWO

Grammar:
SUMMING UP AND PERSPECTIVE

Grammar helps us extend our knowledge and mastery of language.

Practical people are suspicious of theory, of knowledge "for its own sake." They want to know *how* — what button to push, what to do here and now. But a good engineer, or a first-rate doctor, is not satisfied to know the tricks of the trade. He wants to know *why*. He wants to understand what he is doing. This way he is prepared to handle new situations and new problems — not only those for which there are tried-and-true rules of thumb. He can look at "practical" advice given by others, and judge whether it makes sense. Practice not based on sound theory is likely to be bumbling, hampered by superstitions and false alarms.

Grammar provides us with a theory of how language works. It helps us understand how sounds combine into words, and words into sentences, to express an infinite variety of facts, observations, opinions, and feelings. A knowledge of grammar helps us use language with some sense of what we are doing, and why. It helps us *understand* practical advice about language — and it helps us *decide* whether the advice is soundly based.

Modern grammar, like modern mathematics or physics, has gone through a stage of exciting discovery and vigorous controversy. What you read in this chapter may sound newfangled to people who studied grammar many years ago. It may already sound old-fashioned to people who keep up with the latest scholarship and research. Grammars differ because grammarians must make important decisions about what to cover and how. The choices that a grammarian must make come under three major headings:

— HISTORICAL BACKGROUND

The grammar of our language is a *historical fact*. Its ways of operating, its forms and patterns, are things that have come about, like it or not. One way of explaining these facts is to show how they have gradually developed over the centuries. Many features of our language make more sense when we see them in historical perspective. Some of them are isolated survivals of older ways of doing things, now forgotten. For instance, the *-'s* ending in "the *bride's* bouquet" is a remnant of a once elaborate system of showing, by endings, how a noun was related to the rest of a sentence.

Here are some pairs showing historical changes in our grammar over the centuries:

EARLIER: The house is *a-building*.
NOW: The house is *being built*.

EARLIER: *Methought* I heard a voice cry, "Sleep no more!"
　　　　　　　　　　　　　　　　　　　　　(Macbeth)
NOW: *I thought* I heard a voice cry . . .

EARLIER: *Me list* no longer rotten boughs to climb. (Wyatt)
NOW: *I* no longer *want* to climb rotten boughs.

EARLIER: *Me waes gegiefan* an boc. (Old English)
NOW: *I was given* a book.

EARLIER: Many . . . are thy thoughts which are *to us-ward*. (Psalms)
NOW: Many are your thoughts which are (directed) *towards us*.

— CLASSIFICATION

A grammar should arrange the facts of language in clear, simple, and logical *order*. It should put things together that are truly alike. But this is easier said than done. When we sort out a barrel of apples, there is no self-evident system for putting them into separate bins. Should we have one bin for big apples, and one for small? Or one for ripe apples, one for green? Or one for eating apples, one for canning? How we sort things out depends on our *purpose.* Even when we are sure of what we are trying to do, some things are in-between and not easily put with one group or the other. It is easy enough to put horse, donkey, and zebra each in a different class. But what is a mule — a horse, or a donkey?

For a long time, grammarians used a traditional system for sorting out words into different **parts of speech:** noun, pronoun, adjective, verb, adverb, preposition, conjunction, interjection. But in recent years, they have re-examined the purposes this system of classification serves. They have tried to deal with the overlappings that such a scheme must take into account. For example:

(1) In "The house has a *frame,*" *frame* is a noun.
In "the *wooden* house," *wooden* is an adjective.
— What is *frame* in "the *frame* house"? Is it still a noun, or has it become an adjective? Most modern grammarians would still call it a noun, though it is now used to *modify* another noun. In this book, we call it a **modifying noun.**

(2) *Very* is traditionally called an adverb. But it doesn't act like most adverbs we know:

He runs *fast.*   BUT NOT   He runs *very.*
It *suddenly* stopped.   BUT NOT   It *very* stopped.

Very seems to belong with *quite, fairly,* and *extremely:*
quite cold   *fairly* cold   *extremely* cold   *very* cold

Modern grammarians group these special adverbs together as **intensifiers.**

(3) Typical English verbs have four or five different forms: *break, breaks, broke, broken, breaking. Be* is a very unusual verb; it has eight different forms: *be, am, are, is, was, were, been, being. Be* also has special uses not shared by typical verbs. Some modern grammarians therefore do not call it a verb at all, but simply call it a *be.* In this book we call it a verb — always remembering that it is an unusual one, needing special attention.

— COMPLETENESS

Ideally, we would like to test a grammar by choosing any sentence at random and using our grammatical system to classify or explain everything in it. But no school grammar could be complete enough to cover all the possibilities. No one could put a complete outline of how our language works between the covers of one book. In practice, all grammarians pick and choose. They present what they consider most basic, or most common, or most useful. For instance, most school grammars take it for granted that native speakers of English would know when to insert the article *the* in the following pairs. But how much time would you need to explain the unpredictable workings of this article to a foreign student?

He has *the flu.*
He has *cancer.*
We watched an eclipse of *the sun.*
We watched an eclipse of *Jupiter.*
We are having *pork chops* for dinner.
We are having *the pork chops* for dinner.
He is going to *Ethiopia.*
He is going to *the Congo.*
I like *rice.*
I like *the rice.*

To sum up: If the materials in this chapter seem new and different to you, one or more of the following may be the reason:

— *Historical background* is often used to help explain current facts;
— *major categories* are set up to reflect as clearly and usefully as possible the actual workings of our language;
— *coverage* is complete enough to include not only basic principles, but also the most important complications.

G 1 Grammatical Devices and Their History

English employs grammatical devices that have changed in important ways during its history.

The grammar of a sentence carries information over and above the dictionary meanings of words. This "grammatical meaning" is conveyed by devices that vary from one language to another, and that may change from one stage in the development of a language to the next. Grammatical devices add information to the dictionary meaning of a single word. *Sang* adds to the meaning of *sing* the notion of past time. But above all, grammatical devices show how several words in a sentence are related. Grammar causes the differ-

ENGLISH GRAMMAR
A Summary

GRAMMATICAL DEVICES

Inflections	His friend*s* stopp*ed* work*ing.*
Word order	*The man* attacked *the dog.*
Function words	*The* firemen asked *for a* raise.

SENTENCE PATTERNS

S-V	Speed kills.
S-V-O	Lincoln freed the slaves.
S-LV-N	Benedict Arnold was a traitor.
S-LV-Adj	Advice is cheap.
S-V-IO-O	Congress awarded him a medal.
S-V-O-OC	Tom called Juan his friend.
S-V-O-Adj	Macbeth considered Banquo dangerous.

SIMPLE TRANSFORMATIONS

Request	Drop the gun.
Passive	The slaves were freed by Lincoln.
Question	Where have the flowers gone?
Negation	Crime does not pay.
There-is	There is hope.

MODIFIERS

Adjectives	a *treacherous* friend
Modifying noun	a *brick* house
Number adjective	*several* bystanders
Adverb	acted *carelessly*
Prepositional phrase	the girl *in white*
Appositive	Fred Gonzales, *a senior*

CONNECTIVES

Coordinating	She called, *but* I kept walking.
Adverbial	I think; *therefore,* I am.
Subordinating	Catch me *if* you can.
Relative pronoun	He looked for people *who* cared.
Special	Tell me *that* you love me.

VERBALS

Present participle	*Barking* dogs don't bite.
Past participle	He raked up the *fallen* leaves.
Gerund	*Seeing* is *believing.*
Infinitive	*To err* is human.

ence in meaning between "the friend's husband" and "the husband's friend." Before we look at the workings of grammar in detail, we should get an overview of the basic grammatical devices that the language puts at our disposal.

G 1a Inflections

At one time, English was a heavily inflected language.

Inflections change the form of a word to add something to its meaning or to fit it into a particular slot in a sentence. *Man's* and *men* are inflected forms of *man. Sees, saw, seen,* and *seeing* are inflected forms of *see.* In many languages that are close cousins to English, articles, adjectives, nouns, and pronouns all have many separate word forms of this kind. A student of German must learn at least half a dozen different inflected forms for each word in a combination like *the old man* or *my new bicycle.* The same was true in Old English.

Where Modern English has only one form of the definite article *the,* Old English had a number of forms. In a tenth-century version of the biblical story of the sower and the seed, the following inflected forms take the place of the simple *the* (modern spelling is used for *th*):

MODERN ENGLISH	OLD ENGLISH
the weed	*se* coccel
the lord's	*thaes* hlāfordes
the man	*thāēm* menn
the wheat	*thone* hwaete

To discover the "meaning" of the various forms, we check how each of these combination fits into its sentence. We find that each combination plays as part of the whole. Here is a rough scheme:

SUBJECT	*the weed* appeared	*se*
POSSESSIVE	*the lord's* men	*thaes*
OBJECT OF PREPOSITION	like *the man*	*thāēm*
OBJECT OF VERB	you uproot *the wheat*	*thone*

Distinctions such as these, when signaled by different word forms, are called differences in **case.** Old English, like Latin or modern German, had a full-fledged case system. Only a small part of it survives. Here are the facts about the use of case forms and other inflected forms in Modern English:

(1) *English nouns and pronouns have only a few isolated case forms but use inflected forms to indicate number.* English nouns still have a **possessive** case:

PLAIN:	the man	a day
POSSESSIVE:	the *man's* daughter	a *day's* work

Several English pronouns still have a special form for the object of a verb or preposition:

SUBJECT-FORM:	I	he	she	we	they	who
OBJECT-FORM:	me	him	her	us	them	whom

English still relies on inflection to indicate singular and plural — in other words, **number:**

SINGULAR:	bird	house	man	tooth	child	mouse
PLURAL:	birds	houses	men	teeth	children	mice

English *no longer* uses inflection to indicate differences in **gender.** In many languages, these correspond, at least to some extent, to differences in sex. In Spanish, we know that *Roberto* is a boy, *Roberta* a girl. Even if we know little Italian, we are likely to realize that "*La* Traviat*a*" is an opera about a woman, "*Il* Trovat*ore*" an opera about a man. In English, we have separate forms for male and female only for a few words borrowed from Latin or French:

MASCULINE:	alumnus (plural: alumni)	fiancé	actor
FEMININE:	alumna (plural: alumnae)	fiancée	actress

When foreign words are imported, they sometimes bring inflected forms along with them. For instance, the following words preserve their original *Latin or Greek plural forms.* For many of them, Anglicized, "Englished," plurals are now coming into standard use:

	ORIGINAL PLURAL	ANGLICIZED PLURAL
antenna	antennae	antennas
appendix	appendices	appendixes
crisis	crises	
criterion	criteria	
curriculum	curricula	curriculums

	ORIGINAL PLURAL	ANGLICIZED PLURAL
formula	formulae	formulas
genus	genera	
medium	media	
memorandum	memoranda	memorandums
phenomenon	phenomena	
stimulus	stimuli	
thesis	theses	

(2) *Like nouns and pronouns, English verbs have lost many of their distinctive forms.* English, like its continental cousins, originally had a highly developed system of verb inflections. We still typically have four or five forms for each verb: *say, says, said, saying; sing, sings, sang, sung, singing.* For the auxiliaries, we have *can* and *could, will* and *would, shall* and *should.* We have not only *may* but also *might* (which has been called *"may* with the confidence taken out"). But only the verb *be* preserves anything approaching the original full-fledged system of inflections. Here, pieced out with the archaic forms used after *thou,* is a rough scheme:

PRESENT	SINGULAR	PLURAL
First person (speaking)	I *am*	we *are*
Second person (spoken *to*)	(thou *art*)	you *are*
Third person (spoken *about*)	he *is*	they *are*

PAST		
First person	I *was*	we *were*
Second person	(thou *wert*)	you *were*
Third person.	he *was*	they *were*

Of the original system, most verbs preserve three major features. The first is the basic distinction between present and past, which we call a difference in **tense.** For many modern English verbs, the inflectional ending that signals past tense is *-ed:*

PRESENT TENSE:	walk	slip	retreat	write	bring
PAST TENSE:	walked	slipped	retreated	wrote	brought

The second surviving feature is the inflectional ending *-s* that sets apart the "third person singular" from all other uses of the present tense:

(I, you, we, they)	run	walk	sing	bring	decide
(he, she, it)	runs	walks	sings	brings	decides

The third surviving feature is the use of special inflected forms after the auxiliaries *have* and *be*. One of these is the **present participle**, always using the inflectional ending -*ing: walking, slipping, singing.* The other is the **past participle.** Though today this form is often identical with that used in the past tense, originally most English verbs had a separate past participle providing the third form in three-part patterns like the following:

fall	fell	have *fallen*
write	wrote	have *written*
sing	sang	have *sung*
take	took	have *taken*

In many similar verbs, one or more of these distinctive forms have disappeared. Can you see how the forms in brackets have been replaced by others, helping to *simplify* and *regularize* our system of inflections?

shine	shone	have [shinen]
cling	[clang]	have clung
stand	stood	have [standen]
help	[halp]	have [holpen]

Like *who* and *whom,* such alternate forms as *am* and *are, was* and *were, sang* and *sung* are vestiges of an earlier grammatical system. They are *holdovers* from an earlier stage of the language. The farther we go back in our reading of English literature, the greater the number and variety of inflected verb forms. Here, from Shakespeare's plays, are a few of the inflected forms used after *thou:*

(can)   Thou *canst* not say I did it.
(shall)   All hail, Macbeth! that *shalt* be King hereafter.
(will)   If thou *wilt* lend this money, lend it not as to thy friends.
(do)   I care not if thou *dost* for me as much.
(speak) Thou *speak'st* it well. Go, father, with thy son.

Here, from the King James Version of the Psalms, are forms for the past tense and the past participle:

(speak) He *spake* unadvisedly with his lips . . . they have *spoken* against me with a lying tongue.
(help)   I was brought low, and he *helped* me . . . they have *holpen* the children of Lot.

(hold)	Thy right hand hath *holden* me up.
(forget)	They soon *forgat* his works . . . mine enemies have *forgotten* thy words.
(break)	He brought them out of darkness . . . and *brake* their bands in sunder. He hath *broken* the gates of brass.
(swear)	He *sware* unto the Lord . . . the Lord hath *sworn*.
(cleave)	He *clave* the rocks in the wilderness.

EXERCISE 1 Change the form of the word in the left margin to make it fit into the blank space in the sentence. Write the inflected form after the number of the sentence.

1. be Modern English _____ a member of the Indo-European family of languages.

2. speak Indo-European languages are _____ today by about half of the world's population.

3. million But _____ of people speak languages not related to our own.

4. live Sometimes only a few speakers of an almost extinct language are still _____ in isolated communities.

5. man But a language like Chinese is the native tongue of many millions of _____ and women.

6. identify Linguists have _____ several major language families besides the Indo-European.

7. include The Semitic family of languages _____ both Hebrew and Arabic.

8. revive Hebrew has recently been _____ as the national language of Israel.

9. speak Christ _____ Aramaic, a close cousin of Hebrew.

10. be For many centuries, Arabic has _____ the national language of Egypt.

11. write The Holy Scriptures of both Christianity and Islam were first _____ in a Semitic language.

12. know The scholars who first translated the Old Testament _____ both Hebrew and Aramaic.

13. God In the Koran, _____ revelations to Mohammed are recorded in Arabic.

14. African	The language of many _____ belongs to the Bantu family.
15. resemble	In the Far East, Chinese _____ the languages of Tibet and Viẹtnam.
16. we	It comes as a surprise to most of _____ that Chinese and Japanese are not related.
17. use	The Japanese are merely _____ a writing system borrowed from the Chinese.
18. criterion	Languages spoken by close geographical neighbors are often found to be unrelated when the linguist's _____ for what makes languages similar are applied.
19. bring	When the Europeans first _____ English and Spanish to America, there were about forty million American Indians.
20. phenomenon	They spoke many different languages, exhibiting a wide range of different linguistic _____.

EXERCISE 2 Words borrowed from foreign languages sometimes bring some of their inflected forms with them. What is the original *imported plural* of each of the following?

1.	analysis	*11.*	beau
2.	nebula	*12.*	hypothesis
3.	desideratum	*13.*	synthesis
4.	index	*14.*	tempo
5.	seraph	*15.*	cactus
6.	cherub	*16.*	focus
7.	dilettante	*17.*	stigma
8.	virtuoso	*18.*	larva
9.	bandit	*19.*	nucleus
10.	esophagus	*20.*	hippopotamus

EXERCISE 3 As words travel from one language to another, *inflectional forms* sometimes lose their original meaning and function. The following words borrowed from Latin are now all used as English nouns. For each write down a literal translation showing the original meaning and function. Be prepared to explain in class what part of speech and what kind of inflectional form the word originally represented. (Use a collegiate dictionary if it is available.)

EXAMPLE: *facsimile* "make it similar"

1. omnibus   2. recipe   3. interim   4. quorum   5. affidavit
6. imprimatur   7. innuendo   8. agenda   9. addendum   10. placebo

EXERCISE 4 In each of the following quotations from Shakespeare's plays, one *inflected verb form* differs from the form we would expect today. After the number of the passage, write down the more current form. (Where appropriate, write both the auxiliary and the main verb.)

1. I am sorry thou wilt leave my father so.
2.   . . . he rides well;
   And his great love, sharp as his spur, hath holp him
   To his home before us.
3. And for mine own part, I durst not laugh, for fear of opening my lips and receiving the bad air.
4. The clock hath stricken three.
5. What cares these roarers for the name of king?
6. Such men as he be never at heart's ease
   Whiles they behold a greater than themselves.
7. We have not spoke us yet of torchbearers.
8. At this hour lies at my mercy all mine enemies.
9. 'Tis vile . . . and better in my mind not undertook.
10. I have almost forgot the taste of fears.

EXERCISE 5 [Optional] For each of the following inflected forms, dictionaries list a *double, serving the same grammatical function*. Write down this alternative form after the number of the word. (Be prepared to report in class what you can find out about differences in the history, meaning, or use of the two forms in each pair.)

1. brothers   2. dived   3. sank   4. cows   5. waked   6. shone
7. pennies   8. hung   9. proven   10. thrived

G 1b   Word Order

In Modern English, word order has taken over
much of the work done earlier by inflections.

Much of the study of modern English grammar deals with *what has replaced* the extensive system of inflections once employed by our language. Other grammatical devices now do much of the work earlier done by inflected forms. The first of these grammatical

WORDS

INFORM
REQUEST
INVITE
PLEAD
ADMONISH
INSPIRE
DENOUNCE

devices is **word order.** In Modern English, the order in which the parts of a sentence occur is part of their meaning. Here are some typical meanings conveyed by word order:

ACTOR	—	ACTION VERB	—	TARGET		
The batter		hit		the ball.		

SENDER	—	ACTION VERB	—	ADDRESS	—	MISSIVE
The boy		sent		his mother		a letter.

PERSON	—	LINKING VERB	—	LABEL		
Red		looked		happy		

ACTOR	—	ACTION VERB	—	TARGET	—	LABEL
Mary		called		Jean		a bumbler.

Arranged in a different order, the same words would mean something else:

> The ball hit the batter.
> His mother sent the boy a letter.
> Happy looked red.
> A bumbler called Mary Jean.

When we try to do without the signals conveyed by word order, a sentence may become ambiguous. A modern translator of Chaucer wrote the following lines:

> And O ye men, of you naught need be said,
> Except that *ladies men have oft betrayed!*

Does this mean: *"Ladies* have often betrayed *men"?* Or does it mean: *"Men* have often betrayed *ladies"?* (The original makes it clear that women are being warned against treacherous *men.*)

In highly inflected languages, meanings like "this is the target" or "this is the address" are signaled by word forms instead. The following Latin sentence would mean "The boy loves the girl" regardless of how the words are arranged. The *-am* ending in *puellam* says "this is the object" — regardless of changes in word order:

> Puer puellam amat.
> (boy — girl — loves)
> Puer amat puellam.
> Puellam amat puer.

In Old English, word order was similarly *optional*. With the verb *send,* for instance, sender, address, and missive appear in several different combinations:

> *Tham godan casere sende theodosie aerend-gewrit.*
> The good emperor (ADDRESS) sent Theodosius (SENDER) message (MISSIVE)
> *He asende his apostlum thone halgan gast.*
> He (SENDER) sent his apostles (ADDRESS) the Holy Ghost (MISSIVE)

Regardless of word order, inflected forms like *tham* and *apostlum* say "this is *to whom* it was sent."

Remember the following points when you encounter unconventional word order in your reading and writing:

(1) In reading Shakespeare's English, we must be alert to word order using *options no longer available* or only rarely employed. In the following lines from *Macbeth,* can you see how word order varies from typical modern practice?

> *Gentle my Lord,* sleek o'er your rugged looks.
> Now *spurs the lated traveller* apace,
> To gain the timely inn; and near *approaches*
> *The subject* of our watch.
> For them *the gracious Duncan have I murther'd.*
> *So foul and fair a day I have not seen.*

(2) In much later literature, writers employ deviations from normal word order for the sake of *rhythm, rhyme, or variety.* Here are some examples of deliberate **inversion** — a reversal, whole or in part, of the usual subject-verb-complement order:

INVERTED: Who *dainties love* shall *beggars prove.*   (Ben Franklin)
NORMAL: Those who *love dainty things* will *become beggars.*

INVERTED: *Dust thou art,* to dust returnest,
Was not spoken of the soul. (Longfellow)
NORMAL: "*You are dust,* and will return to dust" was not said of the soul.

INVERTED: *Whose woods these are* I think I know. (Robert Frost)
NORMAL: I think I know *whose woods these are.*

(3) In modern English, we vary normal word order *for special emphasis*. We can pull an important word to the beginning of a sentence to make it stand out, or to take up again an idea brought up before, or to line up two important words for contrast:

> *This* I believe.
>
> *Great,* therefore, was the excitement throughout the valley.
> (Hawthorne)
>
> He lifted his sack to the table under the white light and emptied out two dozen common starfish. *These* he laid out side by side on the table. (Steinbeck)
>
> Grief is an artist of powers as various as the instruments upon which he plays his dirges for the dead. . . . *Some natures* it startles; *some* it stupefies. (Ambrose Bierce)

EXERCISE 6 From each of the following sentences, construct a *new sentence* using the same words in a different order. (Do not change the *form* of any of the words.)

1. Gentlemen prefer blondes.
2. The criminal called his lawyer a liar.
3. My friend called the girl charming.
4. Her new friend looked handsome.
5. Police stopped the car.
6. The word spread.
7. The landlord had the roof fixed.
8. I remember the joke that you told.
9. Marilyn loves our guest house.
10. Jim ate only the fish.

EXERCISE 7 Some words are exceptionally versatile, fitting *many different positions* in a sentence. Write *two* additional versions for each of the following sentences. Each time change the meaning by shifting the italicized word to a different position. (Do not change the *form* of any of the words.)

1. Jean took *only* her sweater.
2. The car turned *right* at the corner.
3. The pretty girl walked *very* slowly to this door.
4. His antique car *almost* broke down on every trip.
5. After a *light* meal, the girl in the blue dress turned off the switch.

EXERCISE 8 The following lines are taken from the Psalms in the King James Version (1611). They illustrate possibilities of word order in *Early Modern English*. Rewrite each line to make it follow normal or typical modern word order. (You may modernize archaic forms if you wish.)

1. In the Lord put I my trust.
2. In the net which they hid is their own foot taken.
3. With our tongue will we prevail.
4. In thy presence is fullness of joy.
5. By them is thy servant warned.
6. Good and upright is the Lord.
7. Him shall he teach in the way that he shall choose.
8. Eyes have they, but they see not.
9. One thing have I desired of the Lord.
10. Thou knowest my downsitting and mine uprising, thou understandest my thought afar off.

EXERCISE 9 [Optional] Write two additional versions of each of the following sentences. Each time change the word order to *emphasize* a different part of the sentence. (Be prepared to explain in class how each version might be used — in what context, or with what changes in meaning or implication.)

1. I will never do that.
2. We have already met Fred.
3. He was hungry.
4. He gave the dog the scraps.
5. He was discovered by accident.

G 1c *Function Words*

In Modern English, much of the work formerly done by inflections is done by function words.

A student learning Latin or French memorizes dozens of inflected verb forms. Different forms of the same single word signal not only present and past, but also future and different *kinds* of past. They further signal differences between possibility and fact, and between active and passive. Here is a mere sampling of the different forms of the Latin verb for "love":

amo	I love
amabam	I loved
amabo	I will love
amavi	I have loved
amaveram	I had loved
amavissem	I would have loved
amor	I am loved
amabar	I was loved

Notice that in English the only inflected form used is *loved*. Additional words *(will, have, had, am, was)* have taken over the function of the Latin inflections. Words that perform functions often assigned to other grammatical devices are called **function words.** (Sometimes they are called "structure words.") Function words are to the other words of a sentence as mortar is to brick, or nails to a wooden frame. They help hold the different parts of a sentence together to make up a meaningful whole.

Four important categories of function words are

articles	*the, a, an*
auxiliaries	*be, have, will, may, can, shall*
prepositions	*at, in, by, on, during, under, about*
connectives	*and, but, if, though, because*

Here are the principal facts about the role function words have come to play in Modern English:

(1) *Much of the work of inflected verb forms has been taken over by auxiliaries.* We use *shall/should, will/would, may/might,* and other auxiliaries to make changes in meaning that at a very early stage of our language would have been made by changes in the verb itself. In Shakespeare's English, we still find single word forms doing some of the work now done by auxiliaries:

EARLIER: I know he would not be a wolf
But that he sees the Romans are but sheep;
He were no lion, were not Romans hinds. (Julius Caesar)
NOW: He *would be* no lion, if Romans were not fair game.

EARLIER: the sauce to meat is ceremony;
Meeting were bare without it. (Macbeth)
NOW: A meeting *would be* bare (that is, dull) without it.

EARLIER: *Swear priests and cowards . . .*
       . . . unto bad causes swear
      Such creatures as men doubt; but do not stain
      The even virtue of our enterprise, . . .
      To think that or our cause or our performance
      Did need an oath.   *(Julius Caesar)*
NOW: *May* priests and cowards *swear . . . may* such creatures as
      men doubt *swear* (adherence) to bad causes . . .

(2) *Much of the work of inflected case forms has been taken over by prepositions.* In each of the following, the italicized endings have been replaced by prepositions like *of* and *to:*

OLD ENGLISH: his fēond*a* sum (literally, "his fiends' some")
MODERN: some *of* his enemies

OLD ENGLISH: heofon*a* rīce (literally, "heavens' kingdom")
MODERN: the kingdom *of* heaven

OLD ENGLISH: ic secge th*ǣm* riper*um*
MODERN: I say *to* the reapers

(3) *Though their role has slowly changed over the centuries, function words generally are more stable and permanent than content words.* Nouns and verbs are **content words**—they point to the objects, actions, or ideas that form the content of our experience. As we encounter new things and new ideas, hundreds of new words and meanings come into our language, with old words becoming obsolete. By contrast, function words are part of the basic grammatical machinery. Their main function is to establish *relations* among the different content words in a sentence. These relations often stay the same, even though the things *we talk about* change:

    the driver *of a* buggy
    the engineer *of a* train
    the pilot *of a* jet
    a scabbard *for the* sword
    a cartridge *for the* gun

Linguists call nouns and verbs (like adjectives and adverbs) **open** classes — each new edition of a dictionary lists hundreds and thousands of new ones. Function words are **closed** classes — only rarely does a new preposition or connective make its way into the language.

EXERCISE 10 Rewrite each of the following groups of words as an English sentence. Use *function words* to fill in the blank spaces. Use articles, prepositions, and auxiliaries only. (You may use *more than one* function word to fill one blank space.)

1. _____ police discovered _____ body _____ park _____ accident.
2. Guests _____ shoes _____ barred _____ club.
3. Philip _____ written _____ parents _____ money.
4. _____ sinking _____ *Titanic* came _____ surprise _____ experts.
5. Computers _____ not swayed _____ prejudice.
6. Jim went _____ Egypt _____ studying Arabic _____ years.
7. _____ traffic jam _____ called monumental _____ chief _____ police.
8. _____ beginning _____ World War II _____ last commercial airship _____ gone down _____ flames.
9. _____ teacher _____ not treat _____ students _____ drill sergeant _____ army.
10. _____ bird _____ hand is worth two _____ bush.

EXERCISE 11 In your reading of literature, what function words do you encounter that are *unusual or no longer in common use?* Each of the following passages contains a preposition or connective that is either uncommon or used in an unfamiliar way. After the number of the passage, write down the meaning of the italicized function word.

1. *Ere* the bat hath flown
   His cloistered flight . . . there shall be done
   A deed of dreadful note.   *(Macbeth)*
2. Good things of Day begin to droop and drowse
   Whiles Night's black agents to their preys do rouse.
                                                        (Macbeth)
3. Nay, *an* I tell you that, I'll ne'er look you i' th' face again.
                                                        (Julius Caesar)
4.   . . . *but* he's something stain'd
   With grief . . . thou mightst call him
   A goodly person.   *(The Tempest)*
5. . . . my trust. . . . which had indeed no limit,
   A confidence *sans* bound.   *(The Tempest)*
6. I can love any, *so* she be not true.
                                                        (John Donne)

7. And here, *lest* you should think I am exaggerating, is Hazlitt's own confession. (R. L. Stevenson)

8. Miniver loved the Medici,
   Albeit he had never seen one.
   (E. A. Robinson)

9. *Directly* he could walk without a stick, he descended into the town to look for some opportunity to get home.
   (Joseph Conrad)

10. He finished first in his class, *however* incredible that may sound.

REVIEW EXERCISE 1 In each of the following pairs, the second version uses the same basic group of words but makes somewhat different use of major grammatical devices. In which pairs does the *meaning* of the statement remain the same, with at the most only a change in emphasis? Put *S* for "same" after the number of each such pair. In which pairs does the change in the use of grammatical devices produce a change in meaning? Put *D* for "different" after the number of each such pair.

(Be prepared to point out in class what grammatical devices are employed to bring about the changes in each pair.)

1. My parents called Louisa their pet.
   My parents called their pet Louisa.

2. He had already visited Spain.
   Spain he had already visited.

3. Her mother's family had come from the Caribbean.
   The family of her mother had come from the Caribbean.

4. The Congressman addressed the honor students.
   The Congressman's address honored the students.

5. The Websters had painted their house.
   The Websters had their house painted.

6. Scrooge gave Tiny Tim's family a Christmas turkey.
   Scrooge gave a Christmas turkey to Tiny Tim's family.

7. The secretary called the doctor her boss.
   The secretary called the doctor for her boss.

8. People give advice more freely than money.
   Advice people give more freely than money.

9. With a ferocious roar the lion attacked the natives.
   With a ferocious roar the natives attacked the lion.

10. We like actors to talk about the theater.
    We actors like to talk about the theater.

G 2 The Complete Sentence

***The basic model of the English sentence is a
statement made up of a subject and a predicate.***

Occasionally, a single word, or a single closely linked group of
words, conveys our intended meaning:

> Fire! Silence! My books! What a man!

Much more often, however, we convey meaning by putting together
two major and distinct parts. No matter how varied the topics that
we want to discuss, we focus first on some thing or idea — something that we can point to in the outside world, or something that
we can assign to some logical category in our minds. We start our
two-part utterance with a segment that points, identifies, names: the
subject. We then proceed to a second part that *makes a statement*
about whatever we have identified. This second part we call the
predicate. The two-part structure that calls our attention to a
subject, and then makes a statement about the subject, we call a
sentence.

The following sentences consist *only* of subject and predicate;
they contain only the minimum elements needed to make a sentence
in English:

> Time / flies.
> Bees / sting.
> Our turn / will come.
> The sun / has set.
> Man / will prevail.

Subject and predicate are our terms for the two basic slots we have
to fill when building the typical English sentence. Other terms for
major slots in typical sentences are *complement, object, modifier*
(see **G 3** and **G 5**). When we ask what typically *fills* the major slots
in a sentence, we start talking about the **word classes**, or parts of
speech. The four major word classes are *noun, verb, adjective,* and
adverb. To tell these apart, we have to see what slots they fill in
typical sentences. We have to see what work they do in a complete sentence.

ENGLISH SENTENCES ARE COMPLEX

LINGUISTS USE DIFFERENT KINDS OF DIAGRAMS TO CHART SENTENCES.

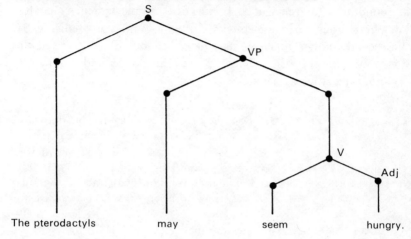

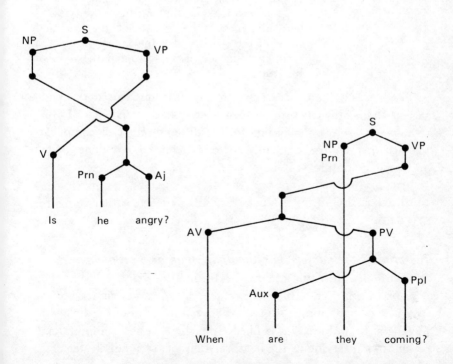

Rarely are actual sentences as simple as the "Time / flies" model. Typically, each of the two parts merely serves as a core around which cluster numerous other elements. To understand such a sentence, we have to find the basic two-part structure that serves as foundation for the whole. In the first sample sentence that follows, numerous further elements cluster around the predicate. In the second, numerous elements cluster around the subject. In the third, numerous further elements both introduce and follow the two-part structure as a whole:

BASIC MODEL: Mr. Dedalus / began.
ACTUAL SENTENCE: *Mr. Dedalus / began* to sway his head to and fro, crooning like a country singer.
(James Joyce)

BASIC MODEL: Any sound / would be picked up.
ACTUAL SENTENCE: *Any sound* that Winston made, above the level of a very low whisper, / *would be picked up* by it. (George Orwell)

BASIC MODEL: He / became mate.
ACTUAL SENTENCE: In time, when yet very young, *he / became* chief *mate* of a fine ship, without ever having been tested by those events of the sea that show in the light of day the inner worth of a man, the edge of his temper, and the fibre of his stuff. (Joseph Conrad)

To develop "sentence sense" means learning to see the basic subject-predicate structure even in a complicated sentence. It further means acquiring a feeling for the different *kinds* of complicating elements that make the difference between the bare-bones model and actual, mature sentences.

G 2a Noun and Pronoun

The core of the subject is typically a noun or a pronoun.

Normally, the subject is the first of the basic sentence parts. The core of the subject — the part that actually names something, or calls it to our attention — is typically a **noun**. In all of the following sentences, the subject slot is filled either by a noun standing alone, or by a noun serving as the **headword** of a short noun cluster:

Rain / falls.
A truck / had stalled.
The pavement / was wet.
Tourists / were passing by.
Your invitation / surprised us.
The conference / had begun.
These interruptions / must end.
Their politeness / was unexpected.

Three major features help us recognize nouns:

(1) *Nouns are often preceded by* **determiners.** These are "noun markers," giving us the signal that a noun will shortly follow. There are three major kinds:

ARTICLES:	*the, a, an*
POSSESSIVE PRONOUNS:	*my, your, his, hers, its, our, their*
DEMONSTRATIVES:	*this, these; that, those*

Notice that proper names, with a few exceptions, are not preceded by determiners. We say "*My country* won" but "*America* entered the war"; "*Her brother* had left" but "*John* joined the army."

(2) *Most nouns have a separate form for* **plural,** *signaling the meaning of "several of a kind."* Normally, the plural form adds to the plain noun the inflectional ending spelled *-s* or *-es*: *trucks, tourists, birds, trees, families, nations, interruptions.* Other ways of forming the plural were common during earlier stages in the history of the language. Here are a few modern survivals:

-en PLURAL:	ox*en,* brethr*en,* childr*en*
VOWEL CHANGE:	m*i*ce, t*ee*th, m*e*n, g*ee*se, f*ee*t
"ZERO"-PLURAL (*no* ending):	deer, sheep

Note that "count nouns" have a plural, but "mass nouns" typically do *not.* We say "two *bricks*" and "three *spoons*" but not "two *earths*" and "three *rices.*"

(3) *Many English nouns consist of some other word plus a noun-forming* **suffix.** Such endings, helping to derive a new word from another, are called "derivational" suffixes. They come *before* any inflectional ending, such as the plural *-s.* Some noun-forming suffixes go back to the common Old English stock and have been employed in English for many centuries:

-dom	kingdom, Christendom, wisdom, stardom
-er	singer, ruler, speaker, fighter, rider
-hood	womanhood, brotherhood, neighborhood, childhood
-ness	likeness, kindness, fondness, aloofness
-ship	friendship, apprenticeship, ambassadorship

Other noun-forming suffixes are common in nouns originally from French or Latin:

-al	approval, removal, referral
-ance	performance, disturbance, ordinance
-ence	independence, conference, reference
-ess	princess, actress, governess, poetess
-ism	organism, optimism, pessimism
-ment	government, improvement, regiment
-tion	determination, compilation, devotion

A few noun-forming suffixes are especially active in contemporary American English. They appear in many new words first used by journalists or advertisers:

-ee	draftee, trainee, addressee, appointee
-eer	racketeer, profiteer, pamphleteer, auctioneer
-ette	kitchenette, dinette, drum majorette
-ster	gangster, mobster, roadster, pollster

By using a determiner, the plural *-s*, or a derivational suffix, we can *turn into nouns* words that usually belong to a quite different class of words. Can you see how such words are turned into nouns in each of the following sentences?

> We were not sure of *the when and where.*
> His reply was full of *ifs* and *buts.*
> One today is worth two *tomorrows.*
> There was always a big *if.*
> He relied on his *cleverness* for *his livelihood.*

In looking for the subject of a sentence (and in looking at other typical noun positions in a sentence), we encounter *substitutes* that do not share any of the three major noun features. In many modern grammars, such **noun substitutes** are referred to as "nominals." Noun substitutes *look* different from nouns, but do the same work in a sentence that a noun would normally do. The words, and groups of words, that serve as doubles for nouns fall into three major categories:

(1) Most of the single words that substitute for nouns are **pronouns.** There are several kinds:

personal pronouns — replace nouns *already mentioned* or understood as part of the situation: *I, you, he, she, it, we, they*

FIRST MENTION: *Jim* called *Bertha* on the phone.
SECOND MENTION: *He* asked *her* to the dance.

reflexive pronouns — replace nouns *already mentioned in the same sentence,* typically when performer and target, or agent and beneficiary are the same: *myself, yourself, himself, herself, itself, ourselves, yourselves, themselves*

Mr. Garcia cut *himself.*
The owners blamed *themselves* for the loss.
My sister wanted the dress for *herself.*

possessive pronouns — use (with the exception of *his*) a special form, different from that used as a determiner: *mine, yours, hers, its, ours, theirs*

DETERMINER: *Her* audition was yesterday.
NOUN-SUBSTITUTE: *Mine* will be today.

DETERMINER: *Your* application has been approved.
NOUN-SUBSTITUTE: *Ours* was rejected.

demonstrative pronouns — use the *same* form that is used as a determiner: *this, these; that, those*

INTRODUCES NOUN: *That* man is my brother.
REPLACES NOUN: *That* is the man.

INTRODUCES NOUN: *These* seats are reserved.
REPLACES NOUN: *These* are available.

indefinite pronouns — do not point to any specific person or thing: *one; somebody (someone), anybody (anyone), everybody (everyone), nobody (no one or none); something, anything, everything, nothing*

Everybody was late for the party.
Nobody had mentioned a fee.
Nothing was said about her trip.

interrogative pronouns — ask questions to be *answered* by nouns:
who, whom, what, which

Who furnished the cake? *My aunt* did.
What are you eating? *A snack.*

Remember that these question-words, like several of the other kinds of pronouns here listed, do other work in sentences besides substituting for nouns.

(2) The second major category of noun substitutes consists of **verbals.** Often these carry further material along with them and together with the additional material make up a verbal phrase. (See **G 7** for a detailed account.) In all of the following, the subject of the sentence is a verbal or a verbal phrase:

To err / is human.
Seeing / is believing.
To ask for her advice / was a mistake.

(3) The third major category of noun substitutes consists of **noun clauses** (see **G 6b**). Noun clauses have *their own* subject and predicate and yet substitute for a single noun. In each of the following, the subject of the sentence is a noun clause:

Whoever did it / was a professional.
That he told you / is unforgivable.
What this means / is obvious.

To sum up: Our answer to "What is a noun?" consists of five major points.
— A noun can serve as the *subject* of a sentence. (It can also serve other functions, to be examined later.)
— A noun may be preceded by a *determiner* like *the, my,* or *this.*
— Most nouns have a *plural* form, typically adding *-s.*
— Many nouns have a noun-forming *suffix* like *-hood, -ness,* or *-ment.*
— A noun can be replaced by a *pronoun* or other noun substitute.

When you look for nouns functioning as subjects, remember *four additional points:*

— Between the determiner and the noun, and immediately following the noun, there may be considerable complicating material that becomes part of the noun cluster or "noun phrase" (see **G 5**):

> *The* handsome young *man* in the convertible / drove off.

— Several nouns, joined by *and* or *or*, may combine to serve as a **compound** subject:

> *The owl* and *the pussycat* / went to sea.
> *The walrus* and *the carpenter* / were walking close at hand.

— The noun used as the subject of the sentence *agrees* with the predicate in **number**. Whenever we have a choice of alternative forms, subject and predicate change from singular to plural together. (See **U 3a**.)

> *The sea* / *was* wet as wet could be,
> *The sands* / *were* dry as dry.
> (Lewis Carroll)

— The noun that serves as subject of a sentence is *not* linked to the rest of the sentence by a preposition:

> (In the afternoon) *the group* / reached a deserted village.
> *The* first *half* (of the afternoon) / had passed.

EXERCISE 12 Which of the following could serve as the subject of a normal English sentence? After the number of each item that is eligible, write *Yes.* Be prepared to explain in class which of the typical noun features the word or group of words illustrates. After the number of each item that could not normally serve as a subject, write *No.*

1. the deep blue sea
2. incredibly beautiful
3. liberty
4. had never been visited
5. our very successful track stars
6. brotherhood
7. silent in the moonlight
8. could have been prevented

9. years of heat and drought
10. a farmer and his two oldest sons
11. this extreme callousness
12. with great ease
13. tall and handsome
14. very little encouragement
15. those familiar excuses
16. may happen again
17. a young girl in a light blue cotton dress
18. on approval
19. my first and last attempt
20. a leisurely walk along the shore

EXERCISE 13 How well do you know your language? After the number of each item, write the answer required by the instructions.

1. Proper names normally do not have determiners: *France, Germany, Austria.* But write the names of three countries or cities that do carry the article *the* with them.

2. When we say "The Andrew Jackson had left," we are not talking about a person but probably about what?

3. The normal plural of *head* is *heads;* of *foot, feet.* Write one sentence in which *head* and another in which *foot* is used as a plural.

4. *Water* and *coffee* are normally mass nouns and therefore "non-pluralizers." They do not normally have a plural form with -*s.* Can you write a sentence for each of these words in which it plausibly and appropriately appears with a plural -*s?*

5. In each of the following pairs, only one of the words normally has a plural form with -*s.* Select this word from each pair and use it in a short sentence: *liberty/slavery; beauty/ugliness; order/chaos.*

6. For each of the following noun-forming suffixes, write down three nouns *not included* on page 100: -*ee,* -*eer,* -*ette,* -*ster.*

EXERCISE 14 Can you distinguish the different kinds of pronouns? After the number of each sentence, write down all italicized words. After each word, write the appropriate abbreviation in parentheses: *Det* for a word used as a determiner; *Per* for personal pronouns; *Ref* for reflexive pronouns; *Pos* for a possessive pronoun *not* used as a determiner; *Dem* for a demonstrative pronoun used *not* as a determiner but as a noun substitute; *Ind* for indefinite pronouns; *Int* for interrogative pronouns.

EXAMPLE: *Who* reserved *this* corner for *himself?*
                           (Answer) who (Int), this (Det), himself (Ref)

1. Some American authors have had *their* books translated into many languages.
2. *They* tell the foreign reader about *themselves* and *their* country.
3. In some countries almost *everybody* knows Mark Twain.
4. Jack London made *himself* equally well known through *his* tales.
5. *These* usually tell *us something* about *his* own experiences.
6. *He* grew up on California ranches and became a sailor in *his* teens.
7. *He* took numerous odd jobs, but never kept ·*these* long.
8. *Nothing* long kept the attention of *this* young wanderer.
9. *He* once found *himself* in jail for thirty days as a vagrant.
10. *He* educated *himself* through private study.
11. During the gold rush, many tried *their* fortunes in the Klondike.
12. Jack London tried *his* but the experience gained *him nothing.*
13. Here the Far North exposed *him* to *its* icy cold.
14. *He* wrote *his* best stories about *its* hardships.
15. In *these* stories the men of the North prove *themselves.*
16. People in many countries immersed *themselves* in *these* tales.
17. *They* cherished *this* American author like one of *theirs.*
18. Have *you* read *anything* by Jack London?
19. *What* appealed to *you* about *it?*
20. *He* is *my* favorite author. *Who* is *yours?*

EXERCISE 15 [Optional]   Write five pairs of related sentences. In the second sentence in each pair, replace as many nouns as possible with appropriate pronouns. Underline the pronouns and the nouns they replace. Make use of several different types of pronouns.

EXAMPLES: 1. *The customer* returned *the boots.*
                        He could not wear *them.*
                   2. *Your sister* failed *the test.*
                        Mine passed *it.*
                   3. *Fred* did not send us *the stamps.*
                        He kept *them* for *himself.*

G 2b   Verb and Auxiliary

**The core of the predicate is the verb,
which may include one or more auxiliaries.**

In simplified model sentences, the **verb** is the second of the two
basic sentence parts. It is the core of the predicate; it is the part of
the sentence that actually "makes a statement." In all of the following sentences, the predicate slot is filled by a verb standing alone,
or by a verb combining with auxiliaries and then serving as the
headword of a short verb cluster or "verb phrase":

> Time / *passes.*
> Your visit / *helped.*
> Times / *have changed.*
> Your turn / *will come.*
> The results / *were announced.*
> A storm / *was brewing.*
> George / *may disagree.*
> A rescue party / *is being organized.*

The following features help us recognize verbs:

(1) *Verbs have a built-in reference to time.* They refer to
actions or events as they happen (or could happen) in time. Verbs
are the only words that can show a change in time by a change
in form:

PRESENT:	I *ask*	we *help*	I *see*	they *teach*
PAST:	I *asked*	we *helped*	I *saw*	they *taught*

(2) *Verbs have preserved a more fully developed inflectional
scheme than any other group of words in English.* Nouns have at
the most four different forms — three of which normally *sound
alike,* but look different when written down: *boy,* several *boys,*
a *boy's* father, several *boys'* fathers. Many English verbs have
five different forms: the plain form (which appears alone or after
the infinitive-marker *to*); the -*s* form (used in the present for agreement with all singular subjects other than *I* and *you* —"third person
singular"); the past form; the -*en* form for use after *have* (some
of these do not have the -*en* ending, but instead have an inflectional
change *in* the word itself); and the -*ing* form. Here are some typical
five-part verbs:

PLAIN	PRESENT SG.	PAST	v-*en*	v-*ing*
(to) break	breaks	broke	(have) broken	breaking
(to) fall	falls	fell	(have) fallen	falling
(to) take	takes	took	(have) taken	taking
(to) sing	sings	sang	(have) sung	singing
(to) know	knows	knew	(have) known	knowing

With many other verbs, the past form does double duty, appearing also after *have* and leaving the verb without a distinct form to correspond to *broken* or *fallen*. With many such verbs, the form thus doing double duty uses the ending spelled -*d* or -*ed*. Here are some typical four-part verbs:

PLAIN	PRESENT SG.	PAST	v-*ing*
(to) help	helps	helped (have) helped	helping
(to) ask	asks	asked (have) asked	asking
(to) regret	regrets	regretted (have) regretted	regretting
(to) educate	educates	educated (have) educated	educating

(For help with usage problems involving the different forms of English verbs see **U 1a** and **U 2d**.)

(3) *Verbs are often preceded by auxiliaries.* Only the first three forms of a four-part or five-part verb can serve as a complete verb without further help:

Birds *sing.*   The bird *sings.*   Birds *sang.*
Dogs *bark.*   The dog *barks.*   Dogs *barked.*

To make a complete statement, the -*en* form ("past participle") and the -*ing* form ("present participle") need a form of *have (has, had)* or *be (am, are, is, was, were, has been,* and so on). Have and *be* are then used as "helping verbs" or **auxiliaries:**

Snow *has fallen.*   Jim *is driving.*
Jim *had known.*   Birds *were singing.*
Cars *are driven.*   I *am eating.*
A letter *was written.*   A crowd *was waiting.*
A leader *had been chosen.*   Fred *has been working.*

The plain form of a verb can serve as a complete verb by itself, or it can combine with one of the **modal** auxiliaries: *can (could), may (might), will (would), shall (should), must:*

Birds *fly.*	Times *change.*
Birds *can fly.*	Times *may change.*
Birds *must fly.*	Times *will change.*
Birds *should fly.*	Times *might change.*

(4) *Many verbs consist of some other word plus a verb-forming suffix.* The following suffixes are still constantly used to make up new words:

-ate   activate, alienate, chlorinate
-ize   organize, standardize, popularize, synchronize
-en   deepen, redden, harden, blacken
-fy   glorify, beautify, indemnify, electrify

Some English verbs make use of typical verb-forming prefixes:

be-   befuddle, bemuse, bewilder
en-   enslave, enrage, enliven, enlist

The first of these was especially active during earlier stages of the language. We find it in many words that have become old-fashioned: *bespeak, behoove, betoken.*

The typical verb features here described help us *turn into verbs* words that normally belong to a quite different class of words. By adding a typical verb ending *(-ed, -ing)*, by putting the word after an auxiliary, or by using an appropriate suffix or prefix, we can "verbalize" nouns, for instance. Edgar, in Shakespeare's *King Lear,* says: "He *childed* as I *fathered.*" This means: "He has the same kind of trouble with his *child* as I have with my *father.*" Can you see "what makes a verb" in the less bold examples that follow?

> She was always *lording* it over me.
> He *encoded* a message for the students to decode.
> You should always *sir* an officer.
>   . . . For her own person,
> It *beggared* all description. (Shakespeare)

When we look for verbs serving as predicates of actual sentences, we must be prepared for a *great variety* of combinations. Combining the possible forms of a verb with one or more of the auxiliaries, we obtain a wealth of actual verb phrases. These nevertheless follow a fairly simple pattern: Modal (if any) first; form of *have* (if any) second; form of *be* (if only *one*) third; *being* (if two forms of *be* are present) immediately before the main verb.

MODAL	HAVE	BE	(BEING)	MAIN VERB
	has			arrived
will				succeed
		was		condemned
		is		changing
		is	being	changed
can		be		improved
	had	been		postponed
might	have	been		overlooked
should	have	been		corrected
		was	being	rebuilt

These different combinations make possible many different shades of meaning. Grammars conventionally take inventory of the possible *time distinctions,* or **tenses.** Note that the names of the tenses may call attention to only *one* possible use out of several:

PRESENT: I *concede.* (now)
I *exercise* regularly. (past, present, and future)
I *leave* tomorrow. (future)
Suddenly I *see* this man... (vivid past)

PAST: He *left.* (past and done with)
If he *left* us tomorrow... (possibility)

PERFECT: She *has applied.* (recently completed, with bearing on the past)

PAST PERFECT: He *had resigned.* (in the more distant past)

FUTURE: She *will preside.*

Note that for all five of these tenses we have alternate forms for *action in progress:*

PROGRESSIVE — present: He *is talking.*
— past: They *were quarreling.*
— perfect: It *has been raining.*
— past perfect: We *had been talking.*
— future: She *will be waiting.*

In addition to the regular and predictable features of English verbs, you should be prepared for a number of *complications:*

(1) *Many English verbs are two-word combinations.* A word like *at, up, on,* or *down* combines with a familiar short verb to form a new grammatical unit. Sometimes indeed *three* words combine to take the place of some other single verb with the same meaning:

ONE WORD:	We *watched.*	I *yielded.*	He *rose.*
TWO WORDS:	We *looked on.*	I *gave in.*	He *stood up.*
ONE WORD:	He was *admired* by all.		
THREE WORDS:	He was *looked up to* by all.		

Not all of these combinations work the same way in a sentence. (For further discussion see **G 5b**.)

(2) *Some auxiliaries double as main verbs. Have* and *be* not only have some additional uses in combination with another verb; each can also serve as a complete verb in its own right. Here is a preview of the major uses of each:

HAVE:	He *has left.*
	He *has to go.*
	He *has it done.*
	He *has them report.*
	He *has* money.

BE:	He *is singing.*
	He *is ignored.*
	He *is to be examined.*
	He *is* here.
	He *is* happy.
	He *is* a friend.

(3) *Numerous familiar combinations precede other verbs to convey shades of meaning similar to those conveyed by the modal auxiliaries:*

FUTURE:	He *will* leave.
	He *is going to* leave.
	He *is about to* leave.
	He *is on the point of* leaving.
OBLIGATION:	We *must* go.
	We *ought to* go.
	We *have to* go.
HABITUAL PAST:	They *would* sit around a fire and sing.
	They *used to* sit around a fire and sing.

(4) *Several verbs may follow the same subject.* Joined by *and* or *or,* they form a **compound** predicate:

> They *laughed* and *tumbled* and *shouted* on the mountain.
>
> (William Golding)

> The great rock *loitered, poised* on one toe, *decided* not to return, *moved* through the air, *fell, struck, turned over, leapt* droning through the air and *smashed* a deep hole in the canopy of the forest.
>
> (William Golding)

EXERCISE 16 Which of the following could serve as the *complete verb* of a normal English sentence? After the number of each item that is eligible, write *Yes.* Be prepared to explain in class which of the typical verb features the word or group of words illustrates. After the number of each item that could not normally serve as the complete verb, write *No.*

1. her invincible hatred	*11.* fell
2. might have failed	*12.* a sudden rain
3. argue	*13.* theorize
4. pushing back his hair	*14.* stopped
5. had been ringing	*15.* being followed
6. roses and carnations	*16.* his annoying laugh
7. varies	*17.* has been confirmed
8. fallen	*18.* should get up
9. had frozen over	*19.* their insistent questions
10. is being repaired	*20.* will soften

EXERCISE 17 Each of the following sentences from William Golding's *Lord of the Flies* shows a different way of making *more than one verb* follow the same subject. Using each sentence as a model, write a sentence of your own on a different topic. For each sentence, follow the grammatical structure of the original as closely as you can.

1. The boys *chattered* and *danced.*

2. He *paused* for a moment and automatically *pushed back* his hair.

3. He *bent down, took up* a double handful of lukewarm water, and *rubbed* the mess from his face.

4. Ralph *said* no more, *did* nothing, *stood* looking down at the ashes round his feet.

5. He *noticed* blood on his hands and *grimaced* distastefully, *looked* for something on which to clean them, then *wiped* them on his shorts and *laughed.*

EXERCISE 18 How well do you know your language? After the number of each item, write the answer asked for in the instructions.

1. Not *all* English verbs change their form when we move from present to past tense. A few verbs would use the same form to fill both blanks in "I _____ something at present, and I also _____ it yesterday." Write down *three* verbs for which the plain form and the past tense are the same.

2. Not all verbs for which the past tense and the *-en* form are the same use the ending spelled *-d* or *-ed*. For instance, we say, "I *taught*" and also "I *have taught*." Write down the past tense of three more such verbs.

3. Use each of the three following words in a short but plausible sentence: *bemuse, behoove, betoken*.

4. In addition to those listed on page 108, list three verbs using the suffix *-fy* and three verbs using the prefix *en-*.

5. In much *spoken* English, a form of *get* replaces a form of *be* or *have* used in combination with another verb. In other words, *get* is used as if it were an auxiliary. Write two sentences to illustrate this use, using *get* once to replace a form of *be* and once to replace a form of *have*.

EXERCISE 19 The following words are most frequently used as nouns. But for each, write a short sentence in which you use it as the *complete verb* or part of the complete verb. Change the form of the word as necessary or appropriate.

   table, structure, author, position, voice, vacation, thumb, service, style, engineer

REVIEW EXERCISE 2 In the following two paragraphs, twenty words have been italicized. Number them from 1 through 20. Write down each word after its number. Mark it *N* if it is used as a noun. Mark it *V* if it is used as a verb or part of a verb. Be prepared to explain in class what *typical noun and verb features* you relied on in classifying these words.

1.   He gave a wild *whoop* and *leapt* down to the pale sand. At once the *platform* was full of noise and *excitement,* scramblings, *screams* and laughter. The assembly *shredded* away and *became* a discursive and random *scatter* from the palms to the *water* and away along the *beach,* beyond nightsight.
                                        —William Golding, *Lord of the Flies*

2.   I *paced* a turn or two on the poop and *saw* him *take* up
his *position* face forward with his *elbow* in the ratlines of the
mizzen-rigging before I *went* below. The *mate's* faint snoring
was still going on peacefully. The cuddy lamp was *burning*
over the table on which stood a vase with flowers, a polite
attention from the ship's provision merchant — the last
flowers we should *see* for the next three months at the
very least.   —Joseph Conrad, "The Secret Sharer"

G 3   Sentence Patterns

**Several common sentence patterns provide the
underlying structure for most English sentences.**

Except when we repeat ready-made slogans, our sentences are
free to exploit the resources of our language in new and varied
ways. Nevertheless, in their basic structure, they tend to follow a
few simple models. When stripped to the bare skeleton, they are
found to consist of two, or three, or at the most, four basic parts.
The most basic model simply splits up into a noun (or equivalent)
and its verb. But often a third and perhaps a fourth basic part
follow the verb. They are needed to complete the predicate and
are called **complements**. A complement is not linked to the rest of
the sentence by a preposition or other connecting word. It is as
essential a part of the basic structure as the third side of a triangle,
or the third and fourth sides of a square.

Can you see that each of the following examples would have a
chopped-off effect without complements?

SUBJECT	VERB	COMPLEMENT	COMPLEMENT
Dinner	is	*ready.*	
The Smiths	had bought	*a trailer.*	
Jim	gave	*the driver*	*instructions.*

To produce or to understand a complicated sentence, we need
a firm grasp on its underlying simple structure. In the following
summary, the *seven most common patterns* are sorted out according
to whether or not the verb carries along any complements, and, if
so, how many and what kind. For each sentence pattern, the summary first shows the simple, bare-bones model. It then shows the

pattern as it might be expanded and varied in actual sentences — first, through the addition of *modifiers* (see **G 5**); second, through the *duplication* of one or more basic parts; and, third, through *inversions,* or variations in word order (see **G 1b**).

PATTERN ONE: Subject—Verb (S-V)

This is the bare-minimum sentence in English. The *verb alone* serves as the complete predicate. Verbs used in this pattern are called **intransitive** — they are not "in transit" to anything; they are not going anywhere.

MODELS: Kites fly.   Mary nodded.   The rain had stopped.

VARIED: *A cat may look* on a king.
She leaned forward and *listened,* smiling.

(Rudyard Kipling)

The long *day wanes; the* slow *moon climbs; the deep Moans* round with many voices.   (Alfred Lord Tennyson)

PATTERN TWO: Subject—Verb—Object (S-V-O)

In this pattern, a **transitive** verb *carries the action of the subject across to a second noun* (or noun substitute). The difference between a transitive and an intransitive verb is like that between a through road and a dead-end street. The second noun becomes part of the basic structure of the sentence and is called the **direct object.** In many sentences, it acts as the target of an action, the result of a performance.

MODELS: Dogs chase cats.
The arrow hit the target.
Familiarity breeds contempt.

VARIED: *The heavens declare the glory* of God.   (Psalms)

The fox condemns the trap, not himself.   (William Blake)

During all those years he *had* never *heard* from any of his masters *a* flippant *word.*   (James Joyce)

He accepted a piece of half-raw meat and *gnawed it* like a wolf.   (William Golding)

Behind him *his men carried* six *bowls* of rice, *a bowl* of palm oil, two *bowls* of broken meat.   (Graham Greene)

Strange *fits* of passion *have I known.*   (William Wordsworth)

PATTERN THREE: *Subject—Linking Verb—Noun (S-LV-N)*

In this pattern, the verb *pins a label on the subject.* The label is a second noun that serves as a description of the first. The second noun in this pattern is often called a **predicate noun.** The verb linking it to the subject is called a **linking verb.**

Most commonly the linking verb is a form of *be.* Occasionally, especially in British usage, the linking verb is a verb like *feel, seem,* or *remain:*

MODELS: Philip is a fool.
            Her father was a mailman.
            George remained my friend.

VARIED: *Man is the measure* of all things.
            A thing of beauty *is a joy* forever. (John Keats)
            Punctuality is the thief of time. (Oscar Wilde)
            The sound must seem an echo to the sense. (Alexander Pope)

PATTERN FOUR: *Subject—Linking Verb—Adjective (S-LV-Adj)*

In this pattern, the linking verb again pins a label on the subject. But this time the label is *not* a second noun. It is rather a word chosen from the third major word class: an **adjective** (See **G 5a**). Adjectives are words like *warm, slender, blue, heavy, beautiful, ladylike, studious.* They typically fit in after **intensifiers** like *very, fairly, extremely:* very short, fairly expensive, extremely beautiful. In comparisons, they use forms with *-er/-est* or are preceded by *more* and *most: older* than my brother; *more difficult* than you think. The adjective that follows the linking verb is often called a **predicate adjective.**

Verbs that may serve as linking verbs in this pattern include *be, seem, appear, become, grow, turn, feel, taste, sound, smell,* and *look:*

MODELS: Men are mortal.
            Grandfather was growing old.
            Dinosaurs had become extinct.
            The soup tasted strange.

VARIED: All *the boys seemed* to him very *strange.* (James Joyce)
            No *man* ever yet *became great* by imitation.
                                           (Samuel Johnson)

All *three were hot, dirty,* and *exhausted.* (William Golding)

He was gentlemanly, steady, tractable, with a thorough knowledge of his duties. (Joseph Conrad)

Pre-eminent among the pigs *were* two young *boars* named Snowball and Napoleon. (George Orwell)

PATTERN FIVE: Subject—Verb—Indirect Object—Object (S-V-IO-O)

In this pattern, a transitive verb makes a *detour through a second complement* before carrying the action across to the direct object. The additional noun (or noun substitute) inserted between the verb and direct object is called the **indirect object.** Typically, the indirect object shows the intended *recipient or destination.* By its position, that is, by word order, it conveys a meaning that at a different point in the sentence would have to be shown by a preposition indicating *to* whom or *for* what.

Verbs that fit this pattern include *give, send, teach, write, buy, leave, lend, offer, show, ask:*

MODELS :   Jim wrote his wife a letter.
The father gave the pair his blessing.
Leonard lent strangers money.

VARIED :   *Thou canst* not every day *give me thy heart.*   (John Donne)

Life still *leaves* human *effort scope.* (Matthew Arnold)

The heat of the tropics, *the descent, the search* for food, and now *this* sweaty *march* along the blazing beach *had given them the complexions* of newly washed plums.

(William Golding)

PATTERN SIX: Subject—Verb—Object—Object Complement (S-V-O-OC)

In this pattern, a transitive verb first carries the action or process across to the object. We then go on to a second complement that *pins a label* on the object. In this pattern, the label pinned on the object is an additional *noun* (or noun substitute), called the **object complement.** The resulting pattern looks the same as Pattern Five but is put together differently. In Pattern Five, there is a triangle relationship of "Sender — Destination — Missive." *What* is sent and *to whom* are two quite different things. In Pattern Six, we have a combination of Pattern Two ("I consider John") and Pattern Three ("John is a fool"). As a result, in "I consider John a fool" John and the fool are the *same person.*

Verbs that fit this pattern include *consider, think, call, make, name, choose, elect, vote, appoint:*

MODELS: I consider John my friend.
Jim called Mr. Greene his mentor.
The parents had named the child Miranda.
The voters elected the actor governor.

VARIED: *A* child's *laughter makes the darkness light.*
The disparagers of culture *make its motive curiosity.*
(Matthew Arnold)
Coleridge called Shakespeare's *plays works* of true genius.

PATTERN SEVEN: *Subject—Verb—Object—Adjective (S-V-O-Adj)*

In this pattern we again have the verb pin a label on the object. This time, the *label is an adjective.* The result is a combination of Pattern Two ("I consider this action") and Pattern Four ("This action is premature"). Combining these two statements, we arrive at "I consider this action premature."

Verbs that fit this pattern include some of the verbs from Pattern Six, but also many others: *consider, think, call, make, find, paint, turn, keep.*

MODELS: I consider John eligible.
His actions kept the voters happy.
You will find the food excellent.
We are painting the roses red.

VARIED: *Winter kept us warm,* covering
Earth in forgetful snow. (T. S. Eliot)

He knew himself the most *unfit*
Of men to herd with Man. (Lord Byron)

When you start looking for the basic patterns that underlie actual sentences, remember the following *cautions:*

(1) *Not all complete utterances fit the subject-predicate pattern.* In spoken English, but also in imaginative writing, we find many units that are grammatically self-contained and yet lack subject or verb or both. Many *exclamations* consist merely of a noun cluster:

What a man!
My ticket!
That impossible Mr. Jones!

Many *casual remarks* sound like a sentence of Pattern Three or Four from which a mere filler subject like *it* and a form of *be* have been omitted:

(It is a) Beautiful day today.
(Is it) Warm enough for you?
(It is) Better late than never.

Subject or verb or both are missing from many *familiar sayings* balancing one thing off against the other:

Like father, like son.
Penny wise, pound foolish.

(2) *Some familiar sentence types fit the basic patterns only imperfectly.* The following sentences use *be* as a main verb (and not as an auxiliary); and *be* does *not* link a noun or an adjective to the subject. We would therefore classify it as an intransitive verb in Pattern One:

Your brother was here.
The President is abroad.

Here and *abroad* belong to the fourth major word class. They are **adverbs** — in this case, adverbs of place (See **G 5b**). Usually we would treat these as optional modifiers added to the basic pattern. But here the *basic pattern* does not seem complete until the adverb has been added. Some grammarians would therefore list a Pattern Eight: Subject — *Be* — Adverb (S-*Be*-Adv).

(3) *Some sentences do not fit the familiar basic patterns at all.* In the following sentences, the verb is an intransitive verb that fits Pattern One, but at the same time it acts as if it were a linking verb that pins a label on the subject:

Grandmother *died* happy.
The dinner guests *rose* hungry.

In the following sentences, the *fourth* element in the basic pattern pins a label on the subject — rather than on the object:

He left the casino *a millionaire*.
Father had left Ireland *penniless*.

In other words, our listing of basic patterns is not intended as a complete inventory of possible sentence types. But it does furnish us with *the most common* among the simple structures that more complicated sentences expand, vary, and combine.

EXERCISE 20 *Which basic pattern* underlies each of the following sentences? After the number of the sentence, write down the appropriate abbreviation:

S-V
S-V-O
S-LV-N
S-LV-ADJ
S-V-IO-O
S-V-O-OC
S-V-O-ADJ

1. In India, English has long been the language of government.
2. The British made English the official language.
3. The schools taught all students English.
4. Now the government is adopting Hindi as the national language.
5. The supporters of this change consider English unpatriotic.
6. Not all Indians speak Hindi.
7. The government recognizes fifteen major languages.
8. Now the schools will teach many people Hindi.
9. A duplicate in English will accompany official documents.
10. English will remain a "link" language.
11. Also, Hindi will absorb many English words.
12. For instance, English gave the Indians the word *motor*.
13. In a modern language, many scientific words are necessary.
14. Hindi lacks many necessary terms.
15. India's translators must translate all laws.
16. Publishers must offer the schools Hindi textbooks.
17. Many people must change their customary ways.
18. The government considers the changeover inevitable.
19. India is a proud new nation.
20. A national language gives people a common identity.

EXERCISE 21 Many English verbs *change their meaning* as they move from one basic pattern to the other. After the number of each sentence, write down a word or phrase that translates the meaning the italicized verb has in the sentence. Be prepared to identify in class the basic pattern used in each sentence.

 1. The governor *stayed* in the capital.
 2. The governor *stayed* the execution.
 3. The speakers *rendered* tribute to his achievement.
 4. The defect *rendered* the machine useless.
 5. Myrtle *washes* her hair every night.
 6. This material *washes* well.
 7. Mr. Greene *walked* to work.
 8. Mr. Greene *walked* his dog.
 9. Uncle Simon *left* his family a fortune.
10. Uncle Simon *left* his family destitute.
11. Isabel *had made* the dress.
12. Isabel *had made* her mother happy.
13. This time the machine *worked*.
14. The new manager *worked* a miracle.
15. Mr. Smith *called* the office.
16. Mr. Smith *called* the office a madhouse.
17. George *found* his mother a taxi.
18. George *found* the party dull.
19. The sentinel *sounded* the alarm.
20. The sentinel *sounded* sleepy.

EXERCISE 22 Many English verbs fit only one or, at the most, two of the basic patterns. Other verbs are more versatile. For each of the following verbs write *four or more* short sentences, each time using the verb in a *different* basic pattern: *make, turn, call, find, keep.*

EXAMPLE: *get*
Fred got help.
The situation was getting difficult.
His father will get me a loan.
Louise was getting the children ready.

EXERCISE 23 [Optional] For each of the following, *write a sentence of your own* modeled as closely as possible on the grammatical structure of the original sentence. Be prepared to explain in class which of the basic patterns each sentence employs, and how the sentence has expanded, varied, or modified it.

1. Inside the floating cloak he was tall, thin, and bony; and his hair was red beneath the black cap. His face was crumpled and freckled, and ugly without silliness.   (William Golding)

2. He couldn't describe the narrow, steep, lost paths, the snakes sizzling away like flames, the rats, the dust, the naked diseased bodies.   (Graham Greene)

3. Striking ideas we have, and well-executed details we have; but that high symmetry which, with satisfying and delightful effect, combines them, we seldom or never have.

(Matthew Arnold)

G 4 *Transformations*

Several familiar sentence types can be derived from the basic patterns by one or more simple transformations.

Actual sentences seldom follow the simple one-two-three order of the basic patterns. If we construct a model of how sentences are generated in the language centers of the brain, we may well assume a first, raw stage at which every future sentence exists in a simple subject-verb or subject-verb-complement form. But to arrive at the finished product, we must assume a number of further operations. When the sentence is ready for use, some of the basic parts may have been *rearranged*. New elements may have been *added* to establish new connections. Parts no longer necessary may have been *deleted*. The operations that transform the simple model sentence into the more elaborate finished product are called **transformations**.

Showing how the parts of a product seem to fit together is one thing. *Reconstructing* the different stages in the process by which it was produced is quite another. A *transformational* grammar, which tries to describe the sentence-generating process, is more ambitious than a *structural* grammar, which describes the finished product. Even with a fairly simple sentence, an attempt to account fully for all necessary stages in the process can lead to formidable complications. But by limiting ourselves to elementary transformations, and by taking them up one at a time, we can learn much about how English grammar works. At the same time, we can build an important bridge from our simplified basic patterns to actual living sentences.

TRANSFORMATION ONE (Requests): Verb—Complement (IMP)

To turn a statement into an order or a request, we start by *deleting the subject*. We then change the verb to the request-form, or **imperative**. The rest of the sentence remains unchanged. Note that the request transformation can be applied to each of the seven basic patterns:

	SUBJECT	VERB	COMPLEMENT	COMPLEMENT
S-V	(John	stopped.)		
		Stop!		
S-V-O	(Jean	opened	the window.)	
		Open	the window!	
S-LV-N	(John	is	a man.)	
		Be	a man.	
S-LV-ADJ	(The boys	kept	quiet.)	
		Keep	quiet.	
S-V-IO-O	(A friend	gave	the boy	a chance.)
		Give	the boy	a chance.
S-V-O-OC	(The voters	elected	Smith	senator.)
		Elect	Smith	senator!
S-V-O-ADJ	(The marshal	kept	the citizens	calm.)
		Keep	the citizens	calm.

If the subject were *not* omitted from a request, it would typically have to be *you*. Notice that this "understood" *you* still appears in Shakespeare's plays and in modern spoken English. It also reappears in the **tag-questions** that we can add to make a request more polite:

EARLY MODERN ENGLISH: *Return you* to my sister.
Go to, *say you* nothing.
Do you but *mark* how this becomes the house.

SPOKEN ENGLISH: Now *you be* careful.
You tell him exactly what I said.

TAG-QUESTIONS: *Give* him this key, will *you?*
Be careful, will *you?*

The following passages make extensive use of the request-form. To what basic pattern has the request transformation been applied in each case?

Love the earth and sun and the animals, *despise* riches, *give* alms to every one that asks, *stand up* for the stupid and crazy, *devote* your income and labor to others, *hate* tyrants, . . . *have* patience and indulgence toward the people, *take off* your hat to nothing known or unknown or to any man or number of men.   (Walt Whitman)

Hope humbly then; with trembling pinions *soar;*
Wait the great teacher Death; and God *adore.*

(Alexander Pope)

TRANSFORMATION TWO (Passive): Ex-Object—Passive Verb (PASS)

The **Passive** Transformation *reverses* the usual Subject-Verb-Object order. The original object is moved in front of the verb and becomes the new subject. The verb is changed to include a form of the auxiliary *be,* followed by the past participle (V-*en*) of the original verb. The original subject is either *deleted* or put after *by* and made to follow the verb. If we label the original subject NP_1 (for "first Noun Phrase") and the original object NP_2 (for "second Noun Phrase"), the complete formula for the passive would be:

$NP_2 + be + V\text{-}en + (by + NP_1)$
The cat is chased (by the dog).

The passive transformation can be applied to all four of the basic patterns that have at least one object after a transitive verb. For Pattern Five, which has *two objects,* two different passives are possible:

s-v-o	The dog chases *the cat.*
	The cat is chased by the dog.
s-v-io-o	The Browne family offered *the city the site.*
	The city was offered *the site* by the Browne family.
	The site was offered *the city* by the Browne family.
s-v-o-oc	The mayor called *the reporter* a liar.
	The reporter was called a liar by the mayor.
s-v-o-adj	The storm had swept *the streets* clean.
	The streets had been swept clean by the storm.

Not all verbs that take objects have passive forms. We say "It *suited* him" but not "He *was suited* by it." Such verbs, in their uses *with* a possible object but *without* a possible passive, are often put in an in-between category between transitive and intransitive verbs and called **middle verbs.** Do you agree that no passive is possible for the following sentences?

> Her new dress *became* her.
> The set *weighed* six pounds.
> His father *has* a ranch.
> Rip had *slept* many years.
> The fair *will cost* millions.

Typically, the passive shifts attention from the active element, that *initiates* or performs an action, to the passive element, that *undergoes* it or is its target. The two different sets of verb forms that mirror this shift in perspective are traditionally called the **active** and the **passive voice.** The passive is often used as a pretentious way of saying something that could be said more simply. (See **U 4a.**) But note that there are at least two major uses where the passive is especially appropriate. We use it when we want to *emphasize the result* rather than the cause. We also use it when the forces initiating an action are large, *impersonal, anonymous* — hard to pin down, or not important enough to be specified.

EMPHATIC PASSIVE: Always darkish in color, *Simon was burned by the sun* to a deep tan that glistened with sweat. (Golding)
Neither *gossip nor slander had* ever *been traced* to her. (Rudyard Kipling)

ANONYMOUS PASSIVE: *It has been* well *observed* that the misery of man proceeds not from any single crush of overwhelming evil, but from small vexations continually repeated. (Samuel Johnson)

TRANSFORMATION THREE (Questions): Aux—Subject—Verb (QUES)

One basic way of turning a statement into a question is to *move all or part of the verb* in front of the subject. This transformation produces simple yes-or-no questions (QUES-yes/no). It turns

"George *is a friend*" into "*Is* George *a friend?*" With the addition of a question-marker, the same transformation produces questions beginning with words like *when, where, what, why,* or *how* (QUES-wh). "George *is happy*" becomes "Why *is* George *happy?*"

To see the question-transformation at work, we have to distinguish four major possibilities:

(1) When the *complete verb is a one-word form of "be,"* the verb simply reverses — that is, trades places — with the subject. Especially in British English, the same simple reversal is possible (but not required) if the complete verb is a one-word form of *have:*

Time *is up.*	_____	*Is* time *up?*
Peter *was absent.*	_____	*Was* Peter *absent?*
You *are a gentleman.*	_____	*Are* you *a gentleman?*
It *was late.*	_____	*Was* it *late?*
You *have a match.*	_____	*Have* you *a match?*

(2) When the *complete verb includes one or more auxiliaries,* the *first* auxiliary reverses with the subject. Especially in British English, *dare* and *need* in front of another verb are often treated as if they were auxiliaries like *can* or *may:*

X was waiting.	_____	*Was* Irma still *waiting?*
X has finished.	_____	*Has* your friend *finished* his work?
X had been paved.	_____	*Had* the road *been paved?*
X will return.	_____	When *will* the boat *return?*
X could have been avoided.	_____	How *could* it *have been avoided?*
(I need say.)	_____	*Need* I *say* more?
(I dare come.)	_____	How *dare* you *come* in here?

(3) When a *verb other than "be" has no auxiliary with it,* we put a form of *do* in its place. In other words, if there is no auxiliary to reverse with the subject, we *make one up.* We use *do* as a filler or dummy to fill the slot left empty by the missing auxiliary. This use of *do* as a special auxiliary makes possible the familiar "switch-the-verb" or "split-the-verb" effect:

X lives here.	_____	*Does* Mr. Greene *live* here?
X collects stamps.	_____	*Do* you *collect* stamps?
X told you his name.	_____	When *did* the driver *tell* you his name?

X had Y for breakfast.	_____	What *did* you *have* for breakfast?
X lives at Y.	_____	Where *do* the Smiths *live?*

(4) *When a question-word like "who," "which," or "what" asks a question about the subject, the question-transformation does not take place:*

X took the car.	_____	*Who* took the car?
X happened.	_____	*What* happened?
X leads to Chicago.	_____	*Which road* leads to Chicago?
X has been tried.	_____	*What remedy* has been tried?

The reversal of verb (or auxiliary) with the subject is an old, established way of asking a question in our language:

> Why *is* my neighebores *wif* so gay? (Chaucer)
>
> *Shall* I *compare* thee to a summer's day? (Shakespeare)
>
> How *do* I *love* thee? Let me count the ways. (E. B. Browning)

But note that the use of *do* to fill in for the missing auxiliary is relatively new. In Shakespeare's plays and in the King James Version of the Bible, the *do* is missing from many questions where it would be required today:

EARLIER: What ring *gave you,* my Lord?
NOW: What ring *did* you *give?*

EARLIER: Wherefore then *serveth the law?*
NOW: Wherefore then *does* the law *serve?*

EARLIER: *Received ye* the spirit by the deeds of the law?
NOW: *Did* you *receive* the spirit?

TRANSFORMATION FOUR (Negation): Aux—not—Verb (NEG)

The *not* (or the more informal *n't*) that turns an affirmative into a negative statement has a "split-the-verb" effect similar to that of the question-transformation. Only when the complete verb is a one-word form of *be* does the *not* simply *follow* the verb:

> Change of mind *is not inconsistency.* (Matthew Arnold)

Otherwise, we put the *not* between the first auxiliary and the rest of the verb. Or we use a form of *do* to fill the slot before the *not* if no auxiliary is present:

X has been solved.	_____	The problem *has* not *been solved*.
X is doing his share.	_____	Your friend *isn*'t *doing* his share.
X will be repeated.	_____	The warning *will* not *be repeated*.
X speaks French.	_____	Fred *doesn*'t *speak* French.
X recognized the state.	_____	The U. S. *did* not *recognize* the state.
X likes tourists.	_____	The natives *do* not *like* tourists.

In Shakespeare's time, this use of *do* also was merely possible, not yet consistently required. Here are some lines from *The Merchant of Venice:*

EARLIER: And for my love, I pray you, *wrong* me *not.*
NOW: *Do* not *wrong* me.

EARLIER: I *like not* fair terms and a villain's mind.
NOW: I *do* not *like* fair terms and a villain's mind.

TRANSFORMATION FIVE (There-is): There—be—Subject (THERE)

This transformation inserts *There* as a sentence opener that makes the subject and the verb reverse their usual order. The resulting **postponed subject** appears most frequently after a verb containing a form of *be*. But especially in literary English, the *there*-transformation is also applied to sentences using other verbs:

Linoleum *was* on the floor.   _____   There *was* loose, bulging *linoleum* on the floor.

There *is* no greater *desert or wilderness* than to be without true friends. (Sir Francis Bacon)

There is *something* behind the throne greater than the king himself. (William Pitt)

In January, there *came* bitterly hard *weather.*
(George Orwell)

As you look back over these five elementary transformations, note a few *additional points:*

(1) *Not* and *there* have traditionally been classified as adverbs. But because of their special role, the modern grammarian prefers to treat each of them simply as one of a kind. That the *there* in the

there-is transformation is different from the "pointing" adverb *there* is clear in Gertrude Stein's remark about a large, colorless city: "There's no *there* there."

(2) The special auxiliary *do* has several other uses in which it serves as a dummy verb. Besides, it can serve as a *main verb* in its own right in several basic patterns. Here is a listing of its major uses:

> That will never *do*. (S-V)
> The sergeant *did* his duty. (S-V-O)
> Your friend *has done* us a favor. (S-V-IO-O)
> What *did* he say? (Ques)
> We *do* not agree. (Neg)
> That *does* look odd. (Emphasis)
> He still lives there, *doesn't* he? (Tag-question)
> She plays the piano and so *does* he. (Repetition)

EXERCISE 24 Which *basic pattern* underlies each of the following sentences? Which *elementary transformation* has been applied to it? After the number of each sentence, put first (in parentheses) the abbreviation for the original sentence pattern. Then put (in capital letters) the abbreviation for the transformation that has been applied to it: IMP, PASS, QUES, NEG, or THERE.

EXAMPLE: Have you seen Laurence Olivier in *Hamlet?*
(Answer) (S-V-O) QUES

(Be prepared to *reconstruct* in class the original sentence as it was before the transformation was applied to it.)

1. There is only one Shakespeare in English literature.
2. He is generally considered the greatest English writer.
3. His plays have been translated into all major languages.
4. They are performed by theater groups all over the world.
5. His characters have been studied by generations of critics.
6. Which plays have you read?
7. Do you know any plays besides *Julius Caesar* and *Macbeth?*
8. Shakespeare's contemporaries did not worship him quite like later generations.
9. He was even called an upstart by a rival.
10. In his time, there were many successful playwrights.
11. Except for Marlowe, his rivals have been almost forgotten.
12. Shakespeare's plays were written for the popular stage.

13. He did not give the printer carefully revised copies.

14. You should not merely read his plays.

15. Attend a live performance.

16. See them on the stage.

17. Be ready for a fast-moving spectacle.

18. There have been movie versions of several plays.

19. Have you seen the film version of *Hamlet?*

20. Did you find it different from the written play?

EXERCISE 25 Put each of the following sentences through its paces. Write *eight different versions* as follows: (a) request; (b) passive; (c) yes-or-no question; (d) *wh*-question; (e) negative with *not;* (f) passive yes-or-no question; (g) passive negative with *not;* (h) passive yes-or-no question in the negative with *n't.*

EXAMPLE: The posse caught the badman.
(Answers)

    a. Catch the badman.
    b. The badman was caught by the posse.
    c. Did the posse catch the badman?
    d. When did the posse catch the badman?
    e. The posse did not catch the badman.
    f. Was the badman caught by the posse?
    g. The badman was not caught by the posse.
    h. Wasn't the badman caught by the posse?

1. John Dryden rewrote Shakespeare's play.

2. Laurence Olivier acted the part of King Richard.

EXERCISE 26 Make up a sentence of your own and *write a dozen different versions,* using the five elementary transformations and the emphatic *do,* both alone and in various combinations. Use a sentence that has both a first and a second passive. After each version, put in parentheses the appropriate abbreviations for the transformations used, for example, (Ques, Pass). Use Emp for the emphatic *do.*

EXERCISE 27 Examine the way elementary transformations have been applied in the following *passages from Shakespeare's plays.* Which sentences are fully in accord with current usage? Which are different, and how? Can you draw any general conclusions about the handling of these transformations in Shakespeare's English?

1. Feed, and regard him not. (*Macbeth,* Act III, Sc. 4)

2. Why, what care I? If thou canst nod, speak too.

(*Macbeth,* Act IV, Sc. 3)

3. I pray you, speak not; he grows worse and worse;
   Question enrages him. At once, good night:—
   Stand not upon the order of your going,
   But go at once.   (*Macbeth,* Act III, Sc. 4)

4. How goes the night, boy? (*Macbeth,* Act II, Sc. 1)

5. Live you? Or are you aught
   That man may question? (*Macbeth,* Act I, Sc. 3)

6. (Lady Macbeth) He has almost supp'd. Why have you left the
   chamber?
   (Macbeth) Hath he ask'd for me?
   (Lady Macbeth) Know you not, he has?
                                       (*Macbeth,* Act I, Sc. 7)

7. (Brutus) What means this shouting? I do fear the people
   Choose Caesar for their king.
   (Cassius)   Ay, do you fear it?
   Then I must think you would not have it so.
                                    (*Julius Caesar,* Act I, Sc. 2)

8. But wherefore do you hold me here so long?
   What is it that you would impart to me?
                                    (*Julius Caesar,* Act I, Sc. 2)

9. Mislike me not for my complexion. *(Merchant of Venice)*

10. What talk you of the posy or the value? *(Merchant of Venice)*

EXERCISE 28 [Optional] For each of the following passages
from the writings of Ralph Waldo Emerson, *write a passage of your
own* modeled as closely as possible on the grammatical structure of
the original. Note that in several of the sentences, *more than one
simple transformation* has been applied to the same basic pattern. Be
prepared to explain in class what transformations have been applied
in each sentence.

1. The new in art is always formed out of the old.

2. Is there no loving of knowledge, and of art, and of design, for
   itself alone?

3. Is not, indeed, every man a student, and do not all things exist
   for the student's behoof?

4. Man is timid and apologetic; he is no longer upright; he dares
   not say "I think," "I am," but quotes some saint or sage.

5. Don't bewail and bemoan. Omit the negative proposition. Nerve
   us with incessant affirmatives. Don't waste yourself in rejection,
   nor bark against the bad, but chant the beauty of the good.

G 5 Modifiers

Modifiers help us expand basic patterns.

Modifiers fill in and develop the basic sentence patterns. They put flesh on the bare bones of the sentence skeleton. Only rarely does an actual statement use only the bare minimum of parts required to make a complete sentence:

COMPLETE: Nature abhors a vacuum.   (S-V-O)

More typically, **modifiers** *expand, restrict, or otherwise qualify* the meaning of the basic sentence parts:

BARE: Something had caught the eye.   (S-V-O)
MODIFIED: *Another rectangular* hole *in a small cleared space among the dusty greenery* had caught *Mr. Lever's* eye.
                                                        (Graham Greene)

BARE: The sea remained still.   (S-LV-Adj)
MODIFIED: *Under the sinister splendor of that sky* the sea, *blue and profound,* remained still, *without a stir, without a ripple, without a wrinkle — viscous, stagnant, dead.*
                                                        (Joseph Conrad)

The basic sentence part to which one or more modifiers are attached is often called the **headword.** Alone, the headword is often general and colorless. Modifiers *specify* and *make concrete.* They make things visible and tangible, giving them shape, texture, and location. They add the odd angles and accidental features that give to an anonymous member of a class a separate identity and a history of its own:

HEADWORD: paper
MODIFIED: smooth creamy paper, a little yellowed by age
                                                        (George Orwell)
HEADWORD: a shop
MODIFIED: a frowsy little junk shop in a slummy quarter of the town   (George Orwell)
HEADWORD: a jacket
MODIFIED: a short jacket of brown corduroy, newer than the remainder of his suit   (Thomas Hardy)

Modifiers make up a large and miscellaneous grammatical category. Technically, this category includes almost anything that can be added to a basic pattern other than the determiners and auxiliaries, and other than the connectives that may tie one pattern to the other (see **G 6**).

G 5a Adjectives

Adjectives typically modify nouns.

Single-word modifiers fall into two major categories: adjectives, whose *most typical* use is to modify nouns; and adverbs, whose *most typical* use is to modify verbs. Such single-word modifiers are an economical means of working into a statement information from added sources:

STATEMENT: The man climbed the steps.
ADDED SOURCE: The man was old.
ADDED SOURCE: The man was tired.
ADDED SOURCE: His climbing was slow.
RESULT: The *tired old* man *slowly* climbed the steps.

Adjectives appear after linking verbs (see **G 3**) but may be shifted to become *directly attached to a noun.* Notice how the use of adjectives in the following sentences bears out the assertion that "the meaning is in the modifiers":

BARE: O'Brien was a man with a neck and a face.
MODIFIED: O'Brien was a *large, burly* man with a *thick* neck and a *coarse, humorous, brutal* face. (George Orwell)

BARE: He had a forehead, eyes with wrinkles, and lips.
MODIFIED: He had a *low* forehead, *small, sharp* eyes, *puckered* about with *innumerable* wrinkles, and very *thin* lips.

(Hawthorne)

The following are *typical adjective features,* though not every adjective shares them all:

(1) Typical adjectives *fit in after linking verbs:* "The man was *burly.*" "His neck was *thick.*" "His eyes were *sharp.*" But notice that some of the adjectives that modify nouns cannot be so used:

olden times	BUT NOT	the times were *olden*
mere lip service	BUT NOT	his lip service was *mere*

(2) Adjectives often refer to *qualities that can change in degree.* As a result, such adjectives fit in after **intensifiers:** *very, extremely, fairly, rather, quite.* They have a **comparative** form — with the inflectional ending *-er* or the word *more.* They have a **superlative** form — with the ending *-est* or the word *most:*

thin	very thin	thinner	thinnest
small	quite small	smaller	smallest
brutal	rather brutal	more brutal	most brutal
humorous	very humorous	more humorous	most humorous

But notice that some adjectives cannot be "intensified":

due respect	BUT NOT	*duer* respect
dental plates	BUT NOT	very *dental*
daily trips	BUT NOT	more *daily*
annual review	BUT NOT	extremely *annual*

(3) Many adjectives are derived from other words through the *addition of adjective-forming suffixes:*

-y	tasty, scary, smelly, rainy, showy, healthy
-al	seasonal, formal, commercial
-able	passable, expendable, changeable
-ous	marvelous, porous, humorous
-ful	wonderful, awful, colorful
-like	childlike, businesslike, warlike, ladylike
-some	handsome, burdensome, frolicsome
-less	childless, penniless, fruitless, colorless

Notice that many of our adjectives were derived from a French or Latin word *before* they were imported into English. Often the root word was left behind. *Annual* was derived from a Latin noun that we encounter only in the combination *per annum* ("yearly"); *royal* was derived from the noun that we encounter in the title of a Greek play: *Oedipus Rex* ("King Oedipus").

(4) Unlike nouns and verbs, *adjectives are not inflected for number.* Notice how the addition of a plural *-s* turns adjectives into nouns: *casuals, commercials, blinds, reds, whites, shorts.*

In many school grammars, any modifier appearing before a noun is put under the general heading of "adjective." In practice, however, we find a number of *different slots in front of the noun*, each filled by a somewhat different type of modifier. Study the following rough chart:

PREDETER-MINER (Predet)	DETER-MINER (Det)	NUMBER ADJ (Num)	ADJECTIVE (Adj)	MODIFYING NOUN (MN)	NOUN (N)
	a		mean		temper
		three	blind		mice
		four	husky	football	players
	this		beautiful	flower	arrangement
		second			prize
both	his		wooden		houses
	my	two	tiny	song	birds
many	a		dusty	dirt	road
half	the				battle
	the	only	available	horse	cart
all	the	chief		tourist	attractions
	our	every			wish
	these	three	valuable	silver	coins

Notice that in this chart three different types of modifiers appear *between* the determiner and noun. In addition, a fourth type of modifier occasionally *precedes* the determiner:

(1) The words in the "Adjective" column are *true adjectives*. Notice that only these can be preceded by an intensifier. We can say "these three *very* valuable silver coins." We cannot say "these *very* three valuable silver coins" or "these three valuable *very* silver coins." We can say "my two *quite* tiny songbirds." We cannot say "My *quite* two tiny songbirds" or "my two tiny *quite* songbirds."

(2) The words that *come before any true adjective* modifying the same noun can be called **number adjectives**. They include actual number words like *one, two, three; first, second,* and *third*. They also include words dealing with number or quantity in a more general way: *few, several, no, all, both, either, neither, some, much, many, enough, any,* and the like. Notice that many of these double as nouns or noun substitutes:

NUMBER ADJECTIVE:	*Three* little pigs lived in a house.
NOUN SUBSTITUTE:	*Three* is a crowd.
NUMBER ADJECTIVE:	*All* empty cans must be returned.
NOUN SUBSTITUTE:	*All* is not lost.

(3) The words that come *between the true adjectives and the headword* are **modifying nouns.** Like adjectives, such modifying nouns serve as modifiers. But this is the only feature they share with them:

a *football* player	BUT NOT	The player is *football.*
	OR	The player is *very football.*
a *horse* cart	BUT NOT	The cart is *horse.*
	OR	The cart is *horser* than the wagon.

(4) A few of the number adjectives can *precede a determiner* and are then called **predeterminers:**

| *many a* summer | *all his* friends |
| *both my* sisters | *half a* loaf |

The prescribed order of modifiers before a noun illustrates well the importance of word order as a basic tool of English grammar. Even when *several true adjectives modify the same noun,* word order is not entirely optional. Can you change the order of the adjectives in any of the following examples? Can you explain what kind of adjectives follow one another in what order?

a	small	oval		plastic	button
a	big		old	wooden	bucket
the	tiny	round		golden	frame
a	huge	tall	bronzed		athlete
a		square	yellow		patch

Though adjectives typically precede the nouns they modify, the reverse is also possible. *Adjectives follow nouns* in many set expressions. Many of these are borrowed from the French, where reverse order is much more common than in English:

court-*martial*	the devil *incarnate*
attorney-*general*	the voters *present*
heir *apparent*	the funds *available*
notary *public*	the only solution *possible*
the body *politic*	God *Almighty*

Adjectives frequently follow nouns when *more than one* adjective modifies the same noun, or when the adjective is *in turn modified* by other material:

> Makola, *taciturn and impenetrable,* despised the two white men.
> (Joseph Conrad)
>
> Her image accompanied me even in places *the most hostile to romance.*
> (James Joyce)

EXERCISE 29 Write down each word that is italicized in the following passages. After each, write the abbreviation that shows how it was used: *Num* for number adjective; *Adj* for true adjective; *MN* for modifying noun. Be prepared to explain what adjective features, if any, each word shares. (Number the words from 1 through 30.)

1. In 1876 the *first great international* exposition was held in America. The *Centennial* Exhibition in Philadelphia was the *greatest* fair ever held anywhere in the world. It cost *six* times as much as the *famous* exposition in the *Crystal* Palace in London in 1851. It was *bigger* even than the *Vienna* Exhibition of 1874 with its *fifty* acres of buildings.

2. Against the *mica* panes of the *small deep* window the *early* daylight showed like fog, *silvery* and *chill.* Luis jumped alive from sleep and went like a *pale* shadow to the *dead* fireplace, where he blew ashes off a *few remote* coals. (Paul Horgan)

3. Down on *River* Street, he could see the *harbor* lights and the light from the stars on the *calm black* water. The Wright-Sherwin plant was a *grim black* shadow on River Street, with the *street* light shining on its *blind brick* façade.
   (John P. Marquand)

EXERCISE 30 Expand each of the following headwords three different ways, using *different kinds of adjectives* (in different possible positions) as well as modifying nouns.

EXAMPLE: a car
    a shiny new sports car
    a decrepit old touring car
    a second car, unpretentious and inexpensive

1. a shop
2. a street
3. birds
4. his gun
5. her hat

EXERCISE 31 The following *model sentences* make ample and varied use of adjectives to fill in detail. For each sentence, write one of your own, preserving as far as possible the grammatical structure of the original.

1. In this manner, from a happy yet often pensive child, he grew up to be a mild, quiet, unobtrusive boy.   (Hawthorne)
2. He was only a little boy, ten years old, with hair like dusty yellow grass and with shy polite gray eyes, and with a mouth that worked when he thought.   (Steinbeck)
3. His hair and long, full beard were white, his gray, lustreless eyes sunken, his face singularly seamed with wrinkles.

   (Ambrose Bierce)
4. The horizon stretched, impersonal once more, barren of all but the faintest trace of smoke.   (Golding)
5. Antiquated war offices, weak, incompetent, or arrogant commanders, untrustworthy allies, hostile neutrals, malignant Fortune, ugly surprises, awful miscalculations — all take their seats at the Council Board on the morrow of a declaration of war.   (Sir Winston Churchill)

EXERCISE 32 Our language has many ways of turning adjectives into nouns or verbs. Sometimes we simply take the same word, putting it to noun or verb uses: "*free* the slaves," "*right* a wrong," "out in the *cold*." Sometimes we add derivational suffixes: "it was a mere *formal*ity," "the countries had *normal*ized their relations." For each of the following adjectives, write two short sentences. In one, turn the word into a noun. In the other, turn it into a verb. Use either the same word or the word plus derivational suffixes:

   tight, wide, dark, strong, neutral, broad, free, right, cool, weak

G 5b   Adverbs

Adverbs modify verbs but also other sentence elements.

When we add adverbs to nouns, verbs, and adjectives, we have four major **form classes.** These form classes have various features in common. Their members often have more than one form: *man, man's, men, men's; fast, faster, fastest.* The form classes are "open" classes. We frequently coin *new* nouns, verbs, adjectives, adverbs: *radar, debrief, radioactive, electronically.* By contrast, the function words making up the remaining word classes are part of the basic language machinery. They are seldom augmented by new prepositions, connectives, and the like.

Like other familiar categories, the class of **adverbs** actually includes a number of *sub-classes* that behave differently in a sentence:

manner adverbs   These are the most typical adverbs: they *modify verbs,* typically telling us *how.* They often have the typical *-ly* ending. They typically have forms with *-er/-est* or *more/most* for comparative and superlative:

The bear approached *slowly.*
(His *approach* was slow.)
He ended the interview *abruptly.*
(The *ending* was abrupt.)
The group left *hurriedly.*
(Their *departure* was hurried.)

space/time adverbs   These often behave like manner adverbs but have some special features of their own. Many of them lack the *-ly* ending: *here, there, away, abroad, now, today, yesterday, tomorrow.* Unlike manner adverbs, such words appear after *be* (occasionally after *stay* or *remain*). These same adverbs can be put directly *after a noun* to modify that noun:

Your friends are *here.*
His *arrival here* went unnoticed.

His uncle was *abroad.*
His *friends abroad* supported him.

The time is *now.*
Its *condition now* is unknown.

intensifiers   These adverbs modify *other modifiers.* They are words like *very, rather, quite, extremely,* and *fairly.* They appear immediately before the adjective or adverb they modify:

Her parents had been *very anxious.*
A *fairly large* crowd was waiting for us.
The meeting ended *quite abruptly.*

sentence modifiers   Words like *certainly* or *generally* typically apply to a statement *as a whole* rather than to any part of it:

> *Certainly,* he cannot hold out much longer.
> (*That he cannot hold out much longer* is certain.)
>
> *Generally,* we leave after lunch.
> (*That we leave after lunch* is generally true.)

Adverbs that modify verbs or the sentence as a whole have more *freedom of movement* than most sentence parts enjoy. This relatively free-floating quality of adverbs makes it possible for a writer to vary sentence rhythm and prevent monotony. Notice how the adverb appears in a different position in each of the following sentences by Robert Graves:

> The stranger smiled *good-naturedly.*
> Richard *suddenly* asked Charles if he would let him hear the shout.
> *Presently* a stranger came up and asked permission to sit down.
> Richard thought that Charles must have gone *suddenly* mad.

When looking for adverbs in your own reading and writing, remember that adjectives and adverbs *overlap in form* (see also **U 2c**):

(1) When both adjective and adverb use *the same root word,* the adverb is typically the form with *-ly.* But remember that many adjectives *also* use the *-ly* ending:

ADVERB: rapidly, similarly, regularly, speedily, successfully, incredibly, mildly, suspiciously, cautiously

ADJECTIVE: a *friendly* smile, a *leisurely* walk, the *early* train

(2) A few *prefixes and suffixes* are often found with adverbs (but not *only* with adverbs):

a-   abed, adrift, askew, aslant, astern, asleep, awake, awash, astraddle, afloat

to-   tomorrow, today, together

-wise   lengthwise, counterclockwise

(3) In some instances, adjective and adverb are *identical:*

ADVERB: ran *fast,* rose *early,* did it *right,* moved *forward*
ADJECTIVE: a *fast* train, *early* notice, the *right* answer, a *forward* movement

In its earlier stages, English had two distinctive adverb forms: one with *-like* (which became *-ly*) and one with *-e* (which became "silent" and dropped off). As a result, words like *slow, loud,* and *quick* have both a marked and an **unmarked** adverb form: "Move *slowly*" and "go *slow.*" Chaucer's Chanticleer "gan to sing *loude.*" Though *slowly* and *loudly* are more common in formal English, both forms survive:

> The children . . . shouted *loud* in the ears of the two men.
> (Robert Graves)
> Then she ran back into the house laughing *loudly.*
> (Robert Graves)

In Shakespeare's English, not only short words like *loud* but also longer words appear in unmarked forms, whereas today we would expect distinctive adverb forms. What would be the modern equivalent of *"grievous* sick," *"wondrous* strange," *"indifferent* cold," or *"passing* fair"?

EXERCISE 33 Sometimes *three or more adjectives and adverbs* are closely related in origin or in meaning. Since the *-ly* ending is not a reliable guide, we have to rely on their role in the sentence to sort them out. After the number of each sentence, put *Adj* if the italicized word is an adjective. Put *Adv* if it is an adverb. Be prepared to explain in class the differences in use and meaning.

1. The *late* Senator Gordon was a friend of labor.
2. The Senate has passed a few labor laws *lately.*
3. The law had been passed *late* in the year.
4. His *homely* little sister had become a beautiful girl.
5. The children had been sent *home* early.
6. We especially enjoyed the *homelike* atmosphere.
7. He considered his chances *good.*
8. He studied the map *well.*
9. A *goodly* number had already arrived.

10. He had been sick, but now he was *well* again.
11. The *right* man has not yet been found.
12. The mayor handled the problem *right*.
13. He has *rightly* been called a friend of the poor.
14. His home county had been a very *backward* area.
15. Jim always did everything *backward*.
16. We considered their action a step *backwards*.
17. His parents had always worked *hard*.
18. His father *hardly* ever worked.
19. His father had been a *hard* worker.
20. His grandfather had been a *hardy* soul.

EXERCISE 34 Rewrite each of the following sentences twice, each time using *different adverbs* to fill the blanks.

1. _____ the _____ fast track star _____ pleased the crowd _____.
2. _____ a _____ large crowd _____ awaits the results.
3. _____ the crew _____ finished its _____ heavy work _____.
4. _____ the _____ peaceable bear _____ attacked the campers.
5. _____ the _____ cheerful girl laughed _____.

G 5c Prepositional Phrases

Prepositional phrases are the most versatile among the modifiers in a sentence.

Prepositions are everywhere in the typical English sentence. Their most basic function is to work into a sentence nouns (or substitutes) other than those that are part of the basic subject-verb-complement structure. Such a noun becomes the **object** of the preposition. The preposition combines with its object in a **prepositional phrase.** Notice how much of the freight in the following sentence is carried by prepositional phrases:

BARE: A German band was playing.

MODIFIED: *In a quiet bystreet* a German band *of five players in faded uniforms and with battered brass instruments* was playing *to an audience of street arabs and leisurely messenger boys.* (James Joyce)

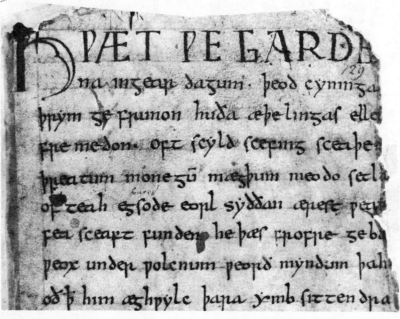

Facsimile of the first page of the Beowulf manuscript (the
Trustees of the British Museum)

After dyuerse werkes made/ translated and achieued/ha
uyng noo werke in hande. J sittyng in my studye where as
laye many dyuerse paunflettis and bookys. happened that
to my hande cam a lytyl booke in frensh .Whiche late was
translated oute of latyn by some noble clerke of fraūce whi
che booke is named Eneydos/ made in latyn by that noble
poet & grete clerke Vyrgyle/ whiche booke J sawe ouer and
rede therin. How after the generall destruccyon of the gre
te Troye. Eneas departed berynge his olde fader anchises
Bpon his sholdres/his lityl son yolus on his honde.his wy

Facsimile of manuscript of the Caxton Preface: the Preface to
the Book of Eneydos, 1490 (Syracuse University Press)

Here is a partial inventory of *common prepositions,* listing first single words and then combinations serving the same function:

> about, above, across, after, against, along, among, around, as, at, before, behind, below, beneath, beside, between, beyond, by, during, except, for, from, into, like, of, off, on, over, since, through, to, toward, under, until, up, upon, with, within, without; aside from, as to, as well as, because of, due to, in spite of, instead of, on account of, out of

Here are some *less common* prepositions:

> amidst, astride, athwart, onto, throughout; by dint of, by virtue of, in behalf of, in lieu of

Prepositional phrases modify nouns, verbs, and adjectives alike. In turn, the object of a preposition may carry with it an array of various modifiers. To speak authentic English, we need a mastery of **idiomatic prepositions** — a knowledge of the preposition *customarily* used with a given noun, verb, or adjective:

NOUNS
anger *at* his remarks; assent *to* a proposal; dissatisfaction *with* a solution; dissent *from* an opinion; surprise *at* a decision

VERBS
abide *by* an agreement; abstain *from* voting; acquiesce *in* an injustice; agree *with* a person, *to* a proposal, *on* a solution; aspire *to* high honors; comply *with* a request; concur *with* someone, *in* an opinion; confide *in* somebody; conform *to* specifications; delight *in* mischief; deprive *of* a privilege; dissuade *from* an action; infer *from* evidence; insist *on* accuracy; interfere *with* a performance, *in* someone's business; object *to* a solution; part *with* one's belongings; persevere *in* a task; prevail *on* someone to help; prevent someone *from* an action; refrain *from* wrongdoing; rejoice *at* good news; resolve *on* a course of action

ADJECTIVES
alarmed *at* the news; capable *of* an action; deficient *in* strength; identical *with* the original; ignorant *of* the facts; inconsistent *with* an overall plan; indifferent *to* praise; inferior *to* the competition; jealous *of* rivals; partial *to* countrymen; rich *in* resources

When you look for prepositions in actual sentences, you will have to be prepared for the usual *overlappings and complications:*

(1) Many prepositions do *double duty as adverbs:*

PREPOSITION	ADVERB
He fell *down the stairs.*	He fell *down.*
Jim came *in a convertible.*	Jim came *in.*
Dora came *up the path.*	The subject came *up.*
We looked *around the corner.*	We looked *aròund.*
The bear came *near the fire.*	The bear came *near.*

(2) When a verb is typically followed by an idiomatic preposition, the preposition often *shifts away from its object and stays with the verb* if the question-transformation or the passive-transformation changes the order of the major sentence parts:

> (You are looking *at a valuable document.*)
> What are you *looking at?*

> (The police should look *into the matter.*)
> The matter should be *looked into.*

(3) Some former prepositions have *blended with a verb* to become the second part of a **phrasal verb.** They then become "particles" that carry the stress when the combination appears together. They can trade places with the object, with the result that the phrasal verb then has an "enclosed object":

PREPOSITION : Jim turned / *in the driveway.*
PARTICLE : Jim turned *in* / his key.
Jim *turned* his key *in.*

PREPOSITION : Jean looked / *up the stairs.*
PARTICLE : Jean looked *up* / a word.
Jean *looked* a word *up.*

(4) Where we would expect a prepositional phrase indicating time or place, we often find simply a noun (or noun phrase) *without a preposition* to tie it to the rest of the sentence:

> The festival will be repeated (during) *this summer.*
> There are few farms (on) *this side of the river.*

Many prepositional phrases must remain next to what they modify. But those that apply to the sentence as a whole share with adverbs considerable *freedom of movement.* Can you see how the different positions possible for prepositional phrases make for great variety in sentence rhythm?

Suspicions *amongst thoughts* are *like bats amongst birds;* they ever fly *by twilight.*
(Sir Francis Bacon)

Outside the fair, in the valleys and woods, all was quiet.
(Thomas Hardy)

In the afternoon, at Mother's request, Father took me *for a walk.*
(Frank O'Connor)

EXERCISE 35 How complete is your knowledge of *idiomatic prepositions*? After the number of each expression, write down the missing preposition.

1. accuse _____ a crime
2. adhere _____ a plan
3. attend _____ his business
4. charge _____ an offense
5. divest _____ all responsibility
6. find fault _____ a gift
7. pertain _____ a subject
8. secede _____ the Union
9. succeed _____ an attempt
10. superior _____ all rivals

EXERCISE 36 Write three simple sentences illustrating different basic patterns. Then write *three different expanded versions,* fleshing out the basic structure with a variety of prepositional phrases.

EXAMPLE: The sergeant talked.

The sergeant *in the shiny new uniform* talked *to the girl from Toledo.*

In a corner of the crowded room, the sergeant *with a bloody bandage around his arm* talked *to the nurse with the graying hair and serious eyes.*

With both hands in his pockets, the sergeant *at the center desk* talked *at the top of his voice about the shortcomings of the United States Army.*

EXERCISE 37 The following *model sentences* make ample and varied use of prepositional phrases to fill in detail. For each sentence, write one of your own, preserving as far as possible the grammatical structure of the original.

1. A maid in a white cap and apron was watering a box of plants on a sill which shone like a slab of limestone in the warm glare.
(James Joyce)

2. At one end of the big barn, on a sort of raised platform, Major was already ensconced on his bed of straw, under a lantern which hung from a beam.
(George Orwell)

3. To the birds of the more soaring kind Casterbridge must have appeared on this fine evening as a mosaic-work of subdued reds, browns, greys, and crystals, held together by a rectangular frame of deep green.　　(Thomas Hardy)

G 5d *Appositives*

A noun may be modified by one or more other nouns serving as appositives.

An **appositive** is a second noun that modifies the noun it follows *by simple juxtaposition.* Unlike the modifying noun that *precedes* another noun, an appositive often carries its own determiners and modifiers with it. Whereas we can work other modifiers into the smooth flow of the sentence, appositives typically cause an *audible break* and are set off in writing by commas.

In effect, appositives provide us with an *additional* way of working further information into an originally meager sentence:

SOURCES:　Crossley had a queer face.
　　　　　His face was not unpleasant.
　　　　　He was a man of forty or fifty.

RESULT:　Crossley, *a big man of forty or fifty,* had a queer, not unpleasant face.　　(Robert Graves)

SOURCES:　Kayerts was short and fat.
　　　　　He was the chief.
　　　　　Carlier was tall.
　　　　　He was the assistant.

RESULT:　Kayerts, *the chief,* was short and fat; Carlier, *the assistant,* was tall, with a large head and a very broad trunk perched upon a long pair of thin legs.　　(Joseph Conrad)

Only when appositives are essential for identification (and in effect become part of a name) do the breaks and the commas disappear:

George *the Third*　　William *the Conqueror*　　my sister *Clare*

More than one appositive may modify the same noun. Appositives may in turn be heavily modified in various ways. They need not always immediately follow the noun, but may sometimes *point forward or back to it* from other positions in the sentence. As a result, appositives add further to our ample resources for sentence variety. Notice the different positions of the appositives in the following sentences:

> *A creature of custom,* George read more from habit than from curiosity.
>
> My eye was caught by a chik-chak, *a little brown house lizard with a large head,* high up on the wall. (W. Somerset Maugham)
>
> Ralph turned involuntarily, *a black, humped figure against the lagoon.* (Golding)
>
> The first had died, *an infant,* when her husband first went out to France. (D. H. Lawrence)

EXERCISE 38 Write three simple sentences, using basic patterns with two or more nouns. Then write *three different expanded versions* of each, making varied use of appositives as well as other modifiers.

EXAMPLE: John stopped the car.
John, *the shy rookie policeman from Buffalo,* stopped the car, *a powerful black limousine with drawn curtains.*
John, *the mild-mannered hitchhiker with the red beard,* stopped the car, *a late-model Continental with a wealthy Republican at the wheel.*
John, *the family's trusted chauffeur,* stopped the car, *a beautiful antique with polished brass trim.*

EXERCISE 39 The following *model sentences* make varied use of appositives. For each sentence, write one of your own, preserving as far as possible the grammatical structure of the original.

1. The girl was alone, a rather short, sullen-looking young woman of twenty-seven. (D. H. Lawrence)
2. Up there, for once, were clouds, great bulging towers that sprouted away over the island. (Golding)
3. At length Maurice rose restlessly, a big obtrusive figure. (D. H. Lawrence)
4. Each time he left a trail of souvenirs — model tanks and Gurkha knives with handles made of bullet cases, and German helmets and cap badges and button-sticks, and all sorts of military equipment. (Frank O'Connor)

5. We had a glimpse of the other youngster, a little, white face, pallid from sweet-eating and over-sapid food, and distorted by evil passions, a ruthless little egotist, pawing at the enchanted pane. (H. G. Wells)

REVIEW EXERCISE 3 Can you tell modifying nouns from adjectives, adjectives from adverbs, adverbs from prepositions? Write down all words italicized in the following passages from a short story by D. H. Lawrence. After each word, put in parentheses the appropriate abbreviations: *Num* for number adjective; *Adj* for all other adjectives; *MN* for modifying noun; *Int* for intensifier; *Adv* for all other adverbs; *Prep* for preposition; *App* for appositive. (Number the words from 1 through 20.)

1. *At* this time Bertie Reid wrote to Isabel. He was her *old* friend, a *second* or third cousin, *a Scotchman.*

2. The *long* dining room was *dim,* with its *elegant* but *rather* severe pieces of old furniture. Only the *round* table glowed *softly* under the light.

3. She looked *automatically* again at the *high,* uncurtained windows. In the last dusk she could just perceive *outside* a huge *fir* tree swaying its boughs.

4. Light came *out* from the open *kitchen* door. She went *forward* and stood in the doorway. The *farm* people were at tea, seated at a *little* distance from her, *round* a long, narrow table.

REVIEW EXERCISE 4 [Optional] A complete account of English modifiers would have to mention some additional possibilities not covered in this book. It would have to describe additional *kinds* of modifiers, additional *uses* of some of the modifiers here described, and uses of some of them as sentence parts *other than* modifiers. *Can you discover some of these possibilities for yourself* by studying the following examples? Take notes and be prepared to present your findings in class. Provide additional examples of your own.

1. The senator was famous for *off-the-cuff* pronouncements.
2. Her *grandfather's* farm was in Vermont.
3. Mr. Petersen is *quite* a man.
4. He called an ambulance for *the sick* and wounded.
5. Only *the very rich* .can afford to live there.
6. *After nine* is too late.
7. All his *behind-the-scenes* maneuvers had failed.
8. The performance was *rather* a bore.
9. The *very* idea was new to him.

10. Everything had changed for *the better*.
11. Charles spoke *hardly* a word.
12. *The wealthiest* are not always *the most charitable*.
13. Even *the bravest* have moments of weakness.
14. The *girl's* father had come from Italy.
15. The *girls'* mothers had been very anxious.

G 6 Connectives

**Connectives help us build up complex,
mature sentences from short, isolated units.**

Actual sentences do not exist in a vacuum. They are a link in
a conversation, a part of a picture, a step in an argument. Only
occasionally do we stop short for a sentence that is meant to stand
by itself — that cuts through to essentials, strips off complications:

> The mind is not a muscle.
> The proper study of mankind is man. (Alexander Pope)

Such sentences can give us the *gist* of an argument. They can
serve to *emphasize* a central point. But they cannot give us the
whole picture. They do not make room for any "yes, but" or any
"maybe yes, maybe no." Often we need a sentence that gives not
only the stark facts, but also some of their causes. We need not just
an opinion, but also some of the necessary conditions and reserva-
tions. We then move away from the kind of sentence we can fit
on a poster or shout through a megaphone. We build the kind of
sentence that *shows a number of facts in their proper relations:*

SIMPLE: The frequency of envy makes it familiar.

COMPLEX: The frequency of envy makes it *so* familiar *that* it escapes
          our notice; *nor* do we often reflect upon its turpitude or
          malignity, *till* we happen to feel its influence.
          (Samuel Johnson)

SIMPLE: The forest protected him from the direct sun.

COMPLEX: The forest protected him from the direct sun, *but* it shut
          out the air, *and* the occasional clearings, shrivelled *though*
          they were in the vertical glare, seemed cooler than the
          shade *because* there was a little more air to breathe.
          (Graham Greene)

SIMPLE: She had slow eyes and parted lips.

COMPLEX: *Though* she was stout in build and stood erect, her slow
eyes and parted lips gave her the appearance of a woman
who did not know *where* she was or *where* she was
going.   (James Joyce)

In these sample sentences, different kinds of **connectives** join
short isolated statements as *parts of a larger whole.* Each subject-
predicate unit that becomes part of a larger sentence is called a
clause. The multiple-clause sentence is indispensable to the writer
who wants to keep from oversimplifying his subject. It is the favorite
tool of a writer like Henry James, whose ideal is to "take everything
in." It is the natural medium for a writer like William Faulkner,
who, if possible, would "capture all of life in one sentence."

The following chart is a preview of the connectives we use to
establish *different kinds of links* between clauses:

1.	COORDINATING CONNECTIVES	and, but, for, or, nor, yet, so
2.	ADVERBIAL CONNECTIVES	however, therefore, moreover, furthermore, nevertheless, besides, indeed, consequently, hence, in fact
3.	SUBORDINATING CONNECTIVES	when, whenever, while, before, after, since, until, as, if, because, unless, provided, though, although, whereas; so that, no matter how, no matter what
4.	RELATIVE PRONOUNS	who, whom, whose; which, that
5.	SPECIAL CONNECTIVES	that, why, whether, how, who, what, whoever, whatever

G 6a Coordination

Coordinating and adverbial connectives join independent clauses.

Some ways of linking two or more clauses leave such word
groups grammatically **independent,** or self-contained. Like freight
cars temporarily coupled together to make up a train, they could

easily be unhitched again to function as separate sentences. We can establish such a loose connection between two clauses by merely putting them next to each other. We then change the *falling* intonation pattern that signals "End of statement" and substitute the *level* pattern that signals "Statement goes on." In writing, we signal this change by putting a *semicolon* in place of the period:

> The Lord is my shepherd; I shall not want. (Psalms)
>
> There was a bit of the magpie about Father; he expected everything to come in handy. (Frank O'Connor)

More typically we join two independent clauses by means of a coordinating or an adverbial connective:

(1) **Coordinating** connectives are *and, but, for, or, nor, yet,* and *so.* These are the true all-purpose connectives in English. We use them to join statements that are roughly on an *equal footing* — two equally important parts of the picture, two equally important steps in an argument:

> For the last two days the crew had had plenty of hard work, *and* the night before they had very little sleep.
> (Joseph Conrad)
>
> The fox provides for himself, *but* God provides for the lion.
> (William Blake)
>
> Ralph did not take the hint, *so* the fat boy was forced to continue. (Golding)

Nor causes a *reversal* of subject and auxiliary similar to that brought about by the question-transformation:

> Youth could not be pleaded as his excuse; *nor could* ignorance *be* his excuse since he was a man who had seen something of the world. (James Joyce)

Connectives like *but, for,* and *so* establish *logical* relations: contrast, cause, result. *And,* however, merely *adds.* It suits the "honest reporter," who concentrates on the action — with no comment, no interpretation:

> Then it crashed again *and* he felt the blow as it hit his lower ribs and ripped on through, blood sudden hot and frothy in his mouth, *and* he galloped toward the high grass where he could crouch and not be seen. (Ernest Hemingway)

But *and* can also suggest the "naive observer," who reports every-thing pell-mell, without sorting it out:

> They had been engaged a long time, but old Jake Woods had objected, *and* so they had run away, *and* were going to Poker Flat to be married, *and* here they were. *And* they were tired out, *and* how lucky it was they had found a place to camp and company. (Bret Harte)

NOTE: All the words used as coordinating connectives *between* clauses also serve various other functions. *And, but,* and *or,* for in-stance, also link elements *within* a clause:

> He went down on hands *and* knees in the dust *and* opened his suitcase. He took out his wife's photograph *and* stood it on the chop-box; he took out a writing-pad *and* an indelible pencil. (Graham Greene)

(2) **Adverbial** connectives are words like *however, therefore, nevertheless, consequently, instead, besides, furthermore, moreover, indeed,* and *in fact.* These generally make for a more noticeable break between the two clauses they join than do coordinating con-nectives. Where *and* and *but* are typically preceded by a comma, *however* and *therefore* typically require a semicolon. Often they are set off from the rest of the second clause by further punctuation:

> I think; *therefore,* I am.
> Winston had never made the smallest effort to verify this guess; *indeed,* there was no way of doing so. (George Orwell)
> I let on not to notice him; *instead,* I pretended to be talking to myself. (Frank O'Connor)

Unlike coordinating connectives, adverbial connectives share with adverbs *freedom of movement within the second clause:*

> The doctor rushed in; *however,* his efforts were useless.
> The doctor rushed in; his efforts, *however,* were useless.
> The doctor rushed in; his efforts were useless, *however.*

Words like *furthermore, however,* and *therefore* are more formal than *and, but,* and *so.* Generally, adverbial connectives are more common in the formal movement and countermovement of argu-ment than in the casual give-and-take of conversation:

The disparagers of culture make its motive curiosity; sometimes, *indeed*, they make its motive mere exclusiveness and vanity. (Matthew Arnold)

So tricky a piece of work would never be entrusted to a single person; *on the other hand,* to turn it over to a committee would be to admit openly that an act of fabrication was taking place. (George Orwell)

EXERCISE 40 Write down all the words italicized in the following passages. After each word, put in parentheses the appropriate abbreviation: *El* for a connective joining elements *within* a clause; *Co* for a coordinating connective actually joining *two clauses; Ad* for an adverbial connective; *No* for "not a connective." (Number the words from 1 through 20.)

Be prepared to point out in class the *subject(s) and verb(s)* of each clause.

1.   In Faith *and* Hope the world will disagree,
     But all Mankind's concern is Charity.
                              (Alexander Pope)
2.   I linger *yet* with Nature, *for* the Night
     Hath been to me a more familiar face
     Than that of man. (Lord Byron)
3. Then all the congregation stopped rustling *and* was still, *so* I turned myself to more fitting thoughts. (Alan Paton)
4. The tears filled his mild eyes; *something* precious had passed away. (Henry James)
5. He looked hard at the book on the end of the bench, *but* he wouldn't have touched it *for* the world. (Henry James)
6. His liberation [was] promised *for* the morrow; meanwhile, *however,* the intensity of his meditations kept him tranquil.
                              (Henry James)
7. Mr. Lever lay in bed *and* his thoughts went round *and* ,round *and* he couldn't sleep. (Graham Greene)
8. I wanted to draw him out, *for* I was interested in his sudden gravity, *and* there was a suggestion of irony in his last remark.
                              (E. M. Forster)
9. I expected to hear a yell of surprise and terror, *and* made a movement, *but* had not the strength to get on my legs.
                              (Joseph Conrad)
10. Moths beat against his lamp; *but* there were no mosquitoes; he hadn't seen *or* heard one. (Graham Greene)

EXERCISE 41 In the following passages, two independent clauses have been joined to become part of a larger sentence. Using these as *model sentences,* write passages of your own in which you preserve the grammatical structure of the original.

1. Always be ready to speak your mind, and a base man will avoid you. (William Blake)
2. Children sweeten labors, but they make misfortunes more bitter. They increase the cares of life, but they mitigate the remembrance of death. (Sir Francis Bacon)
3. A single life doth well with churchmen, for charity will hardly water the ground where it must first fill a pool. (Sir Francis Bacon)
4. The human beings did not hate Animal Farm any less now that it was prospering; indeed, they hated it more than ever. (George Orwell)

G 6b Subordination

Subordinating connectives, relative pronouns, and special connectives make one clause dependent on another.

*Co*ordination strings clauses loosely together. We can unhitch them again by merely changing a comma or a semicolon to a period. *Sub*ordination makes the subordinated clause grammatically **dependent** on the **main clause.** Like a shelf detached from its wall, or a two-wheel trailer detached from a truck, a dependent clause detached from its main clause is incomplete. When it does appear in writing, it suggests a *fragmentary afterthought* rather than a complete statement:

> He was all for Macomber again. *If you could forget the morning.* (Ernest Hemingway)

There are *three major ways* of subordinating a second clause to a main clause:

(1) **Subordinating** connectives are words like *when, whenever, while, before, after, since, until, as, as long as, where, if, because, unless, so that, provided, though, although, whereas, no matter how, no matter what.* They introduce clauses that specify time and place; fill in causes, results, conditions; or establish comparisons and contrasts:

Fools rush in *where angels fear to tread.*   (Alexander Pope)

When the short days of winter came dusk fell *before we had well eaten our dinners. When we met in the street* the houses had grown sombre. . . . The cold air stung us and we played *till our bodies glowed.*   (James Joyce)

I will sing unto the Lord, *because he hath dealt bountifully with me.*   (Psalms)

A sudden breeze shook the fringe of palm trees, *so that the fronds tossed and fluttered.*   (Golding)

Everything had a battered, trampled-on look, *as though the place had just been visited by some large violent animal.*   (George Orwell)

Unlike coordinating connectives, "subordinators" typically introduce clauses that have *freedom of movement* in the larger sentence:

My father recited poems *when he felt well.*
When he felt well, my father recited poems.
My father, *when he felt well,* recited poems.

NOTE: This shifting of the dependent clause is *not* possible with **paired** subordinators like *as . . . as, so . . . that,* or *more . . . than,* where the first connective *hooks back* into the main clause:

These studies had *so* waked him up *that* a new light was in his eyes.   (Henry James)

A wise man will make *more* opportunity *than* he finds.
    (Sir Francis Bacon)

(2) **Relative pronouns** are *who, whom, whose, which,* and *that.* (See U 2b on *who* and *whom.*) They serve a double function: they *link* a dependent clause to one of the nouns in the main clause, with the dependent clause serving as a modifier. At the same time, they *substitute* for one of the nouns within the dependent clause:

STATEMENT: Fred knew the man.
ADDED SOURCE: *The man* had left the message.
RESULT: Fred knew the man *who* had left the message.

STATEMENT: Simon was not in the bathing pool.
ADDED SOURCE: They expected to find *Simon* there.
RESULT: Simon, *whom* they expected to find there, was not in the bathing pool.   (Golding)

The resulting **relative clauses** can appear *at many different points* in a sentence, often with more than one such clause modifying the same noun:

> The evil *that men do* lives after them.　　(*Julius Caesar*)
>
> There was no life at all, except for a few large birds *whose wings creaked overhead through the invisible sky like an unoiled door.*　　(Graham Greene)
>
> She lived in the memory of her mother, *who had died* when she was fourteen, and *whom she had loved.*　　(D. H. Lawrence)

Notice that the relative pronoun *that* is often *deleted* when it would have served as the object in a relative clause:

> Some slighting phrases *she had used* still rankled in his memory.
> 　　(James Joyce)
>
> There is no duty *we so much underrate* as the duty of being happy.　　(R. L. Stevenson)

(3) *That, if, whether,* and question words like *who (whoever), what (whatever), why, where,* and *how* can be used as **special connectives** to introduce a **noun clause.** Such a clause substitutes for one of the nouns in the main clause:

NOUN:	The postman reported *the news.*
NOUN CLAUSE:	The postman reported *that James had left.*
NOUN:	*The informer* is not known.
NOUN CLAUSE:	*Who told the police* is not known.

Noun clauses are versatile, since they may appear in a *variety of noun positions:*

> *What is now proved* was once only imagined.　　(William Blake)
>
> I rather tell thee *what is to be feared*
> Than *what I fear.*　　(*Julius Caesar*)
>
> By the late summer the news of *what had happened on Animal Farm* had spread across half the county.　　(George Orwell)

Notice that *that* is often *deleted* at the beginning of a noun clause:

> The noble Brutus
> Hath told you *Caesar was ambitious.*　　(*Julius Caesar*)

To classify connectives, we have to look, not merely at the word or its meaning, but at the way the word *functions in the sentence*. Words like *that* and *who* function both as relative pronouns and as special connectives. Subordinators like *before, after,* and *until* double as prepositions *(before the meeting, after the fact)*. Notice that a similar *meaning* may be expressed by connectives of quite different types:

CONTRAST: Fred adores Hilda, *but* she detests him.
Fred adores Hilda; she, *however,* detests him.
Fred adores Hilda, *though* she detests him.

REASON: He left the country, *for* his visa expired.
He left the country, *because* his visa expired.

RESULT: The road was icy, *so* the descent was slow.
The road was icy; the descent, *therefore,* was slow.
The road was icy, *so that* the descent was slow.

EXERCISE 42 In the following passages, do you recognize the different kinds of *coordination and subordination* that help combine simple units into more complex sentences? Write down all the italicized words. After each word, put in parentheses the appropriate abbreviation: *El* for a connective joining elements *within* a clause; *Co* for a coordinating connective actually joining two clauses; *Adv* for an adverbial connective; *Sub* for a subordinating connective; *Rel* for relative pronoun; *Spec* for special connective. (Number the words from 1 through 20.)

Be prepared to point out in class the *subject(s) and verb(s)* of each clause.

1. The animals had never heard of anything of this kind before *(for* the farm was an old-fashioned one *and* had only the most primitive machinery), *and* they listened in astonishment *while* Snowball conjured up pictures of fantastic machines *which* would do their work for them *while* they grazed at their ease in the fields *or* improved their minds with reading and conversation. (George Orwell)

2. The great congregation stirred and rustled, *and* with a kind of sigh, *because* this boy could preach. Then they stood up and sang, *and* one or two of the women wiped their eyes, *which* my brother never likes, *because* he says *that* religion is a matter for obedience *and* not for tears. I watched him too, *but* I did not know *what* he thought, *nor* have I ever known what passed in that mind. (Alan Paton)

3. The fond illusion, *while* it lasted, eased the wound of elections never won . . .; it *moreover* lighted the lamp *that* would glimmer through the next eclipse. (Henry James)

EXERCISE 43 The following *model sentences* show different kinds of subordination alone or in combination. For each of these, write a passage of your own, preserving as far as possible the grammatical structure of the original.

1. No man can justly censure or condemn another, because indeed no man truly knows another. (Sir Thomas Browne)
2. Fortune is like the market, where many times, if you can stay a little, the price will fall. (Sir Francis Bacon)
3. When we arrived with our bags at the asylum cricket ground, the chief medical officer, whom I had met at the house where I was staying, came up to shake hands. (Robert Graves)
4. Mr. Browne, whose face was once more wrinkling with mirth, poured out for himself a glass of whisky while Freddy Malins exploded, before he had well reached the climax of his story, in a kink of high-pitched bronchitic laughter. (James Joyce)
5. Perpetual devotion to what a man calls his business is only to be sustained by perpetual neglect of many other things. (R. L. Stevenson)

EXERCISE 44 [Optional] A complete account of subordination would have to describe some *additional* types of dependent clauses not covered in this book. Can you *discover some of these for yourself* by studying the following examples? Take notes and be prepared to present your findings in class. Provide additional examples of your own.

1. There was no doubt that the girl was her daughter.
2. He discovered the reason we had stayed away.
3. It happened on the day they came home.
4. I am glad that you could come.
5. I was surprised that you took the money.
6. He spread the rumor that the bank would fail.
7. Few were aware that a ship had passed the island.
8. It is possible that he missed the train.
9. It is certain that the check was cashed.
10. The charge that the brakes were defective has not been proved.
11. I was surprised you left early.
12. She could never forget the morning she first met him.

13. Are you sure you locked all the doors?
14. It is unfortunate that nobody was at home.
15. It is a fact that he never called back.

REVIEW EXERCISE 5 Can you classify connectives, including some of the *less common* ones, according to how they behave in a sentence? After the number of each sentence, put the appropriate abbreviation in parentheses:

co   coordinating (both connective and clause are stationary)

adv   adverbial (connective may *shift* within its clause)

sub   subordinating (*clause* may shift within the sentence)

rel   relative pronoun (replaces a *noun* in relative clause)

spec special (clause replaces a noun in *main* clause)

1. Many people talk about modern painters, *yet* few buy their works.
2. Some people will buy a painting, *provided* it treats familiar subjects.
3. They welcome art *as long as* it deals with flowers and sunsets.
4. Few ask *whether* the treatment is original.
5. Most prefer realistic art; *accordingly,* they distrust strange colors and shapes.
6. They neglect artists *that* prefer an abstract style.
7. Many modern painters avoid familiar objects *so that* they can freely experiment with lines and angles.
8. They do not reproduce familiar sights, *nor* do they tell a story.
9. They do not paint cheerful scenes, *no matter how* much the public may like optimistic art.
10. Most modern artists are impatient with popular taste; many, *in fact,* do not cater to a commercial public at all.
11. What are the forces *that* have shaped modern art?
12. The modern artist does not repeat *what* everyone else has done.
13. He expresses his own feelings; *otherwise* he feels stifled.
14. He rejects convention *in order that* he may have full creative freedom.
15. He knows the rewards of conformity; *nevertheless,* he travels his own lonely road.
16. Not every artist is a true pioneer, *or* artists would not be human.
17. The true leaders create new styles, *whereas* lesser artists follow current fashions.

18. Some artists merely want to be different, *as if* originality were an end in itself.
19. The true artist wants to be himself; *consequently,* he searches for a truly personal style.
20. The true artist follows *wherever* his genius leads him.

G 7 Verbals

Verbals cannot serve as complete verbs but perform a rich variety of other functions in a sentence.

Language is not a mechanical system of signals but a living, growing thing. If it had been designed by engineers, one kind of part would be clearly different from another, and each would serve a clearly limited function. But language is more like an organism than like a machine. Its elements may serve several different functions at once. Parts originally designed for a quite different function have been assigned new roles. As a result, nouns and verbs and adjectives are not clearly distinct, rigidly separated categories. In various complicated ways, they *overlap* and shade over into each other.

Like a living thing, language draws on its own resources in order to adapt to new and different needs. The best illustration of this resourcefulness is our extensive system of **verbals.** Though *derived* from verbs, verbals are neither true verbs nor true nouns nor true adjectives. Instead, they *share various features* with them all. Their versatility makes verbals a rich additional resource in sentence-building. In each of the following examples, verbals appear at strategic points in the structure of a fully developed, multi-layered sentence:

> He saw himself
> > *saving* people from *sinking* ships,
> > *cutting* away masts in a hurricane,
> > *swimming* through a surf with a line;
> or as a lonely castaway,
> > barefooted and half-naked,
> > *walking* on *uncovered* reefs in search of shellfish *to stave off* starvation.
> > > (Joseph Conrad)

The vastness and strangeness of the life
 suggested to him by the bales of merchandise
  stocked along the walls or
  swung aloft out of the holds of steamers
wakened again in him the unrest
 which had sent him *wandering* in the evening from garden
 to garden in search of Mercedes.   (James Joyce)

They came to a grizzled church,
 whose massive square tower rose unbroken into the *darkening* sky.
  the lower parts *being illuminated* by the nearest lamps
  sufficiently *to show*
   how completely the mortar from the joints of
   the stone-work had been nibbled out by time
   and weather.   (Thomas Hardy)

G 7a   Participles

Participles can serve as modifiers.

Participles are verbals that appear as part of the complete verb after the auxiliaries *be* and *have*. The **present participle,** or *-ing* form, appears after *be:* "is *crying*," "was *waiting*," "are *returning*." The **past participle,** or *-en* form, appears after both *be* and *have:* "was *taken*," "had *helped*," "has *brought*." (See **G 2b.**) We can lift either participle out of its usual place after the auxiliary and use it to modify a noun (or sometimes a whole sentence). Such a participle often carries with it objects or modifiers that accompanied it when it was part of a verb. The resulting grammatical hybrid is a compact way of working added detail or related information into a sentence:

STATEMENT: George went up into the gallery.
ADDED SOURCE: He was *whistling under his breath.*
RESULT: George went up into the gallery, *whistling under his breath.*

STATEMENT: I was left alone with my ship.
ADDED SOURCE: It had been *anchored at the head of the gulf.*
RESULT: I was left alone with my ship, *anchored at the head of the Gulf of Siam.*   (Joseph Conrad)

STATEMENT:	The thin sun appeared.
ADDED SOURCE:	It was *rapidly burning away mist and cloud.*
ADDED SOURCE:	It was *warming the air and the earth.*
RESULT:	By midmorning the thin sun appeared, *rapidly burning away mist and cloud, warming the air and the earth.* (William Faulkner)

Notice that occasionally *more complicated* forms of the participle carry auxiliaries along to show perfect tense or progressive:

STATEMENT:	The authors were listed on the board.
ADDED SOURCE:	They were *being studied.*
RESULT:	The authors *being studied* were listed on the board.

Participles — alone, or combining with other material in a **verbal phrase** — may appear in *many different positions* in a sentence. They thus make possible great variety in sentence style:

(1) The verbal may *immediately precede a noun* being modified:

He was driven to his bed by *nagging* women.
The driver showed us his *badly cut* hands.

(2) One or more verbals may appear *at the end of a sentence:*

The groom at the head looked back, *jerking the leading rope.*
(D. H. Lawrence)
They turned to each other. *laughing excitedly, talking, not listening.* (William Golding)
The ground beneath them was a bank *covered with coarse grass, torn everywhere by the upheavals of fallen trees, scattered with decaying coconuts and palm saplings.* (Golding)

(3) A verbal may *interrupt* a sentence at various points, making possible great variety in sentence rhythm:

Most of the children, *feeling too late the smart of sunburn,* had put their clothes on. (Golding)
He faced about and, *standing between the awnings,* held out his right hand at arm's length toward the sun. (James Joyce)

(4) One or more verbals may *introduce* a sentence, with other verbals possible later:

Gazing up into the darkness, I saw myself as a creature *driven and derided by vanity.*   (James Joyce)

Seizing the sailor's arm with her right hand, and *mounting the little girl on her left,* she went out of the tent *sobbing bitterly.*
(Thomas Hardy)

The verbals in these examples are hybrids between adjectives and verbs: like *adjectives,* they serve as modifiers. Like *verbs,* they carry their own modifiers and objects with them. When they *cross over completely* to become true adjectives, they are no longer modified by such typical verb modifiers as manner adverbs. Instead, like true adjectives, they are preceded by intensifiers like *very:*

VERBAL: a quickly *fading* glow, a badly *leaking* faucet
ADJECTIVE: a very *interesting* story, a very *charming* girl

Many past participles have similarly crossed over to become true adjectives. At one time, English had many more distinctive past participles in *-en,* like *broken, fallen, hidden, driven, forgotten, chosen, woven, bitten.* Many old participles in *-en* now live on only as adjectives, while a new regularized verbal has taken their place as part of the verb:

VERB FORM:	had *melted*	had *swelled*	had *drunk*
ADJECTIVE:	*molten* gold	a *swollen* river	a *drunken* sailor
VERB FORM:	had *shrunk*	had *cleft*	
ADJECTIVE:	a *shrunken* head	a *cloven* hoof	

Some of these old participles still preserve some verb characteristics. We say "a *loaded* question" but "a heavily *laden* boat"; "he hadn't *shaved*" but "a clean-*shaven* face."

EXERCISE 45 Write down all words italicized in the following passages. Number them from 1 through 20. After each word, write the appropriate abbreviation in parentheses:

CV — used as a *complete verb*
PV — used as *part* of a complete *verb*
Mod — used as a *modifier*

1. One night Sergeant O'Neill had *come* to the house and had *stood* in the hall, *talking* in a low voice with his father and *chewing* nervously at the chinstrap of his cap.   (James Joyce)

2. The lamplights now *glimmered* through the *engirdling* trees, *conveying* a sense of great snugness and comfort inside, and *rendering* at the same time the *unlighted* country without strangely solitary and vacant. (Thomas Hardy)

3. The great draught-horses *swung* past. They were tied head to tail, four of them, and they *heaved* along to where a lane *branched* off from the highroad, *planting* their great hoofs floutingly in the fine black mud, *swinging* their great rounded haunches sumptuously, and *trotting* a few sudden steps as they were *led* into the lane. (D. H. Lawrence)

4. Well, my brother went to bed after all. For two or three days he *resisted* it, *grumbling* and *growling*, and *picking* at his food.

(Alan Paton)

EXERCISE 46 Rewrite each of the following pairs as a *single sentence*. Making use of participles, work the material from the second sentence into the first as a verbal or verbal phrase.

EXAMPLE: The child went into the house.
He was crying bitterly.
(Result) Crying bitterly, the child went into the house.

1. Many people read Charles Dickens.
They live in all parts of the world.

2. His books have sold millions of copies.
They have been translated everywhere.

3. His stories usually have a strong moral.
They were written in Victorian England.

4. Dickens reforms his old skinflint Scrooge.
He turns him into a kindly old gentleman.

5. In *David Copperfield*, David does well.
He leads a good life.

6. Steerforth perishes in a shipwreck.
He had strayed from the right path.

7. Dickens deals in extremes.
He puts kindness and loyalty next to brutal evil.

8. Some of his villains are vicious brutes.
They murder without remorse.

9. *A Tale of Two Cities* describes bloodthirsty revolutionaries
They are driven by the spirit of revenge.

10. Dickens still cherished kindness.
He knew the dark side of human nature.

EXERCISE 47 The following *model sentences* illustrate various uses of participles. For each, write a sentence of your own, preserving as far as possible the grammatical structure of the original.

1. Trees, forced by the damp heat, found too little soil for full growth, fell early, and decayed. (Golding)
2. He bumped his elbow against the door at the end and, hurrying down the staircase, walked quickly through the two corridors and out into the air. (James Joyce)
3. They plunged down the bank, slipping and sliding in the thawed earth, crashing through the willows and into the water. (William Faulkner)
4. Roving across the landscape, the doctor's quick eye detected a figure in black passing through the gate of the field, down towards the pond. (D. H. Lawrence)
5. I sat there, fagged out, looking at the curtains, trying to clear my mind of the confused sensation of being in two places at once, and greatly bothered by an exasperating knocking in my head. (Joseph Conrad)

G 7b   *Gerund and Infinitive*

Gerunds and infinitives substitute for nouns; in addition, infinitives serve many other functions.

Verbals may substitute for nouns in most of the typical noun positions in a sentence. When the *-ing* form is used as a noun substitute, it is traditionally called a **gerund,** or, more simply, a verbal noun. When the plain form of the verb is used as a verbal (either to substitute for a noun or to serve some other function), it is called an **infinitive.** Infinitives typically have the "infinitive marker" *to* (*to sing, to ask*). But we also find "unmarked" infinitives without *to*. To indicate perfect or passive, we use infinitives including the plain form of *have* or *be* (*to have asked, to be taught*).

SUBJECT	VERB	OBJECT	OBJECT	PREP. PHRASE
Smoking	endangers	health.		
The guests	hated	*to leave.*		
Linda	had asked	me	*to write.*	
Fred	surprised	us		by *studying.*

In keeping with their hybrid status between verbs and nouns, such verbals may *carry along their own objects and modifiers:*

> *To reason right* is to submit.   (Alexander Pope)
> *To create a little flower* is the labor of ages.   (William Blake)

The infinitive is especially frequent in sentences where it fills in the meaning of the dummy subject *it:*

> *It* is impossible *to please everybody.*
> *It* annoys me *to see such shoddy workmanship.*
> Certainly *it* is heaven upon earth *to have a man's mind move in charity, rest in providence, and turn upon the poles of truth.*
> (Sir Francis Bacon)

In addition to substituting for nouns, infinitives serve several *other major functions:*

(1) The infinitive appears in many *extended verb phrases* using *have to, ought to, am going to, am about to,* and *used to.* Very similar is the use of the infinitive after verbs like *happen, seem, need, dare, hesitate:*

> His friends *had to leave.*
> He *ought to pay* his own bills.
> Her brother *was going to join* the army.
> Big steamboats *used to travel* up the river.
>
> She *seems to have taken* it to heart.
> His aides *hesitated to wake* him up.
> This proposal *needs to be studied.*

(2) The infinitive takes the place of a *second object* after verbs like *ask, cause, want, permit, allow, enable, order, like:*

SUBJECT	VERB	OBJECT	INFINITIVE
Henry	asked	us	*to leave.*
The device	enabled	him	*to see again.*
The director	allowed	spectators	*to sit on the stage.*
Mrs. Holt	wanted	her son	*to become a doctor.*

The *unmarked* infinitive appears in the same position after verbs like *see, hear, let, make, watch:*

No one	saw	him	*leave the house.*
The ending	made	everyone	*cry.*
We	watched	the car	*come up the driveway.*

(3) The infinitive is extremely versatile as a *modifier*. It is used to modify nouns, verbs, adjectives, or a sentence as a whole:

(Noun) a place *to live*
time *to go home*
the point *to remember*
the decision *to turn back*

(Verb) paused *to think*
called *to apologize*
resigned *to return to private practice*

(Adjective) glad *to be back*
eager *to meet him*
hard *to believe*
anxious *to return to work*

(Sentence) *To start the motor,* turn the key.
To be safe, I locked the door.

Infinitives always preserve some of their verb features. Many gerunds, however, *cross over completely* to become true nouns. They then no longer carry objects with them; they can no longer be modified by manner adverbs. Instead, they acquire such noun features as determiners or a plural *-s;* they are modified by adjectives:

VERBAL NOUN: He believed in *eating well.*
NOUN: He believed in *good eating.*
VERBAL NOUN: *Shipping snakes* is illegal.
NOUN: *The shipping of snakes* is illegal.
VERBAL NOUN: *Dwelling further on this point* is useless.
NOUN: *All the dwellings* were substandard.

EXERCISE 48 Write down all *-ing* forms italicized in the following passages. Number them from 1 through 20. After each word, put the appropriate abbreviation in parentheses:

PV — *part* of a complete verb
Mod — participle used as a *modifier*
VN — *verbal noun* preserving verb features
N — form that has lost its verb features to become a true *noun*

1. Piggy was *standing cradling* the great cream shell and the *shouting* died down. (William Golding)

2. Natural abilities are like natural plants, that need *pruning* by study. (Sir Francis Bacon)

3. They had collected there, *coming* from north and south and from the outskirts of the East, after *treading* the jungle paths, *descending* the rivers, *coasting* in praus along the shallows, *crossing* in small canoes from island to island.

   (Joseph Conrad)

4. The *roaring* of lions, the *howling* of wolves, the *raging* of the stormy sea, and the destructive sword are portions of eternity, too great for the eye of man. (William Blake)

5. By *fighting* his wife in the presence of customers and by *buying* bad meat he ruined his business. (James Joyce)

6. People are always astonished at *meeting* each other. All kinds come through the hedge, and come at all times — when they are *drawing* ahead in the race, when they are *lagging* behind, when they are left for dead. I often stand near the boundary *listening* to·the sounds of the road — you know what they are — and wonder if anyone will turn aside. (E. M. Forster)

7. Where was the glory of *having taken* Rome for those tumultuous barbarians, who poured into the Senate-house, and found the Fathers *sitting* silent and unmoved by their success?

   (R. L. Stevenson)

EXERCISE 49 Find all gerunds and infinitives in the following passage. Be prepared to explain orally how each is used or what function it serves.

Though it is a shocking thing to stop walking, I was so tired that I sat down on a milestone to rest. People outstripped me, jeering as they did so, but I was too apathetic to feel resentful, and even when Miss Eliza Dimbleby, the great educationist, swept past, exhorting me to persevere, I only smiled and raised my hat. At first I thought I was going to be like my brother, whom I had had to leave by the roadside a year or two round the corner. He had wasted his breath on singing, and his strength on helping others.

—E. M. Forster, "The Other Side of the Hedge"

EXERCISE 50 Rewrite each of the following sentences *five times,* substituting verbals or verbal phrases for the italicized word. Each time start with simple verbals and work up to extended verbal phrases.

EXAMPLE: *Something* is a pleasure.

Skating is a pleasure.

Popping corn is a pleasure.

To walk slowly down a busy street is a pleasure.

Swimming in a cool lake on a hot summer day is a pleasure.

To see someone try to worm his way to the head of a long line in front of a movie theater, and fail, is a pleasure.

1. *Something* is useless.
2. The stranger started *something.*
3. A friend taught me *something.*

EXERCISE 51 The following *model sentences* illustrate various uses of gerunds and infinitives. For each, write a sentence of your own, preserving as far as possible the grammatical structure of the original.

1. It is a miserable state of mind to have few things to desire and many things to fear. (Sir Francis Bacon)
2. To yield reverence to another, to hold ourselves and our lives at his disposal, is not slavery; often, it is the noblest state in which a man can live in this world. (John Ruskin)
3. Economy is the art of making the most of life. (G. B. Shaw)
4. Cunning is the art of concealing our own defects, and discovering other people's weaknesses. (William Hazlitt)
5. To spend too much time in studies is sloth; to use them too much for ornament is affectation; to make judgment wholly by their rules is the humor of a scholar. (Sir Francis Bacon)

G 7c Absolute Constructions

In absolute constructions, verbals carry along their own subjects.

A verbal worked into a sentence from an added source may carry along *its own subject.* The resulting verbal phrase is less closely tied to the rest of the sentence than most other modifiers. It is called an **absolute** construction:

STATEMENT: Everything had a new look.

ADDED SOURCE: There was *no sun.*

RESULT: *There being no sun,* everything had a new look.

STATEMENT:	He walked on.
ADDED SOURCE:	*His arms* were scarcely swinging at all.
ADDED SOURCE:	*His body* was bent forward a little from the waist.
RESULT:	He walked on, *his arms scarcely swinging at all, his body bent forward a little from the waist.*

STATEMENT:	I was glad I came, because my nephew sat with us.
ADDED SOURCE:	*Nella* had stayed with the children at home.
RESULT:	I was glad I came, because my nephew sat with us, *Nella having stayed with the children at home.*

(Alan Paton)

When the complete verb of the added source is a form of *be,* the verbal is often *omitted* from the absolute construction:

STATEMENT:	The director stood at the window.
ADDED SOURCE:	His back *was* to the light.
RESULT:	The director stood at the window, *his back to the light.*

STATEMENT:	Jack stood up as he said this.
ADDED SOURCE:	The bloodied knife *was* in his hands.
RESULT:	Jack stood up as he said this, *the bloodied knife in his hands.* (William Golding)

Absolute constructions may appear at various points in a sentence. They thus add further to our extended resources for *sentence variety:*

(1) The most typical position for the absolute construction is *at the end,* where it fills in added detail:

> He turned uneasily aside, *the retreating steps of the horses echoing in his ears.* (D. H. Lawrence)
>
> She floated at the starting point of a long journey, very still in an immense stillness, *the shadows of her spars flung far to the eastward by the setting sun.* (Joseph Conrad)

(2) One or more absolute constructions may appear *at the beginning,* serving as a preamble for the main part of the statement:

> *My head bursting with stories and schemes,* I stumbled in next door. (Frank O'Connor)
>
> *Eyes shining, mouths open, triumphant,* they savored the right of domination. (Golding)

(3) One or more absolute constructions may *interrupt* a sentence, making possible variety of sentence rhythm:

He reached the church without observation, and *the door being only latched,* he entered. (Thomas Hardy)

Kayerts, *his round eyes suffused with tears, his fat cheeks quivering,* rubbed his bald head, and declared, "This is a splendid book." (Joseph Conrad)

EXERCISE 52 Write down all the words italicized in the following passages. Number them from 1 through 20. After the number of each word, put in parentheses the appropriate abbreviation:

CV — used as a *complete verb* or part of a complete verb
Mod — used as a *modifier*
Abs — used as part of an *absolute construction*

1. One evening of late summer, before the present century had *reached* its thirtieth year, a young man and woman, the latter *carrying* a child, were *approaching* the large village of Weydon-Priors, in Upper Wessex, on foot.
(Thomas Hardy)

2. Were there always these vistas of *rotting* nineteenth-century houses, their sides *shored up* with balks of timber, their windows *patched* with cardboard and their roofs with corrugated iron, their crazy garden walls *sagging* in all directions?
(George Orwell)

3. He had the strange feeling of one who is *moving,* yet at peace — the feeling of the swimmer, who, after long struggling with *chopping* seas, finds that after all the tide will *sweep* him to his goal.
(E. M. Forster)

4. A man stood upon a railroad bridge in northern Alabama, *looking* down into the swift water twenty feet below. The man's hands were behind his back, the wrists *bound* with a cord. A rope closely *encircled* his neck. It was attached to a stout cross-timber above his head and the slack fell to the level of his knees. Some loose boards *laid* upon the sleepers *supporting* the metals of the railway supplied a footing for him.
(Ambrose Bierce)

5. Dante stared across the table, her cheeks *shaking.* Mr. Casey *struggled* up from his chair and *bent* across the table towards her, *scraping* the air from before his eyes with one hand as though he were *tearing* aside a cobweb. (James Joyce)

EXERCISE 53 The following *model sentences* make varied use of absolute constructions. For each, write a sentence of your own, preserving as far as possible the grammatical structure of the original.

1. She went out of the room with the tray, her face impassive and unchanged. (D. H. Lawrence)
2. The choice made, she could surrender her will to the strange, the exhilarating, the gigantic event. (Graham Greene)
3. Davies' white, indoor face was hard with his intensity, his young-looking eyes shining, his big mouth drawn down to be firm. (Walter V. T. Clark)
4. The light spread upwards from the glass roof, making the theater seem a festive ark, anchored among the hulks of houses, her frail cables of lanterns looping her to her moorings. (James Joyce)
5. On the far side of the room, sitting at a table alone, a small, curiously beetle-like man was drinking a cup of coffee, his little eyes darting suspicious glances from side to side. (George Orwell)

REVIEW EXERCISE 6 Verbals are among the most versatile of grammatical elements. A complete account of their uses would have to describe a number of possibilities not covered in this book. Can you *discover some of these for yourself* by studying the following sample sentences? Which of these uses of verbals are similar to those you have already studied? Which are different? Take notes, and be prepared to present your findings in class. Provide additional sample sentences of your own.

1. We encountered many English-speaking natives.
2. He was uncertain whether to stand up or remain sitting.
3. For the equation to work out right, the several steps must be taken in the right order.
4. He did not know where to look for her.
5. Tim had his glasses adjusted.
6. The islands had once been populated by man-eating savages.
7. He saw himself saving people from sinking ships.
8. He found himself surrounded by eager faces.
9. No one had told us what to do.
10. His car had an air-cooled engine.
11. His arrival had not been a world-shaking event.
12. She found herself supervising girls her own age.
13. Jane loved to have her picture taken.
14. When they had done laughing, Ralph turned back to his work.
15. I had him tell me exactly what had happened.

G 8 Phonology

Writing transcribes the sounds of speech in incomplete and at times misleading ways.

Grammar is often divided into three major parts. **Syntax** deals with the *structure of the sentence;* it shows how we make words work together in sentences. **Morphology** deals with the *shape of words;* it shows how we put roots, prefixes and suffixes, and inflections together to make up words. **Phonology** deals with the *sound system* of English. It shows how we use our sound resources to give sentences and words their spoken form.

Phonology, in other words, deals with the grammar of *speech.* To study it profitably, we have to become fully aware of the difference between speech and writing. In much of our study of grammar, we are actually studying *written* sentences — sentences on a chalkboard, or in a book. When we deal with such matters as the position of a word, the written sentence is indeed a *graphic* demonstration of what we actually speak and hear. But when we deal with something like the inflection spelled *-ed,* we begin to realize that writing only *partially* reflects what goes on in speech. There are three different ways of pronouncing the *-ed* ending:

back*ed,* crack*ed*	*t*-sound	(rhymes with *fact*)
bagg*ed,* lagg*ed*	*d*-sound	(rhymes with *snagged*)
hat*ed,* wait*ed*	*id*-sound	(as in *horrid*)

There are *three major reasons* for this lack of a one-to-one correspondence between speech and writing:

(1) *Speech is historically prior to writing.* Highly developed languages were spoken for many thousands of years before writing was invented — first as a rough means of recording commercial accounts, laws, religious lore. The writing system brought to England by Christian missionaries was an *adaptation* of an alphabet originally designed for languages quite different from English. It goes back to the alphabet of the Phoenician traders of the Mediterranean, who spoke a Semitic language related to modern Hebrew

and outside the Indo-European language family. This alphabet had been adapted and developed by the Greeks and Romans, who spoke languages that were at least distant cousins of Old English. But even so, the Roman alphabet when applied to English is a poor fit. For instance, English spelling had to develop new *combinations* of letters to stand for single sounds not represented in the Roman alphabet at all:

> *th* as in *this, that;* but also in *thing, thought*
> *sh* as in *shy, shore*

(2) *Speech is less conservative than writing.* Spoken English has changed greatly since Chaucer's time, but written English has not kept up with it. Much of our spelling system mirrors the sounds of fifteenth- or sixteenth-century English rather than those of the language of our own time. For instance, the *gh* in *light, knight,* and *night* once stood for an actual sound, related to those still heard in German *Licht* and *Nacht.*

(3) *Speech is less standardized than writing.* English *sounds* differ in different parts of the country (and the world), but most of these differences are not reflected in writing. When we listen to a speech, we may be able to tell whether the speaker is from Scotland or Alabama, from Australia or New Jersey. But in the printed version of the speech, most, if not all, of the distinctive regional features will have disappeared. The student of phonology has to be very cautious in trying to determine what is "normal" or "typical" use of sound resources for speakers of English. He has to recognize considerable *variety* from one part of the country, and one part of the world, to another. A book like this one can at best give a roughly averaged-out version of what is commonly heard in current American speech.

Only recently have grammarians begun to pay detailed attention to the grammar of speech. There are several different systems for describing the sound features of English, and experts disagree on a number of important points. You will have to test what you are told *against your own experience.* Ask yourself: Have I heard it this way? Do I hear it this way in my own speech?

G 8a Consonants and Vowels

English makes use of a limited inventory of consonant and vowel phonemes.

Each language uses only a *limited choice* of the considerable variety of possible speech sounds. In studying foreign languages, we encounter numerous sounds not used in English and therefore rather difficult for the native speaker of English to hear and imitate successfully:

GERMAN: i*ch,* Li*ch*t; a*ch,* Na*ch*t; *ü*ber, g*ü*tig
FRENCH: t*u,* f*u*mer; j*eu*ne, Di*eu; s*on, b*on; un,* Verd*u*n
SPANISH: Me*x*ico, Don Qui*x*ote

In studying those sounds that English *does* use, the linguist's main concern is with those that produce a meaningful contrast. For instance, the *e* and *a* in *pen* and *pan* are very close together in the way they are pronounced. They are hard for many foreign students of English to tell apart. But the change from one to the other clearly *produces a change in meaning* in pairs like *pen/pan, bed/bad, men/man.* Sounds that actually produce a difference in meaning are called **phonemes.** Not every two sounds that are pronounced differently represent two different phonemes. For instance, the *l* in *lip, light,* and *long* sounds different from the one in *all, full,* or *well.* But we do not change the meaning of *lip* by putting at the beginning of the word the fuller *l,* pronounced farther back in the mouth, that we hear in *all.* These two varieties of *l,* (and a third variety sometimes heard in words like *bottle* and *shuttle* are different versions, or **allophones,** of the same phoneme.

Though inventories of the English phonemes differ in some details, most recognize the following groups:

(1) **Consonants** are sounds we produce when lips, teeth, or tongue set up some kind of *obstruction to the flow of speech.* According to the kind of friction or obstruction that produces the consonants, we can sort them out into several types. The symbol used by many linguists for each phoneme appears between diagonal lines:

Lip-sounds — produced by the lips alone or together with the teeth

/b/	*b*id, *b*ed, *b*ait
/f/	*f*ull, *f*it, *f*oe
/m/	*m*ine, *m*eat, *m*ole
/p/	*p*it, *p*en, *p*ut
/v/	*v*eil, *v*ine, *v*iew

Tip-of-the-tongue sounds — produced by the tongue being placed against the teeth or the palate

/č/	*ch*urch, *ch*ink, *Ch*ina
/d/	*d*o, *d*ie, *d*ark
/j̇/	*j*ack, *j*oin, *j*inx
/l/	*l*ip, *l*ight, *l*oad
/n/	*n*o, *n*ine, *n*est
/s/	*s*it, *s*oap, *s*et
/š/	*sh*ine, *sh*ow, *sh*eep
/θ/	*th*in, *th*ick, *th*ought
/ð/	*th*e, *th*at, *th*ose
/t/	*t*en, *t*ip, *t*op
/ž/	*z*ip, *z*oo, *z*ink
/z/	a*z*ure, plea*s*ure, lei*s*ure

Back-in-the-mouth sounds — produced with the tip of the tongue kept down, out of the way

/g/	*g*ood, *g*et, *g*old
/k/	*k*id, *k*een, *c*ut
/ŋ/	lo*ng*, si*ng*, ga*ng*
/r/	*r*ight, *r*ow, *r*ed

Notice that in this list of consonants there are several *pairs* of sounds for which the position of lip and tongue is the same:

*b*et/*p*et	*v*ine/*f*ine	*J*oyce/*ch*oice	*d*o/*t*o
*z*ip/*s*ip	lei*s*ure/*s*ure	*th*is/*th*istle	*g*ood/*c*ould

You can hear the difference best when you first pronounce a long drawn out *f* and then change it to *v*. As you change, you can hear the *voice* being turned on: the vocal cords start vibrating, changing the **unvoiced** consonant *f* to the **voiced** consonant *v*.

(2) **Semivowels** are pronounced with little obstruction to the flow of speech. In this and other ways they are *in-between* consonants and vowels:

/h/	*h*ot, *h*and, *h*eal
/w/	*w*et, *w*ink, *w*ail
/y/	*y*ear, *y*ou, *y*oung

(3) **Vowels** are *unimpeded* sounds given their quality by the size and shape of the sound chamber formed by the mouth. Vowels change in quality as we gradually open our mouths from *half-closed* through *intermediate* to *open,* as in bid — bed — bad. They change as we move them back from the *front* of the mouth, first to the *middle,* and then to the *back,* as in bet-but-bought. Of the resulting possibilities, most speakers of English use roughly the following (see *Chart*):

Front vowels (from half-closed to open)

/i/	p*i*n, b*i*t, l*i*p
/e/	b*e*d, b*e*t, l*e*d
/æ/	m*a*n, b*a*d, h*a*d

Back vowels (from half-closed to open)

/u/	p*u*t, f*u*ll, g*oo*d
/o/	b*o*ne, h*o*me, *o*nly
/ɔ/	b*o*ught, c*au*ght, d*o*g

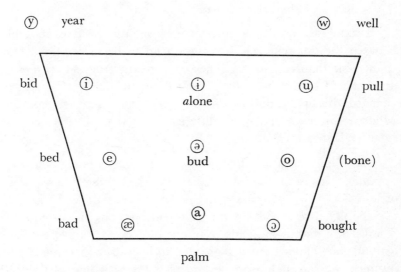

A SIMPLIFIED CHART: Nine Simple Vowels

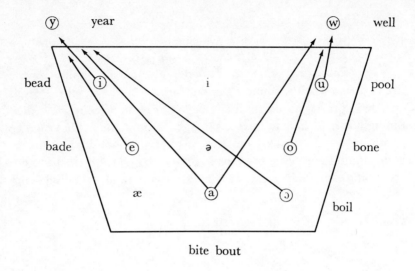

A SIMPLIFIED CHART: Seven Glides (Diphthongs)

Middle vowels (from half-closed to open)

/i/   *a*lone, nos*e*s, rott*e*n
/ə/   b*u*t, b*u*d, ab*o*ve
/a/   f*a*ther, p*a*lm, c*a*rt

Because of the many intermediate mouth positions possible between the different vowels, vowels tend to be more varied and changeable than consonants. They vary greatly from one *region* to another and thus help us to identify different dialects. They have changed drastically during the *history* of our language, making Modern English sound quite different from that of Chaucer's or even Shakespeare's time.

(4) **Diphthongs** are double vowels, more accurately described as *glides*. Because of the intermediate positions possible as we raise or lower our jaws, vowels are not as clearly set apart as the keys of a piano. They are more like the different positions of a trombone. The English diphthongs glide from one position to another the way a trombonist glides from a high note to a low, or vice versa. For instance, we can glide from several of our vowels toward the /y/ of *year*, located high in front of the mouth. We thus change *bid*

to *bead, bet* to *bait, lawn* to *loin.* Gliding toward the /w/ of *well,* high in back of the mouth, we change *full* to *fool.* For most speakers, this glide toward /w/ accompanies the /o/ of *bone* and *home.*

Here is a list of commonly heard diphthongs (see *Chart*):

Front glides

/iy/	h*e*, m*e*, s*ee*
/ey/	m*a*de, l*a*bel, p*ay*
/ay/	b*i*te, *eye*, str*i*de
/ɔy/	l*oi*n, b*oy*, ann*oy*

Back glides

/uw/	f*oo*l, l*oo*se, n*oo*n
/ow/	b*o*ne, h*o*me, *ow*n
/aw/	h*ou*se, c*ow*, n*ow*

Notice that sometimes we get the effect of a *double* glide: We take the /uw/ of *booty* or *food* and then *precede* them with a glide from /y/ to change them to *beauty* and *feud.*

EXERCISE 54 How good a listener are you? On a separate sheet, write down the answers to each of the following questions, filling in the *appropriate phonemes* where required.

1. What are the two common ways of pronouncing the last sound in *garage?* / / or / /.
2. How does the final consonant in *house* change when it precedes the plural ending spelled *-es*? From / / to / /.
3. In various languages, we encounter all four of the following "consonant clusters" at the *beginning* of a word: /spr/ /špr/ /pl/ /pn/. Which two of these are possible at the beginning of an English word? / / and / /.
4. How does the vowel in *the* change when instead of preceding a consonant (th*e* *c*ar) it precedes a vowel (th*e* *a*nt)? From / / to / /.
5. When, in writing, we add a "silent *e*" at the end of *shin* and *sham,* how does the pronunciation of the vowel in each word change? From / / to / /, and from / / to / /.
6. Words that sound alike may be spelled differently. For each of the following, write down two possible different spellings: /siy/ /sən/ /prey/ /baw/.

EXERCISE 55 To take inventory of *your own speech sounds,* you will have to listen in your speech for some of the more common variations. Which of the following occur in your own speech? Compare your own inventory with that of your classmates.

1. /r/ Among the English consonants, /r/ varies most from region to region, and from speaker to speaker. The most distinctive American /r/ is the growled "Western" /r/, with the tongue drawn far back into the mouth. The most distinctive British version is the trilled Scottish /r/. With many speakers of eastern New England and the South, /r/ appears only as a bridge between two vowels. The /r/ is *omitted* in words like *farm, barn, hard; bird, heard, word. Farm* then rhymes with *calm.* Which of your friends "growl" their /r/; which skip the /r/? Make them say the following test sentence:

   He heard his former partner warn him against birds.

2. /æ/ In Eastern New England and Virginia, as in much British English, the vowel of *ask, dance, path,* and *aunt* is often closer to the /a/ of *father* than to the /æ/ of *bad.* Test:

   The class asked my aunt from France to the dance.

3. /a/ In much American English, the vowel of *not, hot, got, stop,* and *lock* is closer to the /a/ of *father* than to the /ɔ/ of *bought.* But in Philadelphia English, as in most British English, /ɔ/ is used. Test:

   It was not too hot on the spot for the cot.

4. /ay/ In the South, several diphthongs tend to lose all or most of their glide. *Time* then very nearly rhymes with *calm; oil* with *call.* Test:

   My kind tries to be refined but I don't mind.

5. /æy/ /ɔu/ /əy/ In various parts of the country, glides are added to sounds more commonly heard as simple vowels. Where would you hear *class* with /æy/, *dog* with /ɔu/, *first* with /əy/?

G 8b Intonation

Contrasts in stress and pitch help determine the meaning of the spoken sentence.

Written English reflects only imperfectly the **intonation** patterns that determine the rhythm and melody of speech. To make a sentence intelligible to the listener, we have to stress the right syllables. We have to make our speech melody rise and fall at the right points; we have to provide the right kind of breaks. The resulting patterns depend on *contrast* between adjoining syllables — stressed and unstressed, high-pitched and low-pitched, and so on. These patterns thus *cut across* the smaller segments of a sentence and are often called **suprasegmental.** Those contrasts in stress and pitch that change meaning are often called "suprasegmental phonemes."

(1) *Every phrase and sentence we utter shows a contrast of stressed and unstressed syllables.* We vary **stress** by pronouncing some syllables *with greater force* than others. Usually we first become aware of stress when we study poetic meter, which regularizes the more variable stress patterns of normal speech:

Tŏ érr ĭs húmăn; tŏ fŏrgíve, dĭvíne.

Meter results from the regular recurrence (with some variation) of *strong* (⁄) as against *weak* (·) stress. In addition, we can recognize *medium* stress (ˎ), seen most clearly in words with four syllables. (Some linguists further subdivide medium stress into two distinct levels.)

díctionàry, élevàtor, ˋoperátion

The most familiar function of contrasts in stress in ordinary speech is to convey *emphasis:*

The uncle gave Phyllis the ticket.
The uncle gave Phyllis the *ticket.*
The uncle gave *Phyllis* the ticket.
The uncle *gave* Phyllis the ticket.
The *uncle* gave Phyllis the ticket.

Here are some other common uses of contrasts in stress:

Noun as against verb

good *con*duct; con*duct* an orchestra
satisfactory *pro*gress; pro*gress*ing slowly
young *reb*els; re*bell*ed against authority
a written *rec*ord; re*cord* a conversation

Adjective as against compound noun

wear a *green belt;* a *green*belt around the city
a completely *black bird;* a *black*bird
a formerly *white house;* moved into the *White* House
carry a heavy *weight;* a well-known *heavy*weight

Participle as against gerund (verbal noun)

*skat*ing *young*sters (the youngsters are skating)
*skat*ing rink (the rink is *for* skating)

*trav*eling *sales*man (the salesman is traveling)
*travel*ing iron (the iron is *for* traveling)

*mov*ing *target* (the target is moving)
*mov*ing van (the van is *for* moving)

Preposition as against phrasal verb

He *turned* on the *bridge.*
He turned *on* the *light.*

She *wrote* in her *diary.*
She wrote *in* for ins*truct*ions.

(2) *Every phrase or sentence has a pitch contour that affects its meaning.* As with the strings of a guitar, the faster our vocal cords vibrate, the higher or shriller the sound. The variations thus produced are called differences in **pitch.** By shifting from one level of pitch to a contrasting one in the middle of a word, we change *John?* to *John.* Typically, such shifts in pitch combine with characteristic *breaks* at the end of a phrase or sentence to convey the intended meaning. The breaks, called **terminals,** or sometimes "junctures," combine with the pitch contours to form characteristic intonation patterns.

The most common intonation patterns utilize three contrasting pitch levels: *low* (1), *normal* (2), and *high* (3):

Complete statement — from normal to high (on stressed syllable) and then *going down to low* — **falling** terminal with a dropping off and fading effect at the end:

^{2}He is ^{3}hungry^1 ⭨

Incomplete statement — from normal to high and *back to normal,* with a **level** terminal that makes us listen for some *continuation* of the sentence:

^{2}If he is ^{3}hungry^2 →

Question rise — from normal to high and *staying high,* with a **rising** terminal that makes us listen for an *answer:*

^{2}He is ^{3}hungry^3? ⭧

Notice that some other question signal may take *the place of* the question rise. "Where are you staying?" and "Do you know him?" are recognized as questions even when pronounced with a falling terminal. A fourth level of pitch (extra high) is used for special emphasis or *contrast:*

(It's not snowing;) ^{2}it's ^{4}raining^1! ↘

EXERCISE 56 What is the meaning of the *intonation features* marked in the following examples? After the number of each example, put the letter indicating the most probable choice.

1. Henry is ill →
   a. speaker is giving information
   b. speaker is questioning previous statement
2. I don't work on the paper, but most *seniors* do.
   a. speaker is a senior
   b. speaker is not a senior
3. I don't work on the paper, but most seniors *do.*
   a. speaker is a senior
   b. speaker is not a senior
4. England *was* named after the Angles.
   a. speaker is expressing doubt
   b. speaker is confirming a statement that has been questioned
5. Can the experiment be repeated ↗
   a. speaker is asking a question
   b. speaker is making a statement
6. Jean introduced me to her *Engl*ish *teach*er.
   a. teacher was from England
   b. teacher taught English
7. The experiment can be repeated →
   a. speaker is asking a question
   b. speaker has been interrupted
8. Jean introduced me to her *danc*ing teacher.
   a. teacher was dancing
   b. teacher taught dancing
9. Jim turned *in* his cot.
   a. he was lying in it and turned around
   b. he was handing it over
10. Jim *turned* in his chair.
    a. he was sitting in it and turned around
    b. he was handing it over

11. Mr. Greene doesn't play golf, but many teachers *do*.
    a. Mr. Greene is a teacher
    b. Mr. Greene is not a teacher
12. "He is teaching in Ethiopia."
    "Where ↘"
    a. questioner wants to know where in Ethiopia
    b. questioner is incredulous
13. "He is teaching in Ethiopia."
    "Where ↗"
    a. questioner wants to know where in Ethiopia
    b. questioner is incredulous
14. We saw many *yell*ow jackets
    a. we saw people in yellow jackets
    b. we saw wasps called "yellow jackets"
15. We saw many *yell*ow *jack*ets.
    a. we saw people in yellow jackets
    b. we saw wasps called "yellow jackets"
16. Pedro does not like pizza, but many *Ital*ians do.
    a. Pedro is Italian
    b. Pedro is not Italian
17. Somebody is *knock*ing down the *hall*.
    a. somebody is knocking
    b. the hall is being demolished
18. We'll try again ↘
    a. speaker has finished his statement
    b. speaker has been interrupted
19. Women can't enter through the front door ↗
    a. speaker is making an announcement
    b. speaker is incredulous
20. "The ship is leaving tomorrow."
    "When ↘"
    a. questioner wants to know exact time
    b. questioner is incredulous

EXERCISE 57 [Optional] Have several people pronounce the following pairs. Then describe as fully as you can the *differences in intonation* and their meanings. If one is available, you and your classmates may want to use a tape recorder in working on this project.

1. Give the blue one to *John.* / Give the *blue* one to John.
2. Smiling, Jim answered. / Smiling Jim answered.
3. Who called, Jean? / Who called? Jean?

4. George is an honor student. / George is an "honor" student.
5. He put it in the oven. / He put it in the *oven!*
6. The cans are for refuse. / I knew he would refuse.
7. The chemical was a nitrate. / The hotel offered a night rate.
8. John Allen, farmer, lived there. / John Allen Farmer lived there.
9. Are you ready, John? / Are you ready? John?
10. Who called Jim? / Who called, Jim?

FURTHER STUDY: *Language and Literary History*

The scientific study of English developed in the nineteenth century, when scholars were rediscovering some of the great documents of our literary past. To read *Beowulf* or Chaucer's *Canterbury Tales*, historical linguists studied the grammar of Old and Middle English. The following assignments ask you to take stock of some of the grammatical difficulties that you would have to deal with in reading early literary documents. They will help you deal with some of the language problems that confront the modern reader (and spectator) of Shakespeare. At the same time, some of these assignments will make you look at how poet, playwright, and novelist go *beyond* ordinary language, bending and stretching its grammar for purposes of their own.

Assignment 1   How far can you go back in history and still find language that you would recognize as English? The following is the beginning of a long "moral poem" as written down *about A.D. 1200.* Can you puzzle out this passage with the help of the words in the Glossary? Point out grammatical features that are roughly the same as in modern English. Point out grammatical features that have changed or disappeared.

(Spelling has been slightly modernized.)

Poema Morale

Ich aem elder then ich wes · a wintre and alore.
Ich waelde more thanne ic dude · mi wit ah to ben more.
Wel lange ic habbe child ibeon · a weorde end ech adede.
Theh ich beo awintre eald · tu yung i eom a rede.
Un nut lif ic habb ilaed · end yet me thincth ich lede.   5
Thane ic me bithenche · wel sore ic me adrede.
Mest al that ic habbe ydon · is idelnesse and chilce.
Wel late ich habbe me bithoht · bute me god do milce.
Fele ydele word ic habbe iqueden · sythen ic speke cuthe.
And fale yunge dede ido · the me ofthinchet nuthe.   10
Al to lome ic habbe agult · a weorche end ec a worde.
Al to muchel ic habbe ispend · to litel yleid an horde.
Mest al thet me licede aer · nu hit me mislichet.
The mychel folyeth his ywil · him sulfne he biswiketh.
Ich mihte habbe bet idon · hadde ic tho y selthe.   15
Nu ich wolde ac ic ne mei · for elde ne for unhelthe.
Ylde me is bistolen on · aer ic hit a wyste.

Ne mihte ic iseon before me · for smeche ne for miste.
Aerwe we beoth to done god · end to yfele al to thriste.
More aeie stent man of manne · thanne him do of criste.   20
The wel ne deth the hwile he mei · wel oft hit hym scael ruwen.
Thaenne hy mowen sculen end ripen · ther hi aer sowen.

GLOSSARY: (l. 2) *waelde* wield, control (oneself) ; *ah* ought (l. 3)
ech "eke," also (l. 4) *theh* though; *rede* wisdom (l. 5) *un nut* useless
(l. 7) *chilce* childishness (l. 8) *milce* "mildness," mercy (l. 9) *fele*
much; *iqueden* spoken; *sythen* since (l. 10) *ofthinchet* displease;
nuthe now (l. 11) *lome* often (l. 13) *aer* "ere," before (l. 14)
biswiketh deceives (l. 15) *tho* then; *selthe* happiness (l. 16) *elde* age
(l. 17) *wiste* knew (l. 18) *smeche* smoke (l. 19) *aerwe* cowardly;
thriste bold (l. 20) *aeie* fear (l. 21) *the* he who (l. 22) *hy sculen*
they shall

Assignment 2   The following passages are two early versions of
the parable of the Sower and the Seed from the Gospel of Matthew
(13: 24-30). The first version is *Middle English*, from the fourteenth
century. The second version is *Old English*, from the tenth century.
Study first the Middle English version, pointing out any features that
make it different from Modern English. Then, going back to the material in **G 1** for an introduction, study the Old English version. Point
out any distinctive grammatical features that you can identify.

(In these passages the original spelling has been largely preserved: g often stands for later *y*, *u* for *v*. In the Old English, the
runic symbol þ stands for later *th*.)

1.   The kyngdom of heuenes is maad lijk to a man, that sewe
       good seed in his feld. And whanne men slepten, his enemy
       cam, and sewe aboue taris in the myddil of whete, and wente
       awei. But whanne the erbe was growed, and made fruyt,
       thanne the taris apperiden. And the seruauntis of the hose-
       bonde man camen, and seiden to hym, Lord, whether hast
       thou not sowun good seed in thi feeld? where of thanne hath
       it taris? And he seide to hem, An enemy hath do this thing.
       And the seruauntis seiden to him, Wolt thou that we goon,
       and gaderen hem? And he seide, Nay, lest perauenture ge in
       gaderynge taris drawen vp with hem the whete bi the roote.
       Suffre ge hem bothe to wexe in to repyng tyme; and in the
       tyme of ripe corne Y shal seie to the reperis, First gadere ge
       to gidere the taris, and bynde hem to gidere in knytchis to be
       brent, but gadere ge whete in to my berne.

2. Heofona rīçe is geworden þǣm menn gelīç þe sēow gōd sǣd on his
æcere. Sōþlīçe, þā þā menn slēpon, þā cōm his fēonda sum, and ofer-
sēow hit mid coccele onmiddan þǣm hwǣte, and fērde þanon. Sōþlīçe,
þā sēo wyrt wēox, and þone wǣstm brōhte, þā ætīewde se coccel hine.
þā ēodon þæs hlāfordes þēowas and cwǣdon: "Hlāford, hū, ne sēowe
þū gōd sǣd on þīnum æcere? Hwanon hæfde hē coccel?" þā cwæþ hē:
"þæt dyde unhold mann." þā cwǣdon þā þēowas: "Wilt þū, wē gāþ
and gadriaþ hīe?" þā cwæþ hē: "Nese: þȳlǣs gē þone hwǣte āwyrtwalien, þonne gē þone coccel gadriaþ. Lǣtaþ ǣgþer weaxan oþ rīptīman; and on þǣm rīptīman iç secge þǣm rīperum: 'Gadriaþ ǣrest
þone coccel, and bindaþ scēafmǣlum tō forbærnenne; and gadriaþ
þone hwǣte intō mīnum berne.' "

OE Glossary: rīce empire ("Reich"); geworden (has) become;
sōþlīce truly ("in sooth"); coccel weed; fērde went ("fared"); þanon
thence; wyrt root, plant; wēox grew ("waxed"); wǣstm harvest;
aetīewde appeared; ēodon went; hlāfordes lord's; þēowas men;
cwǣdon spoke; hwanon whence; unhold evil; þȳlǣs lest; āwyrtwalien
uproot; ǣgþer either; oþ until; rīptīman reaping time; ǣrest first;
scēafmǣlum "a sheaf at a time"

Assignment 3 In the following passages from the Prologue to
Chaucer's *Canterbury Tales* (1386-1400), almost all the words used
survive in Modern English. (Some have changed in spelling, form, or
meaning; others have become archaic, like *lief, wend,* or *wight.*) Make
sure first that you recognize all the words. Then ask: What *grammatical* features of Chaucer's English does the modern reader have
to be prepared for? Pay attention both to the use of major grammatical
devices and to specific matters of structure and form.

1. Thanne longen folk to goon on pilgrimages.

2. And specially from every shires ende
   Of Engelond to Canterbury they wende
   The holy blisful martyr for to seeke
   That hem hath holpen whan that they were seke.

3. Me thinketh it accordant to resoun
   To telle you al the condicioun
   Of eech of hem, so as it seemed me.

4. He nevere yit no vilainye ne saide
   In al his life unto no manere wight:
   He was a verray, parfit, gentil knight.

5. But for to tellen you of his array,
   His hors were goode, but he was nat gay.

6. Short was his gowne, with sleeves longe and wide,
   Wel coude he sitte on hors, and faire ride.
7. Of smale houndes hadde she that she fedde
   With rosted flessh, or milk and wastelbreed;
   But sore wepte she if oon of hem were deed.
8. Another Nonne with hir hadde she
   That was hir chapelaine, and preestes three.
9. And in his harping, whan he hadde songe,
   His yën twinkled in his heed aright
   As doon the sterres in the frosty night.
10. For him was levere have at his beddes heed
    Twenty bookes, clad in blak or reed,
    Of Aristotle and his philosophye,
    Than robes riche.

Assignment 4 What are some of the grammatical features of
Early Modern English that are illustrated in *Shakespeare's plays?*
Point out the grammatical features that make each of the following
passages different from current American English. Pay special attention
to pronoun and verb forms.

1. (Macbeth)   Thou art the best o' th' cut-throats;
                Yet he's good that did the like for Fleance:
                If thou didst it, thou art the nonpareil.
   (Murderer)   Most royal Sir . . . Fleance is scap'd.
   (Macbeth)   Then comes my fit again: I had else been perfect.
                                         (*Macbeth,* Act III, Sc. 4)

2. (Marcellus) Peace, break thee off. Look where it comes again.
   (Bernardo)   In the same figure like the king that's dead.
   (Marcellus) Thou are a scholar; speak to it, Horatio.
   (Bernardo)   Looks 'a not like the king? Mark it, Horatio.
   (Horatio)   Most like. It harrows me with fear and wonder.
   (Bernardo)   It would be spoke to.
   (Marcellus) Question it, Horatio.   (*Hamlet,* Act I, Sc. 1)

3. Are ye fantastical, or that indeed
   Which outwardly ye show? My noble partner
   You greet with present grace and great prediction
   Of noble having and of royal hope,
   That he seems rapt withal: to me you speak not.
                                         (*Macbeth,* Act I, Sc. 3)

4. How far that little candle throws his beams! . . .
   A substitute shines brightly as a king
   Until a king be by.   (*Merchant of Venice,* Act V, Sc. 1)

5. I am not sick, if Brutus have in hand
   Any exploit worthy the name of honor. . . .

   Here will I stand till Caesar pass along
   And as a suitor will I give him this. . . .

   (Julius Caesar, Act II, Sc. 1-3)

6. (Hamlet)   Did you not speak to it?
   (Horatio)   My lord, I did;
   But answer made it none. Yet once methought
   It lifted up its head and did address
   Itself to motion like as it would speak:
   But even then the morning cock crew loud,
   And at the sound it shrunk in haste away.

   (Hamlet, Act I, Sc. 2)

7. Pray to the gods to intermit the plague
   That needs must light on this ingratitude . . .

   Brutus, I do observe you now of late;
   I have not from your eyes that gentleness
   And show of love as I was wont to have.

   (Julius Caesar, Act I, Sc. 1-2)

Assignment 5   Poets adapt the grammatical patterns of ordinary speech in order to meet the special requirements of their art — for instance, those of meter or rhyme. Poetry makes freer and more imaginative use of possible *variations in word order,* for example. Describe as fully as you can the grammatical structure of each of the following passages. Pay special attention to instances of word order departing from that of ordinary current speech.

1. For Fate with jealous eye does see
   Two perfect loves, nor lets them close:
   Their union would her ruin be,
   And her tyrannic power depose.

   — Andrew Marvell, "The Definition of Love"

2. For different styles with different subjects sort,
   As several garbs with country, town, and court.
   Some foreign writers, some our own despise;
   The ancients only, or the modern prize.
   Be thou the first true merit to defend,
   His praise is lost, who stays till all commend.

   — Alexander Pope, *Essay on Criticism*

3. Me though just right, and the fixed laws of Heaven
   Did first create your leader, next, free choice,
   With what besides, in council or in fight,
   Hath been achieved of merit, yet this loss
   Thus far at least recovered, hath much more
   Established in a safe unenvied throne
   Yielded with full consent.

   —John Milton, *Paradise Lost*

4. Full many a gem of purest ray serene
   The dark unfathomed caves of ocean bear;
   Full many a flower is born to blush unseen,
   And waste its sweetness on the desert air.

   —Thomas Gray, "Elegy Written in a Country Churchyard"

5.   Be thou, Spirit fierce,
   My spirit! Be thou me, impetuous one!
   Drive my dead thoughts over the universe
   Like withered leaves to quicken a new birth!
   And, by the incantation of this verse,
   Scatter, as from an unextinguished hearth
   Ashes and sparks, my words among mankind!

   —Percy Bysshe Shelley, "Ode to the West Wind"

Assignment 6   A poem is typically *more deliberately and more elaborately structured* than ordinary speech. Of the following three sentences, the first two were written by a seventeenth-century poet; the third by a twentieth-century poet. Each makes exceptionally full use of the resources of the English sentence. Chart the grammatical structure of each sentence as fully as you can.

1. Death, be not proud, though some have callèd thee
   Mighty and dreadful, for thou art not so;
   For those whom thou think'st thou dost overthrow
   Die not, poor Death, nor yet canst thou kill me.

   —John Donne, Holy Sonnet 10

2. At the round earth's imagined corners, blow
   Your trumpets, angels, and arise, arise
   From death, you numberless infinities
   Of souls, and to your scattered bodies go,
   All whom the flood did, and fire shall o'erthrow,
   All whom war, dearth, age, agues, tyrannies,

Despair, law, chance, hath slain, and you whose eyes
Shall behold God, and never taste death's woe.

—John Donne, Holy Sonnet 7

3. Never until the mankind making
Bird beast and flower
Fathering and all humbling darkness
Tells with silence the last light breaking
And the still hour
Is come of the sea tumbling in harness

And I must enter again the round
Zion of the water bead
And the synagogue of the ear of corn
Shall I let pray the shadow of a sound
Or sow my salt seed
In the least valley of sackcloth to mourn

The majesty and burning of the child's death.

—Dylan Thomas, "A Refusal to Mourn the Death,
by Fire, of a Child in London"

Assignment 7 Much modern poetry, like the poetry of Shakespeare and his contemporaries, *stretches the grammatical resources of ordinary speech.* The bolder the poet, the more freely he will wrestle with the language, twist it into new shapes. Study the following poem by e. e. cummings, a modern American poet famous for the boldness of the games he plays with ordinary language. Can you identify the ways this poem departs from the grammar of ordinary speech? Can you "explain" any of these departures — do they "make sense"?

anyone lived in a pretty how town
(with up so floating many bells down)
spring summer autumn winter
he sang his didn't he danced his did.

Women and men (both little and small)
cared for anyone not at all
they sowed their isn't they reaped their same
sun moon stars rain

children guessed (but only a few
and down they forgot as up they grew
autumn winter spring summer)
that noone loved him more by more

when by now and tree by leaf
she laughed his joy she cried his grief
bird by snow and stir by still
anyone's any was all to her

someones married their everyones
laughed their cryings and did their dance
(sleep wake hope and then) they
said their nevers they slept their dream

stars rain sun moon
(and only the snow can begin to explain
how children are apt to forget to remember
with up so floating many bells down)

one day anyone died i guess
(and noone stooped to kiss his face)
busy folk buried them side by side
little by little and was by was

all by all and deep by deep
and more by more they dream their sleep
noone and anyone earth by april
wish by spirit and if by yes.

Women and men (both dong and ding)
summer autumn winter spring
reaped their sowing and went their came
sun moon stars rain

CONTENTS

CHAPTER THREE

Usage:
UNIFORMITY AND VARIETY

Our language serves as a common medium and yet makes possible variety and individuality.

When we study usage, we shift the emphasis from the resources of language to the behavior of *people*. Why do some people talk differently from others? Why do people speak and write differently on different occasions? What standards do we have to guide our own choices when we have different ways of saying the same thing?

The effective speaker and writer has learned to gauge accurately the probable reactions of listener and reader. He moves ahead with confidence when faced with a choice between *doesn't* and *don't, can* and *may, who* and *whom, boss* and *superior, wireless* and *radio.* To develop this feeling of confidence in your own choices, you will have to understand some basic principles:

(1) *Language is shared in common by a group.* We cannot communicate unless the words we use are recognized and shared by others. Our language is not of our own invention. We have learned it from our parents and friends and teachers. The shared language helps make us a part of the group, and it helps *make the group.* Historically, first the tribe, and then the nation, was a group of people speaking the same language. Part of what makes a Frenchman French, and a German German, is his pride in his language

and the culture it carries. Countries without one single national language often find it hard to establish a national identity and a sense of undivided loyalty. Canadian politics is embittered by the division between English-speaking and French-speaking Canadians. In Belgium, there is conflict between French-speaking and Flemish-speaking Belgians.

(2) *A language tends to develop distinct dialects.* As a language spreads over a large territory, it develops regional varieties or **dialects.** In the earliest stages of our language, there was no "standard English." The Old English chronicles and retellings of Bible stories were written down in the dialects of the different tribal kingdoms. To people in isolated rural villages, England through centuries, in Thomas Hardy's words, "was a continent." The different regional varieties could thus drift far apart. In England, as in France or Germany, a farmer living in the north may not understand at all the dialect of his counterpart living in the south. Among the different English-speaking countries, we find regional variations on a larger scale. Not only does a British automobile have the steering wheel on the right; its parts are called by different names: The hood is the "bonnet," the trunk the "boot."

(3) *In many major languages, a prestige dialect has become the national standard.* Standard French is historically the local dialect of the Paris region. Classical Latin was originally the dialect of Rome. **Standard English** is historically the dialect of London, which in the Middle Ages became a great trading center as well as the seat of the royal court. In order not to appear as country bumpkins, people who came to London to become businessmen or lawyers had to speak like the people of London. No matter what their dialect had been at home, writers began to write London English if they wanted to reach a national audience. Today, what was once London English has become the standard language of education, business, and government in English-speaking countries around the world. It has become a worldwide medium of communication for millions of people in other countries who speak and write it as a second language.

In America, the intermingling of settlers from different regions has prevented the emergence of strong regional dialects. *The important dialect differences in our country today are social rather than regional.* Even in nineteenth-century England, what mattered to the speaker of a rural dialect was *not* that he could not understand a speaker from a farming area two hundred miles away. What mattered was that his dialect was different from that of people who had education, wealth, or status. Then as now, teachers, employers, and parents of marriageable children used a person's speech as a rough indicator of his social standing. In Thomas Hardy's *The Mayor of Casterbridge,* the hay-trusser who has become a prominent citizen of the town sees the dialect words used by his adopted daughter as a threat to his hard-won social status:

> " 'Bide where you be,' " he echoed sharply. "By heaven, are you only fit to carry wash to a pig-trough, that ye use words such as those?" (Ch. 20)

The important dialect difference in America today is the difference between the **nonstandard** English of the blue collar worker and the standard English of the man in the office. The schools teach standard English because it is their job to *enlarge the range of the student's possibilities.* The mechanic's son with a good command of standard English does not have to become a mechanic himself *unless he wants to.* Standard English is his passport to a wide range of other occupations, including those of office worker, teacher, journalist, insurance salesman, business executive, lawyer, engineer, scientist, and physician.

An easy command of standard English is a tremendous asset. But to make standard English serve you well, you will have to steer clear of some common *misunderstandings:*

— *Standard English is not a rigid artificial dialect.* It has **functional varieties,** ranging from the informal language of casual conversation to the more formal language of platform speech and serious writing. You do not produce standard English by making your language always as stiff and unnatural as possible.

— *Standard and nonstandard English do not represent a rigid either-or choice.* In England, many people who use standard English all day at the office slip easily into a more regional language as they loosen their ties at home or at the local pub. In America, many people speak standard English with a lawyer, minister, or business prospect, and nonstandard English with their relatives or close friends.

— Standard English should not make us feel snobbishly superior. London English did not become the national norm because it was more vigorous, more logical, or more beautiful than Liverpool English. It became the national norm because it was *there.*

U 1 Standard and Nonstandard

Recognize the features, and understand the nature, of nonstandard English.

Standard English is the language of school and office. We hear it on radio and television; we see it in print. It is the language of business, law, and government. The private and official business of this nation is transacted in standard English. At home and on the job, however, millions of Americans speak **nonstandard** English. Much of the vocabulary and grammar of standard and nonstandard English are exactly alike. The difference is in forms and constructions that occur frequently in everyday speech and are thus easily noticed. A nonstandard speaker may be very articulate — a good storyteller, conversationalist, and giver of directions. He may be more intelligent and sensitive than you or I. But if he cannot *shift to standard English when necessary,* he is limited in his job opportunities, social contacts, and share in community affairs.

Here are the most distinctive features of nonstandard English. Though there are some regional variations, most of these are characteristic of nonstandard English in all parts of the nation:

VERB FORMS:	he *don't,* you *was,* I *says; knowed, growed, throwed;* have *wrote,* had *went;* I *seen* him
PRONOUN FORMS:	*hisself, theirself; this here* book, *that there* table; *them* coupons
CONNECTIVES:	*without* he pays the rent; *on account of* she was sick; *being as* he lived there
DOUBLE NEGATIVES:	we *don't* have *no* time; *never* hurt *nobody*
VOCABULARY:	*nowheres, nohow*

The following facts about nonstandard English are often misunderstood:

(1) Nonstandard English *follows its own grammatical rules.* A speaker using *hisn* or *hern* is not making "errors" or "mistakes." He is following the rules of nonstandard English. He *always* uses *his, her,* and *our* when the pronoun appears *before the noun.* He always uses *hisn, hern,* and *ourn* when the pronoun appears alone, after the verb:

NONSTANDARD	STANDARD
His friend kept *hisn.*	He kept *his.*
Her 'sister finished *hern.*	She finished *hers.*
Our teacher gave us *ourn.*	We found *ours.*

(2) Nonstandard English *preserves many older features of our language.* Many nonstandard forms are not "blunders" but were once part of the language of Chaucer and Shakespeare. Note the following examples:

DOUBLE NEGATIVE: (*"Can't* give you *none"*):
He *nevere* yit *no* vilainye *ne* said. (Chaucer)
NOUN-PRONOUN (*"My brother, he* left long ago"):
Our father he hath writ, so hath our sister. (Shakespeare)

(3) Nonstandard English *shows patterns of change found elsewhere in our language.* Through the centuries, speakers of English have more and more *regularized* English verbs. In the past tense, we now simply add *-ed* to many verbs that once had a separate past tense form. *Halp* has become *helped; clomb* has become *climbed.* Nonstandard English has continued the same process: *Knew* has become *knowed; grew* has become *growed.* Look for other examples of such regularized verb forms in our earlier literature:

He made a pit, and *digged* it, and is fallen into the ditch which he made. (Psalms)

The following two sections review the standard forms of verbs and pronouns, since here the contrast with nonstandard forms is most extended and systematic. For discussion of other nonstandard forms, see the *Glossary of Usage,* especially the following entries: *a, an; ain't; being as; could of; double negative; irregardless; learn, teach; off of; seeing as how; without, on account of.*

U 1a *Verb Forms*

Be sure of the standard forms of English verbs.

Standard differs from nonstandard English in the forms of many common verbs. Here are some typical contrasts:

NONSTANDARD	STANDARD
we is, you is, they is	we are, you are, they are
we was, you was, they was	we were, you were, they were
ain't right, ain't true	isn't (is not) right, isn't true
ain't been, ain't got	haven't (have not) been, haven't got
he don't	he doesn't (does not)
I says	I say (present), I said (past)
knowed, growed, throwed	knew, grew, threw
have wrote, had went	have written, had gone
I done, I seen, I been	I've (I have) done, I've seen, I've been

Be sure of the *standard forms* in the following charts:

(1) For *be* and a few other common verbs, be sure of the forms that *agree* with different subjects. (For further discussion of agreement, see **U 3a**.)

		FIRST PERSON	SECOND PERSON	THIRD PERSON
be (Present)		I am	you are	he (she, it) is; the boy is
		we are	you are	they are; the boys are
(Past)		I was	you were	he (she, it) was; the girl was
		we were	you were	they were; the girls were
do		I don't	you don't	he doesn't; a man doesn't
		we don't	you don't	they don't; drivers don't
say		I say	you say	he (she, it) says
		we say	you say	they say

(2) For **irregular** verbs — verbs that do not simply use a form with *-ed* for past and perfect — be sure of the *forms for the different tenses:*

PRESENT	PAST	PERFECT
begin	began	have begun
bend	bent	have bent
blow	blew	have blown
break	broke	have broken
bring	brought	have brought
catch	caught	have caught
choose	chose	have chosen
come	came	have come
dig	dug	have dug
do	did	have done
draw	drew	have drawn
drink	drank	have drunk
drive	drove	have driven
eat	ate	have eaten
fall	fell	have fallen
fly	flew	have flown
freeze	froze	have frozen
go	went	have gone
grow	grew	have grown
know	knew	have known
ride	rode	have ridden
run	ran	have run
see	saw	have seen
sing	sang	have sung
speak	spoke	have spoken
swim	swam	have swum
take	took	have taken
throw	threw	have thrown
wear	wore	have worn
write	wrote	have written

NOTE: Up-to-date dictionaries often list *two possible standard forms:*

They *dived* (or *dove*) into the pool.
He *dreamed* (or *dreamt*) of a white Christmas.
They *lighted* (or *lit*) the fire.
The theory was *proved* (or *proven*) wrong.
The ship *sank* (or *sunk*).

EXERCISE 1 Easy competence in the use of standard English results from *constant exposure to standard forms in the appropriate* *context.* If your command of standard verb forms is unsure, use the following passages for *oral drill.* Read each set of forms over several times. Come back to this exercise repeatedly over a number of weeks.

1. He is tall, she is short, it is true; we *are* friends, you *are* right, they *are* wrong; he was here, she was there, it was new; we *were* tired, you *were* rude, they *were* gone; the dog is fed, the story is true, a page is missing; roses *are* red, violets *are* blue, times *are* hard; the meeting was over, the night was warm, the people *were* happy; he was invited, but we *weren't* asked; the car was there, but the boys *were* gone; Jim is polite, but his brothers *aren't;* Jean isn't here, but her sisters *are.*

2. Jim *threw* the ball; I *knew* it all the time; the wind *blew;* I've *known* him for years; I've *driven* his car; he's *done* it again; the dish was *broken;* the spy was *caught;* the story was *written;* the water had *frozen;* he had *dug* a ditch; she had once *grown* flowers in the yard, but now nothing *grew* there; I *knew* his face but had never *known* his name; he *threw* back the ball I had *thrown* to him; we *drove* the same car we had *driven* east; he had always *eaten* what the natives *ate,* and had always *drunk* what they *drank;* we *swam* out to the float to which we had *swum* before.

3. I say yes but my father says no; I *said* tomorrow but my mother *said* today; Jim wants to come but his brother *doesn't;* Jean wants to come but her sisters don't; she *doesn't* speak English, and her parents don't either; Fred *doesn't* dance, but his friends don't care; I *did* what I could; I *have done* nothing wrong; the men *did* their best; they *have done* their duty; your friend *doesn't* realize what we *have done* for him; your friends *don't* realize what they *did* to us.

EXERCISE 2 In each of the following sentences, fill in the appropriate *standard form of the verb* listed at the end. After the number of the sentence, write down the form that would fit into the blank space in the sentence. Do *not* add any auxiliaries not already supplied.

1. The trees had _____ to tremendous height. (grow)
2. He always listens when I _____ something. (say)
3. We _____ having dinner when we heard the news. (be)
4. The lake had not _____ over in many years. (freeze)
5. The girl prayed as the sailors _____ a rope to the tossing boat. (throw)
6. The crowd gasped when George _____ the ball. (catch)

7. If he _____ not call tomorrow, I am going to leave. (do)
8. Candidates today _____ more handsome than they used to be. (be)
9. He met a man he had _____ in the army. (know)
10. Last year's election _____ many surprises. (bring)
11. I had never _____ such a big crowd before. (see)
12. In all these years he had never _____ more than his share. (take)
13. Many students work part-time while they _____ to college. (go)
14. Her uncle had _____ all the way from Indiana. (drive)
15. Pasternak had _____ poetry before he published *Dr. Zhivago*. (write)
16. Your friends came looking for you while you _____ out. (be)
17. When he arrived, the librarian had _____ home. (go)
18. I gave her your message the last time I _____ her. (see)
19. In his family, close relatives kiss when they _____ goodbye. (say)
20. It was dark, and a cold wind _____ outside. (blow)
21. The family had _____ 600 miles in an attempt to reach Dayton by sunset. (ride)
22. The speaker _____ again after the audience had quieted down. (begin)
23. Janice never _____ the aria before. (sing)
24. Yesterday, Ted _____ the 200-meter race in record time. (swim)
25. The boy had never _____ a tie. (wear)

U 1b   Pronoun Forms

Be sure of the standard forms of English pronouns.

Nonstandard English preserves many pronoun uses that have disappeared from standard speech. Here are some typical contrasts:

NONSTANDARD	STANDARD
my brother he left	my brother left
them books, them people	these books, those people
this here trip, that there box	this trip, that box
yourn, hisn, hern, ourn	yours, his, hers, ours
hisself, theirself	himself, themselves
ourself, yourself	ourselves, yourselves (plural)

Be sure of the *standard forms* in the following charts (see also **G 2a**):

demonstrative	*this* book	*that* book
	these words	*those* words
possessive — two sets	*my* turn	it's *mine*
	your friend	it's *yours*
	his face	it's *his*
	her car	it's *hers*
	its crib	it's *its*
	our house	it's *ours*
	their luck	it's *theirs*
reflexive	I congratulated *myself*	
	you distinguished *yourself*	
	(singular)	
	he questioned *himself*	
	she blamed *herself*	
	it speaks for *itself*	
	we think for *ourselves*	
	you distinguished *yourselves*	
	(plural)	
	they fended for *themselves*	
intensive — same as reflexive	he did it *himself*	
	they *themselves* told me	

EXERCISE 3 Reinforce your command of standard pronoun forms by *oral drill*. Read the following passage over several times. If necessary, come back to this exercise repeatedly over a number of weeks.

He told me *himself* that the fault was *his;* they told me *themselves* that the fault was *theirs;* we told them *ourselves* that the fault was *ours;* you boys should make *yourselves* useful; put *this* box on *that* shelf; put *these* boxes on *those* shelves; who brought *those* jars in? Where did you get *those* shoes? We wrapped *ourselves* in our blankets; the stranger considered *himself* fortunate; they failed to protect *themselves* against mosquitoes; you should enter your name *yourself;* you should enter your names *yourselves;* two-thirds is *ours,* and the rest is *hers;* he gave me mine but not *yours;* he *himself* had checked all the doors; they *themselves* had gone looking for help.

EXERCISE 4 In each of the following sentences, fill in the appropriate *standard form* of the missing pronoun. After the number of the sentence, write down the form that would fit into the blank space in the sentence.

1. I am going to pay my share of the bill if you pay _____.
2. Shaving this morning, he cut _____ badly.
3. Both officers had distinguished _____ during the war.
4. Why don't you girls make _____ useful?
5. The Smiths had invited their friends, and we had invited _____.
6. The guest of honor excused _____ early.
7. These things over here are mine, but _____ books over there are my brother's.
8. Jean and I kept our receipt, but Doris threw away _____.
9. No one believed that we had built the cabin all by _____.
10. His brother had made a name for _____ as a scientist.

REVIEW EXERCISE In the following two passages, two *American authors record nonstandard speech* — William Faulkner in the South, Nelson Algren in Chicago. Point out all features of nonstandard English that you recognize. Are there any that have not been discussed in the preceding sections of this book? Are there any that are not common in your part of the country?

1.   We stood there, it was cold, listening to the fellow in the radio talking, only I couldn't make no heads nor tails out of it. Then the fellow said that would be all for a while, and me and Pete walked back up the road to home, and Pete told me what it was. Because he was nigh twenty and he had done finished the Consolidated last June and he knowed a heap: about them Japanese dropping bombs on Pearl Harbor and that Pearl Harbor was across the water.
    "Across what water?" I said. "Across that Government reservoy up at Oxford?"
    "Naw," Pete said. "Across the big water. The Pacific Ocean."
    We went home. Maw and pap was already asleep and me and Pete laid in bed, and I still couldn't understand where it was, and Pete told me again — the Pacific Ocean.
    "What's the matter with you?" Pete said. "You're going on nine years old. You been in school now ever since September. Ain't you learned nothing yet?"
    "I reckon we ain't got as fer as the Pacific Ocean yet," I said.   —William Faulkner, "Two Soldiers"

2.   The fellas begun giv'n me awful razzin' then, ever' day. It was bad, wherever I went around the Triangle, all the neighborhood fellas 'n little niducks 'n oldtime hoods by the Broken Knuckle, whenever they seen me they was pointin'

'n laughin' 'n sayin', 'Hi, Baldy Bicek!' So I went home 'n
got the clippers 'n the first guy I seen was Bibleback Watro-
binski, you wouldn't know him. I jumps him 'n pushes the
clip right through the middle of his hair — he ain't had a
haircut since the alderman got indicted you — 'n then he took
one look at what I done in the drugstore window 'n we both
bust out laughin' 'n laughin', 'n fin'lly Bible says I better finish
what I started. So he set down on the curb 'n I finished him.
When I got all I could off that way I took him back to the
store 'n heated water 'n shaved him close 'n Ma couldn't
see the point at all.

—Nelson Algren, "A Bottle of Milk for Mother"

U 2 Formal and Informal

**Learn to shift from informal conversational English to
the more formal English appropriate in serious writing.**

Within standard English, there are *functional varieties* suitable
for different occasions. **Formal** language goes with public occasions:
official business, serious discussion, writing intended for a general
audience. **Informal** language goes with a small circle of friends,
casual talk, personal letters. To use language effectively, you must
have a firm sense for the difference between formal and informal
language. You must be able to use either where it is appropriate.

What are some of the features that make for the difference
between formal and informal in the following pairs?

FORMAL: I shall be happy to accept your invitation.

INFORMAL: Count me in.

FORMAL: In view of the many conferences that have been held
           on education, it would seem impossible to say anything
           new on the subject.

INFORMAL: I've put up with about as much debate concerning the
           public schools as I can stand quietly, and I'm going to
           get into the act.

FORMAL: Anger blows out the lamp of the mind.

INFORMAL: When a man sees red, he's likely to see little else.

When you select language appropriate to the occasion, remember the following points:

(1) *Writing is generally more formal than speech.* What we write down is generally more important than what we merely mention. It is typically intended for a larger audience. Formal language indicates that we are taking our subject and our audience seriously. Language that is too breezy may make the audience feel that what we say does not merit much attention. When informal language *does* appear in writing, it is often designed to echo speech — the folksy tone of the people being described, or the relaxed storytelling of the narrator:

> Some said it was because he had no wife,
> And hated to be *twitted* on the subject . . . (Robert Frost)

> Sam had made him ride the one-eyed mule which would not *spook* at the smell of blood. (William Faulkner)

> At the sound of my voice he nearly *jumped out of his skin.*
> (Joseph Conrad)

(2) *Effective writers avoid excessive formality as well as breezy informality.* Effective formal English is vigorous and natural. If you always use the most formal word available, you will make your writing stilted, pompous, unnatural. Much effective modern prose moves between the two extremes:

VERY FORMAL	IN-BETWEEN	SLANG
retire	go to bed	hit the sack
fatigued	exhausted	bushed
vanquish	trounce	clobber
wedded	married	hitched
spouse	husband	old man

(3) *Formal English is governed by changing conventions.* Our language, like our national life, has over the decades steadily moved in the direction of greater informality. Men once wore gloves and starched collars to functions where now a suit and tie is entirely appropriate. *Lunch* for *luncheon,* and *dress* for *gown,* were once criticized as too informal. *Mob* was once criticized as slang. Today all these words are entirely appropriate in serious speech and writing.

The following sections review some of the major features that set formal apart from informal English. The *Glossary of Usage* examines many additional words and forms that are often criticized as too informal for serious discussion.

U 2a Word Choice

Learn to recognize words with a limited range of appropriateness.
Many of the words we use are fit for all occasions. No matter
how formal or informal the occasion, we can always call a hand
a hand and a house a house. But many other words are suitable
only in the right context. They seem out of place when used elsewhere. *Beseech* (for *implore*), *edifice* (for *building*), and *bequeath*
(for *hand down*) are very formal words. We might expect to see
them in a scholarly piece of writing or hear them on ceremonial
occasions. Occasionally, a dictionary will label a word like this
literary. *Kids, fake,* and *traipse* are informal words. We expect to
hear them in casual conversation among friends and neighbors.
Many dictionaries label such words **colloquial.** *Loaded, mutt,* and
latch onto are **slang.** They are so informal as to be disrespectful.
We expect to hear young people use them among themselves, but
not to an older person. We might hear these words from the boys
on their night out, or from G.I.s off duty.

The following passages show words representing this whole
range of formality in typical contexts:

VERY FORMAL— *literary or scholarly*

There is an old and perhaps foolish *query* about the
books which one would wish to take with him if he were to
sojourn upon a desert island. But like some other foolish
questions, the problem which it sets us is worth *pondering.*
Upon the *voyage* of life there are few books of which we may
hope to make lifelong companions; and, as in the other relations of life, it *behoves* us, if we hope to avoid *calamity* on
our voyage, to choose our mates with *discretion.*
—Chauncey B. Tinker, *On Going to College*

FORMAL — *generally appropriate to serious discussion*

Man without writing cannot long *retain* his history in his
head. His intelligence permits him to grasp some kind of
succession of generations; but without writing, the tale of the
past rapidly *degenerates* into fumbling myth and fable. Man's
greatest *epic,* his four long battles with the advancing ice of
the great continental glaciers, has *vanished* from human memory without a trace. Our illiterate fathers disappeared and
with them, in a few *scant* generations, died one of the great
stories of all time. This *episode* has nothing to do with the

LANGUAGE RANGES FROM THE VERY FORMAL . . . .

. . . . TO THE VERY INFORMAL.

biological quality of a brain as between then and now. It has to do instead with a device, an invention made possible by the hand. That invention came too late in time to *record* eye-witness accounts of the years of the Giant Frost.

—Loren Eiseley, "The Long Loneliness," *The American Scholar*

INFORMAL — *limited to humorous, chatty writing*

If lost hunters would only *stay put,* they'd be fairly easy to find. But they rarely do. If they're inexperienced enough to lose themselves *in the first place,* they're inexperienced enough to *get panicky.* The *thing to do,* once you know you are lost, is to find a good, safe place to build a little fire, build it, fire three shots, light a cigarette, and sit down and wait. If the shots aren't answered wait a while till you are sure it's late enough for searchers to be out looking for you and shoot again. If you've *plenty of* shells with you, continue to do so every five minutes.

—Louise Dickinson Rich, *We Took to the Woods*

SLANG — *in writing, recording extremely informal speech*

His right name was Frank X. Farrell, and I guess the X stood for "Excuse me." Because he never *pulled a play,* good or bad, on or off the field, without apologizin' for it.

"Alibi Ike" was the name Carey *wished on him* the first day he reported down South. O' course we all *cut out* the *"Alibi"* part of it right away for fear he would overhear it and bust somebody. But we called him "Ike" right to his face and the rest of it was understood by everybody on the club except Ike himself. —Ring Lardner, "Alibi Ike"

In almost all the writing you do in school or office, in practically all public speaking, you will be expected to use *more formal language* than in everyday casual talk. Remember the following advice:

(1) *Limit colloquial words to writing that is either very personal or meant to be humorous and entertaining.* In writing meant to be taken seriously, avoid the following:

COLLOQUIALISMS:	*act up, enthused, fake, flunk, folks, gang up on, goof, gripe, hassle, josh, kid, mean, mess, mope, ornery, pal, skinny, sloppy, stump, swap, wangle*
TRITE, EVERYDAY FIGURES OF SPEECH:	*down to brass tacks, elbow grease, pull all the stops, hold your horses, throw in the sponge, get on the ball, get the show on the road, play ball, polish the apple, lie down on the job*

(2) *Use slang only for special effects.* Routine use of slang makes writing seem juvenile. But many an effective writer shows that he has *learned from slang* about some of the things that make language colorful and vigorous. Much slang has a pointed, no-nonsense quality that keeps language from going soft and sticky. In printer's slang, an exclamation mark becomes simply a "bang." Here are some typical slang words that are short and to the point: *blab, click, fizzle, jell, jibe, scram, wow.* Much of our language is slang that has made the grade: *bogus, boom, carpetbagger, crook, graft, handout, hike, hobo, honky-tonk, racketeer.*

Though much slang comes and goes, some slang terms were first used centuries ago:

grub (food) — 1659; *hick* (rustic) — 1690; *sap* (fool) — 1815

What limits the usefulness of slang is its deliberate *defiance of convention, authority, respectability.* "Head" becomes *bean,* "jail" becomes *jug* or *clink.* Slang metaphors are deliberately extravagant, exaggerated out of all proportion: "that kills me," "hit the ceiling," "fly off the handle," "go whole hog." In your own writing, use slang only when you can give it a witty, original twist, and when you can assume that your readers have a sense of humor.

EXERCISE 5 Which is the *more formal alternative* in each of the following pairs? Write the letter for the more formal choice after the number of each pair — for instance, *7b.*

1.	(a) party	*6.*	(a) snoop	*11.*	(a) yen	*16.*	(a) failure
	(b) shindig		(b) pry		(b) yearning		(b) flop
2.	(a) nap	*7.*	(a) gripe	*12.*	(a) swipe	*17.*	(a) weary
	(b) snooze		(b) complain		(b) steal		(b) fagged
3.	(a) swell	*8.*	(a) dazed	*13.*	(a) dupe	*18.*	(a) impudent
	(b) fine		(b) groggy		(b) patsy		(b) sassy
4.	(a) hoodwink	*9.*	(a) flatter	*14.*	(a) lay for	*19.*	(a) leary
	(b) bamboozle		(b) butter up		(b) waylay		(b) wary
5.	(a) cockeyed	*10.*	(a) bunk	*15.*	(a) horn in	*20.*	(a) frisk
	(b) absurd		(b) nonsense		(b) intrude		(b) search

EXERCISE 6 With the experienced reader, how much formality he requires, or how much informality he welcomes, becomes a matter of personal judgment. Record your own judgments by putting your

reactions after the number of each item: *F* for "formal" if the expression seems generally appropriate in serious writing; *I* for "informal" if the expression seems too colloquial for formal written English.

(You may wish to compare your own judgments with those of others by tabulating the responses of your classmates, and by checking them against the usage labels in dictionaries that use labels like "informal," "colloquial," or "slang.")

1.	snapshot	*11.*	picky
2.	on the go	*12.*	pipe down
3.	lunge	*13.*	goose step
4.	wise up	*14.*	thug
5.	up to snuff	*15.*	pinup
6.	outlaw	*16.*	on the double
7.	sellout	*17.*	nifty
8.	snippy	*18.*	babble
9.	hindsight	*19.*	back talk
10.	beside the point	*20.*	penniless

EXERCISE 7   Many expressions *at first used very informally* prove useful or striking enough to become part of the more formal vocabulary. Would you expect to see any of the following in formal written English? Used where and how? Discuss what you take to be the status of each expression. Check your own impressions against usage labels in available dictionaries.

checkup, con man, bawl out, slip up, pushover, buildup, kickback, pep, big time, panhandle

EXERCISE 8   The best modern prose is *formal without being stuffy.* It has touches of informality that leaven the whole without making it breezy or superficial. Do any of the following passages meet these requirements for a vigorous, natural formal style? Place each of these on a scale of formality — which is the most formal? Which the most informal? In each passage, point out half a dozen specific expressions that help determine the degree of formality of the whole.

1.   In areas where television ownership has spread to the point of virtual universality, viewing reverts to a pattern which resembles that of radio listening in its prime. Viewing is now almost wholly within the family group, with outsiders not normally present. The television set remains the focal point of the family's typical evening activities. However, it

probably no longer occupies the dominant position which it enjoyed in TV's earlier days, when other social activities slackened and even casual conversation was hushed in obedience to the set's demands. —Leo Bogart, *The Age of Television*

2. Now, ordinarily, if you have a few trustworthy men to help you, the moving of a python of any size is simple. Someone grabs the head, someone the tail, and the others hold on to various bits of the body. Keep it well stretched out so that it has no chance to coil round anything, and it is comparatively helpless. All I lacked was the few trustworthy men. To the Africans the python is a poisonous snake, and not only poisons you with its tongue but with the sharp point of its tail as well. Useless for me to protest that I would hold the head, while they held the harmless parts of the anatomy — they would point out that they could easily be killed by the tail. —Gerald M. Durrell, *The Overloaded Ark*

3. Another man made a valuable discovery because he forgot to wash his hands. He knocked off work in a laboratory to eat a roast beef sandwich, took one bite and gagged. The sandwich was sickeningly sweet! In reaching for a glass of water, he noticed his hands were dirty. Could the dirt have anything to do with the unexpected sweetness of that sandwich? He examined the stuff he had been handling in the laboratory before lunch and thereby discovered saccharin.
—W. Furness Thompson, "Why Don't Scientists Admit They Are Human?"

4. To hit the target, a man has to shoot off much ammunition. One of the marks of true genius is a quality of abundance. A rich, rollicking abundance, enough to give indigestion to ordinary people. Great artists turn it out in rolls, in swatches. They cover whole ceilings with paintings, they chip out a mountainside in stone, they write not one novel but a shelf full. It follows that some of their work is better than other. As much as a third of it may be pretty bad. Shall we say this unevenness is the mark of their humanity — of their proud mortality as well as of their immortality?
—Catherine Drinker Bowen, "The Nature of the Artist"

EXERCISE 9 [Optional] Informal language, being around us every day, offers us excellent opportunities for *firsthand investigation* of language in action. Prepare a short paper on *one* of the following topics:

1. What are the favorite *colloquial figures of speech* in your family or circle of friends? What areas are they drawn from? How familiar or how original are they?
2. Recount the same episode first in adult formal English for the benefit of teacher or parent, then in *current teen-age slang.*

U 2b Pronoun Usage

Use pronouns according to the conventions of formal usage.

The use of pronouns has changed considerably during the history of our language. In a poem written before 1542, Sir Thomas Wyatt said, "Blame not my lute, for *he* must sound / Of this and that as liketh *me*." Today we would say, "*it* must sound" and "as *I* like *it*." The changing history of our pronouns has left us with a number of confusing alternatives and overlappings. Remember the following points when choosing pronouns in accordance with the conventions of formal written English:

(1) *Use the object form of a personal pronoun as the object of a verb or preposition.* In formal English the surviving **case** forms of pronouns are used as follows:

SUBJECT	OBJECT (of verb)	OBJECT (of preposition)
I heard	he told *me*	with *me*
he arrived	I saw *him*	around *him*
she denied it	we believed *her*	against *her*
we had hoped	they betrayed *us*	without *us*
they deserve it	we noticed *them*	for *them*

In shifting from informal to formal English, observe these distinctions when the pronoun is part of a *combined subject or object:*

Jim *and I* heard	he told Jim *and me*	between you *and me*
he *and* Fred did	we saw Fred *and him*	for Fred *and him*
she *and* Jill left	I asked Jill *and her*	about Jill *and her*
we seniors did	he asked *us seniors*	against *us seniors*

Fill in the appropriate form even when *part of a sentence has been omitted:*

Jim writes better than *I* (do).
They know Jim better than (they do) *me*.

Few people are as considerate as *he* (is).
She had never liked anyone as much as (she did) *him*.

(2) *Use "who" in subject positions; use "whom" or acceptable alternatives in object positions.* Spoken English increasingly uses only *who* where formal English requires a choice between *who* and *whom*. As a question word, or **interrogative pronoun,** *who* asks a question about the subject, *whom* about the object of a verb or preposition:

> *Who* sent the letter? (*He* did.)
> *Whom* did you ask? (You asked *him*.)
> With *whom* did you discuss it? (I discussed it with *him*.)

As a **relative pronoun,** *who* appears as subject, *whom* as object in the relative clause:

> The people *who* knew him believed him. (*They* knew.)
> Mrs. King, *whom* he had met, introduced him. (He had met *her*.)
> The girl with *whom* I saw him was beautiful. (I saw him with *her*.)

Notice that often *whom* can be omitted or replaced by *that*:

> The man against *whom* he was running was an unknown.
> The man he was running against was an unknown.
> The man *that* he was running against was an unknown.

NOTE: An interpolated *I think* or *I feel* does not affect the choice of *who* or *whom*:

> I vote for the man who *I think* is best qualified.
> (I think *he* is best qualified.)
> I vote for the man whom *I feel* I can trust.
> (I feel I can trust *him*.)

(3) *Use the subject form after linking verbs.* Historically, English requires the subject form for the complement that pins a label on the subject: "It is *I*"; "That is *he*." The linking verb here works like an equal-sign: "Subject equals something else." But increasingly, object forms, usual after transitive verbs, have taken over, as in Shakespeare's "Damned be *him* that first cries, 'Hold, enough!'" Today, "it's *me*" is universally heard in spoken English. "That's *him*" and "it's *her*" are rapidly following suit. Use the subject form in written sentences like the following:

FORMAL: It was *she* who had notified the police.
FORMAL: The police had known from the start it was *he.*

(4) *Use a singular pronoun to point back to indefinite pronouns like "everybody" (everyone), "nobody" (no one), "somebody" (someone), "anybody" (anyone), "one," and "a person."* Informal English uses a singular verb after these but then switches to a plural pronoun: "Everyone *is* bringing *their* own lunch." Formal English consistently uses the singular:

FORMAL: Everybody *is* bringing *his* own lunch.
FORMAL: Somebody *has* left *his* lights on.
FORMAL: A person should not be required to tell *his* innermost thoughts.

(5) *Use "who" in reference to persons, "which" in reference to things and ideas.* But note that *that* may refer to both people and things:

> The people *who* lived there had left abruptly.
> The furniture, *which* they had left behind, was covered with dust.
> We swept up the debris *that* littered the floor.

(6) *Observe agreement in combinations like "this kind of" and "this sort of."* In informal English, the pronoun agrees not with *kind* or *sort* but with the noun that follows the *of:* "*these* kind of *cars.*" In formal English, it is either *this kind* or *these kinds,* either *that kind* or *those kinds:*

FORMAL: The builder recommended *this kind* of reinforcements.
FORMAL: My father knew all *these kinds* of wines.

EXERCISE 10   Reinforce your command of *formal pronoun choices* by reading over the following passages. Repeat your reading until the italicized choices have become familiar and natural to you.

1. My brother *and I* had left; *he and* his brother arrived; he is inviting you *and me;* we saw *him and* his brother; this is strictly between you *and me;* he left a message for you *and her; we Americans* welcome debate; they regarded *us Americans* with suspicion; this is hard for *us Americans* to understand; it was *she* who made the suggestion; it was *they* who recommended it; he plays better than *I;* the barber charged him more than *me;* he can do it as quickly as *I;* the accident injured him as badly as *her.*

2. The people *who* count; the people *whom* he named; the people with *whom* he had talked; people *who* he felt were his friends; people *whom* he knew to be his friends; the people *who* she said were coming; a man *who* knew him; a man *whom* he knew; a man *whom* he thought he knew; a man about *whom* he had read; a man *that* he had read about; the people *that* he had talked with; the man *who* had answered the phone; the phone *which* he was to repair.

3. Everybody brought *his* own food; a person attacking the government should be sure of *his* facts; everyone in *his* dreamworld imagines *himself* the hero beating *his* bullying opponent; no one can be considered happy if *he* hates *his* job; somebody left *his* car lights on; I never liked *this kind* of car; we are all tired of *that kind* of argument; the store carried all *these kinds* of light bulbs.

EXERCISE 11   Test your command of formal pronoun choices by *selecting the alternative appropriate to formal written English*. Write down the formal choice after the number of the sentence.

1. Someone who has always lived in the suburbs will never know what cultural attractions a big city could offer *him/them*.

2. To imagine the view of the world of a peasant in India is hard for *we/us* Americans.

3. My father had always wanted to own one of *that/those* kind of cars.

4. Jim was disappointed that *he/him* and his friends were not selected.

5. Everyone there felt a strong loyalty toward *his/their* family.

6. For my sister and *I/me,* the theater was part of a distant, unknown world.

7. No one enters college quite as eager to learn as graduation speakers expect *him/them* to be.

8. The Irishmen *who/whom* had settled in this part of the town had left Ireland during the Great Famine.

9. Rachel was chosen our first president, because it was *she/her* who first suggested our founding the club.

10. I never read an author *who/whom* I admired more.

11. *This/These* kind of statistics will not convince skeptical readers.

12. A person should not allow others to choose a career for *him/them*.

13. The director must choose an actress *who/whom* he feels can really live the role.

14. He hired handicapped people for *who/whom* a job meant not only a living but renewed self-respect.
15. There were few parts of the world where *she/her* and her sister had not traveled.
16. A professional can do the work better and cheaper than you or *I/me*.
17. Sometimes we meet someone *who/whom* we feel we have known all our lives.
18. Against *who/whom* did King Arthur fight his battles?
19. In all these years, he has never had a friendly word for you and *I/me*.
20. There was no part of my aunt's farm that *we / us* boys had not explored.

EXERCISE 12 [Optional] Literature using the *English of different times and regions* shows us many pronoun uses that vary from the conventions of current formal usage. Explain how the italicized pronouns in the following passages depart from current formal English.

1. How far that little candle throws *his* beam!
   (*Merchant of Venice*, Act V, Sc. 1)
2. And in these fits I leave them, while I visit
   Young Ferdinand, *whom* they suppose is drowned.
   (*Tempest*, Act III, Sc. 3)
3. Thou, *which* hast showed me great and sore troubles, shalt quicken me again. (Psalms)
4.   Give me your hand;
   Conduct me to *mine* host: we love him highly.
   (*Macbeth*, Act I, Sc. 6)
5.   I give my reputation to those
   Which were my friends, *mine* industry to foes. (John Donne)
6.   Three parts of him
   Is ours already, and the man entire
   Upon the next encounter yields *him* ours.
   (*Julius Caesar*, Act I, Sc. 3)
7.   For I
   Have given you here a third of my own life,
   . . . . *who* once again
   I tender to thy hand. (*Tempest*, Act IV, Sc. 1)
8. If the salt have lost *his* savor, wherewith shall it be salted?
   (Matthew 5:23)

9. Al started the motor and backed the truck to the gas pump. "Fill *her* up. *She*'ll take about seven," said Al. (John Steinbeck)
10. "Not likely to rain today. *She's* rained *herself* out."

(John Steinbeck)

U 2c   Verb and Adverb Forms

Use verbs and adverbs according to the conventions of formal usage.

The history of English verbs and adverbs has left us with a number of choices between two possible forms. Typically, the one form is widely heard in informal spoken English. The other is required in serious writing. Some of the spoken forms are occasionally labeled "substandard," or "incorrect," or "ungrammatical." But they are widely used by educated people, and they are often in keeping with historical developments going back many centuries.

Remember the following points when choosing verbs and adverbs in accordance with the conventions of *formal English:*

(1) *Use the formal forms for verbs that have confusing doubles.* In informal English, *lie* and *lay,* and *sit* and *set* long ago began to overlap. Emily Dickinson used *lain* for *laid* in one of her poems:

> I died for beauty, but was scarce
> Adjusted in the tomb,
> When one who died for truth was lain
> In an adjoining room.

Formal English sorts these verbs out as follows:

INTRANSITIVE: (s-v)	I *lie* in the sun (present) he will *lie* in the sun (future) we *lay* in the sun all day (past) we have *lain* in the sun (perfect) she was *lying* in the sun (progressive)
TRANSITIVE: (s-v-o)	I *lay* my burden down (present) he will *lay* the cornerstone (future) we *laid* our cards on the table (past) we have *laid* tile (perfect) I am *laying* bricks (progressive)

INTRANSITIVE:	I always *sit* here (present)
(s-v)	he will not *sit* still (future)
	we *sat* there quietly (past)
	we have often *sat* there (perfect)
	why are you *sitting* here (progressive)

TRANSITIVE:	she *sets* the table (present)
(s-v-o)	he will *set* it down over here (future)
	he *set* up his headquarters (past)
	he has *set* his burden down (perfect)
	he was *setting* a precedent (progressive)

Remember: We *lie* down, but we *lay* something down; we *sit* up, but we *set* something up.

(2) *Use the subjunctive for conditions contrary to fact, or for actions requested or desired.* At one time, English verbs had a separate set of forms for actions merely *possible.* We still have expressions like "if need *be.*" Thoreau said, "An efficient and valuable man does what he can, whether the community *pay* him for it or not." *Be* and *pay* used instead of the factual *is* and *pays* are **subjunctive** forms. The subjunctive is disappearing from spoken English. In formal English, use it in two situations:

— use *were* instead of *is* (or *was*) after *if, as if,* and *as though* if the assumption made is clearly improbable or contrary to fact:

SUBJUNCTIVE: It was very much as though this *were* a great reception and Paul *were* the host.   (Willa Cather)
(But it was not *really* a great reception, nor was he the host.)

SUBJUNCTIVE: I see advertisements for "active" young men, as if activity *were* the whole of a young man's capital.
(Thoreau)
(But it is not *really.*)

— use subjunctive forms after verbs indicating that something is *desirable or necessary* but has not yet come about:

I wish his sister *were* not so talkative.
He requested that the city *repave* the street.
We demand that he *pay* his debt to society.
They moved that the meeting *be* adjourned.

(3) *Use the distinctive adverb form where informal English would use unmarked adverbs.* Historically, English had two possible

adverb forms. One developed into the familiar -*ly* adverbs: *quickly, slowly, loudly.* The other became identical with the corresponding adjective: *quick, slow, loud.* Shakespeare uses "shall make it go *quick* away"; Whittier uses, "The mug of cider simmered *slow.*" Formal English generally prefers distinctive adverb forms. Use the adjective form to modify nouns, and after linking verbs. Use distinctive adverb forms as manner adverbs (see **G 5b**):

ADJECTIVE	ADJECTIVE	ADVERB
easy work	seemed *easy*	won *easily*
loud hurrahs	sounded *loud*	speak *loudly*
careful words	has been *careful*	did it *carefully*
considerable pain	was *considerable*	changed *considerably*
a *good* deed	tasted *good*	worked *well*

NOTE: A few adverb forms are unmarked even in formal English: *fast, right, much, thus.*

a *fast* move	seemed *fast*	acted *fast*
the *right* tone	looked *right*	acted *right*

(4) *Use distinctive adverb forms as intensifiers and sentence modifiers.* In earlier English, and in informal English today, we encounter many unmarked adverb forms that modify other modifiers, or the sentence as a whole:

> Thou hast made him *exceeding* glad with thy countenance.
>
> (Psalms)
>
> He went to the iron gate, for that must be opened too; but that lock went *damnable* hard.
>
> (John Bunyan, *Pilgrim's Progress*)

Current formal English requires distinctive adverb forms in these situations. Remember especially the following contrasts:

INFORMAL	FORMAL
pretty cold	*fairly* cold
real fast	*very* fast
awful slow	*extremely* slow
mighty proud	*very* proud
it *sure* was late	it *certainly* was late

EXERCISE 13   Reinforce your command of *formal verb and adverb forms* by reading over the following passages. Repeat your reading until the italicized choices have become familiar and natural to you.

1. I know better than to *lie* in the sun; last summer we *lay* on the beach all day; the letter had *lain* on his desk for weeks; I want to *lie* down; when I stayed with my uncle, he always *lay* down after lunch for a nap; he should have *lain* down for a rest; hens *lay* eggs; we are now *laying* the foundation; the foundations have been *laid;* the boards have to be *laid* end to end; last year we *laid* new tile; the boards were just *lying* there; the man was just *sitting* there; when we left, he still *sat* there; he had *sat* there all day; come in and *sit* down; we should *sit* in the back of the room; he told us to *sit* still; we have to *set* a deadline; we are *setting* a precedent; he had *set* the load down in the wrong place.

2. He acted as if he *were* my long-lost brother; the bird looked as if it *were* a plane; if I *were* you, I would refuse; if she *were* my friend, she would act differently; if he *were* in town, he would call us; if he *was* in town, we will hear about it; she would not work if she *were* ill; she should not have worked if she *was* ill; I suggest that he *return* the money; we recommend that the contract *be* renewed; I wish the work *were* finished; the workers demanded that the law *be* changed; I insist that she *tell* me herself.

3. A *good* machine works *well;* the car looked *good* and ran *well;* the weather was *good,* and the crowd behaved *well; considerable* expense; their performance had improved *considerably; easy* payments; the doors open and shut *easily;* a *careful* look; he looked at it *carefully;* he is a *real* friend; I like him *very* well; she is a *pretty* girl; it gets *rather* cold; there was an *awful* accident; the police arrived *extremely* fast; he is *sure* of himself; he *certainly* is.

EXERCISE 14 Test your command of formal verb and adverb choices by *selecting the alternative appropriate to formal written English.* Write down the formal choice after the number of the sentence.

1. His mother never learned to speak Spanish very *good/well.*

2. Opposition to the regime had weakened *considerable/considerably.*

3. Our proposals had simply been *lying/laying* on the shelf.

4. The landlords behaved as if the country *was/were* still in the Middle Ages.

5. For the first time, the news from home sounded *good/well.*

6. Thousands were *sitting/setting* in the rain waiting.

7. He had never heard the piece played so *good/well.*

8. People were *lying/laying* odds three to one against his election.

9. We demanded that the matter *was/be* reopened.
10. People were *lying/laying* on benches and along the walls.
11. We refused to *sit/set* there doing nothing.
12. We had *set/sat* up all night waiting for the eclipse.
13. His withdrawal *sure/surely* surprised everyone.
14. We were never *sure/surely* what he would do next.
15. He never succeeded in making the point *real/really* clear.
16. His wife always talked to him as if he *was/were* an obstinate and not very bright child.
17. If the check *was/were* forged, it will be hard to prove the forger's identity.
18. Tim had never had to earn a living in the *real/really* world.
19. Hundreds of dead and wounded still *lay/laid* on the battlefield.
20. Whenever I asked for my allowance, he pretended he did not hear very *good/well*.

U 3 Usage and Logic

Observe relationships between the conventions of usage and the logic of ideas.

Formal English requires careful attention to the relationship between usage and logic, between words and ideas. This relationship is not simple. Ideally, we want to make the language we use as logical as possible — to make it a clear and effective way of communicating ideas. But some scholars feel that our *language* determines what seems logical to us in the first place. Something seems natural to us because it is the way it is usually done. Today, *has* for us naturally goes with singular subjects: "The time *has* come." But Shakespeare just as "naturally" used *has* with a plural subject:

> What, *has* his daughters brought him to this pass? *(King Lear)*

Many of us today use *it*, the neuter pronoun, in reference to ships: "The carrier made *its* way back to port." But it was long usual to use the feminine pronoun (*she* or *her*) instead:

> The mind of the master of a vessel is rooted deep in the timbers of *her*. (Stephen Crane)

As a result, we cannot simply ask: "What would be the most logical way of expressing this idea?" We must ask: "How do the *conventions of our language* handle this problem?" The following sections examine how some of the basic relationships in a sentence are handled according to the conventions of written English.

U 3a Agreement

Solve agreement problems in keeping with the conventions of written English.

Logically and grammatically, a verb is closely tied to its subject. This close relationship is often reflected in matching changes in the forms of subject and verb. Most English nouns and pronouns have one form for singular and another for plural: one *plane/* several *planes;* one *accident/* several *accidents.* When there is a matching change in the form of the verb, the verb and its subject are said to agree in **number:**

SINGULAR	PLURAL
The hour *passes.*	The hours *pass.*
Her boy friend *was* happy.	Her boy friends *were* happy.
She *plays* the flute.	They *play* in the band.

English, like other Indo-European languages, at one time had elaborate sets of verb forms showing agreement in different tenses. Today, agreement survives most noticeably in verb forms involving a form of *be (is/are, was/were)* or of *have (has/have).* With other forms, agreement survives only in the present tense, in speaking about a third party ("third person") : *speaks/speak; admits/admit.*

Most of the time we observe agreement automatically. Handle the following special problems in keeping with the conventions of *written English:*

(1) *Make the verb agree with unusual Latin or Greek plurals* (see **G 1a**) :

SINGULAR	PLURAL
This *phenomenon* is new.	These *phenomena* are new.
The *medium* is the message.	The *media* are powerful.
This *criterion* is irrelevant.	These *criteria* are irrelevant.
His *analysis* was incomplete.	His *analyses* were incomplete.

The word *data,* originally a plural ("pieces of information"), is now also used as a singular:

This *data* means little.   These *data* mean little.

(2) *Make the verb agree with a subject from which it is separated, or which it precedes.* Material that *intervenes* between subject and verb does not affect agreement:

> *The precision* of these exercises *amazes* audiences.
> *Understanding* other nations *is* difficult.
> *The truth* of his predictions *has* been questioned.

Make the verb agree with a *postponed* subject, common after *there:*

> In the box *were thousands* of dollars in old coins.
> There *is* little *hope* for a new beginning.
> There *were dozens* of boxes to be put on the shelves.

NOTE: After *it* used as a dummy subject, the verb always remains singular:

> It *is* a *privilege* to listen to him.
> It *is* his *friends* who set him against us.

(3) *Use a plural verb only with true compound subjects.* Two singular subjects connected by *and* add up to a plural. Make the verb plural even when such a **compound subject** *follows* the verb:

> Hiking and swimming *were* his only recreation.
> There *were* a church and a cemetery at the top of the hill.

But note that *or,* and *either . . . or,* may merely give us a choice between two singular subjects. *As well as, together with,* and *in addition to* introduce prepositional phrases; they do *not* add a second subject and thus leave the number of a singular subject unchanged:

> His brother or a friend *has* always helped him out.
> The design as well as the specifications *has* been changed.
> The colonel together with a few diehards *was* still holding out.

Two possible subjects conected by *and* may be part of the name of a single thing and are then treated as a singular:

> His friend and lifelong companion *has* left him.
> Ham and eggs *was* his favorite breakfast.
> The Stars and Stripes *was* fluttering in the wind.

(4) *Follow convention in handling confusing singulars and plurals.* The **indefinite pronouns** like *each, either, neither,* and *everyone* may seem plural in meaning but are treated as singulars:

> Each of them *is* going to be heard.
> Either *is* entirely acceptable.

But *a number of,* singular in form and plural in meaning, is treated as a plural:

> A number of people *were* still waiting outside.

Amounts, and the names of *fields of study,* may be plural in form and yet be treated as singulars:

> Three dollars *is* too much.
> Five hours *was* more than enough time.
> Physics *has* always fascinated him.

None, once only a singular, and the **collective nouns** like *class, team, police,* and *committee* are acceptable *both* as singulars and as plurals:

> None *has* (or *have*) ever complained.
> The police *has* (or *have*) closed the case.

(5) *Observe agreement in relative clauses.* After *who, which,* and *that,* the verb agrees with whatever noun the relative clause as a whole modifies:

> She despises a man who *plays* with love.
> She despises men who *play* with love.
>
> He is *the only one* of her relatives who really *cares.*
> (Only *one* cares.)
> He always was one of *those people* who really *care.*
> (*Several* care.)

NOTE: Like some other relationships, agreement between subject and verb is treated more loosely in informal than in formal English. The following are widely heard in informal standard speech:

INFORMAL: There *was* a band and a cheering mob at the station.
INFORMAL: The chief as well as his assistants *were* disappointed.
INFORMAL: I am not one of those who *believes* in war.

You may on occasion see these usages in print in the work of a competent writer. But by avoiding them, you protect your writing against criticism.

EXERCISE 15 Reinforce your command of the *conventions governing agreement* in formal written English by reading over the following passages. Repeat your reading until the italicized forms have become familiar and natural to you.

1. The first criterion *is* clarity, but other criteria *are* equally important; the first medium of mass communication *was* the press, but soon other media *were* equally important; the phenomenon *has* attracted much attention, though similar phenomena *have* gone unnoticed; the usefulness of these inventions *is* limited; the implication of his findings *remains* unclear; understanding their motives *is* difficult; finding replacements *takes* time; there *is* a newcomer living there; there *are* newcomers living there; there *are* a newcomer and his wife living there; it *is* a newcomer and his wife who are living there; there *is* a cabin by the lake; there *are* a cabin and small store by the lake; there *are* cabins by the lake; it *is* the cabins that will have to be removed.

2. All *arrive* together, but each *leaves* separately; either *is* eligible, but neither *has* applied; everyone *comes* to the meeting, but a number of people always *leave* early; the sheriff and his deputy *are* conducting the search; the sheriff together with two deputies *is* conducting the search; a number of local citizens *have* joined the search; the mayor as well as several aldermen *has* opposed the plan; Thoreau is one of the writers who *have* preached civil disobedience; he is not the only one who *has* written about it; I am not one of those who *recommend* the use of force; Jean was one of those girls who *enter* every contest; he was one of those politicians who *respond* to every change in the wind.

EXERCISE 16 How would you have handled agreement in the following student-written sentences? After the number of each sentence, *write down the choice appropriate to formal written English.*

1. The time spent traveling, the money spent for lunch, and the wear and tear on one's nerves *makes/make* commuting a poor bargain.
2. There *was/were* no trees, bushes, or any form of shade.
3. More active participation in sports by young people *has/have* been encouraged by public officials.

4. At Christmas time, the children wait impatiently to open the different kinds of presents that *has/have* been put under the tree.

5. Other arguments against early marriage *is/are* low earning power and unexpected children.

6. In the lobby, a rich display of flowers *fills/fill* the air with fragrance.

7. A doctor and nurse *has/have* a great responsibility to live up to the code of ethics of their profession.

8. I found that friendliness and a few casual words *was/were* effective in selling.

9. There *is/are* always several tests coming up at this time of the year.

10. How can anyone remember all the rules that *is/are* listed in the manual?

EXERCISE 17   In the following paragraph, select verb forms in accordance with the conventions of formal English. After the number of each sentence, *write down the choice appropriate to formal written English.*

(1) South Africa is one of those countries that *does/do* not have a single national language. (2) The language of many original settlers *was/were* Dutch. (3) As the result of some decades of British rule, almost everyone among their descendants *has/have* learned English as a second language. (4) Either *is/are* understood by many South Africans today. (5) A number of Dutch words *has/have* become part of South African English. (6) Each of the following words *stands/stand* for some feature of the countryside first settled by the Dutch "Afrikanders": *dorp, kloof, kopje, veldt.* (7) Understanding the problems caused by the country's two languages *helps/help* us understand books like Alan Paton's *Too Late the Phalarope.* (8) Among the characters, there *is/are* an English-speaking police captain and a Dutch-speaking member of parliament. (9) The hero is one of those Afrikanders who *speaks/speak* English well. (10) His father is one of those Dutch Calvinists who *is/are* antagonistic toward the English and their language.

U 3b Pronoun Reference

Make pronouns point clearly to their antecedents.

Pronouns keep our language from becoming impossibly cumbersome. After a first mention, "the Prime Minister" simply becomes *he;* "the third building from the corner" simply becomes *it.* To do its work well, such a pronoun must point back clearly to its **antecedent** — to "what has gone before." When the antecedent is not fresh or clear enough in the reader's or listener's mind, a sentence becomes *vague.* If there are two possible antecedents, the sentence acquires an unintended double meaning. It becomes *ambiguous.*

(1) When there are *two possible antecedents,* rearrange or rewrite the sentence to avoid ambiguity:

AMBIGUOUS: *Mary* was friendly to *my sister* because *she* was going to be a bridesmaid. (Was Mary going to be the bridesmaid, or was the sister?)

CLEAR: Because *my sister* was going to be a bridesmaid, *Mary* was friendly to *her.*

Often the reference of *he, she, it,* or *they* becomes clear when one of two possible antecedents is changed from singular to plural, or vice versa:

AMBIGUOUS: *People* read these *authors* because *they* are fascinated with war.

CLEAR: The *public* reads these authors because *it* is fascinated with war.

(2) Bring out more clearly an antecedent that is *merely implied, or that appears as a modifier* rather than as a major part of the sentence:

CONFUSING: Since my father is a businessman, I have also chosen *it* as a career. (What is *it?*)

CLEAR: Since my father is a businessman, I have also chosen a *business* career.

CONFUSING: He reached for the dog's leash, but *it* ran away. (the leash?)

CLEAR: When he reached for its leash, *the dog* ran away.

(3) A *this* or *which* pointing to a general idea implied in a sentence is often vague. Avoid such vague **idea reference** by making *this* or *which* refer to a specific noun, or by spelling out clearly what is referred to:

CONFUSING: As a teacher, I would try hard not to play favorites. *This* is often the best way to gain the students' confidence. (*What* is the best way — playing favorites, or *not* playing favorites?)

CLEAR: As a teacher I would try hard not to play favorites. Complete *impartiality* is often the best way to gain the students' confidence.

CONFUSING: She refused to scrub the floors, *which* always annoyed her husband. (What annoyed him — the scrubbing, or the refusal?)

CLEAR: Her refusal, *which* always annoyed her husband, kept the floors from being scrubbed.

(4) Limit to informal use the *they* and *you* that stand for "people in general." In formal English, spell out who *they* are. Use *you* only when you actually mean "you, the reader":

INFORMAL: We had just gotten our tickets when *they* announced our flight.

FORMAL: We had just gotten our tickets when *a voice* announced our flight.

INFORMAL: At Oakdale College, *they* require two years of French.

FORMAL: *Oakdale College* requires two years of French.

INFORMAL: *You* have to work full time at being a mother. (Many of your readers are not yet mothers, and many never will be.)

FORMAL: A mother's job is full-time work.

NOTE: For reference to indefinite pronouns (*everybody* took *his*), see **U 2b**.

EXERCISE 18 Check the italicized pronouns for *clarity of reference*. Put *S* (satisfactory) after the number of the sentence if the pronoun points clearly to its antecedent. Put *U* (unsatisfactory) if reference is confusing or informal. Your teacher may ask you to revise the unsatisfactory sentences.

1. It is hard to believe that we are lacking teachers, for *this* should be a field too highly regarded to suffer a shortage.

2. His fiancée refused to return the ring *which* he had given her.

3. Many of us have been depressed, but not all of us know how to rid ourselves of *it*.

4. We stopped at an Indian trading post and bought several items that *they* had made.

5. Herman hated editors, because *they* kept rejecting his manuscripts.

6. City children are cheated when *they* build modern schools only in the suburbs.

7. What makes Marine Corps training different is that its purpose is to turn *you* into a different person.

8. Sky-diving fascinated me because *it* introduced me to a completely new world.

9. The voters turned against the party leaders because *they* believed in private property.

10. We decided on a brick wall because *it* is easier to carry and to handle than concrete blocks.

EXERCISE 19 In the following paragraph, check the italicized pronouns for *clarity of reference*. Put *S* (satisfactory) after the number of the sentence if the pronoun points clearly to what it stands for. Put *U* (unsatisfactory) if reference is confusing or informal. Your teacher may ask you to revise the unsatisfactory sentences.

(1) Have *you* ever heard "paper" pronounced like "piper," or "my shirt" like "me shirt"? (2) In World War II, many American G.I.s heard this kind of pronunciation when *they* were stationed in Australia. (3) In Australia, *they* speak a kind of English similar in many ways to that of Great Britain. (4) The British originally sent convicts there because *they* had no use for the continent. (5) Later, when free immigrants followed, *they* found a climate, plants, and animals different from those of their native England. (6) They learned words like "wombat," "kangaroo," and "boomerang," *which* were taken from the language of the Australian aborigines. (7) Australia is a long trip around the world from England, *which* has made close contacts difficult. (8) But in education and politics *you* follow British models, and everyday language owes much to British slang. (9) In Australia, *you* call a man a "cove" rather than a "guy" or a "fellow." (10) The Australian feels close to the British because he considers *it* his mother country.

U 3c Position of Modifiers

Place modifiers so that they clearly modify one thing rather than another.

Normally, English word order clearly relates a modifier to what it modifies: "a *momentous* discovery," "a *truly* remarkable achievement," "in love *with easeful Death*." Confusion results when a modifier seems to point two different ways at once, or when it does not seem to point to anything actually mentioned in the sentence.

(1) Place words like *only, almost,* and *just* with special care. They can modify almost every major element in a typical sentence:

CONFUSING:	You have to notify the supervisor *only* in an emergency.
CLEAR:	You have to notify *only* the supervisor in an emergency.
CLEAR:	You have to notify the supervisor in emergencies *only.*
CONFUSING:	We had *almost* enough to eat for everyone.
CLEAR:	We had enough to eat for *almost* everyone.

(2) Revise *prepositional phrases and verbals* that seem to point to the wrong thing and thus become **misplaced modifiers:**

MISPLACED:	He sent me a bill for the teeth he had filled *by mail.*
REVISED:	He sent me a bill *by mail* for the teeth he had filled.
MISPLACED:	*Stubbornly refusing to move,* George whipped the mules.
REVISED:	*Stubbornly refusing to move,* the mules had to be whipped.

Keep *appositives and relative clauses* from becoming misplaced. Tie them firmly to the noun they modify:

MISPLACED:	There was only one case before the judge, *a confirmed alcoholic.*
REVISED:	Only one case, *a confirmed alcoholic,* was before the judge.
MISPLACED:	We heard about the boat of a friend *that had capsized.*
REVISED:	We heard about a friend's boat *that had capsized.*

(3) Revise *verbals* modifying something that has dropped from the sentence. Here are some typical **dangling modifiers:**

DANGLING:	*Walking across the yard,* the building seemed deserted.
REVISED:	As *I* walked across the yard, the building seemed deserted.
DANGLING:	*Working silently,* the attempts at rescue continued.
REVISED:	Working silently, *the men* continued their attempts at rescue.

(4) Do not treat as dangling modifiers *familiar expressions* that clarify the intention or attitude of the speaker or writer. In expressions like the following, "I" or "we" is clearly implied:

ACCEPTABLE: *Generally speaking,* there has been little change.
ACCEPTABLE: *Considering his background,* he is doing well.

NOTE: In practice, writers and readers vary considerably in their tolerance of dangling modifiers. Many danglers go unnoticed when the meaning is clear from the context: "*Going down the stairs* his glasses became so dimmed with moisture that he had to take them off and polish them" (James Joyce). Here as elsewhere, however, observance of the formal conventions forestalls criticism.

EXERCISE 20 Check the following sentences for *dangling, misplaced, or confusing modifiers.* Write *S* after the number of the sentence if all modifiers are satisfactory. Write *U* if one or more modifiers are unsatisfactory. Your teacher may ask you to revise the unsatisfactory sentences.

1. He declined the invitation to speak at the meeting with regret.
2. An incurable optimist, Carl was looking for a beautiful, intelligent, and fabulously wealthy girl.
3. Though announced three times, Jean was late for the examination.
4. Having finished my dinner, the waiter removed the dishes.
5. Bleeding from a cut above the left eye, the champion was severely handicapped.
6. I kept calling her Miss Smith after she got married by mistake.
7. Considering his qualifications, his salary is already too high.
8. A high school graduate handicaps himself by not entering college in many different ways.
9. Labeled immoral by the city fathers, large crowds came to see the Swedish movie.
10. Frantically manipulating the controls, he finally succeeded in stabilizing the plane.
11. Painted in three bright colors, we could not make up our minds to buy the car.
12. He steadily applied his file to the steel grille barring the window.
13. The students were unaware of the prowl cars that had appeared on the scene.
14. At the age of twelve, Grandfather invited me to Canada.
15. He had strong feelings about the issues that he could not disguise.
16. Special meals were prepared for tourists only in Spain.

17. He always noted down in his diary all data about the girls he dated.
18. Having taken American history the year before, I saw no need to take it again.
19. Always saying hello to me, I wondered who the handsome stranger was.
20. Half asleep in our jeep, a herd of elephants suddenly blocked the road.

U 3d Mixed Construction

Revise confused or illogical sentences.

In informal speech, we all use sentences that are improvised or half-finished. As we are speaking, we change our minds about what we are going to say, and about how we are going to put it. We interrupt a sentence and start over. We start a sentence one way and finish it another. Part of our task in giving final shape to a piece of writing is to revise sentences that preserve the loose, improvised quality of speech.

(1) *Correct unintentional duplication or omission of grammatical elements.* Check for awkward repetition of grammatical links like *that* or *when* when the clause they start has been interrupted by an aside:

CONFUSED: I know *that* when the chips are down *that* he will be on our side.
REVISED: I know *that* he will be on our side when the chips are down.
REVISED: I know *that* when the chips are down he will be on our side.

Check for inadvertent omission of minor grammatical elements like *a, the, has, be,* or *am.*

(2) Correct *predicates that repeat an idea already expressed in the subject,* or that make a statement that *does not logically apply* to the subject. Here are some examples of **faulty predication:**

CONFUSED: *The choice* of the site *was selected* by a committee.
REVISED: *The choice* of the site *was made* by a committee.
REVISED: *The site was selected* by a committee.

CONFUSED:	*His job* is *an inspector* in Quality Control.
REVISED:	*He* is *an inspector* in Quality Control.
REVISED:	*His job* is *that* of an inspector in Quality Control.

CONFUSED:	*The participation* in club activities *was overcrowded.*
REVISED:	*The club meetings were* always *overcrowded.*
REVISED:	*Participation* in club activities *was* very *lively.*

(3) Correct sentences in which *several possible constructions have become mixed.* Settle for *one* of the several alternatives that have become entangled:

MIXED:	*In case of* an accident *should be reported* to the office.
CLEAR:	*In case of an accident,* notify the office.
CLEAR:	Accidents *should be reported* to the office.

MIXED:	*He worked* as little as possible and *still pass the course.*
CLEAR:	*He tried to work* little and still *pass* the course.
CLEAR:	*He worked* as little as possible while still passing the course.

MIXED:	We made a detour *because of* the bridge *was closed.*
CLEAR:	We made a detour *because* the bridge *was closed.*
CLEAR:	We made a detour *because of* a closed bridge.

In formal English, avoid using a *when*-clause or a *because*-clause as if it were a noun clause (see **G 6b**). Revise the informal *is-when* sentences that use a *when*-clause after the linking verb *be.* Revise the informal sentences that use a *because*-clause as the subject of the sentence:

INFORMAL:	Nepotism *is when* relatives receive special favors.
FORMAL:	Nepotism *is the practice* of giving special favors to relatives.

INFORMAL:	*Because he is your friend* does not mean he is mine.
FORMAL:	*That he is your friend* does not mean he is mine.
FORMAL:	*Just because he is your friend,* he is not necessarily mine.

(4) *Revise illogical or incomplete comparisons.* In informal spoken English, comparisons easily move off the track as they move from the one thing being compared to the other:

ILLOGICAL:	His own *reputation* was equal to his *father.*
REVISED:	His own *reputation* was equal to *that* of his father.
REVISED:	*His* own reputation was equal to his *father's.*

ILLOGICAL:	The science teacher knew more than *anyone* on the staff.

LOGICAL: The science teacher knew more than *anyone else* on the staff.

AMBIGUOUS: I understood the parents better than the boys.
CLEAR: I understood the parents better than the boys *did.*
CLEAR: I understood the parents better than *I did* the boys.

(5) Avoid *excessive telescoping* when different elements in a sentence express similar ideas. When parts of a sentence are joined by *and, or,* or *but,* we can omit elements that are *exactly duplicated:* "he *was* drafted but *(was)* soon released"; "they were respectful *(to)* and loyal *to* their superiors." Such telescoping does not work in formal English when the elements duplicated are merely *similar:*

INFORMAL: He never *has* and never *will admit* his mistake.
FORMAL: He never has *admitted* and never will *admit* his mistake.

INFORMAL: She became *infatuated* and *subservient to* a young stranger.
FORMAL: She became infatuated *with* and subservient *to* a young stranger.

INFORMAL: My work is *as good,* if not *better, than* yours.
FORMAL: My work is as good *as,* if not better *than,* yours.

EXERCISE 21 Check the following sentences for *confused construction, illogical comparisons,* or *unsatisfactory telescoping.* Write *S* after the number of the sentence if it is satisfactory. Write *U* if it is unsatisfactory. Your teacher may ask you to revise unsatisfactory sentences.

1. His kindness was unlike anyone I have ever met.
2. The students demonstrated in favor of higher standards and against overemphasis on athletics.
3. The use of the football helmet today is used not only for protection but also as a weapon.
4. He is being dismissed because he is not now and never has done the job for which he was hired.
5. Accidents can and do happen to people like you and me.
6. Because the cabin was damaged does not mean that we should cancel the trip.
7. A student should be graded in English on the same basis as any other class.
8. His mother's attitude was much more liberal than his father's.

9. I finally saw the play of which he had told me about.
10. It is preferable but not absolutely necessary that a boy's dream girl should share his religious beliefs.
11. Discipline, to me, is a school with teachers who keep the students under control.
12. The purpose of the device was designed to serve as a warning system in case of enemy attack.
13. Parole is when a prisoner is released before he has served his full sentence.
14. Watching the crowd was as entertaining as watching the fight.
15. I believe that with the right attitude that early marriages can be made to work.
16. She has dozens of toy animals which she buys with her own money and places them around the room.
17. Some men just cannot or will not understand the way women feel about a home and children.
18. Few men ever have or ever will equal Emerson as the master essayist of American literature.
19. Young people really conform more readily than adults.
20. The judge blamed the boys more than their parents.

EXERCISE 22 [Optional] If you have tape recording equipment available, *record all or a portion of a discussion* — one lively or even heated enough for people to speak spontaneously and naturally. Select a segment of about 300 to 400 words. First transcribe exactly what you think you hear. Then produce an *edited* second version in which you fashion the material into finished sentences acceptable in formal English. How extensive are the changes that you have to make? What kinds of changes are they? (You may arrange to do this assignment as a group project.)

U 4 *Usage and Style*

Cultivate features that make for a vigorous and effective style.

Much of the study of usage is concerned with things *not* to do. A speaker cannot be effective unless he has some sense of what his listeners would consider stuffy, offensive, or immature. A writer cannot count on the good will of his readers if he ignores their objections to what they consider breezy, or uneducated, or illogical.

Nevertheless, in recent decades, guides to usage have shifted the emphasis away from *what to avoid,* and toward *what to do.* Constant worry over possible objections has an inhibiting effect. No one has ever become a magnificent speaker or a great writer merely as the result of carefully avoiding errors. It is not true that effective language is automatically left over after all possible "mistakes" have been removed. An effective speaker and writer must cultivate the *positive* qualities that give his use of language point, coherence, and force:

(1) *Give clear, direct, and memorable form to key ideas.* True, often you need to give careful, detailed explanation. But do not allow your most important points to be lost in details as in a fog. After a truly effective speech, certain key phrases echo in our minds. After reading an effective article, we can quote phrases that in a memorable way sum up a main point. Here are some lines from a memorable and quotable document of American history:

> We hold these truths to be self-evident: That all men are created equal; that they are endowed by their Creator with certain inalienable rights; that among these are life, liberty, and the pursuit of happiness; that to secure these rights, governments are instituted among men, deriving their just powers from the consent of the governed; . . .
>
> (Thomas Jefferson)

Would these words be as familiar if the key points had been diluted in wordy phrases like the following?

ROUNDABOUT:	survival in a troubled world, the limitation of government authority, and the satisfaction of basic human drives
DIRECT:	life, liberty, and the pursuit of happiness
ROUNDABOUT:	political processes by which the exercise of governmental functions is subjected to the approval or disapproval of the voters
DIRECT:	the consent of the governed

(2) *Set up patterns that your audience can identify and anticipate.* Effective speech and writing help *channel* our expectations. They guide us by setting up consistent perspective; by setting up an

overall pattern and following it through. They use repetition to tie together related points. Notice how the repetition of the same grammatical constructions sets up a pattern in the following famous lines:

> *With malice* toward none;
> *with charity* for all;
> *with firmness* in the right, as God gives us to see the right,
>   let us strive on
>   *to finish* the work we are in;
>   *to bind up* the nation's wounds;
>   *to care* for *him* who shall have borne the battle,
>   and for *his widow,*
>   and his *orphan* —
>   *to do* all which may *achieve*
>   and *cherish* a *just,*
>   and a *lasting* peace,
>   *among* ourselves,
>   and *with* all nations.   (Abraham Lincoln)

(3) *Exploit the resources of our language for richness and variety.* The following lines from a famous speech use the kind of repetition that channels our expectations. But at the same time, these lines have the variety that give them a rhythm not gray and monotonous but powerful and alive. Can you see how the "we shall go on . . . we shall fight" pattern sets up the basic rhythm of the passage? Can you see how the speaker achieves great intensity by even new variations of his basic point?

> Even though large tracts of Europe and many old and famous States have fallen or may fall into the grip of the Gestapo and all the odious apparatus of Nazi rule, we shall not flag or fail. We shall go on to the end, we shall fight in France, we shall fight on the seas and oceans, we shall fight with growing confidence and growing strength in the air, we shall defend our Island, whatever the cost may be, we shall fight on the beaches, we shall fight on the landing grounds, we shall fight in the fields and in the streets, we shall fight in the hills; we shall never surrender, and even if, which I do not for a moment believe, this Island or a large part of it were subjugated and starving, then our Empire beyond the seas, armed and guarded by the British Fleet, would carry on the struggle, until, in God's good time, the New World, with all its power and might, steps forth to the rescue and the liberation of the old.   (Winston Churchill)

Certainly, the patterns and rhythms of language are not as striking in everyday situations as they are in solemn or impassioned moments. But every speaker and writer must develop at least a rudimentary feeling for what gives force, and pattern, and variety to language.

U 4a Directness

Cultivate features that make sentences clear and direct rather than awkward and roundabout.

Good prose, as George Orwell has said, is like a windowpane. It allows us to take a clear and unobstructed look at the object in view. Awkward and roundabout prose is like a fogged-up windshield. It gets in the way. Remember the following advice when trying to make your sentences clear and direct:

(1) *Use active verbs where overuse of nouns would make a sentence static and opaque.* The right verb can help make a sentence go; it can give us actions or events to *visualize.* Try translating what things *are* into what people *do:*

STATIC: Violent *argument* resulted every time there was a *reunion* of the family.

BETTER: Every time the members of my family *met,* they *argued* violently.

STATIC: Our prevailing *tendency* is toward *contempt* for *integrity* and *intelligence* when attended by *poverty.*

BETTER: We *spurn* at virtue and genius in rags, and *lick* the dust in the presence of vice and folly in purple.   (William Hazlitt)

STATIC: An *examination* of the typical ambitious business executive will reveal that the excessive *pressures* of modern life are a primary *cause* of poor mental and physical *health.*

BETTER: *Look at* one of your industrious fellows for a moment . . . He *sows* hurry and *reaps* indigestion; he *puts* a vast deal of activity out to interest, and *receives* a large measure of nervous derangement in turn.   (R. L. Stevenson)

(2) *Use active constructions where the passive would be awkward or too impersonal.* The passive pulls into prominent position, as the subject of the sentence, a noun that would more typically be

the object of the verb (see **G 4**). It is especially appropriate when we want to emphasize the *outcome,* and not the origin, of a process; or the *result,* and not the instigator, of an action:

EFFECTIVE: *Repairs,* except what you could do for yourself, *had to be sanctioned* by remote committees.   (George Orwell)

EFFECTIVE: *The institutions* of policy, *the goods* of fortune, *the gifts* of providence *are handed down* to us, and from us, in the same course and order.   (Edmund Burke)

The passive gets in the way when whoever *makes things happen* is as important as ever but has been shifted to an inconspicuous part of the sentence. The passive becomes evasive and bureaucratic when whoever is responsible for an action has been dropped from the sentence altogether.

AWKWARD: *Preparations are being made* by opponents of the bill for an extended advertising campaign.

BETTER: *Opponents* of the bill *are planning* an extensive advertising campaign.

BUREAUCRATIC: *All* personnel *records will be* periodically *evaluated* in the light of established company policy.

BETTER: *Management will* periodically *evaluate* the records of all employees.

(3) *Remove the deadwood from sentences using impersonal or roundabout constructions.* Often a sentence moves more briskly after you remove fillers like *one, a person,* or *there is:*

AWKWARD: When *one* is a teacher in a big-city school, *he* obtains a firsthand look at our urban problems.

BETTER: *A teacher* in a big-city school can take a firsthand look at our urban problems.

AWKWARD: When *a person* who is still a teenager joins the army, *there is* a tremendous adjustment to be faced.

BETTER: *A teen-ager* who joins the army faces a tremendous adjustment.

(4) *Make sprawling sentences more compact by reducing clauses to phrases, phrases to single words.* A paragraph becomes heavy and lumpy when every sentence is weighed down with more grammatical machinery than is needed to carry the meaning. Often, a verbal can carry the same meaning as a lengthy subordinate clause.

An appositive can carry the same meaning as a relative clause:

LENGTHY: *Because we were living* in a remote part of the state, we hardly ever saw a doctor.

COMPACT: *Living* in a remote part of the state, we hardly ever saw a doctor.

LENGTHY: The mansion, *which had been built* to last hundreds of years, belonged to Mike Fawley, *who was a wealthy rancher.*

COMPACT: The mansion, *built* to last hundreds of years, belonged to Mike Fawley, *a wealthy rancher.*

(5) *Revise or break up sentences in which several dependent clauses crowd, or work against, each other.* Sometimes several similar clauses will follow one another in "house-that-Jack-built" fashion. Sometimes a clause at the end will seem to cancel out a clause at the beginning, producing a teeter-totter effect:

OVERLOAD: We sat watching the waves *that* were driven along by the storm *that* was building up.

BETTER: We sat watching the waves *driven along* by the storm that was building up.

OVERLOAD: *If we finish in time,* we might go walking *if we feel like it.*

BETTER: *If* we finish in time, *and if* we feel like it, we might go walking.

EXERCISE 23 Rewrite the following sentences to make them more *direct* or more *compact.*

1. In being a teacher, it is important not to show any favoritism.

2. After all these requirements are met by the candidate, there is still a personal interview to be faced.

3. My selection of a career has been due in part to my father's influence.

4. We loved to hear the ancient bells which hang in the church towers, which have survived centuries of war and poverty.

5. As a newcomer in politics, one must avoid making charges that are founded on hearsay.

6. My views of marriage have been acquired gradually and have not been shaped by any one instance.

7. The availability of sufficient funds is a prerequisite for the person who desires to go to college.

8. Careful attention should be paid by those who hire a teacher to his emotional stability.

9. A substantial part of my earnings was expended for room and board.

10. The qualifications required of a person who wants to enter a school of nursing vary in different locations.

EXERCISE 24 From your recent writing, select *three sentences* that are indirect, awkward, or roundabout. Write down the original sentence and then a *revised version* that makes the sentence more direct or compact.

U 4b Consistent Point of View

Help your reader find his way by maintaining a consistent grammatical perspective.

We can usually look at people or events from more than one grammatical point of view. Usually, we describe past events in the past tense: "The regiment slowly *fell* back under heavy fire." But to make past events especially vivid, we may use the **historical present** instead:

> All shops, unless it be the Bakers' and Vintners', *are* shut: Paris *is* in the streets. . . . The tocsin, by order, *is* pealing madly from all steeples.
>
> (Thomas Carlyle, *The French Revolution*)

Once we choose the vivid present tense here, we should not confuse the reader by suddenly shifting back to the past. A route full of unexpected twists and turns irritates and confuses the motorist. A sentence or a paragraph with unexpected shifts in perspective irritates and confuses the reader.

(1) *Be consistent in the use of tense.* Normally, we fit time relationships into the following scheme:

PRESENT (also *habitual* action, or past treated *as if* happening now) :
Industry *is* a means and not an end; and mankind *work* only to get something which they *want*.   (T. H. Huxley)

PAST (events past and done with) :
As he *passed* along the ranks of the guards he *saluted* them with a smile, and *mounted* the scaffold with a firm tread.

(T. B. Macaulay)

PERFECT (past events with a bearing on the *present*) :
> The working man *has become* a fighting man; has one want only: that of arms. (Thomas Carlyle)

PAST PERFECT (past events *prior to other* events in the past) :
> Milton was, like Dante, a statesman and a lover; and, like Dante, he *had been* unfortunate in ambition and in love. (T. B. Macaulay)

Avoid sudden shifts from the *past to the present:*

SHIFT: As we *drove* along, the horse suddenly *panics* and almost *overthrows* the cart.

CONSISTENT: As we drove along, the horse suddenly *panicked* and almost *overthrew* the cart.

Avoid shifts in the opposite direction, making events appear *simultaneous* that actually occur at different points in time:

SHIFT: My father *showed* us where he *served* as an apprentice.

CONSISTENT: My father *showed* us where he *had served* as an apprentice.

(2) *Be consistent in the use of pronouns.* If you use impersonal expressions like *one, a person,* or *the reader,* use pronouns like *he* and *himself* to point back to them. Do not suddenly shift to the more personal *I* or *you,* or vice versa.

SHIFT: There are some things a *person* ought to know before *you* travel abroad.

CONSISTENT: There are some things a *man* ought to know about America before *he* sees it. (G. K. Chesterton)

SHIFT: *I* would not want to live in a tract where all *your* neighbors know everything *you* do.

CONSISTENT: *I* would not want to live in a tract where all *my* neighbors know everything *I* do.

(3) *Be consistent in the use of active and passive constructions.* A shift to the passive will confuse your audience if the *same person* or thing continues to make things happen:

SHIFT: Totalitarians *urge* us to give all to the cause, and close personal ties *are considered* a luxury.

CONSISTENT: Totalitarians *urge* us to give all to the cause; they *consider* close personal ties a luxury.

CONSISTENT: Personal relations *are despised* today. They *are regarded* as bourgeois luxuries . . . and we *are urged* to get rid of them, and to dedicate ourselves to some movement or cause instead.   (E. M. Forster)

Note that *necessary changes* in grammatical perspective result when an account actually moves from the present to the past, or from one person to the other. Confusing *shifts* result when there is a switch in tense but not in time, or when pronouns change but the person stays the same.

EXERCISE 25   Which of the following sentences are *consistent* in grammatical perspective? Put *S* (for "satisfactory") after the number of each such sentence. Which sentences show a confusing *shift* in point of view? Put *U* (for "unsatisfactory") after the number of each of these. Your teacher may ask you to revise the unsatisfactory sentences.

1. When I walk past the small neighborhood grocery stores and corner restaurants, I feel at home, among my own people.
2. When one is writing a paper, you must first collect your thoughts.
3. Every young person should go away to college, because there you are exposed to new people and ideas.
4. The Welsh have built themselves some of the ugliest villages in the world, but they love literature, music, and any kind of learning.
5. My uncle had been trained as an architect but made a living selling real estate in New York City.
6. Scientists have already conquered polio and tuberculosis, and the cause of cancer is being searched for in a big way today.
7. In a little shack with a Coca-Cola sign, an old woman sells souvenirs and sweetens the air with popular recordings.
8. Chiropractors believe that most of a person's illnesses are due to dislocated vertebra in your spine.
9. As they cautiously advanced into the cave, the earth begins to tremble and rocks start tumbling down the side of the mountain.
10. When one compares today's language with that of Shakespeare's time, many differences are observed.
11. If a student likes to read, he should be encouraged to become an English major in college.
12. In my childhood, cattle were still rounded up for sale in the fields behind our house, and pigs were herded down our street to the slaughterhouse at the other end of town.

13. At halftime our team had a comfortable lead, but early in the second half the visitors suddenly draw to within three points.
14. On Saturday mornings, we always mowed the lawn, swept the sidewalk, and the car was washed later.
15. If you want to pass the course, all work should be turned in on time.

U 4c Parallel Structure

Line up related ideas in grammatically parallel form.

We can show that two or more ideas are closely related by repeating the same grammatical structure. The repetition of the grammatical pattern signals "more of same"; it prepares the audience to look for additional examples of the same point, for further applications of a key idea. Several phrases or clauses that are thus built the same way are said to be **parallel** in structure. To make parts of a sentence parallel, we may for instance repeat the same basic Subject-Verb-Object pattern; or we may use several combinations of Verb-Prepositional Phrase.

The following sentences use parallel structure to line up several ideas that belong *under the same heading:*

There was *no view,*
  no way out for the eyes,
  no change of scene. (Graham Greene)

We are *all prompted by* the same motives,
  all deceived by the same fallacies,
  all animated by hope,
    obstructed by danger,
    entangled by desire, and
    seduced by pleasure. (Samuel Johnson)

Around us *nothing moved,*
  nothing lived,
    not a canoe on the water,
    not a bird in the air,
    not a cloud in the sky. (Joseph Conrad)

To sit still and contemplate, —
to remember the faces of women *without desire,*
to be pleased by the great deeds of men *without envy,*
to be everything and everywhere in sympathy,

and yet content to remain *where* and
       what you are —
is not this *to know* both *wisdom* and
      virtue, and
   to dwell with happiness?   (R. L. Stevenson)

The following sentences use parallel structure to line up *opposed ideas for contrast:*

People will not *look forward to posterity*
    who never
    look backward to their ancestors.
                            (Edmund Burke)

Gambling promises the poor
   what
property performs for the rich.   (G. B. Shaw)

Democracy substitutes
   selection by the incompetent many for
   appointment by the corrupt few.   (G. B. Shaw)

The following passage uses parallel structure to line up *related ideas in a paragraph:*

> Certainly the prolonged education indispensable to the progress of Society is not natural to mankind. It cuts against the grain. *A boy would like to follow* his father in pursuit of food or prey. *He would like to be doing* serviceable things so far as his utmost strength allowed. *He would like to be earning* wages however small to help to keep up the home. *He would like to have* some leisure of his own to use or misuse as he pleased.   —Sir Winston Churchill, *My Early Life*

Many uses of parallel structure are merely optional. They help the audience follow by giving a sentence or a paragraph a clearer, more distinct pattern. Some uses of parallel structure, however, are *required* if a sentence is not to be thrown off balance:

(1) Two sentence elements joined by *and, or,* or *but* should be in the same grammatical category. For instance, these **coordinating connectives** should not link an adjective to a noun, or a phrase to a clause, or a gerund to an infinitive:

OFF BALANCE: The production was *lavish* but *a disappointment.*
PARALLEL: The production was *lavish* but *disappointing.*

OFF BALANCE:	He left *without a penny* and *after he had lost all his friends.*
PARALLEL:	He left after he had lost *all his money* and *all his friends.*

OFF BALANCE:	He liked *to eat* well and heavy *drinking.*
PARALLEL:	He liked to *eat* well and *drink* heavily.

(2) When three or more elements are joined in a **series,** the last part should not snap out of the established pattern:

OFF BALANCE:	The receiver is *small, compact,* and *uses* flashlight batteries.
PARALLEL:	The receiver is *small, compact,* and *inexpensive.*
PARALLEL:	The receiver *costs* little, *runs* on flashlight batteries, and *fits* into a woman's purse.

OFF BALANCE:	He liked to *swim, play* tennis, and many other *sports.*
PARALLEL:	He liked *swimming, tennis,* and many other *sports.*

(3) Elements joined by **paired connectives** like *either . . . or,* and *not only . . . but also,* should be parallel in structure. Make sure the *either* or the *not only* appears in the most logical position:

OFF BALANCE:	He not only *called* him a liar but also *a thief.*
PARALLEL:	He called him not only *a liar* but also *a thief.*

OFF BALANCE:	We should either *turn back* now or *going ahead* without constant second thoughts.
PARALLEL:	We should either *turn back* now or *go ahead* without constant second thoughts.

EXERCISE 26 Point out and describe as fully as you can all examples of *parallel structure* in the following excerpt from Sir Francis Bacon's essay "Of Studies" (1597).

Studies serve for delight, for ornament, and for ability. Their chief use for delight, is in privateness and retiring; for ornament, is in discourse; and for ability, is in the judgement and disposition of business; for expert men can execute, and perhaps judge of particulars, one by one: but the general counsels, and the plots and marshalling of affairs come best from those that are learned. To spend too much time in studies, is sloth; to use them too much for ornament, is affectation; to make judgement wholly by their rules, is the humour of a scholar: they perfect nature, and are perfected by experience. . . . Crafty men condemn studies, simple men admire them, and wise men use them; for they teach not their own use; but that is a wisdom without them and above them, won by observation. Read not to contradict and confute, nor to believe and take for granted, nor to find talk and discourse, but to weigh and consider. Some books are to be tasted, others to be swallowed, and some few to be chewed and digested; that is, some books are to be read only in parts; others to be read but not curiously; and some few to be read wholly, and with diligence and attention.

EXERCISE 27 Select *three* of the literary sample sentences used to illustrate parallel structure in **U 4c.** Use them as *model sentences.* For each, write a sentence on a subject of your own choice, preserving as far as possible the grammatical structure of the original sentence.

EXERCISE 28 Which of the following sentences are parallel in structure? Put *S* (for "satisfactory") after the number of each such sentence. Which sentences are off balance? Put *FP* (for "faulty parallelism") after the number of each such sentence. Your teacher may ask you to revise the unsatisfactory sentences.

1. The first dictionaries explained words that English had recently borrowed from Latin, French, Italian, Greek, and Hebrew.
2. She wanted to know how one enters the contest, what the rules are, and about the judges who select the winning entry.
3. Teachers, he charged, were expected to take vows of poverty, chastity, and obedience.
4. He returned to pay the rent and because he had left some of his things.
5. The new coach was completely relaxed, cordial, and we felt immediately at ease in his presence.
6. Word books at first gave only the spelling and meaning of hard words.
7. Most of the other passengers were teen-age boys and who considered girls an inferior species.
8. Every morning, my father read not only the local newspaper but also two or three out-of-town dailies.
9. He pulled up a chair to the shelf, took down the family Bible, and began to read.
10. He was falsely accused of treason, imprisoned for life, but then made his escape from a supposedly escape-proof prison.
11. The use of atomic weapons in a war would destroy our cities in their entirety and ruining what is left of our ancient cultures.

12. The dresses she sold were stylish, different, and at a good price.
13. One of the first dictionaries had "choice" words in the first part and not so choice words in the second.
14. The hero of the typical Western loves his horse and stands for right and justice.
15. The new manager was a hard worker and very intelligent.
16. His ambition was to retire from politics and living as a gentleman of leisure.
17. He asked us either to approve his report or to find a new treasurer.
18. The Greeks wrote their dictionaries by hand and called them "lexicons."
19. Her husband is a member of the VFW, the YMCA, and an active supporter of many community projects.
20. A knowledge of Latin is useful not only to physicians and pharmacologists, but also to students of law and theology.

U 4d Sentence Variety

Exploit the rich resources of English grammar for greater sentence variety.

English grammar offers us an almost infinite variety of patterns, combinations, and substitutions. An effective user of the language exploits this wide range of possible choices. He avoids the gray monotony that results when someone uses the resources of language in too tired, too unimaginative "primer prose," or in too timid a fashion.

(1) *Vary the length of your sentences.* Use long, elaborate sentences for careful explanation, detailed information, fully developed examples. Use a short sentence to drive home a key point. Study carefully the alternation of long and short sentences in the following examples:

> *We live in an age of rising seas.* Along all the coasts of the United States a continuing rise of sea level has been perceptible on the tide gauges of the Coast and Geodetic Survey since 1930. . . .
>
> (Rachel Carson)

> He sat down behind his rock and watched while he reloaded, and saw the cat spilling its blood on the snow; and

then gradually he could hear it moaning as his head cleared. *Then it suddenly died.*

(Paul Horgan)

I now saw Death as near as I believe I have ever seen Him. He was swimming in the water at our side, whispering from time to time in the rising wind which continued to carry the boat away from us at about the same speed we could swim. *No help was near. Unaided we could never reach the shore.* I was not only an easy, but a fast swimmer, having represented my House at Harrow, when our team defeated all comers. *I now swam for life.*

(Sir Winston Churchill)

(2) *Vary your sentence openings.* The great majority of English sentences start with the subject and move on to the verb, building up modifiers and dependent clauses as they move along. A writer can keep this pattern from becoming too plodding by simply moving a *modifier* or a dependent clause to the beginning of the sentence:

> *For six years now* he had been a man's hunter. *For six years now* he had heard the best of all talking.

(William Faulkner)

> *On a huge hill, cragged and steep,* truth stands.

(John Donne)

> *Trained by the best educators of the seventeenth century, the Jesuits; naturally endowed with a dialectic grasp and subtlety which even they could hardly improve; and with a passion for getting at the truth which even they could hardly impair,* Descartes possessed in addition a rare mastery of literary expression.

(T. H. Huxley)

The introductory modifier serves as an effective *linking device* when it hooks back into an idea expressed in the preceding sentence:

> The world at present is full of angry self-centered groups, each incapable of viewing human life as a whole, each willing to destroy civilization rather than yield an inch. *To this narrowness* no amount of technical instruction will provide an antidote.

(Bertrand Russell)

Here, and not through a change of heart, is our probable route. *Not by becoming better, but by ordering and distributing his native goodness,* will Man shut up Force into its box.

(E. M. Forster)

Another possible departure from the familiar Noun–Verb sequence is to use a *verbal* or a *noun clause* as the subject:

To describe with precision even the simplest object is extremely difficult.

(Aldous Huxley)

What is good in people — and consequently in the world — is their insistence on creation, their belief in friendship and loyalty for their own sakes.

(E. M. Forster)

(3) *Vary sentence rhythm.* Experiment, for instance, with interrupting elements that break up the familiar Subject–Verb, or Subject–Verb–Object sequence:

Life, *at all times full of pain,* is more painful in our time than in the two centuries that preceded it.

(Bertrand Russell)

Jesus, *in a world of arrogant Pharisees and egoistic Romans,* thought that purity and poverty were one.

(D. H. Lawrence)

EXERCISE 29 From your recent writing, select *three* important and substantial sentences that follow the familiar Subject–Verb sequence. *Rewrite each sentence twice,* each time making use of features that make for sentence variety.

EXERCISE 30 How varied are the sentences in each of the following selections? Describe as fully as you can variations in *sentence length,* in *sentence openings,* and in *sentence rhythm.* Point out any other features that make for sentence variety.

1. Rather than love, than money, than fame, give me truth. I sat at a table where were rich food and wine in abundance, and obsequious attendance, but sincerity and truth were not; and I went away hungry from the inhospitable board. The hospitality was as cold as the ices. I thought that there was no need of ice to freeze them. They talked to me of the age of the wine and the fame of the vintage; but I thought of an older, a newer, and a purer wine, of a more glorious vintage,

which they had not got, and could not buy. The style, the house and grounds and "entertainment" pass for nothing with me. I called on the king, but he made me wait in his hall, and conducted like a man incapacitated for hospitality. There was a man in my neighborhood who lived in a hollow tree. His manners were truly regal. I should have done better had I called on him.

—Thoreau, *Walden*

2. With much interest I sat watching him. Savage though he was, and hideously marred about the face — at least to my taste — his countenance yet had a something in it which was by no means disagreeable. You cannot hide the soul. Through all his unearthly tattooings, I thought I saw the traces of a simple honest heart; and in his large, deep eyes, fiery black and bold, there seemed tokens of a spirit that would dare a thousand devils. And besides all this, there was a certain lofty bearing about the Pagan, which even his uncouthness could not altogether maim. He looked like a man who had never cringed and never had had a creditor.

—Herman Melville, *Moby Dick*

3. Not marble, nor the gilded monuments
    Of princes, shall outlive this powerful rhyme.
    But you shall shine more bright in these contents
    Than unswept stone, besmeared with sluttish time.
    When wasteful war shall statues overturn,
    And broils root out the work of masonry,
    Nor Mars his sword nor war's quick fire shall burn
    The living record of your memory.
    'Gainst death and all-oblivious enmity
    Shall you pace forth. Your praise shall still find room
    Even in the eyes of all posterity
    That wear this world out to the ending doom.
    So, till the judgment that yourself arise,
    You live in this, and dwell in lovers' eyes.

—Shakespeare, "Sonnet 55"

U 5 *Glossary of Usage*

Know the current status of expressions frequently criticized.

The first duty of the effective speaker and writer is to use English that is *true to the language.* His first aim must be to speak and write **idiomatic** English — English that is natural, vigorous, authentic, homegrown. But a second important duty of a speaker and writer is to become aware of the standards and preferences of his audience. The following glossary reviews the current status of expressions that have been frequently criticized. The glossary recognizes three major varieties of usage:

NONSTANDARD: *Spoken* by many Americans at home and on the job, but a definite handicap in most white-collar occupations. Use in writing only when directly quoting the speech of people with relatively little formal education.

INFORMAL STANDARD: The natural *speech* of educated people — the language of casual conversation and of everyday work in the office. Use in writing for personal letters to close friends, or in other writing that is clearly meant to be humorous or casual.

FORMAL STANDARD: The *written* English of serious discussion — the language of news reporting, business correspondence, political argument. Use for all serious writing, but also for the more formal varieties of public speech.

Abbreviations in the entries of the glossary refer to the following authoritative guides to modern usage:

W III: *Webster's Third New International Dictionary* (1961), the unabridged volume from which books like *Webster's Seventh New Collegiate Dictionary* are derived. Published by the G. & C. Merriam Company, whose citation files have been called the "national archives" of the language. Many expressions formerly labeled "incorrect" or "careless" are here recognized as widely used by educated people.

BRYANT: Margaret M. Bryant, editor, *Current American Usage* (1962). Reviews the status of controversial points of usage, drawing on evidence from careful objective studies of current American speech and writing. Recognizes many instances of *divided* usage, with more than one possible form being in wide use among educated people.

PERRIN: Porter G. Perrin, *Writer's Guide and Index to English* (1965). The fourth edition of a pioneering reference guide based on the recognition of different legitimate *varieties* of English usage.

a, an. In standard English, use *a* when the next sound you *pronounce* is a consonant. Use *an* when the next sound you *pronounce* is a vowel:

a   a trip, a board, a house, a cold winter, a useful tool, a *C*

an   an error, an honor, an invitation, an unpaid bill, an *A*

ain't. The best-known, single feature of nonstandard speech, and denounced by generations of teachers as ignorant or illiterate. Sometimes used facetiously in informal writing. In first person questions, many Americans find "ain't I" more natural than "aren't I" ("I'm your friend, ain't I?"). *Ain't I* is used orally "by many cultivated speakers" (W III) and "may perhaps be regarded as Informal" (Perrin). *Advice:* Avoid all uses of *ain't* in speech and writing, but remember that people who *do* use it may be as well educated as you are.

amount, number. *Number* is more exact than *amount* in reference to things that can be individually counted:

EXACT: A large *number* (not *amount*) of people were waiting.

and and **but** at the beginning of a sentence. This construction "is used in the best writing" (Bryant). It is common, for instance, in the prose of Hawthorne and Emerson. Many modern writers prefer the initial *and* or *but* to heavier connectives like *moreover, furthermore,* or *however.*

and/or. This combination is sometimes necessary in commercial or official documents. In ordinary prose it is awkward and annoying.

as. *As* is nonstandard as a substitute for *that* or *who.* As a substitute for *because* it is standard but sometimes criticized as ambiguous:

NONSTANDARD: I don't know *as* I can come.
NONSTANDARD: Those *as* knew her avoided her.

AMBIGUOUS:	*As* we talked about war, I remembered Bill.
UNAMBIGUOUS:	*Because* we talked about war, I remembered Bill.
UNAMBIGUOUS:	*While* we talked about war, I remembered Bill.

being as, being that. Nonstandard when they stand for *because* or *since:*

NONSTANDARD:	*Being as* he was the mayor's son, we invited him.
STANDARD:	*Because* he was the mayor's son, we invited him.

between, among. *Between* is historically related to *two* and *twain*. Traditional handbooks have typically restricted its use to references to two of a kind ("choose *between* right and wrong"); they have required *among* in references to more than two ("choose *among* many candidates"). But *between* is also appropriate when more than two things can be considered in pairs of two:

He had sand *between* his toes.
Bilateral agreements exist *between* many countries.

blame for, blame on. Both *blame for* and *blame on* are standard English, appearing with about equal frequency in publications like *Time* and *The New York Times* (Bryant). But some writers consider *blame on* informal:

STANDARD:	He blamed the disaster *on* his subordinates.
FORMAL:	He blamed his subordinates *for* the disaster.

can and **may.** *Can* in the sense of "have permission" was once labeled careless or incorrect. It is now "used interchangeably with *may*" in standard spoken English (W III). But in formal written English, *can* is used to show ability, *may* to show permission:

INFORMAL:	*Can* I go now?
FORMAL:	Each person *may* (permission) take as much as he *can* (ability) carry.

cannot help but. "Cannot help *but think*" instead of "cannot help *thinking*" is standard and occurs in spoken and written English (Bryant). But some teachers and editors object to *cannot help but* as illogical or confused.

SAFE: I cannot help *admiring* his courage.

could of, might of. To transcribe informal speech, use *could've, might've.* In formal writing use *could have, might have, should have.*

couple of. *A couple of minutes,* in the sense of "several," is informal. *A couple dollars,* without the connecting *of,* is nonstandard.

different than. *Different than* is standard American English, but *different from* is preferred in formal writing.

STANDARD: Things didn't seem any different *than* usual.
(Walter Van Tilburg Clark)
FORMAL: He looked different *from* what I had expected.

disinterested, uninterested. In informal writing, *disinterested* usually means "unswayed by personal, selfish interest": "We were sure he would be a *disinterested* judge." Many readers object to *disinterested* used to mean "uninterested" or "indifferent."

double comparative, double superlative. Adjectives are either inflected for degree (bigg*er,* bigg*est*) or preceded by intensifiers (*more* convenient, *most* convenient). At one time, the ending and the intensifier could duplicate and reinforce each other, as in Shakespeare's "the *most* unkind*est* cut of all." Today, such double comparatives or double superlatives are nonstandard.

double negative. In Chaucer's and Shakespeare's English, several negative words like *not, no,* or *never* reinforce each other in the same sentence. In modern English, such duplication is nonstandard. Less obvious double negatives, in which a word like *hardly* or *scarcely* repeats the negative idea, "are colloquial in nature and at times are used by well-known writers" (Bryant).

NONSTANDARD:	A little rain *never* hurt *no* one.
NONSTANDARD:	It's them that have*n't no* common sense that make trouble on this island.
	(William Golding)
INFORMAL:	We could*n't hardly* get into the house.
INFORMAL:	He could*n't scarcely* walk straight.
FORMAL:	He could *scarcely* walk straight.

due to as a preposition.   *Due to* is generally accepted when *due* serves as an adjective: "His absence was *due to* ill health"; "his absence, *due to* ill health, caught us by surprise." As a preposition meaning "because of," *due to* occurs "in writing produced and edited by unquestionably educated persons" (Bryant) but used to be condemned as ungrammatical.

DEBATABLE:	He canceled his trip *due to* ill health.
SAFE:	He canceled his trip *because of* ill health.

enthuse, enthused.   Informal shortcuts for "become enthusiastic," "show enthusiasm," and the like. Many readers find these words annoying. Avoid.

etc.   *Et cetera* is Latin for "and so on"; therefore, *and etc.* is redundant. *Ect.* is a common misspelling. Avoid this vague and evasive abbreviation altogether.

get hurt, got missent.   *Get* is used in informal English as an emphatic and unambiguous passive auxiliary instead of *be* (Perrin):

INFORMAL:	Several of his colleagues *had gotten* promoted.
FORMAL:	Several of his colleagues *had been* promoted.

hadn't ought to. Used instead of *ought not to have,* this form is widespread in educated speech but often considered nonstandard.

> DEBATABLE: He *hadn't ought to* mention the incident.
>
> SAFE: He *ought not to have* mentioned the incident.

if, whether. People were formerly taught to avoid *if* to express doubt or uncertainty after verbs like *ask, don't know, wonder,* and *doubt.* But modern usage is about equally divided between *if* and *whether,* with *whether* being more common in formal situations.

> FORMAL: I wonder *whether* his information is reliable.

in, into. Formal writing often requires *into* rather than *in* to indicate direction: "He came *into* (not *in*) the room."

infer, imply. In formal usage, *imply* usually means "*point to* a conclusion"; *infer* means "*draw* a conclusion." But in much informal usage, *infer* is used as a synonym of *imply* in the sense of "hint at, point to" ("a horse . . . *infers* only weight and speed while Lion *inferred* not only courage . . . but endurance" — William Faulkner). This informal use of *infer* is strongly condemned by many teachers and editors.

> FORMAL: From what he *implied* throughout his talk, we *inferred* that our chances were nil.

irregardless. Though often heard in informal educated speech, *irregardless* instead of *regardless* is widely considered nonstandard. Avoid.

learn, teach. *Learn* used to mean both "learn" and "teach" ("Unless you could teach me to forget a banished father, you must not *learn* me how to remember any extraordinary pleasure" — *As You Like It,* Act I, Sc. 2). In the sense of "teach," *learn* has become nonstandard.

STANDARD: Students *learn* what teachers *teach* them.

leave, let. *Leave* in the sense of "permit, allow, let" is nonstandard.

NONSTANDARD: You wouldn't *leave* nobody else hug and kiss you.
(Wilbur Daniel Steele)
STANDARD: You wouldn't *let* anybody else kiss you.

less, fewer. People used to be taught to use *fewer* for count nouns ("fewer accidents"), *less* for mass nouns, measured by quantity or bulk ("less water"). But some of the best modern writers use *less* with countable items, and W III simply lists *less* as a possible synonym of *fewer* ("They felt that they would sooner have had *less* figures and more food"—George Orwell). By using *fewer* with countable items, you avoid criticism:

FORMAL: There were *fewer* complaints than we had expected.

like as a connective. *Like* is acceptable in all varieties of English as a preposition: "The girl looked *like* her mother." It is also commonly heard as a connective taking the place of *as, as if,* or *as though* at the beginning of a clause: "Do *like* I tell you." According to Perrin, this use of *like* "is certainly now within the range of Standard English," but since "many people are prejudiced" against it "writers should avoid it except in distinctly informal papers."

INFORMAL: "What's up?" I asked Canby . . . "Lynching, I'd judge," he said, *like* it didn't interest him.
(Walter Van Tilburg Clark)
FORMAL: "Lynching, I'd judge," he said, *as if* it did not interest him.

most, almost. *Most* in the sense of "almost" or "nearly" is informal.

INFORMAL: *Most* everybody was there.
FORMAL: *Almost* everybody was there.

myself. *Myself* has long been a more emphatic substitute for *I* or *me* when the pronoun is one of several subjects or objects: "Front to front / Bring thou this fiend of Scotland, and *myself*" (*Macbeth*, Act IV, Sc. 3); "It was *myself*, my brother, and his son/That brought you home and boldly did outdare / The dangers of the time" (*Henry IV*, Part One, Act V, Sc. 1). Though common in speech and writing, this use of *myself* has sometimes been arbitrarily condemned.

> SAFE: Mrs. Graham and *I* (not *myself*) will expect you in the afternoon.

off of. *Off of* instead of *off* or *from* is common in informal educated speech but considered nonstandard by some teachers and editors. Avoid.

> FORMAL: The storm tore the roof *off* (not *off of*) the building.
> FORMAL: He borrowed the money *from* (not *off of*) his mother.

possessive of inanimate nouns. A traditional rule limited the use of the possessive with *-'s* to nouns referring to living things (the *girl's* purse), and to nouns involving measurement (a *day's* work, a *dollar's* worth). For inanimate nouns, the rule prescribed the construction using *of* (not "the *car's* roof" but "the roof *of* the car"). This rule goes counter to common standard usage as well as to the practice of the best writers and should be ignored:

> Duncan is in his grave;
> After *life's* fitful fever he sleeps well.
> (*Macbeth*, Act III, Sc. 2)

> He leadeth me in the path of righteousness for his *name's* sake. (Psalms)

> This is my *play's* last scene; here heavens appoint
> My *pilgrimage's* last mile; and my race,
> Idly yet quickly run, hath this last pace;
> My *span's* last inch, my *minutes'* latest point;
> And gluttonous death will instantly unjoint
> My body and my soul, and I shall sleep a space.
> (John Donne)

possessives with verbal nouns. A traditional rule, still widely observed in formal writing, required the *possessive* form of noun or pronoun before a verbal noun (gerund) in sentences like the following:

FORMAL: No one objected to *John's* taking the job.

FORMAL: I cannot imagine *his* driving there alone.

INFORMAL: No one objected to *John* taking over the job.

INFORMAL: I cannot imagine *him* driving there alone.

preposition at the end of a sentence. The rule against ending a sentence with a preposition has been abandoned by most teachers and editors. The final preposition has long been idiomatic English and occurs in the work of the best writers:

> Thy blood is cold;
> Thou hast no speculation in those eyes,
> Which thou dost glare *with*.
>   (*Macbeth,* Act III, Sc. 4)
>   I, your glass,
> Will modestly discover to yourself
> That of yourself which you yet know not *of*.
>   (*Julius Caesar,* Act I, Sc. 2)

A writer may, however, move the preposition ahead in order to place another word in an emphatic position at the end:

EMPHATIC: Do not ask *for* whom the bell tolls.
                    (John Donne)

reason is because. The best modern authorities on usage recognize that *reason is because* is "in reputable use though disapproved by some" (W III):

> The quarrels and divisions about religion were evils unknown to the heathen.
> The *reason was because* the religion of the heathen consisted rather in rites and ceremonies than in any constant belief.
>   (Sir Francis Bacon)

But "because of widespread prejudice against the construction" (Perrin), students do well to use *reason is that* instead:

> SAFE: The *reason* we do not have enlightened legislation in this area *is that* no one has the courage to speak out against the inequities of the old law.

seeing as how. Nonstandard for *because:*

> NONSTANDARD: *Seeing as how* he was an old friend, I lent him the money.
> STANDARD: *Because* he was an old friend, I lent him the money.

shall, will. At one time, handbooks of usage stated elaborate rules for the use of *shall* and *will.* They required *shall* rather than *will* to indicate future action after first person pronouns (I *shall* try; we *shall* leave at eight). But *will* has long been the prevailing choice for simple unemphatic future in American English, and is now acceptable in written English to most teachers and editors.

The more emphatic *shall* often indicates strong determination, definite obligation, or authoritative command. It is also common in polite first person questions:

> I *shall* return.
> In no case *shall* such payments exceed five percent.
> *Shall* we dance?

split infinitive. The modifier that comes between *to* and the rest of the infinitive has long been idiomatic English ("He was fool enough to *really* imagine he was going to find that plantation" — Mark Twain). It was once widely criticized but is today accepted without comment by most teachers and editors.

Awkwardness may result when *more than one word* splits the infinitive:

> AWKWARD: He ordered us *to* with all possible speed *return* to our stations.

BETTER: He ordered us *to return* to our stations with all possible speed.

superlative in reference to two. "The *tallest* one of the twins" is often criticized as illogical, and "the *taller* one of the twins" is preferred in formal English:

INFORMAL: Which of the two is the *best* speaker?
FORMAL: Which of the two is the *better* speaker?

unique, perfect, equal. It is often argued that one thing cannot be *more* unique, *more* perfect, or *more* equal than another. If it is unique, it is "one of a kind" and cannot be *more* so; if it is perfect, it cannot be *improved*.

SAFE: Our aim must be to make educational opportunities *more nearly* equal.

used to, didn't use to, used to could. Formal English does not employ *used to* in questions or negative statement with *did:*

INFORMAL: She *didn't use to* live here.
FORMAL: She *used not* to live here.

Used to could is nonstandard for *used to be able.*

wait on, wait for. *Wait on* for *wait for* occurs in speech and writing, but most teachers and editors expect *wait for* in formal English.

INFORMAL: "We might as well sit down," Davies said. "They're *waiting on* Bartlett anyway."
(Walter Van Tilburg Clark)
FORMAL: Recording artists have long *waited for* copyright legislation to protect their rights.

where at, where to. In formal English, *where* takes the place of both *where to* and *where at.*

INFORMAL: Where are you *at?* Where do you want it sent *to?*
FORMAL: Where are you? Where do you want it sent?

Where used instead of *that* ("I read in the paper *where* taxes are going up") is informal.

without, on account of. *Without* and *on account of* are prepositions in standard use. They are nonstandard as connectives, introducing a clause:

NONSTANDARD: I can't let you in *without* you have your ticket.

STANDARD: I can't let you in *unless* you have your ticket.

NONSTANDARD: We missed the show *on account of* the bus was late.

STANDARD: We missed the show *because* the bus was late.

USAGE TEST Achievement tests in English, including those required for admission to college, may ask you to identify usages *inappropriate to formal written English*. In each of the following sentences, *one* of the three italicized expressions is widely considered nonstandard or excessively informal. Put the letter preceding it after the number of the sentence. (Only items listed in the Glossary are included.)

1. A man (a) *like* our governor finds it (b) *hard* to act (c) *like* he had no desire to run for President.
2. (a) *Regardless* of what his story was, the guards (b) *hadn't ought to* let in a (c) *total* stranger.
3. (a) *Without* another word, he (b) *took* his broom and started to sweep the leaves (c) *off of* the sidewalk.
4. When I (a) *left* him, he had only (b) *a couple* dollars left and was (c) *waiting for* a check from home.
5. Jim was (a) *unable* to (b) *leave* town (c) *on account of* he was scheduled to act in an insecticide commercial.
6. She strongly (a) *implied* that she wanted us to (b) *leave,* but we stayed on (c) *irregardless.*
7. (a) *Being as* he was new, we had to (b) *teach* him (c) *where* to store the different kinds of merchandise.
8. I (a) *inferred* from his remarks that at one time he (b) *could of* married the wealthiest and (c) *most* beautiful girl in town.
9. (a) *Most* everybody I knew (b) *used to* come to the station to (c) *wait for* the afternoon train.
10. He had (a) *always* received a fair (b) *number* of complaints, but they (c) *didn't use to* bother him.

FURTHER STUDY: British and World English

English is the national language not only of Great Britain and the United States, but also of Australia, New Zealand, and Canada. In India, English provides a common medium for the political life and educational system of a new nation whose people speak several different languages. Millions of people throughout the world learn English as a second language because it serves as an international language of trade, science, and technology. The following assignments will give you an opportunity to explore some of the range and variety of world English.

Assignment 1 What are some of the differences between American and *British* English? Be prepared to report on any firsthand experience with British English that you might have had. To judge from your own experience or from information in your dictionary, what is the typical British pronunciation of the following words: *blackguard, boatswain, halfpenny, twopence, Southwark, Warwick, waistcoat, schedule, Gloucester, tomato?* For each of the following words, what is an everyday meaning or use that might be unfamiliar to the American visitor to Great Britain?

lift, tube, spanner, torch, minerals, bonnet, boot, chemist, wireless, fender, master, knacker, corn, lorry, dust bin, hoarding, bowler, maize, bobby, guinea

Assignment 2 The *rural dialects* of England, like those of France and Germany, used to be so different as to be sometimes mutually unintelligible. Today, the standardized English of the schools, of radio and television, and of the movies is making its influence felt in the countryside. Most young people speak a nationally intelligible kind of English with more or less strong dialect features. Study the use of rural dialect in one of the novels of Thomas Hardy. He often has people with wealth and status speak standard English with few dialect features, while servants and workingmen make freer use of the local dialect. Report typical features, paying attention to such matters as word choice, verb forms, common idioms. Here are some sample sentences from *The Mayor of Casterbridge:*

> We work harder, but we *bain't* made *afeard* now.
> We *be bruckle* folk here, the best *o'us* hardly honest sometimes
> I've been strolling in the Walks, till I feel quite *leery.*
> I *zeed* that he *wambled,* and could hardly drag along.

(Your teacher will tell you whether to present your findings in a short paper or as an oral report.)

Assignment 3 In his novel *Saturday Night and Sunday Morning* (1958), Alan Sillitoe reproduces the dialect spoken by working-class people in the *industrial Midlands* of England. To judge from the following short excerpts, what features of pronunciation, vocabulary, and grammar help set this dialect apart from standard American English? Have you encountered any of these features in *other* varieties of British English? What features does this dialect share with *nonstandard* American English?

1. Do you think if I won the football pools I'd gi' yo' a penny on it? Or gi' anybody else owt? Not likely. I'd keep it all mysen, except for seeing my family right. I'd buy 'em a house and set 'em up for life, but anybody else could whistle for it. I've 'eard that blokes as win football pools get thousands o' beggin' letters, but yer know what I'd do if I got 'em? I'll tell yer what I'd do: I'd mek a bonfire on 'em.

2. In them days yer could get a packet o' fags for tuppence, and a pint of ale for threepence. And just look at what the sods do to me . . .: "Income tax, two pounds eighteen and a tanner." It ain't right. That's munney I've earned.

3. We's'll see'f Taylors' 'ave sum tuffeys, shall we? But you're a bit of a lead weight, our Bill. What does Margaret feed you on? Cannon-balls? Ye'r a ton-weight, and no mistake. The tuffeys wain't mek yer any lighter, I do know that!

4. It's like living in a different house, when the kids aren't fighting and running over everywhere. Eddie's gone up Clifton with Pam and Mike, and they won't be back till six, thank God. They lead me such a dance all week that I'm allus glad to get shut on 'em at weekend.

5. I used to come up here blackberryin', when I was a young 'un. Once with my cousin Bert we met some kids who'd already bin blackberryin', and Bert took theirn off 'em. I didn't want to, but Bert said it would save us hours o' searchin'.

6. I wish Johnny was here. He's a good lad to me. . . . I've never known him to say a bad word to me. I remember one day a man in Waterway Street said summat to me that worn't nice and Johnny chased him all the way down the street.

7. He looks lonely to me. . . . He should go back to India. I can tell when a bloke's lonely. He don't say owt, see? And that means he misses his pals.

Assignment 4 Scotland was until the Act of Union in 1707 a separate kingdom, with its own traditions in government, religion, language, and literature. If Scotland had remained independent from

England, its language might now be as different from standard British English as Dutch is from German. Today standard British English is spoken in school and office — with some dialect features like the trilled Scotch *r*. Here are some words and meanings that dictionaries list as characteristic of Scottish English: *dub* ("puddle"), *ikla* ("each, every"), *winnock* ("window"), *unco* ("very, extremely"), *canny* ("quiet"), *drouthy* ("thirsty").

These are some of the features that set Scottish English apart from that spoken farther south in the British Isles:

— Old English words that survived in Scotland but not in standard English:
  > *kale* (cabbage), *bairn* (child), *snell* (quick), *lift* (air), *mickle* (much)

— Scandinavian borrowings, as in the following lines from Robert Burns:
  > "I *kent* her heart was a' my ain" (knew)
  > "Poor beastie, thou *maun* live" (must)
  > "An folk begin to tak the *gate*" (road)

— words testifying to centuries of French influence:
  > "For you sae *dounce*, ye sneer at this" (sober, from *doux*)

Have you encountered Scottish English in the dialect poems of Robert Burns? Select 15 or 20 lines from a poem like "Tam O'Shanter" and report on the dialect features you encounter there.

Assignment 5   English came into Ireland with British rule, and from the seventeenth century on gradually replaced the native Irish language, or "Erse." A world-famous Irish author is Sean O'Casey, who wrote about the Irish struggle for independence from the British crown. His play *Red Roses for Me* (1942) is set in Dublin before it became the capital of the independent Irish state. The play deals with the tensions between the Irish working class and their British rulers, and between the predominantly Catholic Irish and Protestants loyal to Britain. In the following short excerpts from the play, the characters speak an **Irish** version of English. To judge from the written text, what features of pronunciation would make Irish English *sound* different from American English? What *words and expressions* are there that would be strange or unfamiliar to an American? What features of *grammar or sentence structure* set these passages apart from oridnary American English?

Have you encountered any of the features of Irish English in the speech of Americans of Irish descent?

1. No answer, eh? An' me afther seein' a light in th' window. Maybe they are out. For their own sakes, I hope they are; for it's hardly an honourable thing to gainsay a neighbour's knock.

2. At long last, afther hard sthrainin', me an' Sammy have got the tune down in tested clefs, crotchets, an' quavers, fair set down to be sung be anyone in thrue time. An' Sammy's below, in his gay suit for the Show, waitin' to be called up to let yous hear th' song sung as only Sammy can sing it.

3. All bark, but no bite! We know him of old: a decent oul' blatherer. Sure, doesn't he often buy violets and snowdhrops, even, for little Ursula, below, tellin' her she mustn't put them before a graven image, knowin' full well that that was th' first thing she'd hurry home to do.

4. Is it dhreamin' I am? Is somethin' happenin' to me, or is it happenin' to you? O, man, it's mixin' mirth with madness you are at thinkin' St. Pathrick ever looped his neck in an orange sash, or tapped out a tune on a Protestant dhrum! Let us only keep silent for a minute or two, an' we'll hear him sayin' that th' hymn St. Pathrick sung an' he on th' way to meet King Laeghaire, an' quench th' fire o' Tara, was Lilly Bullero Bullen a Law!

5. I hold me hand at praisin' th' puttin' of Brian Boru's golden harp on every black porther bottle, destined to give outsiders a false impression of our pride in th' tendher an' dauntless memories of th' past. But it's meself should whisper little against th' bottles, havin' used them as cunnin' candlesticks, year in an' year out, since I lost meself in marriage; an' a fine conthrast is a tall white candle, set firm in th' neck of a slender black bottle, givin' light to all in th' room.

6. Ara, God help your innocence! You should ha' seen them sthrikin' at men, women, an' childher. An' me own friend, Dympna, in hospital gettin' her face laced with stitches, th' way you'd lace a shoe! An' all along of followin' that mad fool!

CONTENTS

CHAPTER FOUR

Composition:
THE WRITER AT WORK

*Study the way a good writer structures
substantial materials in order
to make them serve his purpose.*

How does a writer learn to write?

When we ask how good writers developed their talent, we find almost always that they developed it in close contact with the work of other writers. They *read* — at first much that was good, bad, or indifferent, but gradually working their way to what they found truly worthwhile. They *imitated* — sometimes, like Ben Franklin, by following a model point for point, but more often by merely aping the manner (and ideas) of writers they admired. Even the greatest writers typically did not *start out* original. They learned by becoming thoroughly familiar with the work of other writers, and by trying to do themselves what those writers had done. Gradually, after a long apprenticeship, they found their own way. They developed their own style.

Your own study of writing will be fruitful if you learn from what competent writers have done. As you study their work, look for clues to how they have achieved the three fundamental qualities of good writing:

(1) *Good writing has substance.* It has something to offer. It does not merely repeat ideas that are safe and superficial. No one

will quarrel with statements like the following, but these statements do not *say* anything:

> The future lies ahead.
> Agriculture is an important national asset.
> The automobile is here to stay.
> The boys of today will be the men of tomorrow.
> The invention of glass is proof of man's desire to better himself culturally.

A paper says something when it tells us something we did not know before, or when it points out something that we were too busy to notice. A writer says something when he makes a statement that gives us a chance to agree — or to *dis*agree. A writer says something when he talks in detail about people and events, and when he makes us share in the thoughts and emotions they made him experience. A paper that has substance does not merely repeat secondhand notions about the blessings of liberty or the high cost of crime. When we read a substantial piece of writing, it is as if the writer were saying to us: "This is what I have observed. This is what I have experienced. This is what I have felt. This is what I have thought."

(2) *Good writing has structure.* In a well-written article, we can find our way, just as we can find our way in a well-designed building. As we reach the end of one paragraph, we are ready for the next. We suspect what it will contribute even before we start reading it. If the author has already discussed two types of "student rebels," we are ready to see what the *third* type will be, and whether we will recognize it. If the author has given the arguments on *one* side of an issue, we are ready to look at the arguments on the *other* side.

Here are the kinds of reactions that make the reader of a well-structured paper want to *go on* reading:

— "The author has done a good job on the *external appearance* of the person he is describing. Now let me see whether the person's *behavior* will be in keeping with this external impression."
— "This use of the term *fair play* is interesting, but it is not the most important one. I am sure the author will get around to *more important* uses of this term later on."

— "This is an important objection to a widely held view. Can this objection be *refuted?* I hope the author can show it to be ill-founded."

(3) *Good writing has a purpose.* It is true that sometimes the purpose is only to fill space, or to provide a required number of words. Newspaper editors sometimes fill a gap between two news stories with items like the following:

LIZARD SALE
A Camaroun exporter has offered a large quantity of lizard skins to the highest bidder.

The reader's reaction is likely to be: "What else is new?" Though the reader may not say so out loud, the question in his mind typically is: "Why are you telling me this? Why did you write this down?" Your writing would reflect a sense of purpose if your answer to such a question would be something like the following:

— "This is something that I have passed by hundreds of times, but never really *looked at* before."

— "This is something that made me happy, or angry, or sad, and I had to *tell* someone about it."

— "This is something I have often heard said, and I finally decided to think the matter through and make up *my own mind.*"

— "This is an important *obligation* that people would like to turn their backs on, but I will not allow them to do so."

— "This has often been *misrepresented,* and someone had to set the record straight."

C 1 The Process of Composition

Learn how to gather and organize material in order to present it effectively to your reader.

In the finished product, the various qualities of good prose *go together.* The writer seems to know his subject, and he has laid it out in such a way that we can easily follow him. He moves natural-ly, without strain, from one major point to the next. Though he usually does not know us personally, he seems to be speaking directly to us, anticipating our questions, explaining things that bother us. He holds our attention. When he is through, we say to ourselves: "That was well done!"

As readers, we see *only* the finished product. When we change roles, and become writers ourselves, we have to ask: "How is the product *produced?*" When we want to understand what makes an article successful, we have to ask how it was put together. *We have to reconstruct the process of composition.* We start asking questions like the following:

— What does a writer do when he first starts on a project?
— How does he bring his subject under control?
— How does he decide what to *say?*
— How does he decide what to put first, and what to use later?
— How does he bridge the gap from one section to the next?
— What does he do to attract and hold the attention of the reader?

In short, how does a writer write? The following sections will take you through some of the major steps in the writing process.

C 1a *Focusing on a Topic*

Focus on a limited topic and do it justice.

Effective writing concentrates on one point at a time. When an article covers thirteen miscellaneous grievances, few readers can remember afterward what they were. But if the writer selects the three major ones, each has a chance to sink in. If the writer selects the one outstanding and overriding grievance and gives it exclusive attention, *everyone* will remember the point at issue.

The first thing a writer does is to *limit* the territory he is going to cover. An observer aboard a space satellite has a true bird's-eye view of our planet. But he takes in too *large* a picture to say anything meaningful about the forms of life that might be found here. A traveler in a plane can make out houses, schools, highways. But he still takes in a panorama. To describe well an actual house, with its weeds in the lawn and a broken toy on the stairway, he would have to get down on the ground. He would have to walk up to the house for a *close-up*.

Substantial writing is "close-up writing." Only when we get close to a limited topic can we make the reader feel that we "know" our subject. Whenever we look at a large subject from a distance, the reader is bound to feel: "I know more about this subject than you do!"

As you explore possible subjects, look for a limited area that you can cover in detail. The narrowing process might go something like this:

GENERAL AREA: Cooking
LESS GENERAL: Cooking for special diets
LIMITED: Cooking for vegetarians

To limit this subject still more, you might finally focus on how to cook for those who are vegetarians from *religious* conviction (rather than for health reasons). Typically each large subject will split up into several possible subheadings. These in turn can be subdivided into subjects that come close to being actual limited topics for a magazine article, or the like. In each of the following "topic inventories," a large subject is split, first, into subject areas of intermediate size, and, finally, into limited topics:

LARGE: The life of Darwin
  INTERMEDIATE: Darwin's scientific career
    LIMITED: His voyages of exploration
        How Darwin was led to the theory of evolution
        Darwin's quarrel with another famous scientist

  INTERMEDIATE: Darwin's personal life
    LIMITED: Darwin and his family
        Darwin and his friends
        Darwin and poetry
        Darwin and religion

LARGE: Censorship
  INTERMEDIATE: Moral censorship
    LIMITED: Kissing in the movies
        No dirty jokes on TV
        Playboy corrupts the young

  INTERMEDIATE: Political censorship
    LIMITED: News magazines not in your library
        What students are taught about socialism
        Das Kapital is not for sale

When a teacher or editor *assigns* you a topic, he may already have done most of the narrowing down that a large subject area requires. Even so, you will typically sketch out an area *within* the larger topic, and then cover it in depth. You will concentrate on a limited angle or facet that you can discuss with conviction. Here are some ways of bringing an assigned topic into focus:

(1) *Concentrate on one key term.* Perhaps you have been asked to write about the role of individualism in modern American life. If you look for a type of the self-reliant individual, you may think of the pioneer and his prominent role in American history. You might focus your paper on the way Americans *today* use the term "pioneer." What picture does the word bring to mind? Where do we find the term used? How much of the pioneering spirit actually survives in today's society?

(2) *Ask a "what-is-the-most" question.* There are many ways an American can show that he considers himself a sturdy, self-reliant individual. He can take pride in fixing his own wiring, roofing, and plumbing; or in doing his own bricklaying and carpentering, the way people *had* to in pioneering days. Or he can own a gun and think of himself as a protector of his family and as a rugged outdoorsman "roughing it" during the hunting season. Ask yourself: "Which is the most *typical* or *revealing* expression of such feelings?" Few readers will rush to read a paper titled "Various Expressions of Current American Individualism." But they will be attracted by the promise of a *focused* paper if your title is "A Man and His Gun" (or perhaps, "Do-It-Yourself — the American Way").

(3) *Concentrate on a test case or key example.* Sometimes an important test case will dramatize a familiar issue. In recent years, for instance, there has been much discussion of "civil disobedience." We all have heard arguments declaring it a moral duty to disobey unjust laws. But we have also heard predictions that such disregard of the law will lead to a breakdown of law and order.

A well-focused paper could examine in depth what happened when someone actually did rebel against an "unjust" law. What was wrong with the law? Had attempts been made to change it? What was said in defense of the law? What form did the "disobedience" take? How did the authorities react? What was the end result? Dealing in detail with a real-life situation, the paper could confront the reader with the key question: "Would you have rebelled in the same way?"

REMEMBER: No one can solve the problems of the world in a few hundred words. A writer earns the right to be heard by showing that he can do justice to one limited area at a time.

EXERCISE 1   Much has been written in recent years about the following general subjects. For each of them, write down a more limited topic that you might focus on in a paper of between 400 to 500 words. Compare your topics with those of your classmates. Which of them best stake out a limited territory that could be explored in detail? (Your teacher may ask you to write a short paper on the most promising of your topics.)

1. Our vanishing open spaces
2. The student's voice in his own education
3. Student protest
4. Decay in American cities
5. Teen-age marriage
6. Automation and the unskilled worker
7. Minorities asking for a place in the sun
8. The attitude of young Americans toward business
9. Reform and rebellion in our churches
10. Violence and the entertainment media

EXERCISE 2   Have you ever complained that you have "nothing to write about"? See how many promising subjects you can discover by writing down three or four limited topics under each of the following general subjects.

1. Neighbors
2. Things I like to do
3. Movies
4. Things and people that annoy me
5. Problems

EXERCISE 3 Study the table of contents of several recent issues of general-interest magazines. Write down three titles of articles that seem to promise a well-focused treatment of a clearly limited topic. Be prepared to discuss and defend your choices.

C 1b Making a Point

Pull together related material to support a single point.

Once a writer has marked out an area, he can study it in detail. He can bring together — from his memory, from his reading, from current observation — what he knows about his subject. Suppose a conservationist has decided to write about our rapidly disappearing native wildlife. Here is the kind of inventory he might take of material he could use:

— He may remember reading about the passenger pigeon, which once lived in this country in huge flocks of tens of thousands of birds, but which was hunted till it finally became extinct.

— He may recall seeing prairie dogs live where the prairie is now covered by subdivisions and parking lots.

— He may recall stories his grandfather told about shooting mountain lions in hills where now such animals are never seen.

— He may remember magazine articles about the dangers to fish from industrial wastes in our streams and lakes.

— He may ask himself what small animals he still encounters: lizards, frogs, squirrels, an occasional snake.

These various memories and observations all help tell the same story. The point of that story could be summed up in a single sentence: "Unless man preserves a livable environment for our remaining wildlife, our remaining animal species will soon be extinct." This sentence could become the key idea of a paragraph. We then call it a **topic sentence.** Or, the sentence could become the central idea for a paper or short article. We then call it a **thesis.**

In the following paragraph, a well-known writer has *pulled together* material about our vanishing animal species. He has put the key idea that his observations point to at the beginning of the paragraph as a topic sentence:

We need viable habitats for the species that our expansion threatens. Some, like the passenger pigeon, are beyond our belated friendship. But there are the waterfowl whose nesting and feeding places we have drained or flooded, and the fish whose spawning grounds we have drowned or poisoned with agricultural sprays, and the robins whose decimation Rachel Carson made use of to shock a whole people; and there are also all the frogs, toads, newts, lizards, snakes, skunks, prairie dogs, coyotes, alligators, mountain lions, and nocturnal varmints that are apparently "useless" or "harmful" to man, yet by their enduring in the biotic pyramid give man both the pleasure of their company and the assurance of their biological support.

—Wallace Stegner, "What Ever Happened to the Great Outdoors?"
Saturday Review

The writer who "has a point" is the one who has learned how to make related material add up. Can you see that in each of the following paragraphs the material presented in the rest of the paragraph "adds up" to the point made in the initial topic sentence?

TOPIC SENTENCE:	*Romantic love was not a major theme either in serious American literature on its highest level or in familiar American folklore.* After the first
EXAMPLE:	few chapters, *"Moby Dick"* has no female characters except mother whales. There were not
EXAMPLE:	many women, either, in the *great cycles of myth* that dealt with the wilderness, the river, the cattle ranges, and the mining camps. All consisted of stories about men, working or wandering, hunting, fighting, enduring hardships, getting rich, or running away from civilization, but
EXAMPLE:	seldom or never passionately in love. *Huck Finn* was of course too young for love, but all the
EXAMPLE:	familiar heroes were boys at heart. *Old Leatherstocking* died a bachelor.

—Malcolm Cowley, "American Myths, Old and New,"
Saturday Review

TOPIC SENTENCE:	*Below a certain level no intellectual interests*
SINGLE	*can survive.* In the camp where I had come down
INCIDENT:	with malaria, I had lain with my head on my pack in a kind of coma, only getting up to collect my rice, hardly talking and hardly thinking. But one day I had suddenly realized that inside

my pack I had the works of Shakespeare: and for a week I read them all through with enormous pleasure, and had gone through half way again before relapsing into my previous apathy. It wasn't till many months later that I understood what had happened: the same battalion doctor rejoined me in one of the base camps, and explained that my brief spurt of intellectual energy had begun and ended with a small supply of vitamin B which had come into the camp, and which I'd taken for the few days it had lasted.

—Ian Watt, "The Liberty of the Prison," *Yale Review*

TOPIC SENTENCE:

EXAMPLES:

CAUSES:

Our children are given years of cultural nonparticipation in which they are permitted to live in a world of their own. They are allowed to say what they like, when they like, how they like, to ignore many of the conventions of their adults. Those who try to stem the tide are derided as "old fogies," "old fashioned," "hide bound" and flee in confusion before these magic words of exorcism. This state of discipline is due to very real causes in American society. In an immigrant country, the children are able to make a much better adjustment than have their parents. The rapid rate of invention and change in the material side of life has also made each generation of children relatively more proficient than their parents. So the last generation use the telephone more easily than their parents; the present generation are more at home in automobiles than are their fathers and mothers. When the grandparent generation has lived through the introduction of the telegraph, telephone, wireless, radio and telephotography, automobiles and aeroplanes, it is not surprising that control should slip through their amazed fingers into the more readily adaptable hands of children.

—Margaret Mead, *Growing Up in New Guinea*

Can you see that in the following excerpted versions of short papers, the material in *several different paragraphs* "adds up" to the thesis presented at the beginning?

No Time for Pranks

THESIS: Compared with the demonstrations and solemn demands of today's students, *the student pranks of years gone by seem like innocent amusements.* . . .

EXAMPLE: When my oldest brother went to college, the students showed their defiance of authority by water fights with the campus police. On a hot summer night, they would open fire hydrants, rout the local fire department, and drench the dean of students. . . .

EXAMPLE: But the typical student prank used to be more elaborate. One year, five students in Ohio stole a corpse from an undertaking parlor, transported it a hundred miles, and placed it in front of the union building on their college campus. . . .

EXAMPLE: Only rarely did the pranks of yesterday's students have any political significance. At one Southern school, a group of students once replaced a statue of General Lee with one of General Grant, shipped in a huge crate from an adjoining state. . . .

No End to Violence

THESIS: *New York City is rapidly becoming a place that is not fit for people to live in.* . . .

EXAMPLE: Policemen, who are supposed to protect others from violence, have become the objects of mass assaults. Every week we read news stories about policemen beaten, wounded, or killed in the course of their duty. Only last week a patrolman, age twenty-nine, died of gunshot wounds inflicted when he and another patrolman prevented a hold-up at a Harlem grocery store. . . .

EXAMPLE: No woman of any age is any longer safe to go out alone at night. An old lady we know finally left her apartment in Harlem after she was robbed twice in the elevator. She found a place to stay with the Little Sisters of the Poor. . . .

EXAMPLE: Much of the violence is cowardly and mean. It is hard to think of anything more downright mean than a couple of young hoodlums stealing the watch and wallet left on the wharf by a passerby who is trying to rescue a man drowning in the river. . . .

An effective writer does not simply say whatever comes into his head. Instead, he looks at the material he has collected and asks: "What does this mean?" When he makes his points in the finished paper, he *supports* them by citing the examples and incidents from which they were originally derived. His finished paper answers the two basic questions asked by a serious reader: "What do you think?" "What *made* you think so?"

EXERCISE 4 In each of the following paragraphs, related material has been brought together. About each paragraph, ask yourself: "What is the point?" Then write a statement that could serve as a topic sentence for the paragraph.

1. Huck Finn's father tries to cheat him and then imprisons him. In order to get away from this drunken "mudcat," Huck must set it up so that everyone will think he has been murdered. This is a boy who, although surrounded by Aunt Sallies who want to "sivilize" him, runs off to be himself. He has to protect himself against fraudulent adults like the Duke and the Dauphin. Every time he gets off that raft he is yelped at by dogs and menaced by people.

2. A Dane and a Dutchman meeting in Rome will almost automatically find themselves speaking to each other in English. The pilots of a Russian plane approaching Cairo will use English to ask for landing instructions. Malayan lecturers use English when addressing their Malayan students in Kuala Lumpur. To people in Africa, Asia, and South America English is an important foreign language to master, not merely because it is the language of Britain or the United States, but because it provides ready access to world scholarship and world trade. It is understood more widely than any other language.

3. The other day I happened to look at the dog food shelf in the local supermarket. It turns out that dog food now comes in half a dozen different flavors, including chicken, cheese, and vegetable. It comes in many different shapes and consistencies. Some cans contain little patties like hamburgers. Some make their own gravy, thus saving the housewife all that messy work over the hot stove. Dog food is now enriched with vitamins and extra nutrients, with your choice of bone meal and wheat germ and cod liver oil. These valuable ingredients keep your dog at top form, with a keen eye and a glossy coat. One brand of dog food contains chlorophyll to give your dog a sweeter breath.

4. On a crowded bus, a mother sat by quietly while her five-year-old in various ways disturbed the other passengers — squeezing through the crowded aisle, stepping on people's toes, playing with their luggage. Finally, an older man, speaking carefully in a heavy foreign accent, asked the mother to do something about the child's behavior.

The mother told the man to mind his own business, whereupon several other passengers came to his defense. At the end of the somewhat heated exchange, the mother triumphantly concluded: "At least *I* am an American." At this point, the driver, who had been listening quietly so far, turned around and said: "That's a pity."

5. Some years ago, a girl crashed in a light plane in Alaska. She finally made it back to civilization after severe hardships. These were not "untold hardships," however, for newspapers and magazines all over the country immediately picked up her story. Editors and publisher's agents tried to sign her up for an "authentic firsthand account" of her "real-life adventure." When the book finally appeared, it had been thoroughly worked over by ghost-writers and editors on the basis of numerous tape recordings the girl had made. When the girl appeared on a national television program, she herself seemed no longer sure of the details of what had happened to her. Everything had been edited and "adapted" too many times.

EXERCISE 5 Study each of the following model paragraphs. Can you see that the writer has arrived at his topic sentence by "adding up" the observations listed later in the paragraph? For each topic, gather *observations of your own* that may be very similar but also very different. Then use them in a paragraph of your own, starting with a topic sentence that adds up what *you* have observed.

1. Topic: Manners of young people today

Young people today have very little of what used to be called "manners." Young men today no longer bow or tip their hats. They smoke in the presence of ladies, seldom bothering to ask for permission. We seldom see a young man opening a car door for a girl, or surrendering his seat on a bus to an older person. Parents of teenagers can seldom get them to listen, let alone to give a polite answer. Students talking to their teachers use language that would have gotten them expelled not too many years ago. They use four-letter words freely to show their disapproval of things as they are.

2. Topic: The layman vs. the expert

In a complicated situation, the layman is helpless because nothing stands out for him to act upon. A library, a museum, or a machine shop is merely a maze for the newcomer. The expert sees everything in its place and knows exactly where to turn for what he needs. To the layman, a caterpillar is just skin and squash. A botanist can dissect it and show us the exquisite viscera. In a battle or at a fire, the layman is surrounded by noise and confusion. The veteran takes in the situation and analyzes immediately what is happening and what needs to be done.

C 1c   Organizing the Theme

Work out a pattern of organization that fits your material.

Good writing is organized. It has a pattern that the reader can take in and follow. When he is halfway through a well-organized paper, the reader can say to himself: "We are now nearing the end of the second of three major stages." Or, "The author is now turning to the third and most important of the major categories he has set up." Or, "The author has almost finished explaining the *advantages* of the new plan. He will soon take up the major *disadvantages.*" When such an overall pattern is missing, the reader starts saying to himself: "I cannot discover what this is all about. I can't make out where this paper is headed."

How does a writer organize his material?

When you first jot down possible ideas for a paper, your list will be *miscellaneous.* Things will appear as they come to mind, with no obvious connection between one idea and the next. Here is such a miscellaneous list for a paper taking stock of what the author learned during his high school years:

(1) drafting
(2) algebra and geometry
(3) working with other people
(4) note taking
(5) when to lead and when to follow
(6) meeting schedules, budgeting one's time
(7) how to work hard for grades
(8) how to overcome bad first impression
(9) study habits
(10) learn how to take second place

What goes with what? Obviously (1) and (2) go together as the kind of practical courses that will be useful to someone who plans a career as a technician or engineer. What about the rest? Several points — (9), (4), (6), and (7) — deal not with the subject-matter a student studies but with *how* he studies — his work habits, in other words. To the student who goes on to college, being able to plan his own work, and to keep at it, may prove just as important as any course content he has covered. The remaining points — (3), (5), (8), (10) — deal with the kind of education for which there are no tests and grades: working and living with other people.

After you *sort out* the material in such a list, you may arrive at an outline like the following:

You Can Take It with You

I. Career skills
   A. Drafting
   B. Algebra and geometry
II. Study habits
   A. Note taking
   B. Meeting schedules
   C. Concentrating on a definite goal
III. Social skills
   A. Teamwork
   B. Being a good loser

To give his reader a clear sense of direction, a writer will often summarize briefly at the *beginning* of his paper the categories he has set up. Such a preview starts the reader thinking along the right lines. It creates a set of expectations that the rest of the paper will satisfy. Here is how Samuel Johnson, writing in 1751, started an essay describing different kinds of jealous gossips:

> As the industry of observation has divided the most miscellaneous and confused assemblages into proper classes, and ranged the insects of the summer, that torment us with their drones or stings, by their several tribes, the persecutors of merit, notwithstanding their numbers, may be likewise commodiously distinguished into Roarers, Whisperers, and Moderators.

By the end of this introduction, the reader will be ready to hear more: first, about the "roarer" (who comes right out and makes accusations in a strong voice); then, about the "whisperer" (who circulates jealous gossip with an air of importance and great secrecy); and, finally, about the "moderator" (who puts on a reasonable front by always seeming to *excuse* the people he gossips about, or by seeming to *doubt* the rumors he circulates).

How you sort out your material depends both on your subject and on what you are trying to do with it. A good pattern of organization seems tailor-made. It makes the reader feel: "This is a good way to tackle *this particular subject.*" Even so, some common patterns of organization are frequently used because they fit many similar situations. You will often have the opportunity to use or *adapt* one of the following:

(1) *Divide a mechanical or historical process into major stages.* When you trace a process, you usually find many small steps. When you first study the history of jazz, for instance, you find that it developed gradually, with many byways and dead alleys. But if you just present your findings step by little step, your reader will feel completely lost. The names and dates you mention will just become a blur in his mind. He will begin to feel that he is finding his way if you can mark off some major *phases:*

    I. Dixieland
    II. Big-band swing
   III. Bebop
   IV. Modern "concert" jazz

(2) *Work out a classification that serves a clear purpose.* A Congressman writing an article about the mail he receives might just chat amusingly about various unusual letters. At the end, though, he would realize that he has told the reader little about how a Congressman — and Congress — works. In an *organized* article, he could talk about how he classifies his mail in order to decide *what to do* with it. The following might be a rough scheme for the article:

    I. "Lobby mail" urges the special cause of some organized group, with numerous letters almost identical in content and wording. Such letters can be tabulated to provide a rough guide to public opinion.

    II. "Fan mail" requests autographs or photographs and applauds stands taken by the Congressman (sometimes a fan letter proposes marriage). Most of these should receive a pleasant reply that may look personalized but is often typed on an automatic typewriter.

   III. "Case mail" asks for assistance in dealing with government agencies, or for support for important projects. Letters in this category, if they are considered justified or important, are acted upon by the legislator's staff.

Notice that the article would not try to cover *everything*. It would not cover "crank mail," with threats of violence or tales of imaginary persecution. It would not cover "school mail," letters from students asking for help with social studies projects, and the like. By concentrating on the three major types, the author could give his readers a clear picture of the kinds of "feedback" a legislator may expect from his constituents.

(3) *Select several key points for fruitful comparison and contrast.* Suppose a college freshman were to write a paper on the differences between high school and college. Obviously, there are *many* differences, and also many similarities. In order to produce a focused paper, the writer might decide to concentrate on one striking observation: Though beginning college courses often cover areas similar to those covered in high school, the *work* expected of the student may be much more demanding. The outline of the finished paper might look as follows:

> THESIS: In college, the former high school student is expected to work and think on his own.
>
> I. Material assigned
>   A. In high schools, materials for study are often carefully screened to eliminate controversial treatments of sex or political ideology.
>   B. In college, courses in literature or the social sciences may concentrate heavily on "taboo" subjects.
>
> II. Preparation expected
>   A. In high school, the student may have become used to fairly short reading assignments, with much help provided by "study questions" and "study guides."
>   B. In college, the student may be asked to read large chunks of material on his own, with few or no questions to serve as a guide.
>
> III. Performance expected
>   A. In high school, the student often feels that there is one approved view or conclusion he is supposed to reach.
>   B. In college, the student is often bombarded with opposing views on the same subject and left to make up his own mind.

Notice that in such a **point-by-point comparison** *one* feature of high school work is described (with examples) and then *immedi-*

ately compared with the corresponding situation in college. This way the reader can immediately see the similarity or the difference involved. In a **parallel-order comparison,** the writer would first describe *several* major features of high school work and then take up the corresponding features of college work *in the same order.* Can you see what the advantages and disadvantages of each method of comparison might be?

I. High school work
    A. Noncontroversial materials
    B. Short assignments with many study helps
    C. Conformity to "approved" opinions

II. College work
    A. Controversial subject-matter
    B. Long assignments with few guides
    C. Opposed views

(4) *Weigh evidence for and against in order to reach a balanced conclusion.* When you evaluate a proposal, or take a stand on an issue, a fair-minded reader will welcome a study of the major arguments on both sides. A "pro-and-con" paper has more built-in suspense than a paper that makes a flat assertion at the beginning. The reader becomes a spectator who looks on as the evidence is weighed and the issue decided. When you discuss a proposal for a new kind of school or program, you can list the *advantages* first, then point out *disadvantages,* and finally suggest a *modified* proposal that promises to achieve the benefits without the drawbacks. Here is a possible scheme for such a paper:

I.   People often ask for more vocational courses, which give both the student and his parents the feeling that he is getting a "practical" education.

II. But some vocational courses prepare the student for jobs that automation and a changing technology are about to eliminate.

III. Vocational courses today should teach a student how to acquire *new* skills as jobs change.

REMEMBER: Whatever scheme of organization you select must fit your *subject.* You have to study your material before you can decide how to order it. Furthermore, your scheme of organization must become clear to your *audience*. You may have to size up your audience before you can decide on an effective approach.

EXERCISE 6   Suppose you have jotted down the following points for a paper on "The Hallmarks of Cheap Fiction." How would you sort out these points into major categories? Prepare an outline, using Roman numerals for major headings and capitals for subheadings.

1. The villains are all black, with no shades of gray.
2. The hero and heroine ride off into the sunset to live happily ever after.
3. The hero succeeds in hairbreadth escapes and last-minute rescues that would never succeed in real life.
4. The heroine flowers from an ugly duckling into a ravishing beauty.
5. The red-blooded American boy triumphs over his enemies.
6. By a marvelous coincidence, the hero meets a long-lost friend on a South Sea island.
7. In the nick of time, the villain gets his amply deserved comeuppance.
8. The orphan is found to be the son (or daughter) of a rich businessman.
9. The hero accidentally discovers documents that help him expose the villain.
10. In a chest in the attic, the poor heroine discovers documents that show her family to be the real owners of land worth a fortune.
11. In New York City, the heroine accidentally discovers her much-loved sister, believed dead but actually living under an assumed name.
12. The hero is mistaken for a famous outlaw, who looks and talks amazingly like him.

EXERCISE 7   Study the overall plan revealed in each of the following excerpted (and adapted) versions of substantial articles. How has the writer structured his material? How clear does the overall plan become to the reader? Can the reader see *why* the different points follow each other in the order the author has chosen? Prepare a *rough outline* for each of these articles.

1.   The Hungry World

It is difficult for the English-speaking peoples to assess the real meaning of hunger. Those who spent years in enemy prison camps are perhaps the only ones who have had to stare starvation in the face. . . .

To a great degree, hunger is usually associated with war. Farms are deprived of the necessary manpower and equipment. Military campaigns devastate the countryside; retreating troops destroy food supplies. . . .

But the basic causes of starvation are independent of such relatively short-range developments. Perhaps the greatest single factor that has contributed to the present food problem is man's inability to conquer the forces of soil erosion. Huge areas of the earth in the past have been devastated by bad farming; by plowing steep slopes and thus permitting rain to wash soil away; by permitting cattle to overgraze and thus destroying the grass roots which prevent wind erosion; by letting spring rains rush off land which has been stripped of trees. . . .

But even if the world's farmers were to triumph over soil erosion, the world would still be without enough food to feed its people. Not until new farmlands have been developed will the world be out of its present dilemma. . . .

There will have to be an enormous increase in productivity of land. This means better crops — such as high-yield hybrid corns. Dams will have to provide irrigation for arid areas. Scientists will have to seek hardier grains that can withstand desert drought and arctic cold. . . .

2.   Guilt by Association

No more pernicious doctrine has ever found its way into American law or into popular acceptance than this doctrine of guilt by association. . . .

First, then, the doctrine of guilt by association is unsound in logic, and this for a variety of reasons. It is unsound because it assumes that a good cause becomes bad if supported by bad men. . . .

Second, the doctrine is wrong legally. In Anglo-American law, guilt is personal, not collective. It does not spread, by a process of osmosis, from guilty to the neighboring innocent. . . .

Third, the doctrine is wrong practically, and this for a variety of reasons. It is wrong practically because when we try to apply it as a yardstick it changes on us like Alice's Cheshire cat. . . .

Fourth, the doctrine of guilt by association is wrong historically, for it flies in the face of our experience and of the experience of the English-speaking peoples. If there is one thing that has always distinguished the English and the American peoples, it is their faith in voluntary associations as the way to get things done. . . .

Finally, the doctrine of guilt by association is wrong morally. It is wrong morally because it assumes far greater power in evil than in virtue. It is based therefore on a desperate view of mankind. It rests on what may be called the rotten-apple theory of society — the theory that one wicked man corrupts all virtuous men, and that one mistaken idea subverts all sound ideas. . . .

—Henry Steele Commager, *Freedom, Loyalty, and Dissent*

3.   Going to School in Britain

It is difficult to make a valid comparison between British and American high school education. British high schools still enroll a relatively small number of selected students. Entrance exams are given at an early age. . . .

The British system is not at all ideal. The early entrance exams penalize the "late bloomer". . . .

Especially in the final years, instruction still moves in a very formal pattern. Compared with American high schools, there is little student participation. . . .

There are, however, values in British education that Americans could usefully study. First of all, there is a greater uniformity of standards throughout the country. Students in different areas are assured of more nearly equivalent preparation. . . .

In Britain, basic subjects are covered according to a more definite plan as the student moves from year to year. . . .

In recent years, schools in both countries have shown signs of becoming more alike. In many British schools, there is now more emphasis on student initiative and free discussion. In many American schools, students are expected to cover more subject-matter than they were ten years ago. . . .

EXERCISE 8 How good are you at working out a definite plan for a paper? Prepare the following outlines, showing what material you would use and how you would arrange it. (Your teacher may ask you to write a paper following the most promising of your outlines.)

1. Divide a *process* into its major stages. Choose a hobby, manufacturing process, building project, or the like. Write an outline showing the major stages *and* intermediate steps.

2. Write an outline for a paper in which you *classify* one of the following: kinds of homes in your community; kinds of cars owned

by your neighbors; popular songs currently favored by your friends.

3. Write an outline for a *comparison and contrast* of one of the following: interests or attitudes of teen-age boys as against teen-age girls; the way young people and older people dress today; movies you like as against those you dislike; attitudes or prejudices of two newspaper columnists with differing views.

4. Select a proposal, scheme, or project that is currently being debated in your community. Write an outline for a paper in which you would weigh the *evidence pro and con*.

C 1d Carrying the Reader Along

Help your reader follow you from point to point.

How does a writer carry his readers along?

An effective writer sets his signals so that his readers know from the beginning: "This is where we are headed." Then, while they are reading, he makes them feel: "We are getting somewhere." At the end, he makes them feel: "We have covered the ground. We have done justice to the topic. We have accomplished what we set out to do." An effective writer creates *expectations* in his readers' minds, and then proceeds to satisfy these expectations. If he asks a question at the beginning of a paper, he will have answered it by the time the paper is finished. If he mentions a term like "intelligent conservatism," he will have defined and illustrated it by the time he is through.

In large part, what the reader expects is determined by the overall pattern of a paper or article. When we have a clear sense of what the paper *as a whole* is trying to do, we read with a sense of direction. But an effective writer also makes sure that the reader does not get lost *on the way*. He employs devices that give his writing **coherence.** He makes sure his ideas "hang together" as his readers move from one sentence, and one paragraph, to the next.

If your readers cannot easily follow you from one part of your paper to the next, try these remedies:

(1) *Make a paragraph, or a longer section of your paper, follow a clear logical pattern.* The reader is prepared to move easily from one example to a second *similar* example that strength-

ens the point already made. He moves easily from one step in a process to the next. He moves easily from a cause to its effect, or from the situation "then" to the situation "now."

Can you see how naturally each of the following passages makes the reader move along?

SERIES OF EXAMPLES

I had not thought it possible that boys could work so hard. *Cricket and football, the collection of moths and butterflies,* though not forbidden, were discouraged. . . . In place of a dozen *lines of Virgil* with a dictionary, I was expected to learn with the help of a crib a hundred and fifty lines . . . what could I, who never worked when I was not interested, do with a *history lesson* that was but a column of seventy dates? . . .   —W. B. Yeats, *Autobiographies*

EVENTS IN CHRONOLOGICAL ORDER

One afternoon while we were there at that lake a thunderstorm came up. . . . The whole thing was so familiar, the first feeling of oppression and heat and a general air around camp of not wanting to go very far away. *In midafternoon* . . . a curious darkening of the sky, and a lull in everything that had made life tick; *and then* the way the boats suddenly swung the other way at their moorings with the coming of a breeze out of the new quarter, and the premonitory rumble. *Then* the kettle drum, *then* the snare, *then* the bass drum and cymbals, *then* crackling light against the dark, . . . *Afterward* the calm, the rain steadily rustling in the calm lake, . . . And the comedian who waded in carrying an umbrella.

—E. B. White, *One Man's Meat*

FROM CAUSE TO EFFECT

. . . I tried to explain what has happened, unfailingly, whenever a significant body of Negroes move North. *They do not escape Jim Crow:* they merely encounter another, not-less-deadly variety. They do not move to Chicago, they move to the South Side; they do not move to New York, they move to Harlem. *The pressure within the ghetto causes the ghetto walls to expand,* and this expansion is always violent. White people hold the line as long as they can, and in as many ways as they can, from verbal intimidation to physical violence. But inevitably *the border which has divided the ghetto from the rest of the world falls back* bitterly before the black horde;

the landlords make a tidy profit by raising the rent, chopping up the rooms, and all but dispensing with the upkeep; and *what has once been a neighborhood turns into a "turf".* . . .

—James Baldwin, *Nobody Knows My Name*

CONTRAST

Yesterday, African history, shutting out the colored man and all his cultures, began with Livingstone, Stanley, Cecil Rhodes, . . . *Today,* beginning with the arts of prehistoric peoples, it mentions explorers and European annexations as but tiresome, trivial interruptions.

(2) *Strengthen the network of synonyms and related terms that holds together a passage developing systematically the same topic.* When in charting a paragraph we find a network of terms like "justice," "fair distribution," "earned reward," and "equal shares," we know that the author is dealing with one point at a time. We do not have to find our way through a maze of unrelated ideas. When we find such synonyms and related terms, it is as if the author were saying to us: "Let's stay on this subject until we have explained the problem, or settled the issue."

Study the italicized terms in the following passages. Can you see how they help hold each passage together?

It is said that a *poet* has died young in the breast of the most stolid. It may be contended rather that a (somewhat minor) *bard* in almost every case survives, and is the spice of life to his possessor. Justice is not done to the versatility and the unplumbed childishness of men's *imagination.* His life from without may seem but a rude mound of mud: there will be some *golden chamber* at the heart of it, in which he dwells delighted.

In those days after the Civil War, it was the *good women, wives and schoolmistresses,* who bought the books and read the magazines; most men read only the newspapers. To be successful an author had to please a *feminine audience. Women* liked *love stories* and hence the magazines were full of them, while all the popular novels ended to the peal of a *wedding march.*

Buying and selling is a function *particularly disdained.* Some years ago there was a hit comedy on Broadway that pictured a junk dealer as a sort of *parasite,* growing rich on a nation's trouble. Another prize-winning play had as its theme the thought that the life of a salesman is a life *tragically mis-spent*. In novels, in movies, in television the man of business may be either hero or villain, but there is *never any sugges-tion that* by running a furniture factory the men in the executive suite are *performing a social service*.

Can you see how the coherence of the following passage is graphically revealed by the continued references to the essay being discussed, and to the man who wrote it?

It was in 1893 that a *young and unknown historian* appeared before the American Historical Association and read *a paper* entitled "The Significance of the Frontier in American History." *That paper* made him a scholar with honor in his own country, for, brief though *his essay* is, it is recognized as the most influential single piece of historical writing ever done in the United States. *It* altered the whole course of American historical scholarship. The *young man* was Frederick Jackson Turner of the University of Wisconsin. Following *Turner's* lead, there arose in the United States a whole school of frontier historians who have worked out in many directions the rich mine that *Turner* opened up. It is not necessary here to elaborate *Turner's* famous thesis except to reiterate that it expounded the overwhelming importance of the frontier as the dominant force in creating a democracy and making the individual free from Old World restrictions.

(3) *Use transitional expressions to steer the reader in the right direction.* These are like directional signals that say "now for the reason," or "here is an additional example," or "now let me draw the conclusion." Notice how *unobtrusively* these signals do their work in the following passages:

A DISTINCTION MADE:	Language is indispensable to human thinking, *but* this does not mean that mental ability is the same thing as having a large vocabulary. A limited vocabulary, *it is true,* restricts the range of our thinking. And this may lead us, mistakenly, to think of people as being unintelligent merely because certain words are unfamiliar to them. The children in an underprivileged neighborhood, *for example,* did very poorly in an intelligence test which contained questions such as this: "A hand is to an arm as a
AN OBJECTION GRANTED:	
AN EXAMPLE GIVEN:	

foot is to a _____." Only a few children filled the blank with "leg" and most of them scored low in intelligence. *But* later it was learned that the expression "is to" was unfamiliar to these children. They would have said "goes with," that is, a hand "goes with" an arm, and when "goes with" was substituted for "is to" in the same test, they did very well, and scored high in "intelligence."

AN OBJECTION RAISED:

—Lionel Ruby, *The Art of Making Sense*

A REASON GIVEN:

You do not have to travel to find the sea, *for* the traces of its ancient stands are everywhere about. Though you may be a thousand miles inland, you can easily find reminders that will reconstruct for the eye and ear of the mind the processions of its ghostly waves and the roar of its surf, far back in time. *So,* on a mountain top in Pennsylvania, I have sat on rocks of whitened limestone, fashioned of the shells of billions upon billions of minute sea creatures. *Once* they had lived and died in an arm of the ocean that overlay this place, and their limy remains had settled to the bottom. *Then,* after eons of time, they had become compacted into rock and the sea had receded; *after yet* more eons the rock had been uplifted by bucklings of the earth's crust and *now* it formed the backbone of a long mountain range.

A RESULT GIVEN:

EVENTS PLACED IN CHRONOLOGICAL ORDER:

—Rachel Carson, *The Sea Around Us*

A REASON GIVEN:

AN ALTERNATIVE PROPOSED:

ADDITIONAL FACTS:

LOGICAL CONCLUSION DRAWN:

The total sale of Horatio Alger's books will probably never be known, *for* he had numerous publishers, many of which did not stay in business very long. *But* one can get a clue from the fact that one of the firms, which did not begin publishing the books till after Alger's death, estimates its total at close to ten million copies. *Another* company estimates its total sales at five million. It is *therefore* safe to assume that the grand total was well over twenty million copies.

REMEMBER: The connection between one point and the next is usually more obvious to the writer than it is to his readers. The experienced writer has learned to go back over a paper or a paragraph to ask: "Have I done enough to help my reader follow?"

EXERCISE 9   In the following passages, point out all features that help carry the reader along. Is there a clear, *logical pattern* for the reader to follow? Is there any repetition of *synonyms or related terms?* What use does the author make of *transitional expressions?*

1.   The checker, or researcher, is usually a girl in her twenties, usually from some Eastern college, pleasant-looking but not a *femme fatale.* She came from college unqualified for anything, but looking for an "interesting" job. After a few years, she usually feels, bitterly and rightly, that *nobody* appreciates her work. Her work consists of assembling newspaper clippings and other research material early in the week and then checking the writer's story at the end of the week. The beginning of the week is lackadaisical, and so is the research, but toward the end, when typewriters clack behind closed doors and editors snap at intruders, there are midnight hamburgers and tears in the ladies' room. For the checker gets no credit if the story is right, but she gets the blame if it is wrong. It doesn't matter if the story is slanted or meretricious, if it misinterprets or misses the point of the week's news. That is the responsibility of the editors. What matters — and what seems to attract most of the hostile letters to the editors — is whether a championship poodle stands thirty-six or forty inches high, whether the eyes of Prince Juan Carlos of Spain are blue or brown, whether the population of some city in Kansas is 15,000 or 18,000.
　　　　—Otto Friedrich, "There are 00 Trees in Russia," *Harper's*

2.   Some spring the white man came, built him a house, and made a clearing here, letting in the sun, dried up a farm, piled up the old gray stones in fences, cut down the pines around his dwelling, planted orchard seeds brought from the old country, and persuaded the civil apple tree to blossom next to the wild pine and the juniper, shedding its perfume in the wilderness. Their old stocks still remain. He culled the graceful elm from out the woods and from the river-side, and so refined and smoothed his village plot. And thus he plants a town. He rudely bridged the stream, and drove his team afield into the river meadows, cut the wild grass, and laid bare the homes of beaver, otter, muskrat, and with the whetting of his

scythe scared off the deer and bear. He set up a mill, and fields of English grain sprang in the virgin soil. And with his grain he scattered the seeds of the dandelion and the wild trefoil over the meadows, mingling his English flowers with the wild native ones. . . . The white man's mullein soon reigned in Indian corn-fields, and sweet scented English grasses clothed the new soil.

—Henry David Thoreau,
A Week on the Concord and Merrimack Rivers

3.   Our churches are all private voluntary associations, and have been ever since the Revolution and its aftermath broke the connection between church and state. Our political parties are private voluntary associations, unknown even to the law until recent years. Our labor unions, fraternal orders, clubs, business and professional societies — the bar associations and medical associations and chambers of commerce, the associations of scholars and of librarians, of artists and musicians, of alumni and of veterans — all are voluntary. Most of our colleges and universities are the products of such voluntary associations. Most of our reforms, too, have been carried through by just such organizations — many of them regarded as disreputable or subversive by their respectable contemporaries. Call the list of those reforms that have given the United States its most distinctive character over the past century and a half and you will discover that almost all of them had their inception in, and were carried to completion by, associations of individuals. Thus the abolition of slavery, temperance, women's rights, prisons and penal reforms, educational reform, slum clearance, the peace movement, the protection of Indians, of Negroes, of the foreign-born from exploitation — these and a hundred others belong in this category.

—Henry Steele Commager, *Freedom, Loyalty, Dissent*

4.   Since only seven per cent of the earth's surface is under cultivation, it would appear that the task of expanding the world's food producing areas would be simple. But no two qualified people will agree on the validity of this. Approximately half of the earth's land surface is covered with ice, tundra, mountains, or desert. It is estimated, however, that there are still remaining 1.3 billion acres which might be brought under cultivation. A billion of these are in the tropics. None of them would be simple to cultivate. Man has already ploughed the easy acres. Nevertheless, if the human race is to survive, these unproductive wastelands must be brought into service. Can it be done? The most brilliant of farming experts think it can; but not cheaply.

EXERCISE 10 How successfully does the author of the following magazine article carry the reader along from paragraph to paragraph? Are there clear, logical connections? What use does the author make of related terms and transitional expressions?

... It is a severe shock, after living in South Africa, to visit the American South. For with all the differences of the continents, the resemblance is astonishing. ...

There are strong resemblances in the character of the American Southerner and the Afrikaner in South Africa; they were molded by the same kind of history. ... Both societies have developed from the isolation of the frontier, with the gun, the Bible, and the ox-cart as their powerful symbols. ...

Even more striking is the resemblance in their wars — the Civil War and the Boer War — which still dominate their present. The Yankees in the South and the British in South Africa were the same kind of intruders — rich, industrial, detribalized and committed to the extinction of slavery; and the continuing resentments against them were also similar. ...

In places, their history is so similar that even the outward appearance of the towns is very close. The oil city of Dallas, with its sheer skyscrapers rising suddenly out of the Texas prairie, with ramshackle Negro huts in the middle of town and white suburban mansions outside, has the same higgledy-piggledy mixture of concrete and gingerbread, boom city and hick town, that you find in the gold metropolis of Johannesburg. ...

But the most reminiscent sight I discovered in the South was West Ninth Street, Little Rock — the main Negro street in the city. Just next to a white street, it makes a spectacular contrast to the city center. ...

It seemed at first sight an almost exact reproduction of Sophiatown, the condemned Negro township in Johannesburg which has been the setting of so much writing about South Africa. ...

—Anthony Sampson, "Little Rock and Johannesburg," *The Nation*

C 1e *Titles, Introductions, Conclusions*

Know how to attract and channel your reader's attention.

An effective writer knows how to attract attention. He makes people feel: "This I want to read." He knows how to get them *involved* in a topic. He leaves them at the end with a strong, unified impression. When they look back over the piece they have just finished reading, they do not have to ask: "What was this all about? What does it all prove? Why was I told all this?"

Remember the following when you try to start a paper right and to finish it on a strong note:

(1) *Make your title both attractive and informative.* Like the sign saying "EAT" above a roadside restaurant, an effective title beckons to the reader and says "READ." But at the same time, a good title gives the reader a clue as to what he will find. Often, the title stakes out the *territory* to be covered:

> How Words Are Born
> The New St. Louis
> On Respecting the Americans

Often, in addition, the title conveys the *key point* to be supported:

> You Can't Live in New York
> My Crusade Against Football
> The Case for Early Marriage

And very commonly the title shows the attitude of the writer, the *tone* he is going to adopt:

> Cheating: American Disgrace
> The Ad and the Id
> TV or Not TV

Weak titles are too pretentious, too general, or too dull:

PRETENTIOUS:	Facing the Challenge of Tomorrow
MORE HONEST:	I Was Taught by a Computer
	The Crash Program that Stalled
	Why Schools Don't Stay Integrated
GENERAL:	My Autobiography
MORE FOCUSED:	Growing Up Confused
	Confessions of a Mouse
	How I Learned to Love
DULL:	Government and the People
MORE LIVELY:	I Helped Elect the Mayor
	Don't Write Your Congressman
	Don't Bite the Politicians

(2) *Use your introduction to draw your readers into the topic.* After your reader has read the first few sentences of a short paper, he should have the answers to questions like the following: "Why should I read this? What are you trying to do? How are you going to do it?" The introduction may make it clear that the author will

— discuss a *topic often neglected* or treated inadequately:

On Being the Right Size

The most obvious differences between different animals are differences of size, but for some reason the zoologists have paid singularly little attention to them. In a large textbook of zoology before me I find no indication that the eagle is larger than the sparrow, or the hippopotamus bigger than the hare, though some grudging admissions are made in the case of the mouse and the whale. (J. B. S. Haldane)

— relate an *incident that has a special meaning* for him:

Shooting an Elephant

In Moulmein, in lower Burma, I was hated by large numbers of people — the only time in my life that I have been important enough for this to happen to me. . . .

(George Orwell)

— discuss a topic of *direct concern to the reader:*

Our Vanishing Countryside

Some morning drive out past the edge of town, turn off into a back road and go for a spin through the open countryside. Look well at the meadows, the wooded draws, the stands of pine, the creeks and streams, and fix them in your memory. This may be about the last chance you will have. . . .

(William H. Whyte, Jr.)

— appeal to the reader's *interest in the unusual:*

A Glimpse of India

Unpacking my suitcase in London after a fortnight in India I noticed a violent smell of spice. It came from my socks. A little of India sinks in a long way. . . . (V. S. Pritchett)

— take a position that *differs from familiar views:*

The Duty of Society to the Artist

A great deal has been said about the duty of the artist to society. It is argued that the poet, the novelist, the painter, the musician, has a duty to the community; he is a citizen like everyone else; he must pull his weight, he must not give himself airs, or ask for special terms, he must pay his taxes honourably, and keep the laws which have been made for the general good. That is the argument and it is a reasonable one. But there is another side: what is the duty of society to the artist?

(E. M. Forster)

— develop a striking *contrast:*

Aging and Everyman

Throughout human history until recent times, most human beings have died in infancy, and no more than a very small percentage survived to ripe old age, carrying with them the wisdom of their experience or the foolishness of their years. Now all is changing, thanks to antibodies, antibiotics, the surgeon's knife, and the welfare state.

(N. J. Berrill)

— discuss a familiar topic in a *lively or provocative manner:*

Teen-age Tyranny

Teen-age, like birth and death, is inevitable. It is nothing to be ashamed of. Nor is it a badge of special distinction worthy of a continuous birthday party. . . .

(Grace and Fred M. Hechinger)

Note that a good introduction heads straight for the topic without making defensive or apologetic remarks. It does not merely present a vague program for the rest of the paper but often gives a capsule preview of the results:

DEFENSIVE: The youth of America today are living on borrowed time. To the casual observer this statement may seem over-exaggerated and even fallacious. The casual observer does not see how terribly true this statement is. . . .

DIRECT: We no longer allow children to be children. In a recent issue, *American Girl* discussed the problems of girls who use their first lipstick and wear their first nylons years earlier than did girls in years gone by. . . .

VAGUE: In this paper, I am going to examine the basic similarities and some important differences between Shakespeare's Julius Caesar and Macbeth. . . .

DIRECT: Though both Caesar and Macbeth are tyrants, Macbeth is a tyrant haunted by a guilty conscience. . . .

(3) *Use your conclusion to reinforce your major point and show why it was important.* A conclusion is not the same thing as a summary. Sometimes a summary is indeed needed: When you

have described a complicated process, you may want to summarize by looking back over the major steps. When you have studied important objections, you may need a strong summary of your own point of view. But often a summary is merely lame *repetition*. The reader's reaction is "You just told me!"

Do not use a summary that merely restates what is already quite clear. Experiment with alternatives like the following:

— Apply your major point to a *current situation:*

> (an article on Washington's personality) . . . There are times to smile and times to scowl. Washington lacked one of the basic qualities we have come to expect in the head of a chamber of commerce or the public relations director of a large company. He did not try to please everybody, all the time.

— Use an *anecdote* to sum up or reinforce your main point:

> (an article on the frustrations and humiliations suffered by the courting male) . . . A certain male (homo sapiens) of my acquaintance . . . one night after dinner asked his wife to put down her detective magazine so that he could read her a poem of which he was very fond. She sat quietly enough until he was well into the middle of the thing, intoning with great ardor and intensity. Then suddenly there came a sharp, disconcerting *slap!* It turned out that all during the male's display, the female had been intent on a circling mosquito and had finally trapped it between the palms of her hands. The male . . . went over to Tim's and had a flock of drinks and recited the poem to the fellas. I am sure they all told bitter stories of their own about how their displays had been interrupted by females. I am also sure that they all ended up singing "Honey, Honey, Bless Your Heart."
>
> —James Thurber, "Courtship Through the Ages"

— Use a *quotation* to give added force to your own position:

> (a paper on the shortcomings of "respectability") . . . William Hazlitt said, "There is not any term that is oftener misapplied, or that is a stronger instance of the abuse of language, than this same word *respectable*." The trouble with respectable people is that they are too timid to do the things that would win our respect.

Take special care to avoid the kind of vaguely inspirational conclusion that really adds nothing. Never use a conclusion that could be used *interchangeably* with many other papers on similar subjects:

WEAK: ... There were many great writers at this time — some of the greatest. Each of these writers had his own reason or purpose for writing. Each one did his or her job well and effectively. Certainly this era in literature's history will not be forgotten.

(Can you tell whether the paper was about colonial American writers? English Romantic writers? Can you tell what kind of literature the author loves — or hates?)

WEAK: ... The teen-agers who are concerned only with tomorrow night's date are going to have to become the adults who will run businesses, seek offices, and decide world policies. If we are not able to respond to the challenge of tomorrow, we shall find ourselves ill-prepared and ill-equipped to deal with the jobs that must be done.

(Was this a paper asking for support for the Boy Scout movement? Or advocating more homework? Or suggesting a new kind of curriculum?)

REMEMBER: Avoid elaborate introductions that "beat around the bush." Avoid padded conclusions that repeat for the third time something you have already said. Take your reader into your topic by the shortest possible route, and keep your conclusion short and pointed enough to be remembered.

EXERCISE 11 How attractive and informative are the following *titles*? Which of them make you want to read what the author has to say? Which of them could serve as a model for the title of a student theme? Explain and defend your answers.

1. Hope for the Blind
2. Detective Agencies
3. The Shame of Our Cities
4. The Spirit of Democracy
5. Bemused in Buffalo
6. An Open Letter to the New Mayor
7. Death at an Early Age
8. How to Get Along with People
9. Beat the Drum Slowly
10. A Warning to the Rich White World

EXERCISE 12 Describe how each of the following *introductions* leads the reader into the topic. In each case, would you want to go on reading? Why, or why not?

1. Whatever Happened to the Great Outdoors?

    About conservation, which next to the Bomb is the subject of greatest importance to every person in the world, there is nothing new to say. In every aspect it is an old problem — which is to say an unsolved one. The basic fact is known to anyone who thinks at all: man's impact on his environment, on the total natural endowment of earth, air, and water, animal, vegetable, and mineral, has been bad, and is getting rapidly worse, and will get worse yet.

2. Hunting Deer-Hunters

    The real excitement of the deer-hunting season isn't hunting deer, it's hunting deer-hunters. It's always the same, every year. . . .

3. Adults Only

    Some months ago, the president of the Motion Picture Association of America announced in Hollywood that his organization was reconsidering its policy on classifying films. . . .

4. The Glory of Age

    There is a legend abroad that America is a land of young people. We are pictured in the advertisements as blooming, smooth-skinned, forever under thirty-five. We are always reaching forward to next year's faster car, with little to remind us of the old, the tired, and the wise. This picture is countered, however, by certain statistics which are only beginning to be general news. . . .

5. Dickens and His Critics

    "He has gone up like a rocket," wrote Abraham Hayward in 1837, "and he will come down like the stick." It was the most wildly erroneous prediction ever made even by a literary critic. Charles Dickens never did come down; the rocket is still circling the earth, a luminary visible to all men's eyes.

EXERCISE 13 Which of the following passages sounds to you as if it would make a strong, pointed *conclusion* to a paper or article? What, in detail, would make it a strong or a weak conclusion?

1. . . . This problem of anti-intellectualism is an important one. Perhaps it should be looked into a little further. In this fast-growing nation of ours, nothing is more important than the development of our minds.

2. ... The philosophy of Plato began in words and ended in words — noble words indeed, words such as were to be expected from the finest of human intellects exercising boundless dominion over the finest of human languages. The philosophy of Bacon began in observations and ended in arts.

3. ... The press was given its privileged status in order to question and, if necessary, counteract the exercise of government power. In that function it is defaulting. Writing in the *New York Review of Books,* Andrew Kopkind has described the real sources of news suppression: "In ways which journalists themselves perceive only dimly or not at all, they are bought, or compromised, or manipulated into confirming the official lies: not the little ones, which they delight in exposing, but the big ones, which they do not normally think of as lies at all, and which they cannot distinguish from the truth."

4. ... knowing the investment that this nation makes in the education of the young, we students of America will strive to be worthy of the trust put in us by our parents. With the knowledge and training we receive, we will become not only better students, but also better citizens.

5. ... When Christ was on the cross, the story goes, His persecutors were preparing a fourth spike made of silver to pierce his heart. Some Gypsies stole the spike, and Christ was spared the additional agony. God was so grateful that he gave the Gypsies permission to steal thereafter. I asked my hostess whether she believed the story. "How else can you explain it?" she replied. "Why can a Gypsy steal but he'll never get caught? The Gypsies don't have a church, and they don't have a country, but God made them free and He watches over us."

EXERCISE 14 [Optional] Look through current issues of general-interest magazines and find *three* articles that are exceptionally successful in attracting the reader's attention and leaving him with a strong, unified impression at the end. Choose articles from magazines like *Harper's, Atlantic, Saturday Review, National Review, New Republic, Commentary,* or *Commonweal.* Discuss each author's title, introduction, and conclusion. (Your teacher will tell you whether to present your findings as an oral report or in a short paper.)

REVIEW EXERCISE 1: Evaluating Student Writing
The following short *student themes* were written by high school seniors as writing samples for a college entrance examination. How would you rate them on a three-point scale going from "Good" to

"Satisfactory" to "Poor"? Ask the following basic questions about each paper:

(1) How successfully has the author pulled together authentic *material* to support his points? Does he use good details, and do they fit in?

(2) Has the author successfully *organized* his material? Is there a clear, overall scheme, with clear transitions from point to point?

(3) How successfully has the author reached his *readers?* Does he get (and keep) you interested in his subject? How? Does he make you agree with him? Why, or why not?

NOTE: These papers have been edited lightly for spelling and punctuation. Otherwise they remain as first written.

1.   Ideals on Madison Avenue

There are many ways to express a nation's ideals. The Greeks expressed theirs in their sculpture and writings, the English by their colonialism, and the Americans by their advertisements. "How," you ask, "can advertisements express ideals?" I will show you, and I will also show you *what* exactly American ideals are, anyway.

First of all, our advertisements express wealth. This is quite evident from the fact that advertisements are usually demonstrative of the more expensive items of American culture, such as automobiles, homes, expensive kitchen and home appliances, et al. From this we can assume that Americans are desirous of wealth, for one cannot buy expensive things without wealth.

After wealth, we can place beauty, for it is quite obvious from all the Lux, Palmolive, Ivory, and other advertisements that Americans like to be beautiful. Americans must despise ugliness, for we never see advertisements for deforming products, do we? We are forever *barraged* by advertisements for all sorts of health foods, beauty aids, reducing equipment, and other beauty-producing paraphernalia that we can also assume that another great American ideal is beauty.

One more subtle, but prominent, American ideal is happiness. Happiness is not in itself a product that is advertised, but, nevertheless, we find it is included in almost every advertisement. These advertisements stress that we will be happy in our new cars, happy with Brand X cigarettes, happy with Palmolive care, and happy in B.V.D.'s. Can we not also assume that happiness is another American ideal? I think we can. Most of all, though, I think that we can assume that

Americans, all Americans, have as an ideal the ideal of equality.

Yes, equality above all is what American manufacturers are advertising and selling to the American public. In our advertisements we can see that this is so, for do not the advertisements say, — "Everyone else has one, so should you!" — This is a dominant theme in all advertising. Our society is the first of its kind; it is a society of the masses, thus the advertising does not appeal to the intellectuals and the leaders, for they reject it, but the advertising appeals to Joe Doe, John Q. Public, you and me. That is where we find the greatest American ideal of all: equality.

In their advertisements the American people demonstrate their desire for equality. Everyone wants to be the same, and since the Joneses up the street have a Ford, can't we have one, too? Yes! the man on TV said last night we could. Aren't we just as good as Sam Jones and his wife? You bet your boots we are! The man on TV *said* we are, or at least he implied it. He said *everyone* could afford a new Thunderbird, didn't he? As a matter of fact, he did, because he knows that conformity is one of the most powerful ideals in America, and he appealed to it.

We have thus seen how advertising in America expresses some of the ideals of the American nation. We have thus seen how advertising expresses the ideals of wealth, beauty, happiness, and, above all, the ideal of equality. May Madison Avenue endure forever, glorious center of American ideals!

2.   Money

If I were a foreigner coming into the United States, judging from its billboards, television commercials, and newspaper and magazine advertisements, I would say that the Americans are very materialistic. They have all sorts of things on their billboards across the states. They are mainly telling the passerby to come on in and buy this item that you can't do without. But, of course, all of this salesman talk is untrue. They have to tell their buyers a few lies in order to sell their products.

On the television commercials the only thing that the advertiser is trying to do is sell. He tells his viewers to buy this or that because they need it. In other words, he is trying to say "keep up with your neighbor, buy this." The advertiser knows that in order to sell he has to have a real good commercial. He knows that he has most of the American people watching TV. All he has to do is sell.

In newspaper and magazine advertising, the advertiser is the same as any other advertiser. He is trying to sell his product, to get money.

Still looking at the U.S. through the eyes of a foreigner, everywhere you go you hear the sound of money. From looking at television, billboards, magazines, listening to the radio, all you hear is "buy this," "get this new time-saving device."

One false idea that a foreigner might get of Americans is that they are all rich. From hearing and seeing all of their different advertisements, one can say "The Americans can afford to get these things; they must be rich."

A foreigner might also get the idea that the Americans don't work, they are lazy, they don't know how to handle their children, etc.

I believe that the advertisements are really hurting the American people. They are giving the foreigners a wrong impression of Americans.

When I myself think about it, I do believe that the Americans are entirely too materialistic.

3.   Look Around

"Education is the key to a nation." Television, radio, the newspaper, magazines, in fact, all forms of communication which "inform" sound this phrase. What are the young people of today subject to derive from this? One suggestion might be that the minds of the young will guide the nation of tomorrow. Therefore, these minds must be cultivated with the tools of knowledge, stimulated with desire to learn so that the possessors of these delicate instruments can lead the nation in fulfilling its ideals with strong, yet wise patriotism.

A better standard of living. What do the billboards describe but more resistant siding for houses, safer and more efficient housing facilities, easier ways of doing things, in short, luxury. Transportation now provides moving pictures, stereophonic sound in music, all the comforts of home. The more complete TV dinners make life easier on mother. Sanforized garments and the new fabrics make ironing a joy! What do we have to do today but follow instructions and enjoy life!!?

Forms of entertainment. The stately opera, "Harrah's" at Lake Tahoe where the celebrities perform, the new resorts where "life is like living on a cloud." The exotic weeks in Europe, South America as advertised by "National Airlines, the only way to fly."

Beauty. The new eye liner that is waterproof, the two-tone lipstick, the permanent permanent, the hair color that won't wash out, the stockings which give any woman's legs luxurious comfort. With a little know-how, the homeliest girl can be charming and desirable. But what's it all for? Why the luxury, comfort, and modernized living? Surely, primitive man got along with his crude knives and forks. Everything man does today stems from a built-in characteristic in his make-up: man's constant and never-ending search for perfection and happiness. All of the standards, the knowledge, easier living, desires for beauty are a source of temporary happiness and perfection for man. He has a feeling of accomplishment at having reached the summit of perfection. This desire is good. If this wish were non-existent, if man had perfect happiness, there would be no stimulae or purpose for living. Therefore, no matter how temporary or incomplete these joys may be, they are good when taken in the right sense, and they make the nation's ideals more purposeful.

C 2 Writing from Experience

Draw on your own observation and experience to give substance to your writing.

A good writer does not merely repeat other people's impressions and opinions. He forms his own impressions on the basis of close, firsthand observation. What he knows and believes is anchored firmly to his firsthand experience. He has learned to pay attention to what happens around him. As a result, his writing has *authentic substance*. It is as if he were telling his readers: "What I say is not just words. Instead, it is related to what people actually see, hear, say, do, think, and feel."

In your own apprenticeship as a writer, writing focused on your own observation and experience is an essential stage. Writing is no good unless the reader feels: "This is real. This has something to do with actual living people." When you try to make your own writing real and substantial, remember requirements like the following:

(1) *Draw on what people actually see.* Bring in the specifics that help your readers visualize what you describe. It is harder to

visualize a man who merely *walks* than a man who *shuffles, strides, limps, hops,* or *trots.* It is hard to visualize ordinary, anonymous tree branches or telephone poles. It is easier to visualize trees that wave their branches like angry arms in the November wind, or telephone poles dotting a subdivision like the masts of sunken ships.

(2) *Draw on what people actually say.* We always get one important step closer to reality when a writer can reproduce what was *said* as well as what was done. In the following passage, the writer helps us follow him to the Scotland of his childhood by making us hear the voices of the people he describes:

> We cross Melville Drive, climb over the iron railings that separate it from the Meadows (there are several open entrances, but we prefer to climb) and find ourselves amid heaps of stacked piles of wood. There are several children swarming around these, and we join them, clambering up and slipping down, chasing each other between the stacks, shouting at the top of our voices. Then one of the workmen, who are busy further down the field, sees us and shouts: *"Hey, get oot o' that!"* We shout louder than ever, and the workman makes a threatening gesture. I find myself among a chorus of children chanting: *"Ha, ha, ha, ye canna catch me! Ha, ha, ha, ye canna catch me!"* I am not happy about this defiance of the workman, but I am encouraged by being a member of a group, and chant as loud as anyone. Then a shrill whistle blows, and the cry goes up: *"The parkie! The parkie!"* and we all stream off toward the Middle Meadow Walk as the parkkeeper, in his official uniform, whistles and waves at us.
>
> —David Daiches, *Two Worlds*

(3) *Draw on what people actually feel.* The real feelings of people are usually less spectacular than the emotions inspired by a horror movie or a passionate love story. A good novel often seems real to us because the author knows how to make us share the ordinary emotions of ordinary people. Bernard Malamud, for instance, in *The Assistant,* makes us share the feelings of a Jewish neighborhood grocer struggling against poverty and crime. Can you spell out the feelings the reader is made to share in the following passage from the first page of the book?

The front door opened and a girl of ten entered, her face pinched and eyes excited. His heart held no welcome for her.

"My mother says," she said quickly, "can you trust her till tomorrow for a pound of butter, loaf of rye bread and a small bottle of cider vinegar?"

He knew the mother. "No more trust."

The girl burst into tears.

Morris gave her a quarter-pound of butter, the bread and vinegar. He found a penciled spot on the worn counter, near the cash register, and wrote a sum under "Drunk Woman." The total now came to $2.03, which he never hoped to see. But Ida would nag if she noticed a new figure, so he reduced the amount to $1.61. His peace — the little he lived with — was worth forty-two cents.

C 2a Description

Give your writing authentic substance by doing justice to the sights and sounds around you.

In writing description, a writer looks around him at the world in which he lives. He does not merely repeat what "people always say." He takes things in at first hand. He *notices* — the outlines of a building, the features of a face, the texture of a piece of cloth. The descriptive writer is like someone who goes out with a camera and a tape recorder and then comes back to say: "Look at what I have seen. Listen to what I have heard."

A good observer finds things to point out and to marvel at where ordinary people pay little or no attention. He looks at things as though he were seeing them for the first time. This way they *register* — and he can later share them with his readers.

Study and practice the basic skills needed in descriptive writing:

(1) *A good descriptive writer has an eye for detail.* He cannot make his readers visualize actual scenes or objects by merely giving them a general impression: "The room was cluttered"; or "The shelves were neatly arranged." His first job is to bring in enough of what was there, and how it looked, for the reader to say, "I am beginning to get the picture." Can you see that the authors of each of the following thumbnail sketches had an eye for detail?

(the office of a student newspaper)

>a grubby, ill-lit room full of pencil stubs, shreds of paper, paste, ink, broken chairs, typewriter ribbons, and candy wrappers

(an old-fashioned pantry)

>shelves laid out with rows of jelly glasses and brown jugs and white stone-china jars with blue whirligigs and words painted on them: coffee, tea, sugar, ginger, cinnamon, allspice

>(Katherine Anne Porter)

(a sea slug)

>a snail without a shell — a soft, shapeless brown body spotted with dark-edged circles and fringed with flaps and folds of skin, so that as it creeps over the weed in search of prey it can scarcely be distinguished from the vegetation   (Rachel Carson)

The writing of the inexperienced writer too often stays on the surface. It asks us to accept everything on the writer's mere say-so. It lacks the rich detail that *shows* the reader instead of merely *telling* him. Contrast the passages in each of the following pairs:

BARE: Each housing unit had prepared an elaborate float or display. Each float must have taken much time and energy to prepare. They were very ingenious.

DETAILED: Each housing unit had prepared an elaborate float or display. One prize-winner was an *enormous red bull* (the home team) *towing a corn cutter which mowed down cornstalks* (the opposing team) *and delivered them in bags.* Another winner was a *gigantic Indian whose eyes lighted up and moved from side to side, whose head moved on a swivel, and whose chest heaved.*

BARE: From my window, I could see a young man working in his apartment across the street. He was polishing a long table top. He was really working at it, giving it everything he had.

·DETAILED: Framed in a lighted window level with mine in the apartment house across the street, I saw a young man *in a white T-shirt and white shorts* at work polishing a long, beautiful dark table top. It was obviously his own table in his own flat, and he was enjoying his occupation. He was *bent over* in perfect concentration, *rubbing, sandpapering, running the flat of his palm over the surface, standing back now and then to get the sheen of light on the fine wood.*   (Katherine Anne Porter)

(2) *A good descriptive writer has a word for it.* Rachel Carson, in her books about the sea, described many small sea animals — their strange shapes and colors and motions. How could she have described their shapes without words like *disc, tentacle, fringe, flap, fold,* or *tube?* These words are specific — they bring to mind a definite shape. We all know that there are hundreds of species of birds that all look and sound different. Note the words Miss Carson used for the appearance and cries and motions of different birds:

> gulls hovering with eager, mewing cries
>
> the dry twitter of the phalaropes, small brown birds, wheeling and turning, dipping and rising
>
> a small heron in gray and rusty plumage — a reddish egret that waded across the flat with the stealthy, hesitant movements of its kind

A routine writer relies too much on all-purpose words like *building, thing,* or *move.* The word *move* does not make us see a particular kind of motion. The English language has hundreds of words that would create a more vivid picture in the reader's mind: *lurch, jerk, stagger, slide, leap, hop, shift, totter, sway, glide, crawl, slip, shift, veer, careen,* and the like. Notice in the following excerpt from a Hemingway story the many words that make the reader take in specific objects, sights, sounds, and motions:

> The car was going a wild forty-five miles an hour across the open and as Macomber watched, the buffalo got bigger and bigger until he could see the gray, hairless, *scabby* look of one huge bull and how his neck was a part of his shoulders and the shiny black of his horns as he galloped a little behind the others that were *strung out* in that *steady plunging gait;* and then, the car *swaying* as though it had just *jumped* a road, they drew up close and he could see the plunging hugeness of the bull, and the dust in his sparsely haired hide, the wide *boss* of horn and his outstretched, wide-nostrilled *muzzle,* and he was raising his rifle when Wilson shouted, "Not from the car, you fool!" and he had no fear, only hatred of Wilson, while the brakes *clamped* on and the car *skidded, plowing* sideways to an almost stop and Wilson was out on one side and he on the other, *stumbling* as his feet hit the still speeding-by of the earth, and then he was shooting at the bull as he

moved away, hearing the bullets *whunk* into him, emptying his rifle at him as he moved steadily away, finally remembering to get his shots forward into the shoulder, and as he *fumbled* to re-load, he saw the bull was down.

—Ernest Hemingway, "The Short Happy Life of Francis Macomber"

(3) *A good descriptive writer has an eye for similarities.* We are not really helped to visualize the body shell of a beetle when we are told what exactly it is made of. But we can begin to picture it when we are told whether it looks more like leather, or hard rubber, or a certain kind of metal. In the following passages, can you point out the comparisons that help us imagine an animal that we may have never seen before?

From the deck of a vessel you may look down, hour after hour, on the shimmering discs of jellyfish, their gently pulsating bells dotting the surface as far as you can see.
(Rachel Carson)

There are fierce little dragons half an inch long, the sharp-jawed arrowworms. There are gooseberry-like comb jellies, armed with grasping tentacles, and there are the shrimp-like euphausiids that strain food from the water with their bristly appendages.
(Rachel Carson)

Notice how naturally and effectively the author of the following passage compares the motions of a half-tame mouse (which few readers are likely to have observed) to the motions of more *familiar* animals:

It probably had never seen a man before; and it soon became quite familiar, and would run over my shoes and up my clothes. It could readily ascend the sides of the room by short impulses, *like a squirrel,* . . . when at last I held still a piece of cheese between my thumb and finger, it came and nibbled it, sitting in my hand, and afterward cleaned its face and paws, *like a fly,* and walked away.

—Henry David Thoreau, *Walden*

(4) *A good descriptive writer makes detail add up.* He does not merely point to one interesting detail here and another there. He *selects* those details that help him create a unifying, overall impression. If he wants to create a bustling street scene, he will

select details that contribute movement and color. If he wants to describe a nervous person, he will stress those movements and gestures that make the person seem fidgety, ill at ease.

Can you see how in the following passage all the italicized words and phrases help build up the same **dominant impression?** Can you show how some of the remaining details help reinforce the same prevailing mood?

> We pass'd quite a number of tramps, singly or in couples — one squad, a family in a *rickety* one-horse wagon, with some baskets evidently their work and trade — the man seated on a low board, in front, driving — the *gauntish* woman by his side, with a baby well bundled in her arms, its little red feet and lower legs sticking out right towards us as we pass'd — and in the wagon behind, we saw two (or three) *crouching* little children. It was a queer, taking, rather *sad* picture. If I had been alone and on foot, I should have stopp'd and held confab. But on our return nearly two hours afterward, we found them a ways further along the same road, in a *lonesome* open spot, haul'd aside, unhitch'd, and evidently going to camp for the night. The freed horse was not far off, quietly cropping the grass. The man was busy at the wagon, the boy had gather'd some dry wood, and was making a fire — and as we went a little further we met the woman afoot. I could not see her face, in its great sun-bonnet, but somehow her figure and gait told *misery,* terror, *destitution.* She had the *rag-bundled, half-starv'd* infant still in her arms, and in her hands held two or three baskets, which she had evidently taken to the next house for sale. A little *barefoot* five-year old girl-child, with fine eyes, trotted behind her, *clutching* her gown. We stopp'd, asking about the baskets, which we bought. As we paid the money, she kept her face hidden in the recesses of her bonnet. Then as we started, and stopp'd again, Al., (whose sympathies were evidently arous'd,) went back to the camping group to get another basket. He caught a look of her face, and talk'd with her a little. Eyes, voice and manner were those of a *corpse,* animated by electricity. She was quite young — the man she was traveling with, middle-aged. Poor woman — what story was it, out of her fortunes, to account for that inexpressibly scared way, those *glassy eyes,* and that *hollow voice?*
> —Walt Whitman, *Specimen Days*

(5) *A good descriptive writer brings life into a static scene.* He arranges his details so that they form a pattern. He makes the reader move forward systematically in time or in space. In describ-

ing a high school campus, he might take an imaginary visitor through the main entrance to the principal's office, from there to a typical classroom and the library, then to the cafeteria at lunchtime, and finally to the gym and playing fields in the afternoon.

Study the following prose model. Can you show how it illustrates the various features of good descriptive writing? In this passage, an experienced writer describes the subdivision in which she lives. She gives her readers an idea of what it *feels like* to live there. Note how she gives life and movement to what could be a static scene. Rather than describe the subdivision already built up, she shows it in the *process* of being built. Can you show how her following of this process gives a clear, overall pattern to this piece of writing? (Your teacher may ask you to prepare a rough outline.) Study the passage carefully, and prepare to answer the questions that follow it.

PROSE MODEL 1

LOIS PHILLIPS HUDSON

Springtime in the Rockies

For anybody who grew up on the prairie, it was and is a remarkable experience to watch three or four hundred acres of fields and pasture becoming city. During the springs of my childhood I roamed alone over a half section — about the acreage of our Table Mesa subdivision, which is now populated by about ten times as many people as there were in the town where I went to school three miles from our farm. That town once seemed to me to be bursting with people; I suppose it would look quite different to me now. One street was paved, because it was also U.S. Highway 10, and there were a few blocks of cement sidewalk. But cement was never part of my idea of a prairie spring.

Nevertheless, when I looked out of my picture window my first spring in Table Mesa, what I saw was cement — cement on the move. We lived in the last completed house on our loop, and what seemed like the biggest fleet of cement trucks in the world rumbled by us, headed for the bulldozed lots between us and the prairie. Our house is called the Metropolitan, which seems a significant appellation, the two other "big-value" models are called the Trojan and the Apollo, and the largest and most expensive is called, also significantly, the Americana. Day after day, sidewalks, basements, patios, foundations, and driveways rolled by in their emulsive state, revolving in oblong tubs over howling engines and shuddering transmissions. Behind the cement trucks came the steel girder trucks and the lumber trucks loaded with prefabricated walls and gables. Then came the roofing trucks, the plumbers' trucks, the painters' trucks, and Melvin the Landscaper's trucks. Hot on their exhaust fumes came the trucks from the businesses in the new Table Mesa Shopping Center — the wall-to-wall rug trucks and the floor-to-ceiling drapery trucks, from shops that are now out of business, theirs being a relatively short-lived boom, not unlike the booms of the gold and silver ghost towns all around us, with collapsing roads called Bonanza, El Dorado, or Wall Street.

No sooner had the first parade of shiny trucks of prosperous subcontractors begun to dwindle than a second parade began — a parade of independent small businessmen, in ten-year-old pickups, scarred and dented Volkswagen buses, and fenderless, paintless panel trucks. Our neighbors, I thought, looking out of my picture window, are now free of the subcontractors and they are shopping around. This second parade brought, and still brings, the touches with which my neighbors "individualize" their homes. For example, a panel truck parked in front of the Trojan two doors down from us, and when it left two hours later, that Trojan had a brilliant red front door. Across the street a pickup arrived with a ten-foot blue spruce rooted in about three hundred pounds of burlap-wrapped dirt. I had been watching the man of the house for three weekends while he dug a vast hole in the lawn he had worked on every weekend before that, and I had been waiting for the dénouement. The sinewy, undernourished nursery-man and the sweating, overnourished accountant dragged the tree across the lawn and managed to set it upright in the hole. There will be blue lights on it come Christmas, I thought. That will be the dénouement. All blue lights.

To the Americana on our northern side, trucks brought great loads of fill, topsoil, and fertilizer, all dumped in conical piles in the driveway. Then came boulders, bulldozers to move the boulders, and men to build and plant terraces, borders, walks, and patios. I watched to see if spotlights would be installed under the boulders, as they were at the house on the corner, but instead our neighbor chose a white plaster rabbit with two white babies, an orange deer, three white ducks with orange bills, and a little black jockey in white shirt and orange pants. The yard ornaments repeat the color scheme of the Americana, which is built of black bricks and white siding trimmed with orange shutters.

During our first spring in Table Mesa we endured the worst windstorms in the recorded meteorological history of Colorado. The first storm came the night after we moved into our new house and registered gusts of over a hundred miles an hour. One of these gusts demolished a nearly completed building behind us, and all night long, sizable pieces of the wreckage blew into our house. All the windows in the children's bedroom were shattered, spraying glass over both sleeping girls. Our eight-foot picture window and the sliding glass doors of our patio bowed in and out as though they were made of cellophane, and the reflected light of our candle undulated with the glass as though it shone over waves of water. The next morning we found that parts of our new roof had been torn away and some of our siding was ripped, revealing to our apprehensive gaze the fact that it was not wood, but a kind of extra-heavy cardboard painted to look like wood, that stood between us and the hurricane.

I left my picture window that first spring and went out to see if I could still find my idea of prairie spring. . . . One block west of our new house, the bulldozers were still digging basements. I could see the world being newly made or unmade. The next block was roughly graded and set with stakes that seemed, with the expanse of the prairie behind them, oddly and frighteningly close together, even though the stakes marked out lots the size of our own. We were circumscribing ourselves in tiny bits of the earth, while the whole earth still called to us from beyond our imaginary lines.

—from *The Reporter*

1. Explain briefly each of the following words: *appellation, emulsive, dénouement, conical, undulate, expanse, circumscribe*. What uses of the word *Americana* do you know?

2. Suppose that for each of the phrases in the first column the author had substituted the more general expression in the second column. Explain what is *missing* from the second version.

I *roamed* over	I *moved* around in
our *loop*	our *street*
collapsing roads	roads *in poor condition*
howling engines	*noisy* engines
shuddering transmissions	*trembling* transmissions
parade of shiny trucks	*traffic* made up of shiny trucks
sinewy, undernourished nurseryman	*lean,* undernourished nurseryman

3. Point out several uses of specific detail that help *individualize* something — that set it apart from other similar things.

4. In the first two paragraphs, the author uses the word *cement* six times. Can you explain why this word is a key word in the essay? When you look at the essay as a whole, what does cement symbolize? How does the use of the word reflect the attitude of the author toward what she describes?

5. Show how and where the author makes use of comparison and contrast.

6. Write a paragraph in which you describe something by showing it in the *process* of being produced. You might describe, for instance, a special kind of cabinet, an ingenious toy, or a new and unusual article of clothing.

EXERCISE 15 Write *thumbnail sketches* (each no more than one sentence) of half a dozen items in a group. For instance, you might sketch:

— strange objects a tourist might bring back from a trip to Mexico or an Indian reservation;
— tropical plants not familiar to all readers;
— offbeat costumes for a masquerade or play;
— unusual carpenters' or shoemakers' tools;
— unusual fish in a home aquarium.

EXERCISE 16 Write a paragraph in which you describe one of the following *processes* in exact detail:

— tying a bowknot in a shoelace;
— playing a violin;
— doing a currently popular dance with complicated motions or steps.

EXERCISE 17 Assume that you are exploring your own familiar neighborhood as the scout for a landing party coming from an entirely different culture. Write a report *tracing a familiar route* (such as your daily route to school) merely by identifying in concrete detail major landmarks or points of reference. How, for instance, would you make sure that people who have never seen a gas station will recognize one if they see it — and tell one from another? (Write as if all signs, house numbers, and the like, had been mysteriously wiped out.)

THEME TOPICS 1 A. Write a paper on close firsthand observation of one of the following: an industrial section of town; an angry or hostile crowd; the crowd at a concert or dance; people you saw in a hospital; people in a bus or subway. Work toward a unifying over-all impression.

B. Write about some sight that represents a way of life about to pass out of existence. Here are some examples:

— a once splendid mansion about to be torn down, or up for sale;
— a passenger train now discontinued (or about to be);
— a once busy railroad station now deserted;
— a formerly elegant resort;
— a famous park, museum, or the like, that has seen better days.

C. Are billboards as ugly as their opponents claim? Are they all different, or can you identify basic types? Describe as graphically as you can three or four current billboards that seem to you especially striking or representative. Concentrate on making the reader *visualize* the billboards you describe.

D. Is it true that public buildings — city halls, schools, libraries — express the spirit of a community? Select one such building. Describe it as graphically as you can, concentrating on features that make it in some way representative or symbolic of the community and its people.

E. People who study the outer surface of American life reach many different and contradictory conclusions. Some claim that the American scene is shaped by our emphasis on the *practical,* with no respect for beauty or tradition. Others claim that Americans like the gaudy and extravagant, shown in the *im*practical and wasteful design of our cars, for instance. Still others find in the skylines of our big cities and in the sweeping arcs of our freeways an exhilarating, futuristic beauty. Concentrate on one major area — big-city architecture, freeway design, car design, kitchen appliances, or the like. What is the relationship between "practical" and "aesthetic" factors? Make use of graphic description.

C 2b Autobiography

Give your writing authentic substance by taking stock of your own experience.

When you complain that you have nothing to write about, one obvious reply is: "Write about yourself." Write about what is closest to you and what you know best: your own background, your own interests, your own problems. Write about people and events that helped shape your outlook, your personality. Such writ-

THE STORY OF THE ALPHABET

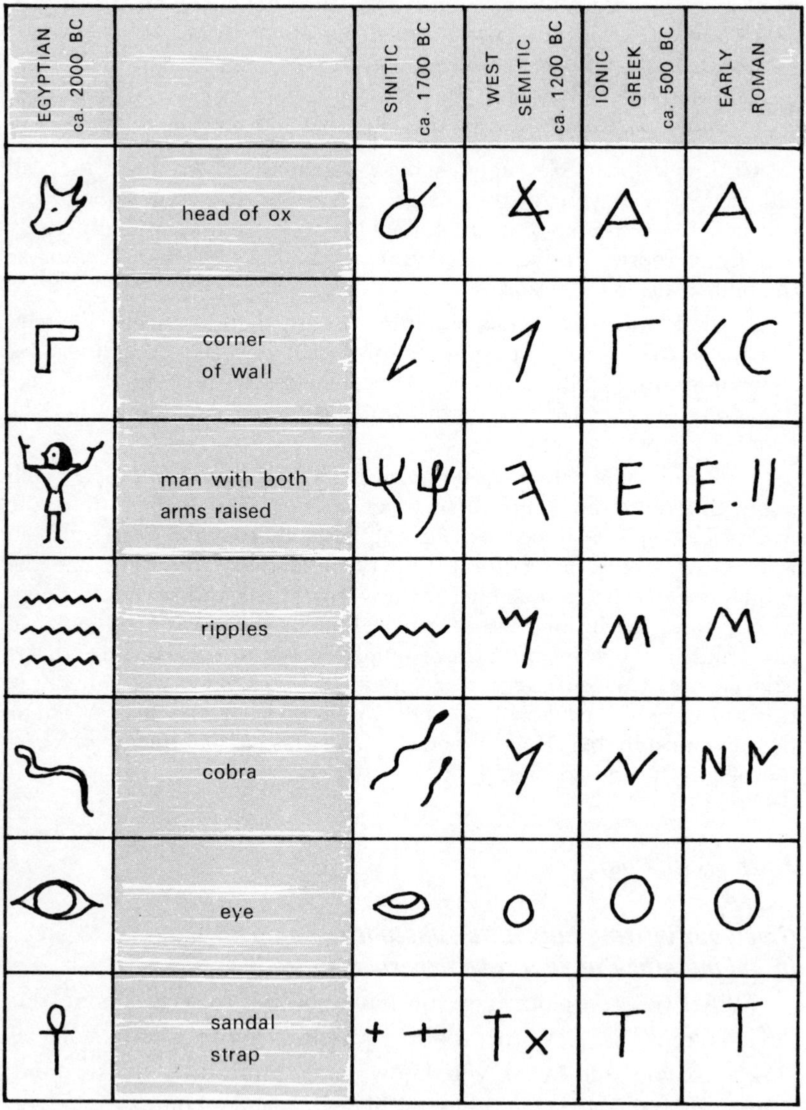
EGYPTIAN ca. 2000 BC
SINITIC ca. 1700 BC
WEST SEMITIC ca. 1200 BC
IONIC GREEK ca. 500 BC
EARLY ROMAN
head of ox
corner of wall
man with both arms raised
ripples
cobra
eye
sandal strap

ing is autobiographical; it deals with the author's own life. In writing autobiography, a writer *looks back* over his own experience. He tries to remember, and he tries to understand.

What you write and say has its full meaning only when you show how it is related to your own experience. Your ideas will mean something when you tie them to events you have witnessed, people you have known, problems you have confronted. The same words and ideas may mean quite different things to people with different experiences. The word *welfare,* for instance, meant one thing to the journalist who wrote about a Hollywood actress collecting unemployment compensation when she could not find a TV part just right for her:

> In Hollywood the quaint idea that the dole line is a squalid place, steeped in the shadow of shame, is dramatically dispelled. Here it is the most lighthearted joblessness, not to say larceny, within the boundless reaches of the welfare state. Here, they receive the dole and it's like an honorary degree. . . . They tell of movie luminaries pulling up in Rolls-Royces and Bentleys. While master gets in line inside, chauffeur retires to the donut shack on the corner to have a hot dog. . . . They tell of the mink-clad wives of producers in the $50,000 bracket, who, as sometime actresses, also qualify for compensation and stride in to collect their $65 a week without blinking a lash.   —Jordan Bonfante, "Cash on the Line," *Life*

But "welfare" means something completely different to thousands of other people. It meant something completely different to a famous comedian when in his autobiography he described what it meant to his family to be on relief:

> I remember how the social worker would poke around the house, wrinkling her nose at the coal dust on the chilly linoleum floor, shaking her head at the bugs crawling over the dirty dishes in the sink. My Momma would have to stand there and make like she was too lazy to keep her own house clean. She could never let on that she spent all day cleaning another woman's house for two dollars and carfare. She would have to follow that nasty woman around those drafty three rooms, keeping her fingers crossed that the telephone hidden in the closet wouldn't ring. Welfare cases weren't supposed to have telephones . . . she couldn't explain that while she was out spoon-feeding somebody else's kids, she was worrying about

her own kids, that she could rest her mind by picking up the telephone and calling us — to find out if we had bread for our baloney or baloney for our bread, to see if any of us had gotten run over by the streetcar while we played in the gutter, to make sure the house hadn't burnt down from the papers and magazines we stuffed in the stove when the coal ran out.

—Dick Gregory, *Nigger*

When words are not tied to what someone has experienced, they remain just words. Writing becomes real when the author shows by the way he writes: "This means something to me personally. This is not just theory; it has something to do with how I live and what I am."

When you write an autobiographical paper, you are trying to answer three questions at the same time. These three questions are: "What was it like?" "How did it feel?" and "What did it mean?"

(1) *"What was it like?"*

The writer of autobiography in effect turns to his reader and says: "Imagine yourself in my place in a little town in Ohio ten years ago." The reader's natural reaction is "How *can* I?" The answer is "I will help you by conjuring up the actual setting, by recreating scenes and events as concretely as I can. I will try to make them so real that you feel as if *you* were the person seeing and doing these things."

To make good on this promise, the writer has to practice the first rule of autobiographical writing: Don't tell everything, but what you tell, tell concretely. Pick out the scenes and incidents most likely to take the reader from where he is to *that* place, *that* time. Then describe them in such concrete detail that the reader can imagine himself participating in what is going on.

Can you show what the authors of the following passages have done to help their writing meet this first basic rule? Can you point out the kind of detail that only someone who *lived through* the incidents described would know?

On the way to school in late spring and early fall, we would crack open watermelons in the growers' fields and eat just the hearts out of them, arriving at school all stuck together down the front with pink mud. Or we would detour around by Johansen's loquat tree, dump out the plain bread-

and-butter sandwiches from our lunch bags, and fill up the sacks with dead-ripe, honey-sweet fruit. We kept the hard-boiled egg, though. —Dolly Connelly, "Game's End," *Atlantic*

At mealtime we ate ravenously in the mess hall. There were steaming platters of pork and beans and cabbage and stew. As we walked to the long clapboard building with our hair freshly combed and water glistening on our faces, which we washed at the flowing pipe of a big artesian well, we existed in a transport of driving hunger. In the steamy fragrance of the mess hall we set up a clatter of knives and forks and china, and afterward we went to our cabins and flopped on the bunks in a state of drowsy satisfaction. Somehow, fat never formed on our skinny frames. We ran too much. We paddled in the boats. We swam. We cut firewood and played softball after supper. When there was nothing else to do we climbed in the rafters of our cabins, trying to invent complicated monkey swings that no one else could do.

—Thomas Sancton, "The Silver Horn," *Harper's*

As I go back to the block now the back wall of the drug-store still rises up to test me. Every day we smashed a small black viciously hard regulation handball against it with fanatical cuts and drives and slams, beating and slashing at it almost in hatred for the blind strength of the wall itself. I was never good enough at handball, was always practicing some trick shot that might earn me esteem, and when I was weary of trying, would often bat a ball down Chester Street just to get myself to Blake Avenue. I have this memory of playing one-o'-cat by myself in the sleepy twilight, at a moment when everyone else had left the block. . . . I would throw the ball in the air, hit it with my bat, then with perfect satisfaction drop the bat to the ground and run to the next sewer cover. Over and over I did this, from sewer cover to sewer cover, until I had worked my way to Blake Avenue and could see the park.

—Alfred Kazin, *A Walker in the City*

(2) *"How did it feel?"*

A reporter is expected to take in scenes and events, but he looks at them from the outside. We do not expect him to laugh or cry. We do not expect him to feel sorry for himself, or to bubble over with good cheer. The basic difference between a newspaper report and an autobiographical paper is the author's feeling: "This is happening to *me*." An important part of his job is to make his readers understand his attitudes and share his emotions.

How can you make your reader share in something you felt? Try not just to *talk* about what you felt. Make what you felt grow out of the situation, out of the actual incident you describe. Keep your feelings anchored to the people, objects, and scenes that originally brought them about. Stress what you did that *showed* your emotions. We know a person is angry if we see him *act out* his anger — by his frown, his cutting remarks, the way he slams the door on the way out.

Would you agree that in each of the following passages the author does not ask you to take his feelings on trust? *How* does each author help you feel what he felt?

There is only one way to find out accurately human sensations in a ship two or three thousand feet up when the motor quits, and that is actually to experience that gone feeling at the pit of the stomach and the sharp tingling of the skin from head to foot, followed by a sudden amazing sharpness of vision, clear-sightedness, and coolness that you never knew you possessed as you find the question of life or death completely in your own hands. It is not the "you" that you know, but somebody else, a stranger, who noses the ship down, circles, fastens upon the one best spot to sit down, pushes or pulls buttons to try to get her started again, and finally drops her in, safe and sound. And it is only by such experience that you learn likewise of the sudden weakness that hits you right at the back of the knees after you have climbed out and started to walk around her and that comes close to knocking you flat as for the first time since the engine quit its soothing drone you think of destruction and sudden death.

—Paul Gallico, *Farewell to Sport*

Little things that happened during these years seemed of great importance. I remember that in my first year at camp I wore an ill-fitting Boy Scout hat. One of the councillors, a boy five years my senior who seemed to me to belong already to the grown-up world of brilliance and authority, began, in a pleasant way, to tease me about the hat. Every morning for a week he led us to the abandoned logging road and clocked us as we walked and trotted a measured mile. My hat was anchored down by a heavy chin strap; it flopped and sailed about my head as I ran to the finish line. The boy began to laugh at me. He waved his arms and called out, "Come on, you rookie!" The other kids took it up and Rookie became my first nickname. I loved it. I tingled when someone called it out.

I painted it on my belt, carved it in my packing case, inked it into my hatband, and began to sign it to my letters home. Years later when we were grown I knew this camp officer again. The gap between our ages had vanished and in real life now he seemed to me a rather colorless young lawyer. He did not remember about the hat.

—Thomas Sancton, "The Silver Horn," *Harper's*

(3) *"What did it mean?"*

Autobiography gives the author a chance to relive scenes almost forgotten. But it does not merely give him a chance to feel nostalgic. It gives him a chance to *think*. It makes him think about himself, the people close to him, and the society into which he was born. In good autobiographical writing, the author is trying to understand himself. He is writing for an audience, but he is first of all explaining things *to himself*.

When a writer selects one autobiographical incident among many, we assume that it *meant* something. Perhaps it made him understand something important about his parents. Or it made him change his mind about a custom, an institution. Or it revealed something to him about his own weaknesses or strengths.

In the following passage, a well-known American biographer tells about her aged parents. Each of them has come to represent something to her — a way of looking at things, an attitude toward life. Can you see how she stays close to things that actually happened, and yet shows what these things meant to her?

To my father old age spelled tranquillity; he who had been the most active and ambitious of men sat quietly by his window rereading the books he loved best — *Treasure Island, Vanity Fair, The White Company, Moby Dick* — and he read them not for their philosophy or "symbolism" but for the story pure and simple. "Have you read *Captain Fracasse* lately?" he would ask me gravely. "It is delicious. Let me just read you this page, where Agostino sets up the scarecrows in the field. . . . Can you sit down, have you time?"

His absorption and his pleasure in *Aztec Treasure Houses* and *Quentin Durwards* irritated my mother, whose years only increased her native intensity, her relish for each small domestic detail of living. Her hubsand's withdrawal I believe she looked on as something slightly immoral. Once a year my mother's sister (herself in her early eighties) came from New

York to spend a week with us. My mother contrived to make the day of arrival a turmoil such as only visiting queens can look for. Every car that passed our door was Aunt Cecilia's car. I remember one such day when my mother refused her much relished five o'clock cup of tea because the act of setting down the cup would slow her welcoming rush to the front door. My father who for days had been the victim of this mounting excitement of preparation, raised both arms to me across the room and waggled his fingers, smiling resignedly.

For me there was continual fascination in observing these two as they walked slowly toward their end, the one quieter, ever more remote, the other possessed of a kind of ferocious joy — or grief — in each passing moment as though she must savor it wholly, wholly, for it would not come again.

—Catherine Drinker Bowen, "The Magnificence of Age," *Harper's*

As you work on your own autobiographical papers, remember the following cautions:

— *Be selective.* In 400 or 500 words, you cannot write the "story of your life." You *can* tell in detail the story of one major incident that marked a stage in your growing up. Or you can trace two or three key events that changed your mind about a person close to you. Or you can deal with a major stage in the development of one of your beliefs or attitudes: your attitude toward the church in which you grew up, your knowledge of people from backgrounds other than your own.

— *Do not promise your reader more than you are going to deliver.* Some autobiographical papers are all advertising and no product. They keep assuring the reader that the author had a wonderful or hilarious time. But they do not re-create that wonderful time for the reader to share. The following two passages are too much like checks not covered by sufficient funds — they promise much, but they deliver little:

> Late in September the football games begin. No one misses these if possible. It's such a thrill to see our band march down the center of the field and put on a great performance. Of course Bucky Badger is always seen at this time, darting here and there on the field. The climax of the halftime and the band performance is our school song. Everything is quiet while the students sing their song, and end it with a big Rah-Rah.

(What makes the performance of the band so great? Can you describe a specific maneuver that they executed and that impressed you? What does the school song say—and what does it sound like? Did you ever attend a football game when you did *not* feel like shouting Rah-Rah?)

Thanksgiving and Christmas vacations come very quickly. Then everyone is in his happiest moods, wishing everyone a wonderful vacation and saying farewell for a while. Coming back from vacation is almost more fun than the real thing because everyone is anxious to hear and tell what the students did while away from school.

(What actually happened to you during one such "wonderful" vacation? And are vacations *always* fun?)

— *Do not turn your reader against you by being too one-sided.* It is true that your reader will expect you to look at things from your personal point of view. He will expect your paper to reflect *your* likes and dislikes, *your* standards. But even so, you want your reader to put himself in your shoes. You want him to say, "I know how you must have felt." A fair-minded reader will find this hard to do if you *always* blame difficulties on other people, if you *always* call other people self-centered or ignorant — but never yourself.

The following autobiographical passage tells the story of what happened to a Negro boy when, as a senior in high school, he won a prize in a literary contest. The selection concentrates on a single day — on part of an afternoon. The author is setting out to respond to an invitation to meet the other winners at the Arts Club that sponsored the competition. As you read the selection, ask yourself how successfully it answers the questions: "What was it like?" "How did it feel?" "What did it mean?"

PROSE MODEL 2

M. CARL HOLMAN

The Afternoon of a Young Poet

I left school on a hazily bright afternoon alive with the tarry tang of smoke and the green smell of growing things which I associate still with spring in St. Louis. It was good to be a privileged truant with the whole block in front of the school to myself, the typewriters clicking behind me in the principal's office and the unheeded voices of the teachers floating out of the classroom windows overhead. The first trolley was a long time coming. When I got on I remembered to ask for the transfer, and though over half the seats were empty on both trolleys, I stood up all the way. But when I got off the second car I found that I had managed to lose the directions my mother had given me. I could not remember whether I was to go north or south from the trolley stop. My palms promptly began sweating and I took out the letter from the Arts Club, reading the address again as if that would give me a clue. In my neighborhood most of the houses were row houses, or were separated from each other by nothing more than a narrow passageway. Even houses like the one we lived in, though not flush with the pavement, were close enough so that the addresses could be easily read from the sidewalk. But out here the houses were set back from wide lawns under shade trees and there was no way of making out the addresses without going up a long walk to the front door. No small children were playing outside, there were no stores into which a stranger might go and ask directions, and the whole neighborhood was wrapped in a fragrant but forbidding stillness. Remembering that my mother had said the club was only two blocks away from the trolley stop, I started walking south, deciding that if it turned out I was going the wrong way I could always come back and go two blocks in the other direction. I walked three blocks for good measure without finding Westmoreland Place, then turned and started back.

A red-faced old man with bushy military whiskers that reminded me of pictures I had seen of the Kaiser came down one of the walks with a bulldog on a leash. I braced myself to ask him where Westmoreland Place was, but before I could speak, his china blue eyes suddenly glared at me with such venomous hatred that I had the feeling he was about to set the dog on me. I averted my eyes and walked on, trembling suddenly with an answering hatred as senseless as his. Not noticing where I was going, I was about to cross into the next block when I looked up at the street sign and found that I was on Westmoreland Place. It was a street of thick hedges and houses which, if anything, were more inaccessible than those I had already passed. I walked up the street in one direction, then crossed and reversed my course. By now the letter was wilting in my hand. The trolley ride had taken longer than I had estimated and I was sure I was already late. One of the last things my mother had said to me that morning was, "Now try to be sure not to get out there on Colored People's Time." My mind groped for a plausible lie that would let me give up the whole business and go home. I thought of saying that the meeting had been called off, that the place was closed when I got there, that I had caught the wrong car and gone too far out of the way to get back in time. At one point, I almost convinced myself that I should go back to the trolley stop and catch a car that would take me downtown to my old refuge, the main public library. I could stay there reading for an hour or two, then claim I had actually attended the tea. But my spirit quailed at the prospect of inventing answers to all the questions that would follow. And what if in the meantime someone from the club had already called my home or the school? I hated myself for entering the competition and felt sick with envy when I thought of my schoolmates who by now were idling down the halls on free period or dreaming their way through the last classes before the liberating bell.

I was plodding down the same block for the second time when around the corner of a big stone house across the street came an unmistakably colored man in work clothes, uncoiling a garden hose. We might have been the only two living souls on a desert island. Almost faint with relief I angled across the street toward him. But the handyman, his high shiny forehead furrowed in elaborate concentration, adjusted the nozzle and began playing rainbow jets of spray across the grass. I halted at the edge of the lawn and waited for him to take note of my presence. In due time he worked himself close enough so that I was able to ask him if he knew where the Arts Club was. I held out the letter as I asked him, but he merely turned his rusty deepset eyes on me with a look that plainly said, *I hope to God you ain't come out here to make trouble for the rest of us.* In later years I have seen that look in the eyes of Negro businessmen, schoolteachers, college presidents, reverend ministers — and a trio of cooks and dishwashers peering through the swinging doors of a restaurant kitchen at the dark-skinned students sitting at counters where no one of their color ever presumed to sit before.

But I was of another generation, another temperament and state of mind from those students. So when the handyman flicked one hand in the direction from which I had just come and said, "There 'tis, over there," I thanked him — rather thanked his back, which was already turned to me.

I would never have taken the two-story brick building at the end of the flagstone walk to be anything other than the residence of a comfortably well-off family. Just before I pushed the button beside the broad door it occurred to me that the handyman might be playing his notion of a joke on me. Then I looked down at the thick mat on which I was standing and saw the letters "A-C." I pressed the button, waited and was about to press it again when the door swung open. The rake-thin white maid standing there had composed for her plain freckled face a smile of deferential welcome. The smile faded and her body stiffened in the neat gray uniform. For an instant I thought she would close the door in my face, but she braked it so that it was barely ajar and said, "Yes?" I mumbled something and held out the letter. She squinted at the envelope and said, "You wait here." The door closed and I stood there with my face burning, wanting to turn and go away but unwilling to confront the expression of sour satisfaction I expected to see on the face of the handyman across the street. After what seemed fifteen full minutes a gray-haired woman in a blue uniform with starched cuffs came to the door. "All right, what is it now?" she said, sounding like a very busy woman. I held out the letter and she took it, measured me up and down with her shrewd eyes and said to the younger woman hovering behind her, "I'll be right back." The freckle-faced thin one looked miles above my head toward the street but we shared the unspoken understanding that I was not to move from where I stood and that she was to watch me.

I stood rooted there, calling myself every kind of black fool for coming in the first place, my undershirt cleaving to my damp skin. It had become clear to me that I had received the invitation by mistake. And now that I had surrendered the letter, the only proof that I had been invited, my sole excuse for being there at all was gone. I pictured them huddled inside, talking in whispers, waiting for me to have the good sense to leave. Then I heard voices coming toward the door. My keeper faded back into the gloom of the hallway and an attractive woman in her forties held the door open and smiled at me. Everything about her, her fine-textured skin, the soft-colored dress and the necklace she was wearing, her candid gaze, defined an order of relationships which did away with any need for me to deal further with the other two women. "Hello," she said. "So you're the boy who came over to tell us Mr. Holman couldn't come?"

I stared dumbly at her, wondering how I could have been fooled into thinking she was one of those white women my mother would have described approvingly as "a real lady, as nice as they come."

"Please tell him we hope he'll be feeling better soon," the woman said. "We had so hoped to meet him."

"I'm — I got the letter saying to come out here," I blurted. We stood there for a minute staring at one another and then her pink skin flushed red. "Oh, you mean you — oh, I *am* so sorry," she said. "Please do come in. I didn't know." She glanced back at the maids. "I mean, we thought —"

It was finally clear to all of us what she had thought. That the white boy who wrote the poem had been unable to come so his family had thoughtfully sent their colored boy to tender his regrets.

"You come right on in," the woman said. "I'm your hostess. All the others are already here and we've been waiting for you." She drew me inside the cool, dim hallway and guided me up the stairs like an invalid. I could not remember ever walking on such thick carpets. I had a hazy impression of cut flowers in vases, and paintings hanging along the walls like those I had seen in the Art Museum in the park. As she went up she kept on talking, but I made very little of what she was saying because now I could hear the murmur of other voices and laughter coming from the floor above us. I had the feeling that an intimate and very pleasant family party was in progress which we were about to ruin and I wanted to ask my hostess if I might not be excused after all. Instead I let myself be piloted into a sunny high-ceilinged room which at one and the same time seemed as spacious as a playing field and so intimate that no one could move without touching the person beside him. A blur of white faces turned toward us, some of them young, some middle-aged, some older, but all of them clearly belonging to a different world from that of the uniformed women downstairs. A different world from mine. For a flickering moment there was a drop in energy like that sudden dimming of lights during a summer storm and then I was being introduced in a flurry of smiles, bobbing heads and a refrain seeming to consist of variations on "Delightful . . . delighted . . . so good you could come . . . a pleasure."

Whenever I have tried to recollect that afternoon since, the faces in that upstairs room elude me like objects seen through sunlit water. I remember that one of the girls was blonde and turned eagerly from one speaker to another as if anxious not to miss one word, that there was a boy there from a school out in the country who talked and moved with the casual, almost insulting assurance which for a long time afterward I automatically associated with private schools. All of the other students there who had won prizes or honorable mentions in the area-wide competition were either from private schools or from white high schools whose very names were new to me. One of the girls was from a Catholic school and one of the sisters from the faculty had come along with her. I discovered that other winners were accompanied by their teacher and I mentally kicked myself for not realizing that I might have been buttressed by the presence of Miss Armstrong or Mr. Blanton. Certainly they would have been much more at home in this company than I was. Gradually, as cookies, tea and punch were passed and the talk again swirled back and forth, I began to relax somewhat, content to be on the periphery of that closed circle. I kept stealing glances around the room, taking in the wide fireplace and the portrait above the mantel of some famous man whose identity kept eluding me, the rows of books in the recessed shelves along the wall, and the magazines scattered tantalizingly just out of reach on the long oaken table in the center of the room. . . .

Toward the end of the long afternoon, it was proposed that the young writers read their poems. Once again I was plunged into sweaty-palmed agony. My torment only increased as the first two readers read their poems like seasoned professionals, or so it seemed to me. When my turn came I tried to beg off, but the additional attention this focused upon me only increased my discomfort and I plunged in, at first reading too fast and almost inaudibly but finally recollecting some of the admonitions my teachers had dinned into my head in preparation for "recitations" before Negro school and church audiences as far back as the second grade. I had not realized how long a poem it was when I was writing it and I was squirmingly conscious of certain flaws and failures which had never before loomed so large. The applause and praise that followed when I finished, if anything, exceeded that given the others; a situation which, even then, aroused the fleeting suspicion that the dancing bear was being given higher marks than a man might get for the same performance. One of the older women murmured something about Paul Laurence Dunbar. Someone else asked me if I liked Pushkin. I could only look blank, since at that time I knew almost nothing about the great Russian's poetry and even less about his Negro lineage. Inevitably, there was a flattering and irrelevant comparison to Langston Hughes. A wavy-haired gentleman took his pipe out of his mouth to ask if I didn't think "The Negro Speaks of Rivers" was a marvelous poem. I said I certainly did.

—from *Anger, and Beyond*

1. Explain briefly each of the following: *venomous, avert, inaccessible, quail* (vb.), *trio, presume, deferential, tender* (vb.), *elude, periphery, tantalize, lineage.* For which of these can you provide an exact synonym that would fit the context where the word was used? For which of these words is an exact synonym hard to find? Why?

2. How good an observer is the author? Point out half a dozen details that help make the account authentic. Which details help especially to give the passage an "I-was-there" quality?

3. Study the thumbnail portraits of the different persons that appear briefly in this passage. What does the author do to make them seem like real people? Write *three* similar portraits of people you know well or have recently encountered — use no more than three or four sentences for each portrait.

4. Real experiences often turn out different from what we expect. The feelings they produce in us are often contradictory or confused. Point out several striking examples of unexpected or contradictory events, thoughts, and feelings. How real or convincing does the author make them?

5. Much of the author's account is concerned with the thoughts that pass through the boy's mind. Is there any one passage where you felt: "I once felt very much this way myself"? Write a paragraph about a situation that made you experience a similar thought or feeling.

6. What do you think the author learned from this experience? What would you have learned if you had been in his place?

THEME TOPICS 2   A. A German proverb says, "The unhoped-for often happens." Narrate an event (or a series of closely related events) where things went contrary to expectation. For instance, you might write about a childhood prank that turned serious, a project that turned out in an unexpected way, a holiday that departed from tradition, a sporting event or other competition in which you participated and which took an unexpected turn.

B. Lord Chesterfield said in one of his letters that "loud laughter is the mirth of the mob, who are only pleased with silly things; for true wit or good sense never excited a laugh since the creation of the world." Did your own experience ever make you think about the role humor plays in people's lives? Are you the kind of person who makes jokes — or who is the butt of the joke? What do the people you know laugh at — and do you laugh *with* them? Concentrate on one especially meaningful experience, or on several closely related ones.

C. Many nineteenth-century writers deplored idleness and glorified work, which they considered an ennobling experience. But many later writers have stressed the drudgery of work, the dull, deadening fatigue produced by continuous and supervised manual work, and its tendency to drain off all surplus vitality. What does the word *work* mean to you? Draw only on your own experience and observation.

D. British teacher and writer David Daiches, well known in this country, once wrote about his experiences as a Jewish boy in a Scots Presbyterian school. Here is part of what he said:

> At school I did not join in the hymns with which the day's proceedings opened (in the elementary school we did not have prayers in hall, as we were to do in the senior school, but sang an opening hymn in class), though I got to know them perfectly well — "Onward Christian Soldiers," "Once in Royal David's City," and many others. I knew, from my tenderest years, that the theology of these hymns was all wrong and that the Jewish religion was of course *right;* but it was one's duty to be tolerant, and one had a friendly pity for one's non-Jewish companions who actually believed in the divinity of Jesus and dirtied their stomachs with *treife* food. As for my teachers and schoolmates, they had the Presbyterian respect for the People of the Book and regarded me with interest and sometimes even with a touch of awe. —*Two Worlds*

Have you ever been in a situation where you, or someone you came into contact with, were "different" because of religious beliefs or religious affiliations? Or were you, or someone you observed closely, ever an "outsider" in a group for some other reason? What does it feel like to be "different"? Or, what does it feel like to be part of a group that reacts to an "outsider"? Draw on authentic firsthand experience.

E. Margaret Mead, famous for comparisons of primitive and modern ways of life, said twenty-five years ago that there is "great contrast in the lives of the majority of Americans between the pattern of human relationships which they learn at home and the pattern they learn at school and out in the world. In many cases this contrast is a contrast between cultures, between homeways which are Polish or Italian or Irish, or at least stem from a completely different part of the United States, and school and outer-world ways which represent the more standard American culture." Does this contrast still exist to any large extent? Did you experience any such contrast in your own upbringing? Or were the "ways" of home and those of school very closely related? Focus on one major area or possible source of conflict.

F. One of the most famous autobiographical novels in English is Samuel Butler's *The Way of All Flesh*. It traces the bitter quarrel and break between a self-righteous, sanctimonious Victorian father and a son that envied a man who "had been born an orphan, without father, without mother, and without descent." Today again we hear much about the conflicts between parents and their children, about the gap between the generations. Write a paper in which you answer one major question that an objective observer might ask about such conflicts. For instance, is it possible for young people to judge fairly the generation to which their parents belong? Is it possible for young people to "understand" their parents? Why are older people often unsuccessful in explaining their point of view to younger people? Concentrate on one key question, and draw on evidence from your own experience and observation.

G. Phyllis McGinley once said, "When you ask a question of life, it isn't often that you get a straight and immediate answer." Have you ever found this to be true? Have you ever had a serious question to which the answer was hard to find? What kind of answer *did* you find or work out? Discuss the question concretely — bring in the actual incidents, people, or relationships involved.

C3 Writing and Thinking

Make your writing show that you can think a subject through.

The best compliment we can pay a writer is "This has made me think." When we read an article about teen-age marriage, or about unemployment, we want to feel that the writer has taken it seriously. We want him to show that he has thought about it. A good writer has faith that a subject will become more intelligible if he takes a serious look at it. If he seriously thinks about a subject, he knows that he can clarify it somewhat. He can help his readers understand it at least a little better.

How can we tell that a writer has done some serious thinking? How can we tell he is the kind of writer who can help us understand his subject?

(1) *A serious writer uses his own mind.* He shows that he has studied and thought *for himself.* He makes us say, "I didn't think of that. I wasn't aware of that, but now that you point it out, I can

see that it deserves attention." Many people have set ideas about unemployment — mostly they deplore the fact that money has to be "doled out" to people out of work. But the author of the following passage has taken a *new look* at the subject. He asks, not "What does it cost?" but, "What does it do to people?" Can you restate his answer in your own words? Can you see that it is different from what "everybody says"?

> The man who has lost his job is not just out of luck economically; in fact, in a rich country such as ours, the direct economic consequences of unemployment can be minimized almost to the vanishing point. But he is incapable of producing anything, of being effective in society; in short, he is incapable of being a citizen, he is cast out. For he derives his productiveness, his function in the community, his citizenship — at least his effective rather than purely formal citizenship — from his position in the group effort, in the team, in the productive organism. It is this social effect of unemployment, rather than the economic effect, that makes it the major catastrophe it is. That unemployment endangers people's standards of living is, of course, bad enough; but that it endangers their citizenship and self-respect is its real threat.
>
> —Peter F. Drucker, "Henry Ford: Success and Failure"

(2) *A serious writer can show important relationships.* When we report miscellaneous facts to him, he will try to tie them together. He will try to show how they *relate to each other.* He knows how to present two ideas in such a way that we can see the logical link between the two:

— an *effect* and its *cause:*

> Just about everyone likes biography. The *reason* for this is not hard to find. It is the pleasure we get in identifying ourselves with real people who have attained eminence of some sort. By the magic of biography we are transported out of ourselves into kings and queens, generals, poets, lovers, and bankers.

— a general *rule* and a specific *example:*

> Experience has made it quite apparent that marriage calls for mutual sacrifice. Most of the marriages that fail, marriage counselors tell us, fail because the partners lack this quality. Dishwashing, by general agreement, is a classic *example* of

domestic drudgery that requires a sacrifice of the husband who shares in it. It is an excellent test of his willingness to do his share.

— opinions *pro* with opinions *con:*

> Fluoridation of water supplies, a good thing *in my opinion* and that of many experts, has been strongly *opposed by some* nutritionists of considerable reputation, such as Robert Harris, director of the Nutritional Biochemistry Laboratory at M.I.T.

(3) *A serious writer weighs his words.* If we want to decide whether today's students lack "school spirit," we have to agree on what "school spirit" is, and how it is shown. If we want to show that an action taken by a student council is "undemocratic," we must be able to show what *democracy* means — not only in theory, but in practice. We can tell that a writer has done some serious thinking when he can give exact meanings to the key terms connected with his subject.

C 3a Definition

Give exact meaning to key terms by careful definition.

When we start on a difficult job, we make sure that our tools are in good working order. We make sure they are right for the task. The most skillful surgeon cannot perform a delicate operation with a blunt knife. When we start on a difficult *verbal* task, we examine the words we are going to use. We make sure our key terms carry the right message — no less, and no more.

The process of sharpening terms to make them carry the right message is the process of definition. Definition sets exact limits. When we define our terms, we give them exact meanings, so that writer and reader can focus clearly on the point at issue.

Here are typical situations that remind a writer of the need to define key terms:

— A term is not in wide use and is likely to be *unfamiliar* to the average reader. The writer has to ask himself: "Since this term is likely to be a blank for my reader, how can I *fill it in* as fully and clearly as possible?" The most obvious examples of completely unfamiliar terms are words the author has borrowed from another language:

> Some of the intensely close feeling a Mexican Indian child has for his mother is traceable to the omnipresent *rebozo, an oversized, hand-woven stole* that his mother is seldom without. The infant, carried about on her back *in that snug improvised hammock,* is always close to the warmth of his mother's body, and he remains close to her emotionally the rest of her life.

— A *technical* term serves as a convenient label but needs to be made clear to the layman. For instance, an article on conservation of our natural resources may distinguish between "extractable resources"—coal, gas, oil—and "renewable resources"—soil, water, grass, timber, air. The short label is convenient because the writer need not list everything included each time the subject comes up. But without a brief explanation of the key terms, many readers will be confused.

— A *familiar* term covers a whole range of meaning. It remains *vague* unless we specify the exact point on a scale. When we accuse someone of "negligence," we must define what *degree* of carelessness constitutes negligence. Perhaps we would agree that the owner of an apartment house was negligent when he installed a swimming pool without a fence, so that toddlers could fall in and drown. But what if there was a fence, but someone had left the gate unlocked? Would we still call the landlord negligent? When we use the term "anarchy," *how much* absence of regulation constitutes anarchy? Are we going to speak of anarchy if high school students are allowed to grow their hair long, and dress as they please? Would we use the term if students could attend class when they choose, but do something else if they prefer? When *would* such a strong term be justified?

— A familiar term is used by different people in *different ways.* Do the different uses of the word have anything in common? Even if the uses of the word *are* different, are they in some important way related? Here are some passages using a term that seems to mean different things:

> His position on the team reminded him of the story of the man who maintained that the Harvard crew was *democratic*

because after three years everyone in the boat spoke to him
except number seven.   (John P. Marquand)

The strength of *democracy* is its interest in individuals.
                                              (Mark Van Doren)

Democracy is a word which . . . can be made to accommodate almost any collection of social facts we may wish to
carry about in it. In it we can as easily pack a dictatorship
as any other form of government. We have only to stretch the
concept to include any form of government supported by a
majority of the people, for whatever reasons and by whatever
means of expressing assent, and before we know it the empire
of Napoleon, the Soviet regime of Stalin, and the Fascist systems of Mussolini and Hitler are all safely in the bag.
                                              (Carl Becker)

The basis of the Athenian democracy was the conviction
of all democracies — that the average man can be depended
upon to do his duty and to use good sense in doing it. *Trust
the individual* was the avowed doctrine in Athens, and expressed or unexpressed, was common to Greece.
                                              (Edith Hamilton)

— An important term is often *misunderstood,* misapplied, or
abused. What is the right way to use it? The author of the following
passage was bothered by what he thought was a common misunderstanding of "freedom of speech":

While the right to talk may be the beginning of freedom,
the necessity of listening is what makes the right important
. . . What matters is not the utterance of opinions. What matters is the confrontation of opinions in debate. No man can
care profoundly that every fool should say what he likes.
Nothing has been accomplished if the wisest man proclaims
his wisdom in the middle of the Sahara Desert. This is the
shadow. We have the substance of liberty when the fool is
compelled to listen to the wise man and learn; when the wise
man is compelled to take account of the fool, and to instruct
him; when the wise man can increase his wisdom by hearing
the judgment of his peers.   (Walter Lippmann)

How do we go about defining a term that is unclear, or that
has become too vague or contradictory for effective use? As you
work up your own definition of an important term, remember the
following requirements:

(1) *Relate the word to the thing.* An experienced writer instinctively shows us a word in action — he shows us where, when, by whom, and to what it is applied. If you are going to stake out the exact territory that a term covers, you must at least *reach* that territory first. Do you agree that in each of the following passages the author quickly reaches the territory that his key term covers?

Part of the educational program of the high school is carried on outside classrooms, in *"extracurricular"* activities — stamp, chess, art, French, math, Future Farmers, Future Teachers and similar clubs; student government activities and student publications; the school orchestra and band and glee club and Little Players, which give public performances; athletic teams and so forth. —Martin Mayer, *The Schools*

Modern life requires a certain amount of *regimentation.* Individuals obviously cannot be allowed to run amuck. At least the great majority of persons must adapt themselves to other persons. Mechanical contrivances, such as traffic lights, must replace individual judgment; laws are to some extent substitutes for individual choice.

(2) *Look for the common denominator.* Once you have discovered authentic examples of a word in action, you can ask: "What do these different instances have in common?" Sometimes, there may be *one* key feature; in other cases, more. Here, for instance, is a list of examples a writer drew up when he tried to define the term *excellence.* Could you identify one or more features that the examples on this list might have in common?

Confucius teaching the feudal lords to govern wisely . . . Leonidas defending the pass at Thermopylae . . . Saint Francis preaching to the birds at Alviano . . . Lincoln writing the second inaugural "with malice toward none" . . . Mozart composing his first oratorio at the age of eleven . . . Galileo dropping weights from the Tower of Pisa . . . Emily Dickinson jotting her "letters to the world" on scraps on paper . . . Jesus saying, "Father, forgive them; for they know not what they do." . . . Florence Nightingale nursing the wounded at Balaclava . . . Eli Whitney pioneering the manufacture of interchangeable parts . . . Ruth saying to Naomi, "Thy people shall be my people." —John W. Gardner, *Excellence*

Often, a good definition heads straight for the common *element* that the writer has identified. Can you restate in your own words the "common element" identified in each of the following definitions?

The *American Way,* if it means any one thing more than another, means diversity, many powers, no concerted plan, no interest in putting over on anybody else the final strait jacket of a system so as to extort the miserable advantage of lip-service to catchwords. Not that there aren't some few million people among . . . our population who would like to do just what I deny. They may even succeed in their little corner — their family, office, shop or village. The impulse is age-old and will not die in our generation. But on our soil it has a harder time thriving than in most places.

—Jacques Barzun, *God's Country and Mine*

What do I mean by *narrow-mindedness?* I have seen it in many different situations, all of which reveal a preoccupation with the idea of moral standards. Narrow-minded people from what I have observed have one idea of good and another completely different one of what is bad. Everything that happens from day to day will fall either into their strict category of good or the category of bad. There is no between, no median. If something is good, all possibilities of bad are immediately removed. The narrow-minded person is so affected by one small sign of something bad that he fails to remain objective in viewing a situation. He greatly exaggerates the degree of badness that exists. This tendency to misjudge characterizes a narrow mind. Inevitably there will be bad as well as good, and the narrow-minded person as a result will view life from the bad side. —Student Theme

(3) *Pay attention to the attitudes and values built into words.* Pay attention not only to what words are *about,* but also to what they are *for.* Many important terms have a built-in agenda — a call to action, a nudge toward an attitude approved by the author. Usually, we define *integrity, democracy,* or *liberty* to show that they are desirable — and a good definition shows why (or why not). People who define *expediency, anarchy,* or *subversion* usually assume that these are *un*desirable — and again a good definition would show cause.

Can you show that the following definitions of *politics* and *science* reveal attitudes that might differ from those of other speakers or writers?

I have always defined *politics* to mean the science of government, perhaps the most important science, because it involves the art and ability of people to live together.

(Harry Truman)

I define *science* as the organization of our knowledge in such a way that it commands more of the hidden potential in nature. What I have in mind therefore . . . admits no sharp boundary between knowledge and use. There are of course people who like to draw a line between pure and applied science; and oddly, they are often the same people who find art unreal. To them, the word useful is a final arbiter, either for or against a work; and they use this word as if it can mean only what makes a man feel heavier after meals.

(J. Bronowski)

(4) *Try to sum up clearly and exactly what you have found.* A **formal definition** makes the writer sum up in one brief, exact statement the meaning of his key term. It thus makes him pull together what he has discovered. It gives the result to his readers in capsule form, so that they can focus on it, remember it — and argue with it, if necessary.

A formal definition first places the term in a class, or *general category*. It thus tells us what kind of thing we are defining. It then narrows the choices by giving us the *distinctive features* of what we are defining. It thus sets it apart from other things of the same kind. A chipmunk is a type of squirrel (general category) that is smaller than most squirrels and has stripes down its back (distinctive features). A sonnet is a short lyrical poem (general category) that has fourteen lines, usually iambic, and an interlacing rhyme scheme (distinctive features).

Formal definitions therefore use two businesslike steps to stake out the territory a term covers. Such definitions are most effective when the general category does much of the work of narrowing down the term. The distinctive features then rule out similar things that are *not* included. Here are some additional examples:

TERM:	History	
CLASS:	is a recital in chronological order of events	(so is a novel)
FEATURES:	known to have occurred.	(but now fiction is ruled out)

TERM:	Alliteration	
CLASS:	is the repetition of the same or a similar sound	(so is rhyme)
FEATURES:	when it occurs at the beginning of a word or syllable.	(but now rhyme is excluded)
TERM:	A paradox	
CLASS:	is a statement that seems at first glance self-contradictory,	(so is much mere nonsense)
FEATURES:	but that is then found to express a truth.	(now nonsense is excluded)
TERM:	Democracy	
CLASS:	is a form of government	(so are dictatorship and theocracy)
FEATURES:	in which major decisions are made by elected representatives of the people.	(authoritarian governments are ruled out)

(5) *Make your definition clear and convincing with supporting material.* An **extended definition** brings in the examples that show what the definition means in practice. It supplies background; it anticipates possible misunderstandings or confusions. Here are typical kinds of material that a writer might draw on in developing an extended definition of an important term:

HISTORICAL BACKGROUND

In its primary historical significance, *democracy* refers to a form of government and only to government. A government is democratic to the extent that those who are affected by its decisions — leaving aside children — have a share, direct or more often indirect, through election of its agents or representatives, in determining the nature of the decisions.

(Sidney Hook)

KEY EXAMPLE

Galileo hypothesized an experiment which proved that a marble rolling down one slope and then up another could never reach a point higher than its original elevation. Under ideal conditions, Galileo showed, however, that the marble would reach a height equal to its original elevation. This is what we now think of as *conservation of energy* in its simplest form. The energy of position which the marble possesses — because of its elevation — is transformed into energy of motion as it rolls down, and then back to energy of position as the marble rolls up the opposite slope. (Sir George Thompson)

RELATED USES OF THE TERM

Conformity implies agreement and harmony in any endeavor, not merely in the sense of "going along with the crowd." In mathematics the word has the same meaning as *congruity;* one may refer to two geometric figures which are equal in every respect as being "congruous" or "conforming." The term is used in religion to denote religious compliance, especially compliance to a prescribed church ritual.

(Student Theme)

CONTRAST WITH RELATED TERMS

Sentimentality is the evocation of a greater amount of feeling or emotion than is justified by the subject. It must not be confused with *sentiment,* which is merely another name for feeling or emotion, and which lacks the bad connotations of *sentimentality.* Some students confuse these two nouns because the adjective *sentimental* seems to be derived from both. *Sentimental* goes with *sentimentality,* not with *sentiment.* The poet who adopts a sentimental tone becomes more tearful or more ecstatic over his subject than it deserves. The sentimentalist is addicted to worn-out baby shoes, gray-haired mothers, and small animals — subjects certain to evoke an automatic response in a particular kind of reader. (College Textbook)

Writing devoted to definition typically deals with words that are hard to define. We would not feel the *need* to define a word if it had not given us trouble. In the following prose model, an American scholar tries to define one essential quality of popular art and entertainment — as represented, for instance, by slick magazines, Christmas cards, Tin Pan Alley, and the usual Hollywood movie. This passage originally was part of a much longer article. It illustrates a kind of writing that depends on careful distinctions, and that uses words with great care. Study the selection carefully with the help of the questions that follow it. Take your time.

PROSE MODEL 3

ABRAHAM KAPLAN

Sentimentality

Superficial, affected, spurious — this is the dictionary meaning of *sentimental*. So far as feeling goes, it is sentimentality that is most distinctive of popular art. There is a sense, I suppose, in which we could say that all feeling starts as sentiment: however deep down you go you must begin at the surface. The point is that popular art leaves our feelings as it finds them, formless and immature. The objects of sentiment are of genuine worth — cynicism has its own immaturity. But the feelings called forth spring up too quickly and easily to acquire substance and depth. They are so lightly triggered that there is no chance to build up a significant emotional discharge.

Dewey has criticized sentimentality as being disjoined from action, but it is only action within the experience itself that is relevant here. Maintaining a certain psychic distance is essential to the aesthetic attitude. In another connection William James tells of the Russian aristocrat who weeps at the tragedy on the stage while her waiting coachman is freezing to death outside the theater. What makes her tears sentimental is not that she does not hurry to his relief, but that she is incapable of more than the very beginnings of pity even at the play: her eyes are dry within. She is not experiencing a catharsis, for there is scarcely anything there to be purged. She does not participate in the action of the drama but only reacts to it, that is, reenacts feelings she has not made truly her own. The tears are real enough, but they have no reason — only a cause.

In the eighteenth century a "sentiment" meant a moralistic apothegm (as in *The School for Scandal*). The words are full of feeling, but the speaker is not. The object of the sentiment so well defines the feelings called for that the definition itself is mistaken for the feeling. The true man of sentiment is far from being a hypocrite; his feeling is sincere enough as far as it goes, but it goes nowhere. Sentimentality is a mark always of a certain deficiency of feeling; it is always just words, a promise that scarcely begins to move toward fulfillment.

Yet, paradoxically, there is also something excessive about sentimentality. Stephen Pepper has characterized it as a violation of "emotional decorum," an abandonment of proper restraint. But it is easy for us to beg the question of how much is excessive. There are no a priori limits to the intensity of feeling that art can encompass. There is boundless depth in David's cry, "O my son Absalom, my son, my son Absalom! Would I had died instead of you, O Absalom, my son, my son!" No doubt there are those who would find it excessive; undeniably it does not express an Anglo-Saxon attitude, but it is also undeniably free from sentimentality. Cultures may differ in their tolerance for sentimentality, or even proclivity towards it, but the quality itself is not wholly a cultural variable.

It is only an excess of a special kind that is in question here. We must distinguish sentimentality from sensibility, that is, a ready responsiveness to demands on our feelings. Art has no purchase at all on insensibility. Unless a man is capable of being moved, and moved deeply, in circumstances where his antecedent interests are not engaged, art has nothing for him. Of such a man we may well ask, "What's Hecuba to him or he to Hecuba, that he should weep for her?" Sensibility becomes sentimental when there is some disproportion between the response and its object, when the response is indiscriminate and uncontrolled. Emotion, Beethoven once said, is for women, and I think we all understand him; but we are to keep in mind the difference between such women as Elizabeth Bennet and her mother.

It is this difference that we want to get at. Dewey comes very near the mark, I believe, in characterizing sentimentality as "excess of receptivity without perception of meaning." It is this lack of meaning, and not intensity of feeling, that makes the receptivity excessive. Popular art is not sentimental because it evokes so much feeling, but because it calls for so much more feeling than either its artist or audience can handle. The trouble is not too much feeling but too little understanding; there is too little to be understood. The tear-jerker provides an occasion for the tears it invites, but *why* we weep lies outside the occasion and beyond our perception. In art, apprehensions are enlarged; we feel in more detail and in broader perspective. It is in this sense that there is a catharsis: emotions are transcended as we move along the dimension of their meaning from a subjective state to the objective forms in which feeling has become patterned.

The sentimentalist makes himself the standard of proportionality of feeling; the only meaning that matters to him is what he has stored up within. As R. H. Blythe has beautifully

said (in his treatise on *haiku,* I think), sentimentality is loving
something more than God does. It is viewing things in their
significance only for the viewer; his emotions are decisive, and
they are their own justification. . . .

Sentimentality moves in a closed circle around the self.
The emotions released by a stimulus to sentiment satisfy a
proprietary interest, and one which is directed inward. The
important thing is that they are *my* feelings, and what is more,
feelings about *me.* The prototype of sentimentality is self-pity.
Popular art provides subjects and situations that make it easy
to see ourselves in its materials. We await only a signal to rush
into identification. All art invites the self, but it does so in a
way that draws us out of ourselves. Art enlarges and transforms the self that has been brought to the aesthetic encounter.
The aesthetic experience begins with empathy: we must give
ourselves to it. But in the consummation art repays our willing
identification by giving us an identity. We do not see ourselves
in art but truly *find* ourselves there, become what before was
only a bare potentiality. Popular art accepts and discharges
the obligation on our own recognizance. It takes us at face
value, but leaves us to contemplate our own empty features.
Narcissus, W. H. Auden conjectured, was probably a hydrocephalic idiot, who stared into the pool and concluded, "On
me it looks good!" The self-centeredness of popular art is the
measure of our own diminishing.

—from *The Popular Arts: A Critical Reader*

1. Explain briefly each of the following: *spurious, cynicism, aesthetic, catharsis, moralistic, apothegm, decorum, a priori, encompass, proclivity, antecedent, proprietary, empathy, hydrocephalic.*
   Several of the names mentioned in the passage are those of the
   author's fellow scholars. Who are William James, W. H. Auden,
   Narcissus?

2. State in your own words the full meaning of each of the following
   sentences. Pay special attention to the way the author has used
   the italicized terms. In this context, does each term mean something *different* from a more common or more familiar use?

   "Sentimentality is not wholly a cultural *variable.*"
   "Art has no *purchase* at all on insensibility."
   "In art, *apprehensions* are enlarged."
   "The *prototype* of sentimentality is self-pity."
   "In the *consummation* art repays our willing identification by
   giving us an identity."

3. *How* does the author go about pinning down his key term? Identify three different tasks he performs, or different avenues he explores, in trying to give exact meaning to the term *sentimentality*.
4. Does the author succeed in identifying one key feature of *sentimentality?* Or are several *related* features necessary? Sum up in your own words the results of the author's investigation.
5. In other parts of the same article, the author used the following terms: *soap opera, sensational, highbrow, romance, escapist.* Write a formal definition for each of these, making it as clear and exact as you can. Compare your definitions with those of your classmates.
6. Write a paragraph in which you restate in your own words the author's distinction between *sentiment, sensibility,* and *sentimentality.* (You may wish to compare the definitions of these terms given in your dictionary.)

EXERCISE 18 In the following passages, what do you think would be the full meaning of the italicized terms? For each term, write a brief definition that would fit the *context*.

1. The many clubs that form part of the extracurricular activities in high school are essentially *middle-class;* they mirror typical features of the community's culture.
2. The truth is rarely *pretty,* though often *beautiful.*
3. The principal insisted on *conservative* dress for high school students.
4. Much literature of the Middle Ages shows people in the grip of *superstition.*
5. There are some situations in which democratic processes may be inappropriate to the proper performance of function, e.g., in an army. Yet even here we know what we mean to impart by the term when we say that one army is or could be more *democratic* than another. (Sidney Hook)
6. There is nothing immoral about adapting one's style of conversation so as to please different people. A person who humors different people is not a hypocrite. To adapt oneself to the expectations of others is a matter of *manners,* not of *morals.*

EXERCISE 19 How, and how successfully, do the authors of the following passages give a full and clear meaning to the italicized key terms?

1. To most Americans, *conservation* is the attempt to preserve parks and open spaces, so that man living in an industrial society can keep in contact with nature. The more crowded our cities, the

more cluttered our roadsides, the more choking and eye-smarting the air, the more we need grass and trees, birds, running streams, and quiet woods.

2. Up to only a generation ago, most villages were to a great extent *self-sufficient* communities. Every trade was represented by its local technician; the local produce was consumed or exchanged in the neighborhood; the inhabitants worked on the spot. If they desired instruction or entertainment or religion, they had to mobilize the local talent and produce it themselves.

3. *Figurative language* . . . does not merely embellish or decorate a thought. A figurative statement is not a more effective or more vivid way of saying something that could be just as well said literally. Compare, for instance, "Shut up!" (an implicit metaphor that likens a human being to a box and thus takes from him all his humanity) and "Stop speaking!" These two commands do not say the same thing; they are not interchangeable. Similarly, the command "Don't butt in!" compares a human being with a goat and is thus not the equivalent of "Don't interfere in my affairs."

4. For this is not the liberty which we can hope, that no grievance ever should arise in the commonwealth — that let no man in this world expect; but when complaints are freely heard, deeply considered, and speedily reformed, then is the utmost bound of *civil liberty* attained that wise men look for. (John Milton)

5. A reporter doesn't have to be a philosopher to know that *"the facts"* do not necessarily represent the *truth,* and that neither one of them necessarily represents the *news.* That men should live at peace with one another might be described as truth, but it is not a fact, nor is it news. That a certain number of children were born yesterday in Chicago is a fact, and the truth, but not news. Journalism involves an effort to discover, select, and assemble certain facts in a way that will be not only reasonably true but reasonably interesting — and therefore reasonably salable.

THEME TOPICS 3   A. What is your idea of a truly "feminine" woman — or of a truly "masculine" man? For instance, is there one indispensable feminine quality that a true woman must have? Should she depend on masculine support and protection as a member of the "weaker sex"? Or, is it unmanly for a man to be charming, graceful, polite, kind, forgiving? Must a truly manly man be athletic or an outdoor type?

   B. Have you ever tried to draw a clear line between two overlapping terms? Try to distinguish clearly between the two terms in one of the following pairs: "love" and "affection"; "vanity" and "pride"; "faith" and "bigotry."

C. A term like *crime* is a very general label covering many different kinds of activities. When we talk about "crime statistics," we lump all of these activities together. But, in the words of one sociologist, "if we asked instead for the cause of crime, we should at once realize that *crime* is an umbrella term held over the heads of some extraordinarily different kinds of things." Can you show that *crime* is indeed such an umbrella term? Can you nevertheless identify one or more important common elements? Or, if you wish, write about another umbrella term that is applied to a great variety of different things. Choose one of the following: *controversial, modern, bad taste.*

D. American historians like Frederick Jackson Turner have identified "individualism, working for good and for evil," as a dominant trait of the American national character, inherited at least in part from the days when the life of the frontier put a premium on self-reliance. How would you define *individualism* as it works in American life today? What role does it play in the life of the average person? Use detailed examples from your own observation and experience.

E. H. L. Mencken once defined radicals as "humorless persons who take the platitudes of democracy seriously." What did he mean? Write your own definition of a "radical," taking issue — or agreeing — with Mencken.

F. [Optional] In recent years, many young people have taken to using words like the following as loosely defined terms of abuse: *racism, fascism, imperialism, colonialism, capitalism.* Select one of these. What does the term mean? What is its history? How appropriate is its use in current political controversy?

C 3b Generalization

Formulate careful generalizations and support them effectively.

Much of the thinking that a writer does goes into his setting up of generalizations. Another large part of his thinking goes into his supporting the generalizations he has set up. The following are examples of the generalizations we encounter when we study a writer's work:

— An early traveler to the United States reports that many educational opportunities are open to American women and that they are free "to go out of the home to agitate for temperance, anti-slavery, and other reforms."

— An English writer, criticizing his countrymen, writes that in England military leaders are more admired than scientists or poets.

— An American playwright says in a magazine article that the cowboy in American Westerns does not stand for the actual historical past, but for what people *want* to believe the past was like.

— A prominent educator claims that students who want to do well in high school are ridiculed or otherwise discouraged by their less ambitious classmates.

These statements and claims are not concerned with individual instances. They do not report incidents like "Smith said that he admired General Eisenhower" or "Fred called me a grind for wanting an A on my geography test." Instead, each statement represents a generalization that someone has produced by *totaling* up many individual observations.

The kind of thinking that produces generalizations from individual observations is called inductive thinking, or **induction.** Induction is part of the standard procedure not only of the writer but also of the scientist, the market research specialist, and many another expert. Here is how a famous British scientist described the inductive process:

> Suppose you go into a fruiterer's shop, wanting an apple — you take up one, and, on biting it, you find it is sour; you look at it, and see that it is hard and green. You take up another one, and that too is hard, green, and sour. The shopman offers you a third; but, before biting it, you examine it, and find that it is hard and green, and you immediately say that you will not have it, as it must be sour, like those that you have already tried.... You found that, in two experiences, hardness and greenness in apples went together with sourness. It was so in the first case, and it was confirmed by the second. True, it is a very small basis, but still it is enough to make an induction from; you generalize the facts, and you expect to find sourness in apples where you get hardness and greenness. You found upon that a general law, that all hard and green apples are sour; and that, so far as it goes, is a perfect induction.
>
> —T. H. Huxley, "The Method of Scientific Investigation"

In order to recognize generalizations in your own writing, you will have to distinguish between the *process* of induction, and the end *result*. In the process of induction, we typically gather the different observations first, and then total them up. Here, for instance, are observations that a zoologist might have collected concerning the migrations of fish. When these observations are put together, they add up to a general pattern:

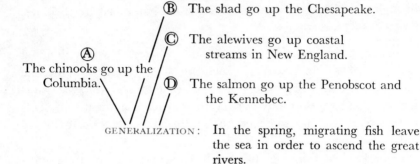

Ⓑ The shad go up the Chesapeake.

Ⓒ The alewives go up coastal streams in New England.

Ⓐ
The chinooks go up the
Columbia.

Ⓓ The salmon go up the Penobscot and the Kennebec.

GENERALIZATION: In the spring, migrating fish leave the sea in order to ascend the great rivers.

In writing, we usually present the *result* first. We usually give the sum first — and then show what we have added up. Here is a paragraph that follows the familiar pattern of "generalization-first":

GENERALIZATION:

OBSERVATION A:

OBSERVATION B:

OBSERVATION C:
OBSERVATION D:

In the *spring the sea is filled with migrating fishes, some of them bound for the mouths of great rivers, which they will ascend to deposit their spawn.* Such are the spring-run chinooks coming in from the deep Pacific feeding grounds to breast the rolling flood of the Columbia, the shad moving in to the Chesapeake and the Hudson and the Connecticut, the alewives seeking a hundred coastal streams of New England, the salmon feeling their way to the Penobscot and the Kennebec. For months or years these fish have known only the vast spaces of the ocean. Now the spring sea and the maturing of their own bodies lead them back to the rivers of their birth.

—Rachel Carson, *The Sea Around Us*

We usually write as if the reader had said to us: "Tell me first how it *comes out*. You can tell me later how you *arrived* there." Here are two additional passages that follow the pattern of "generalization-first":

GENERALIZATION: *One of the most interesting and engaging char-
                     acteristics of island species is their extraordinary
                     tameness* — a lack of sophistication in dealings
                     with the human race, which even the bitter teach-
                     ings of experience do not quickly alter. When
A: Robert Cushman Murphy visited the island of
                     South Trinidad in 1913 with a party from the brig
                     Daisy, terns alighted on the heads of the men in
                     the whaleboat and peered inquiringly into their
B: faces. Albatrosses on Laysan, whose habits include
                     wonderful ceremonial dances, allowed naturalists
                     to walk among their colonies and responded with
                     a grave bow to similar polite greetings from the
C: visitors. When the British ornithologist David Lack
                     visited the Galapagos Islands, a century after Dar-
                     win, he found that the hawks allowed themselves
                     to be touched, and the flycatchers tried to remove
                     hair from the heads of the men for nesting mate-
                     rial. "It is a curious pleasure," he wrote, "to have
                     the birds of the wilderness settling upon one's
                     shoulders, and the pleasure could be much less rare
                     were man less destructive."

                                  —Rachel Carson, *The Sea Around Us*

GENERALIZATION: *All artists quiver under the lash of adverse
                     criticism.* Rachmaninoff's first symphony was a
A: failure. So Rachmaninoff took sick (and I mean,
                     took sick) and lay around on sofas for a year,
                     without writing one measure of music. He was
                     twenty-two at the time. But he recovered, and
                     wrote much music. When Beethoven heard that
B: a certain conductor refused to perform one of his
                     symphonies, he went to bed and stayed there until
C: the symphony was performed. Charles Dickens was
                     forever defending himself against criticism, writing
                     letters to the press and protesting that he was mis-
                     understood. Yet neither criticism nor misunder-
                     standing stopped his output. "Dickens," said G. K.
                     Chesterton, "was the character whom anybody can
                     hurt and nobody can kill."

               —Catherine Drinker Bowen, "The Nature of the Artist," *Atlantic*

Your basic task in presenting a generalization is to convince
your readers that it resulted from a genuine process of induction.
You have to show that your general statement is an *earned* gen-

eralization. You do so by producing at least some of the observations on which it was originally based. Since often generalizations are the end result of countless individual observations, you are in the position of a coach at a football game: You can pull your most promising players off the bench. You can support your generalizations with those specific observations most likely to strike your reader as authentic, relevant, and important.

Here are typical kinds of supporting material for the generalizations that you might present to your reader:

GENERAL IDEA: Nobody is perfect.

SPECIFIC   That's why the pencil manufacturer equips pencils
APPLICATION: with erasers.

GENERAL IDEA: British schoolboys used to be subjected to strict discipline.

DETAILED   When I was eight or so, we were given weekly arith-
EXAMPLE: metic tests in preparation for the examinations two
                years later, which would grant or forbid us high-
                school careers. School began at eight-thirty, but we
                were encouraged to begin earlier (more overtime!)
                and some of my schoolmates were so intimidated
                that they would come at six o'clock in the morning.
                While we worked, the headmaster would move
                along unceasingly behind the rows of seats, slapping
                us with great vigor if we made a mistake or were
                in the process of making one. At ten-thirty he took
                the papers away, and came back in the afternoon to
                work through the problems with us. We got a cut
                with the cane for each one wrong.

GENERAL IDEA: There is no point in inflicting harsh punishment on
                adolescents who have been subjected to irrational
                violence all their lives.

CASE HISTORY: The judge's voice boomed through the courtroom
                as he said, "I'm going to put you on probation in
                the custody of your parents. But I'll tell you this —
                if any boy of mine ever got caught smoking mari-
                juana in the school washroom, I'd flog the hide off
                him with a horsewhip." The boy before the judge
                slowly rolled up the sleeve of his shirt. On his upper
                arm was a cluster of livid welts and blue-black

bruises. "There's more of the same," the boy said, "on my back and shoulders, Judge. My old man's been doing just what you said twice a week for the last five years."

GENERAL IDEA: In America, pleasure and entertainment are big business.

STATISTICAL EVIDENCE: Leaders of our entertainment industry are the best paid men and women in the United States. Last year, the American people spent nearly thirty billion dollars for alcoholic beverages, theater and movie tickets, tobacco, cosmetics, and jewelry. We spend as much for moving pictures as for churches, more for beauty shops than for social service.

GENERAL IDEA: We are too afraid to rely on ourselves as our own authorities.

SUPPORTING ANECDOTE: There is a story about Thomas Hardy using the word "smalling" while writing something, and then wondering whether there was any literary warrant for the word. So he went to the big Oxford Dictionary and found that one well-known writer had used it previously: Thomas Hardy.

When you generalize, you expect your reader to say: "Yes — on the basis of the experience you describe, or the evidence you cite, your general conclusion seems justified." When your reader *refuses* to accept one of your generalizations, it is likely to suffer from one of the following shortcomings:

(1) *Beware of sweeping generalizations.* Many generalizations go too far too fast. It is hard to formulate generalizations that are really true of *all* Americans, *all* teen-agers, *all* businessmen. American high schools being as diverse as they are, it is hard to generalize about "the American high school." The *less* we know about Puerto Ricans, or Englishmen, or Swedes, the more tempted we are to make sweeping generalizations about all of them. The *more* we find out about a group, the more aware we become of important differences that set its members apart.

Can you see why each of the following statements would make a skeptical reader say, "Not so fast"? Can you think of exceptions that would make a cautious writer restate the generalization more cautiously?

SWEEPING: Teen-agers today become aware of adult problems sooner than they used to. In the leisurely world of our grandparents, children were allowed to remain children for a few years longer than is the case today.

SWEEPING: The typical hero of the modern novel, story, or play is a drunk, a dope addict, or a sex pervert. He suffers from one or many neuroses and has a persecution complex and an overprotective mother. He is, in fact, a type of anti-hero.

SWEEPING: The average American is unwilling to assume responsibility for the state of the rest of the world. While news commentators discuss famine or civil war abroad, he thinks about what type of fall suit to buy or speculates about the outcome of next Saturday's football game.

(2) *Beware of repeating ready-made generalizations at second hand.* The following statements are of the kind that will make many readers say: "Where have I heard this before? Have you really checked this general idea against your own experience and observation? Can you think of important instances where this turned out to be true?"

Money cannot buy happiness. The harried business executive who thinks only in financial terms is not a happy man.
We did not shape this world; we are merely the products of an environment we never made.
Americans are passionately dedicated to the cause of freedom.
People who want to enjoy freedom must first learn to shoulder responsibility.

(3) *Beware of presenting several undeveloped generalizations at one time.* Some writing skips too easily from one general statement to another. The reader feels like saying: "Stop! Keep your 'abstraction count' down! Give us one general term, or one general idea, at a time — and then follow it up with a 'for instance'!" Here is the kind of writing that is all generalization and no support:

Yes, only through my ancestors' *courage, hardships,* and many struggles have I gained my *freedoms.* Only through their *stoutness of heart* and *soul* has my America become the *great* and *true* land it is today. My eyes, as they see the *beauty* and *wonder* of this *beautiful* land, are amazed by the *magnificence* of it all. They see Indian Summer with its *beautiful* colors over all the land, and it becomes more of a reality to me that had it not been for those *courageous* and struggling people I would not have my great American *heritage.*

The following prose model shows a responsible writer in the process of working out carefully limited generalizations. George Orwell, author of *Animal Farm* and *1984,* wrote the following account of English national traits in 1941. At the time, totalitarian regimes in Germany, Italy, Japan, and Russia offered a striking contrast with the traditional ways the British have cherished over the centuries. As you study the selection, look for the generalizations the author presents. How has he arrived at them? How does he support them? Answer the questions that follow the selection.

PROSE MODEL 4

GEORGE ORWELL

England Your England

National characteristics are not easy to pin down, and when pinned down they often turn out to be trivialities or seem to have no connection with one another. Spaniards are cruel to animals, Italians can do nothing without making a deafening noise, the Chinese are addicted to gambling. Obviously such things don't matter in themselves. Nevertheless, nothing is causeless, and even the fact that Englishmen have bad teeth can tell one something about the realities of English life.

Here are a couple of generalisations about England that would be accepted by almost all observers. One is that the English are not gifted artistically. They are not as musical as the Germans or Italians, painting and sculpture have never flourished in England as they have in France. Another is that, as Europeans go, the English are not intellectual. They have a horror of abstract thought, they feel no need for any philosophy or systematic "world-view." Nor is this because they are "practical," as they are so fond of claiming for themselves. One has only to look at their methods of town-planning and water-supply, their obstinate clinging to everything that is out of date and a nuisance, a spelling system that defies analysis and a system of weights and measures that is intelligible only to the compilers of arithmetic books, to see how little they care about mere efficiency. But they have a certain power of acting without taking thought. Their world-famed hypocrisy — their double-faced attitude towards the Empire, for instance — is bound up with this. Also, in moments of supreme crisis the whole nation can suddenly draw together and act upon a species of instinct, really a code of conduct which is understood by almost everyone, though never formulated. The phrase that Hitler coined for the Germans, "a sleep-walking people," would have been better applied to the English. Not that there is anything to be proud of in being a sleepwalker.

But here it is worth noticing a minor English trait which is extremely well marked though not often commented on, and that is a love of flowers. This is one of the first things that one notices when one reaches England from abroad, especially if one is coming from southern Europe. Does it not contradict the English indifference to the arts? Not really, because it is found in people who have no esthetic feelings whatever. What it does link up with, however, is another English characteristic which is so much a part of us that we barely notice it, and that is the addiction to hobbies and spare-time occupations, the *privateness* of English life. We are a nation of flower-lovers, but also a nation of stamp-collectors, pigeon-fanciers, amateur carpenters, coupon-snippers, darts-players, crossword-puzzle fans. All the culture that is most truly native centres round things which even when they are communal are not official — the pub, the football match, the back garden, the fireside and the "nice cup of tea." The liberty of the individual is still believed in, almost as in the nineteenth century. But this has nothing to do with economic liberty, the right to exploit others for profit. It is the liberty to have a home of your own, to do what you like in your spare-time, to choose your own amusements instead of having them chosen for you from above. The most hateful of all names in an English ear is Nosey Parker. It is obvious, of course, that even this purely private liberty is a lost cause. Like all other modern peoples, the English are in process of being numbered, labelled, conscripted, "coordinated." But the pull of their impulses is in the other direction, and the kind of regimentation that can be imposed on them will be modified in consequence. No party rallies, no Youth Movements, no coloured shirts, no Jew-baiting or "spontaneous" demonstrations. No Gestapo either, in all probability.

But in all societies the common people must live to some extent *against* the existing order. The genuinely popular culture of England is something that goes on beneath the surface, unofficially and more or less frowned on by the authorities. One thing one notices if one looks directly at the common people, especially in the big towns, is that they are not puritanical. They are inveterate gamblers, drink as much beer as their wages will permit, are devoted to bawdy jokes, and use probably the foulest language in the world. They have to satisfy these tastes in the face of astonishing, hypocritical laws (licensing laws, lottery acts, etc., etc.) which are designed to interfere with everybody but in practice allow everything to happen. Also, the common people are without definite religious belief, and have been so for centuries. The Anglican Church never had a real hold on them, it was simply a preserve of the landed gentry, and the Nonconformist sects only influenced minorities. And yet they have retained a deep tinge of Christian feeling, while almost forgetting the name of Christ. The power-worship which is the new religion of Europe, and which has infected the English intelligentsia, has never touched the common people. They have never caught up with power politics. The "realism" which is preached in Japanese and Italian newspapers would horrify them. One can learn a good deal about the spirit of England from the comic coloured postcards that you see in the windows of cheap stationers' shops. These things are a sort of diary upon which the English people have unconsciously recorded themselves. Their old-fashioned outlook, their graded snobberies, their mixture of bawdiness and hypocrisy, their extreme gentleness, their deeply moral attitude to life, are all mirrored there.

The gentleness of the English civilisation is perhaps its most marked characteristic. You notice it the instant you set foot on English soil. It is a land where the bus conductors are good-tempered and the policemen carry no revolvers. In no country inhabited by white men is it easier to shove people off the pavement. And with this goes something that is always written off by European observers as "decadence" or hypocrisy, the English hatred of war and militarism. It is rooted deep in history, and it is strong in the lower-middle class as well as the working class. Successive wars have shaken it but not destroyed it. Well within living memory it was common for "the redcoats" to be booed at in the street and for the landlords of respectable public-houses to refuse to allow soldiers on the premises. In peace-time, even when there are two million unemployed, it is difficult to fill the ranks of the tiny standing army, which is officered by the county gentry and a specialized stratum of the middle class, and manned by farm labourers and slum proletarians. The mass of the people are without military knowledge or tradition, and their attitude towards war is invariably defensive. No politician could rise to power by promising them conquests or military "glory," no Hymn of Hate has ever made any appeal to them. In the 1914-18 war the songs which the soldiers made up and sang of their own accord were not vengeful but humorous and mock-defeatist. The only enemy they ever named was the sergeant-major.

In England all the boasting and flag-wagging, the "Rule Britannia" stuff, is done by small minorities. The patriotism of the common people is not vocal or even conscious. They do not retain among their historical memories the name of a single military victory. English literature, like other literatures, is full of battle-poems, but it is worth noticing that the ones that have won for themselves a kind of popularity are always a tale of disasters and retreats. There is no popular poem about Trafalgar or Waterloo, for instance. Sir John Moore's army at Corunna, fighting a desperate rear-guard action before escaping overseas (just like Dunkirk!) has more appeal than a brilliant victory. The most stirring battle-poem in English is about a brigade of cavalry which charged in the wrong direction. . . .

And yet the gentleness of English civilisation is mixed up with barbarities and anachronisms. Our criminal law is as out of date as the muskets in the Tower. Over against the Nazi Storm Trooper you have got to set that typically English figure, the hanging judge, some gouty old bully with his mind rooted in the nineteenth century, handing out savage sentences. In England until recently people were still hanged by the neck and flogged with the cat o' nine tails. Both of these punishments are obscene as well as cruel, but there has never been any genuinely popular outcry against them. People accept them (and Dartmoor, and Borstal) almost as they accept the weather. They are part of "the law," which is assumed to be unalterable.

Here one comes upon an all-important English trait: the respect for constitutionalism and legality, the belief in "the law" as something above the State and above the individual, something which is cruel and stupid, of course, but at any rate *incorruptible*.

It is not that anyone imagines the law to be just. Everyone knows that there is one law for the rich and another for the poor. But no one accepts the implications of this, everyone takes it for granted that the law, such as it is, will be respected, and feels a sense of outrage when it is not. Remarks like "They can't run me in; I haven't done anything wrong," or "They can't do that; it's against the law," are part of the atmosphere of England. The professed enemies of society have this feeling as strongly as anyone else. One sees it in prison-books like Wilfred Macartney's *Walls Have Mouths* or Jim Phelan's *Jail Journey,* in the solemn idiocies that take place at the trials of Conscientious Objectors, in letters to the papers from eminent Marxist professors, pointing out that this or that is a "miscarriage of British justice." Everyone believes in his heart that the law can be, ought to be, and, on the whole, will be impartially administered. The totalitarian idea that there is no such thing as law, there is only power, has never taken root. Even the intelligentsia have only accepted it in theory.

An illusion can become a half-truth, a mask can alter the expression of a face. The familiar arguments to the effect that democracy is "just the same as" or "just as bad as" totalitarianism never take account of this fact. All such arguments boil down to saying that half a loaf is the same as no bread. In England such concepts as justice, liberty, and objective truth are still believed in. They may be illusions, but they are very powerful illusions. The belief in them influences conduct, national life is different because of them. In proof of which, look about you. Where are the rubber truncheons, where is the castor oil? The sword is still in the scabbard, and while it stays there corruption cannot go beyond a certain point. The English electoral system, for instance, is an all but open fraud. In a dozen obvious ways it is gerrymandered in the interest of the monied class. But until some deep change has occurred in the public mind, it cannot become *completely* corrupt. You do not arrive at the polling booth to find men with revolvers telling you which way to vote, nor are the votes miscounted, nor is there any direct bribery. Even hypocrisy is a powerful safeguard. The hanging judge, that evil old man in scarlet robe and horsehair wig, whom nothing short of dynamite will ever teach what century he is living in, but who will at any rate interpret the law according to the books and will in no circumstances take a money bribe, is one of the symbolic figures of England. He is a symbol of the strange mixture of reality and illusion, democracy and privilege, humbug and decency, the subtle network of compromises, by which the nation keeps itself in its familiar shape.

—from *A Collection of Essays*

1. Explain briefly: *communal, conscripted, inveterate, intelligentsia, anachronism, legality*. Who or what are the "landed gentry," "Nonconformist sects," "public-houses," "stationers' shops," the "Tower"? Are there any other references that would have to be explained to a reader not familiar with British institutions?

2. Identify several of the author's most significant generalizations and show how they are supported. Can you identify one or two that are *not* supported?

3. Can you point out one or more striking examples of *cautious* generalization? Look for general statements that are especially carefully qualified — with exceptions or complications carefully noted.

4. Orwell cites typically "British" expressions like "They can't do that; it's against the law." Can you collect half a dozen typically "American" expressions? Do they have anything in common? (Your teacher may ask you to write a paper discussing the expressions you have found.)

5. Orwell describes the "hanging judge" as a typical English figure. Write a paragraph about a similar representative figure in *American* life.

6. Orwell knows how to call attention to surface characteristics and then give them a deeper significance. Note for instance what he says about the Englishman's love of flowers. Write a paragraph about a surface characteristic of American life that to you reveals something important about Americans or their way of life.

7. Does this selection have an overall plan? Prepare a rough outline of the major points covered by the author.

EXERCISE 20 What kind of material would you look for if you were asked to support (or challenge) the following generalizations? What difficulty would you expect to encounter in trying to find relevant and convincing material? Which of these generalizations would be the hardest to support?

1. Over the years, nonfiction books have more and more replaced the novel as the favorite reading matter of the general public.

2. The young are so completely fascinated by their own monologues that they have to approach thirty before they even stop long

enough to notice that nobody is listening. All young people use monologue, particularly young males, more than young females.

3. Public opinion almost always supports the President against Congress.

4. Children who have been conditioned to listen passively most of the day to the warm verbal communications coming from the TV screen, to the deep emotional appeal of the so-called TV personality, are often unable to respond to real persons because they arouse so much less feeling than the skilled actor.

5. School districts with a large proportion of children from Spanish-speaking families now welcome teachers who are themselves bilingual.

6. Experience makes us see an enormous difference between piety and goodness. (Blaise Pascal)

7. The Roosevelt administration for many years was unwilling to antagonize the Nazi regime.

8. When a first offender is sentenced to a long prison term, he is likely to return to society as a hardened criminal.

9. Most young people get married on the basis of physical attraction.

10. Most people who go to church on Sunday live the rest of the week without letting religious ideas or principles influence their lives.

EXERCISE 21 The following passage is an excerpt from Ralph Waldo Emerson's "English Traits." Study the single-minded way it supports the initial generalization with a massive array of examples. Using this paragraph as a model, write an account of one common trait of a group you know well: high school students, policemen, farmers, farm workers, dropouts, immigrants, or the like.

The bias of the nation is a passion for utility. They love the lever, the screw and pulley, the Flanders draught-horse, the waterfall, wind-mills, tide-mills; the sea and the wind to bear their freight ships . . . . They are heavy at the fine arts, but adroit at the coarse; not good in jewelry or mosaics, but the best iron-masters, colliers, wool-combers and tanners in Europe. They apply themselves to agriculture, to draining, to resisting encroachments of sea, wind, travelling sands, cold and wet sub-soil; to fishery, to manufacture of indispensable staples — salt, plumbago, leather, wool, glass, pottery and brick — to bees and silkworms — and by their steady combinations they succeed. A manufacturer sits down to dinner in a suit of clothes which was wool on a sheep's back at sunrise. You dine with a gentleman on venison, pheasant, quail, pigeons, poultry, mushrooms and pine-apples, all the growth of his estate. They are neat husbands for ordering all their tools pertaining to house and field. All are well kept. There is no want and no waste. They study use and fitness in their building, in the order of their dwellings and in their dress. The Frenchman invented the ruffle; the Englishman added the shirt. The Englishman wears a sensible coat buttoned to the chin, of rough but solid and lasting texture. If he is a lord, he dresses a little worse than a commoner. They have diffused the taste for plain substantial hats, shoes and coats through Europe. They think him the best dressed man whose dress is so fit for his use that you cannot notice or remember to describe it.

THEME TOPICS 4 A. Write an imaginary portrait of one of the following: "The man the typical American voter would trust"; "the man the typical American high school girl would like to marry"; "the ideal minister for the typical American congregation"; "the woman most likely to succeed in American business (or politics)."

B. An actor who had starred in many Hollywood Westerns once said: "I think Westerns have fed the public a false concept of the West. Kids around the world are growing up thinking one man will always ride into town to fight their battles while the rest of the community sits on its collective hands. In many of the television shows and Western movies, the hero is a kind of father-figure who fights alone for justice against the entire community." What general idea of "justice" would a viewer derive from current Western movies and television shows? Or, what general ideas about "crime" would a viewer derive from crime movies and shows? Use detailed examples.

C. Among the qualities that the British have often claimed as national traits are fairness, practicality, and common sense. Select *one* of these. Show whether it could be justly claimed as a typical feature of *American* life as you know it. •

D. Among the *un*favorable traits that the English are accused of, the most frequently mentioned is hypocrisy. What would you select as the most typical unfavorable trait of Americans? Make sure your paper will strike an impartial reader as a *fair* account. Use detailed examples.

E. Arthur Miller once said, "Any people has a conventional idea of what they are like. Americans fancy themselves, for instance, to be openhanded, on the side of justice, a little bit careless about what they buy, wasteful, but essentially good guys, optimistic." In your experience, what is the trait that Americans most often claim for themselves? Use evidence from speeches you have heard, editorials you have read, conversations you have participated in, and the like.

F. About the national symbols of England, E. M. Forster once said that "the national figure of England is Mr. Bull with his top hat, his comfortable clothes, his substantial stomach, and his substantial balance at the bank. Saint George may caper on banners and in the speeches of politicians, but it is John Bull who delivers the goods." Examine and discuss two or three national symbols that reveal different (and perhaps contradictory) aspects of *American* life.

G. Young people are often accused of a "lack of respect for authority." In your own experience, has authority been worthy of respect? What qualities do you require in the kind of authority that you would respect? Refer in detail to actual incidents and experiences on which your generalizations are based.

C 3c Argument

Learn how to present a convincing argument to the reader.

Argument shows relationships between ideas. It examines general idea *A* and general idea *B* and then shows how the two ideas, put together, help us reach general idea *C*. When someone presents an honest argument, his attitude is: "Here are certain things we know — certain things we can agree on. Now here are the logical conclusions that we should draw from what we know." An argument has reached its goal when a writer can honestly say *"Therefore,* we must conclude...," or *"Thus* we see...," or *"Hence,* it follows that...."

Aldous Huxley, the author of *Brave New World,* once wrote an article on how more citizens could take an active part in democratic self-government. He structured his argument as follows:

BASIC PRINCIPLE (accepted by most of his readers):
> Practice in self-government is necessary for men who want to be truly free. There can be no true democracy if people do not assume responsibility; if they are used to passive obedience.

MAJOR OBJECTION (could easily be shown to be true, and is known to most readers):
> Most voters are not really informed about the long-range issues of national economic policy and foreign affairs. Many of them can take an intelligent interest only in short-range, small-scale problems.

LOGICAL CONCLUSION (results when we balance off the apparently opposed first two points):

> To make democracy work, we should provide many opportunities for citizens to participate in *local* self-governing groups — in their church, in a consumers' cooperative, or in their profession. Democracy is not just a matter of national policies; it must be a participatory democracy on the local level.

The test of such an argument is whether it takes the reader along to the logical conclusion at which the writer aims. Often the writer will *begin* by stating the logical conclusion he has reached. That conclusion then serves as his **thesis.** He then devotes the rest of the paper to showing the steps by which he has reached his conclusion. An argument is convincing if the reader says at each major step: "Yes, I can see how you got from *A* to *B*." It is unconvincing if the reader keeps saying: "I don't see how this *follows.*"

Remember the following advice when you try to present a convincing argument to your reader:

(1) *Identify a limited issue and do it justice.* If you want your argument to convince your readers, you have to take clear aim. We do not expect someone to solve a limited problem if he always flails out wildly at everything. We know that an argument will lead nowhere if someone starts out by saying, "I disagree with you on *everything*" instead of saying, "I disagree with you on *this particular point.*"

The advantage of stating a strong thesis at the beginning is that both writer and reader know from the start: This is the point at issue. Both writer and reader can concentrate on one basic question: Is the argument strong enough to support this point?

Notice that each of the following paragraphs is focused on a clear-cut issue. The first answers the question: "Is U.S. Negro music primarily 'American' or 'African'?" The second answers the question: "Is it true that so-called immoral books contribute to juvenile delinquency?" In each case, the writer has asked himself: "What am I trying to prove?" All the material he presents is directly relevant to the point at issue:

> *U.S. Negro music is mainstream.* This music, far from being simply Afro-American (whatever that is, the continent of Africa being as vast and varied as it is), is, like the U.S.

Negro himself, All-American. This is why so many other American musicians, like Paul Whiteman, George Gershwin, Benny Goodman, Woody Herman, Gerry Mulligan and all the rest, identify with it so eagerly. The white American musician (excluding hill-billies, of course) sounds most American when he sounds most like an American Negro. Otherwise he sounds like a European. White Americans may strike Negroes as being almost embarrassingly awkward on the dance floor, but all Americans, even those committed to segregation, are, culturally speaking, closer to the blues than any song-and-dance group or tribe anywhere in Africa. The blues tradition is not indigenous to Africa. It is a U.S. Negro tradition, and it is indigenous to the United States.

—Albert Murray, "Something Different, Something More," *Anger, and Beyond*

It would not be easy to find a responsible professional expert who sees any significant relation at all between the greater frankness of contemporary general literature and juvenile delinquency or misbehavior. As a matter of fact, most juvenile delinquents exhibit serious reading disabilities, averaging three years or more behind what is normal for their age-level. It is unusual to find in serious trouble with the authorities a youth whose capacity for sustained reading is adequate for an adult novel. Whatever creates juvenile delinquency, it is not the reading of works by John O'Hara or D. H. Lawrence or Vladimir Nabokov or, for that matter, Grace Metalious. In fact, it is the *inability* to do sustained reading, frustrating the youth at school and cutting off a major avenue of escape from the limits of what is usually a mean and sordid environment, that tends to breed rebellious delinquency.   —Dan Lacy, "Obscenity and Censorship"

We judge the good faith of a writer by how close he stays to the central issue. Suppose you want to ask, "How widespread (or how serious) is dishonesty among police officers?" Perhaps you have studied reports of pay-offs, or of a police burglary ring in a major city. Even a reader who respects and supports the police will grant you the right to take an impartial look at the evidence of any wrongdoing. But he will draw the line if your argument suddenly shifts to charges that policemen tend to be gun-lovers and prone to violence. You are now *ignoring the issue* and instead engaging in a general attack on the group of people under discussion. Fair-minded readers become suspicious when an argument suddenly shifts ground: from the mayor's policies to his home life, from a teacher's teaching ability to his political views.

(2) *Weigh the evidence pro and con.* To convince an intelligent reader, you have to do more than merely collect all the evidence that favors your *own* point of view. You have to convince him that you looked at favorable and *unfavorable* evidence. You have to show that you were willing to change your mind, if necessary.

Suppose you have become interested in arguments concerning American immigration policies. At the moment, you are not concerned with whether immigration itself is a good or a bad thing. You are trying to answer the question: Is the present quota system, limited as it is, a fair attempt to preserve the current ethnic and racial balance of the country? On the affirmative side, you might find evidence that quotas to European countries are parceled out on a roughly proportionate basis. A majority of people in this country are of Anglo-Saxon origin, and England and Ireland are allotted a major share of the immigration quota. Fewer Americans are of Scandinavian or German origin, and their home countries receive a proportionately smaller share of the quota. And so on.

Is there any evidence on the negative side? You may find an article claiming that a child born of mixed British and Chinese parents in London would have to wait for a place on the almost nonexistent Chinese quota. Why? Though the ancestors of twenty million Americans came from Africa, there seems to be no proportionate quota for African countries. Why? An impartial observer would study the relevant statistics and the key provisions of current immigration laws. He might finally conclude that there is a rough attempt to do justice to the different *national* origins of Americans, but no attempt to do justice to their racial origin.

(3) *Draw justified conclusions from what you know.* We interpret current events by relating them to previous experience. During a downpour, we see two badly damaged cars pulled over to the side of the highway. We are likely to think that one of the drivers lost control of his car on the rain-slick road. We relate the present incident to a general rule we have previously formed about accidents in the rain:

GENERAL RULE:	In the rain, cars tend to skid on slick pavement and thus cause accidents.
SPECIFIC INCIDENT:	This car has had an accident in the rain.
CONCLUSION:	*Therefore,* this car must have skidded on the wet pavement.

When we carefully examine this conclusion, we will change the *must* to *may*. The conclusion is *probably* true. But, rain or no rain, *other* factors also cause accidents: defective steering wheels or inattentive drivers, and so on. The present instance may well be an exception to the general rule.

Much argument applies our general knowledge to individual cases. In a way, we thus turn the process of generalization upside down. When we generalize, we look at many individual cases and reach a general conclusion. But then, when still another individual case comes along, we are ready to say: This is merely another example of the general rule we already know. The kind of reasoning that *applies* the general rule to the new example is called deductive reasoning, or **deduction**.

The more ironclad the general rule is, the more reliable the conclusions we can draw from it. When the general rule has the word *all* or *only* or *no* in it, it does not allow exceptions. We can confidently apply it to the individual case at issue:

GENERAL:	Only persons over 21 were allowed to vote in the recent election.
SPECIFIC:	Jim voted in the recent election.
CONCLUSION:	Jim must be over 21.

GENERAL:	No unaided human being can survive without air.
SPECIFIC:	There is no air on the moon.
CONCLUSION:	No unaided human being could survive on the moon.

When we draw such conclusions in the course of an argument, we should not try to get out of a general rule more than went into it. Learn to ask: How far exactly does the rule go — what ground does it cover? Look at the following argument:

GENERAL:	All Communists read Karl Marx.
SPECIFIC:	John Smith reads Karl Marx.
CONCLUSION:	John Smith is a Communist.

Here, the conclusion goes *farther* than the rule. There is nothing in the rule to exclude the possibility that, in addition to Communists, a great many *other* people also read Karl Marx. We could rewrite the rule as follows: "All Communists (and, for all we know, also many *non*-Communists) read Karl Marx."

Not all arguments follow a clear three-step pattern. But much argument in one way or another applies general rules to specific situations. Would you agree that the specific conclusion drawn at the end of the following passage follows from the general principles that the author presents first? Can you state these principles in your own words?

> Under primitive agricultural conditions the farmer had few insect problems. These arose with the intensification of agriculture — the devotion of immense acreages to a single crop. Such a system set the stage for explosive increases in specific insect populations. Single-crop farming does not take advantage of the principles by which nature works; it is agriculture as an engineer might conceive it to be. Nature has introduced great variety into the landscape, but man has displayed a passion for simplifying it. Thus he undoes the built-in checks and balances by which nature holds the species within bounds. One important natural check is a limit on the amount of suitable habitat for each species. Obviously *then,* an insect that lives on wheat can build up its population to much higher levels on a farm devoted to wheat than on one in which wheat is intermingled with other crops to which the insect is not adapted.
>
> —Rachel Carson, *Silent Spring*

(4) *Recognize important distinctions.* The old-fashioned patent medicine provided the same remedy for coughs, liver trouble, and appendicitis. We no longer put much faith in medicines that treat everybody and everything alike. To do justice to any serious problem, we have to recognize features that set the problem *apart* from other similar ones. For instance, a person who wants to promote equal educational opportunity for all students may have to take into account distinctions like the following:

> The prosperous citizen can afford a house in an expensive suburb which has a fine school. The good suburban schools are sociologically not unlike the good independent prep

schools. The chief difference is that in the suburb, establishing residence is a part — and a very expensive part — of the price of admission (the other part being heavy school taxes). In a way the private prep school is more democratic because *it takes in a number of scholarship students of truly impoverished parents.* There is no possibility of such an arrangement in Scarsdale. A youngster cannot attend the Scarsdale schools unless his parents live in Scarsdale; and that is something that impoverished parents do not commonly do.

—John W. Gardner, *Excellence*

This kind of argument shows why often a *simple* solution to a problem won't work. In this case, for instance, someone aiming at more "democratic" schools might have advocated the abolition of private schools. But then he finds that some private schools are more "democratic" than many suburban *public* schools. In a carefully developed argument, we expect the author to take into account complications such as these. We soon become wary of a writer who *oversimplifies* every issue.

(5) *Consider important alternatives.* Often, an argument remains unconvincing because the reader is presented with a very narrow range of choice. He is pushed toward a "yes" or "no" answer when he really wants to say "maybe" or "that depends." He is asked to choose *either* one solution *or* the other when he really wants to ask: "Aren't there *other* solutions that are also possible?"

When a mechanic is given a choice of only two monkey wrenches for a job, he has little hope that one of them will fit. When he has a selection of six or seven, he will approach the job with more confidence. Similarly, when a reader is presented with a simple *either-or* choice, he may well reply: "Neither of these two alternatives fits the situation. You are presenting me with a *false dilemma*: You make me choose between two undesirable solutions, when actually there is a third way out."

Before you present your reader with an *either-or* argument, see whether there is a third possibility that presents a way out. For instance, people often talk as if children are made to learn *either* by fear of punishment or by the hope of reward — whether a good grade, a pat on the back, or a place on the honor roll. But there is also a third possibility that may be very important. The good student in math is often the one who *enjoys* solving problems. The best student in a Spanish class is often the one who likes to study a foreign language and to try it out. Many educators feel that children learn best when they enjoy what they are doing.

Before you present your reader with a clear-cut choice, see whether the answer might not really be a matter of *degree*. Does our country really have an *either-or* choice between unregulated "free enterprise" and state-controlled "socialism"? When we look at different countries, we find that there are different *degrees* of state control or government regulation. Here are some countries, each with a list of some major activities run by the government:

RUSSIA	POLAND	ENGLAND	USA
education	education	public education	public education
transportation	transportation	(but some	(but also
industry	industry	private)	private)
farms	(but not all	medicine	post office
	farms)	some industry	some health and
		TV and radio	old age
		(but not	insurance
		newspapers)	
		airlines	
		railways	

In addition to the more specific requirements for a sound argument, remember one general rule: Do not feel obliged to commit yourself strongly on every issue. Everyone must learn to *suspend judgment* when necessary. Many issues of public interest are too complicated to permit easy solutions. Racial prejudice, equal opportunity, or delinquency and crime are issues that have baffled and defeated many first-rate minds. An honest, *limited* contribution to such a problem is more valuable than a panacea, advertised with much fanfare and soon forgotten.

The following prose model is an example of an editorial arguing an *un*popular position. The author is known for his strong views, and his emotions are aroused by his topic. Nevertheless, he is aiming his argument at an *intelligent* reader. Can you show that he respects the reader's judgment? Study the selection carefully and answer the questions that follow it.

PROSE MODEL 5

NORMAN COUSINS

Who Killed Benny Paret?

I once had an interview with Mike Jacobs, the prize-fight promoter. I was a fledgling reporter at that time; my beat was education but during the vacation season I found myself on varied assignments, all the way from ship news to sports reporting. In this way I found myself sitting opposite the most powerful figure in the boxing world.

There was nothing spectacular in Mr. Jacobs' manner or appearance; but when he spoke about prize fights, he was no longer a bland little man but a colossus who sounded the way Napoleon must have sounded when he reviewed a battle. You knew you were listening to Number One. His saying something made it true.

We discussed what to him was the only important element in successful promoting — how to please the crowd. So far as he was concerned, there was no mystery to it. You put killers in the ring and the people filled your arena. You hire boxing artists — men who are adroit at feinting, parrying, weaving, jabbing, and dancing, but who don't pack dynamite in their fists — and you wind up counting your empty seats. So you searched for the killers and sluggers and maulers — fellows who could hit with the force of a baseball bat.

I asked Mr. Jacobs if he was speaking literally when he said people came out to see the killer.

"They don't come out to see a tea party," he said evenly. "They come out to see the knockout. They come out to see a man hurt. If they think anything else, they're kidding themselves."

Some years ago, a young man by the name of Benny Paret was killed in the ring. The killing was seen by millions; it was on television. In the twelfth round, he was hit hard in the head several times, went down, was counted out, and never came out of the coma.

The Paret fight produced a flurry of investigations. Governor Rockefeller was shocked by what happened and appointed a committee to assess the responsibility. The New York State Boxing Commission decided to find out what was wrong. The District Attorney's office expressed its concern. One question that was solemnly studied in all three probes concerned the action of the referee. Did he act in time to stop the fight? Another question had to do with the role of the examining doctors who certified the physical fitness of the fighters before the bout. Still another question involved Mr. Paret's manager; did he rush his boy into the fight without adequate time to recuperate from the previous one?

In short, the investigators looked into every possible cause except the real one. Benny Paret was killed because the human fist delivers enough impact, when directed against the head, to produce a massive hemorrhage in the brain. The human brain is the most delicate and complex mechanism in all creation. It has a lacework of millions of highly fragile nerve connections. Nature attempts to protect this exquisitely intricate machinery by encasing it in a hard shell. Fortunately, the shell is thick enough to withstand a great deal of pounding. Nature, however, can protect man against everything except man himself. Not every blow to the head will kill a man — but there is always the risk of concussion and damage to the brain. A prize fighter may be able to survive even repeated brain concussions and go on fighting, but the damage to his brain may be permanent.

In any event, it is futile to investigate the referee's role and seek to determine whether he should have intervened to stop the fight earlier. That is not where the primary responsibility lies. The primary responsibility lies with the people who pay to see a man hurt. The referee who stops a fight too soon from the crowd's viewpoint can expect to be booed. The crowd wants the knockout; it wants to see a man stretched out on the canvas. This is the supreme moment in boxing. It is nonsense to talk about prize fighting as a test of boxing skills. No crowd was ever brought to its feet screaming and cheering at the sight of two men beautifully dodging and weaving out of each other's jabs. The time the crowd comes alive is when a man is hit hard over the heart or the head, when his mouthpiece flies out, when the blood squirts out of his nose or eyes, when he wobbles under the attack and his pursuer continues to smash at him with pole-axe impact.

Don't blame it on the referee. Don't even blame it on the fight managers. Put the blame where it belongs — on the prevailing mores that regard prize fighting as a perfectly proper enterprise and vehicle of entertainment. No one doubts that many people enjoy prize fighting and will miss it if it should be thrown out. And that is precisely the point.

—from the *Saturday Review*

1. Explain briefly *bland, colossus, adroit, concussion, futile, mores.* Study the words the author uses to describe what the crowd sees during a fight. Would you say he is writing about boxing from hearsay, or from close, firsthand observation? How can you tell?

2. Is this editorial clearly focused on a central issue? Can you state it in your own words?

3. Can you point out one or more examples of a general principle being applied to a specific instance? How acceptable or convincing are the general assumptions from which the author argues?

4. Can you point out an important distinction that is crucial to the author's argument? How clearly or how fully is it worked out?

5. What is the author's attitude toward people who do *not* share his view?

6. Have you ever listened carefully to the spokesman for a view *opposed* to your own? Write a paragraph in which you present as fully and impartially as you can a point of view with which you strongly disagree.

7. How convincing is the author's argument as a whole? Does it convince *you?* Discuss his overall strategy, pointing out its strengths or weaknesses.

EXERCISE 22 Study the following short passages. How sound, effective, or convincing is the argument presented in each? Are there any points at which you *refuse* to follow the author's reasoning? Why?

1. To me, American democracy is based on the right to choose a leader and to have a voice in the adoption of laws that will govern one. In the military, one does not choose a leader, nor does he have any voice in the preparation of regulations. The army is designed to reduce each individual to a cog in a huge and complex machine. This is not democracy. Yet, democracies have been forced in times of crisis to adopt military standards to preserve democracy. When these military standards are preserved in peacetime, I feel that the state is held more important than the individual. This is the very idea that our nation fears. Continuing the draft in peacetime goes counter to the ideals of our democracy.

2. In recent years, many bills have been introduced in legislatures in order to restrict a citizen's right to own firearms. I assume the purpose is to reduce the number of casualties caused by human violence. If so, why stop at firearms? We should also advocate the barring of windows, since people have been known to jump out of

them. We should also come out against knives, beer bottles, frying pans, razor blades, and silk stockings. All of these have been used as lethal weapons. However, our best bet would be to abolish old age. Then we would all live forever.

3. According to the Bill of Rights, a person is free to choose any religion he desires without pressure from the government in any way affecting his choice. I think it would be logical to say that if he is free to choose any, he should also be free to choose none. Public schools are supported by the government. If a person who is not religious is denied a job in one of these schools, he is being punished by the government for exercising the freedom given him by it.

THEME TOPICS 5 A. Write a paper in which you seriously re-examine familiar assumptions or your own thinking on *one* of the following topics:

(a) How serious (and how widespread) is the practice of cheating in order to obtain better grades? Is cheating a minor transgression ("everybody does it") or is it serious dishonesty? Can (and does) a typical student avoid ridicule and ostracism from his peers if he cooperates with school authorities determined to punish cheaters?

(b) Who is to blame for "juvenile delinquency"? Old-fashioned teachers and judges blame the individual; parents blame bad company; social workers often blame the family; sociologists often blame society. Whom or what do *you* blame?

B. The price of self-government is a loss in efficiency. Important decisions are held up while the issues are debated; the final result may be a deadlock or a weak compromise. Furthermore, poorly informed laymen vote on issues that require extensive technical knowledge. For these reasons, soldiers are not allowed to vote on battle plans; students usually are not allowed to vote on the curriculum of their school. Select one limited area, like military service, high school education, highway planning, city government, urban renewal, or factory management. Write a paper defending the position that there should be either *more* or *less* reliance on democratic processes in the area of your choice.

C. Emerson said about the Fugitive Slave Law in 1851, "This filthy enactment was made in the nineteenth century, by people who could read and write. I will not obey it, by God." At what point would *you* grant people the right to say about a law, "I will not obey it, by God"?

D. Attack or defend the following statement: "It is not the business of the legislature to pass laws assuring equal employment opportunities for minority groups. Our relations with minority groups are a question of morality. There will be changes in our behavior only if there first is a change of heart. You cannot legislate morality."

E. Americans used to be criticized for excessive pride in their country. Rudyard Kipling, for instance, after watching a Fourth of July celebration on a trip to America, said: "What amazed me was the calm with which these folks gathered together and commenced to belaud their noble selves, their country, their 'institootions' and everything else that was theirs." Today we are often told the opposite: Americans seem obsessed with their country's shortcomings and faults. Younger people, especially, often stress the darker side of American history, the injustices of American society. What do you think is the attitude a young American should take toward his country? Why? Limit your discussion to one major issue or one major area of American life.

C 4 The Writer and His Audience

Learn how to make your writing produce the right effect on the reader.

First and last, a writer's business is with his reader. It is true that during much of the writing process the writer has to concentrate on his subject. He has to find and interpret information. He has to work out the connections between different sets of facts. But the final question is: "Will this mean anything to the reader?"

The transactions between a writer and his reader are of three major kinds:

(1) *A good writer effectively conveys his message.* He knows how to make his points *clear.* He knows how to make his readers *grasp* what may be difficult or new. His first question is: "Am I being understood?" He knows that it is not enough to state a fact — it must be stated in words that the reader can comprehend, and in a manner that will make it *sink in.* Can you see that in each of the following passages the author helps the reader understand?

> There is just the same kind of difference between the mental operations of a man of science and those of an ordinary person as there is between the operations and methods of a baker or of a butcher weighing out his goods in common

The Tragedie of Hamlet

Ham. How long will a man lie i'th earth ere he rot ?

Clow. Fayth if a be not rotten before a die, as we haue many pockie corfes, that will fcarce hold the laying in, a will laft you fom eyght yeere, or nine yeere. A Tanner will laft you nine yeere.

Ham Why he more then another ?

Clow. Why fir, his hide is fo tand with his trade, that a will keepe out water a great while ; & your water is a fore decayer of your whorfon dead body, heer's a fcull now hath lyen you i'th earth 23. yeeres.

Ham. Whofe was it ?

Clow. A whorfon mad fellowes it was, whofe do you think it was ?

Ham. Nay I know not.

Clow. A peftilence on him for a madde rogue, a pourd a flagon of Renifh on my head once ; this fame skull fir, was fir *Yoricks* skull, the Kings Iefter.

Ham. This ?

Clow. Een that.

Ham. Alas poore *Yoricke*, I knew him *Horatio*, a fellow of infinite ieft, of moft excellent fancie, hee hath bore me on his backe a thoufand times, and now how abhorred in my imagination it is: my gorge rifes at it. Heere hung thofe lyppes that I haue kift I know not howe oft, where be your gibes now ? your gamboles, your fongs, your flafhes of merriment, that were wont to fet the table on a roare, not one now to mocke your owne grinning, quite chopfalne. Now get you to my Ladies table, & tell her, let her paint an inch thicke, to this fauour fhe muft come, make her laugh at that. Prethee *Horatio* tell me one thing.

Hora. What's that my Lord ?

Ham. Dooft thou thinke *Alexander* lookt a this fafhion i'th earth ?

Hora. Een fo.

Ham. And fmelt fo pah.

Hora. Een fo my Lord.

Ham. To what bafe vfes wee may returne *Horatio* ? Why may not imagination trace the noble duft of *Alexander*, till a find it ftopping a bunghole ?

Hor. Twere to confider too curioufly to confider fo.

Ham. No faith, not a iot, but to follow him thether with modefly enough, and likelyhood to leade it. *Alexander* dyed, *Alexander* was

---

Facsimile of manuscript of the Hamlet Quarto of 1604 (the Folger Shakespeare Library)

scales, and the operations of a chemist in performing a difficult and complex analysis by means of his balance and finely
graduated weights.

—T. H. Huxley, "The Method of Scientific Investigation"

Being in tune with a remote period is like listening to a
radio station while motoring. As you approach the limit of its
range the program begins to fade. You turn up the volume
higher and higher, and when you can turn it no higher you
strain to hear. At last you go around a bend in the road or
down a long hill and there is silence. So it is as we travel away
from our own time into the past. We who were born in the
last century can tune in on the eighteenth century (we, too,
were born in a horse-drawn age), but it will be very hard for
those born after 1930 to do so: too much has happened in
the past fifty years.

—Wilmarth S. Lewis, "The Difficult Art of Biograph," *Yale Review*

(2) *A good writer knows how to change the reader's mind.*
Sometimes a writer is content to provide background information,
or to tell the reader things that are good to know. But a serious
writer soon begins to ask himself: "Will this make any difference
to the way my readers think and act?" Can you see that the following passage effectively conveys a sense of *urgency?* Can you see
that in effect it says to the reader: "This concerns *you.* This should
be part of *your* agenda"?

According to the projections of demographers, the present
world population of 3.3 billion will double by 2000 A.D. Then
our planet will have to harbor two New Yorks instead of one,
two Londons, two Tokyos, two Calcuttas, two Hong Kongs,
one .more of every existing human congregation. There will
be double the highways and freeways to link them, double
the consumption of oxygen by human and industrial and auto-
motive combustion, double the air and water pollution, half
the elbow room, a shrunken area of cropland that will have to
be more and more intensively mined, a limited amount of
parkland and open space trampled flat by the millions wanting
to smell mown grass or show their children a squirrel.

(3) *A good writer makes reading a pleasure for his readers.*
A good writer does not expect his readers to read from a sense of
duty. He wants them to keep saying to themselves, "That was well
said!" or "I wish I had thought of that!" or "A memorable sent-

ence!" With some writers, in fact, the reader runs the danger of being *carried away* by their sheer delight in words, their pleasure in putting our language through its paces:

> My education was the liberty I had to read indiscriminately and all the time, with my eyes hanging out. I never could have dreamed there were such goings-on, such do's and argie-bargies, such ice blasts of words, such love and sense and terror and humbug, such and so many blinding bright lights breaking across the just awaking wits and splashing all over the pages, as they can never quite do again after the first revelation. . . . It was then, in my father's brown study before homework, usually the first botched scribblings of gauche and gawky heart-choked poems about black-bloomered nymphs, the jussive grave and the tall, improbable loves of the sardine-packed sky, poems never to be shown to anyone except on pain of death, that I began to know one kind of writing from another, one kind of badness, one kind of goodness. I wrote endless imitations, though I never at the time of writing thought them to be imitations but rather colossally original, things unheard of, like eggs laid by tigers, imitations of whatever I happened to be golloping then. . . . Nothing in those days was too much for me to try. If *Paradise Lost* had not already been written, I would have had a shot at it.
>
> —Dylan Thomas, "A Few Words of a Kind," *Mademoiselle*

C 4a Persuasion

Study the strategies that will help you persuade a skeptical reader.

The kind of writing that depends most directly on the reaction of the reader is persuasion. The aim of the persuasive writer is to make someone else share his view — and to make him *act* accordingly. Effective persuasion changes attitudes and behavior. The copywriter who writes advertising, and the ghost-writer who writes a campaign speech, are working toward a tangible goal. They are aiming their writing directly at the audience, and they expect results.

In order to succeed, a persuasive writer must know his reader. He must relate what he says to the interests and standards of his audience. He must find some kind of common ground. His attitude toward the audience is: "This is what I want you to believe and do — and you yourself will agree that it is right, or necessary, or in your own best interest." In each of the following passages, an author appeals to basic interests or convictions that he shares with his audience. Can you spell out in full what these common interests or convictions are?

> Parks like Golden Gate Park in San Francisco or the beautiful parks of Denver are the result of the citizens' investment in their city's future. We are now enjoying the dividends of the money that earlier generations spent in making these cities beautiful. Therefore, we should in turn invest in the parks that will make our growing cities beautiful places to live for our children and children's children.

> Clubs, fraternities, nations — these are the beloved barriers in the way of a workable world, these will have to surrender some of their rights and some of their ribs. A "fraternity" is the antithesis of *fraternity*. The first (that is, the order or organization) is predicated on the idea of exclusion; the second (that is, the abstract thing) is based on a feeling of total equality. Anyone who remembers back to his fraternity days at college recalls the enthusiasts in his group, the rabid members, both old and young, who were obsessed with the mystical charm of membership in their particular order. They were usually men who were incapable of genuine brotherhood, or at least unaware of its implications. Fraternity begins when the exclusion formula is found to be distasteful. The effect of any organization of a social and brotherly nature is to strengthen rather than to diminish the lines which divide people into classes; the effect of states and nations is the same, and eventually these lines will have to be softened, these powers will have to be generalized.

> —E. B. White, *One Man's Meat*

What can a writer do to present his appeal as forcefully and effectively as possible? What are some of the features that help make a piece of writing persuasive? In writing persuasive papers of your own, remember the following advice:

(1) *Use language that strongly conveys the right attitudes and emotions.* It is hard to raise the reader's generous enthusiasm for the preservation of our forests and wildlife in the neutral, clinical language of the botanist and geologist. Note how effectively the words in the following passage convey the author's strong emotions:

The *tragedy* of the oceanic islands lies in the *uniqueness,* the *irreplaceability* of the species they have developed by the slow processes of the ages. In a *reasonable* world men would have treated these islands as *precious* possessions, as natural museums filled with *beautiful* and *curious* works of creation, *valuable beyond price* because nowhere in the world are they duplicated. W. H. Hudson's lament for the birds of the Argentine pampas might even more truly have been spoken of the islands: "The beautiful has vanished and returns not."

—Rachel Carson, *The Sea Around Us*

Can you explain how and why the italicized terms in the following passage help steer the reader's reactions in the right direction?

We have much studied and much perfected, of late, the great civilized invention of the division of labor; only we give it a false name. It is not truly speaking, the labor that is divided; but the men: Divided into mere *segments of men* — broken into small *fragments* and *crumbs* of life; so that all the little piece of intelligence that is left in a man is not enough to make a pin, or a nail, but exhausts itself in making the point of a pin, or the head of a nail.

—John Ruskin, *The Stones of Venice*

(2) *Use analogies and comparisons that effectively steer the reader's reactions.* Can you show that the analogies in the following passages do not merely carry information but also suggest *attitudes?*

The parents who are trying to force their children *with an academic shoehorn* into colleges with academic standards way beyond the students' capacities are doing lasting harm.

A high school commencement should be an occasion of importance and meaning. Like all effective goals, it should be kept in a veil of doubt about its attainability. There is little satisfaction in *aiming at a target that is so close that anybody can score a bull's-eye* without skill, training, or suspense.

We are living like the irresponsible *heirs of a millionaire uncle.* At an ever accelerating rate, we are now squandering the capital of metallic ores and fossil fuels accumulated in the earth's crust during hundreds of millions of years. How long can this spending spree go on? (Aldous Huxley)

(3) *Go from the simple to the difficult, or from the obvious to the new.* Reassure your reader by starting from what he already

knows or understands. Then take him step by step toward the new, the difficult, the controversial. Many a reader will not budge if he is directly contradicted; if his cherished ideas and commitments are frontally attacked. But he may follow you at least part of the way if you make it possible for him to take one small step at a time.

Can you see how the following rough outlines proceed from the less important to the more important, from what is easy to what is harder to accept?

(the definition of a "gentleman")
    — knows which fork to use first at a gala dinner;
    — is considerate and helpful toward women and older people;
    — is not embarrassed to introduce friends from lowly former days to high-class, new acquaintances.

(a policeman's right to strike)
    — the factory worker's right to strike is an established part of the American way of life;
    — white-collar workers are organizing and using the strike as a legitimate weapon;
    — in recent years, teacher strikes have dramatically improved the working conditions of teachers;
    — it is hard to see how policemen can be denied a right granted to private and public employees alike.

(4) *Bring out the weaknesses in an opponent's view.* Point out telling contradictions or absurdities. The following passage is part of an article attacking hunting as a sport. Can you show in detail what the author does in order to demolish his opposition?

> Let it be supposed that all hunters obey all regulations. Let it be supposed that no whiskey bottle is dropped to pollute any glen or dingle, no fence is broken, no fawn is shot, no forest is set afire, no robins are massacred in mistake for pheasants and no deer-hunters in mistake for porcupines (or possibly chipmunks), and no meditative philosopher, out to enjoy the loveliness of autumn, is ever plugged through the pericardium. The question persists: Is it a spectacle of manhood (which is to say of our distinctive humanness), when on a bracing morning we look out upon the autumn, draw an exhilarating breath, and cry "What a glorious day! How golden the light of the sun, how merry the caperings of creatures; *Gloria in excelsis Deo!* I will go out and kill something"?
>   —Alan Devoe, "On Hunting," *The American Mercury*

(5) *If you can, balance negative criticism with positive, constructive suggestions.* Readers easily tire of the writer who is always ready to discover a grievance but seldom suggests a feasible solution. In the following passage, the author deplores the purely *negative* direction of attempts to censor the reading materials available to adolescents:

> In the specific area of juvenile delinquency a basic problem is the serious reading difficulties experienced by most delinquent children, the barren cultural environments in which they are reared, and their meager opportunities to envision a kind of life richer and better than that surrounding them. For those whose concern for the troubled and rebellious youths we call delinquent is genuine, giving aid to remedial reading programs and making efforts through school programs, boys' clubs, youth centers, police athletic leagues and similar organizations to *place in the hands of youngsters good books — books within their reading grasp, yet ones which can excite and enlarge their view of life and lead them upward and out of the narrow bounds they live in —* can be infinitely more rewarding, if more difficult, than issuing manifestoes about "objectionable books." Local librarians and youth agencies can suggest dozens of useful projects of this kind in every community.
>
> —Dan Lacy, "Obscenity and Censorship," *The Christian Century*

REMEMBER: With an experienced reader, persuasive devices cannot take the place of sound arguments based on relevant evidence. Many such devices do not really strengthen the *substance* of the author's case. They merely help him present his case *to advantage.* Persuasive techniques can give an argument the right send-off, a welcome boost. But, when overdone, they can also make a reader suspect that the author's message is all "sales talk," with little factual substance.

A persuasive writer defeats his own purpose when he tries *too hard* to persuade. The experienced reader soon begins to feel: "You are pushing me! Let me study your arguments and your evidence — and give me a chance to make up my own mind!" When persuasion becomes too aggressive, it becomes **polemics.** Polemical writing defeats its own purpose when it puts the reader on the defensive.

To keep from putting your reader on the defensive, try to keep your writing free of the following:

UNCONVINCING SUPERLATIVES The experienced reader is weary of exaggeration, overemphasis, overstatement. He has heard words like *tremendous, terrific, glamorous, thrilling,* and *unique* so many times that he is no longer impressed by them. Passages like the following, designed to rouse his enthusiasm, may well have the *opposite* effect:

> The most tremendous cultural advance in the city's long history nears completion with the impending opening of the new Center for the Performing Arts.
> The student at the new school participates in a highly cultural community, gains unlimited instruction and inspiration from an outstanding faculty, studies a planned curriculum unsurpassed by any other school of its kind, and has the assurance that he is receiving the ultimate techniques of education.

LOADED LANGUAGE An intelligent reader refuses to be carried away by words that are *mere* words. What to one observer is "boisterous," "obstreperous," "exuberant," and "rolicking" behavior, showing the "high spirits" of those involved, is to another observer "noisy," "unruly," "undisciplined," "riotous" behavior by a group of youthful "vandals." What to one writer is the "steadily growing *burden* of school taxes" is to another writer "society's steadily growing *investment* in education." The experienced reader knows that in practice the words in each of the following pairs often mean much the same thing, with the choice depending on the intentions of the writer:

crony	trusted friend
bureaucrat	administrator
brutality	firmness
agitator	advocate
deal	settlement
regimentation	discipline

MISLEADING ANALOGIES The experienced reader knows that all analogies are only *partial* analogies. When he is told that "a tide of indignation is sweeping the country," he remembers that a real tide sweeps *back out* to sea as irresistibly as it first swept *in*. As a result, the skeptical reader often feels: "You are pushing the analogy *too far.*" Would you agree that an analogy is pushed too far in each of the following passages? Can you explain where each analogy *breaks down?*

Our mistake is to put juvenile delinquents in institutions where they are exposed to other juvenile delinquents. You can't put a bunch of bad apples together in a barrel and expect them to improve. Probation should be used in all cases where it can safely be employed.

I am going to ask you to begin our study of Democracy by considering it first as a big balloon, filled with gas or hot air, and sent up so that you shall be kept looking up at the sky whilst other people are picking your pockets. When the balloon comes down to earth every five years or so you are invited to get into the basket if you can throw out one of the people who are sitting tightly in it; but as you can afford neither the time nor the money, and there are forty millions of you and hardly room for six hundred in the basket, the balloon goes up again with much the same lot in it and leaves you where you were before. (George Bernard Shaw)

CHEAPENED IDEALS OR STANDARDS   Love of country is a powerful motive. But we cheapen it when we use it to help promote a pet scheme, or sell soap ("true American values . . . special money-saving coupons inside"). The prestige of science depends on its impartiality. The scientist's first loyalty is to *truth.* We cast doubt on that loyalty when we claim that "Science" has discovered a new skin cream, or a new miracle diet.

The following prose model is an excerpt from an attack that John Milton wrote over three hundred years ago on the *prior* censorship of books. To this day, people concerned over freedom of speech or freedom of the press quote Milton's ringing words. What makes them exceptionally powerful or persuasive? Study the selection carefully, and answer the questions that follow it.

PROSE MODEL 6

JOHN MILTON

A Plea for Unlicensed Printing

I deny not but that it is of greatest concernment in the church and commonwealth to have a vigilant eye how books demean themselves, as well as men, and thereafter to confine, imprison, and do sharpest justice on them as malefactors. For books are not absolutely dead things, but do contain a potency of life in them to be as active as that soul was whose progeny they are; nay, they do preserve as in a vial the purest efficacy and extraction of that living intellect that bred them. I know they are as lively, and as vigorously productive, as those fabulous dragon's teeth; and being sown up and down, may chance to spring up armed men. And yet, on the other hand, unless wariness be used, as good almost kill a man as kill a good book: who kills a man kills a reasonable creature, God's image; but he who destroys a good book, kills reason itself, kills the image of God, as it were, in the eye. Many a man lives a burden to the earth; but a good book is the precious life-blood of a master spirit, embalmed and treasured up on purpose to a life beyond life. 'Tis true, no age can restore a life, whereof, perhaps, there is no great loss; and revolutions of ages do not oft recover the loss of a rejected truth, for the want of which whole nations fare the worse. We should be wary, therefore, what persecution we raise against the living labors of public men, how we spill that seasoned life of man preserved and stored up in books; since we see a kind of homicide may be thus committed, sometimes a martyrdom and if it extend to the whole impression, a kind of massacre, whereof the execution ends not in the slaying of an elemental life, but strikes at that ethereal and fifth essence, the breath of reason itself, slays an immortality rather than a life.

If we think to regulate printing, thereby to rectify manners, we must regulate all recreations and pastimes, all that is delightful to man. No music must be heard, no song be set or sung, but what is grave and Doric. There must be licensing dancers, that no gesture, motion, or deportment be taught our youth, but what by their allowance shall be thought honest; for such Plato was provided of. It will ask more than the work of twenty licensers to examine all the lutes, the violins, and the guitars in every house; they must not be suffered to prattle as they do, but must be licensed what they may say. And who shall silence all the airs and madrigals that whisper softness in chambers? The windows also, and the balconies, must be thought on; there are shrewd books, with dangerous frontispieces, set to sale: who shall prohibit them, shall twenty licensers? The villages also must have their visitors to inquire what lectures the bagpipe and the rebec reads, even to the balladry and the gamut of every municipal fiddler, for these are the countryman's Arcadias and his Monte Mayors.

Next, what more national corruption, for which England

hears ill abroad, than household gluttony? Who shall be the rectors of our daily rioting? And what shall be done to inhibit the multitudes that frequent those houses where drunkenness is sold and harbored? Our garments also should be referred to the licensing of some more sober work-masters, to see them cut into a less-wanton garb. Who shall regulate all the mixed conversation of our youth, male and female together, as is the fashion of this country? Who shall still appoint what shall be discoursed, what presumed, and no further? Lastly, who shall forbid and separate all idle resort, all evil company? These things will be, and must be; but how they shall be least hurtful, how least enticing, herein consists the grave and governing wisdom of a state.

To sequester out of the world into Atlantic and Utopian polities, which never can be drawn into use, will not mend our condition; but to ordain wisely as in this world of evil, in the midst whereof God hath placed as unavoidably. Nor is it Plato's licensing of books will do this, which necessarily pulls along with it so many other kinds of licensing as will make us all both ridiculous and weary, and yet frustrate; but those unwritten or at least unconstraining laws of virtuous education, religious and civil nurture, which Plato there mentions as the bonds and ligaments of the commonwealth, the pillars and the sustainers of every written statute; these they be which will bear chief sway in such matters as these, when all licensing will be easily eluded. Impunity and remissness, for certain, are the bane of a commonwealth; but here the great art lies, to discern in what the law is to bid restraint and punishment, and in what things persuasion only is to work. If every action which is good or evil in man at ripe years were to be under pittance, and prescription, and compulsion, what were virtue but a name, what praise could be then due to well-doing, what gramercy to be sober, just, or continent?

Many there be that complain of divine Providence for suffering Adam to transgress. Foolish tongues! When God gave him reason, he gave him freedom to choose, for reason is but choosing; he had been else a mere artificial Adam, such an Adam as he is in the motions. We ourselves esteem not of that obedience, or love, or gift, which is of force: God therefore left him free, set before him a provoking object ever almost in his eyes; herein consisted his merit, herein the right of his reward, the praise of his abstinence. Wherefore did he create passions within us, pleasures round about us, but that these rightly tempered are the very ingredients of virtue? They are not skillful considerers of human things, who imagine to remove sin by removing the matter of sin; for, besides that it is a huge heap increasing under the very act of diminishing, though some part of it may for a time be withdrawn from some persons, it cannot from all, in such a universal thing as books are; and when this is done, yet the sin remains entire. Though ye take from a covetous man all his treasure, he has yet one jewel left: ye cannot bereave him of his covetousness. Banish all objects of lust, shut up all youth into the severest discipline that can be exercised in any hermitage, ye cannot make them chaste that came not thither so: such great care and wisdom is required to the right managing of this point.

—from *Areopagitica*

1. Explain briefly: *progeny, vial, ethereal, madrigal, frontispiece, rebec, garb, ligament, gramercy, bereave, hermitage, thither.* Can you explain *"Doric* songs," *"Arcadia," "Atlantic* and *Utopian* polities"? What, in context, is the meaning of each of the following?

    "how books *demean* themselves"
    "they are *shrewd* books, with dangerous frontispieces"
    "who shall be the *rectors* of our daily rioting?"
    "the mixed *conversation* of our youth"
    "all idle *resort*"
    "if every action . . . were to be under *pittance*"
    "to be sober, just, or *continent*"
    "*suffering* Adam to transgress"
    "as he is in the *motions*"

2. What basic standards, commitments, or interests does Milton appeal to in his audience? What preferences or attitudes does he take for granted? Write a brief, composite portrait of Milton's ideal reader. (Compare your own version with those prepared by your classmates.)

3. Can you point out half a dozen words that carry a strong emotional charge? Choose the words Milton most strongly relies on in steering the reader's reactions in the right direction.

4. What use does Milton make of analogies and comparisons? How effective are they?

5. Apart from his use of language and analogies, what persuasive strategies or techniques does Milton rely on? Are they familiar or unfamiliar to the modern reader?

6. Explain one major change you would make if you were to bring Milton's plea against censorship up to date for the modern reader. For instance, has there been a drastic change in the basic assump-

tions that a modern writer could appeal to? Or, is one major part of the strategy that Milton employs *un*likely to work with a modern audience?

EXERCISE 23 The following passages are adapted from articles in which a well-known news magazine deals with people currently in the news. In each case, can you tell whether the editors approve or disapprove of the person? How? Using the same information that is contained in the passage, could you give a *favorable* description of one of the people here treated unfavorably, or vice versa? How would you have to change the wording of the passage?

1. (About a former general now heading a foreign government) To nearly every question put to him in the brief audience, the General coldly professed ignorance. "I can't tell you anything," he snapped apropos of the U.S. Ambassador's conference with him earlier in the day. Had the General any plan to meet the President? "If I knew of one, I wouldn't tell you," the General replied icily. Would he travel in the coming year? "I don't know," he grumped.

2. (About the two chief negotiators in a labor dispute) The two men facing each other across the conference table could not have been more different. One was an intransigent, fork-tongued man, always close to blowing his 5 ft., 1-in. top. The other was an articulate, patrician product of the Ivy League, who during the recent campaign had traveled to every corner of the country expounding his political philosophy.

3. (About a Washington figure under indictment for tax evasion in connection with an influence peddling scandal) The sharp, ferret-eyed kid who had left South Carolina at fourteen to become a Senate page still showed himself in Washington like an elegant boulevardier, his jowls freshly barbered, his darting eyes hidden behind a pair of grotesquely tinted sunglasses, each arm frequently sporting a giggling girl.

EXERCISE 24 How would you react to each of the following passages? Do you find each passage persuasive? Why, or why not?

1. It is often said that an occasional speech by a subversive speaker has little influence on people who are able to hear both sides, and that therefore such speeches should not be banned. We should remember, however, that often a large avalanche starts out as a little snowball — once it has become an avalanche, it is too late.

2. Did you ever see a man who spends his time and money feeding deer, then stands on the highway crying, "He killed my deer," while a big six-footer is dumping a dead fawn no larger than a dog into his truck? Did you ever have rifle-slugs whizzing past your ears, women and children doing the driving, a hunter crawling on his hands and knees out of the line of fire? Did you ever see a hunter cutting off the hindquarters of a wounded doe while she watched him? Why can a child obtain a hunting license to go into the woods with a lethal weapon, yet he cannot vote until he is twenty-one because of immaturity? When the book of life is closed on those who sanction the cruelties of hunting, they may pray for more merciful judgment than they are giving our wildlife, who have no voice of their own to plead their cause.

3. For years, there has been much tearing down and rebuilding in the downtown section. These massive redevelopment programs have been compared to emergency surgery. Considerable pain is involved, and sometimes shock. Sometimes the operation is a failure. But the patient is undoubtedly sick, or he wouldn't be there.

THEME TOPICS 6 A. Have you ever strongly objected to a custom, practice, or institution that is popular with other high school students? Write a paper in which you try to change their minds.

B. Have you ever had occasion to question one major feature of the American educational system as you know it? Select what to you seems a major shortcoming, or defect. Then write a paper designed to convince teachers and administrators of the need for a change. Use convincing evidence from your own experience.

C. Have you ever seen a promising reform or innovation rejected or inadequately carried out? Or, have you ever seen a worthwhile tradition or institution abolished or unduly neglected? Write a paper in which you persuade your audience to give the project or institution in question a second chance.

D. Suppose voters in your state were considering laws designed to (a) make it easier for younger people to get married; or (b) make it easier for married people to get divorced. Take a position pro or con on one of these, and try to persuade an audience that is strongly committed to the *opposite* view.

E. Schools differ greatly in how closely administrators supervise a school newspaper, literary magazine, yearbook, and the like. Could you persuade adults that they should adopt a strict "hands-off" policy toward such student publications? (Would you be willing to take the position that "anything goes"?) Or, could you persuade your fellow students that some basic restrictions and supervision by adults are necessary? (Where would you draw the line?)

F. In your judgment, how tolerant (or intolerant) of unpopular views is the "average newspaper reader" in your community? Write a paper in which you try to make him understand and respect (though not necessarily share) the convictions of a conscientious objector, a Marxist, a black nationalist, or some other type of dissenter from majority views.

G. In recent decades, the following books have been among those widely read by young people but often banned or removed from high school libraries: *1984, Catcher in the Rye, Brave New World, Animal Farm, Catch-22*. Select one of these, or another book that has more recently been the center of censorship controversies. Show why, or why not, the book of your choice should be read by American high school students.

C 4b Style

Use the stylistic resources that give writing force and variety.

We are often told that *what* a writer says is more important than *how* he says it. But in practice, what he meant to say reaches his readers only the way he actually did say it. A writer may have strong convictions and yet sound undecided or confused. He may mean to be personal and friendly and yet sound cold, pompous, or bureaucratic to his readers. Through the study of **style,** we learn to use the resources of language to produce the results we *want* to produce.

In each of the following passages, part of the writer's aim was to put the reader in a characteristic mood, to convey a typical attitude. John Donne, in the first passage, wants to put the reader in a *solemn* frame of mind. Charles Dickens, in the second passage, wants to put us in a *facetious* mood — humorous, indulgent, tolerant, amused. The anonymous writer in *Time,* in the third passage, allows us to feel *clever* — superior to the dim-witted, more sophisticated than ordinary people. Would you agree that in each case the desired effect on the reader is produced not only by what is said, but also by how it is said?

SOLEMN

No man is an island, entire of itself; every man is a piece of the continent, a part of the main. If a clod be washed away by the sea, Europe is the less, as well as if a promontory were, as well as if a manor of thy friend's or of thine own were: any man's death diminishes me, because I am involved in mankind, and therefore never send to know for whom the bell tolls; it tolls for thee. —John Donne, Meditation XVII

FACETIOUS

Smuggins, after a considerable quantity of coughing by way of symphony, and a most facetious sniff or two, which afford general delight, sings a comic song, with a fal-de-ral — tol-de-rol chorus at the end of every verse, much longer than the verse itself. It is received with unbounded applause, and after some aspiring genius has volunteered a recitation, and failed dismally therein, the little pompous man gives another knock, and says "Gen'l'men, we will attempt a glee, if you please." This announcement calls forth tumultuous applause, and the more energetic spirits express the unqualified approbation it affords them, by knocking one or two stout glasses off their legs — a humorous device; but one which frequently occasions some slight altercation when the form of paying the damage is proposed to be gone through by the waiter.
—Charles Dickens, *Sketches by Boz*

CLEVER

Writing an exciting biography about Warren Gamaliel Harding is like filming a chase sequence with a wooden Indian. Harding's instincts were all for posture. Like a suntanned Roman, he struck his Midwest Ciceronian pose and held it, occasionally delivering himself of the sort of speech that instantly self-destructs upon reaching the brain. Francis Russell, historian of Sacco and Vanzetti *(Tragedy in Dedham)*, keeps his camera circling the 29th President of the United States and sometimes almost creates the illusion the body is twitching with life. . . . But he is up against one of the great political still lifes of modern times. The personal portrait that emerges reveals a man notable mainly for his mediocrity of mind and spirit — a rather lazy fellow for whom somebody else always had to open the door when opportunity knocked.
—"Kiss Me, Harding," *Time*

In imaginative literature, writers draw freely on the whole range of possible effects that differences in style can produce. In more practical kinds of writing, the range of choice is more limited. In writing designed to inform or persuade, the basic question that the author asks himself about style is simple: If there are two ways of saying roughly the same thing, which is going to be more *effective?* Which version is more likely to make the reader pay attention, to help him fully understand, and to make him *go on* reading?

Would you agree that the second version in each of the following pairs says roughly the same as the first — but says it more effectively, more memorably? In each case, can you point out some of the features that *make* the second version more effective?

ROUTINE: In modern war, civilian populations are drawn into a struggle aimed at complete mutual destruction and as a result play a prominent role in the total statistics of a war's casualties.

EFFECTIVE: We now have entire populations, including even women and children, pitted against one another in brutish mutual extermination, and only a set of blear-eyed clerks left to add up the butcher's bill.

(Sir Winston Churchill)

ROUTINE: We assume that man learns from experience. We thus assume that Americans have learned from the serious errors made in the exploitation of our natural resources earlier in our history, and that we have learned to make appropriate and economical use of what remains.

EFFECTIVE: It is said of the boy who twisted the mule's tail that he isn't as pretty as he once was, but he knows more. And it is assumed by many Americans that having made catastrophic errors in land use during our occupation of this continent, we have now learned to take care, and conserve, and preserve, and use wisely.

(Wallace Stegner)

ROUTINE: We all go through periods of high and low vitality. Sometimes we seem to have an exceptionally zestful attitude toward life and make the most of our experience.

EFFECTIVE: The life in us is like the water in the river. It may rise this year higher than man has ever known it, and flood the parched uplands; even this may be the eventful year, which will drown out all our muskrats. It was not always dry land where we dwell.

(Henry David Thoreau)

What are some of the secrets of an effective style? Why are some books or articles that we know to be important nevertheless almost unreadable? And vice versa, what makes some authors a pleasure to read even when they deal with relatively unimportant matters? The following advice should help you in your own attempts to develop a more effective style:

(1) *Develop your ear for the common idiom.* Idiomatic language preserves the rhythm and vigor of natural speech. Writing, it is true, is generally more formal than speech — more exact, more polished, more finished. But writing becomes stilted and unnatural when it moves *too far* away from what would sound natural if it were read aloud. When we study the great masters of American prose, we can imagine their sentences being read by a living voice. Though in some ways their language may have become old-fashioned to our ears, it is often surprisingly close to the common language and common experience of their own time:

> Nature made ferns for pure leaves, to show *what she could do in that line.* (Thoreau)

> If the finest genius studies at one of our colleges, and is not installed in an office within one year afterwards, in the cities or suburbs of Boston or New York, it seems to his friends and to himself that he is right in being disheartened and in complaining the rest of his life. A sturdy lad from New Hampshire or Vermont, who in turn tries all the professions, who *teams it, farms it, peddles,* keeps a school, preaches, edits a newspaper, goes to Congress, buys a township, and so forth, in successive years, and always *like a cat falls on his feet,* is worth a hundred of these *city dolls.* (Emerson)

> The table was a greasy board on stilts, and the table-cloth and napkins had not come — and *they were not looking for them, either.* A battered tin platter, a knife and fork, and a tin pint cup, were at each man's place, and the driver had a queensware saucer that *had seen better days.* . . . There was only one cruet left, and that was a stopperless, fly-specked, broken-necked thing, with two inches of vinegar in it, and a dozen preserved flies with their heels up and *looking sorry they had invested there.* (Mark Twain)

(2) *Learn to sum up key ideas in brief, memorable form.* A short, pointed saying has more *impact* than an involved, rounda-

bout sentence. If you want your reader to remember your major points, try to strip them to their essentials. Sum them up in one or two sentences that are striking enough to be noticed, compact enough to be memorized. Then follow them up with supporting sentences that are more detailed, more leisurely, more elaborate.

Can you see what makes each of the following sentences striking, pointed, memorable?

> Life is a banquet, and most of the people at it are starving.

> Greatness is a dream, which is what makes it enduring.

> That men do not learn very much from the lessons of history is the most important of all the lessons that history has to teach.
>
> (Aldous Huxley)

> The reasonable man adapts himself to the world; the unreasonable one persists in trying to adapt the world to himself. Therefore all progress depends upon the unreasonable man.
>
> (George Bernard Shaw)

(3) *Translate the abstract into the concrete.* A good writer dislikes gray, averaged-out, neutral words like *personnel, resident, occupant, situation, factor.* He draws freely on the resources of figurative language and imaginative comparison to make us see actual shapes and textures, to make us share in feelings and attitudes. When a writer describes a boy as "cradling" a young bird in his hands, we get a vivid picture and a wealth of associations. When he compares Yosemite Valley on a summer weekend to "Times Square without electric signs," we get a vivid picture of an anonymous, jostling crowd and are helped to *feel* what it's like to be there.

A good writer almost habitually brings into general statements things that we can *imagine* — things that we can see and hear, feelings that we can share. Can you see how the authors of the following two passages repeatedly use language to bring in scenes that can be visualized, and events that can be mentally acted out?

> My hope for the city's freedom from the curse of street disorders lies not so much in splendid constructions as in the humble, busy neighborhoods, in the type of people I see passing daily to and fro on nearby Upper Broadway or even *enjoying the sunshine as they sit on the mid-traffic street benches.*

. . . I look for the solution of this question to the silent, unpretending efforts of public-school teachers and nuns and to cops and decent city officials and reasonable architects and friendly corner store keepers, and innumerable good persons, male and female, *who tap typewriters in the ever mushrooming office buildings that madly crowd our limited space.*

—John LaFarge, "Brutality and the City," *Saturday Review*

There is less difference than the intelligentsia would have us believe between the daily grind of the "serious" novelist or biographer *in his cloister* and the reporter filing his daily dispatch with *the wind of the world in his face.* They are both writing "pieces." The *monkish pro* has a scene to finish or a chapter to *defeat;* the secular pro has an *event to trap, a flavor to identify.* They are, whatever the theoretical conditions of their freedom to pause and *polish,* both working *in spurts and against a measured mile.* The disparity between the quality of their stuff is still no more or less than that between two men of different talent; it has very little to do with the *accidental binding of one man's pieces into a book* and the *scattering of* the other man's pieces into a hundred issues of his paper.

—Alistair Cooke, "Journalists Who Make History," *Atlantic*

(4) *Make use of purposeful repetition to channel the reader's attention.* Purposeful repetition of words and grammatical patterns calls the reader's attention to closely related ideas. Similar repetition can line up opposite ideas for pointed contrast. When such repetition becomes very noticeable, it approaches the regular rhythms of poetry or the solemn rhythm of the sermon:

> *Who casts not up his eye to the sun* when it rises? *but who takes off his eye from a comet* when that breaks out? *Who bends not his ear to any bell* which upon any occasion rings? *but who can remove it from that bell* which is passing a piece of himself out of this world? (John Donne)

In businesslike modern prose, repetition is kept unobtrusive. It does its job without calling attention to itself. Can you see how in the following sentence all the details that are part of the author's self-portrait appear in the same grammatical construction?

I myself was an ardent literary little girl in an Episcopalian boarding school on the West Coast,

getting up at four in the morning to write a seventeen-page
medieval romance before breakfast,
smoking on the fire escape and thinking of suicide,
meeting a crippled boy in the woods by the cindery athletic
field,
composing a novelette in study hall about the life of a middle-
aged prostitute . . .
when the name *Vassar* entered my consciousness through the person of
an English teacher.

(Mary McCarthy)

In the following passage, the second and third sentence each
give an example of steps the author took after she decided on the
college she wanted to attend. Can you see how closely parallel the
two sentences are in grammatical structure?

The idea of going to Vassar and becoming like Miss
A—— immediately dominated my imagination. *I gave up a
snap course in domestic science and registered for Latin. I
tutored in Caesar during the summer and coaxed my family.*
To go east to college was quite a step in Seattle.

(Mary McCarthy)

(5) *Exploit the leavening effect of humor and irony.* An inexperienced writer often knows only one way of giving his words
added force: to turn up the volume. With experience, he learns
that there are other ways of getting his readers' attention, and of
winning them over to his side. Here are some ways of avoiding an
excessively earnest, solemn, literal style:

VERBAL HUMOR: A skillful writer delights in the echoes and cross
references among words that make possible word
play of different kinds. He appreciates remarks like that of the five-
year old who had just been told about Fire Prevention Week: "When
is *Police* Prevention Week?" Word play plays off against each other
words related in sound, history, or meaning: A student writer called
a trial accompanied by sensational newspaper publicity not "trial by
jury" but "trial by fury." A book reviewer called a book by an elderly
author "delightful antics by a delightful antique."

IRONY: We know that someone is having fun with language when a columnist attacking questionable
deals by city politicians calls City Hall the "Temple of Civic Virtue."
An ironical statement says the *opposite* of what is meant. An ironical
situation carries with it the opposite of what would be expected or
fitting. The following lines from Shakespeare's *Julius Caesar* point to
an irony in Caesar's character:

But when I tell him he hates flatterers,
He says he does, being then most flattered.

(Act III, Scene i)

SATIRE: We feel like saying "touché" when a student writer in a spoof of Christmas commercials writes "Be the first in your neighborhood to sing Christmas carols with a glycerine tear in your eye." Satire exposes shortcomings to ridicule. It attacks not with the cudgel of outright denunciation but with the fencing thrusts of wit. Can you see how, in the following excerpt from one of his *Fables for Our Time,* James Thurber satirizes the bigotry of a bullying majority?

Within the memory of the youngest child there was a family of rabbits who lived near a pack of wolves. The wolves announced that they did not iike the way the rabbits were living. (The wolves were crazy about the way they themselves were living, because it was the only way to live.) One night several wolves were killed in an earthquake and this was blamed on the rabbits, for it is well known that rabbits pound on the ground with their hind legs and cause earthquakes. On another night one of the wolves was killed by a bolt of lightning and this was also blamed on the rabbits, for it is well known that lettuce-eaters cause lightning. The wolves threatened to civilize the rabbits if they didn't behave, and the rabbits decided to run away to a desert island. But the other animals, who lived at a great distance, shamed them, saying, "You must stay where you are and be brave. This is no world for escapists. If the wolves attack you, we will come to your aid, in all probability."

PARODY: We parody something when we imitate it in such a way as to exaggerate its ridiculous traits. Like any clever mimic, the writer of parody has to know what he imitates quite well — especially its weaknesses. Here is Stephen Leacock's parody of what he calls the "English anecdote":

There is another form of humor which I am also quite unable to appreciate. This is that particular form of story which may be called, par excellence, the English Anecdote. It always deals with persons of rank and birth, and, except for the exalted nature of the subject itself, is, as far as I can see, absolutely pointless.

This is the kind of thing that I mean.

"His Grace the Fourth Duke of Marlborough was noted for the open-handed hospitality which reigned at Blenheim, the family seat, during his régime. One day on going in to luncheon it was discovered that there were thirty guests present, whereas the table only held covers for twenty-one. 'Oh, well,' said the Duke, not a whit abashed, "some of us will have to eat standing up.' Everybody, of course, roared with laughter."

My only wonder is that they didn't kill themselves with it. A mere roar doesn't seem enough to do justice to such a story as this. —*Further Foolishness*

REMEMBER: The more distinctive your style becomes, the greater the chance that it will not suit all of your readers. One reason that much business and office prose is gray and colorless is that a neutral, dull style is *safe*. By sampling the reactions of different readers, a writer learns how to write effectively for readers about whose judgment he really cares.

The following prose model was written by a Welsh poet who loved words. He knew how to use them to stir up, tantalize, and enchant his reader. He knew how to do things with them that made the language of other writers seem tame and secondhand by comparison. Study the passage carefully, and answer the questions that follow it.

PROSE MODEL 7

DYLAN THOMAS

A Fire on Christmas Eve

It was on the afternoon of the day of Christmas Eve, and I was in Mrs. Prothero's garden, waiting for cats, with her son Jim. It was snowing. It was always snowing at Christmas; December, in my memory, is white as Lapland, though there were no reindeers. But there were cats. Patient, cold, and callous, our hands wrapped in socks, we waited to snowball the cats. Sleek and long as jaguars and terrible-whiskered, spitting and snarling they would slink and sidle over the white back-garden walls, and the lynx-eyed hunters, Jim and I, fur-capped and moccasined trappers from Hudson's Bay off Eversley Road, would hurl our deadly snowballs at the green of their eyes. The wise cats never appeared. We were so still, Eskimo-footed arctic marksmen in the muffling silence of the eternal snows — eternal, ever since Wednesday — that we never heard Mrs. Prothero's first cry from her igloo at the bottom of the garden. Or, if we heard it at all, it was, to us, like the far-off challenge of our enemy and prey, the neighbor's Polar Cat. But soon the voice grew louder. "Fire!" cried Mrs. Prothero, and she beat the dinner-gong. And we ran down the garden, with the snowballs in our arms, towards the house, and smoke, indeed, was pouring out of the dining-room, and the gong was bombilating, and Mrs. Prothero was announcing ruin like a town-crier in Pompeii. This was better than all the cats in Wales standing on the wall in a row. We bounded into the house, laden with snowballs, and stopped at the open door of the smoke-filled room. Something was burning all right; perhaps it was Mr. Prothero, who always slept there after midday dinner with a newspaper over his face; but he was standing in the middle of the room, saying "A fine Christmas!" and smacking at the smoke with a slipper.

"Call the fire-brigade," cried Mrs. Prothero as she beat the gong.

"They won't be there," said Mr. Prothero, "it's Christmas."

There was no fire to be seen, only clouds of smoke and Mr. Prothero standing in the middle of them, waving his slipper as though he were conducting.

"Do something," he said.

And we threw all our snowballs into the smoke — I think we missed Mr. Prothero — and ran out of the house to the telephone-box.

"Let's call the police as well," Jim said.

"And the ambulance."

"And Ernie Jenkins, he likes fires."

But we only called the fire-brigade, and soon the fire-engine came and three tall men in helmets brought a hose into the house and Mr. Prothero got out just in time before they turned it on. Nobody could have had a noisier Christmas Eve. And when the firemen turned off the hose and were standing in the wet and smoky room, Jim's aunt, Miss Prothero, came downstairs and peered in at them. Jim and I waited, very quietly, to hear what she would say to them. She said the right thing, always. She looked at the three tall firemen in their shining helmets, standing among the smoke and cinders and dissolving snowballs, and she said: "Would you like something to read?"   —from *Quite Early One Morning*

1. Dylan Thomas was known for his mastery of expressive language that conjures up a graphic picture before the reader's eye. Point out half a dozen words that are more concrete than you would find in more routine prose.

2. Thomas had the kind of imagination that transforms the commonplace into something strange and wonderful. Can you show this kind of imagination at work in this selection?

3. How would you describe the author's kind of humor? How much of it is in the situations he describes? How much of it is in his use of language? Can you compare or contrast it with other kinds of humor with which you are familiar?

4. The author has a sense for the dramatic that gives life and movement to his account of an incident or scene. Can you point out features of the selection that help dramatize the author's account?

5. Write a paragraph in which you make a scene that is quite familiar to your readers into something strange and new.

6. Write two paragraphs, each describing the same authentic incident from your own observation or experience. Make the first version serious, the second facetious.

EXERCISE 25   Write half a dozen "modern proverbs," summing up a general observation in pointed, memorable form. Here, from the British humor magazine *Punch,* are some possible models:

> It's a long street that has no parking meter.
> He who laughs last will never be part of a studio audience.
> Where there's muck there's headlines.
> A watched bus never comes.
> A pound earned is eight-and-threepence owed.
> What goes up is most unlikely to come down.

EXERCISE 26   In each of the following passages, point out all features that make its style different from that of routine, ordinary, uninteresting prose. (Your teacher may ask you to write a paragraph modeled very closely on one of these.)

1.   Writers from the Middle West have kept most of the New York publishers in business for years. Without the Heartland, there would be no American literature. Where did Hemingway come from? And Dos Passos? And Fitzgerald and Lewis? MacLeish and Van Doren came from Illinois, not Long Island. Dreiser came out of Terre Haute, not Westchester County. Where did Sandburg come from? And Hart Crane? And William Dean Howells and Mark Twain? From the Midlands, that's where. Even T. S. Eliot blew his first soap bubble in St. Louis, and Tennessee Williams grew up in the same city.   —letter to the editor

2.   A major television network last night premiered the only new live music-and-dance program of the season. The opening half hour presented six musical acts of varied accomplishment that came and went so fast even the emcee was swamped. The musical quality is as transparent as the producer's intent, but everything moves with hysterical precision. The appeal will be exclusively to teen-agers, a not too demanding audience. Occasionally, one gets the eerie feeling that these are all little dolls come to life and they're going to catch hell when the toymaker comes back. A word should be said about the dancers. The word is "appalling," I would say. But the dances are cunningly choreographed with wild abandon to conceal the fact that the dancers cannot dance. It almost works. Flashy, noisy fun for the kids who have finished their homework — or, more likely, those who aren't planning to do any.   —newspaper column

3.   A wearisome catalogue of items and activities has now been proscribed — not by mums and dads but by highly educated ladies and gentlemen — as "bad for you." Food, for example. A widening waist-line was once something which came naturally with the years, like greying temples or going to sleep after dinner. Then the ghouls with the slide-rules, employed by life insurance companies, put beyond doubt that stout parties were more liable to collapse (permanently) than thin ones. So now we are obsessed with cutting down our weight, preferably without cutting down our eating. With laughable ease fortunes are made by imprisoning people in country mansions and feeding them orange-juice. Chemists' shops are lined with slimming foods, so attractively packaged some look good enough to eat. Our model girls have long ago passed from a bewitching slimness to an absolutely fascinating emaciation.   —column in *Punch*

4.   The bowerbird is another creature that spends so much time courting the female that he never gets any work done. If all the male bowerbirds became nervous wrecks within the next ten or fifteen years, it would not surprise me. The female bowerbird insists that a playground be built for her with a specially constructed bower at the entrance. This bower is much more elaborate than an ordinary nest and is harder to build; it costs a lot more, too. The female will not come to the playground until the male has filled it up with a great many gifts: silvery leaves, red leaves, rose petals, shells, beads, berries, bones, dice, buttons, cigar bands,

Christmas seals, and the Lord knows what else. When the female finally condescends to visit the playground, she is in a coy and silly mood and has to be chased in and out of the bower and up and down the playground before she will quit giggling and stand still long enough even to shake hands. The male bird is, of course, pretty well done in before the chase starts. —James Thurber, *My World — and Welcome to It*

THEME TOPICS 7 A. How do older people talk to teen-agers? How much of the "lack of communication" between the generations can be blamed on the *language* adults use when talking to people your own age? Study typical expressions, sayings, ways of saying things. How do teen-agers react to these? What impression do they get of the adult's attitude toward adolescents?

B. What style óf talking is popular among high school students you know well? Is there any kind of talk that is considered especially sophisticated? Can you give detailed illustrations? Or are there several *different* styles — popular with different groups? What does the way a teen-ager talks reveal about the kind of person he is — or wants to be?

C. Do you know a place that makes you daydream, or that is full of associations with the past? Write a paper about it in which you make a special effort to make your reader share in your own mood or moods.

D. Write two letters in which you describe the same event as seen through the eyes of two quite different observers. Make sure the way each letter is written gives the reader a vivid impression of the kind of person you imagine yourself to be.

E. Write two versions of a love letter addressed to an imaginary person. Each time, imitate a writer known for his distinctive style. For instance, you might select as models Elizabeth Barrett Browning and e. e. cummings, or Charles Dickens and Ernest Hemingway.

F. Study the letters to the editor in your local newspaper. Are there several predictable types of letters? Write three or four short letters that parody the most characteristic types. Or, do a similar parody of letters to columnists offering advice.

G. Are you aware of any current controversy that is conducted with especially grim seriousness? Can you write a paper in which you bring out some humorous sidelights, or try to get the parties involved to see at least some aspect of the controversy in a humorous light?

H. Are you aware of any kind of writing or type of publication that especially annoys you? Write a satirical paper in which you attack its ridiculous or objectionable traits. Make sure your satire has a clear target; try to make it effective with a fair-minded reader.

C 5 Writing About Literature

Learn to write papers in which you interpret and evaluate imaginative literature.

Among the English themes that a student is asked to write in high school or in college, many deal with topics drawn from imaginative literature. Such themes test your skill both as a reader and as a writer. Typically, they will require you to answer one or more of the following questions about a poem, story, novel, or play:

(1) "What do I make of this?" When you answer this first and most basic question, you engage in **interpretation.** When you interpret a work of literature, you tell the reader: "This is what I think this poem or story says. This is what I think the author is trying to do." In interpreting a work, you try to do justice to what is in front of you on the printed page (or what is acted out in front of you on the stage). You show that you have tried to take in what a story has to offer, that you have tried to get into the spirit of a poem or a play. To be fair to the poet or playwright, we try to interpret a work *before* we pronounce judgment. Before we agree or disagree, before we show our likes and dislikes, we try to *understand.*

(2) "How do I react to this?" A poem or a play does not simply give us information that we store for future use. It speaks to us as people. It makes us *think and feel.* When we engage in **evaluation,** we show whether we considered the experience meaningful, or valuable, or worthwhile. Sometimes, we cannot see any real point in a poem or story, and we try to explain the breakdown in communication. Sometimes, we resist the thoughts and feelings a work suggests to us, and we try to explain our antipathy or disapproval. Sometimes, finally, we feel that a work powerfully speaks to us, and we try to explain what gives it its power and meaning.

(3) "How does this compare with other works I have read?" Comparison and contrast helps us *understand and judge.* The first time we read a seventeenth-century sonnet, it may be utterly strange

to us. But after we study several such poems, we begin to detect certain patterns. We begin to see what the poet expects of his reader. A reader who is bewildered or confused can begin to make headway if he can say to himself: "This reminds me of something else I have read."

When you write about literature, you show how much of your reading you can make truly your own. You show how *active* a reader you are — how fully you participate in the kind of imaginative experience that literature makes possible.

C 5a The Critical Paper

Help your reader understand and enjoy a poem, short story, novel, or play.

What is the difference between literature and reading matter intended merely for entertainment? Literature is worth *rereading*. A short story like Hemingway's "The Killers" has been read and enjoyed by thousands of readers. But it has also been read *several times* by people who each time enjoy it again, and *think* about it again. In a critical paper, you have a chance to discuss such a story — to tell your readers how it made you feel, and what you thought about it.

When you write about a story, a poem, or a play, what is there to say? If you do nothing else, you may want to tell your readers "what happens." The following paragraph summarizes what happens in a famous story about a former college football player:

> Irwin Shaw's "The 80-Yard Run" is the story of an appallingly uninteresting fellow who was distinguished only by his talent as broken-field runner. In his sophomore year during a practice session he gets the ball and goes beautifully, perfectly, for a 80-yard touchdown. It is a real moment of truth, in which things fit together and life, in a brilliant flash, has order and meaning. But before his junior year he injures himself and his career is never the same. He carries the ball again but there is always someone in the way to disturb the consummation of the run; things don't open up. He marries a woman who worshipped him as a halfback, gets bored with him in later life, and takes on a lover. The halfback-husband takes a

job as a traveling clothing salesman for colleges, returns to his own school and goes to the empty field to relive the moment of the 80-yard run.

—Dan Wakefield, "In Defense of the Fullback," *Dissent*

If we have never read the story, this summary of the action will give us a good idea of what the story is about. Even if we have read the story, this summary will remind us of the highlights. But at the same time, this summary leaves us with questions like the following:

— *Why* do things happen the way they do in this story?
— What kind of *person* is this former halfback — would the same kind of thing have happened to someone else?
— How does the story make us *feel?*
— What does it make us *think?*
— How does the writer *make us* think and feel the way we do?

When you try to answer such questions, you go beyond a mere plot summary — a mere summary of the action. You begin to talk about what the story means. You begin to talk about how the writer gave the story its meaning. You help your readers understand and enjoy the story when they read it themselves.

Even a short poem or story may raise many different questions in a reader's mind. To give unity to a short critical paper, focus on one of the following:

(1) *Examine a writer's use of language.* A poet (and also a novelist or a playwright) uses language *imaginatively.* He makes it do things we did not know it could do. Normally, for instance, words like *pompous, hate, incompetent, barbaric, supercilious,* and *arrogant* all would create a strongly negative picture. We would call someone "pompous" or "incompetent" or "barbaric" to show that we *dis*approve of him. But the opposite is true when Helene Johnson uses the same words in her defiant "Sonnet to a Negro in Harlem." She uses all these words, but she makes them serve her in her expression of loyalty and admiration for the person to whom they apply. Could you explain in a short paper *how* she does this? Could you show how she changes the *connotations* of these words as she uses them in the poem?

You are disdainful and magnificent—
Your perfect body and your *pompous* gait,
Your dark eyes flashing solemnly with *hate*,
Small wonder that you are *incompetent*,
To imitate those whom you so despise—
Your shoulders towering high above the throng,
Your head thrown back in rich, *barbaric* song,
Palm trees and mangoes stretched before your eyes.
Let others toil and sweat for *labor's* sake
And wring from grasping hands their meed of gold.
Why urge ahead your *supercilious* feet?
Scorn will efface each footprint that you make.
I love your laughter *arrogant* and bold.
You are too splendid for this city street.

(2) *Discuss a major character.* When we first read a good story, we may be carried along by our interest in the action. John Steinbeck's story, "Flight," for instance, keeps us in grim suspense as the boy Pepé is hunted down in the mountains after he has killed a man in a fight. But as we look back over the story, we realize that this is *Pepé's* story. It is the story of a boy who *wanted to be* a man, proudly going on a man's errands for his widowed mother:

> "Adiós, Mama," Pepé cried. "I will come back soon. You may send me often alone. I am a man."

It is the story of a boy who tried to *act* like a man when finding himself suddenly in a man's world:

> "I am a man now, Mama. The man said names to me I could not allow."

It is the story of a boy who *died* like a man when he finally turned to face his pursuers:

> It was a long struggle to get to his feet. He crawled slowly and mechanically to the top of a big rock on the ridge peak. Once there, he arose slowly, swaying to his feet, and stood erect. . . . There came a ripping sound at his feet. A piece of stone flew up and a bullet droned off into the next gorge. The hollow crash echoed up from below. Pepé looked down for a moment and then pulled himself straight again.
> His body jarred back. His left hand fluttered helplessly toward his breast. The second crash sounded from below.

Pepé swung forward and toppled from the rock. His body struck and rolled over and over, starting a little avalanche. And when at last he stopped against a bush, the avalanche slid slowly down and covered up his head.

As you reread the story of Pepé, you might ask yourself questions like the following:

— What kind of general description does the author give of the person? (Steinbeck describes Pepé as a "gentle, affectionate boy.")
— What does the person *do* that reveals something about his character? (Pepé spends hours practice-throwing the long, heavy knife he has inherited from his father.)
— What do other people say about him? And what do they really *think* about him? (Pepé's mother "thought him fine and brave, but she never told him so.")

In a short critical paper, you could tell your reader what Pepé looked like, what he said, what he did, how he seemed to other people. You could help your reader understand *why* things happened in Steinbeck's story the way they did.

(3) *Examine the structure of a literary work.* What holds the different parts of a poem, or a short story, or a play together? In a novel or a play, we can see structural relations on a large scale. Just as an architect builds on a firm foundation, a novelist or a playwright may at the beginning do the groundwork on which to build the rest of his story. Often when you look back at the end, you can say: "This scene, early in the book, helped prepare the reader for something that happened later."

In the last act of Shakespeare's play, Othello, goaded to fury by *false* accusations of infidelity brought against his wife, destroys her in the name of "justice." Earlier in the play we have seen Othello in a *parallel* situation: Incited by *false* reports of a drunken brawl, Othello turns against a faithful subordinate in the name of "order." This repetition of a similar situation, with similar results, is obviously not accidental. The earlier incident **foreshadows** the final catastrophe. It helps build up our understanding of Othello's *double* nature: He is a person of great dignity and high moral standards, and yet capable of unleashed ferocity and destructive, misguided passion. By showing your reader such parallels or other similar connections, you can help explain the strong, unified impact of a great play.

In a short poem, we can study structural relations on a more limited scale. A poet may give unity to a poem by carrying through in detail one, single, imaginative analogy. For instance, we are all familiar with the idea of comparing love to a fever. But in the following sonnet, Shakespeare shows in *how many ways* love is similar to a fever. The analogy thus becomes a structural metaphor that helps give shape to the poem as a whole. Can you show in detail how this structural metaphor is "carried through" in the poem as a whole?

> My love is as a fever, longing still
> For that which longer nurseth the disease,
> Feeding on that which doth preserve the ill,
> The uncertain sickly appetite to please.
> My reason, the physician to my love,
> Angry that his prescriptions are not kept,
> Hath left me, and I desperate now approve
> Desire is death, which physic did except.
> Past cure I am, now reason is past care,
> And frantic-mad with evermore unrest.
> My thoughts and my discourse as madmen's are,
> At random from the truth vainly expressed,
> For I have sworn thee fair, and thought thee bright,
> Who art as black as Hell, as dark as night.
>
> (Sonnet CXLVII)

(4) *Trace a unifying theme.* When we read an announcement, we expect to find a clear and simple message, directly stated. When we read a story or see a play, we may still look for the writer's message, but we expect to find it *acted out.* We come to know the characters, and we witness events, and we gradually begin to sense what it all means. When we trace the **theme** of a story or a play, we try to sum up the overall meaning as it gradually unravels or falls into place.

Suppose we are reading (and rereading) a story like Stephen Crane's "The Open Boat." How would we proceed in order to identify its major theme? As we see the four shipwrecked men in their absurdly small lifeboat, we might ask ourselves: Is there any question raised in our minds — and then *kept alive* by what happens in the rest of the story? Does any idea suggest itself to the reader again and again as he watches these men in their back-breaking struggle to reach the shore?

One idea that enters our minds again and again is that nature, far from being man's real home, is really not made for man. This is our first reaction as we see the men in their boat, not much larger than a bathtub, surrounded by jagged and "barbarously abrupt and tall waves." The men have no eyes for the wild splendor of the shining, storm-tossed sea; they are absorbed in their efforts that take all their limited strength. They are angered by the sea birds, unruffled and at home in a setting that threatens to destroy these exhausted human beings. The men's natural constitution is ill adapted to the toil required of them in rowing the boat, since "the human back can become the seat of more aches and pains than are registered in books for the composite anatomy of a regiment."

When the men finally sight land, the surf keeps them from reaching shore. In their last desperate attempt to make it to safety, the oiler, a strong swimmer and seemingly best adapted for survival, is drowned. The injured captain, seemingly doomed, survives. Again and again, the story makes us feel that man lives in a world not made for him; that man must look for warmth, friendship, and support to other human beings rather than to an indifferent universe, which does not care whether he lives or dies. A well-organized critical paper could present this idea as the central theme, and then show the many ways this theme is echoed, implied, or acted out in different parts of the story.

(5) *Examine the role of a key symbol.* A symbol gives a visible shape to an idea. The cross is a familiar symbol of the Christian faith. Many related thoughts and emotions cluster around it. It brings to mind the passion of Christ, the blood of Christian martyrs, the ardor of generations of true believers.

A writer often chooses his *own* symbols, gradually building up their meanings and associations. He may build a whole poem or story around one or more symbols that become focal points for our attention. By examining closely the role of one such symbol, we can learn much about what the writer wants us to think and to feel. In Ralph Ellison's novel *Invisible Man,* the narrator repeatedly encounters symbolic objects that vividly sum up for him major elements in the history of his own people. Here, for instance, is his first look at a "keepsake" kept by an older man who spent nineteen years on a chain gang before he finally broke the chain and escaped:

> I took it in my hand, a thick dark, oily piece of filed steel that had been twisted open and forced partly back into place, on which I saw marks that might have been made by the blade of a hatchet. It . . . bore the marks of haste and violence, looking as though it had been attacked and conquered before it stubbornly yielded.

In a short critical paper, you could trace the way such a symbol works in its context. How is it first introduced? How do different people react to it? What does the author say about it? Does it play a role in any of the major events of the plot? How does it fit into the story as a whole? In Ellison's novel, the leg-iron from the chain gang becomes one of the things that makes the young Negro feel united with the members of his own race and divides him, for instance, from the white radicals who want him to be their political ally. It becomes a symbol of the solidarity he feels with his black brothers and the alienation he feels from the white man's world.

As you work on critical papers of this kind, remember a few basic requirements:

— *Keep the reader in close contact with the actual work.* When you make general points, support them by referring directly to the work in front of you. Quote the actual words used by a poet; point to specific events in a story; refer in detail to the actions and words of a character in a play. Study carefully the following excerpt from a student paper about Antigone, the central character in the play of the same name by the Greek poet, Sophocles. Can you see how the student author has brought together short quotations from *different* parts of the play to support her estimate of Antigone's character? Can you see how she has chosen a *longer* quotation at a crucial point to show the key motive that makes Antigone act the way she does?

> The chorus, in one instance, gives us a clue to her personality by declaring, "the maid shows herself passionate child of passionate sire, and knows not how to bend before troubles."

Later, when Antigone is on the way to her doom and is lamenting her fate, the chorus replies, "thy self-willed temper hath wrought thy ruin." It also refers to Antigone as mistress of her own fate, indicating that it feels it is nobody's fault but her own that she finds herself facing inevitable death. When Antigone tells her sister, Ismene, of her plans to bury Polyneices, Ismene calls her "over-bold." Creon is more vehement in describing her. He calls her a proud and "o'er-stubborn" spirit. He says, too, that she is "versed in insolence." However, Creon may perhaps be too prejudiced against his niece to see her clearly.

Let us then examine the conflict which makes this passionate and self-willed girl choose the path that leads to her destruction. A famous scholar has said that Antigone's tragic fate illustrates "the devotion to a higher unseen law, resulting in revolt against, and destruction by, the lower visible law." Antigone's religious motivation is very intense. This becomes evident when she tells her sister: "I owe a longer allegiance to the dead than to the living; in that world I shall abide forever. But if thou wilt, be guilty of dishonoring laws which the gods have established in honor." When she is arrested by the guards and brought to Creon, he asks her why she dared to transgress his edict and she replies:

> It was not Zeus that had published me that edict; not such are the laws set among men by the Justice who dwells with the gods below; nor deemed I that thy decrees were of such force that a mortal could override the unwritten and unfailing statutes of heaven. For their life is not of today or yesterday, but from all time, and no man knows when they were first put forth. Not through dread of any human pride could I answer to the gods for breaking these.

— *Define and illustrate key critical terms you use in interpretation and evaluation.* Try not to rely on ready-made labels. When you call a play "propaganda," you may raise more questions than you answer. Is it propaganda for a good cause — or a bad? Is it powerful propaganda — or ineffectual? Where do you draw the line between propaganda and persuasion? Is all preaching "propaganda"? Is everyone who speaks up strongly for a cause a "propagandist"? When you start applying these questions directly to your "propaganda play," the reader will learn about the play itself.

When you simply apply a ready-made label like "propaganda," or "sentimental," or "escapist" to a poem or a play, your reader may feel like asking: "Have you really tried to find out what this poem has to offer? Have you really tried to find out what makes it different from other poems on a similar theme?" Notice how carefully the author of the following passage from a student paper explains what he means by "sensationalism" — instead of using the term as a handy label to paste on a play:

A play is designed to act out a certain fictitious or real occurrence in life. This occurrence, which in reality may have taken days, months, or years to happen, must be condensed into two or three short hours in the play. In this condensation, only the most significant points of the real-life occurrence can be included. Because only these action-packed, emotion-filled, exciting points of many days or months are being squashed into two short hours, we unavoidably have a great deal of dramatic effect. When handled correctly, this dramatic, exciting action can impress very vividly upon the mind of the audience the thoughts that the author is trying to impress. This dramatic, vivid effect alone does not make the play "sensational."

However, a play can be *too* full of action, emotion, and excitement. A play can be dramatically overdone. For example, a death or a murder or a love affair can give a play its expected and necessary amount of excitement, and it can be useful in bringing out the theme of the play. On the other hand, when we have a few assaults, a couple of murders, a love affair, a heart attack, a marriage, two deaths, and a subpoena from the House Un-American Activities Committee all rolled into one play, we lose interest and begin to wonder if perhaps four or five lifetimes, rather than four or five weeks or months, are being considered. Thus when a play is dramatically overdone, it becomes sensational, and interest in the theme is lost.

— *Focus your paper on one key question or major point.* When a critic is famous for his ability to explain difficult works, we might be willing to attend a lecture that is titled merely "Notes I Made While Reading *Hamlet.*" Even if the notes are miscellaneous, we are likely to learn *something* important about a difficult play. But most critics receive basically the same reaction as the salesman who comes to our door. Our question is: "What do you want? What do you have to offer? What is the point?"

Try to make clear early in your paper what you have to offer. Then, in the rest of your paper, concentrate on making that offer good. Can you see how the author of the following short student paper has concentrated on doing one clearly limited task? Can you point out the features that make this an exceptionally well-unified paper?

The Anxieties of Beret Hansa

Beret Hansa, one of the main characters in O. E. Rölvaag's novel, *Giants in the Earth,* was a woman filled with anxieties. These anxieties, nurtured by her guilt complex, later led to her insanity. Beret was not a woman suited to pioneer life. She was a "fine-grained" person, and could not easily endure the hardships of the frontier.

To begin with, Beret was a very devout person. While still living in Norway, she had committed a sin which haunted her mind the rest of her days. Ole, her oldest child, had been conceived out of wedlock. To be sure, Beret later married the child's father, Per Hansa. Although Beret dearly loved her husband, she felt that God was punishing her by casting Satan's hands upon her and her family. Part of Satan's evil plan was to send her and her dear ones away from their beloved home in Norway, to a strange and foreign land where no human being could possibly survive.

As a result, Beret believed that the vast emptiness of the prairie was a part of her punishment. For on the prairie, where few trees or living animals survived, there was no place to hide. All that surrounded her was an endless sea of grass planted on a flat, never-ending surface. Beret felt that she needed some place where she could hide her sins instead of bearing their scars out in the open. But there in the prairie there was no such place — there was no place to hide.

The following prose model was written by an American critic who is at the same time an exceptionally good writer. The passage discusses the American poet Walt Whitman and traces one of the major themes in his poetry. Study the passage carefully, and answer the questions that follow it.

PROSE MODEL 8

ALFRED KAZIN

The Writer and the City

In the nineteenth century the profoundest moralists and poets, and most of the good novelists, felt unrelated to great American cities. Yet there was already one exception in the nineteenth century who was to be prophetic: both of the importance of New York as a world capital of many races and peoples, and of the importance of poetry in shaping twentieth-century epics of the big city. Uniquely among gifted American writers of his time and place, Whitman found himself as man and artist by identifying with New York. None of the talented writers born and bred in New York — not Melville or James or Edith Wharton — was to make of New York such an instrument of personal liberation, such a living glowing fable of democratic possibility. Old patrician New York still speaks in Melville's poem "The House-Top," written July 1863, in his rage against the largely immigrant mobs who were burning and looting in the streets below in their protest against the draft. Melville speaks of the riot as "the Atheist roar of riot," and complains bitterly that "The Town is taken by its rats — ship-rats/ And rats of the wharves." But Whitman, his exact contemporary, did not yet despair of the identification of democracy with the masses that the modern city revealed to him. He found himself by finding the city to be the great human stage. Only through participation by the masses, he felt, would America fulfill the sacred purpose manifest in what even the conservative Tocqueville had felt to be the miracle of God's keeping the New World in reserve for man. The masses, already visible in New York's population of over a million, were the evidence Whitman needed to ground his intuitive and radical gospel. Walt Whitman, poet, formerly a school-teacher, formerly a printer, formerly a newspaperman, formerly a carpenter, a failure at many occupations born into a family of failures and psychic cripples, felt that he had come out of the big anonymous city crowd, with its unspoken griefs and hopes, to speak for it: *"One's self I sing, a simple separate person./ Yet utter the word Democratic, the word En-Masse. . . . Of Life immense in passion, pulse and power,/ Cheerful, for freest action form'd under the laws divine,/ The Modern Man I sing."*

Whitman, it can be said, found the model and form of his book, the one book he wrote all his life, in the city, its volume and mass, its mobility, excitement, danger. Years ago I lived just across from the corner in Brooklyn Heights where Whitman himself first printed *Leaves of Grass.* Every Sunday, by way of Brooklyn Bridge, I walked over the East River that was for him the most significant waterway in the world. I realized then how much Whitman's long single lines, each a complete journey in itself, was formed on his ferry journeys back and across that estuary. Equally, Whitman's idea of his book as a dense, numerous world, that would express "the pending action of this Time & Land we swim in, with all their large fluctuations of despair and hope," found in New York all the sanction he needed for trying to put everything into his book and also for seeking to make his book everything to all men. His instinct in composition was to enter into such free association with himself that every thought, every image, might be a link to everything else.

Whitman was a true prophet of the coming interrelations between the individual spirit and the social body. His image of the city is free from despair and hatred; he is not a determinist; for him the city is still a voluntary community created by vital people choosing to live in the same space; the individual is still in touch with nature, which is God; with his *own* nature, where God is revealed. Whitman's New York is a city of joys and possibilities, of easy afternoons riding next to the drivers of the great omnibuses tearing down Broadway, of ecstatic walks on empty ocean beaches at Coney Island. It is a city rich in sexual excitement — a city for lovers. Yet at the same time it is the city of young men from the crowd awakening to their possibilities as observers, thinkers, writers. Cities, as people still have to be told, are among the greatest inventions of man; are creative deeds and peculiarly centers of creativity. Whitman's best poem of New York, *Crossing Brooklyn Ferry,* identifies the glowing, creative consciousness of the poet with the energy of the crowd at the rush hour and the primal energies of the universe vibrating along the river. It is this feeling for the constant movement of modern life, as it culminates in the unending stir of city life, that makes *Leaves of Grass* anticipate so many twentieth-century social novels equally founded on the human richness of city life.

1. Explain briefly: *moralist, patrician, estuary, determinist, primal.* What are the meanings of the following italicized words in context? *"Found* himself as a man and artist"; "born and *bred* in New York"; "a living glowing *fable* of democratic possibility"; "the purpose *manifest* in what . . . Tocqueville had felt"; "found all the *sanction* he needed."

2. Where in this passage does the critic point to the symbolism in external things that come to stand for ideas? As fully as you can, explain these symbolic relationships in your own words.

3. How would you define the word *democracy* as it is used by Kazin in this passage? Write a paragraph in which you fully define the word as here used, and compare and contrast this use with familiar or current uses of the term.

4. Read "Crossing Brooklyn Ferry," one of the best known and most widely reprinted of Whitman's poems. Can you find in it some of the things Kazin says are typical of Whitman's poetry? Do you find in it anything that would cause you to *dis*agree with Kazin? Report your findings.

5. Whitman wrote in the nineteenth century. How do Americans today think and feel about their big cities? How has the attitude described by Kazin changed since Whitman's time? How much of it survives — how and where? (Have you read a work of literature in which a big city, or life in a big city, plays a major role? Your teacher may ask you to write a paper comparing and contrasting Whitman's treatment of New York in some of his poems with the treatment of a city in the other work you have read.)

6. Whitman wrote many of his poems about the kind of nation he wanted this country to become. Write a paragraph about something that is a symbol of what you would want this country to become.

EXERCISE 27 Much literary criticism deals with classics, or at least with authors generally recognized. Even when it points out shortcomings, it tends to do so respectfully. But a relatively unknown and living author does not always get courteous treatment. Study the following modern poem and the two critical reactions that were published with it. Can you explain the critics' reactions? Do you share them? Do you think they are too harsh? (Or too lenient?) Write a short critical reaction of your own. Feel free to express your likes and dislikes, but support them by pointing to specific things in the poem.

Can A Merry-Go-Round Horse
Gallop in a Straight Line?

As a kid on a merry-go-round
you could point at the whole
world by sticking one finger
out. Rings must have been
on rich kids' merry-go-rounds,
but there was lots of sky,
and mom's wave of new courage
always followed the popcorn
stand. The blind man would
squeeze your last ticket
into his brown hand while
Sousa's "Stars and Stripes
Forever" would come around
again like a red and white

goose after a blue elk and
you came to expect things.
Like the popcorn stand and mom.
Will a policeman who is used
to waving stop and go at anonymous
cars let a green and blue horse
on a yellow pole run a red light
on its way to the rainbow?

(Daniel Ort)

No: this doesn't work for me at all. Unlike "Shower of Small Praise" (also published in this issue), where the charm is danced along with music and form, this is labored and heavy: cotton-candy stuffed with lead. For me, it never gets past cuteness, never gets past prose. And it's filled with sloganized nonsense: the "brown hand" of the ticket-taker (God: the thing might just as well be "weather-beaten"); the Sousa-music (for Colorful Nostalgia); and — egh — Mom. mom. Stuffed down a tuba, I hope.

No. My sympathies are all with the cop, who ought to take that green and blue little teensy horse and break both its legs.

(Stanley Cooperman)

A poem is nothing for me unless it purges my sensitivities. Once it accomplishes this I give it an automatic ear-notch for having quality. Then I go back to the work and single out finer aspects, but keeping in mind that the poem has already done its job.

"Can a Merry-Go-Round Horse Gallop in a Straight Line?" has the ear-notch. It brings back a sensitivity of my youth. It is the excitement and wonder and mouth-gaping curiosity found at a carnival. It is wild imagination bounded by mother's pessimism and the authority of the traffic cop.

The poem is lacking in craft. A close examination reveals mulberry stains on the quilt. The sentence beginning "The blind would . . ." is very awkward. "Would" is a vague verb and using it twice in the same sentence to show simultaneous actions weakens the structure. Going from the blind man's squeeze through the "Stars and Stripes Forever" and "like a red and white goose after a blue elk" is too much to swallow in one gulp.

Just one more thing. I can understand why a kid who spent his last nickel for a ride on the merry-go-round is jealous of the rich kids, but where can I see one of these "rich kids' merry-go-rounds"?

(Tom E. Knowlton)
—from Poet and Critic

THEME TOPICS 8 A. In a good poem, every word counts. Can you show that this is true of many of the words in the following poem? One critic, in discussing this poem, talked about how the words *favored, imperially, arrayed,* and *glittered* help shape our impression of Richard Cory. What other words are different from what you might expect? Can you show what they mean in this poem?

Richard Cory

Whenever Richard Cory went down town,
    We people on the pavement looked at him:
He was a gentleman from sole to crown,
    Clean favored, and imperially slim.

And he was always quietly arrayed,
    And he was always human when he talked;
But still he fluttered pulses when he said,
    "Good-morning," and he glittered when he walked.

And he was rich — yes, richer than a king,
    And admirably schooled in every grace:
In fine, we thought that he was everything
    To make us wish that we were in his place.

So on we worked, and waited for the light,
    And went without the meat, and cursed the bread;
And Richard Cory, one calm summer night,
    Went home and put a bullet through his head.

—Edwin Arlington Robinson

B. Discuss the use of language in a sonnet by Shakespeare, a poem by Emily Dickinson, or a short poem by a modern poet of your choice.

C. Have you recently encountered a fictional character whom you would call a "rebel"? Write a character study in which you try to explain the nature and sources of his rebellion. Here are some possible choices:

— Heathcliff in *Wuthering Heights;*
— Jack in *Lord of the Flies;*
— Holden in *The Catcher in the Rye;*
— Stephen in *A Portrait of the Artist as a Young Man.*

D. In a melodrama, we cheer the hero, and we hiss the villain. But in a truly great play, we are often asked to understand characters who may be a mixture of good and evil. Have you ever tried to understand fully, and perhaps to sympathize with, one of the more *un*popular or *un*heroic characters in a great play? Have you ever looked for the traits that make an evil or unsympathetic character at the same time human or understandable? Write a character study of one such dramatic figure. Here are some possible choices:

— Claudius in *Hamlet;*
— Iago in *Othello;*
— Edmund in *King Lear;*
— The Reverend Parris in *The Crucible;*
— Creon in *Antigone.*

E. Write a letter in which you pretend to be a character from a novel who protests against the treatment he received at the hands of the author. For instance, the letter might be from Steerforth or from Uriah Heep (Charles Dickens, *David Copperfield*) ; or from Eustacia Vye, telling her side of the story (Thomas Hardy, *Return of the Native*) ; or from the "whiskey priest" in Graham Greene's *The Power and the Glory;* or from Comrade Napoleon in George Orwell's *Animal Farm.*

F. Have you read a story, novel, or play where two parallel situations in different parts of the work help develop a similar point? Trace the parallel in detail, showing its significance in the work as a whole.

G. What major changes would a modern playwright have to make who wanted to *adapt* a familiar play in such a way as to be able to change the title from

— *Julius Caesar* to *Brutus;*
— *Macbeth* to *Lady Macbeth;*
— *Hamlet* to *Gertrude;*
— *Othello* to *Desdemona;*
— *Antigone* to *Creon;*
— *The Taming of the Shrew* to *The Taming of the Boor.*

You may wish to write your paper in the form of an outline-script for the adapted play.

H. Have you read a novel or play whose major theme derives from the conflict between generations? What does it say about the sources of misunderstanding or lack of communication? Here are some possible choices:

— Samuel Butler, *The Way of All Flesh;*
— Arthur Miller, *Death of a Salesman;*
— Alan Paton, *Too Late the Phalarope.*

I. In recent years, there has been much concern about the "American image." Assume that you have a chance to send to a friend abroad one American novel that would give him a true feeling for what this country is like. Defend your choice, making use of detailed references to the novel you have chosen.

J. Have you read a story, novel, or play in which a recurrent symbol played a major role? Discuss the author's use of the symbol in the work as a whole.

Interpret and evaluate evidence from several different sources.
What is research?

Research means finding out for yourself. When you do research, you conduct your own independent investigation. You are no longer satisfied with what you have heard other people say. You are no longer satisfied to rely on an encyclopedia or a textbook, which often merely digests or summarizes the results of the investigations of others. When you write a paper based on your own independent research, remember the following minimum requirements:

— *Go to the source.* When you are told that one of our early Presidents liked music, or that one of our great writers believed in the depravity of man, your attitude should be: "Let me see for myself." Whenever possible, consult **primary sources** — eyewitness accounts, letters, contemporary newspaper reports, and the like. When you write on a historical subject, you ask again and again: "Is there any *documentary* evidence for this?" When you write on a literary subject, you ask again and again, "Can I point to evidence of this in the author's *actual text?*"

Notice how habitually a famous American biographer identifies the *firsthand source* on which she has drawn:

> In 1835, Carlyle was in London working on his history of the French Revolution — two volumes filled with life, color, movement. "The great difficulty," Carlyle *wrote in his diary,* "is to keep oneself in right balance, not despondent, not exasperated, defiant, free and clear."
>
> Nineteenth-century romanticists indulged, I believe, in the loudest moans on record. Among these romantics, Wagner yelled more agonizingly than any. Have you read *his letters to Liszt,* written when Wagner was young, living in exile? Here is a sample: "Everything seems so waste, so waste, so waste! Dearest friend, art, with me, after all, is a pure stopgap, nothing else. A stopgap in order to live at all."
>
> —Catherine Drinker Bowen, "The Nature of the Artist," *Atlantic*

— *Weigh conflicting evidence from several different sources.*
Research starts when you no longer accept as gospel truth the

opinion of one single expert who has all the answers. Experts disagree. Witnesses give conflicting testimony. When you write a research paper, you will often weigh the conflicting testimony of different authorities. You will try to see where they agree, and where they disagree. You will try to fill in the gaps in one source with evidence from another.

Note the following excerpt in which a student writer is weighing different interpretations of Melville's short story, "Billy Budd." He is using *contrary* evidence from the text itself to challenge one critic's claim:

> In Melville's story, Billy's adversary is
> Claggart, the master-at-arms, in whom
> Melville saw "the mania of an evil nature, not
> engend'ered by vicious training or corrupting
> books or licentious living, but born with him
> and innate, in short, 'a depravity according
> to nature.'" One of Melville's critics uses
> this quotation as proof that Melville sees
> evil as "immanent" in life itself. Because
> one character in the tale is depraved, does
> Melville want us to conclude that all men are?
> Such a conclusion is discouraged by Melville
> himself when he defines "natural depravity"
> as "by no means" involving "Calvin's dogmas
> as to total mankind" and "applicable but to
> individuals."

— *Make your evidence available for inspection.* Identify your sources so that the reader, in turn, can "see for himself." Detailed **documentation** directs your reader to the exact page in an article, book, or collection of documents where you found your evidence. By identifying your sources, you are telling your reader, "You are welcome to check the original source to see whether I have quoted it accurately and represented it fairly."

Note how the footnote that goes with the following passage tells the reader exactly *where* the author found the quotation:

> Darwin's theory of evolution--that "species
> originated by means of natural selection, or
> through the preservation of the favored races
> in the struggle for life"[1]--was hotly debated
> by his contemporaries.
>
> ---
>
> [1]These are Darwin's words, quoted by
> T. H. Huxley, "The Darwinian Hypothesis,"
> Collected Essays, II: Darwiniana (New York,
> 1895), p. 1.

— *Give credit where credit is due.* Never pass someone else's findings off as your own. When you write down someone's exact words, make sure to put them in quotation marks. When you borrow someone's ideas, identify him: "According to C. P. Snow . . ." or "As Karl Marx has pointed out, . . ." Borrowing without acknowledgment is **plagiarism.** When someone is accused of plagiarizing, he is accused of stealing from someone else's writing. You are welcome to repeat facts and theories that have become widely known. They are "common knowledge." But if someone else had to dig up these facts for you, or if the ideas are his brainchild, you should give him credit.

In your English courses in high school or college, the research papers you write will often deal with literary subjects. Such a paper will typically move through several major stages:

(1) *Find a subject you can investigate by studying several different sources.* A literary research paper might study the way the same central theme is treated in two or more different works. Or it might study the difference between historical accounts of a person or event and the imaginative treatment of the same person or event in a work of literature. Or it might investigate the way different critics or reviewers have reacted to the same work. Do not make such a paper merely an inventory of many possible similarities and differences. *Limit* your subject by identifying one key question or key problem within your general subject area. The answer to your key question should provide you with a unifying **thesis** for your paper as a whole.

Here are some general subject areas. Find your own limited topic by investigating in detail one key question or key problem that arises in your mind as you study some of the relevant materials:

HISTORY AND DRAMA. What is the difference between a historian's treatment of facts and a playwright's imaginative or creative adaptation of them? What is the difference between historical and imaginative "truth"? Here are some possible materials for study:
— Plutarch's *Lives* and Shakespeare's *Julius Caesar*
— Holinshed's *Chronicles* and Shakespeare's *Macbeth*
— The Salem witch trials in American history books and in Arthur Miller's *The Crucible*

— a historical figure (Lincoln, Roosevelt, Churchill) as seen by one or more biographers and by a modern playwright

THE SUCCESS ETHIC IN LITERATURE. Businessmen sometimes complain that their treatment in imaginative literature is unfavorable or unfair. Are there any common trends in the way writers you have read treat the attitudes, practices, and standards of modern business? Look at two or more of the following books:

— Charles Dickens, *Hard Times*
— Sinclair Lewis, *Babbitt*
— Arthur Miller, *Death of a Salesman* (or *All My Sons*)
— John P. Marquand, *Point of No Return*
— John Braine, *Room at the Top*
— F. Scott Fitzgerald, *The Great Gatsby*
— Upton Sinclair, *The Jungle*

AMERICA THROUGH FOREIGN EYES. In the past, America was the land of opportunity and of liberty to millions of oppressed and disadvantaged people abroad. In recent years, we have heard much about "anti-Americanism" abroad. How do foreign (or foreign-born) writers look at this country? What do they expect? What do they criticize? Look at two or more of the following:

— G. B. Shaw, *The Devil's Disciple*
— Graham Greene, *The Quiet American*
— Elia Kazan, *America, America*
— Evelyn Waugh, *The Loved One*
— D. H. Lawrence, *Studies in Classic American Literature*
— Jean-Paul Sartre, *The Respectable Prostitute*

THE WRITER AND WAR. A major theme in the work of some of the best known modern writers has been the nature of war and its challenge to man's moral values. Study the treatment of war and conflict in several works by *one* writer: Stephen Crane, Ernest Hemingway, George Orwell, Norman Mailer, Antoine de Saint-Exupéry, or Graham Greene. Where possible, include in the material to be studied a biography, autobiographical essays, letters, and other material that would throw light on the author's firsthand experience with war. Focus your paper on one major issue or problem, or on one major aspect of war.

BLACK POETRY AND BLACK IDENTITY. The Negro playwright LeRoi Jones once claimed that middle-class black Americans used to resent any reference to their separate identity as Negroes. But a new generation has actively promoted the black American's pride in his own identity, in his own culture. Study the treatment of the theme of black identity or black pride in the work of several American Negro poets. Where possible, include in the material to be studied some critical studies of Negro poetry, essays on Negro poets by writers like LeRoi Jones. Focus on one major issue, one major problem, or one major trend.

UTOPIA AND ANTI-UTOPIA. A "utopia" used to be an ideal society of the future as described in detail by a writer. But many modern accounts of the future are really anti-utopias, warning us against what the future holds in store for us. What accounts for this difference? Look at some of the following:

— Plato, *The Republic*
— Sir Thomas More, *Utopia*
— Jonathan Swift, Book IV of *Gulliver's Travels*
— Aldous Huxley, *Brave New World*
— E. M. Forster, "The Machine Stops"
— George Orwell, *1984*

THE WRITER AND HIS CRITICS. Some books go unnoticed, but others create a storm of controversy. Study one such controversial book and the reception it got from reviewers and critics. What can you learn from their reactions and disagreements? Among novels, some possible choices are J. D. Salinger's *The Catcher in the Rye,* Jack Kerouac's *On the Road,* or Ernest Hemingway's *The Old Man and the Sea.* Among plays, possible choices include plays by Thornton Wilder, Samuel Beckett, Rolf Hochhuth, Edward Albee, and LeRoi Jones. To study critical reactions to modern poetry, you might investigate the reception of T. S. Eliot's *The Waste Land* or the poetry of e. e. cummings.

REMEMBER: Make sure that your topic offers you a *challenge.* No one wants to read a paper that dutifully piles up evidence in which the writer himself was not particularly interested. Halfway through a research project, you may suddenly stop to ask yourself:

"*Why* am I doing this?" You should be able to give an answer like the following:

— "I am trying to puzzle this out." You will feel satisfied at the end of your project if you have explained something difficult, if you have solved a *problem*. Hundreds of books and articles have been written about Shakespeare's Hamlet because again and again a writer has said to himself: "I want to solve the riddle of Hamlet's personality."

— "I am trying to set the record straight." A writer feels satisfied when he has corrected a common *misunderstanding*, when he has helped revise a popular stereotype. The author of the following passage was writing in order to do justice to a neglected and misrepresented American classic:

> *Uncle Tom's Cabin,* like Mark Twain's weather, is talked about by millions who do nothing about it; that is, "Uncle Tom" is a term of contempt used by everybody today, yet hardly anybody bothers to read the book anymore. The picture of the humble and obedient slave is derived not from the novel but from the "Tom Shows" that toured America for a generation before the First War. Uncle Tom is in no sense an "Uncle Tom." He is by far the strongest person in the book.
>
> —Kenneth Rexroth, "Uncle Tom's Cabin," *Saturday Review*

— "I am trying to show why this matters." A true classic may have been written hundreds of years ago, but it means something to people today. Put off by old-fashioned language or an unfamiliar setting, the modern reader may at first miss much of what such a book has to tell him. A writer can take satisfaction in showing his readers the *relevance* of something that otherwise would have stayed unread on their shelves.

(2) *Keep a record of your sources, for use during your project and in a final bibliography.* The books you draw on in writing your paper may come from your school library, a nearby public library, or even a paperback bookstore. (See Chapter 7 for a guide to library resources.) Write down a full description of every book, magazine article, or pamphlet on which you decide to draw for material. For a book, note the full name of the author; the complete title; where published, by whom, and what year; whether edited,

revised, translated, and by whom. For an article, note author, title, issue of magazine, and page numbers. For a short comparative paper drawing only on two or three major sources, you may record all this information simply on a single sheet of note paper. For a larger project, put the information for each source on a separate 3x5 **bibliography card.** These you can then easily alphabetize for use in your final bibliography at the end of your paper.

Use the following system to identify your sources both on your bibliography cards and in your final bibliography. Use *abbreviations and punctuation* exactly as here illustrated unless your teacher gives you other instructions:

1. STANDARD ENTRY FOR A BOOK:

    Harrison, G. B.   Introducing Shakespeare.
    New York: The New American Library, 1947.

2. BOOK WITH A SUBTITLE:

    Miller, Arthur.   Death of a Salesman: Certain
    Private Conversations in Two Acts and a
    Requiem.   New York: The Viking Press, 1958.

3. BOOK WITH SEVERAL AUTHORS:

    Main, C. F. and Peter J. Seng.   Poems.
    Belmont, California: Wadsworth Publishing
    Company, Inc., 1961.

4. BOOK COMPILED BY EDITOR:

    Halio, J. L., ed. Approaches to Macbeth.
    Belmont, California: Wadsworth Publishing
    Company, Inc., 1966.

5. NEW EDITION OF OLDER BOOK:

    Perrine, Laurence.   Sound and Sense: An
    Introduction to Poetry.   2nd ed. New York:
    Harcourt, Brace & World Inc., 1963.

6. TRANSLATION:

    Camus, Albert.   The Stranger, trans. Stuart
    Gilbert.   New York: Vintage Books, Inc.,
    1958.

7. WORK WITH SEVERAL VOLUMES:

Trevelyan, G. M. History of England. 3 vols.
Garden City, N. Y.: Doubleday & Company,
Inc., 1956.

8. BOOK NEWLY EDITED BY OTHER THAN AUTHOR:

Browne, Sir Thomas. Religio Medici, ed.
James Winny. Cambridge: University Press,
1963.

9. STANDARD ENTRY FOR ARTICLE:

Morrison, Theodore. "The Agitated Heart,"
The Atlantic, July 1967, pp. 72-79.

Rosenberg, Marvin. "Elizabethan Actors:
Men or Marionettes?" PMLA, LXIX (September
1954), 915-927.

NOTE: For scholarly magazines, the Roman numeral is the volume number (usually for all issues published during one year). Note that the abbreviation "pp." for "pages" is omitted when the volume number appears. In some fields of study, Arabic numerals are preferred, separated from the page numbers by a colon — 69:915-927.

10. ANONYMOUS NEWSPAPER ARTICLE:

"A Shakespeare Festival," The Oakdale
Register, July 17, 1969, p. 4, col. 3.

11. ARTICLE IN A COLLECTION:

Ornstein, Robert. "The Mystery of Hamlet,"
in Hamlet: Enter Critic, ed. Claire Sacks
and Edgar Whan. New York: Appleton-Century-
Crofts, Inc., 1960.

12. ARTICLE IN ENCYCLOPEDIA:

"Drama." Encyclopaedia Britannica, 1958,
VII, 576-616.

On your bibliography cards (but not in your final bibliography) include *the library call number* for books you have obtained from a library:

---

917. 3   Barzun, Jacques.
B 279g   God's Country and Mine.
            Boston: Little, Brown and Company,
                        1954.

---

(3) *Take notes to record all information and quoted material that you intend to use in your finished paper.* At first, your reading will be mainly exploratory. In various articles or books, you will be trying to identify the passages that bear most directly on the issue you want to discuss. Take detailed notes whenever you say to yourself: "This will help me prove a point." "This will provide essential background material for my readers." "This quotation shows exceptionally well the author's attitude on an important issue."

Many teachers recommend that you take notes on 4x6 cards. Note at the top the tentative *subtopic* under which the material on the card would fit. Note at the bottom, in shortened form, author, title, and *exact page number.* Limit each card to one point, one step in an argument, one set of data — material that you will not have to *split up* for use in different parts of your paper.

Most of the notes you take will be of three major kinds:

Summary or paraphrase — use when you summarize background information, sum up the events of a plot, or give in your own words the gist of an argument:

1

Man and catastrophe

    The play shows Wilder's faith in the
ability of humanity to survive the
catastrophes it encounters. Although
crushing setbacks are suffered, mankind is
never beaten, but makes a fresh start.
First, man survives the Ice age. Next, he
scrapes through decadence and the Flood.
Finally he survives fascism and war.

Thornton Wilder, The Skin of Our Teeth

Direct quotation — use for important passages that reveal a key motive, state a major theme, or illustrate strikingly a characteristic attitude:

Linda about Willi

"I don't say he's a great man. Willy Loman
never made a lot of money. His name was
never in the paper. He's not the finest
character that ever lived. But he's a human
being, and a terrible thing is happening to
him. So attention must be paid. He's not
to be allowed to fall into his grave like an
old dog. Attention, attention must be
finally paid to such a person. "

Death of a Salesman, p. 56

Combination paraphrase and quotation — use to summarize and interpret important passages, while at the same time preserving directly quoted phrases and sentences that give your summary the authentic touch:

```
Majority rule

    Thoreau questions the democratic system of
majority rule.  In practice, the majority
rules not "because it is most likely to be
in the right" but because it is strongest.
A man should let his conscience decide what
is right and wrong.  "Must the citizen ever
for a moment, or in the least degree, resign
his conscience to the legislator?  Why has
every man a conscience, then?"


"Civil Disobedience," p. 37
```

As you write your note cards, ask yourself: "How *usable* will this be when I start writing the actual paper?" In a typical paragraph of your paper, you will *bring together* material from several, closely related cards. For instance, you might take the material giving Thoreau's view on majority rule and combine it with material from two other cards: one giving Thoreau's view on military service (as an *example* of how the majority can make the individual go counter to his conscience); the other giving the view of majority rule held by a famous contemporary of Thoreau (to serve as a *parallel* to Thoreau's view). Here is the kind of paragraph that would combine material from these three note cards:

> Thoreau questions the democratic system of majority rule. In practice, the majority rules not "because it is most likely to be in the right" but because it is strongest. John Stuart Mill, a famous British contemporary of Thoreau, refers to such rule as the "tyranny of the majority." Thoreau feels that a man should let his conscience decide what is right and wrong. He asks: "Must the citizen ever for a moment, or in the least degree, resign his conscience to the legislator? Why has every

man a conscience, then?" The extreme example of a man "resigning his conscience" occurs in the military service. Thoreau describes the soldiers "marching . . . to the wars, against their wills, ay, against their common sense and consciences, which makes it very steep marching indeed."

(4) *Work out a strong, overall pattern of organization.* When you draw on several different sources, you have to make a special effort to bring your material under control. Early in your project, set up a working outline that will guide you in taking notes. Adjust and elaborate your outline as necessary in the light of your findings. As you go along, keep asking yourself: "What is my strategy for tackling this subject?" "What do I want each part of the paper to contribute to the whole?" Remember that your final product should be a *unified* paper that will carry the reader along from point to point.

Make sure your scheme of organization will help you make the *connections* that will tie together material from your different sources. Study carefully the following outline for a paper comparing the treatment of a major theme in two American short stories. Can you see how the author's point-by-point comparison allows him to mesh material from his two major sources?

Two Views of Guilt

THESIS: In both Stephen Crane's "The Blue Hotel" and Shirley Jackson's "The Lottery," innocent people die as the result of man's inhumanity toward his fellowman. But Crane puts the blame on individuals, while Shirley Jackson blames society.

I. Our modern tendency to blame society for evil

II. Individual and society in the two stories

    A. The social setting in both stories
        1. Crane's characters each behave differently toward the victim.
           a. The hospitable landlord
           b. The belligerent son
           c. The disdainful gambler
        2. In "The Lottery," people act the same as members of a faceless mob.

B. The victims in both stories
  1. The Swede turns people against
     him by his mixture of frantic
     suspicion and bullying bravado.
  2. In "The Lottery," all the towns-
     people "took the same chance"
     when the victim is selected by
     lot.

C. The aftermath in both stories
  1. In Crane's story, the Easterner,
     a "bystander," recognizes his
     share of the guilt and points
     out the guilt of others.
  2. In "The Lottery," the killing is
     a customary ceremony in the
     community, and the people feel
     no guilt.

III. Crane's view of guilt is more convincing
because his characters seem like real
people.

The following outline charts the overall plan of a paper on the historical facts behind Shakespeare's *Macbeth*. Can you see how again the author's plan allows him to *draw together* at each step material from his different sources?

The Historical Macbeth

THESIS: In the chronicles from which
Shakespeare drew his story, Macbeth appears
in a more favorable light than in
Shakespeare's play.

I. Shakespeare and the chronicles

II. The play and the historical Macbeth

  A. Duncan's performance as king
    1. Shakespeare's noble and effective
      Duncan
    2. The chronicler's "feeble and
      slothful" king

  B. Macbeth's motives
    1. Shakespeare's Macbeth and
      ambition
    2. The chronicles and Macbeth's
      "just quarrel"
      a. Macbeth as cousin to the
        king
      b. The laws of succession
      c. Duncan's attempt to
        circumvent the law

  C. Macbeth's usurpation of the throne

       1.   Macbeth's conspiracy with Lady
            Macbeth
       2.   The historical Macbeth and his
            fellow conspirators
  D.   Macbeth as king
       1.   The tyranny of Shakespeare's
            Macbeth
       2.   The historical Macbeth and
            "wholesome laws"

III. Shakespeare's other tyrants

Note that in a parallel-order comparison, the author would have to make sure the reader can see how the second set of data contrasts with the first:

  A.   The chronicles
       1.   Duncan as a feeble king
       2.   Macbeth's just quarrel
       3.   Macbeth and his fellow conspirators
       4.   Macbeth and "wholesome laws"

  B.   The play
       1.   Duncan as a "most sacred" king
       2.   Macbeth's ambition
       3.   Macbeth's plotting with his wife
       4.   Macbeth the tyrant

(5) *In writing your paper, identify your sources in footnotes, using conventional footnote form.* At the end of the sentence (or paragraph) that contains borrowed information or quoted material, insert a *raised* footnote number. Number all footnotes consecutively. At the bottom of the page, leave room for a footnote identifying the source of the borrowed or quoted material. (In a short paper or in a manuscript to be sent to the printer, simply put the footnotes on a separate sheet of paper at the end.)

Use the following system for full identification the *first time* you mention a source:

1. STANDARD FOOTNOTE FOR A BOOK:

     [6]Frederick Douglass, Life and Times of Frederick Douglass (New York: Collier Books, 1962), p. 398.

2. BOOK WITH SUBTITLE:

     [3]R. M. Weaver, Herman Melville: Mariner and Mystic (New York: Pageant Press, Inc., 1960), p. 381.

3. BOOK WITH SEVERAL AUTHORS:

[7]Rene Wellek and Austin Warren, Theory of Literature (New York: Harcourt, Brace and Company, 1949), p. 287.

4. BOOK COMPILED BY EDITOR:

[13]Norman Rabkin, ed. Approaches to Shakespeare (New York: McGraw-Hill Book Company, 1964), pp. 9-10.

5. NEW EDITION OF OLDER BOOK:

[8]Albert C. Baugh, A History of the English Language, 2nd ed. (New York: Appleton-Century-Crofts, Inc., 1957), p. 115.

6. TRANSLATION:

[11]Eugene Ionesco, Three Plays, trans. Donald Watson (New York: Grove Press, Inc., 1958), p. 103.

7. ONE OF SEVERAL VOLUMES:

[2]G. B. Harrison, ed. Major British Writers (New York: Harcourt, Brace and Company, 1954), I, 135.

8. BOOK NEWLY EDITED BY OTHER THAN AUTHOR:

[19]Thomas Bulfinch, The Age of Fable, ed. Edward E. Hale (New York, 1894), p. 14.

NOTE: The publisher's name is often omitted from footnotes, especially if there is a full description of all sources in a final bibliography.

Abbreviations Found in Footnotes

© *1965*	the copyright date, usually found on the *back* of the title-page (unless the copyright on a book has been *renewed,* the copyright date is the official year of publication)
ca. or c.	Latin *circa,* "approximately"; used for approximate dates and figures (*ca.* 1952)
cf.	Latin *confer,* "compare"; often used loosely instead of *see* in the sense of "consult for further relevant material" (Cf. Ecclesiastes xii. 12)

et al.	Latin *et alii,* "and others"; used in references to books by several authors (G. B. Harrison *et al.*)
f., ff.	"and the following page," "and the following pages" (See pp. 16f.)
ibid.	Latin *ibidem,* "in the same place"; always points back to the last source cited (with an added page number, it means "in the same source, but on a different page": *Ibid.,* p. 83)
loc. cit.	Latin *loco citato,* "in the place cited"; used without page reference
MS, MSS	manuscript, manuscripts
n.d.	"no date," date of publication unknown
op. cit.	Latin *opere citato,* "in the work already cited," usually preceded by the author's name: Baugh, *op. cit.,* p. 37
passim	Latin for "throughout"; "in various places in the work under discussion" (See pp. 54-56 *et passim*)
q.v.	Latin *quod vide;* "which you should consult"

9. STANDARD FOOTNOTE FOR ARTICLE:

    ⁷Ray B. West, Jr., "The Unity of Billy Budd," Hudson Review, V (Spring, 1952), 124.

10. ANONYMOUS NEWSPAPER ARTICLE:

    ⁸"Albee's Powerful New Play," The Allandale Times, June 17, 1969, p. 3, col. 2.

11. ARTICLE IN COLLECTION:

    ¹¹Honor M. V. Matthews, "Character and Symbol in Macbeth," in Approaches to Macbeth, ed. Jay L. Halio (Belmont, California: Wadsworth Publishing Company, Inc., 1966), p. 89.

12. ARTICLE IN ENCYCLOPEDIA:

    ³"Symbol," Encyclopaedia Britannica, 1965, XXI, 701.

Note how the footnote differs from the bibliography entry: The footnote does *not* put the last name first; it does *not* use periods to separate the major parts; it does not always include the name of the publisher. It *does* provide an exact page number. (In references to a Shakespeare play, you may substitute act and scene; in references to the Bible, chapter and verse as well as book: *Hamlet* III.ii or Judges 13:5.)

The *second time* and subsequent times you refer to a source, identify it by the author's last name. If you are using several sources by the same author, add a shortened version of the title:

1. ONE SOURCE BY AUTHOR:

> [7]Baugh, p. 78.

2. SEVERAL SOURCES BY SAME AUTHOR:

> [4]Baugh, History, p. 78.

3. SAME PAGE AS LAST FOOTNOTE:

> [8]Ibid.

REMEMBER: In working on a research paper, you will spend much of your time exploring sources, copying quotations, and writing footnotes. By the time you finish your first draft, you may be too absorbed in details to judge your paper as a piece of writing. If possible, let your first draft lie a day or two and then go over it to see how it *reads.* You will then be better able to judge what final revisions are necessary as you prepare your final draft.

EXERCISE 28 What books in your school or public library deal with the history of the English language or with the history of English or American literature? Select six books dealing directly with these subjects. Write a bibliography card for each, recording all information that you would need to identify the book in a footnote or final bibliography.

EXERCISE 29 Can you interpret all the information provided in the following footnotes? Point out anything that is unusual or difficult in these notes.

[3]William Hazlitt, Characters of Shakespear's Plays, in The Complete Works of William Hazlitt, IV (London: J. M. Dent and Sons, Ltd., 1930), p. 257.

[7]Walter Raleigh, ed. Johnson on Shakespeare (London: Oxford University Press, 1952), p. 156.

[11]Edith Sitwell, "King Lear," Atlantic Monthly, CLXXXV (May 1950), 58.

[2]Sholom J. Kahn, "'Enter Lear Mad,'" Shakespeare Quarterly VIII (1957), 311–312.

[5]Samuel Taylor Coleridge, Lectures and Notes on Shakespere, ed. T. Ashe (London, 1890), pp. 3–5.

[1]Fred M. Mackenzie et. al. The American Literary Tradition, 3rd ed. (New York: Hayden Press, 1968), p. 89.

EXERCISE 30 In your school library, find a scholarly magazine that prints *documented* articles. Choose a magazine that deals with language or literature. Prepare a report on one representative article. Answer the following questions:

1. What *kind* of sources has the author drawn on?

2. What *use* does he make of them? How well does he work them into a coherent argument? How effectively does he draw on them to support major points?

3. How much use does he make of *summary, paraphrase,* or *quotation?*

4. To what extent do his *footnotes* conform to the system you have just studied? Point out similarities and differences.

5. If there is a *bibliography,* does it observe the conventions outlined in this chapter?
   (Your teacher may choose an article for all members of the class to work on.)

REVIEW EXERCISE 2: Sample Research Paper
   The following student research paper was rated highly by a group of English teachers. Can you see why? What did the author set out to do? How successfully did he bring together material from different sources? What use did he make of summary, quotation, and paraphrase?

God in Three Dramatic Poems

While the book of Job and Robert Frost's Masque of Reason, through their exploration of man's quest for understanding of his existence, develop the concept of God as power, Archibald MacLeish's play J. B., by showing that man's soul transcends the force of power, redefines God as love.

Job, far removed in time from the other works, presents the more primitive concept: the individual is obscured by the cosmic power of God. Believing firmly in his righteousness, which God himself asserts in the prologue to the book, Job is unable to justify his afflictions, for the early Hebraic law allows only that good is rewarded by good and evil by evil. Job must, if he is to find life meaningful, either give up his faith in his knowledge of his own righteousness or break away from the statutes of justice in which his ideas are rooted and by which his comforters judge him. At first, confined by the tradition of justice, Job demands of God that he show him his sin. "Teach me, and I will hold my tongue: and cause me to understand wherein I have erred."[1] Job's dilemma is such that he cannot cling to one idea; he fleetingly believes in his righteousness, in justice, in the meaninglessness of his existence. During the climaxes of his perception, however, he asserts that he is clean and that he must discount the words of his comforters and live in a new understanding of God.

> Behold, I cry out of wrong, but I am not heard: I cry aloud, but there is no judgment.[2]

> Though he slay me, yet will I trust in him: but I will maintain my ways before him. He also shall be my salvation: for a hypocrite shall not come before him.[3]

> For I know that my redeemer liveth, and that he shall stand at the latter day upon the earth: and though after my skin worms destroy this body, yet in my flesh shall I

---

[1]The Book of Job, 6:24.
[2]Job 19:7.
[3]Job 13:15–16.

see God: whom I shall see for myself, and mine eyes shall behold, and not another, though my reins be consumed with me. [4]

For he is not a man, that I should answer him, and we should come together in judgment. [5]

Job's inspirations are confirmed, then, when the Voice in the Whirlwind shows him the greatness of God's power; he realizes that man's perception is so limited by his humanity that he ought not presume to understand the motivations of God's actions. He realizes that God is beyond man's understanding.

Frost, presenting a complement to the Job theory, in his "chapter forty-three of Job," shows that a God within the limits of human understanding would reduce life to a superficial and gaudy masque, ironically, a masque of unreason. Frost's hypothetical God, in contrast with the cosmic power of Job, is easily recognized by man, just as he is easily portrayed by human media. "It's God. /I'd know Him by Blake's picture anywhere." He is ludicrous in his lack of splendor and power: his court is constituted by Burning Bushes and Christmas Trees, by ornaments and gold-enameled nightingales, and his throne, "a plywood flat, prefabricated," collapses on the fifth page of the poem. [6] Not only does God allow Job's wife (who "charms" him) to lodge a protest with him, but, when Job demands again the reason for his suffering, He answers in the human terms of temptation and pride.

The front of being answerable to no one
I'm with You in maintaining to the public.
But, Lord, we showed them what. The audience
Has all gone home to bed. The play's played out.
Come, after all these years—to satisfy me.

[4] Job 19:25-27.
[5] Job 9:32.
[6] Robert Frost, Complete Poems of Robert Frost (New York, 1949), p. 588.

I'm curious. And I'm a grown-up man:
I'm not a child for you to put me off
And tantalize me with another 'Oh,
because!'[7]

I was just showing off to the Devil, Job.
As is set forth in chapters One and Two.

Job, you must understand my provocation.
The tempter comes to me and I am tempted.[8]

This is a God with human characteristics, one
perhaps more human than Job himself, not only
tempted, but unable to withstand temptation.
When Job becomes fully aware of the humanness
of that to which he had formerly aspired,
confused, he tries to rationalize his discovery.

'Twas human of You. I expected more
Than I could understand and what I get
Is almost less than I can understand.
But I don't mind. Let's leave it as it
stood.
The point was it was none of my concern.[9]

From this point, the play falls into a dis-
illusioned meaninglessness of playing charades
with Satan and of taking group pictures of
God and Job and the devil.

...I hold rays deteriorate to nothing,
First white, then red, then ultrared,
then out.[10]

If man's highest aspirations were within his
own understanding, his purpose would
deteriorate to nothing.

MacLeish's God, however, is not that force
which controls man's suffering, which teaches
him to abhor himself, either for reasons in-
conceivable to man or for the human reasons
of pride and weakness in temptation. God is a
force within man himself which transcends the
viciousness of power and gently, like the
forsythia in the wreckage of former life,
restrains man from utter despair, inspires him
with the will to live. Thus, having lost all
that meant life to him, his children, his

---

[7]Frost, p. 597.
[8]Frost, pp. 600-601.
[9]Frost, p. 600.
[10]Frost, p. 601

wife, his material wealth, because of a
contest between the force called god and its
antithesis, Satan, J. B. seeks to justify his
fate by some guilt of his own, that he might
respect that force which had destroyed him.

> ...If I
> Knew . . . If I knew why!
>
> What I can't bear is the blindness--
> Meaninglessness--the numb blow
> Fallen in the stumbling night. [11]
>
> God will not punish without cause.
> God is just.
>   He
> Knows the guilt is mine . . .
>
> I have no choice but to be guilty . . .
>
> God is God or we are nothing--
> Mayflies that leave their husks behind--
> Our tiny lives ridiculous--a suffering
> Not even sad that Someone Somewhere
> Laughs at us as we laugh at apes.
> We have no choice but to be guilty.
> God is unthinkable if we are innocent. [12]

J. B. calls on God to show him the sin he
believes must be unthinkably great to cause
the loss of all, even love. In the midst of
distress come the answers of J. B.'s day:
Christianity, psychology, and Communism.
Before J. B. has time to consider these
answers fully, however, the Distant Voice,
dispersing the Comforters and invalidating
their reasoning, sounds to J. B. to show him
the power of the Voice and to force him into
the dust. Before the unknown entity, J. B. is
as nothing; he prays for death. Thus, that
God which is only power destroys any purpose
in life as completely as the God who is fall-
ible and human. But with the return of his
wife--love--who could not take her life
because of a piece of forsythia she had
found among the ashes of destruction, J. B.
again finds hope. Re-evaluating life, he
finds love to supersede power, and by his new

---

[11] Archibald MacLeish, J. B. (Boston, 1961),
p. 108.
[12] MacLeish, pp. 109-111.

definition, God is neither force nor justice, but love:

> Sarah: I loved you.
> I couldn't help you anymore.
> You wanted justice and there was none--
> Only love.
>
> J. B.: He does not love. He
> Is.
>
> Sarah: But we do. That's the wonder. [13]

J. B. realizes that the soul within man is the key, the essential good of life: God.

> J. B.: It's too dark to see.
>
> Sarah: Then blow on the coal of the heart
> my darling.
>
> J. B.: The coal of the heart . . .
>
> Sarah: It's all the light now.
>
> Blow on the coal of the heart
> The candles in the churches are out.
> The lights have gone out in the sky.
> Blow on the coal of the heart
> And we'll see by and by . . . [14]

Thus, while both the author of Job and Robert Frost hold that God in his glory must not be made answerable to man's reason, MacLeish shows that God, transcending suffering and destruction and reason, is the love within the human soul.

---

[13]MacLeish, p. 151.
[14]MacLeish, p. 153.

FURTHER STUDY: *Creative Writing*

We often draw a rigid line between workaday prose and creative writing. We act as if a journalist could never be a poet. We act as if a scientist could never be in his spare time a successful novelist. But in practice, even "practical" writing is likely to be poor writing if it does not have an imaginative touch. The best expository prose shows that the writer has an ear for language, a sense of drama, an eye for a good story, and the ability to look at the same problem from different points of view.

How much experimenting have you done with creative writing? The following assignments will give you a chance to experiment with its shapes and forms and effects. They will provide you with materials to discuss and evaluate with your classmates.

Assignment 1   Read to yourself (and also, if possible, aloud) examples of American *free verse:* the longer poems of Walt Whitman; Carl Sandburg, "The People, Yes"; Karl Shapiro, "Auto Wreck." What are some of the features and effects such different examples share? Try your hand at a page or two of free verse of your own.

Assignment 2   Study the way some of e. e. cummings' best known poems produce a pattern on the printed page. How do you reproduce this almost dance-like movement when you read such a poem out loud? Write a poem that dances out a similar pattern on the written page.

Assignment 3   Many Renaissance poets used the *sonnet* to express their feelings about love. Could one write a sonnet on a different and modern theme? Would the result still be a sonnet? What are some of the key features of such a poem, and could you reproduce some of them in a sonnet of your own? For your study and possible imitation, here are three sonnets from Shakespeare, Sidney, and Spenser, all of whom used the sonnet to express the theme of love.

Sonnet 29

> When, in disgrace with fortune and men's eyes,
> I all alone beweep my outcast state,
> And trouble deaf heaven with my bootless cries,
> And look upon myself, and curse my fate,
> Wishing me like to one more rich in hope,
> Featured like him, like him with friends possessed,
> Desiring this man's art and that man's scope,
> With what I most enjoy contented least;
> Yet in these thoughts myself almost despising,

Haply I think on thee — and then my state,
Like to the lark at break of day arising
From sullen earth, sings hymns at heaven's gate;
For thy sweet love remembered such wealth brings
That then I scorn to change my state with kings.

—William Shakespeare

Sonnet 16

Having this day my horse, my hand, my lance
Guided so well that I obtained the prize,
Both by the judgment of the English eyes
And of some sent from that sweet enemy, France;
Horsemen my skill in horsemanship advance,
Town-folks my strength; a daintier judge applies
His praise to sleight with from good use doth rise;
Some lucky wits impute it but to chance;
Others, because of both sides I do take
My blood from them who did excel in this,
Think nature me a man of arms did make,
How far they shot awry! The true cause is,
     Stella looked on, and from her heav'nly face
     Sent forth the beams which made so fair my race.

—Sir Philip Sidney

One Day I Wrote Her Name

One day I wrote her name upon the strand,
     but came the waves and washed it away:
     Again I wrote it with a second hand,
     but came the tide, and made my pains his prey.
Vain man, said she, that dost in vain assay
     a mortal thing so to immortalize,
     for I myself shall like to this decay,
     and eek my name be wiped out likewise.
Not so, (quoth I) let baser things devise
     to die in dust, but you shall live by fame:
     my verse your virtues rare shall eternize,
     and in the heavens write your glorious name.
Where whenas death shall all the world subdue,
     our love shall live, and later life renew.

—Edmund Spenser

Assignment 4   How do you write a short story? Some teachers
of creative writing analyze the various elements of a story; they show
how different kinds of stories follow a definite formula. Does the following student-written story follow a formula? Try to describe it as
fully as you can. Then write a story of your own that follows the same
formula.

Civil Rights

Corporal Bowman was six feet, three inches tall, from his kinky black hair to his shiny brown boots. His skin matched the deep coffee-color of his boots, as if it too was aged and colored by many layers of carefully-applied shoe polish.

He jockeyed the three-quarter ton truck through the heavy Board Street traffic as if he were driving a Maserati in the Grand Prix. His big brown hands cradled the wheel like a toy as we roared away from the Fifth Street stop light and shot down bumpy Savannah Road toward the Augusta, Georgia, plant of the Olin Chemical Co.

Someone back at the base had discovered that the chemical plant produced a byproduct which could be used as white-wash, to paint logs, rocks, and other inanimate objects in an effort to give them a military appearance. So there we were, the grim Negro corporal and his detail of one (me, a Yankee formerly acquainted with whitewash only through the pages of Tom Sawyer).

Six G.I. cans rattled in the rear of the truck as we bounced down the road, careened around a corner, shook our way over four sets of railroad tracks, and began to stir up dust on a narrow dirt road lined with gray, weather-beaten houses. Two blocks farther on, several blasts on the horn shook me out of a daydream in time to see a colored girl stick her head out of the open door of one of the unpainted shacks and wave.

We rolled on with our dust cloud, the dirt changed to blacktop, and the chemical company loomed ahead. Its smell preceded it by half a mile.

Bowman looked at me out of the corner of his eye; he saw my question, declined to answer, changed his mind, and said grudgingly, "My girl. Back there." It was the first he had spoken to me since we had left camp. I nodded. We drove up to the lime pit in silence.

For the next half hour, the silence was unbroken except by occasional curses when the white soup we ladled out of the pit would spill on shiny boots or splatter on starched trousers. We worked fast, lifting the heavy cans on the truck after they were filled.

Finally, the last can was loaded; as I started to get into the truck, Bowman pointed at my face contemptuously. I twisted the mirror around, somehow a white circle of white-wash had formed around my right eye. On impulse, I dipped a finger in the white mud and solemnly drew a matching circle around the other eye.

Suddenly the brown face opposite mine dissolved in a toothy grin, disappeared, and reappeared around the corner of the truck, spotted with white; we both collapsed in laughter.

"Oh my gosh," he said, ". . . white measles! I got white measles!"

We admired our whitewashed countenances a moment longer, mounted the truck, and lurched toward the street.

"You in a hurry?" he asked.

"I'm with you, remember?" I shook my head.

"C'mon, Ah'll buy you a coke," he said.

"No, I'll get 'em."

"Huh-uh. Ah'm in charge of this detail. Ah buy the cokes." And we churned up another dust cloud.

I felt out of place as we braked in front of a decayed, unpainted wooden building in the middle of Augusta's colored section. I wondered if I had three eyes, or something, when two urchins stared at me as we opened the worn screen door.

The interior was dimly-lit and dingy; windows refused to admit the bright sunlight from outside; holes in the dirty plank flooring were nailed over with old metal soft-drink signs. Two bare tables stood against the far wall, with several wire-backed chairs. A grizzled old Negro sat in overalls and frayed cap on an upturned milk can. He ran his fingers through his salt-and-pepper beard as he stared at a can of Black Label.

Bowman walked to the linoleum-topped counter and I tried to follow as inconspicuously as possible. I felt acutely embarrassed, as in the dream where you are in the middle of a crowd without any clothes on.

Out of the gloomy depths of a back room, a pimply-faced Negro materialized behind the counter. His eyes darted from the corporal to me and back again.

"We'll have two cokes," Bowman said.

"Only got one," The pimply man frowned.

In a flash, I knew what was happening. Bowman didn't; he answered, "Ah'll take Seven-Up, then."

"For you, okay. Not him." The little man stared through me, as if I didn't exist.

Bowman still didn't understand.

I wanted to get out.

"What?" The big corporal stirred, realized then.

Proudly, the pimply-faced little black man drew himself up behind his shabby counter. His eyes flashed, and, as if he had carefully rehearsed all his life for this moment, he recited: "We reserve the right to refuse service to anyone."

Bowman stared.

I looked fiercely at an Orange-Crush bottlecap imbedded in the floor.

The old man on the milk can studied his beer and ran his fingers through his salt-and-pepper beard.

Assignment 5   In some modern fiction, the same story is told in turn by several different characters. Each one tells us what he has experienced and felt, in his own words. Have you ever read a story or novel that employs this "multiple-reflector" technique? (William Faulkner's *The Sound and the Fury* is a famous example.) What special effects does this technique achieve? Write a story that is really several different versions of the same story as told by different participants or observers.

Assignment 6   If you were a modern playwright, what kind of play would you want to write? On what kind of theme? With what kind of characters? Do one or both of the following: (1) Write a plot outline for a play you would like to write. (2) Write the dialogue for one key scene from the play. (You may be able to arrange a trial staging in which some of your classmates read or act out the scene you have written.)

CONTENTS

Mechanics:
FUNCTION AND CONVENTION

*An effective writer needs an easy
command of the English writing system.*

A good tennis player no longer worries about how to grip the racket. A competent musician no longer has difficulty reading music. An effective writer is no longer distracted by the mechanics of getting words on paper. If he must worry about how to spell the next word, or how to punctuate the next sentence, he can hardly concentrate on what he is trying to say. An experienced writer spells and punctuates as effortlessly as an experienced driver handles the steering wheel, the accelerator, and the brakes.

Mastering the mechanics of writing is harder than driving a car, mainly because our writing system is not strictly *functional.* When we study spelling and punctuation, we do not say: "This is the most efficient, or the most logical, way of using written symbols to communicate meaning." Instead, we say: "This, as the result of countless historical accidents, is *what* we have to work with. Once we master its more arbitrary features, it works *amazingly well.*"

Our present writing system is the result of thousands of years of trial and error. It is the result of much adaptation and improvisation. Here are some of the historical facts that help explain what made our writing system what it is:

(1) *Our alphabet was originally developed to write down languages quite different from our own.* The earliest writing systems

had used picture symbols for whole words. Alphabetic writing developed when people started to use symbols for the sounds *making up* a word. Our own alphabet goes back to a syllabic kind of sound-writing developed by the Phoenician traders of the Mediterranean — the people who built Carthage and fought the Romans in three bloody and disastrous Punic Wars. The Phoenicians spoke a Semitic language related to the Hebrew of modern Israel. The Greeks took over this writing system and developed it into a true alphabet, using separate letters for the different Greek vowels and consonants.

One direct descendant of the Greek alphabet is the **Cyrillic** alphabet of modern Russia, taken there originally by Greek Orthodox missionaries. Here are some lines from a textbook printed in Russian:

Господин Браун очень много курит. Здесь нельзя курить, но он курит. Госпожа Грин тоже курит. Преподаватель просит не курить здесь, но они всё-таки курят.

The Romans adapted the Greek alphabet to their own use, changing the shape of the letters, dropping some, and adding others. It was this Roman version of the alphabet that Catholic missionaries brought to England (and most other European countries). English, like the other European languages, had to develop ways of writing down sounds that were not part of the Latin sound system. Our modern *th,* our uses of *v* and *w* (originally literally a double *u*), are the result of attempts to make a *foreign* alphabet fit a language for which it was not designed.

(2) *For many centuries, our writing system has changed more slowly than the spoken language.* Since books were first printed in English (after 1475) speech has changed considerably, but spelling has tended to stay the same. As a result, modern spelling comes closer to mirroring the sounds of Chaucer's English than the sounds of our own. We still use many spellings that once stood for sounds but now are merely "empty" or silent:

initial *k:* *k*night, *k*nife, *k*nob
gh: throu*gh,* ni*gh*t, li*gh*t, ou*gh*t
final *e:* hav*e,* liv*e*

We use many spellings that show how the sounds of English have changed:

ea:	*tea* (used to have the same vowel sound as st*ea*k)
ou:	h*ou*se (used to have the same vowel sound as y*ou*th)
oo:	g*oo*d (used to have the same vowel sound as f*oo*d)

This general *conservatism* of our spelling system is reinforced by the thousands of Greek, Latin, and French words that preserve their original spelling, regardless of their current pronunciation. We still use the Latin *ti* spelling in words like *nation* and *devotion,* though the *t* in these words has not been pronounced in English for hundreds of years. We preserve the Greek initial *p* in *pneumonia* and *psychology,* though it long ago dropped from the spoken language.

(3) *Over the centuries, our writing system has developed features that are merely conventional.* They are not absolutely necessary to carry meaning but are merely customary, like the businessman's tie. German gets along *without* the apostrophe for the possessive: "des *Bruders* Haus" (the *brother's* house). Capital letters sometimes *do* make a difference in meaning. But we know that e.e. cummings was a person even though he refused to use capital letters with his name.

M 1 *Spelling*

Master your spelling problems by regular spelling work.

Poor spelling puts a barrier between your message and the reader. Whenever there is competition for the reader's attention, the poor speller puts himself at the end of the line. If you have a spelling problem, you will have to do something about it by regular spelling work. Remember the following advice:

(1) *Identify words that cause trouble for you.* Some common words are misspelled over and over again: *believe, definite, athlete.* Keep a spelling log. Include among the common spelling demons all those that you have had trouble with. Add other words that you tend to misspell on quizzes, exams, themes.

(2) *Solve your spelling problems by building the right habit.* A word ceases to be a spelling problem when the correct spelling has become *automatic.* Over and over again, run your eyes over

the individual letters and the shape of the word as a whole. Give the word a chance to become firmly imprinted in your mind. Spell the letters out loud, so that your ears will remember the word, as well as your eyes. Trace the word repeatedly, in exceptionally large letters. Go back over the same word at the next session, and at the next.

(3) *Do not just copy a difficult word from the dictionary.* You will have to go back to the dictionary the next time the word comes up. Take a minute or two then and there to *fix the word in your mind.* Copy it over a few times. Add it to your list of new or difficult words.

M 1a Sounds and Signs

Take inventory of the different ways the same sound may be spelled.

In a phonetic alphabet, one letter would, as far as possible, always stand for one sound. When the Latin alphabet was first used in writing down English, this requirement was partially met. Today, as the result of many changes in the spoken language, there is only a very imperfect "fit" between sign and sound. Many sounds are spelled several different ways:

a (as in *lane*)	also	*ai:*	vain, constrain, maid
		ei:	vein, sleigh, weigh
		ay:	bray, clay, stray
		ey:	they, whey
		ea:	break, steak
e (as in *me*)	also	*ee:*	deed, creed, keen
		ea:	beam, team, steam
		ei:	receive, ceiling, leisure
		ie:	believe, retrieve
f (as in *father*)	also	*ph:*	phone, phrase, emphatic
		gh:	laugh, cough, enough
g (as in *go*)	also	*gh:*	ghost, ghastly, burgher
		gu:	guess, guest, brogue
h (as in *hot*)	also	*wh:*	whole, who

i (as in *hit*)	also *y:*	hymn, gymnasium, cryptic
	ui:	build, guild
i (as in *hide*)	also *ai:*	aisle
	ei:	height, stein
	ey:	eye
	uy:	buy, guy
	y:	sky, defy, rye
j (as in *jam*)	also *g:*	gypsy, oxygen, logic
	dg:	budget, knowledge, grudge
k (as in *kin*)	also *c:*	castle, account, coat
	ch:	chemist, chlorinate, chrome
	qu:	clique, oblique
n (as in *noon*)	also *gn:*	gnat, gnarled, gnash
	kn:	knife, knave, knight
	pn:	pneumonia, pneumatic
o (as in *tone*)	also *oa:*	toad, shoal, foal
	ou:	soul, though,
	ow:	low, crow, stow
	ew:	sew
r (as in *run*)	also *rh:*	rhythm, rhapsody, rhubarb
	wr:	wrong, wrangle, wry
s (as in *sit*)	also *c:*	cent, decide, decimate
	sc:	scent, descent, science
	ps:	psychology, psalm, pseudonym
sh (as in *shine*)	also *ce:*	ocean
	ch:	machine, chef
	ci:	special, vicious, delicious
	si:	impression, possession, tension
	ti:	notion, imagination
	sci:	conscious, conscience, luscious
u (as in *use*)	also *eu:*	feud, queue
	ew:	few, curfew, dew
	ue:	cue, barbecue
	iew:	view, review
z (as in *zero*)	also *x:*	xylophone

M 1b Memory Aids

Use memory aids to help you with common spelling problems.
Many of the spelling errors in student writing are caused by a few dozen common words. Make a resolute attack on these and master them once and for all. Fix them in your mind by association — link them to some similar or related word. Fit them into a jingle or saying. Here are some words you cannot afford to spell wrong:

GROUP ONE

accept
: When you *accept* a gift or an invitation, you are taking something *in*. When you make an *exception,* you are taking something *out:* "Everyone *except* you and me." REMEMBER: The boy with *acc*ent *acc*epted the blame for the *acc*ident.

a lot
: Two separate words (we can say "a *whole* lot"). REMEMBER: a lump, a little, *a lot.*

all right
: Two separate words. REMEMBER: *All right* means ALL is RIGHT.

beginning
: *Begin* has a single *n; beginning* has a double *n*. REMEMBER: There is an INNING in begi*nn*ing.

believe
: One of the most frequently misspelled words in the language. Use *ie* in *believe* and *belief*. REMEMBER: EVE and STEVE beli*eve*.

business
: The *i* in *business* is not pronounced but must be written. REMEMBER: Put an *i* in bus*i*ness.

choose
: We *now* cho*o*se something (with a double *o*); in the *past,* we ch*o*se something (with a single *o*). REMEMBER: Cho*o*se rhymes with OOZE; ch*o*se rhymes with HOSE.

coming
: Never double the *m* in coming.

conscience
: Someone who has been badly hurt may still be *conscious* when the doctor gets there; someone who has stolen a wallet may be bothered by his *conscience*. Both words have the *sc*.

definite
: The problem is the *i* in the *-ite* ending. Compare this word with related words like defin*i*tion and infin*i*te.

REMEMBER: Spell ITE as in KITE to get *definite* right.

disastrous   The *e* drops out of the word *disaster* when we change it to *disastrous*.

friend   Make sure you have *ie*. REMEMBER: His best *friend* was a FIEND.

government   Preserve the *n* at the end when you change *govern* to *government*. REMEMBER: Men who GOVERN are a *government*.

grammar   It's *ar* at the end. REMEMBER: MARgaret loves *grammar*.

hoping   When you have hope, you are *hoping* (with a single *p*); when you hop about, you are *hopping* (with a double *p*). REMEMBER: *Hoping* rhymes with MOPING: *hopping* rhymes with STOPPING.

GROUP TWO

its   *Its* is a pronoun and points back to a noun: "The *horse* bared *its* teeth." *It's,* with the apostrophe, shows that something has been *omitted;* the complete version is *it is*. Never use the apostrophe unless you can substitue *it is:* "*It's* (it is) a shame that you had to miss the party."

library   Notice the *r* that follows the *b*. REMEMBER: The liBRarians BRought BRicks for the BRanch liBRary.

lose   When you have a losing streak, you lose all the time (single *o*). When a car door rattles, something has come loose (double o). REMEMBER: *Lose* rhymes with WHOSE; *loose* rhymes with GOOSE.

necessary   First a *c,* then double *ss*. REMEMBER: The reCESS was necessary.

occasion   Watch for the double *c* and the *s*. REMEMBER: oCCur, oCCupy, occasion; invaSion, occasion.

occurred   Single *r* in *occur* and *occurs;* double *r* in *occurred* and *occurring*. REMEMBER: Double *r* occurred in occurred.

perform   It's *per* in *per*form and *per*formance. REMEMBER: PERcent, PERmit, *perform*.

prejudice	People with prejudices have made *ju*dgments *pre*maturely; they *preju*dge people and ideas without giving them a fair hearing.
principle	A basic idea or rule is a princi*ple* (with *ple* at the end); the person who runs a school is a princi*pal* (with *pal* at the end). REMEMBER: He paid us trIPLE on princi*ple*.
privilege	There is a second *i* in the middle, and a single *g* toward the end. REMEMBER: sacrIleGe, priv*i*lege.
probably	The *ab* in prob*ab*le is preserved in prob*ab*ly. REMEMBER: ABly, capABly, prob*ab*ly.
quantity	Make sure to put in the first *t*. REMEMBER: enTity, quan*t*ity.
quite	The word with *ite* means "entirely" (you are *quite* right). The word with *iet* means "silent" (keep *quiet*). REMEMBER: *Quite* rhymes with KITE; *quiet* rhymes with DIET.
receive	One of the three or four most common spelling problems. It's *e* after *c*. REMEMBER: CEIling, deCEIve, re*ce*ive.
recommend	Double *m*. REMEMBER: Double *m* is recoMMended in reco*mm*end.
GROUP THREE	
referred	Single *r* in re*fer* and re*fers;* double *r* in re*ferred* and re*ferring*. REMEMBER: Refer spells like HER; referring spells like HERRING.
separate	It's *ate* at the end. (This is one of the most ferocious of all spelling demons.)
similar	Concentrate on the *-lar* ending. REMEMBER: circuLAR, popuLAR, simi*lar*.
studying	The *y* in *study* is kept in *studying*. REMEMBER: Stud*y*ing is done in a STUDY.
succeed	Double *c* in su*cc*eed and su*cc*ess. REMEMBER: ACCelerate if you want to su*cc*eed.
surprise	The first syllable is *sur-*. REMEMBER: When the SURfer SURfaced we were *sur*prised.

than	Use the *a* in comparisons (brighter *than*). Use the *e* in talking about time (now and *then*).
there	Use the *-eir* spelling only when you talk about what *they* do or what belongs to *them* (*their* car, *their* behavior). Use the *-ere* spelling when pointing to a place (over *there*) and in the *there is/there are* combination (*there* is time). Use *they're* only when you can substitute *they are*. REMEMBER: Th*eir* car was not th*ere*.
to	*To* indicates direction (*to* church, *to* school) and occurs in the to-form of the verb (He started *to* run). *Too* shows that there is *too* much of something, but then it means "also," *too*. REMEMBER: *Too* late, he *too* came *to* school *to* learn.
together	When people g*a*ther (with *a*), they are tog*e*ther (with *e*).
tries	It's *y* in *try,* but *ie* in *tries* and *tried*. REMEMBER: cry, fly, try; cries, flies, tri*es*.
villain	The *a* is first, then the *i*. REMEMBER: The vill*ai*n went to SP*AI*N.
whose	"Wh*ose* house?" means "belonging to whom?" Use *who's* only if you can substitute *who is*. REMEMBER: Who's the girl wh*ose* book you found?
women	It's one wom*a*n (with *a*), but several wom*e*n (with *e*).
writing	Single *t* in wri*t*e and wri*t*ing, double *t* in wri*tt*en. REMEMBER: Wri*t*ing rhymes with BI*T*ING; wri*tt*en rhymes with BI*TT*EN.

EXERCISE 1   After studying the words in this section, have someone dictate them to you. (When two words sound the same, he will have to indicate *which* of the two you are supposed to spell — for instance, *whose* as in "whose car.") Make a list of the words you misspelled and give this list special attention.

M 1c Spelling Rules

Spelling rules help us memorize words that follow a common pattern.

English spelling does not follow simple rules. However, some groups of words do follow a common pattern. The rule that applies to them will usually have exceptions, but it will help you memorize many words that you would otherwise have to learn one by one.

I before E

In some words the *ee* sound is spelled *ie,* in others *ei.* When you sort out these words, you get the following pattern:

ie: believe, achieve, grief, niece, piece (of pie)
cei: receive, ceiling, conceited, receipt, deceive

In the second group, the *ei* is always preceded by *c.* REMEMBER: It is *i* before *e except* after *c.* Exceptions:

ei: either, neither, leisure, seize, weird
cie: financier, species

Doubled Consonant

In many words the final consonant is doubled before the verb endings *ed* and *ing,* or the adjective endings *er* and *est.* This doubling happens when two conditions are met:

(1) A single final consonant follows a *single vowel* — not a combination (diphthong) signaled by a double letter (oe, ou, ee, ea), or a silent *e* at the end of the original word (kit*e,* hop*e,* hat*e*). Study how the spelling reflects the difference in pronunciation in the following pairs:

plan — pla*nn*ed	plane — plane*d*
hop — ho*pp*ing	hope — ho*p*ing
run — ru*nn*ing	rain — rai*n*ing
scrap — scra*pp*ed	scrape — scra*p*ed
slip — sli*pp*ed	sleep — slee*p*ing
red — re*dd*er	read — rea*d*ing
hot — ho*tt*est	neat — nea*t*est

(2) The syllable with the doubled consonant must be the one *stressed* when you pronounce the word. If the stress shifts away from the final syllable, doubling does *not* take place:

DOUBLING	NO DOUBLING
adMIT, adMITTed	BENefit, BENefited
overLAP, overLAPPing	deVELop, deVELoping
reGRET, reGRETTed	exHIBit, exHIBited
beGIN, beGINNing	WEAKen, WEAKening
forGET, forGETTing	ORbit, ORbiting

```
reFER, reFERRed          REFerence
preFER, preFERRing       PREFerable
```

Y as a Vowel

Y appears as a *single* final vowel in words like *dry* and *try,* *hurry* and *carry.* This *y* changes to *ie* before *s*, to *i* before all other endings. The *y* remains *un*changed, however, before *ing*.

ie: try—tries, dry—dries, family—families, quantity—quantities, carry—carries, hurry—hurries

i: easy—easily, beauty—beautiful, happy—happiness, dry—drier, copy—copied

y: carrying, studying, copying, hurrying

When it follows another vowel, the *y* usually remains unchanged: *played, joys, delays, valleys, grayness.* Exceptions: *day — daily, pay — paid, say — said, gay — gaily, lay — laid.*

Final E

A silent *e* appears at the end of words like *hate, love, like.* This final *e* drops out before an ending that starts with a vowel. (It stays in before an ending that starts with a consonant.)

	VOWEL	CONSONANT
hate	hating	hateful
love	loving	lovely
like	likable	likely
bore	boring	boredom

Exceptions: *argue — argument, true — truly, due — duly, mile — mileage, whole — wholly.* Notice also that this rule does not apply to the *e* that accounts for the *dge* sound in chang*e*able, courag*e*ous, or the *ss* sound in noti*ce*able.

Changed Plurals

A number of common words change their spelling when we go from one to several, from singular to plural:

Singular *o:*	hero	potato	tomato	veto	Negro
Plural *oes:*	heroes	potatoes	tomatoes	vetoes	Negroes
Singular *man:*	man	woman	freshman	postman	fireman
Plural *men:*	men	women	freshmen	postmen	firemen
Singular *f (fe):*	life	knife	calf	wife	half
Plural *ves:*	lives	knives	calves	wives	halves

Some of the less common words ending in *o* or *f* do not change their spelling in the plural: *solo — solos, soprano — sopranos, cello — cellos; hoof — hoofs* (or *hooves*), *scarf — scarfs* (or *scarves*). Check your dictionary when you are in doubt.

EXERCISE 2   On a separate sheet, write down the words called for in the following instructions.

1. Fill in *ei* or *ie:* dec--ve, conc--t, n--ce, bel--f, rec--ve, c--ling, bel--ve, s--ze, ach--vement, conc--vable.
2. Write the *plural* of the following words: quantity, postman, parody, Negro, fly, hero, family, freshman, woman, knife, potato, quality, valley, property, veto.
3. Write the *past tense* of the following verbs: shun, hope, permit, edit, plan, cheat, play, tip, float, say, stop, regret, pay, blot, entrap.
4. Add *-ing* to the following words, making the necessary changes in spelling: like, prefer, orbit, commit, wipe, overlap, carry, dry, run, hurry, benefit, study, hate, drop, plan.
5. Add *-er* to the following words, making the necessary changes in spelling: red, sad, swim, lonely, busy, hot, carry, dim, write, white.
6. Add *-able* to the following words, making the necessary changes in spelling: change, notice, envy, regret, enjoy, break, admire, love, pay, debate.

EXERCISE 3   Of the two possible words, write down the one that fits the context.

1. We had *planed/planned* the attack carefully.
2. The immigration law *barred/bared* Orientals.
3. The choir boys were *robed/robbed* in white.
4. We *scraped/scrapped* our plans for a big reception.
5. We were *hoping/hopping* against hope for an end to the rain.
6. Hungry travelers used to look forward to *dining/dinning* on the train.
7. He had *planed/planned* and sanded the wood himself.
8. The noise of the engine was *dining/dinning* in his ears.
9. The late show was a *griping/gripping* suspense drama.
10. After the loss of her lover, she had *pined/pinned* away.

EXERCISE 4   [Optional]   Look up the plural forms of the following words in your dictionary: *buffalo, cargo, cello, Eskimo, mosquito, motto, piano, solo, soprano, wharf.*

M 1d *Confusing Pairs*

Make a special effort to master confusing pairs.

Learn to distinguish the words in three major types of confusing pairs:

(1) The *same root word* in different uses.

court*eou*s	but	court*e*sy
curi*ous*	but	curi*o*sity
descri*be*	but	descri*p*tion
f*ou*r, f*ou*rteen	but	f*o*rty
gener*ous*	but	gener*o*sity
ni*ne*, ni*ne*ty	but	ni*n*th
pron*ou*nce	but	pron*u*nciation
sp*ea*king	but	sp*ee*ch
ti*ll*	but	unti*l*

Remember the following:

We advi*s*e you to try. (verb)
He gave us advi*c*e. (noun)
We pa*ss*ed the turn-off. (verb)
Let us forget the pa*s*t. (noun)
We found little prejudi*c*e. (noun)
He was extremely prejudi*c*ed. (adjective)
We us*e* cardboard and tape. (present)
We us*ed* to meet in the hall. (past)

(2) Words that *sound similar* or alike.

accept: he *acc*epted my apology; his terms are not *acc*eptable; I cannot *acc*ept the money

except: everyone *exc*ept Judy; he made an *exc*eption for us; to *exc*ept (exempt, exclude) present company

adopt: to ad*o*pt a proposal (in its present form); put a child up for ad*o*ption

adapt: to ad*a*pt a plan to one's needs (to make it fit better); an ad*a*ptable worker (who knows how to fit in); an ad*a*ptation of the story

capital: Paris is the capit*a*l of France; a bank needs capit*a*l; print it in capit*a*l letters

capitol:	the Capitol is the building where the legislature meets
censor:	in wartime letters are censored; object to censorship
censure:	he was censured (blamed, condemned) for his behavior; a vote of censure
cite:	he was cited for bravery; he cited several books by experts
site:	the site of the new school (it's situated there)
counsel:	the counseling staff counsels or gives advice (its members are counselors)
council:	a city council is a governing board or committee (its members are councilors)
desert:	we drove through the desert; he deserted his friends; he got his just deserts
dessert:	we had pie for dessert
effect:	he effected many changes (he brought them about, produced them); far-reaching effects; an effective speech
affect:	it affected my grade (had an influence on it); the bill won't affect (change) your status; he spoke with an affected (artificial) British accent
personal:	these are my own personal affairs; he got too personal
personnel:	the manager hired additional personnel; the organization had a personnel problem
presents:	he bought us presents (gifts)
presence:	your presence is essential (opposite of absence)
principal:	his principal (main) argument; a school principal (chief administrator)
principle:	principles (rules, standards) of conduct; he acted on principle
quiet:	be quiet; a quiet neighborhood
quite:	the house was quite old; not quite ready
weather:	stormy weather; to weather the storm
whether:	whether or not

(3) Words with *parts that sound similar* or alike.

-able:	accept*a*ble, avail*a*ble, indispens*a*ble (as in dispens*a*ry)
-ible:	poss*i*ble (also poss*i*bility), plaus*i*ble, irresist*i*ble
-ance:	attend*a*nce, perform*a*nce, acquaint*a*nce,ˋguid*a*nce
-ence:	occurr*e*nce, experi*e*nce, exist*e*nce, excell*e*nce
-ant:	attend*a*nt, brilli*a*nt, abund*a*nt, predomin*a*nt
-ent:	excell*e*nt, promin*e*nt, independ*e*nt, differ*e*nt
-cede:	pre*ce*de, se*ce*de, con*ce*de
-ceed:	suc*cee*d, pro*cee*d (but pro*ce*dure)

NOTE: Make sure to spell out the *have* that sounds like *of* in the following combinations:

could *have* come, should *have* stayed, would *have* written

EXERCISE 5 After the number of each phrase, write down the word that fits the context.

1. cannot *accept/except* the invitation
2. did not *affect/effect* his seniority
3. listen to my *advise/advice*
4. ask him *whether/weather* he knows
5. taught the *principles/principals* of mathematics
6. no one *except/accept* my brother
7. was never *prejudice/prejudiced* against Catholics
8. where he *use/used* to live
9. had *affected/effected* his hearing
10. in the *presents/presence* of witnesses

EXERCISE 6 Write down the following words, inserting the missing letter (or letters).

indispens—ble, permiss—ble, attend—nt, emin—nt, perform—nce, occurr—nce, abund—nce, exist—nce, succ—d, irresist—ble, curi—sity, plaus—ble, proc—d, experi—nce, pron—nciation

EXERCISE 7 [Optional] For each of the following pairs, write two short sentences using the words in context: *cast/caste, cue/queue, aid/aide, aisle/isle, key/quai, queen/quean, dying/dyeing, singing/singeing.*

M 1e Spelling Lists

*Study a list of words frequently misspelled
in order to avoid predictable errors.*

The following list contains several hundred words frequently misspelled by student writers. If your spelling problem is serious and general, you will profit from studying this list, taking up between ten and twenty words at each sitting. If your spelling problem is more limited, you may have someone dictate this list to you. Then give special attention to the words that have given you trouble.

absence	already	attack	character
abundance	altar	attendance	chief
accessible	altogether	audience	choose
accidentally	always	authority	chose
accommodate	amateur		clothes
accompanied	among	bargain	coarse
accomplish	amount	basically	column
accumulate	analysis	basis	comfortable
accurately	analyze	beauty	comfortably
accuses	annual	becoming	coming
accustom	anticipate	before	commercial
achievement	anxiety	beginning	committed
acknowledgment	apologize	belief	committee
acquaintance	apparent	believe	companies
acquire	appearance	beneficial	competition
acquitted	applies	benefited	competitor
across	applying	breath	completely
actuality	appreciate	brilliant	conceivable
address	approach	Britain	conceive
adequate	appropriate	burial	concentrate
admit	approximately	busy	condemn
adolescent	area	business	confident
advantageous	argue		confidential
advertisement	arguing	calendar	conscience
afraid	argument	candidate	conscientious
against	arising	career	conscious
aggravate	arrangement	careless	considerably
aggressive	article	carrying	consistent
allotted	ascend	ceiling	continually
allowed	assent	cemetery	control
all right	athlete	challenge	controlled
		changeable	

convenience
convenient
coolly
courageous
course
courteous
criticism
criticize
curiosity

dealt
deceit
deceive
decision
definite
definitely
definition
dependent
describe
description
desirable
despair
desperate
destruction
develop
development
device
difference
different
difficult
dilemma
dining
disagree
disappearance
disappoint
disastrous
discipline
disease
disgusted
dissatisfaction
dissatisfied
doesn't
due
during

ecstasy
efficiency
efficient
eighth
eliminate
embarrass
embarrassment
eminent
emphasize
endeavor
enough
entertain
environment
equipped
especially
etc.
exaggerate
excellent
exceptionally
exercise
exhaust
existence
experience
explanation
extraordinary
extremely

familiar
families
fashion
favorite
foreign
forward
friend
fulfill
fundamentally
further

gaiety
generally
genius
government
governor
grammar
group

guaranteed
guidance

happily
happiness
height
heroes
heroine
hindrance
hopeful
huge
humorous
hundred
hungry
hurriedly
hypocrisy
hypocrite

ignorant
imaginary
imagination
immediately
immensely
incidentally
indefinite
independent
indispensable
inevitable
influence
ingenious
intellectual
intelligence
interest
interpret
interrupt
involve
irrelevant
irresistible
itself

jealous

knowledge

laboratory
laid
leisure

likely
literature
livelihood
loneliness
losing

magnificent
maintain
maintenance
maneuver
manufacturer
marriage
mathematics
meant
medicine
medieval
method
mileage
miniature
minute
mischievous
morale
muscle
mysterious

naïve
necessarily
necessary
ninety
noticeable

obstacle
occasion
occasionally
occurred
occurrence
omit
operate
opinion
opponent
opportunity
optimism
original

paid
parallel

paralysis	precede	resource	subtle
paralyze	prejudice	response	succeed
particularly	prepare	reveal	successful
passed	prevalent	rhythm	sufficient
past	primitive	ridiculous	superintendent
peace	privilege		surprise
peculiar	probably	sacrifice	
perceive	procedure	safety	temperament
perform	proceed	satisfactorily	tendency
performance	professional	schedule	therefore
permanent	prominent	seize	thorough
persistent	propaganda	sense	together
persuade	psychology	separate	tragedy
pertain	pursue	several	transferred
phase		shining	tremendous
philosophy	quantity	significance	
physical	really	similar	undoubtedly
piece	recognize	simple	unnecessary
playwright	recommend	sincerely	useful
political	regard	sophomore	using
possess	relief	speech	
possession	relieve	sponsor	various
possible	religion	strength	villain
practice	repetition	stretch	
practical	representative	strictly	weird
			writing

REVIEW EXERCISE 1 Test your mastery of common spelling problems by having someone dictate the following sentences to you. They contain *100 frequently misspelled words* included in the preceding section.

1. *Successful propaganda* requires a *thorough knowledge* of *psychology.*
2. The *performance* of *amateur athletes* is *occasionally disappointing.*
3. The *sponsor interrupted* the *tragedy* with *ridiculous commercials.*
4. *Optimism* makes us *seize* on *hopeful* signs in *disastrous occurrences.*
5. His *irresistible strength* made him *approach* the *obstacle confidently.*
6. The *heroine coolly* led the *naive manufacturer* to the *altar.*
7. He *always accuses* his *opponents* of *prejudice* and *hypocrisy.*
8. *Intellectual discipline* is as *necessary* as *genius* or *imagination.*

9. The *candidate addressed* his *arguments* to a *courteous audience.*
10. Our *writing course dealt* with *description* and *definition.*
11. We did not *anticipate* the *extraordinary anxiety* of our *adolescent friend.*
12. The *authorities consistently emphasize* the *influence* of the *environment.*
13. The *efficient villain laid* the *sophomore* out for *burial.*
14. Her *peculiar character* made her *choose beauty* over *convenience.*
15. His *business* was *eliminated* by the *aggressive advertisements* of the *competition.*
16. Her *changeable* and *jealous temperament* drove her *acquaintances* to *despair.*
17. *Disgusted* with *marriage,* he was *beginning* a new *career* in *mathematics.*
18. The *dissatisfied committee condemned* his *careless analysis.*
19. The *governor continually criticized* those with *different opinions.*
20. He *accidentally* met *destruction during* a *speech* on *safety.*

M 2 Capitals and Special Marks

Learn how to use capital letters, apostrophes, and hyphens.

When we transfer spoken words to the written page, we use not only the ordinary alphabet, but also capital letters and special marks. These do not have an exact equivalent in speech — they are not "pronounced" in any way that would give us a clear signal when to put them in. We therefore have to study and practice the several different uses to which these devices are put.

M 2a Capital Letters

Capitalize the first word of a sentence and proper names.

A capital letter appears at the beginning of each new sentence. The pronoun *I* is always capitalized. In addition, we use a capital at the beginning of a **proper name** — a name used to set one person or thing apart from other members of the same group. Remember the three kinds of names that should be capitalized:

(1) Single words, such as the names of people, places, ships, days of the week, months (but not seasons), religions: *John, Mary, Chicago, Russia, California, S.S. Independence, Tuesday, May, Hinduism.* We capitalize not only the proper name itself, but also words derived from it:

England	English grammar
Brazil	Brazilian coffee
Christ	Christian, Christianity
Paris	Parisian fashions
France	French pastry
Buddha	Buddhism

When people forget that a word was derived from a proper name, the lower-case letter replaces the capital as the generally acceptable spelling:

Pasteur (a French scientist)	but	pasteurized milk
India (the country)	but	india ink

Some words are used two different ways: They serve as a *general* term, used to describe several different examples of the same thing. Or they serve as a proper name that picks out *one* example among all the others.

Ancient Greece developed *democratic* institutions. (examples of a type)

He voted for the *Democratic* party. (name of one party)

He moved from *south* of Chicago to *south* of Detroit. (general direction)

He had been born in the *South*. (name of one region)

Several of our *presidents* have been assassinated. (men holding the same office)

The *President* held a press conference. (identifies one person)

"A *p*resident," "a *q*ueen," or "a *p*ope" means "one of several." "The *President*," "the *Queen*," or "the *Pope*" means "the only one"; we use the capitalized forms the same way we would "President Harding," "Queen Elizabeth," or "Pope Pius." This difference also explains why we write "my *m*other" but "Yes, *M*other"; "his *f*ather" but "I know *F*ather was right." We use the lower-case letter when we rely on *my* or *his* to single out one mother or father;

we capitalize the word when we use it like a proper name, instead of *Jim* or *Joan*.

(2) Combinations in which a general term *combines* with a proper name. We then capitalize not only the proper name but also the word that indicates a title, rank, a type of institution, and the like:

a mayor	but	Mayor Brown
a general	but	General Wainwright
a high school	but	Oakdale High School
a college	but	West Valley College
a square	but	Washington Square

(3) Names of books, titles of articles, names of paintings and other works of art. When these consist of more than one word, we capitalize the *first* word and all other words *except* articles *(a, an, the)*, prepositions *(at, with, for, of)*, and connectives *(and, but, when, if)*. We capitalize even the prepositions and connectives, however, when they have *five* or more letters *(through, without, about, around, because)*:

Up from Slavery
Notes of a Native Son
The Grapes of Wrath
Much Ado About Nothing
The Old Man and the Sea

Capitalize words this way when you write the title of your *own* theme and when you mention a book or article *in* your theme. (The titles you mention, but not the title of your own theme, should also be *italicized*. See **M 6b**.)

EXERCISE 8 Use the following exercise for *habit-building*. Read it over several times, paying special attention to pairs where the same word is used once with, and once without, a capital letter.

a village street, Greenwich Village; a city in Kansas, Kansas City; a county courthouse, Santa Clara County; an island in the Pacific, Staten Island; an alderman, Alderman Smith; a Ford sedan, the Ford Motor Company; a side street, a shop on Main Street, the main shopping street; *Much Ado About Nothing, The Mayor of Casterbridge, The Power and the Glory, The War of the Worlds, The Man Without a Country;* Greek gods, the Christian God, the Mosaic law, the

Old Testament, the Bible, a Buddhist temple, a Methodist minister, the Wesleyan movement; civil wars, the Civil War; republican institutions, the Republican candidate; a democratic country, Democratic voters; catholic interests, Catholic beliefs; moved from California to the South, drive south from Los Angeles; the Middle Ages, the Victorian period, the Elizabethan stage, Jeffersonian democracy; the Bill of Rights, the Fourth of July, the Declaration of Independence, the U.S. Senate, the U.S. Army, the Congressional Record; last spring, this fall, in June and September, every Wednesday.

EXERCISE 9 After the number of each sentence, write down (and capitalize) each word that should start with a capital letter. (You need not include the first word of the sentence.)

1. The history of europe has often been dominated by powerful individuals, from charlemagne through frederick the great and napoleon through hitler and stalin.

2. In america, history has often been made by groups of anonymous people.

3. The first spanish explorers and conquerors were followed by jesuit priests aiming to convert the indians to christianity.

4. Later, the fur traders — french, british, and russian — pushed in for beaver and other pelts.

5. Members of protestant minorities — the puritans, the quakers — colonized new england and pennsylvania.

6. In books like *the scarlet letter* and *the house of the seven gables,* hawthorne has recorded the somber spirit of the puritans, whose ancestors came to tame the wilderness with bible and gun.

7. In the war of independence, a citizen army put democracy and republican institutions in the place of the government of king george.

8. After the louisiana purchase, the mississippi gradually became the center of a now vanished way of life for the traders and boatmen immortalized by mark twain in *life on the mississippi.*

9. In the great plains of the west, the wild horses and cattle were rounded up and driven to kansas or texas by a new breed of cowboys and cattlemen, many of them former citizens of the confederacy who were impoverished as the result of the civil war.

10. The gold fields of california and the comstock lode brought new yorkers, southerners, and midwesterners across the rocky mountains or into san francisco harbor to join in the race for quick fortunes.

M 2b   The Apostrophe

Use the apostrophe for contractions and the possessive.

There are three major uses of the apostrophe:

(1) *Use the apostrophe to show the omission of sounds or letters.* Spoken English (and informal written English) makes frequent use of **contractions.** These are shortened forms of *be, have,* and auxiliaries like *will (would), can (could),* and the like.

> "As long as *there's* light *we're* brave enough . . . So we *can't* have a signal fire . . . *"We're* beaten."
>
> (William Golding)

Many contractions contain a shortened form of *not: can't, haven't, don't, isn't, wouldn't, won't.* Take care not to misspell these, especially *doesn't (does not).* Some contractions *sound* exactly like other forms that have different uses. Make sure to spell them differently:

it's *(it is)*	*It's* too early.
its *(of it)*	The ship kept *its* course.
who's *(who is)*	*Who's* next?
whose *(of whom)*	*Whose* coat is that?
they're *(they are)*	*They're* right.
their *(of them)*	*Their* cabin was deserted.

NOTE: Limit your use of contractions to personal letters and informal or humorous themes. Feel free to use an occasional *don't* or *it's* even in more serious papers. But avoid contractions in formal reports, research papers, letters of application.

(2) *Use the apostrophe for the possessive of nouns and some pronouns.* The **possessive** shows where something belongs, what it is part of, who performs an action, and similar close relationships. It typically shows a relationship that could also be shown by the preposition *of.* The most usual form of the possessive consists of the singular noun followed by the apostrophe plus *s:*

SINGULAR: *Greg's* father (the father *of* Greg), his *sister's* graduation (the graduation of his sister), Mr. *Brown's* store (the store *of* Mr. Brown), the *prophet's* beard (the beard *of* the prophet)

When the plain form of the noun already has an *s* at the end, do not *add* a second *s* to make the possessive. This rule applies to all *s* plurals:

PLURAL: the *girls'* pool (the pool of the *girls*), the *slaves'* revolt (the revolt of the *slaves*), the *teachers'* records (the records of the *teachers*)

Notice the use of the possessive in many expressions dealing with *time, price, or measurement:*

a *day's* work, an *hour's* wait, *today's* paper, last *year's* meeting, a *moment's* notice, a good *night's* sleep, a *dollar's* worth; two *weeks'* pay, three *dollars'* worth, six *weeks'* notice

Remember the following complications:

— *Not all plural nouns* have the plural *s.* They then form the regular possessive with apostrophe plus *s:*

women's clubs, the *children's* hour, the *firemen's* ball

— For *proper names* ending with *s,* the use of a second *s* for the possessive is *optional:*

Charles' birthday (or *Charles's* birthday)
Charles *Dickens'* novels (or Charles *Dickens's* novels)

— Only *indefinite pronouns* use the apostrophe; never use the apostrophe with possessive pronouns like *its, hers, ours, theirs, yours* (see **G 2a**):

INDEFINITE: *one's* relatives, *someone's* uncle, *anybody's* guess, *no one's* fault
POSSESSIVE: it's *hers;* it was either *ours* or *theirs;* has run *its* course

Can you see these principles at work in the following passages?

Slowly the red drained from *Jack's* cheeks . . . his gaze avoided the embarrassment of linking with *another's* eye.
(William Golding)
It is a *woman's* business to get married, and a *man's* to keep unmarried as long as he can. (G. B. Shaw)

They separate the grain from the chaff by tossing the straw in the air. This was their *fathers'* method. And it is likely it will be their *sons'*. (William O. Douglas)

Language has made possible *man's* progress from animality to civilization.
(Aldous Huxley)

(3) Use the apostrophe to separate the plural "s" from the name of a letter or of a number, or from a word discussed as a word:

> His record showed all A's and B's.
> His number consisted of seven 3's in a row.
> It was a speech with many if's and but's.
> He taught us to mind our p's and q's.

EXERCISE 10 Write down the right choice after the number of the sentence.

1. Through his illness he lost several *week's/weeks'* pay.
2. He felt that his private life was *nobodys/nobody's* business.
3. Over the years he had collected about ten *dollar's/dollars'* worth of nails.
4. It must be nerve-racking to be a test *pilot's/pilots* wife.
5. We watched the *spectator's/spectators* and their reactions.
6. He was worried about his *children's/childrens'* future.
7. Several new *family's/families* had moved in.
8. It was all in a *day's/days* work.
9. We have the man *who's/whose* fingerprints match those on the gun.
10. We can never be absolutely sure *who's/whose* to blame for an accident.
11. Carl loved to send people on a *fools/fool's* errand.
12. Nobody can be *everybodys/everybody's* friend.
13. You always give me good advice when *it's/its* too late.
14. People look for a scapegoat when *they're/their* angry or hurt.
15. It seems as if *everyones/everyone's* grandfather had to walk ten miles barefoot to school.
16. The minister always called all of us *Gods/God's* children.
17. Peter had always been his *family's/families'* black sheep.
18. The wives commiserated with each other over their *family's/families'* misfortunes.
19. The mayor accepted the Police *Commissioners/Commissioner's* resignation.
20. The board refused to rescind *it's/its* earlier decision.

Use the hyphen in compound words that have not yet merged into a single word.

The hyphen is conventionally used in compound numbers from *twenty-one* up to *ninety-nine*. In addition the hyphen is used in three major ways to tie together words or parts of words.

(1) When two or more words form a single word unit, they are called **compound words.** Many of these are both pronounced and spelled as single words — without a break or a hyphen. Contrast the members of the following pairs:

a black bird (black BIRD)	a blackbird (BLACKbird)
a dark room (dark ROOM)	a darkroom (DARKroom)

However, other words pronounced the same way are still spelled with the parts separated:

a high price (high PRICE)   a high school (HIGH school)

Still other words are at the halfway stage, with a hyphen used to tie the parts together. Many words that used to be hyphenated are now written solid. Others are used either way. When you are in doubt, use the word the way it is listed in your dictionary. Remember some of the more common words in each major category:

ONE WORD: bellboy, bridesmaid, gunman, headache, highway, newspaper, stepmother, typewriter

TWO WORDS: bus boy, commander in chief, goose flesh, high school,
(or more)   labor union, second cousin

HYPHEN: able-bodied, bull's-eye, cave-in, court-martial, great-grandfather, gun-shy, merry-go-round, mother-in-law, place-kick, smoke-filled

Make sure to get the following right:

ONE WORD: today, tomorrow, nevertheless, nowadays
TWO WORDS: all right, a lot (of time), be able, no one

(2) A part of a word that can be put in front of many different words is called a **prefix.** Most prefixes combine with the word that follows into a single unit. Put a hyphen after the prefix in the following situations:

After *all-*, *ex-* (when it means "former"), and *self-:*
all-knowing, all-powerful; ex-champion, ex-president; self-conscious, self-respect

Before a *capital* letter:
all-American, pro-British, anti-German, non-Catholic

Between two *identical vowels:*
anti-intellectual, semi-independent

(3) Several words that are normally kept separate may combine to form a **group modifier** that is put *in front of a noun.* Use hyphens whenever such a group of words takes the place of a single adjective:

SEPARATE: He described the process *step by step.*
HYPHENS: We wanted a *step-by-step* account.

SEPARATE: The speech was followed by *questions and answers.*
HYPHENS: There was a *question-and-answer* period.

SEPARATE: The meal was *well balanced.*
HYPHENS: She served a *well-balanced* meal.

SEPARATE: We decided to *wait and see.*
HYPHENS: He adopted a *wait-and-see* attitude.

Do not use hyphens when one part of the group modifier is an adverb ending in *-ly:* a *rapidly growing* city, a *carefully prepared* demonstration.

EXERCISE 11 *Read over the following exercise several times* to fix in your mind words and expressions that are conventionally hyphenated.

Grandmother, stepfather, mother-in-law, in-laws, great-grandmother; ex-husband, ex-senator, self-styled, self-confident; un-American, pro-British, anti-German, neo-Nazi; drive-in, cave-in; travel first class, send it by first-class mail; he brought us up to date, an up-to-the-minute summary; he was tired of his father's smile-and-the-world-will-smile-with-you routine; wall-to-wall carpets, a heart-to-heart talk, a left-of-center government, middle-of-the-road policies, below-the-surface facts; English-speaking nations, freedom-loving citizens, world-shaking events; first-rate, high-class ore, a well-earned rest, a hard-hitting account, a smoothly running engine, happily smiling listeners; thirty-six, eighteen, ninety-four, eighty-three

EXERCISE 12 In each sentence, find the combination that needs one or more hyphens. *Write the hyphenated expression* after the number of the sentence.

1. He was surprised at the anti Americanism of his Japanese friends.
2. He explained step by step how to make a person to person call.
3. What had been a strictly spontaneous movement turned into a well organized campaign.
4. The ex governor had had strong support from the labor unions.
5. Up to the minute news coverage seldom examines any event in depth.
6. The candidate promised to conduct a down to the grassroots campaign.
7. The quickly formed committee promised an in depth study of the problem.
8. Jim was changing from a happy go lucky young man to a typical junior executive.
9. His self confidence was badly shaken by her curt reply.
10. A government with almost equally powerful branches is preferable to a single all powerful executive.

Punctuation Marks

COMMA

before coordinating connectives	M 4a
with adverbial clauses	M 4b
with relative clauses	M 4c
with nonrestrictive modifiers	M 5a
after introductory modifiers	M 5a
with adverbial connectives	M 4a
with *especially, namely, for example*	M 3b
with *after all, of course,* and other sentence modifiers	M 5a
between items in a series	M 5b
in a series of parallel clauses	M 4a
between coordinate adjectives	M 5b
with dates, addresses, and so on	M 5b
with direct address and other light interrupters	M 5c
between contrasted elements	M 5c
with quotations	M 6a

M 3 End Punctuation

Use end punctuation to show that an utterance is grammatically complete.

Punctuation marks do some of the work done in spoken English by intonation. (**See G 8b.**) There are several ways of saying "This is John." When we let our voice drop off at the end (falling terminal), we show that we have *completed* a statement: "This is John." When we make the pitch rise at the end (rising terminal), we are *asking* a question: "This is John?" If pitch stays level at the end (level terminal), we show that we are going to *continue* the sentence: "This is John, who lives next door." These and similar differences are signaled in writing by punctuation.

The most basic punctuation marks are those that bring an utterance to a complete stop: the exclamation mark, the question mark, the period. They signal that a group of words (or sometimes just one single word) stands grammatically by itself — that it is grammatically complete and self-contained.

M 3a Exclamations and Questions

Use the exclamation mark and question mark after single words and groups of words.

The **exclamation mark** conveys emphasis. Use it for orders, shouts, expressions of strong emotion. Use it to signal anger, surprise, indignation:

> Stop!   Come back!   What a man!
>
> Jim answered another question and was tempted to cry out, "What's the good of this! What's the good!"
>
> (Joseph Conrad)
>
> They wanted facts. Facts! They demanded facts from him, as if facts could explain anything!   (Joseph Conrad)

The **question mark** shows that an utterance asks for a reply. Sometimes the grammatical structure of the sentence shows it to be a question. Sometimes the question mark *turns* it into a question the way a rising terminal does in speech:

> What did he say?   Did he tell the truth?
>
> John?   It's closed?   They get *paid*?
>
> In such a society of big organizations, the need becomes urgent for new answers to the old questions: "Who am I?" "What am I?" "What should I be?"   (*Harper's*)

In using exclamation marks and question marks, remember the following points:

(1) *Too many exclamation marks* make your writing seem juvenile. Avoid using the exclamation mark after statements that

will seem trivial to a serious reader. Avoid using *several* exclamation marks in a row:

JUVENILE: Right there, in the corner, were three spotted puppies!
JUVENILE: We found we had actually won first prize!!!

(2) Make sure not to forget the question mark after questions that are *long or involved:*

> Where does obligation to truth stop and poetic license begin? Should we attribute to great men what they actually said or did, or what they should have said and done?

(Saturday Review)

(3) Use the question mark even after **rhetorical** questions, which merely *seem* to ask for a reply. Actually, the right answer is already built in in the way the question is asked:

> Is it fair that boys are sent out to fight but denied the right to vote?
>
> Do we want brilliant women to waste their talent bent over a stove?

(4) Feel free to use either the question mark or the period after requests worded as questions for the sake of *politeness:*

> Will you please return to the office at three o'clock?
> Will you please return to the office at three o'clock.

EXERCISE 13 Most of the following sentences illustrate acceptable end punctuation. Put *S* for "satisfactory" after the number of each such sentence. Find the two or three sentences that are unsatisfactory. Put *U* after the number of each of these.

1. What could have brought a man like him to this out-of-the-way place?
2. Wasn't it Charles Dickens who wrote *A Tale of Two Cities.*
3. Will you please fill in the attached form and return it to our office.
4. These are the people who represent us in Congress!
5. How well he knew every nook and cranny of the old house!
6. What can a man do if his own family turns against him.
7. Why does he always have to quote Ayn Rand?
8. Don't you ever show your face in this house again!
9. Would you kindly pass this information on to your friends.
10. How are we going to make up for the wrong already done.

M 3b   Sentences and Fragments

Use the period at the end of statements that are grammatically complete.

The **period** separates one grammatically complete sentence from another. To be complete, the normal sentence must have its own subject and predicate. It must *not* be subordinated to another sentence by a subordinating connective *(if, when, because, whereas)* or a relative pronoun *(who, which, that)*. When the period sets off a group of words that is not a complete sentence, the result is a **sentence fragment.** Avoid the sentence fragment in serious writing, and learn to recognize it on tests. To many readers, it is the single, most serious defect of student writing.

Typically, what makes a fragment a fragment is the lack of all or part of the verb. Often, both the verb and a possible subject are lacking:

FRAGMENT: We had a big surprise. *My brother from Chicago.*
COMPLETE: We had a big surprise. My brother *arrived* from Chicago.

FRAGMENT: We listened to Jim. *Singing the blues.*
COMPLETE: We listened to Jim. *He was* singing the blues.

To learn to avoid sentence fragments, first learn to recognize some of the sentence parts that commonly turn into fragments when set off by a period:

Appositives
      He had bought a secondhand car. *A convertible.*
      They were looking for Jim. *The best man.*

Adjectives, Adverbs
      It was a beautiful day. *Clear but cold.*
      We are changing the policy. *Gradually.*

Prepositional Phrases
      He tried to eat his rice. *With chopsticks.*
      She found the missing gloves. *In the back seat.*

Verbals
      He turned the boat around. *To head for shore.*
      She was busy in the kitchen. *Baking her own bread.*

Dependent Clauses
      Heat makes metal expand. *Whereas cold makes it shrink.*
      We went to Buffalo. *Which is his hometown.*

Study the major ways a sentence fragment may be revised:

(1) Tie most adverbs and prepositional phrases, and many verbals, into the preceding sentence *without any punctuation:*

> We are changing the policy *gradually.*
> He tried to eat his rice *with chopsticks.*
> He turned the boat around *to head for shore.*

(2) Use a **comma** rather than a period to set off most appositives, and many verbals and dependent clauses. (See **M 4** and **M 5** for detailed instructions.)

> He had bought a secondhand car, *a convertible.*
> She was busy in the kitchen, *baking her own bread.*
> We went to Buffalo, *which is his hometown.*

Use this comma when you add examples to a more general statement after *such as, especially, for example, for instance,* and *namely.* (In formal writing, use a *second* comma after the last three.)

> He kept exotic fish, *such as Japanese carp.*
> Her friend loved Europe, *especially France.*
> All students take a second language, *for instance, French.*

(3) Use a **colon** to tie a *list, description, or explanation* to the more general statement that came before:

> Only two of us were given a scholarship: *Martha and Boyd.*
> The bison was life to the, Plains Indians: *The Sioux, the Cheyenne, the wild-riding Comanches.*
> My mother lacked one essential trait: *patience.*

(4) Use a **dash** when you actually want to keep something separate as an *afterthought:* (See also **M 5c.**)

> We are changing the·policy — *gradually.*
> He tried to eat his rice — *with chopsticks.*
> He left Newton Jail — *a free man.*

Sometimes it is impossible to tie a sentence fragment into the preceding sentence. Turn such a fragment into a *complete separate sentence:*

FRAGMENT: We tried to change his mind. *Being a futile effort.*
REVISED: We tried to change his mind. *It was a futile effort.*

NOTE: **Permissible fragments** occur in writing when the writer deliberately reproduces the incomplete units that are part of disconnected, spontaneous speech or thought. You will find them in the following instances:

(1) Written records of *conversation,* or prose that reproduces the give-and-take of dialogue:

> "I'd rather be myself," he said. *"Myself and nasty. Not somebody else, however jolly."* (Aldous Huxley)

> Where do I start? *With personal relationships.* Here is something comparatively solid in a world full of violence and cruelty. (E. M. Forster)

(2) *Narrative* or informal essays that reproduce naturally rambling thought:

> Now, as she lay cleared for sea, the stretch of her main deck seemed to me very fine under the stars. *Very fine, very roomy for her size, and very inviting.* (Joseph Conrad)

> I don't think it's fortunate to write. *Or clever.* It's cleverer to converse. (Sylvia Ashton-Warner)

(3) *Description* that takes stock of impressions the way they would move through the mind of the observer:

> The plains vary here even more than usual — sometimes a long sterile stretch of scores of miles — then green, fertile and grassy, an equal length. *Some very large herds of sheep.* (Walt Whitman)

You yourself may use such permissible fragments when reporting a conversation or writing a story. Avoid them in serious writing unless otherwise instructed by the teacher or editor who is to evaluate your work.

EXERCISE 14 What would be the appropriate punctuation at the break that occurs in each of the following passages? On a separate sheet, put the appropriate abbreviation after the number of each passage: *P* for period; *Cm* for comma; *Cl* for colon; *No* for "no punctuation required." Limit yourself to these four choices.

(Your teacher may ask you to write these sentences out with their correct punctuation. When you do, remember to capitalize the first word after a period.)

EXAMPLE: *3. We read several novels ____ for example, Jane Eyre.
(Answer) 3. Cm*

1. Opinions differ on many things ____ for instance, human nature.
2. Some writers admire mankind ____ they consider men good.
3. Man naturally treats his fellowmen ____ with tolerance and love.
4. Wrongdoing is caused by social conditions ____ poverty, or oppression.
5. Man is innocent and benevolent ____ in his natural state.
6. Other writers believe in the opposite ____ man's tendency toward evil.
7. They discover in man two basic qualities ____ selfishness and cruelty.
8. Man learns to be good ____ through education and fear of punishment.
9. He soon forgets the rules of civilization ____ in an emergency.
10. This view prevails in a book ____ read by many high school students.
11. The book is a British novel ____ namely, Golding's *Lord of the Flies.*
12. Golding describes a group of boys ____ relapsing into savagery.
13. The place is a solitary island ____ the time is after a nuclear war.
14. There are no adults left ____ to impose discipline.
15. At first the boys hold on to civilized procedures ____ for example, the election of a leader.
16. They carry on their British traditions ____ such as respecting differences of opinion.
17. Gradually their savage heritage appears ____ under the civilized surface.
18. Soon they are ruled by two primitive forces ____ violence and superstition.
19. The book may be a parable ____ the story has a larger meaning.
20. Perhaps the same thing could happen ____ on a larger scale.

EXERCISE 15 Which of the following passages contain a *sentence fragment?* Put *Frag* after the number of each such passage. Put *S* after the number of each satisfactory passage. (Your teacher may ask you to revise the fragments you have identified.)

1. Rudyard Kipling named his wolf-man Mowgli. Shere Khan was Mowgli's rival and most dangerous enemy.

2. The private followed the corporal's order. Swearing under his breath all the way.
3. Our Constitution registers the desires of our forefathers. The desires for freedom from remote rulers.
4. His name was Charlie Mears. He was the only son of his mother.
5. Most driving tests are the same. Driving through the middle of town, stopping and starting at signals, and parking.
6. At first Mowgli climbed trees like a sloth. Afterwards he flung himself through the branches like the apes.
7. Hawaii is an island with contrasting parts. One part covered with black sand and volcanic rock, and the other with flowers and trees.
8. Fred had gone to Mexico City. To live with a wealthy aunt.
9. The old woman had dozens of cats. Caring for them kept her busy and happy.
10. Kipling wrote about faraway countries. The British Empire east of Suez.

M 4 *Punctuation Between Clauses*

Know when to put the semicolon or the comma between two clauses.

The typical complete sentence has its own subject and predicate. (In requests, the subject may be omitted or "understood.") When two such subject-predicate units become sub-sentences in a larger combined sentence, we call them clauses. (See **G 6.**) Each of the following sentences is a combination of several clauses, with the subject and verb of each clause in italicized print:

> *The quality* of these men *did* not *matter*; *he rubbed* shoulders with them, but *they could* not *touch* him.
>
> (Joseph Conrad)

> *Jim went on* smiling at the retreating horizon; *his heart was* full of generous impulses, and *his thought was contemplating* his own superiority.
>
> (Joseph Conrad)

> *The ship moved* so smoothly that *her* onward *motion was* imperceptible to the senses of men, as though *she had been* a crowded planet speeding through the dark spaces of ether behind the swarm of suns.
>
> (Joseph Conrad)

STYLES DIFFER

𝕰𝖑𝖊𝖈𝖙𝖗𝖎𝖈𝖆𝖑 𝕷𝖆𝖒𝖕𝖑𝖎𝖌𝖍𝖙𝖊𝖗𝖘

National Bank of the Republic

Neighbourly Association for Common Protection

Unprecedented Attractiveness

MARRIAGE CERTIFICATES, BAPTISMAL RECORDS
FIRST MORTGAGE BONDS

To punctuate such combinations, you have to recognize different types of clauses, and different ways of relating them to each other.

M 4a Independent Clauses

Use the semicolon between independent clauses unless they are joined by a coordinating connective.

(1) *Two statements may be closely related even though there is no connective to tie them together.* A **semicolon** may then replace the period. (In this case, the first word of the second statement is *not* capitalized.) Two clauses joined by a semicolon remain grammatically independent:

> The room was empty; papers littered the floor.
> The men stood in stony silence; the women wept.

Can you see the close relationship between the two clauses in each of the following pairs?

> Nothing is wasted in the sea; every particle of material is used over and over again. (Rachel Carson)
>
> His brain was as energetic as his arms and legs; he thought with the rapidity of lightning. (Ambrose Bierce)
>
> All the boys except Piggy started to giggle; presently they were shrieking with laughter. (William Golding)

Notice that *more than two* independent clauses may join in a longer sentence, with semicolons keeping them apart:

> The Little Russian of the Ukraine is unintelligible to the citizen of Moscow; the Northern Italian can scarcely follow a conversation in Sicilian; the Low German from Hamburg is a foreigner in Munich; the Breton flounders in Gascony.
>
> (H. L. Mencken)

(2) *Two clauses may be joined by an adverbial connective.* This category includes *however, therefore, nevertheless, consequently, hence, besides, moreover, furthermore, accordingly, instead, indeed, in fact, and others.* Again, the **semicolon** may replace the period between the two clauses:

The door was locked; *however,* the lights were still on.
We all had doubts; *therefore,* we tabled the motion.
He likes to read; *in fact,* he does little else.

Adverbial connectives may *shift their position* in the second clause (see **G 6a**). The semicolon, however, stays at the point where the two clauses join:

My uncle had moved out; *however,* his son still lived there.
My uncle had moved out; his son, *however,* still lived there.
My uncle had moved out; his son still lived there, *however.*

In formal writing, a **comma** keeps the adverbial connective apart from the rest of the second clause. *Two* commas are needed if the connective appears in the middle of the second clause. In much informal writing, this additional punctuation is omitted:

FORMAL: Emerson did not look for truth only in great books and great men of the past; *instead,* he found truth in the world around him every day.

INFORMAL: Jim never came to the meeting; he went home *instead.*

(3) *Two clauses may be joined by a coordinating connective.* The seven words in this group are true, all-purpose connectives and are found everywhere in ordinary prose: *and, but, so, for, yet, or,* and *nor.* The **comma** is the most typical punctuation when one of these words joins two clauses. (Several of these connectives also link words or phrases.)

Paul had slept very little, *and* he felt grimy and uncomfortable.
(Willa Cather)

She exacted perpetual attention, *but* it was impossible not to like her.
(Henry James)

He was no bigger than I was, *so* I thought him fair game.
(Winston Churchill)

Something strange was happening to Piggy, *for* he was gasping for breath.
(William Golding)

The sand dunes of Cape Cod are as accessible and linked with city life as any suburb, *yet* they stretch most of the time as empty as the desert.
(Jacques Barzun)

Notice the *inversion* of subject and verb caused by *nor* (see **G 6a**):

Jim never volunteered a comment, *nor* did he ever ask a question.

More than two independent clauses may be linked by coordinating connectives in the same sentence:

> America comes out of Europe, *but* these people have never seen America, *nor* have most of them seen more of Europe than the hamlet at the foot of their mountain.
>
> (James Baldwin)

NOTE: In your own writing, the safe practice will be to use the *semicolon with no connective or with an adverbial connective;* the *comma with a coordinating connective.* However, you will encounter the following variations:

(1) In informal writing, a comma may appear even when there is *no connective* or adverbial connective. The result is a **comma splice,** or **run-on** sentence, condemned by many teachers and editors as incorrect:

COMMA SPLICE: The doctor washed his hands, he was dead tired.
COMMA SPLICE: He built another magnificent tomb, this one was of black marble.

In some formal writing, the comma appears between clauses exceptionally closely related in meaning, or closely parallel in grammatical structure. *Avoid* this use of the comma in your own writing unless *three or more* such parallel clauses combine in the same sentence:

DEBATABLE: His love grew thin and faint as the morning mist, his doubts alone had substance.
DEBATABLE: It had not come to him easily, it had been backward and roundabout.
SAFE: The drums rumbled, the bugles called, the fifes shrilled.

(2) A **colon** may join two clauses when the second is the *explanation or result* of the first:

> There was complete silence over the town: everybody was asleep. (Graham Greene)
>
> A few buzzards looked down from the roof with shabby indifference: he wasn't carrion yet. (Graham Greene)

(3) *And, but,* and *or* appear *without punctuation* between clauses that are very short or very closely related:

He had been walking all day *and* he was very tired.

(Graham Greene)

(4) A **semicolon** is possible with all coordinating connectives, especially if the clauses they join are *long or involved:*

The two boys faced each other. There was the brilliant world of hunting, tactics, fierce exhilaration, skill; *and* there was the world of longing and baffled common-sense.

(William Golding)

(5) Both adverbial and coordinating connectives leave the two clauses they join grammatically independent. It is therefore possible to use the **period** for a *more definite break:*

All that year the animals worked like slaves. *But* they were happy in their work; they grudged no effort or sacrifice.

(George Orwell)

EXERCISE 16 What would be the most typical punctuation at the numbered breaks in each of the following sentences? Put *C* for comma after the number of the break if a *coordinating* connective joins two clauses. Put *S* for semicolon if an *adverbial* connective joins two clauses. Put *No* if the break occurs *within* a clause rather than between two clauses. (Your teacher may ask you to point out places where you would insert optional commas.)

A. Canada is a country of powerful minorities _____(1) and can be governed _____(2) only in a spirit of compromise.

B. Canadians differ in language _____(3) and culture _____(4) therefore they have long lacked a strong national identity.

C. They long avoided all national symbols _____(5) in recent years however they have developed a new passion _____(6) for asserting themselves as Canadians.

D. Much of Canada has been settled by the English _____(7) and the Scots _____(8) the Maritime Provinces in fact have long been inhabited mostly by dyed-in-the-wool Britishers.

E. These provinces were always the British stronghold _____(9) for many United Empire Loyalists had left the United States _____(10) for this part of Canada.

F. Toronto is the most American of the big Canadian cities _____(11) yet most of the natives still think of it _____(12) as the most British town on the continent.

G. The French lost their Canadian territories long ago _____(13) but French culture to this day flourishes in the province of Quebec.

H. Many French Canadians have become bilingual _____(14) most however have never given up French _____(15) nor are they likely to do so in the near future.

I. Not only their common language _____(16) but also their European pattern of life gives French Canadians a strong sense of unity _____(17) their political and cultural influence is consequently strong.

J. The province of Quebec is old France and new France _____(18) it is still North America nevertheless.

K. American economic influence is felt everywhere _____(19) and many families have relatives _____(20) across the border in the New England states.

EXERCISE 17 Many of the sentences in this exercise illustrate *typical punctuation between independent clauses.* Put S for "satisfactory" after the number of each such sentence. Other sentences illustrate the kind of comma splice that you should avoid in your own writing. Put CS after the number of each of these. A few of the sentences illustrate the "fused sentence" — two independent clauses with no punctuation or connective between them at all. Put FS after the number of each of these. (Your teacher may ask you to revise the unsatisfactory sentences.)

1. Children need a feeling of security; otherwise, no amount of discipline will help.

2. Harold's dog never spends a whole day in peace, he engages in at least one fight with the neighborhood mongrels.

3. All at once classes begin, and the realities of college life become all too evident.

4. The first theme is written; the first history test is taken; the first physics experiment is done.

5. Age has nothing to do with safe driving, often a person over 21 is a less responsible driver than his younger brother.

6. The average student simply does not read enough books; consequently, long reading assignments make him throw up his hands.

7. Their faces were different, but they were dressed like twins.

8. Some student groups do almost nothing some are concerned with activities outside of school.

9. Friendship is like marriage, you have to work together for success.

10. The campus is a study in contrasts, for the new architecture makes the old more noticeable.

11. The teacher never went into anything he just told us to write and hand in our papers at the end of the period.

12. We five girls live together, not one of us knew any of the others before.

13. A home is no longer just a home; it is expected to be a showplace.

14. There was no sign of recent occupancy in the cabin, nor was there any message.

15. The report does not give a complete account of the concentration camps, one would have to turn to other sources for that.

16. There was something wrong with the airport, it was under water.

17. Black coral grows like a tree up to heights of ten feet; the branches of the coral tree are thin and delicate.

18. The serum must be administered within an hour, or the poison will have run its course.

19. Our society is founded on reason and the spirit of compromise, therefore force should be used only as a last resort.

20. The new principal announced strict new rules; however, he soon learned when and how to allow exceptions.

EXERCISE 18 [Optional] Study punctuation between independent clauses in several articles in a recent issue of *Harper's, Atlantic, The New Republic,* or *National Review.* Collect ten sample sentences illustrating different possibilities. How closely do the authors (or editors) of the magazine you have chosen follow established conventions?

M 4b Adverbial Clauses

Use the comma to set off nonrestrictive adverbial clauses.

Subordinating connectives do not merely join a second clause loosely to the first. They subordinate it, turning it into a grammatically dependent clause. (See **G 6b.**) The clauses thus subordinated are typically **adverbial clauses.** Like adverbs, they give us the time, place, reasons, or conditions of the action or event described in the rest of the sentence.

To make sure you are dealing with a subordinating connective, try putting the adverbial clause *in front of* the main clause:

NORMAL:	We were miles from the camp *when the storm broke.*
REVERSED:	*When the storm broke,* we were miles from the camp.
NORMAL:	The game will be canceled *if the rain continues.*
REVERSED:	*If the rain continues,* the game will be canceled.

Some adverbial clauses require no punctuation; others are set off by a comma. Remember three major possibilities:

(1) *Use no punctuation when you add a restrictive clause.* Most subordinating connectives deal with time, place, or conditions: *when, while, before, after, since, until, where, if, unless, as long as.* The clause they introduce often makes all the difference to the meaning of the whole statement. Such a clause *narrows down* the meaning of the main clause in an important way. It is called a **restrictive** clause.

Can you see how the dependent clause in each of the following examples *restricts* the meaning of the original statement in an important way?

> You can have the day off.
> You can have the day off *if you find a substitute.*
>
> The town was safe.
> The town was safe *until the dam broke.*
>
> It is dangerous to be sincere.
> It is dangerous to be sincere *unless you are also stupid.*
>
> (G. B. Shaw)

A combination like *only when* or *only if* makes it especially clear that the adverbial clause is restrictive and should not be set off by punctuation:

> A man is a man *only as* he makes life and nature happier to us.
>
> (Emerson)

(2) *Use a* **comma** *when you add a nonrestrictive clause.* Some subordinating connectives set up a contrast: *though, although, whereas, no matter what, no matter how.* The clause they introduce does *not* change the meaning of the main clause. It merely points out that something else is *also* true. Such clauses are **nonrestrictive.** They are set off by a characteristic break in the spoken sentence, and by a comma in writing:

> We enjoyed the trip, *though* the weather was bad.
> He was a British subject, *although* he lived in Spain.

English is a Germanic language, *whereas* French derives from Latin.

He always failed, *no matter how* hard he tried.

(3) *Use a* **comma** *when the dependent clause comes first.* Use this comma to show where the main clause starts, regardless of whether the adverbial clause is restrictive or nonrestrictive. The comma then points up the structure of the sentence and often prevents misreading:

> *Where the stream came out of the canyon,* the trail left it.
>
> *While the bubbles were yet sparkling on the brim,* the doctor's four guests snatched their glasses from the table. (Hawthorne)
>
> *As they struggled to and fro,* the table was overturned.
>
> (Hawthorne)

NOTE: A few subordinating connectives may introduce either a restrictive or a nonrestrictive clause. With. *because* and *so that,* use *no* punctuation if the major point of the sentence *follows* the connective. Use the **comma** if the major point is in the main clause, with the adverbial clause merely giving further information. Listen for the break signaled by the comma in the following pairs:

> (Why are you leaving?) I am leaving *because I have to study.*
>
> (What are you doing?) *I am leaving,* because I have to study.
>
> A house can be designed *so that it utilizes all available sunshine.* (Dependent clause states the *purpose.*)
>
> *The house had been built close to the river,* so that water kept seeping into the basement. (Dependent clause *adds* an unintended result.)

EXERCISE 19 What would be the most typical punctuation at the break in each of the following sentences? Put *C* after the number of the sentence if the *dependent clause should be set off* by a comma. Put *No* if no comma is required.

1. Although Australia is a large country _____ Australian speech is remarkably uniform.

2. People sound the same in Queensland and New South Wales _____ whereas in England rural speech varies widely from one region to another.

3. We can see the reason for this difference _____ if we consider the country's history.

4. Australian speech is relatively uniform _____ because local dialects take centuries to grow.

5. They develop _____ where people live in secluded, small communities.

6. But few people settled down in isolated communities _____ after they came to Australia.

7. Ever since the continent was opened up _____ there has been a large, shifting population.

8. Most of them move _____ because their jobs require them to.

9. People cannot work in sheep-shearing and harvesting _____ unless they are prepared to move with the seasons.

10. Teachers and clergymen have to go _____ where they are needed.

11. There has been even less chance for the development of regional dialects _____ since radio and television made their appearance.

12. People listen to many of the same programs _____ no matter where they live.

13. But language differences do exist in Australia _____ though they do not follow geographic boundaries.

14. Many educated people consider British English the best or the purest kind _____ so that the language of the schools is close to Standard British English.

15. But at home most Australians speak "Broad" Australian _____ no matter how much their teachers frown on this form of popular speech.

16. Speakers of Broad Australian say *piper* _____ when they mean paper.

17. When they mean piper _____ they say *poiper*.

18. As you would expect _____educated Australians differ in their attitude toward popular speech.

19. Some believe good English to be the same everywhere _____ so that any departure from British English is automatically corrupt.

20. Others do not object to differences in pronunciation _____ as long as such differences do not interfere with communication.

M 4c *Relative and Noun Clauses*

Use the comma to set off nonrestrictive relative clauses.

Many dependent clauses are simply joined to the main clause by a subordinating connective. But two additional types of dependent clauses are built into the larger sentence in more complicated ways:

— **Relative clauses** are joined to the main clause by a relative pronoun: *who (whom, whose), which, that.* This pronoun at the same time takes the place of one of the nouns in the relative clause (see **G 6b**):

> (The mayor was reelected. *The mayor* had skirted the issues.)
> The mayor, *who* had skirted the issues, was reelected.

> (She was wearing the necklace. He had sent her *the necklace.*)
> She was wearing the necklace *that* he had sent her.

— **Noun clauses** take the place of one of the nouns in the main clause. They are introduced by *that, why, how, where, when,* and other words used as special connectives (see **G 6b**):

> (Jim told us *the truth.* The house was empty.)
> Jim told us *that* the house was empty.

Like other dependent clauses, relative and noun clauses are sentence fragments when kept separate from the main clause by a period. As with other dependent clauses, our choice is typically between the comma or no punctuation.

(1) *Set off relative clauses only when they are nonrestrictive.* Use *no* punctuation when the clause is used to help identify, when it narrows something down in an important way; in short, when it is **restrictive.** Use the **comma** when the relative clause merely gives further information about something already identified. Use *two* commas when such a nonrestrictive clause *interrupts* the main clause:

> RESTRICTIVE: We looked for the man *who had parked the truck.*
> NONRESTRICTIVE: We looked for Jim, *who had parked the truck.*

> RESTRICTIVE: The actor *who played Hamlet* was outstanding.
> NONRESTRICTIVE: Laurence Olivier, *who played Hamlet,* was outstanding.

Can you see the difference between restrictive and nonrestrictive in the following examples? Can you *hear* the breaks that set off nonrestrictive material in speech?

> The vague news of his loss at sea a little later on solved a problem *which had become torture to her meek conscience.*
> (Thomas Hardy)

The sun shone in at the door upon the young woman's head and hair, *which was worn loose,* so that the rays streamed into its depths as into a hazel copse. (Thomas Hardy)

The agricultural and pastoral character of the people *upon whom the town depended for its existence* was shown by the class of objects displayed in the shop windows. (Thomas Hardy)

Note that relative clauses using *that* are almost always restrictive. Clauses from which the relative pronoun has been *omitted* are always restrictive:

The company *that had sold us the car* had gone out of business.

The sun in the west was a drop of burning gold *that slid nearer and nearer the sill of the world.* (William Golding)

The poems *he wrote* were all about flowers and sunsets.

The regimental history described in detail each battle *the regiment had fought.*

(2) *Do not set off noun clauses.* These become part of the sentence without a break in speech, and without punctuation in writing:

He asked us *why we were late.*

Americans believe *that wisdom must be practical.*

No one knew *where the equipment had been stored.*

The woman had long perceived *how zealously and constantly the young mind of her companion was struggling for enlargement.* (Thomas Hardy)

(3) *Punctuate all clauses that modify a noun the way you do relative clauses.* Not all clauses starting with *where, when, after,* and similar words are adverbial clauses. Instead, they may modify a noun in the main clause. Set them off if they are nonrestrictive:

He took us to the spot *where he had buried the treasure.*

She had been taken off to Canada, *where they had lived several years without any great wordly success.* (Thomas Hardy)

There was a time *when Henchard and Farfrae were close friends.*

We went there in the fall, *when the leaves were just turning color.*

NOTE: The difference between restrictive and nonrestrictive is not always clear-cut. Dependent clauses, like other kinds of complicating material in a sentence, are sometimes borderline and may be punctuated either way. Can you show that this would be true of sentences like the following?

They had a small boy *who kept them awake at night.*

They came to a grizzled church, *whose massive square tower rose unbroken into the darkening sky.* (Thomas Hardy)

EXERCISE 20 What would be the most typical punctuation at the breaks in each of the following sentences? Put *C* after the number of the sentence if a *nonrestrictive clause* requires one or more commas. Put *No* after the number of the sentence if no comma is required.

1. Americans _____ who seldom master foreign languages _____ usually read the great masterpieces of world literature in English.
2. Critics _____ who studied available translations _____ used to complain of their poor quality.
3. Robert Frost said flatly _____ that poetry is lost in translation.
4. But we should remember _____ that some of our greatest poets have been fascinated by the translator's art.
5. The writers _____ who produced the masterpieces of English and American literature _____ were often well versed in other languages.
6. The author of *The Canterbury Tales* was Geoffrey Chaucer _____ who had translated a long love poem from the French.
7. John Milton _____ who wrote *Paradise Lost* _____ had written some of his sonnets in Italian.
8. Coleridge _____ whose "Ancient Mariner" is known to every American student had studied the German Romantic poets and philosophers.
9. Anyone _____ who wants to exploit the resources of his own language _____ learns much from studying other languages.
10. Ezra Pound is one of the greatest poets _____ America has produced.
11. Some of the poems _____ that made him famous _____ were translated from Latin and other languages.
12. He translated from Provencal and Chinese _____ which are rarely studied in this country.

13. American writers in their turn are read in translation by the millions abroad _____ who love American literature.
14. Edgar Allan Poe _____ who wrote "The Tell-Tale Heart" and similar stories _____ was translated by the French poet Baudelaire.
15. Mark Twain has been read by millions in the Soviet Union _____ which does not always encourage the reading of foreign authors.
16. Young Frenchmen _____ who know Faulkner and Hemingway _____ have usually read them in French translations.
17. Many people feel _____ that the great foreign classics need to be translated all over again for each new generation.
18. They ask _____ why Socrates should sound like a nineteenth-century Englishman to modern American readers.
19. Many of the Greek classics _____ that students are required to read _____ are available in several excellent modern translations.
20. You may be surprised to find _____ how different a recent translation can be from an older version.

REVIEW EXERCISE 2   In each of the following passages, *more than two clauses* combine in a larger sentence. Point out in detail how the authors have applied or modified familiar conventions governing punctuation between clauses. Do any of these passages present unfamiliar or unusual problems?

1. Mr. Henchy snuffled vigorously and spat so copiously that he nearly put out the fire, which uttered a hissing protest.
   (James Joyce)
2. Now her voice was the sweetest Robin had heard that night, yet he could not help doubting whether that sweet voice spoke Gospel truth. (Hawthorne)
3. A smell of damp came up all round him; it was as if this part of the world had never been dried in the flame when the world was sent spinning off into space. (Graham Greene)
4. It had come to be accepted that the pigs, who were manifestly cleverer than the other animals, should decide all questions of farm policy, though their decisions had to be ratified by a majority vote. (George Orwell)
5. The human beings did not hate Animal Farm any less now that it was prospering; indeed, they hated it more than ever.
   (George Orwell)
6. The rock-pools which so fascinated him were covered by the tide, so he was without an interest until the tide went back.
   (William Golding)

M 5 Internal Punctuation

Know when to use commas or other internal punctuation.

Within a single clause, there is normally no punctuation between the most basic elements: the subject and the verb, the verb and its complements. But even when modifiers are added, they may become an essential part of what the sentence says, and blend into it without a break. Neither of the following sentences requires any internal punctuation:

> Work expands so as to fill the time available for its completion.
>
> (C. Northcote Parkinson)
>
> Love is as necessary to human beings as food and shelter.
>
> (Aldous Huxley)

A writer must learn to distinguish between complicating elements that blend into a sentence without a break, and those that should be set off by commas or other internal punctuation.

M 5a Modifiers

Use commas to set off nonrestrictive modifiers.

Modifiers fill in and develop the basic sentence patterns. (See **G 5.**) In deciding which modifiers to set off, make the following distinctions:

(1) *Distinguish between restrictive and nonrestrictive modifiers.* A modifier that follows a noun may help us single out one thing among several, or one kind of thing among several kinds. It narrows down the possibilities; it helps us *identify* something. Such a modifier is **restrictive** and requires *no punctuation:*

> The girl *in the blue dress* asked me your name.
> (Which girl? The one *in the blue dress*)
>
> Newspapers *critical of the régime* were shut down.
> (Which newspapers? Those *critical of the régime*)
>
> He stopped the man *entering the gate.*
> (Which one? The one *entering the gate*)

When something has already been identified, the modifier merely adds further information. It does not single something out; it is **nonrestrictive**. Such a modifier is set off by a **comma**, or *two* commas if the sentence continues after the modifier:

> Jane, *in a blue dress,* met us at the door.
> He introduced me to Mrs. Brown, *the new librarian.*
> His red convertible, *parked illegally,* had been towed away.
> Europeans, *living on a crowded continent,* envy our wide open spaces.

The following passages all illustrate the kind of modifier that adds further information:

> They had a child, *a little girl.*　　　　(William Faulkner)

> The face of the presiding magistrate, *clean shaved and impassible,* looked at him deadly pale between the red faces of the nautical assessors.　　　　(Joseph Conrad)

> He stood stiffly in the shade, *a small man dressed in a shabby dark city suit, carrying a small attaché case.*　　(Graham Greene)

> He sat there like a black question mark, *ready to go, ready to stay, poised on his chair.*　　　　(Graham Greene)

(2) *Set off sentence modifiers.* Modifiers that seem to apply to the sentence as a whole are set off by one or more **commas** when they are stressed enough to be set apart in speech by slight breaks. Set off *any verbal or verbal phrase* at the beginning of a sentence. Set off any verbal or verbal phrase that appears later in the sentence but applies to the sentence as a whole:

> *Smiling,* she dropped the match into the tank.
> *Overcome with gratitude,* he shook everyone's hands.
> *To make rabbit stew,* first catch the rabbit.
> *Considering the risk,* the price seems reasonable.

> It was the right decision, *all things considered.*
> Hunting, *to be frank,* has never appealed to me.
> He did quite well, *considering his lack of experience.*

With *introductory modifiers* other than verbals, practice varies. As a rule of thumb, use the comma with any introductory modifier of more than three words:

For a man of his talents, it was an easy task.
More than twenty years ago, he had asked her to marry him.
With the aid of a scholarship and a job, Emerson finished Harvard.

(3) *Set off transitional expressions and the like in formal writing.* Here are some of the expressions set off by one or more commas in formal writing, but used without commas in more informal writing: *after all, of course, unfortunately, on the whole, as a rule, certainly, on the other hand, for example.*

The performance, *on the whole,* was not a success.
The money will have to be returned, *of course.*
As a rule, we consider only written applications.
The resolution, *unfortunately,* had already been passed.

EXERCISE 21 In which of the following sentences would you insert *one or more commas* at the break (or breaks) indicated? Put *C* after the number of the sentence if you would use a comma to set off the modifier appearing at the beginning or at the end of the sentence. Put *C* also if you would use *two* commas to set off a modifier appearing in the middle of the sentence. Put *No* after the number of the sentence if use of the comma would be inappropriate.

1. To please their audience _____ popular novelists and playwrights often use stock characters.

2. The men and women _____ populating the pages of a novel _____ sometimes seem strangely familiar.

3. Characters _____ proving popular with audiences _____ may reappear in play after play.

4. Imitated over and over _____ such stock characters may become mere stereotypes.

5. Audiences _____ flocking to the theaters of ancient Rome _____ expected to see on the stage the miser and the braggart soldier.

6. Shakespeare _____ the creator of unforgettable individual characters _____ at the same time used stock figures like the mooning lover and the railing cynic.

7. Charles Dickens _____ writing in nineteenth-century England _____ made use of the kindly old capitalist befriending the unfortunate.

8. Hollywood _____ dream capital of the world _____ has acquainted millions with the stock characters of the Western novel.

9. The cynical badman _____ whiskey-eyed and unshaven _____ brutalizes the citizens of a small Western town.

10. To save the hero _____ the prostitute with a heart of gold throws herself in the path of the deadly bullet.

11. Readers of the old English ballads remember Robin Hood _____ the merry outlaw.

12. Robbing the rich and helping the poor _____ Robin is one of a long line of idealized scofflaw heroes.

13. Stock characters _____ used in the literature of the past _____ can tell us much about the ideals and prejudices of earlier periods.

14. The Romantics believed in the superior nobility of people _____ living close to nature.

15. James Fenimore Cooper _____ the author of the Leatherstocking tales _____ reflects this belief in his portraits of noble Indians.

16. Another familiar stock character of American fiction is Uncle Tom _____ the faithful slave.

17. His head surrounded by a white halo of lamb's wool _____ Uncle Tom smiles gratefully at his master.

18. The noble savage and Uncle Tom are more unreal than most stock characters _____ found in literature.

19. In the hands of a master _____ a stock character may come gloriously to life.

20. Shakespeare's Falstaff is only one of a long line of military men _____ living on credit and telling outrageous lies about their exploits.

M 5b   Coordination

**Use commas where necessary when several elements
of the same kind appear together in a sentence.**

In the typical sentence, the place of any one part may be taken by two or more parts *of the same kind*. Such grammatically "parallel" parts may be coordinated by a connective like *and* or *or*. Often there are punctuation marks in addition to, or in place of, such a connective:

> *Jim* came to say goodbye.
> *Jim, Chad, and Jeremy* came to say goodbye.

> It was a *warm* night.
> It was a *warm, cloudless* night.

(1) *Three or more elements of the same kind form a series.*
Typically, **commas** appear between the elements of a series, with
the last comma followed by a connective that ties the whole group
together:

> His face appears on *monuments, coins,* and *stamps.*
> *Drought, floods,* and *diseases* had damaged the crops.

The slots in a series may be filled by single words, groups of
words, or whole clauses. Study the typical "A, B, and C" pattern
in the following examples:

> She was a middle-aged woman, very *knowledgeable, gossipy,* and *pious.*
> (Frank O'Connor)

> *Cabot, Frobisher,* and *Davis sought* the passage to the
> northwest, *failed,* and *turned back.* (Rachel Carson)

> In the far distance a helicopter *skimmed* down between
> the roofs, *hovered* for an instant like a bluebottle, and *darted*
> away again with a curving flight. (George Orwell)

> *He reads* much,
> *He is* a great observer, and *he looks*
> Quite through the deeds of men. (*Julius Caesar* I, ii)

Note the following variations:

— A series can be expanded to accommodate *more than three
items:*

> Ford showed that one could *raise* wages, *cut* prices, *produce*
> in tremendous volume, and still *make* millions.

— The *last comma* in a series is optional. Use it in your own writing,
but be prepared to see it omitted in much modern literature:

> Mr. Lyons *sat* on the edge of the table, *pushed* his hat towards
> the nape of his neck and *began* to swing his legs. (James Joyce)

— Some authors vary the rhythm of the series by *omitting the
connective:*

> The day there hadn't yet begun with *that first* sleepy *slap*
> of a shoe on a cement floor, *the claws* of a dog scratching as
> it stretched, *the knock-knock* of a hand on a door.
> (Graham Greene)

— **Semicolons** take the place of commas at the major breaks in a series when its parts *already contain commas* of their own:

> Three witnesses testified for the defense: *Claire,* the accused's wife; *Jim,* his best friend; and *Mr. Brown,* his foreman at the plant.

(2) *Dates, addresses, page references, and the like, may have several parts.* Use **commas** between the different elements. Use another comma after the whole group unless the last word of the group ends the sentence:

> The date was *Monday, December 17, 1967.*
> The gold rush at *Cripple Creek, Colorado,* was the last really big one south of Canada.
> He lived at *39 Pine Street, Oakland, California.*
> *Chapter 5, Volume II,* deals with regional history.
> Look at *Chapter 3, page 45.*

Commas also separate the parts of measurements using *more than one unit of measurement.* Here no additional comma is used after the last item:

> The frame was *two feet, three inches* wide.
> He entered *six pounds, two ounces* as the net weight.

(3) *Two or more adjectives may modify the same noun.* When they come in different layers, their order cannot be reversed, and there is no punctuation: *a loyal public servant.* (*A public loyal servant* would not make sense.) But when two adjectives are interchangeable, they may be coordinated by *and* or by a **comma:**

> a tall *and* handsome stranger   a *tall, handsome* stranger
> (a handsome and tall stranger)
>
> a friendly *and* happy crowd   a *friendly, happy* crowd
> (a happy and friendly crowd)

Notice the "coordinate adjectives" in the following:

> A *deep, harsh* note boomed under the palms . . . Ralph continued to blow *short, penetrating* blasts.   (William Golding)
>
> The *shivering, silvery, unreal* laughter of the savages sprayed out and echoed away.   (William Golding)

(4) *A second word or phrase may repeat, reinforce, or explain the first.* A **comma** appears between the two:

> We told him *to improvise, to be flexible.*
>
> He wants players who are *alert, quick in body and mind.*
>
> He *tried to keep* his mind from running ahead, *tried to keep* it absolutely motionless.
> (John Steinbeck)

EXERCISE 22 At which of the numbered breaks in the following sentences would you insert a comma? After the number of each break, put *C* for comma, *S* for semicolon, or *No* if no punctuation is required. *Include all optional commas.*

A. The typical _____(1) Yankee was a tall _____(2) loose-jointed figure with sallow cheeks _____(3) a sharp nose _____(4) and an eye _____(5) to the main chance.

B. The slit-eyed _____(6) lean-jawed _____(7) soft-spoken _____(8) gambler carried two six-guns beneath the frock coat made in Omaha _____(9) Nebraska.

C. Quantrill _____(10) Jesse James _____(11) and Sam Bass _____(12) are among the leaders of famous _____(13) outlaw _____(14) bands.

D. The best-known figures of American folklore are Daniel Boone _____(15) the woods ranger in his coonskin cap _____(16) Davy Crocket _____(17) the backwoods boaster _____(18) and Paul Bunyan _____(19) the prodigious lumberjack.

E. Davy Crocket could outboast any man alive _____(20) grin the bark off a tree _____(21) and hug a bear _____(22) too close for comfort.

F. The stereotyped _____(23) Southern colonel wears a black _____(24) slouch hat _____(25) and shoestring tie while sitting in the familiar _____(26) rocking chair drinking mint juleps.

G. A good Western novel has gunfighters _____(27) law officers _____(28) cattle kings _____(29) Indian chiefs _____(30) gamblers _____(31) sheepmen _____(32) miners _____(33) and scouts.

H. The Pilgrims _____(34) the Quakers _____(35) and the Mormons _____(36) undertook long _____(37) arduous migrations to escape organized _____(38) religious persecution.

I. Carson City _____(39) Nevada _____(40) is the center of a famous mining district in the American West.

**Use commas and other appropriate marks
to set off parenthetic elements.**

Parenthetic elements interrupt a sentence without becoming part of its grammatical structure. There are three major ways of setting off such interrupters:

(1) *Light interrupters blend into the sentence with only a slight break.* They are set off by **commas** — two commas when they appear in the middle of a sentence, one comma when they are moved to the beginning or the end. Use these commas when you

— *address the listener or the reader:*

Your record, *Ralph,* is appalling.
Here are the books, *Mrs. Brown.*
Friends, Romans, countrymen, lend me your ears.

(Julius Caesar III, ii)

— *show how true something is, or who thought so:*

His appeal, *it seems,* was not successful.
They will refund the money, *I am sure.*
He was a man, *I realized,* in poor physical condition, unexercised and sedentary.   (Henry James)

— *start a sentence with "oh," "yes," "well," "no," "why," "all right," and the like:*

Yes, we heard all about it.
Why, he never even mentioned it.
"Well, Julio," said his brother with desperate charm.
All right, if everybody was older than he was, let them parade and give orders.   (Paul Horgan)

— *follow a statement with a tag-question:*

He is your friend, *isn't he?*
So he locked the door, *did he?*

— *insert something for contrast after "not" or "never":*

He always mentioned his children, *never his wife.*
I come to bury Caesar, *not to praise him.*

(Julius Caesar III, ii)

— *shift something to an unusual position in a sentence:*

Bureaucracy, *in a technical age like ours,* is inevitable.

(E. M. Forster)

Now and then we had a hope that, *if we lived and were good,*
God would permit us to be pirates. (Samuel Clemens)

(2) *Heavy interrupters cause a very definite break in speech.*
They are set off in writing by **dashes.** Overuse of the dash makes
for jerky, disconnected writing. Use dashes when you

— *set off a phrase or whole sentence by a thoughtful pause:*
He had come across that man before — *in the street perhaps.*

The compass, the sailing chart, the ship's chronometer — *the
latter was not invented till the eighteenth century* — made
possible the era of exploration.

She had
A heart — *how shall I say?* — too soon made glad,
Too easily impressed. (Robert Browning)

— *insert a modifier that is exceptionally long or contains commas:*
Noise — *hums, hisses, rumbles, pops, clicks, and the like* —
has ruined many a recording.

The hero of a democracy — *unlike the Stuarts, Bourbons, and
Napoleons of the Old World* — cannot invite public opinion
to go to blazes. (Dixon Wecter)

— *make something stand out for a strong effect:*
This is what he left behind — *a country in ruins.*

On the floor of the Capitol is a pattern made from six flags
— *the flags of Spain, Mexico, France, the United States, the
Confederacy, and Texas.*

(3) *Less important information is often given in a lower tone
of voice.* It appears in writing in **parentheses.** Use parentheses instead of dashes when you

— *insert or add something as an aside:*
Jamaica *(I went there last June)* is a fascinating place.
During the rains the village *(it was really no more)* slipped
into the mud. (Graham Greene)

— *provide page references, dates, and other supplementary information:*

The anecdote about the two tramps *(p. 67)* seemed familiar.
The anniversary *(October 15)* will be a gala event.

Samuel Clemens *(better known as Mark Twain)* was a caustic satirist.

When a whole sentence appears *separately* in parentheses, it carries its own end punctuation with it:

Exactly how many volumes Alger wrote is not known. *(One biographer ran the total up to 119.)*

EXERCISE 23 Most of the following sentences illustrate typical punctuation of *parenthetic elements*. Put *S* for "satisfactory" after the number of each such sentence. Put *U* for "unsatisfactory" after the number of each sentence that needs to be revised. Be prepared to explain in class what went wrong.

1. English spelling, we all know, is haunted by ghosts.
2. The *h* in *ghost* (as well as in *ghastly* and *aghast*) stands for nothing.
3. Three of the letters in *through* — a perfectly ordinary word — do not stand for any sounds.
4. Many less common words — *knight, thoroughfare, knickknack* — have three or more silent letters.
5. Our alphabet was tailored to fit the sounds of Latin not English.
6. And much of our written language mirrors Chaucer's or Shakespeare's pronunciation, not ours.
7. British spelling, believe it or not, is even more conservative than American.
8. The British still spell *gaol* (pronounced *jail*).
9. Some progress, it is true, has been made toward modernized spelling.
10. Noah Webster (the American lexicographer) helped us get rid of the *k* in *musick* and *logick*.
11. The word *programme* (still often seen in England) is now spelled *program*.
12. Other modernized spellings *catalog, plow, thru* have met with varying degrees of success.
13. Has no one tried, you might ask, to develop a streamlined spelling system for our language?
14. Yes, there have been many schemes for spelling reform.
15. George Bernard Shaw — always eager to badger his countrymen was a strong champion of modernized spelling.
16. But the arguments against any really thorough reform are obvious aren't they?

17. We cannot simply reprint all existing books, can we?

18. Well, students then would have to learn both the new spelling system and the old.

19. Why every typewriter in the English-speaking countries would have to be equipped with the new letters the reformers have invented.

20. Neither you, dear reader, nor I will see the day when a stream-lined modern spelling system is universally adopted.

REVIEW EXERCISE 3 [Optional] Point out in detail how the authors of the following passages have *used or adapted* different kinds of internal punctuation.

1. He was a tall, slender young man with a light brown moustache . . . The other man, who was much younger and frailer, had a thin, clean-shaven face. (James Joyce)

2. One oil-lamp was lit in the bows, and the girl whom Mr. Tench had spotted from the bank began to sing gently — a melancholy, sentimental, and contented song about a rose which had been stained with true love's blood.
(Graham Greene)

3. In Alaska, man is an uneasy intruder. Jagged black mountains geometric with snow, rivers bloated from glacial silt, impenetrable ice wastes, and tangled northern jungles conspire to dwarf human beings. Rivers are wider, mountains are higher (more than sixty-five peaks exceed 10,000 feet), valleys are vaster than eyes can encompass. *(Saturday Review)*

4. Governments, politicians, newspapers, writers, advertisers, agitators, zealots of all kinds, and just plain talkers pour out a stream of advice, admonition, instruction, and propaganda, using all the known and some unheard-of tricks in their anxiety to tell us what to think, do, eat, wear, smoke, and believe.
(Atlantic)

5. Below the roof of awnings, surrendered to the wisdom of white men and to their courage, trusting the power of their unbelief and the iron shell of their fire-ship, the pilgrims of an exacting faith slept on mats, on blankets, on bare planks, on every deck, in all the dark corners, wrapped in dyed cloths, muffled in soiled rags, with their heads resting on small bundles, with their faces pressed to bent forearms: the men, the women, the children; the old with the young, the decrepit with the lusty — all equal before sleep, death's brother.
(Joseph Conrad)

M 6 *Quotation*

Know how to work quoted material into your text.

We often must make it clear that we are repeating words and ideas not our own. We must make it clear by punctuation and other appropriate means that we are recording what someone else said, or copying what someone else wrote.

M 6a *Direct Quotation*

Use quotation marks to set off passages you quote verbatim.

When you repeat someone's exact words, you are using **direct** quotation. Material quoted word for word is enclosed in **quotation marks.** Usually a **comma** separates the quotation from the introductory statement — the credit tag that identifies its source:

> He said, "We have found your father."
> "You are very kind," the girl replied.

> It was Pascal who wrote, "Men never do evil so completely and cheerfully as when they do it from religious conviction."

Note that the comma is used regardless of whether the credit tag appears at the beginning or at the end. If the credit tag *splits a complete sentence,* you need two commas. If the credit tag *separates* two complete sentences, you need a comma before it and a **period** after it:

> "No human intelligence," he wrote, "could have read the mysteries of his mind."
> "Our faith comes in moments," Emerson said. "Our vice is habitual."

When a quotation ends or is interrupted, commas and periods stay *within* the quotation, *before* the final quotation mark (as in all the above examples). Semicolons conventionally go *outside* the quotation; they follow the final quotation mark:

> He said, "It's perfectly safe"; besides, we had no choice.

Question marks and exclamation marks go *inside* the quotation if the quoted part asks a question or makes a strong point.

They go outside the quotation if the question is asked, or the strong point made, *about* the quotation:

> Everyone asked, "Where is the rest of the crew?"
> He shouted, "You will be as sorry for this as a man can be!"

> Wasn't it Browning who wrote, "Grow old along with me"?
> And this is the man who said, "We all have to make sacrifices"!

When the credit tag follows a question or exclamation, do *not* use a comma in addition to the terminal marks:

> "What's the use of it?" he asked.

In papers on literary topics and in research papers, you will often have to make extended and varied use of quoted material. Be prepared to handle the following *variations:*

(1) *Short quotations* often appear *without a comma* to set them off, especially when they are built into the grammatical structure of a larger sentence. Short quoted phrases built into your own sentences help give your writing an authentic touch by relating it closely to firsthand sources:

> He said "Buenos Días" to a man with a gun who sat in a small patch of shade against a wall. (Graham Greene)

> The other day there was sent to me a California newspaper which calls all the Easterners "the unhappy denizens of a forbidding clime." (Matthew Arnold)

(2) *Long quotations* are often introduced by a **colon** rather than a comma. When they run to more than ten lines of prose, they are treated as **block quotations.** These are *not* set off by quotation marks. They are indented and, in a typed paper, single-spaced. (See Chapter Four for examples of block quotations used in research papers and research reports.)

> The current issue of *Punch* quotes a saying that contains a great deal of truth: "There is always a Jones ahead of the Jones you keep up with."

(3) *Lines of poetry and of dialogue* are set off in special ways. A full line or more of poetry is set off as a block quotation. In the following passage, the author quotes a line and a half from Tennyson's poem "Ulysses":

At their best, epigrams are short but profound observations about human nature, making us feel that their authors are men who have seen

> cities of men
> And manners, climates, councils, governments.

In quoting dialogue, we start a *new paragraph* for each change of speaker:

> "Mr. Lorry, look upon the prisoner. Was he one of those two passengers?"
> "I cannot undertake to say that he was."
> "Does he resemble either of these two passengers?"
> "Both were so wrapped up, and the night was so dark, and we were all so reserved, that I cannot undertake to say even that."
> (Charles Dickens)

(4) *Quotations within a quotation* are shown by **single quotation marks**:

> Voltaire says, "I never made but one prayer to God, a very short one: 'O Lord, make my enemies ridiculous.'"

(5) *Omissions from a quotation* are shown by three spaced periods, called an **ellipsis**. Use four periods if the omission follows the period at the end of a sentence. Comments or corrections *added* to a quotation are inserted between **square brackets**:

> As John Gardner has said, "Favoritism . . . judges the individual on the basis of his relationships rather than on ability and character."
> He said, "The mayor of one Western city [Portland?] was attacked for having placed fourteen relatives in city jobs."

NOTE: The first word of a quotation is *capitalized* if it was the first word of a sentence in the original text.

EXERCISE 24 Explain in detail how each of the following passages illustrates *conventional punctuation* of quotations.

1. "Right you are, Crofton!" said Mr. Henchy fiercely. "He was the only man that could keep that bag of cats in order. 'Down, ye dogs! Lie down, ye curs!' That's the way he treated them."
(James Joyce)

2. The public can never forget that Hamilton once exclaimed, "Your people, sir, is a great beast!"

3. "Sir," said the honest young newsboy, "you have given me a dime by mistake. The newspaper costs only a penny."

4. She softly laid the patient on a sofa, and tended her with great skill and gentleness, calling her "my precious!" and "my bird!" and spreading her golden hair aside over her shoulders with great pride and care. (Charles Dickens)

5. Edgar Allan Poe — who wrote, "I love fame . . . I would have incense arise in my honor from every hamlet" — died in poverty, in delirium, in a Baltimore hospital.

6. "The sense of uselessness," said Thomas Huxley, "is the severest shock which our system can sustain."

7. Free men must cherish what Whitehead called "the habitual vision of greatness."

8. The phrase "I'm just a country boy" has become the favored gambit of sophisticated and wily men. (John W. Gardner)

9. Was it Woodrow Wilson who observed that democracy "releases the energies of every human being"?

10. Mencken defined conscience as the "inner voice which warns us that somebody may be looking"!

M 6b   Indirect Quotation and Words Set Off

Use no punctuation with indirect quotations, but set off words and phrases quoted verbatim.

We do not — and cannot — always quote someone verbatim, word for word. Often we merely repeat his ideas in *our own words.* Often we condense and summarize, giving only the gist of what someone has said. Such **indirect** quotation often takes the form of a noun clause introduced by the special connectives *that, why, how, where, when,* and others. (See **G 6b.**) These noun clauses fit into the sentence *without* punctuation — no comma, no quotation marks:

> It is often said *that every nation has the government it deserves.*
>
> (Matthew Arnold)

A direct quotation looks at things from the point of view of the *speaker,* at the time he was talking. An indirect quotation looks at things from the point of view of the person who *quotes,* at the time he is quoting. Note how references to persons and to time change in the following pairs:

DIRECT:	He asked, "Why *do you* hate *me?*"
INDIRECT:	He asked why *she hated him.*
DIRECT:	She asked him, "Where *have you* been?"
INDIRECT:	She asked him where *he had* been.
DIRECT:	The inspector said, "But no one *saw you* leave."
INDIRECT:	The inspector said that no one *had seen me* leave.

Even in indirect quotation, you may preserve *some of the original words* — because they are striking, or typical of the speaker, or especially important. Enclose such words and phrases (but not the rest of the quotation) in **quotation marks:**

> She said she did not want her son to marry "below his station."
>
> Bret Harte said that the native idiom of Americans was full of the "saber-cuts of Saxon."

In addition to such directly quoted phrases, *set off* the following from your own text:

(1) Put *technical or unusual terms* in **quotation marks** to show that they are new, important, or unusually apt:

> The engine had an "afterburner" especially designed for this plane.
>
> The new pioneers would be the "backtrailers," as Hamlin Garland called them, moving from the Plains States to Chicago, Boston, San Francisco, and New York. (Malcolm Cowley)

(2) Use **italics** to set off *words discussed as words,* as in a discussion of word history or word meanings. (Underlining takes the place of italics in typed and handwritten papers.)

> *Legacies* is the term applied by some fraternities to prospects for membership that are relatives of present members.
>
> The English, seeking a figure to denominate the wedge-shaped fender in front of a locomotive, called it a *plough;* the Americans, characteristically, gave it the far more pungent name of *cow-catcher.* (H. L. Mencken)

(3) Use **italics** to indicate *words borrowed from foreign languages* and still considered foreign. Many terms in law, science, and philosophy belong in this category:

The lawyer entered a plea of *nolo contendere.*

The killer whale *(Orcinus orca)* is a fierce animal 20 to 30 feet long.

The colonists left the old patterns behind them, and found in America a *tabula rasa* on which to sketch the character of a new society. (John W. Gardner)

(4) Use **italics** to set off *titles of complete publications,* such as books and magazines. Use quotation marks to set off titles for *separate parts* of a publication, such as a chapter in a book, an article in a magazine, a poem in an anthology.

Lord Bryce, writing his *American Commonwealth,* included a chapter called "Why Great Men Are Not Chosen Presidents."

NOTE: Students often use quotation marks to set off words — often slang terms — for humorous effect (I was happy to see all my "chums" again). This practice is much overdone and annoys many readers.

EXERCISE 25 The following passages illustrate conventional ways of setting off *words and phrases.* Explain why each was set off the way it was. Point out any variations from familiar practice.

1. The classic works in which this wager *motif* is worked out are the Book of Job and Goethe's *Faust.* (Arnold J. Toynbee)
2. Kings, magicians, smiths and minstrels are all "specialists" — though the fact that . . . Homer, the poet of Hellenic legends, is blind, suggests that in primitive societies specialism is abnormal and apt to be confined to those who lack the capacity to be "all-round men" or "jacks of all trades." (Arnold J. Toynbee)
3. The name *Alaska* comes from the Aleut word *Alayeska,* meaning "the great land."
4. Books like *Risen from the Ranks* and *Bound to Rise* showed generations of American boys the road to fame and fortune.
5. Montaigne set up as his ideal of effective style "a succulent and nervous speech, short and compact."
6. The inferior man must find himself superiors, that he may marvel at his political equality with them, and in the absence of recognizable superiors *de facto* he creates superiors *de jure.*
   (H. L. Mencken)
7. "The Emperor of Ice-Cream" is included in *Poems by Wallace Stevens.*

M 7 Manuscript Form

Hand in neat and legible copy, observing standard form.

The outward appearance of your paper shows *what you think of your reader.* It shows whether you care about his convenience, his eyesight, his standards of neatness. Most readers find it hard to give friendly attention to a paper whose outward form says in so many words: "I couldn't care less."

M 7a Preparing Copy

Write or type your papers neatly, legibly, and in standard form.

Pleasing, legible **handwriting** is the result of deliberate effort and constant practice. Keep the loops open in letters like *e;* keep the dots right over each *i* and cross your *t*'s. Do not run together combinations like *mm, mn, ing, tion.* Avoid excessive slanting and excessive crowding; use letters of standard size and proportion. Flourishes and squiggles do not impress the reader; they annoy him. If your teacher does not require any special type of theme paper, use paper of *standard size,* ruled in *wide* lines.

Competent **typing** is a skill that a high school student (let alone a college student) can hardly do without. Type the original copy on *nontransparent* paper — unlined, of standard size. Semitransparent sheets (onionskin) are for carbon copies.

Observe the following instructions in order to produce acceptable typed copy:

(1) *Double-space* all material except block quotations and footnotes. Leave two spaces after a period or other end punctuation. Use two hyphens--with no space on either side--to make a dash.

(2) *Leave adequate margins.* Leave about an inch and a half on the left and at the top. Leave about an inch on the right and at the bottom. *Indent* the first line of a paragraph — about an inch in longhand, or five spaces in typed copy.

(3) *Capitalize words in the title* of your paper as you would in a title you merely mention (see **M 2a**). Observe the three *don'ts*

for the title you give to your own theme: Do *not* underline or italicize it; do *not* enclose it in quotation marks (unless it is indeed a quotation); do *not* put a period at the end (but use a question mark or exclamation mark where needed).

> How to Become Extinct
> Is War Inevitable?
> Help Prevent Crime!

Proofread a first draft carefully for hasty misspellings or typographical errors. The following last-minute **corrections** are permissible on the final copy if they are neat and few in number:

(1) Draw a line through words or phrases you want to omit. Do *not* use parentheses or square brackets for this purpose.

> this side ~~of~~ idolotry

(2) To correct a word, draw a line through it and write the corrected word in the space immediately above. Do *not* cross out or insert individual letters:

> *implied*
> He ~~inferred~~ we were cheating.

(3) To add a missing word, insert a caret (∧) and write the word immediately above:

> *is*
> A new census ∧ being planned.

(4) To change the paragraphing of a paper, insert the symbol ¶ to indicate an additional paragraph break. Insert *no* ¶ in the margin to indicate that an existing paragraph break should be ignored.

Divide words as recommended by your dictionary. Most dictionaries use centered dots to show the possible breaks (com·pli·ment). Divide words only if otherwise you would have an extremely uneven right margin. Remember the following points:

(1) Do not set off single letters, as for instance in *about, alone, many, via.* Do not set off the *-ed* ending in words like *asked* and *complained.*

(2) When a word is clearly a combination of other meaningful parts, divide at the point where the original parts are joined: *blue·bird, harm·ful.*

(3) Divide hyphenated words only at the point where the hyphen occurs, for instance in *un-American* or *sister-in-law.*

(4) Do not divide the last word on a page.

Underline (or italicize) *for emphasis,* but use this device only rarely, when clearly appropriate:

> The teacher was expected to present the evaluation to the parent *in person.*
>
> "I know *exactly* what you mean," he replied.

M 7b Abbreviations and Numbers

Use abbreviations and figures only where they are appropriate.

Abbreviations and figures save much time and space. In ordinary writing, however, you will have to avoid excessive shortcuts. The following **abbreviations** are *generally acceptable* in ordinary writing:

(1) Before or after names, the titles *Mr., Mrs., Dr., St.* (Saint); the abbreviations *Jr.* and *Sr.;* degrees like *M.D.* and *Ph.D.:*

> We were introduced to Mr. and Mrs. Gilbert Jones.
> The sign identified him as John A. Gielgud, Jr., M.D.

(2) Before or after numerals, the abbreviations *No., A.D.* and *B.C., A.M.* and *P.M.* (or *a.m.* and *p.m.*), and the symbol $:

> The battle of Actium was fought in 31 B.C.
> The plane leaves at 9:25 A.M.

(3) Initials standing for the name of agencies, business firms, technical processes, and the like, providing these initials are in common use:

> Mr. Smith had been an agent for the FBI.
> We studied an article about UNESCO.

(4) Latin abbreviations such as *e.g.* (for example), *etc.* (and so on), *i.e.* (that is), though the modern tendency is to use the corresponding English expressions instead:

> The writer ignored important new resources, e.g. nuclear energy.

Other abbreviations are acceptable in addresses, business records, and the like, but are *spelled out* in ordinary writing:

(1) Names of countries, states, streets, and the like (with a few exceptions: *U.S.S.R.*, Washington, *D.C.*):

> His first stop in the United States was Buffalo, New York.
> His office was on Union Street in Pittsburgh, Pennsylvania.

(2) Units of measurements like *lb.* (pound), *oz.* (ounce), *ft.* (foot), with the exception of *mph* and *rpm:*

> The first fish he caught weighed three pounds, two ounces.

Figures are *generally acceptable* in references to dates and years, street numbers and page numbers, exact sums and technical measurements, especially those referring to percentages or including decimal points:

> He was born on May 13, 1922.
> They lived at 1078 Washington Avenue.
> The town had 23,456 inhabitants.
> The rate had gone up 17.5 per cent.

The following are usually *spelled out:* numbers from one to ten; round numbers requiring no more than two words; a number at the beginning of a sentence. Notice that when they are spelled out, compound numbers from 21 to 99 are hyphenated.

> The first issue of our paper sold about three hundred copies.
> Twenty-five years ago he was not even born.
> The nursery school was for children from two to six years old.

FURTHER STUDY: History of Writing

Writing, like many other human activities, is to a large extent governed by convention. The conventional way of doing things seems natural and right to us because we are *used to it*. On various pages of this book, you have seen photographed passages showing written English in some of its earlier forms. The following short selections give you an opportunity to study in some detail the way written English has changed over the centuries.

Assignment 1 Many of the conventions we follow in our writing reflect customs that developed at one point or another in the *history of printing*. Have you ever looked at a text printed two or three hundred years ago? The following is a short passage by Cotton Mather, first published in 1702. Point out in as much detail as you can how the conventions of spelling and punctuation differ from our own.

It was another Property of his *Preaching,* that there was evermore much of CHRIST in it; and with *Paul,* he could say, *I determined to know nothing but Jesus Christ;* having that Blessed Name in his Discourses, with a Frequency like that, with which *Paul* mentions it in his *Epistles.* As 'twas noted of Dr. *Bodly,* that whatever Subject he were upon, in the Application still his Use of it would be, *to drive Men unto the Lord Jesus Christ;* in like manner, the Lord Jesus Christ was the Loadstone which gave a touch to all the Sermons of our *Eliot;* a Glorious, Precious, Lovely *Christ* was the Point of Heaven which they still verged unto. From this *Inclination* it was, that altho' he Printed several *English* Books before he dy'd, yet his Heart seemed not so much in any of them, as in that serious and savoury Book of his, Entituled, *The Harmony of the Gospels, in the Holy History of Jesus Christ.*

Assignment 2 Modern editors of early English texts often modernize punctuation (and sometimes the use of capitals and hyphens) but leave the *original spelling* essentially unchanged. The following passages are from the late fourteenth century (Chaucer), the late sixteenth century (Shakespeare), and the late seventeenth century (Milton). Study the spelling in these passages in detail. To judge from these selections, how early in the history of our language did some of our modern spelling conventions become fixed in their present form?

1.   A knyght ther was, and that a worthy man,
       That, fro the tyme that he first bigan
       To riden out, he loved chivalrye,

Trouthe and honour, fredom and curteisye.
Ful worthy was he in his lordes werre,
And ther-to hadde he riden, no man ferre,
As wel in Christendom as in hethenesse,
And evere honoured for his worthyness.

(*werre* war; *ferre* farther; *hethenesse* heathendom)

—Chaucer, *Canterbury Tales*

2. From fairest creatures we desire increase,
    That thereby beauties *Rose* might neuer die,
    But as the riper should by time decease,
    His tender heire might beare his memory:
    But thou contracted to thine owne bright eyes,
    Feed'st thy lights flame with selfe substantiall fewell,
    Making a famine where aboundance lies,
    Thy selfe thy foe, to thy sweet selfe too cruell:
    Thou that are now the worlds fresh ornament,
    And only herauld to the gaudy spring,
    Within thine owne bud buriest thy content,
    And tender chorle makst wast in niggarding:
        Pitty the world, or else this glutton be,
        To eate the worlds due, by the graue and thee.

(*chorle* churl, miser; *niggarding* being niggardly)

—Shakespeare, "Sonnet I"

3.   The mind is its own place, and in it self
    Can make a Heav'n of Hell, a Hell of Heav'n.
    What matter where, if I be still the same,
    And what I should be, all but less then he
    Whom Thunder hath made greater? Here at least
    We shall be free; th' Almighty hath not built
    Here for his envy, will not drive us hence:
    Here we may reign secure, and in my choyce
    To reign is worth ambition though in Hell:
    Better to reign in Hell, then serve in Heav'n.
    But wherefore let we then our faithful friends,
    Th' associates and copartners of our loss
    Lye thus astonisht on th' oblivious Pool,
    And call them not to share with us their part
    In this unhappy Mansion, or once more
    With rallied Arms to try what may be yet
    Regaind in Heav'n, or what more lost in Hell?
        So *Satan* spake.

(*astonisht* overwhelmed)

—Milton, *Paradise Lost*

CONTENTS

CHAPTER SIX

Speech:
THE ORAL TRADITION

An effective speaker understands and uses the power of the spoken word.

Speech and writing are closely related. The same principles of composition apply whether we prepare a short speech to a group or write a letter to the editor of a newspaper. We could say, in fact, that the requirements for effective communication apply more forcefully in oral than in written composition. A reader can slow down to ponder a passage. He can retrace his steps. But a listener has to take in what a speech has to offer *while* it is being offered.

Here are some of the qualities effective speech and writing share:

(1) *Like effective writing, effective speech has focus.* An effective speaker learns to take clear aim; he learns not to scatter his shots. If he has an important proposal to present, he makes sure it does not get lost among various other points. When trying to show whether a widely used drug is dangerous or harmless, he limits himself to material that is directly related to this central issue.

(2) *Like effective writing, effective speech is clearly organized.* In listening to an effective speaker, we can follow the order in which he presents his ideas. Often the outline of a speech is *simpler* than that of an article. To give his listeners a clear sense of direc-

tion, a speaker may limit himself to three or four major points. He may present in order

— three major stages in the civil rights movement;
— four reasons this country joined the United Nations;
— three major objections to a new system of metropolitan government, each carefully analyzed and refuted.

(3) *Like an effective writer, an effective speaker knows how to use the resources of language.* He knows how to sum up a key idea in a striking phrase that people will repeat and remember. He knows how to take an abstract idea and give it figurative expression that brings a sharp image to the listener's mind.

In spite of these close parallels, however, a speech is not simply a written composition read aloud. Not everyone who writes well speaks well, and vice versa. As Pascal said, "There are some who

---

Six Hints for Speakers

RELAX. Write at the top of your notes in large block letters: "This too shall pass."

TAKE IN YOUR SURROUNDINGS. Look around before you start talking. Arrange your notes, the lectern, and the mike the way you want them *before* you start.

MOVE NATURALLY. Feel free to use your arms and hands for gestures that reinforce what you say. Step back half a step, raise your head, look at your audience as you ask an important question.

WATCH FOR THE NERVOUS TIC. Fight any tendency to start any regular nervous motion — drumming of fingers, tapping of feet, swaying of the body.

KEEP IT CURRENT. Make your talk sound live by working in last-minute examples: "On my way to class I noticed. . . ." "We all saw yesterday's headline: . . ."

CUT WHERE NECESSARY. Don't race the clock. If you run overtime, omit examples or detailed explanations. Make sure you don't have to stop before you reach your main point.

---

speak well and write badly. For the place and the audience warm them, and draw from their minds more than they think of without that warmth." Speech is more *spontaneous* than writing. It tests our ability to think on our feet, to improvise. Speech brings the *whole person* into play. A speaker does not simply send out a finished message from the privacy of his study. He presents himself live to his audience. Finally, speech tests our ability to *relate to other people*. It makes us show how sensitive we are to the expectations of the audience, how successfully we can break the ice, how we can capitalize on the listeners' response.

S1 Speaker and Audience

A good speaker knows how to reach out to his audience.

Listening to a good speaker is an experience. The listener does not remain a passive spectator. He is drawn in; he participates. We can see the frowns on the listeners' faces as the speaker poses a problem. We can feel the silence deepen in the hall as he admonishes them concerning a solemn obligation. We share in the sudden release of laughter as the speaker relieves the tension with a flash of wit.

Have you ever studied a transcript made from the tape recording of an exceptionally successful talk? Many of the speaker's unique traits will have been filtered out: appearance, personality, voice, reputation. What remains can offer us clues to the speaker's *strategy,* his way of approaching and holding his audience. Here are some of the elements you are likely to find when you analyze a successful speaker's approach.

NOTE: Most of the examples for the following points are taken from an actual talk by Bergen Evans, one of the most popular and successful speakers among authorities on the English language.

(1) *An effective speaker makes himself understood.* His ambition is to convey his message to his audience, regardless of how difficult his points, or how poorly prepared his listeners. He does

not say to himself: "If my audience cannot follow what I am saying, too bad for them!" Instead, he hunts for examples that will make a general point concrete and graphic. He looks for analogies that will bring a technical point closer to the layman. If he talks about the way our memory works, he might use the example of someone trying to remember a name. He might compare the necessary "memory check" to the work of a file clerk looking for something in a filing cabinet.

Suppose a lecturer wanted to make the point that language is shaped by the *culture* of a people, that it reflects where and how they live. Would you agree that examples like the following would help make this point clear to his listeners?

> Arabic has many words relating to the sicknesses of camels, because Arabs have many camels, and camels have many sicknesses. English is almost destitute of words relating to the sickness of camels, because if they are sick, we leave it to the zoo. When the Lord's Prayer was first translated into Eskimo, it read, "Give us this day our daily fish," because Eskimos didn't have bread in those days and wouldn't have understood.

(2) *An effective speaker identifies with his audience.* He asks himself: "What do I and my audience have in common?" He asks: "How can I relate my topic to the background and interests of my listeners?" A speaker who asks himself such questions is able to establish *rapport;* he does not remain an outsider.

Suppose a lecturer is making the point that differences in language develop naturally; that they are a normal, everyday thing. If he is lecturing in Missouri, he might look for an example *from* Missouri: Old-timers pronounce the name of the city "Saint Louie;" others "Saint Louis." If he is lecturing in Illinois, he might point out that people from Vienna, Illinois, call it "Vīenna," with the *i* pronounced "eye." (A man trying to cash a bogus check was caught because he claimed to be from Vienna but did not pronounce it right.)

(3) *An effective speaker keeps his material up to date.* He links his subject to what is current and topical. His speech is a "live" talk — it is related to what is happening *now.* By using current examples, he shows that he is still *thinking* about his material,

that he is open to new impressions and new evidence. If his topic is obstacles to communication, he might look for examples currently in the news:

— the problems of diplomats trying to understand each other at an important conference then in progress;
— a recent disturbance caused by misunderstanding or lack of communication;
— a recent report on the barriers to communication between social workers and welfare recipients.

(4) *An effective speaker varies his pace.* He does not simply cover his points in a dead monotone. He lets his audience see that he is human. When he talks about injustice, his indignation shows in his more insistent, more emphatic pronunciation and gestures. Even when he talks about a serious topic, he shows that he has a sense of humor. Lack of communication, for instance, is a serious matter, but it would take a speaker with a tin ear to ignore its funny side:

> I doubt that animals can mis-communicate. Suppose a bee comes in and does the "clover one-mile north" dance. The whole hive doesn't buzz with "What did he say, what did he say? Alfalfa, two miles south?" But that's what would happen if they were human beings. Human beings tend to get mixed up. A child used to pray "Hallohan be thy name" because Hallohan was the local baker. (This helped make sense of the passage about giving us this day our daily bread.) Another child had always heard the nursery rhyme "Higgledy, piggledy, my son John" as "mice on John." A student listened to a lecture on the New Testament and came away talking about "B-attitudes" instead of "beatitudes."

(5) *An effective speaker gets his audience involved.* He communicates his infectious enthusiasm about his subject. He changes the attitude of his audience from "I am here only because I *have* to be" to "This I want to hear." A good speaker shows that his topic matters to him — by the care with which he has worked up his subject, by the satisfaction he obviously derives from presenting it to others. An audience finds it hard to resist a speaker who is as fascinated with his topic as the author of the following passage:

Human speech is to me the most amazing thing in the entire cosmos. . . . That inorganics should have become organics, that the organics should have become sentient, that they should then become self-conscious and that we should have created this remarkable thing, speech, is the most amazing thing there is. It's the most amazing thing in the cosmos because speech created thought, which is the measure of the universe. It's through speech that we are able to conceptualize, objectify, classify, transmit, and deduce one generation's knowledge and pass it on to another. It's to speech that we owe our glory, our wisdom, our learning, our powers of research and humanity.

EXERCISE 1 Prepare a brief talk in which you explain a *difficult subject* to a group that has little relevant background and needs all the help you can give. For instance, explain a difficult concept in the natural sciences to a group of seventh or eighth graders. Or, explain a crucial part of our system of government to a group of recent immigrants who want to become citizens. Or, explain a new approach to high school mathematics to a group of parents who had their own schooling in math many years ago. Try to make your presentation truly helpful and instructive without making it condescending.

EXERCISE 2 Prepare a brief talk on one of the following topics of general and lasting interest: water pollution, traffic safety, street violence, educational opportunity, or integration vs. segregation. But relate your speech throughout closely to the *current* situation and the *local* scene. Draw on local newspapers and similar sources for recent material of local interest.

EXERCISE 3 Prepare a brief talk in which you try to draw on a full range of moods. Select a topic on which you have strong feelings, but which at the same time has a lighter side. Your classmates may want to vote on whose speech is most *dramatic* — combining informative substance with a successful appeal both to the emotions and to the listener's sense of humor.

EXERCISE 4 Have you ever tried to adapt the same talk to two *different audiences?* Prepare two versions of a speech supporting a definite proposal on an issue of current interest to students. For instance, support a proposal concerning a new approach to student government, career counseling, choice of courses, censorship of student publications, or the like. Address one version to your classmates, the other to a group of teachers or parents. How would you change your examples, your supporting arguments?

S 2 The Power of Words

Study the way an eloquent speaker sways and inspires his listeners.

The spoken word has great power for good and evil. It is true that its everyday uses are often unspectacular: a salesman's praise of his product, a commentator's analysis of the news. But in times of crisis, the spoken word often plays a decisive role in the affairs of men. The eloquence of a leader can make a nation forget old divisions and inspire powerful feelings of loyalty and common purpose. The eloquence of a revolutionary can make men challenge and overturn institutions. The eloquence of a lawyer can mean the difference between freedom and imprisonment, life and death.

The following excerpts are from famous speeches from history and literature. They will give you a chance to study the way an eloquent speaker can help shape the course of events. You will be able to reenact famous addresses, immersing yourself in the occasion, trying to reconstruct from the printed text the personality of the speaker. You will be able to analyze what gives an exceptional speaker his power. You will have a chance to prepare talks of your own on exceptionally serious subjects.

S 2a The Eulogy

Study the way an eloquent speaker builds morale.

One of the oldest uses of the spoken word is to fire up the courage of warriors, the determination of a people at war. In the earliest literature of Greece, of England, of France, the best-known passages are the words in which a speaker exhorts his countrymen to fight on to victory. A famous example is the funeral oration of Pericles, delivered in honor of Athenian soldiers who died in the war against Sparta. This speech was given 2400 years ago and is reported to us by a Greek historian of that time. The following excerpt is a eulogy to the city of Athens and the empire it had built. The speaker praises the institutions and customs of his native city. He tries to show that the men who died fighting for Athens died for a country deserving of their love and sacrifice.

Study the passage carefully and then answer the questions that follow it.

Let me say that our system of government does not copy the institutions of our neighbors. It is more the case of our being a model to others, than of our imitating anyone else. Our constitution is called a democracy because power is in the hands not of a minority but of the whole people. When it is a question of settling private disputes, everyone is equal before the law; when it is a question of putting one person before another in positions of public responsibility, what counts is not membership of a particular class, but the actual ability which the man possesses. No one, so long as he has it in him to be of service to the state, is kept in political obscurity because of poverty. And, just as our political life is free and open, so is our day-to-day life in our relations with each other. We do not get into a state with our next-door neighbor if he enjoys himself in his own way, nor do we give him the kind of black looks which, though they do no real harm, still do hurt people's feelings. We are free and tolerant in our private lives; but in public affairs we keep to the law. This is because it commands our deep respect.

We give our obedience to those whom we put in positions of authority, and we obey the laws themselves, especially those which are for the protection of the oppressed, and those unwritten laws which it is an acknowledged shame to break.

And here is another point. When our work is over, we are in a position to enjoy all kinds of recreation for our spirits. There are various kinds of contests and sacrifices regularly throughout the year; in our own homes we find a beauty and a good taste which delight us every day and which drive away our cares. Then the greatness of our city brings it about that all the good things from all the world flow into us, so that to us it seems just as natural to enjoy foreign goods as our own local products.

Then there is a great difference between us and our opponents in our attitude towards military security. Here are some examples: Our city is open to the world, and we have no periodical deportations in order to prevent people observing or finding out secrets which might be of military advantage to the enemy. This is because we rely, not on secret weapons, but on our own real courage and loyalty. There is a difference, too, in our educational systems. The Spartans, from their earliest boyhood, are submitted to the most laborious training in courage; we pass our lives without all these restrictions, and yet are just as ready to face the same dangers as they are. Here is proof of this: When the Spartans invade our land, they do not come by themselves, but bring all their allies with them; whereas we, when we launch an attack abroad, do the job ourselves, and, though fighting on foreign soil, do not often fail to defeat opponents who are fighting for their own hearths and homes. As a matter of fact, none of our enemies has ever yet been confronted with our total strength, because we have to divide our attention between our navy and the many missions on which our troops are sent on land. Yet, if our enemies engage a detachment of our forces and defeat it, they give themselves credit for having thrown back our entire army; or, if they lose, they claim that they were beaten by us in full strength. There are certain advantages, I think, in our way of meeting danger voluntarily, with an easy mind, instead of with a laborious training, with natural rather than with state-induced courage. We do not have to spend our time practising to meet sufferings which are still in the future; and when they are actually upon us show ourselves just as brave as these others who are always in strict training. This is one point in which, I think, our city deserves to be admired. There are also others:

Our love of what is beautiful does not lead to extravagance; our love of the things of the mind does not make us soft. We regard wealth as something to be properly used, rather than as something to boast about. As for poverty, no one need be ashamed to admit it: the real shame is in not taking practical measures to escape from it. Here each individual is interested not only in his own affairs but in the affairs of the state as well: even those who are mostly occupied with their own business are extremely well-informed on general politics—this is a peculiarity of ours: we do not say that a man who takes no interest in politics is a man who minds his own business; we say that he has no business here at all. We Athenians, in our own persons, take our decisions on policy or submit them to proper discussions: for we do not think that there is an incompatibility between words and deeds; the worst thing is to rush into action before the consequences have been properly debated. And this is another point where we differ from other people. We are capable at the same time of taking risks and of estimating them beforehand. Others are brave out of ignorance; and, when they stop to think, they begin to fear. But the man who can most truly be accounted brave is he who knows the meaning of what is sweet in life and of what is terrible, and then goes out undeterred to meet what is to come.

Again, in questions of general good feeling there is a great contrast between us and most other people. We make friends by doing good to others, not by receiving good from them. This makes our friendship all the more reliable, since we want to keep alive the gratitude of those who are in our debt by showing continued goodwill to them: whereas the feelings of one who owes us something lack the same enthusiasm, since he knows that, when he repays our kindness, it will be more like paying back a debt than giving something spontaneously. We are unique in this. When we do kindnesses to others, we do not do them out of any calculations of profit or loss: we do them without afterthought, relying on our free liberality. Taking everything together then, I declare that our city is an education to Greece, and I declare that in my opinion each single one of our citizens, in all the manifold aspects of life, is able to show himself the rightful lord and owner of his own person, and do this, moreover, with exceptional grace and exceptional versatility. And to show that this is no empty boasting for the present occasion, but real tangible fact, you have only to consider the power which our city possesses and which has been won by those very qualities which I have mentioned. Athens, alone of the states we know, comes to her testing time in a greatness that surpasses what was imagined of her. In her case, and in her case alone, no invading enemy is ashamed at being defeated, and no subject can complain of being governed by people unfit for their responsibilities. Mighty indeed are the marks and monuments of our empire which we have left. Future ages will wonder at us, as the present age wonders at us now.

1. Early in this speech, Pericles refers to Athens as a "free country." Are there parts of this excerpt that sound as though they could have been taken from a speech made by an American patriot about the United States? Explore in detail any possible similarities and parallels. Are there parts that you would *not* expect in a patriotic speech by an American? Again, explore the differences in detail.

2. After two great wars and several bloody minor wars, many modern listeners have become suspicious of patriotic oratory. They expect it to be trite, pompous, or insincere. On the evidence

of this excerpt, could any of these charges conceivably have been brought against this speech? Why, or why not?

3. One observer of the American scene claimed that ever since World War I "Americans have been shy at expressing their deepest convictions and have been verbally cynical about Fourth of July oratory. Yet devotion to the American way has been none the less passionate." How shy, or how open, are Americans today about expressing patriotic feelings? What form does the expression of their patriotic sentiments take — what *style* does it follow? Use evidence from such sources as editorials, letters to the editor, political speeches, and the like.

EXERCISE 5 In recent years, the attitude of Americans toward their country has ranged from uncritical praise of everything American to bitter rejection of many of our practices and institutions. Select an area or feature of the American way of life about which you have strong positive feelings. Prepare a speech in which you *praise or defend* it before a skeptical or critical audience.

EXERCISE 6 When a glowing, ideal picture is contrasted with inadequate reality, disillusionment sets in. The following excerpt is from a Fourth of July speech made in 1852 by Frederick Douglass, the former slave who escaped to the North and became one of the leaders in the struggle for the abolition of slavery in America. Study and describe the excerpt as an example of a speech that eloquently registers *protest or dissent*. Then ask yourself: What kind of speech would a modern Frederick Douglass prepare for the Fourth of July? Prepare a speech that registers your own protest against a failure of American reality to live up to its ideals, or that expresses your dissent from one of the ideals traditionally celebrated by Fourth of July speakers. (Or, prepare a speech in which you register your protest against some current manifestation of protest or dissent.)

What to the American slave is your Fourth of July? I answer: a day that reveals to him, more than all other days in the year, the gross injustice and cruelty to which he is the constant victim. To him your celebration is a sham; your boasted liberty, an unholy licence; your national greatness, swelling vanity; your sounds of rejoicing are empty and heartless; your denunciation of tyrants, brass-fronted impudence; your shouts of liberty and equality, hollow mockery; your prayers and hymns, your sermons and thanksgivings, with all your religious parade and solemnity, are, to him, more bombast, fraud, deception, impiety and hypocrisy — a thin veil to cover up crimes which would disgrace a nation of savages. . . .

You boast of your love of liberty, your superior civilization, and your pure Christianity, while the whole political power of the nation (as embodied in the two great political parties) is solemnly pledged to support and perpetuate the enslavement of three millions of your countrymen. You hurl your anathemas at the crown-headed tyrants of Russia and Austria and pride yourselves on your democratic institutions, while you yourselves consent to be the mere *tools* and *bodyguards* of the tyrants of Virginia and Carolina.

You invite to your shores fugitives of oppression from abroad, honor them with banquets, greet them with ovations, cheer them, toast them, salute them, protect them and pour out your money to them like water; but the fugitive from your own land you advertise, hunt, arrest, shoot, and kill. You glory in your refinement and your universal education; yet you maintain a system as barbarous and dreadful as ever stained the character of a nation — a system begun in avarice, supported in pride, and perpetuated in cruelty.

You shed tears over fallen Hungary, and make the sad story of her wrongs the theme of your poets, statesmen and orators, till your gallant sons are ready to fly to arms to vindicate her cause against the oppressor; but, in regard to the ten thousand wrongs of the American slave, you would enforce the strictest silence, and would hail him as an enemy of the nation who dares to make these wrongs the subject of public discourse!

S 2b The Political Speech

Study the way an eloquent speaker mobilizes support and guides men's aspirations.

Through recorded history, the political speech has been a major weapon in the battle for men's minds. Our political convictions are often in a confused and latent state. A powerful speaker can mobilize sympathies before only dimly felt. He can bring into focus ideas that were "in the air" but not yet widely understood.

Antony's speech in Shakespeare's *Julius Caesar* is a famous literary demonstration of the power of the spoken word to sway an audience, to change the loyalties of a crowd. After the assassination of Caesar, Brutus, the leader of the conspirators, and Antony, the slain dictator's friend, both speak to the citizens of Rome. Compare and contrast carefully the way they try to bring the citizens over to their side. Then answer the questions that follow the selection.

Brutus. Romans, countrymen, and lovers, hear me for my cause, and be silent, that you may hear. Believe me for mine honor, and have respect to mine honor, that you may believe. Censure me in your wisdom, and awake your senses, that you may the better judge. If there be any in this assembly, any dear friend of Caesar's, to him I say that Brutus' love to Caesar was no less than his. If then that friend demand why Brutus rose against Caesar, this is my answer: Not that I loved Caesar less, but that I loved Rome more. Had you rather Caesar were living, and die all slaves, than that Caesar were dead, to live all free men? As Caesar loved me, I weep for him; as he was fortunate, I rejoice at it; as he was valiant, I honor him; but, as he was ambitious, I slew him. There is tears, for his love; joy, for his fortune; honor, for his valor; and death, for his ambition. Who is here so base, that would be a bondman? If any, speak; for him have I offended. Who is here so rude, that would not be a Roman? If any, speak; for him have I offended. Who is here so vile, that will not love his country? If any, speak; for him have I offended. I pause for a reply.

All. None, Brutus, none!

Brutus. Then none have I offended. I have done no more to Caesar than you shall do to Brutus. The question of his death is enrolled in the Capitol; his glory not extenuated, wherein he was worthy, nor his offenses enforced, for which he suffered death.

Enter Mark Antony, with Caesar's body.

Here comes his body, mourned by Mark Antony, who, though he had no hand in his death, shall receive the benefit of his dying, a place in the commonwealth, as which of you shall not? With this I depart, that, as I slew my best lover for the good of Rome, I have the same dagger for myself, when it shall please my country to need my death.

All. Live, Brutus! Live, live!

. . . .

Antony. Friends, Romans, countrymen, lend me your ears;
I come to bury Caesar, not to praise him.
The evil that men do lives after them,
The good is oft interrèd with their bones;
So let it be with Caesar. The noble Brutus
Hath told you Caesar was ambitious.
If it were so, it was a grievous fault,

And grievously hath Caesar answered it.
Here, under leave of Brutus and the rest
(For Brutus is an honorable man,
So are they all, all honorable men),
Come I to speak in Caesar's funeral.
He was my friend, faithful and just to me;
But Brutus says he was ambitious,
And Brutus is an honorable man.
He hath brought many captives home to Rome,
Whose ransoms did the general coffers fill;
Did this in Caesar seem ambitious?
When that the poor have cried, Caesar hath wept;
Ambition should be made of sterner stuff.
Yet Brutus says he was ambitious;
And Brutus is an honorable man.
You all did see that on the Lupercal
I thrice presented him a kingly crown,
Which he did thrice refuse. Was this ambition?
Yet Brutus says he was ambitious;
And sure he is an honorable man.
I speak not to disprove what Brutus spoke,
But here I am to speak what I do know.
You all did love him once, not without cause;
What cause withholds you then to mourn for him?
O judgment, thou art fled to brutish beasts,
And men have lost their reason! Bear with me;
My heart is in the coffin there with Caesar,
And I must pause till it come back to me.

First Plebeian. Methinks there is much reason in his
    sayings.
Second Plebeian. If thou consider rightly of the matter,
    Caesar has had great wrong.
Third Plebeian.   Has he, masters?
    I fear there will a worse come in his place.
Fourth Plebeian. Marked ye his words? He would not
    take the crown,
    Therefore 'tis certain he was not ambitious.
First Plebeian. If it be found so, some will dear abide it.
Second Plebeian. Poor soul, his eyes are\ red as fire with
    weeping.
Third Plebeian. There's not a nobler man in Rome than
    Antony.
Fourth Plebeian. Now mark him, he begins again to
    speak.

Antony. But yesterday the word of Caesar might
    Have stood against the world; now lies he there,
    And none so poor to do him reverence.
    O masters! If I were disposed to stir
    Your hearts and minds to mutiny and rage,
    I should do Brutus wrong and Cassius wrong,
    Who, you all know, are honorable men.
    I will not do them wrong; I rather choose
    To wrong the dead, to wrong myself and you,
    Than I will wrong such honorable men.
    But here's a parchment with the seal of Caesar;
    I found it in his closet; 'tis his will.
    Let but the commons hear this testament,
    Which, pardon me, I do not mean to read,
    And they would go and kiss dead Caesar's wounds,
    And dip their napkins in his sacred blood;
    Yea, beg a hair of him for memory,
    And dying, mention it within their wills,
    Bequeathing it as a rich legacy
    Unto their issue.
Fourth Plebeian. We'll hear the will; read it, Mark
    Antony.
All. The will, the will! We will hear Caesar's will! . . .
Antony. You will compel me then to read the will?
    Then make a ring about the corpse of Caesar,
    And let me show you him that made the will.
    Shall I descend? And will you give me leave?
All. Come down.
Second Plebeian. Descend.   [*Antony comes down.*]
Antony. If you have tears, prepare to shed them now.
    You all do know this mantle, I remember
    The first time ever Caesar put it on:
    'Twas on a summer's evening, in his tent,
    That day he overcame the Nervii.
    Look, in this place ran Cassius' dagger through;
    See what a rent the envious Casca made;
    Through this the well-belovèd Brutus stabbed,
    And as he plucked his cursèd steel away,
    Mark how the blood of Caesar followed it,
    As rushing out of doors, to be resolved
    If Brutus so unkindly knocked, or no;
    For Brutus, as you know, was Caesar's angel.
    Judge, O you gods, how dearly Caesar loved him!
    This was the most unkindest cut of all;

For when the noble Caesar saw him stab,
Ingratitude, more strong than traitors' arms,
Quite vanquished him. Then burst his mighty heart;
And, in his mantle muffling up his face,
Even at the base of Pompey's statue
(Which all the while ran blood) great Caesar fell.
O, what a fall was there, my countrymen!
Then I, and you, and all of us fell down,
Whilst bloody treason flourished over us.
O, now you weep, and I perceive you feel
The dint of pity: these are gracious drops.
Kind souls, what weep you when you but behold
Our Caesar's vesture wounded? Look you here,
Here is himself, marred as you see with traitors.
First Plebeian. O piteous spectacle!
Second Plebeian. O noble Caesar!
Third Plebeian. O woeful day!
Fourth Plebeian. O traitors, villains!
First Plebeian. O most bloody sight!
Second Plebeian. We will be revenged.
[*All.*] Revenge! About! Seek! Burn! Fire! Kill! Slay!
     Let not a traitor live!
Antony. Stay, countrymen.
First Plebeian. Peace there! Hear the noble Antony.
Second Plebeian. We'll hear him, we'll follow him, we'll
     die with him!
Antony. Good friends, sweet friends, let me not stir you
     up
     To such a sudden flood of mutiny.
     They that have done this deed are honorable.
     What private griefs they have, alas, I know not,
     That made them do it. They are wise and honorable,
     And will, no doubt, with reasons answer you.
     I come not, friends, to steal away your hearts;
     I am no orator, as Brutus is;
     But (as you know me all) a plain blunt man
     That love my friend, and that they know full well
     That gave me public leave to speak of him.
     For I have neither writ, nor words, nor worth,
     Action, nor utterance, nor the power of speech
     To stir men's blood; I only speak right on.
     I tell you that which you yourselves do know,
     Show you sweet Caesar's wounds, poor poor dumb
        mouths,
     And bid them speak for me. But were I Brutus,

And Brutus Antony, there were an Antony
Would ruffle up your spirits, and put a tongue
In every wound of Caesar that should move
The stones of Rome to rise and mutiny.

All. We'll mutiny.

First Plebeian. We'll burn the house of Brutus.

Third Plebeian. Away, then! Come, seek the conspirators.

Antony. Yet hear me, countrymen. Yet hear me speak.

All. Peace, ho! Hear Antony, most noble Antony!

Antony. Why, friends, you go to do you know not what:
Wherein hath Caesar thus deserved your loves?
Alas, you know not; I must tell you then:
You have forgot the will I told you of.

All. Most true, the will! Let's stay and hear the will.

Antony. Here is the will, and under Caesar's seal.
To every Roman citizen he gives,
To every several man, seventy-five drachmas.

Second Plebeian. Most noble Caesar! We'll revenge his
death!

Third Plebeian. O royal Caesar! . . .

Antony. Moreover, he hath left you all his walks,
His private arbors, and new-planted orchards,
On this side Tiber; he hath left them you,
And to your heirs forever: common pleasures,
To walk abroad and recreate yourselves.
Here was a Caesar! When comes such another?

First Plebeian. Never, never! Come, away, away!
We'll burn his body in the holy place,
And with the brands fire the traitors' houses.

1. What motives, assumptions, or standards does Brutus appeal to?
    What motives, assumptions, or standards does Antony appeal to?
    Could a contemporary speaker use some of the same appeals,
    adapting them to our own contemporary setting and issues?

2. In what *order* does Antony proceed? Could this order be changed,
    or is it part of his strategy?

3. Would you call Antony a "demogogue"? Where and how do you
    draw the line between demagoguery and legitimate persuasion?
    Can you use current examples to clarify the point?

4. Was Brutus' defeat in the contest with Antony inevitable?

5. Assume that after Antony's speech Brutus had an opportunity for
    rebuttal. Prepare a short speech in which you think of yourself as
    Brutus addressing himself a second time to the audience, trying
    to undo the damage already done.

EXERCISE 7 Have you ever felt that something you believed in represented a *lost cause?* Prepare a speech in which you try your best to get a favorable hearing for an unpopular or unfashionable point of view. For instance, you might try to advocate

— church membership to a group of young people indifferent to religion;
— socialism, or a modified form thereof, to an audience of middle-class Americans;
— nonviolence to a group committed to militant action.

EXERCISE 8 [Optional] In your study of history, have you ever wondered what would have happened if eloquent people had intervened at the right time and swayed the opinion of influential people in order to avert disaster? Imagine yourself present at one of history's *lost opportunities.* Prepare the kind of speech that you think might have helped prevent the worst. For instance, you might imagine yourself speaking to

— members of the British Parliament shortly before the final break between Great Britain and her American colonies;
— a group of influential Southerners shortly before secession and the war between the Union and the Confederacy;
— a group of German writers and journalists shortly before Germany's invasion of Poland and the beginning of World War II.

S 2c The Plea for Justice

Study the way a speaker's eloquence affects our determination of guilt and innocence.

In a courtroom, a speaker's power to persuade has immediate and grave consequences. For the accused man, much, or even all, may be at stake. But much is also at stake for a society that aims at justice for its citizens. How much depends on the eloquence and skill of the people speaking for the prosecution or for the defense.

The following is a passage from a plea for justice delivered by Emile Zola, the famous French novelist. Zola was on trial for libel because of certain statements he had made in his vigorous defense of Alfred Dreyfus. Dreyfus was a French army officer who happened to be Jewish. He was accused and convicted of selling military secrets to Germany in 1894, but was later cleared of false charges. Although Zola was on trial, his famous speech was actually a defense of Dreyfus. Study the excerpt carefully, and answer the questions that follow it.

So I do not defend myself. But what a blunder would be yours if you were convinced that by striking me you would reestablish order in our unfortunate country. Do you not understand now that what the nation is dying of is the obscurity in which there is such an obstinate determination to leave it? The blunders of those in authority are being heaped upon those of others; one lie necessitates another, so that the mass is becoming formidable. A judicial blunder was committed, and then to hide it a fresh crime against good sense and equity has had daily to be committed! The condemnation of an innocent man has involved the acquittal of a guilty man, and now to-day you are asked in turn to condemn me because I gave utterance to my pain beholding our country embarked on this terrible course. Condemn me, then! But it will be one more fault added to the others — a fault the burden of which you will bear in history. And my condemnation, instead of restoring the peace for which you long, and which we all of us desire, will be only a fresh seed of passion and disorder. The cup, I tell you, is full; do not make it run over. . . .

The Dreyfus case! ah, gentlemen, that has now become a very small affair. It is lost and far-away in view of the terrifying questions to which it has given rise. There is no longer any Dreyfus case. The question now is whether France is still the France of the rights of man, the France that gave freedom to the world, and that ought to give it justice. Are we still the most noble, the most fraternal, the most generous nation? Shall we preserve our reputation in Europe for equity and humanity? Are not all the victories that we have won called in question? Open your eyes, and understand that, to be in such confusion, the French soul must have been stirred to its depths in face of a terrible danger. A nation cannot be thus upset without imperiling its moral existence. This is an exceptionally serious hour; the safety of the nation is at stake.

And when you shall have understood that, gentlemen, you will feel that but one remedy is possible, — to tell the truth, to do justice. Anything that keeps back the light, anything that adds darkness to darkness, will only prolong and aggravate the crisis. The rôle of good citizens, of those who feel it to be imperatively necessary to put an end to this matter, is to demand broad daylight. There are already many who think so. The men of literature, philosophy, and science are rising on every hand in the name of intelligence and reason. And I do not speak of the foreigner, of the shudder that has run through all Europe. Yet the foreigner is not necessarily the enemy. Let us not speak of the nations that may be our adversaries to-morrow. Great Russia, our ally, little and generous Holland; all the sympathetic peoples of the north; those lands of the French tongue, Switzerland and Belgium, — why are men's hearts so full, so overflowing with fraternal suffering? Do you dream then of a France isolated in the world? When you cross the frontier, do you wish them to forget your traditional renown for equity and humanity?

Dreyfus is innocent. I swear it! I stake my life on it — my honor! At this solemn moment, in the presence of this tribunal, which is the representative of human justice: before you, gentlemen, who are the very incarnation of the country, before the whole of France, before the whole world, I swear that Dreyfus is innocent. By my forty years of work, by the authority that this toil may have given me, I swear that Dreyfus is innocent. By the name I have made for myself, by my works which have helped for the expansion of French literature, I swear that Dreyfus is innocent. May all that melt away, may my works perish, if Dreyfus be not innocent! He is innocent. All seems against me — the two Chambers, the civil authority, the most widely-circulated journals, the public opinion which they have poisoned. And I have for me only the ideal, — an ideal of truth and justice. But I am quite calm; I shall conquer. I was determined that my country should not remain the victim of lies and injustice. I may be condemned here. The day will come when France will thank me for having helped to save her honor.

1. In an encyclopedia or history text, read an account of the famous Dreyfus case. Do the facts help to explain Zola's obvious emotion?
2. Do you consider Zola's plea effective? Why or why not? How do you think the court reacted? How would *you* have reacted, and why?
3. Zola appeals to the values, standards, and beliefs of his audience. What are these standards? Point out as many different instances as you can?
4. It is sometimes claimed that minority groups cannot expect to obtain equal justice in our courts. We are also sometimes told that juries are likely to be prejudiced against certain groups. Prepare a brief speech in which you try to counsel a group of prospective jurors against the dangers of prejudice.

EXERCISE 9 Lawyers sometimes complain that a client's case has been "tried in the newspapers." During the last year or so, do you recall a court case that has been exceptionally fully reported in the newspapers? From the published accounts, what conclusion did you reach concerning the probable guilt or innocence of the accused? Prepare a talk in which you support your conclusion as effectively as you can. Your classmates will sit as a jury called to judge the effectiveness or persuasiveness of your presentation.

(If you can find a classmate interested in taking the opposite side, you may be able to reenact in your classroom part of the courtroom drama.)

EXERCISE 10 [Optional] Study a famous court case in which someone widely considered innocent was found guilty. You might choose the case of Dreyfus, Sacco and Vanzetti, or a more recent, widely reported example. If possible, study *more than one* account of the trial. Do you find yourself siding with the prosecution or the defense? Prepare a brief speech in which you sum up the case for the side you choose.

S 3 *The Tradition of Debate*

Study the conditions for fruitful debate on serious issues.

Much of our political life carries on the Anglo-Saxon tradition of parliamentary debate. Whether in a club meeting or in the state legislature, we allow spokesmen for *different* proposals to present their views. We invite *discussion* before we take a vote. We believe that people will make more responsible decisions after they have examined the alternatives. We believe that the public will be better informed if we encourage the presentation of contrary evidence and conflicting arguments.

Though we tend to take our traditions of discussion and debate for granted, the conditions that make them possible are by no means easy to maintain. People with strong convictions are often intolerant of dissent. In the heat of controversy, righteous anger keeps them from listening to the other side. In times of crisis, people desperate for a solution grow impatient with the elaborate give-and-take that true discussion requires.

Here are some of the conditions that are necessary if fruitful debate is going to take place on serious issues:

THE RIGHT TO BE HEARD. Free speech is not simply a matter of being able to speak out. The speaker has to be able to get a *fair hearing*. He has to be able to find an audience that is used to listening to evidence and argument. No serious discussion is possible when opponents are shouted down, discredited in advance by ugly rumors, or intimidated by threats of reprisal.

AN OPEN MIND. The test of an educated person is that he does not consider a challenge to his *views* an insult to his *person*. We recognize an educated person by his ability to say: " I was wrong. I have changed my mind." This is what makes excerpts from some of the great parliamentary debates of nineteenth-century England exciting reading: on some of the great issues of the day, we find people changing their minds. In the great debates on the people's right to vote, or on the limitation of child labor, we find people crossing the line, following the integrity of their own consciences:

> When I voted . . . I deliberately adopted a new and bold principle of legislation. I exposed myself to the charge which is thrown out against all who voted with the majority, that they were voting against all principle; for I voted, I am quite aware, against the principle on which legislation on these matters has hitherto been conducted; a legislation which . . . paid no attention to the revolutions which the progress of time brings about in the social condition of nations. New evils require new remedies. A new social state, such as that of England has become in the present century, requires new principles of legislation.
>
> (Sir Charles Buller in support of the ten-hours bill)

RESPECT FOR DISSENT. Discussion is not designed to produce a totalitarian unanimity of opinion. It is designed to make us understand the alternatives, to help us accept responsible majority decisions, and to help us understand and respect minority views. Thomas Paine once said, "I have always strenuously supported the right of every man to his opinion, however different that opinion might be to mine." As long as we respect the right of every man to his opinion, we make it possible for people of different views to work and live together.

Assuming that the conditions are right for fruitful discussion, how do you "hold your own"? Remember that you are involved in a two-way or three-way exchange. Remember advice like the following to help your own contribution come through clearly and effectively:

(1) *State your main point (or points) clearly and forcefully.* Sometimes, it is true, you can score a point by merely asking a provocative question. But do not simply give a rambling survey of evidence without making it clear what the evidence is supposed to prove. State your point forcefully at the beginning, and *restate* it at the end. If several other positions have become identified in the course of the discussion, you may want to show how your position *differs,* and why.

(2) *Use striking supporting material.* Try to use the kind of statistics, and the kind of testimony from authorities, that people will remember *after* other speakers have had their say. Would you agree that the following passages from nineteenth-century debates on child labor laws offer memorable and striking supporting material?

> Remember what has been shown to be the comparative duration of life in Manchester, for instance, and in the county of Wilts, an agricultural district. In Wiltshire, the average duration of life is thirty-three years; in Manchester, it is only seventeen. I do not mean to say that this difference in the duration of human life springs solely or mainly from the nature of factory labor, but it clearly must arise from the circumstances taken all together under which that labor is carried out in the great towns. . . .

> Near Huddersfield the sub-commissioner examined a female child. He said, "I could not have believed that I should have found human nature so degraded. Mr. Holroyd, and Mr. Brook, a surgeon, confessed that although living within a few miles they could not have believed that such a system of unchristian cruelty could have existed."

(3) *Protect yourself against damaging counterattacks.* When you make a hasty generalization, a skillful opponent can deflate it by citing one important exception. When you question someone's patriotism, a skillful opponent may arouse against you the aud-

ience's sense of fair play. When you act superior to the views of others, a skillful opponent can make you seem arrogant.

(4) *Look for weaknesses in the position of your opponents.* Look for evidence of obvious *slanting* — the omission of important facts. Look for attempts to evade the issue — show that evidence or testimony is not really relevant to the point being discussed.

(5) *Do not lose your self-control.* When you turn a discussion into a shouting match, you are likely to arouse personal antagonism rather than strengthen your cause. When you engage in personal abuse, you are likely to arouse the sympathy of the audience for the underdog. The more heated a discussion becomes, the more tempted you will be to make exaggerated statements. Even in the heat of debate, try not to say things that you will regret in more sober moments.

EXERCISE 11 How good are you at participating in the kind of *informal discussion* that gives people a chance to state but also to rethink and develop their views? Prepare to participate in an informal discussion of the points raised in the following passage. (Your teacher or your class may decide to base the discussion on a different passage of their own choice.) After the discussion, take stock of how much actual give-and-take took place. Did people listen to each other? Was anything accomplished?

> There is, of course, nothing wrong with dating as such. It is or ought to be, the natural way for young people of the opposite sex to get to know each other. What is wrong about it today is the aura of frantic compulsion and the rushing of the season. Girls who have their "sweet sixteen parties" or, a few years later, their "coming out" debuts actually have been "out" for six years, and there is no longer any real occasion to be festive.
>
> In line with the hothouse approach to making children grow up, summer resorts encourage parents to have their children, and certainly their teen-agers, attend night clubs until the early morning hours. Other resorts, carrying the trend a little further, advertise teen-age night clubs as a novelty. As a result of this stress on early "maturing," dating becomes a forced, not a natural activity for adolescents.
>
> Margaret Mead, the anthropologist, said in an article for the Associated Press: "Instead of letting boys and girls go their separate ways, in late childhood and adolescence, we

are forcing them to practice, not how to be individuals, but how to be spouses and parents; catapulting them into premature, half-baked adulthood before they have a chance to grow up as individuals."

—Grace and Fred M. Hechinger, *Teen-age Tyranny*

EXERCISE 12 Have you ever participated in a *formal debate*, with one or more speakers on each side taking opposed views on a clearly defined issue, and with opportunity for rebuttal as well as for the original presentation of the conflicting views? Prepare to participate in a debate on one of the following propositions:

1. Political ideas or social ideologies should be kept out of a high school student's education.
2. The American Negro is asking for too much and advancing too fast.
3. Property rights come before human rights.
4. Women's special biological and social functions will always keep them from full equality with men.
5. There should be no censorship of any kind to limit the freedom of literature and the arts.

FURTHER STUDY: Speeches in Literature

A speaker can learn much about his craft by reenacting some of the speeches or sermons that are part of our imaginative literature. The following list provides a brief sampling of possibilities. You may want to memorize a short excerpted passage, or prepare for a reading of a longer selection.

— Henry V's speech before the battle of Agincourt (Shakespeare, *Henry V,* Act IV, Scene 3);
— Richard III's wooing of Anne (Shakespeare, *Richard III,* Act I, Scene 2);
— one of Hamlet's soliloquies;
— Othello's account of his courtship (*Othello,* Act I, Scene 3);
— Romeo's speech under Juliet's window (*Romeo and Juliet,* Act II, Scene 2);
— Major's speech in Chapter 1 of George Orwell's *Animal Farm;*
— Satan's speech to his defeated legions in the opening pages of Milton's *Paradise Lost;*
— one of the sermons from Chapter 3 of James Joyce's *A Portrait of the Artist as a Young Man;*
— a speech from a play or novel you have recently read.

CONTENTS

Resources:
A. THE LARGE LIBRARY
B. TAKING TESTS

R 1 The Large Library

Learn to utilize the facilities of a large library.

Once you graduate from high school, you will probably begin to use larger libraries. The public library systems in many areas have become large and comprehensive. At a college or university, you would find yourself using a library which houses thousands or hundreds of thousands of volumes, depending upon the size of the institution. It will be helpful for you to familiarize yourself with the system employed by most large libraries.

R 1a Systems of Classification

Learn how to locate or order books by their call numbers.

While all libraries employ a basic system of classification and organization which is essentially the same, there are differences which are important. Most high school libraries, for example, employ the Dewey Decimal System of classification. Most large libraries, however, employ a system that is better suited to their needs. The system used by a growing number of large libraries is called the Library of Congress Classification System.

Unlike the Dewey Decimal System, which uses numbers for its base and is therefore limited to ten general categories, the Library of Congress System employs letters. As a result, the system has a base of twenty-six general categories. In actuality, only twenty-one letters have been used so far, leaving some room for eventual expansion as new fields of knowledge develop. The system's ability to expand accounts in large part for its acceptance by so many libraries.

The letters used by the Library of Congress system and the fields of knowledge which they represent are given below. Note that I, O, W, X, and Y are held for future use.

A	General Works	M	Music
B	Philosophy, Religion	N	Fine Arts
C	History	P	Language and Literature
D	History and Topography (except America)	Q	Science
		R	Medicine
E	America (general) — U. S. (general)	S	Agriculture (plant and animal industry)
F	United States (local) and America (except U. S.)	T	Technology
		U	Military Science
G	Geography—Anthropology	V	Naval Science
H	Social Sciences	Z	Bibliography and Library Science
J	Political Science		

In the Library of Congress system, specific categories are designated by placing a second letter after the first. Again, since letters are used, twenty-six specific categories can be registered for every general category, rather than the ten specific categories provided for in the Dewey system. Here, for example, are some specific categories under the general category of Language and Literature.

P	Language and Literature (general)
PA	Classical languages and literature
PB	General works and Celtic languages and literature
PC	Romance languages
PD	Germanic languages
PE	English
PF	Dutch, Flemish, Afrikaans

PG Slavic, Lithuanian — Lettish, Albanian
PH Finno-Ugrian and Basque
PJ Egyptian, Coptic, Hamitic, Semitic
PK Indo-Iranian, Indo-Aryan, Iranian
PL Eastern Asia, Oceania, Africa
PM American (Indian) languages, Artificial languages
PN Literary history and collections (general)
PQ Romance literatures
PR English literature
PS American literature
PT Teutonic literature
PZ Juvenile literature

Numbers are also used in the Library of Congress system to subdivide the specific categories. These numbers appear after the pair of letters. Numbers are used consecutively for each subdivision of a specific category, but some have been reserved for later expansion.

The call number under the Library of Congress system usually appears on three lines at the upper left-hand corner of the catalog card. It consists of the class designation (a pair of letters followed by a series of numbers indicating a specific subdivision), the year of publication, and an author, or book, number. The author, or book, number consists of the first letter of the author's last name followed by a number. The author, or book, number is an aid to the librarian for shelving the book. Books are shelved first by the class number and then by the author, or book, number. Sometimes, the author, or book, number is placed on the second rather than the third line of the call number. Study the following sample card:

```
BF 121  Swift, William Porter, 1914-
  1968       General psychology (by) W. Porter Swift.
S 975      New York,
           McGraw-Hill (1969)
             xii, 381 p.   illus.   23 cm.
           Includes bibliographies.


           1. Psychology.
           BF121.S975              150        68–55276
           Library of Congress    (10-2)
```

EXERCISE 1   All books (except elementary and high school textbooks) receive a Library of Congress catalog number. Choose ten titles from your library or own collection and assign to each the first letter of its call number. If your school library uses the Library of Congress system, you can readily check your answers. If your school library uses the Dewey Decimal system, you can still check your answers by consulting the card catalog. Even on Dewey Decimal cards, the Library of Congress designation will usually be given at the bottom.

EXERCISE 2   If you encountered the following Library of Congress designations, what could you tell about the books to which they were assigned?

BG 105	EP 82	JJ 960	PM 590	N 5300
K-1	A-4	J-5	I-15	R-56
1888	1969	1926	1910	1953

R 1b   Reference Books

Reference books are valuable aids to research.

A large library has a wealth of general and specialized reference books:

(1) ENCYCLOPEDIAS. Encyclopedias are attempts to summarize all of the world's knowledge between the covers of a few volumes. Although they cannot provide you with exhaustive current information, they can serve as jumping-off points for your research.

The information contained in reliable encyclopedias is assembled from various sources. The articles on relatively unimportant topics may be written by editors on the staff of the encyclopedia. An article, for example, on George II, King of Greece, will probably be rather brief. It will most likely be written by one of the editors from standard biographical sources. On the other hand, an article on England's Henry VIII will generally be quite substantial and will be signed with the initials of the authority who wrote it. In some volume of the encyclopedia (usually at the beginning of volume one), there will be a list of each contributor's full name and title.

In addition to providing the researcher with an overview of a topic, a good encyclopedia usually provides an extensive bibliography at the end of each signed article. This bibliography can serve as a guide at the beginning of your research. Checking the books listed there helps you to begin your research.

Among general encyclopedias, the following might prove useful to you:

Collier's Encyclodpedia (P. F. Collier & Son). 20 volumes (Kept current with an annual volume, *Collier's Year Book Covering National and International Events.*)

Encyclopaedia Britannica (Encyclopaedia Britannica Inc.). 24 volumes (Kept current with an annual volume, *Britannica Book of the Year.*)

Encyclopedia Americana (Americana Corporation). 30 volumes (Kept current with an annual volume, *The Americana Annual.*)

New International Encyclopedia (Dodd, Mead & Company). 25 volumes (Kept current with an annual volume, *New International Year Book.*)

Encyclopedia of the Social Sciences (The Macmillan Company). 15 volumes.

(2) GENERAL DICTIONARIES. Dictionaries are important reference tools which merit frequent use. Not only is a dictionary useful in checking the spelling, pronunciation, and meanings of a word, but it is also helpful in establishing the common meanings of words during specific historical periods. Such information is especially useful in researching many literary topics. The following general English language dictionaries are worth noting:

Funk and Wagnalls New Standard Dictionary of the English Language

The Random House Dictionary of the English Language

Webster's Third New International Dictionary of the English Language

The Oxford English Dictionary. 13 volumes (This dictionary will be found only in larger libraries. It defines words historically, offering illustrations of meanings during various periods.

The Shorter Oxford English Dictionary is based on the O. E. D. It is primarily a dictionary of British English.)

(3) PERIODICAL INDEXES. Magazines of all kinds, since they are published daily, weekly, or monthly, are usually the best sources of current information. To up-date your information on any topic, you will probably find it worthwhile to consult one of the following indexes to periodicals:

Readers' Guide to Periodical Literature. Supplements are issued monthly and eventually bound into volumes covering a two-year period. At present about 110 periodicals are indexed. Each article indexed is referred to by author and by subject.

The Social Sciences and Humanities Index (formerly International Index to Periodicals). This index is organized like the Readers' Guide, but it also covers non-American periodicals.

New York Times Index. This index covers the contents of the last edition of each day's Times, America's most comprehensive newspaper. The index goes back to 1913. In many libraries, The New York Times is kept on microfilm.

(4) SPECIALIZED REFERENCE BOOKS. In research, the need for specialized information arises frequently. There is a specialized reference book for almost every area of study. The following is but a partial list, containing those books which you will probably need most often.

Biography:

Current Biography (H. W. Wilson Company). This is probably the most important source of information on current notables, containing extensive biographies on eminent contemporary Americans: About 300 or 400 notables are added each year.

Webster's Biographical Dictionary (G. & C. Merriam Company). This work contains more than 40,000 biographical entries of famous people of all times and nationalities.

World Biography (Institute for Research in Biography). This book contains about 15,000 biographical sketches of living persons throughout the world, with special emphasis upon Americans and Europeans.

Geographic Information:

The Columbia Lippincott Gazetteer of the World (Columbia University Press). This reference work contains about 130,000 entries on virtually every geographical place name of any importance in the world.

Webster's Geographical Dictionary (G. & C. Merriam Company). This is an alphabetical listing of about 40,000 place names throughout the world.

Language Study:

Roget's International Thesaurus (Thomas Y. Crowell Co.). This is a dictionary of synonyms grouped under subject headings.

Webster's Dictionary of Synonyms (G. & C. Merriam Company). This work lists synonyms and antonyms in a dictionary format. It clearly distinguishes shades of meaning.

Dictionary of American English Usage, Margaret Nicholson (Oxford University Press).

Statistics:

The World Almanac (Doubleday). This and other general almanacs are storehouses of general information.

The Statesman's Yearbook (St. Martin's Press). This is a statistical and historical compendium of the states of the world.

Statistical Abstract of the United States. This work contains a wealth of statistical information on all phases of American life.

NOTE: Since there are so many reference books, the need for a reference book on reference books is obvious. One of the most convenient to use is *How and Where to Look It Up* by Robert W. Murphy (McGraw-Hill). In addition to listing thousands of reference works under appropriate topics, the book contains advice on researching a topic.

R 2 Taking Tests

Tests measure what students have learned or remembered.

A good test gives the student a chance to show what he has learned. Memory of specific facts may not be all that is tested; frequently the student's ability to *apply* facts is more important.

The more tests you take, the more practice you will get in showing your true achievement. Your "testmanship" will improve with practice, and you will not lose points unnecessarily. Here are some things to remember as you prepare for and actually take tests:

(1) *Work regularly.* If you do your work regularly, you have no need to fear quizzes and tests and examinations. But, if for some reason, you get behind, plan to catch up as soon as possible. Don't put off such make-up work until the last minute. Spread it out over several days. This goes for reviewing, too. Periodic, leisurely reviews help you to digest what you have studied and to organize it. Cramming is better than no study at all, but it will often leave you nervous and overworked — in poor shape to do yourself justice.

(2) *Write as neatly as you can on written tests.* An illegible test will make it hard to determine what you are saying. A teacher usually has to grade many test papers at one sitting; he usually does not have time (or patience) to ponder a poorly written sentence. Indent your paragraphs. Use complete sentences unless the test instructions call for other forms.

(3) *Consider other purposes for tests besides just earning a grade.* Some tests will show your teacher (and you!) where you need more help, or what you are ready to take up next, or whether to slow down the pace or accelerate it. Other tests which you will take will enable you to demonstrate that you are ready for college, or that you have special abilities in certain fields, or that you have aptitudes for special training — perhaps in a profession you want to make your life's work.

Think of each test as an opportunity to give a fair picture of you to yourself and to others who want to know about you.

R 2a The Written-Answer Examination

Learn to answer questions which call for essay-type answers fully and intelligently.

"Written-answer" questions generally provide a good indication of a student's ability to explain and interpret what he has learned and absorbed. You can make the job of answering such questions easier by practicing the following procedures:

(1) *Preview your task and plan your attack.* If the examination consists of more than one question, scan each carefully. Determine which of the questions you can answer most easily and which will require more time. Then decide whether or not you want to answer the easier questions first or to save them for last. Budget your time carefully so that you won't have to rush through any part of the test.

(2) *Make certain that you answer the question that is asked.* Essay answers frequently go astray because the student has not read the question carefully. To insure that you have read and understood the question, convert the question into a statement which can serve as a kind of topic sentence for your answer. If, for example, a history question asks, "What were three causes of_____," your answer might begin, "Three important causes of _____ were ——, ——, and ——." Naturally, it may take several subsequent sentences to explain each cause; but if such a sentence is written at the beginning of your answer, it will be a guide as you work through your paragraph or paragraphs.

(3) *Make certain that you understand key words in a question.* Questions which call for fully developed answers typically use words like *name, list, discuss,* and *explain.* The terms *name* and *list* generally call for rather brief answers. On the other hand, *discuss* and *explain* may call for an answer of several paragraphs, depending on what is to be discussed or explained. (Some questions may, of course, ask you first to list and then to explain.)

(4) *Organize your answers.* If time permits, outline the answer to a question before you begin to write your answer. A few minutes spent in outlining an answer can help to insure that you touch all of the points you should cover. Many student answers omit important material which probably would have been included had outlining come before the writing of the answer. Naturally, a formal outline is not necessary. Brief jottings will do.

(5) *Write as much and only as much as the question demands.* Length is not a substitute for knowledge. If your answer contains

the necessary information called for by the question, its length will be adequate. To "pad" it serves no useful purpose. Contrary to popular opinion, teachers are not as much impressed by length as they are by pertinent, well-organized material.

EXERCISE 3 Use the following question for practice. (Your teacher might wish to substitute another.) Provide a well-organized answer in about 300 words.

List three contributions which teen-agers make to the life of your community. Explain the importance of each contribution, pointing out what each is and who benefits from it.

EXERCISE 4 Your teacher will shuffle the papers of Exercise 3 and pass them out to the class. Consider the answer on the paper you receive. Be prepared to read it aloud and criticize it constructively. In evaluating it, ask yourself the following questions: Does it answer the question asked? Does the answer stick to the point? Is it well organized? Be ready to make concrete suggestions for any improvements which may be needed.

R 2b   Other Kinds of Tests

Tests follow various forms, used for different purposes.

Tests vary. A quick quiz question will show whether you have gone over assigned material. A "problem-solving" test may ask you to apply detail in a thought-provoking situation. Such a test examines your reasoning powers. You may be asked to draw logical conclusions or predict probable results or figure out relationships.

Here are some types of tests that you probably have taken and will take again:

The open book test. The open book test tests two things: whether you are familiar with the textbook material which has been assigned, and what you know about the structuring of paragraphs and series of paragraphs.

To find the answer to a question quickly, you must remember where it was covered and know how to find this place. If necessary, make use of the author's organization of a book when you are trying to locate information. Here is a summary of such helps:

(1) Use the table of contents of a book to locate the chapter which applies to your topic.

(2) Skim the chapter rapidly.

(a) Look at beginnings (or ends) of paragraphs to see what the paragraph is about. That is, look for topic sentences.

(b) Read paragraphs which will probably give you the information you want.

(3) Use section heads and side heads to help you locate what you want.

(4) Use the index (found in the back of the book) to locate specific information.

The objective test. An objective test is designed to cover much more ground than the written-answer type. One type of question that may be used is the *True-False* kind, where the student simply marks either *true* or *false* as his response to each of a series of statements. If you can, find out before starting a true-false test whether you will be penalized for guessing. No one item should use up too much time; one single item does not have this much value in an objective test. This is also true of other objective-type answers. In an objective test there are so many items to be answered that no one item counts too heavily in the total score.

For word meanings, mathematical detail, terminology, dates, and such factual materials, multiple-choice is a good form for a test. You simply indicate the one of several items that you consider the correct answer. Papers can even be checked cooperatively on the spot.

In taking such a test, read the directions carefully. If they say, "Cross out the word which does not belong," do exactly that. You must use your best judgment when making your choice, but be sure of *what* is asked for.

Standardized tests. These tests have been prepared by experts, tested out, revised, and evaluated until they can be used as valid measures of achievement in a given subject area. Usually there is more material in such a test than can be finished by everyone. The test is taken under standard time limits and standard conditions.

The amount you finish, as well as its quality, determines your standing. This standing is given as a rating which compares the way you performed with the way thousands and thousands of other students in your age group or school group performed.

Standardized tests are usually of the objective type, planned for machine scoring. Often a special pencil is provided, and you are asked to underline or otherwise mark your response. The papers are then run through a machine, which picks up electrically the marks which are correct responses and totals them for a score.

In taking such a standardized test, begin at the beginning and work straight through. If you are not sure of a response, make an educated guess. Do not leave any question unanswered. Work thoughtfully, but steadily, and go just as far as you can in the time allowed. There is no such thing as a "perfect score," only a rating which compares you with other students.

EXERCISE 5 Make up a test which will cover material in a section of a textbook recently assigned to the class. Will answers to your questions give your classmates a chance to show what has been learned — in a fair way? Discuss your questions with the class.

GUIDE TO MANUSCRIPT REVISION

HANDBOOK KEY

INDEX

Guide to Manuscript Revision

ab .... Spell out abbreviation (M 7b)

adv .... Use abverb form (U 2c)

agr .... Make verb agree with subject
           (or pronoun with antecedent) (U 3a, U 3b)

ap .... Use apostrophe (M 2b)

cap .... Capitalize (M 2a)

coh .... Strengthen coherence (C 1d)

coll .... Use less colloquial word (U 2a)

CS .... Revise comma splice (M 4a)

d .... Improve diction (W 4)

dev .... Develop your point (C 1b)

div .... Revise word division (M 7a)

DM .... Revise dangling modifier (U 3c)

frag .... Revise sentence fragment (M 3b)

FP .... Revise faulty parallelism (U 4c)

gr .... Revise grammatical form or construction (U 1)

awk .... Rewrite awkward sentence (U 4a)

lc .... Use lower case (M 2a)

MM .... Shift misplaced modifier (U 3c)

p .... Improve punctuation (M 3-6)

¶ .... New paragraph (C 1b)

no ¶ .... Take out paragraph break (C 1b)

ref .... Improve pronoun reference (U 3b)

rep .... Avoid repetition (U 4a)

shift .... Avoid shift in perspective (U 4b)

sl .... Use less slangy word (U 2a)

sp .... Revise misspelled word (M 1)

st .... Improve sentence structure (U 4)

t .... Change tense of verb (U 1a)

trans .... Provide better transition (C 2c)

w .... Reduce wordiness (U 4a)

HANDBOOK KEY

INDEX

Italicized page numbers indicate that the material referred to is in a summary chart.

Ambiguity
in comparisons, 55–57
of pronoun reference, 229
resulting from misplaced modifiers, 230
American Indian languages, 19
Americanisms, 20
Amount, number, 255
Analogy, 55, 57–58, 63, 387–388
effective use of, 57–58
figurative, to clarify an abstract idea, 63
in figurative language, 55
misleading, in persuasive writing, 387–388
Anonymous passive, *see* Voice
Antecedent, pronoun agreement with, 229
Apostrophe, 76, 261, 475–477
in contractions, 475
history of, in possessive forms, 76
with inanimate nouns, to show possession, 261
its, it's, 475
omitted in possessive pronouns, 476
for plural of numbers and words discussed as words, 477
for possession, 76, 261, 475–476
their, they're, 475
whose, who's, 475
Appositive, 146–147, 230, 484–485
defined, 146
misplaced as modifiers, 230
modifiers and noun markers with, 146
position in sentence, 146–147
punctuation with, 146–147
as sentence fragment, 484–485
Arabic language, 8
Argument in writing, 367–374
deduction in, 371–372
function of, 367
justified conclusions in, 370–371
pros and cons in, 370
Argumentative writing, *see* Persuasive writing
Articles, 92, 99
as function words, 92
as noun markers, 99
use of *the, a, an,* 99
As for *because,* 255
Autobiography, 321–334
emotion in, 326
questions to be answered in, 324–328
selectivity and concreteness in, 324–325
Auxiliaries, 92–93, 106–111, 123, 125, 259
be as, 107

to determine tense, 109
do, in questions and negative statements, 128
doubling as main verb, 110
as function words, 92–93
have as, 107
modal, 108
of for *have,* 467
with participles, 161–162
in perfect tense, 109
in transformations, 123, 125
in verb phrases, 106, 107–111
Awful for *extremely, 221*

Be
in absolute constructions, 170
as auxiliary, 107, 123
highly inflected in Modern English, 82
-ing form of participle with, 161–162
as main verb, 110
in negation transformations, 126
in passive transformations, 123
in question transformations, 125
subject form of personal pronoun after, 215
usage problems with *is, are, was, were, 200*
when-clause after, 235
Because-clause as subject, 235
Being as, being that, 256
Bengali language, 9
Better than me, 214–215
Between, among, 256
Between you and me, 214
Bibliography, 429–432
Blame for, blame on, 256

ca. or *c.,* meaning of, 438
Call number of card catalogue entries, 553–554
Can, may, 256
Cannot help but, 257
Capital, capitol, 465–466
Capitals, 471–474, 516
first word of a sentence, 471
proper adjectives and nouns, 471–472
in quotations, 516
in theme titles, 473
in titles of books, articles, works of art, etc., 473
in titles of persons, 472–473
Card catalogue, 553–555
library call number in, 432
Case forms, *see* Personal pronoun
Celtic language, 9–10
Censor, censure, 466
Changed plurals, 463–464
Choose, chose, 458

Chronological order in paragraph
and theme, 293
Cite, site, 466
Clauses, 150–157, 490–502
adverbial, 495–497
connectives to distinguish types
of, 150–154
definition of, 150
dependent or subordinate, 154,
157, 495–501
independent (main), 150–157,
490–493
noun, 102, 156, 498–501
punctuation between, 490–501
relative, 156–157, 498–501
Cliché, 58
Cognate forms, 8
Coherence
cause and effect for, 293–294
chronological order for, 293
contrast for, 294
in paragraph and theme, 278–282,
292–297
synonyms and related terms for,
294–295
transitional expressions for, 295
use of examples for, 293
Collective nouns, 226
Colloquial English, 210
Colloquialisms, *210*
Colon, 431, 485, 492–493, 515
between clauses, 492–493
before lists, 485
before quotations, 515
Comma, 146–147, 485, 491–493,
495–497
with adverbial clauses, 495–497
with adverbial connective, 492
with *after all, of course,* etc., 503
with appositives, 146–147, 485
between coordinate adjectives, 508
with coordinating connectives, 492
to correct sentence fragments, 485
with dates, addresses, etc., 508
with direct address and other
interrupters, 510, 511
between elements of a series,
506–508
after introductory modifiers,
504–505
to join short, parallel clauses with
no connective, 492
with nonrestrictive modifiers,
503–504
omitted with short quotations, 515
with quotation marks, 514, 515
with relative clause, 498–500
Comma splice, 492
Comparison
illogical or incomplete, 235–236
parallel order, 288

point-by-point, 287–288
Comparison and contrast
in paragraphs, 294
in themes, 287
Complements, 113–128
adjectives as, 117
in basic sentence patterns,
96, 113–121
direct object, 114, 116–117
indirect object, 116
object complement, 116–117
as part of predicate, 113
predicate adjective, 115–116
predicate noun,115
in transformations, 121–128
see also Object complement
Composition, *see* Research paper,
Theme, Writing
Compound predicate, *see* Predicate
Compound subject, 103
Concrete details, 57–58, 312–317
in comparison and analogy, 57–58
in descriptive writing, 312–317
unity of, 315–316
versus general labels, 28
Concrete words, *see* Figurative language, Specific words
Conditional clauses, *see* Adverb
clauses
Confusing pairs, 465–467
Conjunctions, *see* Connectives
Conjunctive adverbs, *see* Adverbial
connectives
Connectives, 149–160, 490–497
adverbial, 150, 152–154, 490–493
coordinating, 150, 152–154,
490–493
definition and functions of, 149–150
to express various meanings, 157
as function words, 92
joining dependent to main clause,
154–155
joining independent clauses,
150–151
punctuation with, 151–152, 490–
497
relative pronouns, 150, 155–157
special, 150, 156, 157
subordinating, 150, 154–155,
495–497
Connotation, 49–52, 343–344
awareness of in word choice,
343–344
changes during the history of a
word, 51
definition of, 49–50
different for different audiences, 51
different for various meanings of
the same word, 51
favorable and unfavorable judgments in, 50–51

Conscience, conscious, 458
Consistency
  of point of view, 243–245
  of verb tense and voice, 243–244
Consonants, 175–176, 178
  back-in-the-mouth sounds, 176
  compared with vowels, 178
  defined, 175
  kinds of, 176
Content words, 93
Context, 33–35, 51
Contractions, 475
  apostrophe in, 475
  its, it's; they're, their, 475
Contrast, *see* Comparison and
    contrast
Coordinating connectives, 150–152,
    247–248, 506, 507–508
  in compound subject, 103
  correct use of, in parallel structure,
    247–248
  to join coordinate elements,
    151–152
  to join independent clauses,
    150–151
  to join items in a series, 517
  list of, 150, 151
  position of, 152
  punctuation with, 151, 491–493
Could of, 199, 257
Couldn't hardly, 258
Couldn't scarcely, 258
Couple of, 257
Counsel, council, 466
Critical writing, 407–420
  close contact with original work in,
    414–415
  defining and illustrating critical
    terms in, 415–416
  discussing major literary characters
    in, 410–411
  examining a key symbol in, 413–
    414
  examining structure of a literary
    work in, 411–412
  focusing on one topic, 416–417
  purposes of, 408–409
  requirements of, 414–417
  tracing a unifying theme in, 412–
    413
  unity in, 409–415
  see also Theme, Writing
Czech language, 9

Dangling or misplaced modifiers,
    230–231
Danish language, 9
Dash, 485, 511
  for breaks in thought, 485
  to set off interrupters, 511
Debate, 547–550

  analysis of opponents' position in,
    550
  conditions necessary for, 548
  effective procedure in, 549–550
  keeping an open mind, 548
  respect for dissent in, 548
  self-control in, 550
Definition in expository writing, 339–
    349
  common elements in, 342–343
  extended, 345–346
  of familiar terms, 340–341
  formal, 341, 344–345
  relating the word to the thing, 342
  of technical terms, 340
Definitions, *see* Word meanings
Demonstrative pronouns, 99–101,
    198, 203
  listed, 99
  as noun markers, 99
  as noun substitutes, 101
  that there box, 203
  this here book, them people, 198,
    203
Denotation
  definition of, 48, 50
  functions of, 48
Dependent or subordinate clauses,
    154–157, 495–501
  adverbial clause, 495–497
  noun clause, 498–501
  position in sentence, 155
  punctuation with, 495–501
  relative clause, 498–501
  as sentence fragments, 484, 485
  subordinating connectives for,
    154–155
  see also Adverb clause, Noun
    clause, Relative clause
Descriptive writing, 312–319
  comparison and similarities in, 315
  concrete details in, 312–313, 315–
    316
  specific terms in, 314–315
  unity of descriptive details, 315–
    316
Desert, dessert, 466
Detail, 62, 312–316
  with abstract terms, 62
Determiners, 100
Development
  of paragraph, 292–297
  of theme, 292–294
Dialects, 5–6, 9, 196–197, 311
  American, as social, 196–197
  as beginnings of new languages, 5–
    6, 9
  examples and history of, 196–197
  methods of development, 5
  prestige dialect as national stand-
    ard, 196

adverbs, 219–221
agreement of subject and verb, 224–227
confusing doubles in, 219–220
equivalents of informal expressions, 214–227
function words, 91–93
glossary, 253–265
illogical construction, 234–236
position of modifiers, 231–233
pronoun forms, 203–204, 214–216
pronoun reference, 228–230
subjunctive in, 220
usage and logic in, 223–224
verb forms, 200–201, 219–221
who, whom, 215
word choice in, 208–210
Four-part verbs, 107
see also Verb, Verb forms
Fragments, 484–486
correcting, 485
kinds of sentence parts that cause, 484
permissible, 486
French language
derived from Latin, 9
dictionary abbreviations for, 6
influence on development of English, 11–12, 19
member of Indo-European family, 8
Function words, 91–93
articles, 92
auxiliaries, 92–93
connectives, 92
definition and categories of, 92
prepositions, 92–93
replacing inflections in Modern English, 91–93
stability of, 93
as "structure words," 92
used in a sentence, 93

Gaelic language, 10
German language, 9–10
Germanic language, 8–9, 11–12, 18
Germanic tribes, 9–11
Gerunds, 165–167
becoming true nouns, 167
definition of, 165
determiners with, 167
modified by adjectives, 167
as noun substitutes, 165
-s plural form, 167
see also Verbals
Glides, *see* Diphthongs
Glossary of usage, 253–265
Grammar, 75–193, 490–497, 503–510
the complete sentence, 96–98
connectives, 149–160, 490–497

differences in grammars, 76–78
function of grammar in language, 75–80
function words, 91–95
historical background, 76
inflections in, 80–84
major parts of, 173
modern, changes and discoveries in, 75–76
modifiers, 131–233, 481, 503–510
morphology in, 173
phonology in, 173
of speech, 173
summary chart of, 79
syntax in, 173
transformations, 121–130
verbals, 160–171
word order, 86–91
Grammatical devices, 78–95
functions of, 78–80
history of, 78–95
see also Grammar, History of English
Greek language, 9, 13, 35–39
plural forms of words in Modern English, 81–82
prefixes as clues to word meaning, 37–38
roots as clues to word meaning, 35–39
source of current English words, 33
Growed for grew, 198, 199
Guide to Manuscript Revision, 565

Had went, 200
Hadn't ought to, 259
Handbook Key, 566–567
Has
with plural subjects in Shakespearean English, 223
with singular subjects, 223
Have
as auxiliary, 107
with infinitives, to show perfect or passive, 165
participles after, in complete verb, 161–162
past or *-en* form of participle with, 161–162
in question transformation, 125
Have wrote, 200
Head word, 131
see also Modifiers
Hebrew language, 8
He don't, 198, 200
He. him, 8, 214
"Helping verbs," *see* Auxiliaries
History of English, 4–28
changes in pronunciation, meaning, grammar, 5

cultural exchange as influencing, 6
development of dialects, 5
effects of changes in cultural styles upon, 18
effects of foreign languages upon, 6–20
Germanic roots, 9
as living record of history, 18
major stages in, 6–14
wars as influencing development of, 6
word resources resulting from, 27–28
History of Grammar, *see* Grammar
History of our writing system, 453–455
History of words, 3–26
    as aid to recognition of overtones and associations of words, 4
    changes in connotations of words, 51
    changes in meanings of words, 21–24
    effects of changing cultures on, 18
    to explain richness and variety of word resources, 4
    as mirror of history, 18–20
    as organizational aid to the study of words, 3
    shown in dictionary, 6
Hyphen, 478–479, 521–522
    in compound numbers, 478
    in compound words, 478
    to divide words at end of line, 521–522
    in group modifier, 479
    after prefixes, 478–479

I before *e*, 462
Ibid., meaning of, 439
Idiom, 30–31
Idiomatic English
    definition of, 253–254
    glossary, 253–265
If, whether, 259
Imagery, *see* Figurative language
I, me, 81, *214*
Imperative sentence, *see* Request transformation
Imperative verb, *see* Verb
Impersonal use of *they, you,* 230
In, into, 259
Incomplete comparison, 235–236
Indefinite pronouns, 101–102, 216, 226
    as noun substitutes, 101–102
    singular number of, 216, 226
Independent (main) clauses, 150–154, 490–491, 493
    joined by adverbial connective, 150, 152–154

joined by coordinating connective, 150–151
joined by semicolon, 151, 152, 490–491, 493
punctuation between, 151, 152, 490–493
Indirect object, 116, 122–124
    in basic sentence pattern, 116
    in passive transformations, 123–124
    in request transformations, 122–123
    verbs used with, 116
Indirect quotation, 517–518
Indo-European language family, 8–9
Infer, imply, 259
Infinitive marker, 165
Infinitives, 165–167
    with *be* or *have,* 165
    definition of, 165
    in extended verb phrases using *have to, ought to, used to,* etc., 166
    functions of, 165–167
    as modifiers, 167
    modifiers with, 166
    objects with, 166
    as second object, 166
    to as infinitive marker, 165
    unmarked, 165
    after verbs like *happen, seem, need,* etc., 166
Inflections, 80–95, 106–107
    history and functions of in English, 80–86
    in parts of speech other than verbs, 80–86
    replaced in Modern English by word order, function words, etc., 86–95
    in verbs, 106–107
Informal standard English, 200–236, 253–265
    adverbs, 219–221
    agreement of subject and verb, 224–227
    glossary, 253–265
    illogical or mixed constructions, 234–236
    incomplete comparisons, 235–236
    is-when sentences, 235
    position of modifiers, 231–233
    pronoun agreement with antecedent, 228–230
    pronouns, 214–216
    subjective disappearing from, 220
    verb forms, 200–201, 219–221
    when-clause, *because*-clause as noun clause, 235
    written, to echo speech, 207

Literal versus figurative, 49
Loc. cit., meaning of, 439
Loose, lose, 459
Loud, loudly, 140
-*ly* ending on adverbs, 221

Main clauses, *see* Independent
   clauses
Manuscript form, 520–523
   abbreviations and numbers, 522–
      523
   division of words, 521–522
   proofreading marks, 521
   typing, 520–521
Mechanics, 453–523
   abbreviations and figures, 522–523
   apostrophe, 475–477
   capitals, 471–473
   hyphens, 478–479
   manuscript form, 520–523
   punctuation, 480–519
   sentence fragments, 499
   spelling, 455–470
Melioration in semantic change, 24
Metaphor, 56, 58, 211
   effective use of, 56, 58
   slang, 211
   trite and mixed, 58
Methods of development, 284–304
   for paragraph, 292–297
   for theme, 284–304
Middle English, 6, 11–13
Middle verbs, 124
Might of, 257
Mighty for *very, 221*
Misplaced modifier, 230
Mixed construction, 234–236
Modal auxiliaries, *see* Auxiliaries
Modern English, 10–11, 81–95
   basic vocabulary of Old English,
      Germanic stock, 11
   function words supplanting in-
      flected forms in, 91–95
   inflected word forms in, 81–86
   word order supplanting inflected
      forms in, 86–91
   word similarities with German, 10
Modern Grammar, *see* Grammar
Modifiers, 131–233, 499, 503–505
   adjectives as, 132–137
   adverbs, 221
   appositives as, 146–149, 230
   dangling, 230–231
   functions of, 131
   group modifiers, headword with,
      131
   infinitives as, 167
   to introduce sentences, for variety,
      251–252, 504–505
   misplaced, 230
   nonrestrictive, defined, 504

with objects of the preposition, 143
with participles, 161–162
participles as, 161–162
position in sentence, 96, 231–233
predeterminers, 135
prepositional phrases as, 141–143
restrictive, defined, 501
restrictive versus nonrestrictive,
   503–504
as sentence fragments, 499
variety of, with nouns, 134
verbals as, 230
of the whole sentence, 502
word order in, 135–136
see also Adjectives, Adverbs
"Modifying nouns," 77, 135
Morphology, 173
Most for *almost,* 260
MS, MSS, meaning of, 439

Negation transformation, 126–127
   be in, 126
   do in, 126–127
   position of *not* in, 126–127
Negative statements, *see* Negation
   transformation
N.d., meaning of, 439
Never hurt no one, 258
Nohow, 198
None has, none have, 226
Nonrestrictive clauses, 496–500
   comma with, 496–497, 498–500
   definition of, 496
   no punctuation with, 497
Nonrestrictive (nonessential) elements, 496, 504, 510–512
   adverbial clause, 496–497
   interrupters, 510–512
   modifiers, 504
   relative clause, 498–500
Nonstandard English, 197–200
   connectives, 197
   double negatives, 197
   glossary, 253–265
   grammatical rules, 198
   misunderstood facts about, 197–
      198
   pronoun forms, 197, 203–204
   verb forms, 197, 200–201
   vocabulary, 197
Norman Conquest, 11–12, 19
Norse language, 11
Norsemen, *see* Germanic tribes
Norwegian language, 9
Not classified alone; not an adverb,
   127–128
   see also Negation transformation
Note cards for research paper, 432–
   435
Noun, 81–82, 98–105, 115–124, 224–
   227, 475–476

summary to aid, 285
"thesis" on central idea, 278, 280–282, 368
use of pros and cons, 288
working outline to aid, 435
see also Paragraph, Theme
Ourn, ourself, 199, 203
Outline, 285–289, 435–437
examples of, 435–437
parallel structure of, 288, 437
point-by-point comparison in, 287, 435
for pro-and-con development, 288
for research paper, 435–437
working outline, 285, 435

Paired subordinators, *see* Subordinating connectives
Paper, *see* Theme
Paragraph, 57–58, 278–280, 292–297
use of analogy in, 57–58
coherence in, 292–297
use of comparison in, 294
logical pattern in, 292–294
methods of development, 292–297
topic sentence, 278–280
transitional expressions, 295
see also Organization, Theme
Parallel structure in sentences, 246–248
with coordinating connectives, 247–248
optional, 246–247
with paired connectives, 248
required, 247–248
in a series, 248
Paraphrasing for research paper, 433
Parentheses, 511–512
Parenthetic elements, *see* Interrupters
Participles, 161–163
to add detail or related information to a sentence, 161–162
auxiliaries with, 161
definition of, 161
as modifiers, 161–162
modifiers with, 161–162
objects with, 161–162
as part of the complete verb after *be* and *have,* 161
past, or *-en* form with *be* or *have,* 161–162
past, or *-en* form, history of, 163
past, in passive transformation, 123
to show perfect tense, 162
present, or *-ing* form with *be,* 161–162
to show progressive tense, 162
verb characteristics in, 163
see also Verbals
Participial phrase, 162–163, 504
position in sentence, 162–163

punctuation with, 504
see also Verbal phrase
"Particles," *see* Prepositions
Parts of a sentence, *see* Complements, Predicate, Subject
Parts of speech
as traditional system of sorting out word functions, 77
see also Adjectives, Adverbs, Nouns, etc.
Passed, past, 465
Passim, meaning of, 439
Passive transformation, 123–124
be as auxiliary in, 123
object in, 123
past participle in, 123
reversal of subject and verb in, 123
transitive verb in, 123
verb form in, 123
word order in, 123–124
Passive voice, *see* Voice
Past tense, 106–107, *109,* 161–162
Patterns of organization, 284–289
to fit topic, 284–289
suggested types, 286–289
for theme, 286–289
Pejoration in semantic change, 24
Perfect tenses, 162
Period, 483–484, 486, 493, 512, 514, 516, 522–523
with abbreviations, 522–523
ellipsis, 516
at end of sentence, 484, 486
with material in parentheses, 512
after polite request, 483
with quotation marks, 514
to separate compound sentence into simple sentence, 493
Persian language, 9
Personal, personnel, 466
Personal pronoun, 81–82, 98, 199, 214–216
case forms of, 81–82, 214–215
as core of subject, 98
correct use of, 214–216
after linking verb, 215
as noun substitute, 101
object form, 214
possessive forms, 101, *204*
repetition of, after subject, *199*
subject form, *81*
Persuasive writing, 382–388
analogies and comparisons in, 384
effects of, 382
exaggeration and overstatement in, 387
loaded language in, 387
logical development in, 384–385
misleading analogies in, 387–388
use of emotion in, 383–384
Phonemes, 175–181

in combined subject or object, 214
demonstrative, 101, *204*
intensive, *204*
interrogative, 102, 215
with linking verbs, 215
nonstandard, 197, *203,* 204
object, *81,* 214
personal, 101
possessive, 101, *204*
reflexive, 101, *204*
singular with *everybody, nobody,*
    etc., 216
standard, 203–204, 214–216
subject, *81*
with *this kind of,* etc., 216
who, which, 216
who, whom, 215
see also Pronoun reference
Pronoun reference, 228–230
agreement with antecedent, 229
ambiguity of, 229
implied antecedent, 229
they, you with unclear reference,
    230
this, which with no antecedent,
    229–230
with two antecedents, 229
Pronouns, 81–82, 98–99, 101–102,
    214–216, 226, 230
agreement of verb with, 226
as antecedent, 230
case and inflected forms of, 81–82,
    214–215
as core of subject, 98
indefinite, 101–102, 216
with linking verbs, 215
as noun markers, *99*
as noun substitutes, 101–102
repetition of, after subject, *199*
usage problems with, 214–216, 226
see also Pronoun forms, Pronoun
    reference
Pronunciation
of *-ed* ending, 173
regional differences in, 174
see also Phonology
Proofreading the composition, 521
Proper nouns and adjectives, 472–473
Punctuation, 146–147, 180–183, 475–
    501, 510–521
apostrophe, 475–477
brackets, 516
chart summarizing uses of, 480–481
colon, 485, 492–493
comma, 146–147, 485, 491–492,
    495–497
dash, 485
with dependent clauses, 495–501
at end of sentence, 481–484
exclamation mark, 482–483, 514,
    515

function of intonation and pitch in,
    180–183
between independent clauses, 490–
    493
with interrupters, 510–512
parentheses, 511–512
period, 484, 486
question mark, 482–483
semicolon, 151, 152, 490–491, 493
with series, 507–509
underlining or italics, 518–519

Question marks, 482–483
after polite questions, 483
in question transformation, 125
with quotation marks, 514–515
with rhetorical questions, 483
after single words and groups of
    words, 482
Question transformation, 124–126
auxiliaries in, 125
be in, 125
do in, 125
have in, 125
question-marker in, 125
word order in, 124–126
yes-or-no questions in, 124–125
Quite, quiet, 466
Quotation, 63, 153, 514–519
block form for long, 153
brackets in, 516
capitalization of first word, 516
colon before, 515
direct, 514–516
direct versus indirect, 518
ellipsis in, 516
indirect, 517–518
lines of poetry and dialogue, 515–
    516
overuse of, for slang expressions,
    519
punctuation with, 514–516
within quotation, 516
in research paper, 514–516
short, without comma, 515
use of, in summary of theme, 303
see also Quotation marks
Quotation marks, 514–519
for direct quotation, 514–516
distinguishing between direct and
    indirect quotation, 518
omitted in long quotations, 515
for original words preserved in in-
    direct quotation, 518
with other marks of punctuation,
    514–515
quotation within quotation, 516
single, 516
for slang expressions, 519
for technical terms, 518
q.v., meaning of, 439

effectiveness of, 527–529
eloquence in, 533–537
organization in, 527
varied pace in, 531
Speeches, types of, 533–546
eulogy, 533–536
inspirational, 533
persuasive, 536–546
political, 538–543
protest and dissent, 537–538
Spelling, 174, 455–470
-able, -ible, and other similar
sounding endings, 467
changed plurals, 463–464
confusing pairs, 465–467
of contractions, 475
different spellings of same sound,
456–457
doubled consonant, 462–463
final e, 463
Greek, Latin, and French words,
455
i before e, 462
list, 468–470
memory aids for common problems, 458–461
of for have, 467
rules, 461–464
several ways to spell one sound,
456–457
steps to improve, 455–456, 458–464
y as a vowel, 463
see also Hyphen
Split infinitive, 263
Standard English, 196–220
adverb forms, 219–221
agreement of subject and verb, 103,
200, 224–227
functional varieties in, 197, 206–
207
pronoun forms, 203–204, 214–216
subjunctive in, 220
verb forms in, 200–201, 219–221
Standard forms, see Standard English
Stress, 180–182
contrasts in, 180–182
described, 181
method of variation, 181
regularized in poetic meter, 181
uses of contrasts in, 181–182
Structural grammar, see Transform-
tional grammar
Structure
of paragraph, 292–297
of sentence, 96–172
of theme, 284–304
"Structure words," see Function
words
Style
consistent grammatical patterns
in, 238–239

elements of effective, 397–404
emphasis on key ideas, 238
richness and variety in, 239–240
word choice to reveal, 208–211
see also Sentence style, Stylistic
resources
Stylistic resources, 397–404
brief, impactful statements, 397–398
common elements of effective style,
397–404
humor and irony, 400–401
idiomatic language, 397
imaginative and figurative language, 398–399
parody, 401–402
purposeful repetition, 399–400
satire, 401
Subject, 96–105, 113–127, 214–215,
224–230
agreement of other elements with,
226–230
agreement with predicate, 103,
224–227
combined, pronoun forms in, 214
compound, 103
as core of sentence, 98
defined, 96
form of pronoun, after linking verb,
215
nouns and pronouns as, 96–105,
113–121
of sentence beginning with there,
127
in sentence patterns, 96–105, 113–
121
in transformations, 122, 123, 127
see also Noun, Pronouns
Subject form of pronouns, 81
Subjunctive, 220
Subordinate clauses, see Dependent or
subordinate clauses
Subordinating connectives, 150, 154–
155, 495–497
definition and functions of, 154–
155
dependent clauses with, 154–155
doubling as prepositions, 157
listed, 150, 154
main clause with, 154–155
paired, 155
Suffixes, 37–38, 99–100, 108–109, 133,
139
adjective-forming, 133
with adverbs, 139
Latin and Greek, 37–38
noun-forming, 99–100
verb-forming, 108–109
Summary, 285, 302–304
contrasted with conclusion, 302–303
function of, 302–304
styles of, 303–304

To-forms of verbs, *see* Infinitives
Topic, selection of, for research
    paper, 426–429
Topic sentence, 278–280
  to achieve unity and coherence of
    details in paragraph, 279
  key idea in, 278
  to state purpose of paragraph,
    278–280
Transformational grammar versus
    structural grammar, 121–122
Transformations, 121–130
  explanation of, 121
  negation, 126–127
  passive, 123–124
  question, 124–126
  request, 122–123
  "there-is," 127
Transitional devices, 295–297
  in cause-and-effect paragraphs, 296
  examples of, 295–297
  in fact-to-conclusion paragraphs,
    296
  in paragraphs that present contrast-
    ing points of view, 295–296
  in pro-and-con paragraphs, 296
  in themes, 288
Transitive verbs, 114, 116–117
Turkish language, 8

Unity, 292–297, 315–316
  in descriptive details, 315–316
  in paragraph and theme, 292–297
  see also Coherence
Usage, 195–265
  colloquial, 210
  conventions of, 224–236
  formal standard English, 197,
    219–236
  glossaries, 253–265
  informal standard English, 197,
    219–236
  and logic, 223–224
  nonstandard English, 197–200
  slang, 208–211
  standard English, 196–200
  and style, 237–252
  see also Sentence style
Used to, 264
Used to could, 264

Variety in sentence structure, 89
Verb, 82–83, 106–111, 114–117, 122–
    124, 144, 160–171, 200, 201,
    219–220, 224–227
  active voice, 124
  agreement with subject, 103,
    224–227
  auxiliaries doubling as, 110
  auxiliaries with, 82, 83, 106, 107–
    111

  compound, 109–111
  as core of predicate, 106
  do as a main verb, 128
  forms to show tenses, 109–111
  idiomatic prepositions with, 143
  intransitive, 114
  linking, 115
  "middle verbs," 124
  modifiers of, 138
  passive voice, 124
  phrase, 106–111, 144
  in sentence patterns, 106, 116–117,
    122–124
  shifts in tense, 106–107, 109–111
  singular and plural of, 82–83
  suffixes of, 161–162
  tense, 82, 106–111, 162
  in transformations, 122–124
  transitive, 114, 116–117, 122–124
  usage problems, 200–201, 219–220
  variety of forms in predicate,
    108–111
  as verbal, 160–171
  voice, 124
  see also Verb forms
Verb cluster ("verb phrase"), 106–
    111
Verb-forming prefixes, 108–109
Verb-forming suffixes, 108–109
Verb forms, 83, 106–111, 123–124,
    160–171, 200–201, 219–220
  complications in, 109–111
  confusing doubles in, 219–220
  -en form, 106–107, 161–162
  imperative (request) form, 122
  inflections in, 82–86
  -ing form, 106–107, 161
  irregular, 200–201
  lie, lay, 219–220
  "middle verbs," 124
  nonstandard, 197, 200–201
  of for *have,* 467
  passive, 123–124
  past participle, 161–162
  phrasal, 106–111, 144
  present participle, 83, 161–162
  progressive, 109
  sit, set, 219–221
  standard, 200–201
  subjunctive, 220
  tenses revealed by, 106–107,
    109–111
  to-form, 165
  variety of, in predicate, 108–111
  verbals, 160–171
  see also Verb cluster
Verbal noun, 165–167
  see also Gerunds, Infinitives
Verbal phrase, 162–163, 169, 504
  absolute construction, 169

Acknowledgments

We are indebted to the following for permission to reprint copyrighted material:

The Bodley Head of London, England, the author's representative, and Penguin Books, for permission to reprint an excerpt from Rex Warner's translation of Thucydides' *Peloponnesian War.*

Christian Century Foundation for permission to reprint an excerpt from "Obscenity and Censorship" by Dan Lacy from the May 4, 1960 issue of *The Christian Century.* Copyright 1960 Christian Century Foundation.

Mrs. Joseph (Dolly) Connelly and The Atlantic Monthly Company, Boston, Mass., for permission to use an excerpt from "Game's End" which appeared in the June, 1962 issue of *The Atlantic Monthly.*

David Daiches for permission to use passages from *Two Worlds* by David Daiches.

The Dial Press, Inc., for permission to reprint an excerpt from *Nobody Knows My Name* by James Baldwin, copyright © 1954, 1956, 1958, 1959, 1960, 1961 by James Baldwin.

Dissent Magazine for permission to reprint an excerpt from "In Defense of the Fullback" by Dan Wakefield, from *Dissent Magazine,* Summer, 1957.

Dodd, Mead & Company for permission to reprint an excerpt from *Further Foolishness* by Stephen Leacock.

Doubleday and Company, Inc., for permission to use an excerpt from the *Thorndike-Barnhart High School Dictionary,* copyright © 1962 by Scott, Foresman and Company.

E. P. Dutton & Company, Inc., for permission to reprint a passage from *Nigger* by Dick Gregory with Robert Lipsyte.

Farrar, Straus & Giroux, Inc., for permission to reprint a passage from *The Assistant* by Bernard Malamud.

Otto Friedrich and *Harper's Magazine* for permission to use a passage from "There are 00 Trees in Russia" by Otto Friedrich; copyright Otto Friedrich.

Mrs. William P. Gwinn for permission to reprint an excerpt from "On Hunting" by Alan Devoe from *The American Mercury,* February, 1951.

Harcourt, Brace & World, Inc., for permission to use an excerpt from *A Walker in the City* by Alfred Kazin; a passage from "England Your England" from *Such, Such Were the Joys* by George Orwell, copyright 1945, 1952, 1953, by Sonia Brownell Orwell; and to reprint "anyone lived in a pretty how town" by e. e. cummings from *Modern American & Modern British Poetry,* copyright 1955 (Rev. shorter ed.) by Harcourt, Brace & World, Inc.

Harper & Row, Publishers for permission to reprint excerpts from *Excellence* by John W. Gardner (Harper, 1961); from *The Schools* by Martin Mayer (Harper, 1961); from pages 143-149, 150, 151 of "The Afternoon of a Young Poet" by M. Carl Holman in *Anger, and Beyond,* edited by Herbert Hill, copyright © 1966 by Herbert Hill, and from Gary Jennings, "Pidgin: No Laughing Matter," © 1963 by Harper and Row.

Harper's Magazine, Inc., and Russell & Volkening for permission to reprint excerpts from "The Silver Horn" by Thomas Sancton, copyright © 1944 by Harper's Magazine, Inc. From the February, 1944 issue of *Harper's Magazine.*

Hill & Wang, Inc., for permission to reprint an excerpt from *The Stones of Venice* by John Ruskin.

Holt, Rinehart, and Winston, Inc., for permission to reprint the upper diagram on page 97 from Owen Thomas: *Transformational Grammar and the Teacher of English;* copyright © 1965 by Holt, Rinehart & Winston, Inc.; and for the alphabet chart on page 322 adapted from *Exercises* to accompany *Historical Linguistics:* An Introduction, by Winfred Lehmann; copyright © 1962 by Holt, Rinehart and Winston, Inc.

Houghton Mifflin Company for permission to reprint an excerpt from *Silent Spring* by Rachel Carson.

Lois Phillips Hudson for permission to reprint a passage from her "Springtime in the Rockies."

Iowa State University for permission to use material from "The Snow Also Freezes" and "Civil Rights" from *Three Quarters, A Magazine of Freshman Writing,* Vol. XIX, Department of English and Speech, Iowa State University, Ames, Iowa, 1965. For the poem "Can a Merry-go-Round Horse Gallop in a Straight Line" by Daniel Ort; for critical comments by Tom E. Knowlton and Stanley Cooperman, from *Poet and Critics,* p. 3, Winter 1967-68, Iowa State University Press, Ames, Iowa 50010.

Abraham Kaplan for permission to reprint passage from his article "The Aesthetics of the Popular Arts" from *Journal of Aesthetics and Art Criticism,* XXXIV, Spring, 1966.

Alfred Kazin for permission to use passage from his "The Writer and the City," copyright © 1968 by Harper's Magazine, Inc. Reprinted from the December, 1968 issue of *Harper's Magazine* by permission of the author.

Alfred A. Knopf, Inc., for permission to use an excerpt from *Farewell to Sport* by Paul Gallico.

Life Magazine for permission to reprint an excerpt from "Cash on the Line," by Jordan Bonfante, November 22, 1968, © 1968 Time Inc.

J. B. Lippincott Company for permission to reprint excerpts from *To Kill A Mockingbird* by Harper Lee, copyright © 1960 by Harper Lee; from *The Art of Making Sense*, A Guide to Logical Thinking, second edition, J. B. Lippincott Co., Philadelphia and New York, copyright © 1968, 1954 by Lionel Ruby.

Little, Brown & Company for permission to use an excerpt from *God's Country and Mine* by Jacques Barzun and for permission to use passages from "The Magnificence of Age" by Catherine Drinker Bowen.

G. & C. Merriam Company for permission to use excerpts from *Webster's New Students Dictionary* © 1969, and from *Webster's Seventh New Collegiate Dictionary* © 1969.

William Morrow & Co. for permission to reprint excerpts from *Growing Up in New Guinea* by Margaret Mead and from *Teen-Age Tyranny* by Grace and Fred M. Hechinger, copyright © 1962, 1963 by Grace and Fred M. Hechinger.

Albert Murray for permission to reprint excerpt from "Something Different, Something More" by Albert Murray from *Anger, and Beyond*.

The Nation Magazine for permission to use an excerpt from "Little Rock and Johannesburg" by Anthony Sampson, from *The Nation*, January 10, 1959.

New Directions Publishing Corporation for permission to reprint a passage from *Quite Early One Morning* by Dylan Thomas, copyright 1954 by New Directions Publishing Corporation; and for "In My Craft or Sullen Art" and "A Refusal to Mourn the Death, by Fire, of a Child in London" from *Collected Poems*. Copyright 1946 by New Directions Publishing Corporation. Copyright 1952 by Dylan Thomas. Reprinted by permission of New Directions Publishing Corporation.

Harold Ober Associates, Inc., for permission to reprint an excerpt from *On Reading His Poetry* by Dylan Thomas, copyright © 1956 by Street and Smith Publications, and from "The Nature of the Artist" by Catherine Drinker Bowen, copyright © 1961 by Catherine Drinker Bowen.

Oxford University Press for permission to reprint abridged passages from *Freedom, Loyalty, Dissent* by Henry Steele Commager. Copyright 1954 by Oxford University Press, Inc. for permission to reprint passages from *The Sea Around Us* by Rachel L. Carson. Copyright © 1950, 1951, 1961 by Rachel L. Carson.

Saturday Review, Inc., for permission to reprint "Who Killed Benny Paret?" by Norman Cousins from *Saturday Review*, May 5, 1962, copyright 1962 Saturday Review, Inc., and for quotes from "American Myths, Old and

New" by Malcolm Cowley (September 2, 1962 *Saturday Review*), copyright 1962 Saturday Review, Inc.; from "Uncle Tom's Cabin" by Kenneth Rexroth (January 11, 1969 *Saturday Review*), copyright 1969 Saturday Review, Inc., and from "Brutality and the City" by John LaFarge (October 21, 1961 *Saturday Review*), copyright 1961 Saturday Review, Inc.

Charles Scribner's Sons for permission to reprint the poem "Richard Cory" from *The Children of the Night* by Edwin Arlington Robinson, excerpts from *The Yearling* by Marjorie Kinnan Rawlings, and from "The Short Happy Life of Francis Macomber" by Ernest Hemingway, and the two lower diagrams on page 97 from Markwardt and Cassidy's *The Scribner Handbook of English*.

Mrs. James (Helen) Thurber for permission to reprint excerpts from "Courtship Through the Ages" in *My World — and Welcome to It,* published by Harcourt, Brace & World, New York. Originally printed in *The New Yorker*. Copyright © 1942 James Thurber. For a fable from "The Rabbits Who Caused All the Trouble" in *Fables for Our Time,* published by Harper and Row; originally printed in *The New Yorker;* copyright © 1940 James Thurber, copyright © 1968 Helen Thurber.

Mr. Ian P. Watt for permission to reprint an excerpt from "The Liberty of the Prison" by Ian P. Watt from *The Yale Review,* © 1956 by Yale University Press.

The World Publishing Company for permission to reprint an excerpt from *Webster's New World Dictionary of the American Language,* College Edition. Copyright 1968 by The World Publishing Company, Cleveland, Ohio.

The Yale Review for permission to use an excerpt from "The Difficult Art of Biograph" by Wilmarth S. Lewis, copyright © 1954 by Yale University Press.

HANDBOOK KEY

HANDBOOK KEY